LEAN BUSINESS SYSTEMS AND BEYOND

IFIP – The International Federation for Information Processing

IFIP was founded in 1960 under the auspices of UNESCO, following the First World Computer Congress held in Paris the previous year. An umbrella organization for societies working in information processing, IFIP's aim is two-fold: to support information processing within its member countries and to encourage technology transfer to developing nations. As its mission statement clearly states,

> *IFIP's mission is to be the leading, truly international, apolitical organization which encourages and assists in the development, exploitation and application of information technology for the benefit of all people.*

IFIP is a non-profitmaking organization, run almost solely by 2500 volunteers. It operates through a number of technical committees, which organize events and publications. IFIP's events range from an international congress to local seminars, but the most important are:

• The IFIP World Computer Congress, held every second year;
• Open conferences;
• Working conferences.

The flagship event is the IFIP World Computer Congress, at which both invited and contributed papers are presented. Contributed papers are rigorously refereed and the rejection rate is high.

As with the Congress, participation in the open conferences is open to all and papers may be invited or submitted. Again, submitted papers are stringently refereed.

The working conferences are structured differently. They are usually run by a working group and attendance is small and by invitation only. Their purpose is to create an atmosphere conducive to innovation and development. Refereeing is less rigorous and papers are subjected to extensive group discussion.

Publications arising from IFIP events vary. The papers presented at the IFIP World Computer Congress and at open conferences are published as conference proceedings, while the results of the working conferences are often published as collections of selected and edited papers.

Any national society whose primary activity is in information may apply to become a full member of IFIP, although full membership is restricted to one society per country. Full members are entitled to vote at the annual General Assembly, National societies preferring a less committed involvement may apply for associate or corresponding membership. Associate members enjoy the same benefits as full members, but without voting rights. Corresponding members are not represented in IFIP bodies. Affiliated membership is open to non-national societies, and individual and honorary membership schemes are also offered.

LEAN BUSINESS SYSTEMS AND BEYOND

First IFIP TC 5 Advanced Production Management Systems Conference (APMS'2006), Wroclaw, Poland, September 18-20, 2006

Edited by

TOMASZ KOCH
Wroclaw University of Technology
Poland

Springer

Lean Business Systems and Beyond

Edited by Tomasz Koch

p. cm. (IFIP International Federation for Information Processing,
a Springer Series in Computer Science)

ISBN: 978-1-4419-4582-2   e-ISBN: 978-0-387-77249-3

Printed on acid-free paper

Printed in the United States of America.

9 8 7 6 5 4 3 2 1

springer.com

CONTENTS

Preface   *xi*

PART ONE – Lean Production Systems for Dynamic Marketplaces

Planning and scheduling

A Basic Study of Auction-based Planning and Scheduling for Cell
Manufacturing.   3
Fujii S., Kaihara T., Sashio K., Yokose H., Kurahashi M., Hayashi N.

Sizing of Heijunka-controlled Production Systems with Unreliable
Production Processes.   11
Lippolt C. R., Furmans K.

A New Approach for Finite Capacity Planning in MRP Environment.   21
Na H-b., Lee H-G., Park J.

Preemptive Jobs Scheduling on Parallel Machines with Setup Times
and Renewable Resources.   29
Śliwiński T., Toczyłowski E.

Dynamic Production Management Architecture Considering Preparative
Operation.   41
Tsumaya A., Koike M., Wakamatsu H., Arai E.

Planning and Balancing of Disassembly Systems.   49
Zülch G., Schwarz R.

Demand Planning & Control – Handling Multiple Perspectives Through
a Holistic Approach to Hierarchical Planning.   57
Nielsen P., Steger-Jensen K.

Review of an ERP System Supporting Lean Manufacturing.   67
Steger-Jensen K., Hvolby H-H.

Orders Loading and Release in Flow Shops including Outsourcing Networks.   75
Tatsiopoulos I.P., Batsis A., Papadopoulos, G.

Information systems

A Service Oriented Architecture to Support Industrial Information Systems.   93
Biennier F., Legait A.

Development of Promise Data Structure.   101
Cassina J., Tomasella M., Taisch M., Marquard M., Metin A., Matta A.

Streamlining Asset Maintenance throughout Analysis of its Usage Data.   111
Jun H-B., Ruibal M., Kiritsis D., Xirouchakis P.

Development of an Information-interoperable Environment Based
on Open Technologies for Lean Production Systems.   121
Kimura T., Tezuka H., Kanda Y.

Performance measurement

The Operations Excellence Audit Sheet.   129
Alfnes E., Dreyer H., Strandhagen J.O.

Comparing Performance Measures for the Trade Off of Flow Time
and Throughput in Complex Manufacturing Systems.   143
Macchi M.

A Method for Measuring Operational and Financial Performance
of a Production Value Stream.   151
Sobczyk T., Koch T.

Modeling concepts for enterprise and process improvement

Reference Models for Mass Customisation Production of High Fashionable
Products: Application to the Shoe Manufacturing Domain.   165
Ducq Y., Vallespir B.

Lean Manufacturing Systems Optimisation Supported by Metamodelling.   175
Gregor M., Štefánik A., Hromada J.

Integration of Factory Planning and ERP/MES Systems: Adaptive   185
Simulation Models.
Mertins K., Rabe M., Gocev P.

Using Simulation-Generated Operating Characteristics Curves
for Manufacturing Improvement.   195
Olhager J., Persson F.

Experimental Exploration of Decision Making in Production-inventory
System.   205
Rydzak F., Sawicka A.

Building a Reference Model for the PLM Processes in Engineering
and Contracting Sector.   215
Tucci M., Bandinelli R., Carli D.

Surveys

Integration in Manufacturing Systems.   223
Santarek K.

Which Manufacturing Logistics Decisions are Supported by Operational
Research? A Literature Survey.   231
Semini M., Fauske H., Strandhagen J.O.

Lean implementation

The Selected Problems of Lean Manufacturing Implementation
in Mexican SMEs.   239
Bednarek M., Niño Luna L.F.

Experiences with Lean Management.   249
Frick J.

Implementing Lean Manufacturing in High-mix Production Environment.   257
Horbal R., Kagan R., Koch T.

Implementing Lean Management in the Romanian Industry.   269
Marinescu P., Toma S. G.

Lean Transformation of Multinational Concerns.   277
Matthiessen R. V., Johansen J.

Orchestrating Lean Implementation.   285
Riis J.O., Mikkelsen H., Andersen J.R.

Set-up Reduction for Lean Cells and Multi-Machine Situations.   295
Van Goubergen D.

Lean and Self Directed Teamwork – Differences, Difficulties and Future
Developments – A Case Study.   305
Goller I., Kehr M., Lindinger C.

PART TWO – Bridging Production Process with Sales and Distribution

Gathering Production Processes of Services and Goods: Towards
the Mixed Enterprise.   317
Alix T., Vallespir B.

Lifecycle Simulation Framework for Production Systems.   327
Nakano M., Noritake S., Ohashi T.

From Order to Delivery: An Integrated Process Approach for Customer
Satisfaction.   337
Neubert G., Crestan A. W., Bouras A.

Lean Information Processing in the Specification Process. Using
operational data to enable real mass customization.   347
Svensson C.

PART THREE – Value Chains

Exploring Competitive Advantage through Lean Implementation
in the Aerospace Supply Chain.   357
Crute V., Wickham A., Johns R., Graves A.

Intercultural Communication Management and Lean Global Supply
Chains- a conceptual approach.   365
Hamacher B.

Building Global Workflow From The Scratch. An Approach Based
on Integration of Heterogenic Workflows by Mediators.   373
Jaber M., Badr Y., Biennier F.

Review of After-Sales Service Concepts.   383
Rolstadaas A., Hvolby H-H., Falster P.

Reducing Turbulences in Industrial Supply Chains.   393
Strzelczak S.

Improving Performance of Supply Chains by Leveraged Hard Solutions
and Business Cultures.   403
Strzelczak S, Huang H.

Architectural Frameworks for Business Information System Analysis
and Design.   413
Trienekens J.H., Hvolby H-H., Steger-Jensen K., Falster P.

The Lea®n Extended Enterprise: The Art of continuously achieving
benefits through Value Adding Communities.   423
Tsigkas A., Freund R.

Modelling Demand-driven Chain Networks using Multiple CODPs.   433
Verdouw C.N., Beulens A.J.M., Bouwmeester D., Trienekens J.H.

Critical Aspects of Information and Communication Technology
in Vendor Managed Inventory.   443
Vigtil A., Dreyer H.C.

Hybrid Modeling Approach for Supply-Chain Simulation.   453
Umeda S., Zhang F.

Concept for Quality Control Management Services in Distributed
Design Networks – Conceptual Paper.   461
Thoben K-D., Seifert M., Sitek P., Emde M., Tarditi R.

PART FOUR – Improving Service Processes

Need to Develop Best Practices for Business Related Services (BRS). 475
Garg A., Gudergaan G.

Lean Healthcare. An Experience in Italy.   485
Portioli-Staudacher A.

Working Time Configuration in Hospitals Using Personnel-oriented
Simulation.   493
Zülch G., Stock P., Hrdina J.

Index   503

Preface

Lean Manufacturing has proved to be one of the most successful and most powerful production business systems over the last decades. Its application enabled many companies to make a big leap towards better utilization of resources and thus provide better service to the customers through faster response, higher quality and lowered costs.

Lean is often described as "eyes for flow and eyes for muda" philosophy. It simply means that value is created only when all the resources flow through the system. If the flow is stopped no value but only costs and time are added, which is muda (Jap. waste).

Since the philosophy was born at the Toyota many solutions were tailored for the high volume environment. But in turbulent, fast-changing market environment and progressing globalization, customers tend to require more customization, lower volumes and higher variety at much less cost and of better quality. This calls for adaptation of existing lean techniques and exploration of the new waste-free solutions that go far beyond manufacturing.

This book brings together the opinions of a number of leading academics and researchers from around the world responding to those emerging needs. They tried to find answer to the question how to move forward from "Spaghetti World" of supply, production, distribution, sales, administration, product development, logistics, accounting, etc. Through individual chapters in this book authors present their views, approaches, concepts and developed tools. The reader will learn the key issues currently being addressed in production management research and practice throughout the world.

This book is composed of four parts, each focused on specific theme whereas the first theme was divided into six subtopics:

- Lean production systems for dynamic marketplaces
  - Planning and scheduling
  - Information systems
  - Performance measurement
  - Modelling concepts for enterprise and process improvement
  - Surveys
  - Lean implementation
- Bridging production process with sales and distribution
- Value chains
- Improving service processes

Each of the chapters in this book have been peer reviewed and presented by the authors at the Advanced Production Management Systems Conference – AMPS'2006, held in Wroclaw, Poland on 18th through 20th of September 2006. The conference was supported by the International Federation for Information Processing and was organised by Working Group 5.7 (Integration in Production Management) of the Technical Committee 5 from within IFIP. The conference was hosted by Wroclaw University of Technology.

As the book editor I would like to thank all of contributors for preparing and presenting their papers to a high standard. I would also like to thank 50 members of APMS'2006 Technical Programme Committee who stand for over 50% of WG5.7 members:

Bjorn Andersen, Norway	Kai Mertins, Germany
Frederique Biennier, France	Jan Olhager, Sweden
Umit Bititci, UK	Ioannis A. Pappas, Greece
Jim Browne, Ireland	Henk Jan Pels, Netherlands
Luis M. Camarinha-Matos,	Edward Radosiński, Poland
Portugal	Jens O. Riis, Denmark
Stephen J. Childe, United Kingdom	Asbjorn Rolstadas, Norway
Eero Eloranta, Finland	Schoensleben Paul, Switzerland
Peter Falster, Denmark	Riitta Smeds, Finland
Jan Frick, Norway	Kathryn E. Stecke, USA
Susumu Fujii, Japan	Volker Stich, Germany
Masahiko Fuyuki, Japan	Richard Lee Storch, USA
Marco Garetti, Italy	Jan Ola Strandhagen, Norway
Robert W. Grubbstroem, Sweden	Stanisław Strzelczak, Poland
Tom Gulledge, USA	Marco Taisch, Italy
Gideob Halevi, Israel	Ilias Tatsiopoulos, Greece
Bernd Hamacher, Germany	Klaus-Dieter Thoben, Germany
Hans-Henrik Hvolby, Denmark	Mario Tucci, Italy
Ichiro Inoue, Japan	Gunduz Ulusoy, Turkey
Christopher Irgens, UK	Shigeki Umeda, Japan
John Johansen, Denmark	Bruno Vallespir, France
Dimitris Kiritsis, Switzerland	Agostino Villa, Italy
Ashok Kochhar, UK	Matt Williamson, USA
Andrew Kusiak, USA	Hans Wortmann, Netherlands
Jan-Peter Lechner, Germany	Gert Zuelch, Germany
Charles R. McLean, USA	

for their support in reviewing and selecting each of the papers.

Tomasz Koch
Wroclaw University of Technology
Poland

PART ONE

Lean Production Systems for Dynamic Marketplaces

A Basic Study of Auction-based Planning and Scheduling for Cell Manufacturing

Susumu Fujii[1], Toshiya Kaihara[2], Kentaro Sashio[2], Hiroko Yokose[2],
Masasi Kurahashi[3] and Nobuhiro Hayashi[3]

1.   Sophia Univeristy, Department of Mechanical Engineering
` 7-1, Kioi-cho, Chiyoda-ku, Tokyo, 102-8554 Japan
2.   Kobe University, Dept. of Computer and Systems Engineering
1-1, Rokkodai, Nada, Kobe 657-8501 Japan
3.   Omron Corporation, Industrial Automation Company,
Production Management &System Engineering Group,
2-2-1, Nishikusatsu, Kusatsu, 525-0035 Japan

Abstract. Cell manufacturing is widely introduced to cope with the dynamically changing market demands. This study considers a scheduling method for a cell assembly system for the products that are characterized by the type and specification. A major set up is required at a cell for the change of types and a minor one for the change of specification within the same types. The scheduling will be made in three folds. Firstly, the scheduling for the orders with due dates of the day is made before the processing of the day starts. If cells have slack times for the production of the orders of the day, express orders to be completed within the day will be accepted in a prespecified time period or until no cells become available for the production. If slack times still exist, advanced production of orders with future due dates will be considered. Auction-based algorithms are proposed for the scheduling and their effectiveness is investigated by simulation studies.

1 Introduction

Cell manufacturing is widely introduced in assembly shops especially in the assembly of electronic devices enabling to keep the agility and the flexibility of the system and to respond the dynamically changing market demands [1]. A cell manufacturing system is constituted of several cells each of which may be also constituted of some stations. One product is assembled in a cell moving from station to station devised with appropriate tools and/or equipments. The product kinds can be changed relatively easily by changing the setups at each station. To attain the high performance out of the system, it is important not only to provide hardware with

Please use the following format when citing this chapter:

Fujii, S., Kaihara T., Sahio, K. Yokose, H., Kurahashi, M. and Hayashi, N., 2008, in IFIP International Federation for Information Processing, Volume 257, Lean Business Systems and Beyond, Tomasz Koch, ed.; (Boston: Springer), pp. 3–10.

high flexibility but also to have a planning and scheduling systems which is also easy to cope with the dynamic changes of the demands in the market.

In this study, an assembly system for electronic devices is considered to be redesigned into cell manufacturing. The products are largely classified into kinds, each of which is further classified into types. The objective system needs to process a large number of orders per day. Most of orders are ordinary orders received before the day starts, but some express orders requiring the shipping in the same day are also received and accepted if possible. To improve the customers' satisfaction, the primary objective of the new system is set to ship out all ordinary orders without any delay with a limited number of cells and then to accept express orders as many as possible as the secondary objective. To cope with these objectives, the planning and scheduling procedures based on the auction are proposed for agile manufacturing.

This paper describes the outline of the objective manufacturing system and the frame of the auction based planning and scheduling procedures. Then the basic design of the planning and scheduling procedures is discussed using a numerical example. The effectiveness of the proposed system will be also demonstrated in conjunction with the designing procedure of the frame.

2   Outline of Objective Manufacturing System

The conceptual configuration of the cell manufacturing system in this study is shown in Fig. 1. The system has N cells and each cell is constituted by some stations, six stations in this study. The products are largely classified into some kinds and products in a same kind are further classified into some types. All products are processed at each station for a pre-determined fixed cycle time regardless to the kinds and types, 15 seconds in this study. For the change in the product kind, each cell needs to stop for a large setup change, 10 minutes in this study, and for the change in the type within the same kind, the setup at one station is made station to station, and one cycle time at a station, 15 seconds in this study, will be required for the setup change.

The orders usually received in advance specifying the product kind and type, the number of products (order size) and the due date for delivery. These orders are called ordinary orders in this study. The shipping date is estimated based on the distance and the due date for delivery and the shipping date becomes the due date at the factory. In this study an order whose completion time is before T, 17:00 in this study, can be shipped out by the last truck scheduled on the day and the order is considered to be in time or without delay. Because of a short processing time of the product in this study, most of the ordinary orders are scheduled for manufacturing on the day of shipping. Such ordinary orders whose shipping date is same as the manufacturing date are called today's order hereafter. In addition, special orders, express orders in this study, will be accepted by the sales department and are also expected to be completed for the shipping of the day. Since today's orders have the first priority, express orders will only be accepted up to the total capacity of the system.

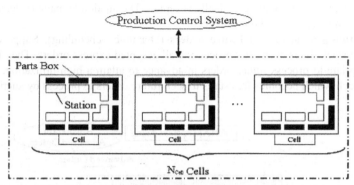

Fig. 1. Conceptual Configuration of Objective Cell System

3   Frame of Daily Planning and Scheduling

For the customers' satisfaction, the primary objective of the system is to complete all ordinary orders without any delay and the secondary one is to accept the express orders as many as possible under the constraint of given number of cells and the regular working hours. Every day, by T0 before the operation of the day starts, say 9:00, the ordinary today's orders are to be assigned to cells. This is a static scheduling of a given set of orders. At T0, all cells starts their operation based on the schedule of today's orders. The express orders received by the sales department are assigned to some cells based on some scheduling rules dynamically. If the system has some slacks even after accepting all express orders in addition to the today's orders, the system can process the future orders, whose shipping dates are tomorrow or later, in advance.

A scheduling system pursuing the optimum may be developed to produce a schedule which minimizes the setup times for today's orders in advance and can inform the available time for express orders to the sales department. It will however take a long time for scheduling a large number of orders and will not be practical to re-run the scheduling system every time the express orders are received to obtain the optimum schedule.

To solve these problems, a new auction based planning and scheduling procedures are proposed taking the advantage of cell manufacturing system into consideration. The procedures for today's, express and future orders are separately developed and then integrated as briefly described below and shown in Fig. 2. The working hour of one day starts at T0 and ends at T. The orders completed by T can be shipped out in this day.

Scheduling of today's orders (Static Scheduling): At the beginning of the day, T0, today's orders are scheduled by the auction. This is called planning auction in this study.

Scheduling of express orders (Dynamic Scheduling): Express orders will be received after the daily operation starts. As far as any cell has a slack to process

them, the express order will be basically accepted. The auction is made to determine
when the order is processed on which cell.

Scheduling of advanced future orders (Dynamic Scheduling): Suppose that
cells have slack times even after processing all accepted express orders. Then it will
be appropriate to process future orders in advance to attain a high utilization. After
T1, each cell which becomes free starts to seek future orders to process by auction.

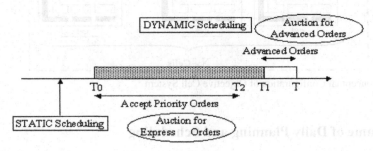

Fig. 2. Time Chart for Daily Planning and Scheduling

4   Basic Design of Objective Manufacturing System

To develop an efficient scheduling system, it is necessary to customize the basic
policy and parameters to the objective manufacturing system. In this study, the
scheduling system is developed for the manufacturing system with 10 cells. The
products are classified into 27 kinds and 1035 types in total. The number of products
in each order, i. e., order size, ranges from 1 to 100. Order sizes are grouped into
three groups; G1=[1-9], G2=[10-60] and G3=[61-100], where the size in one group
is assumed uniformly distributed. Orders for each day are generated so that the
number of orders with order size in each group will become P1={80%:15%:5%}.
For each order the product kind is firstly assigned randomly and then its type are
randomly assigned. To investigate the effect of ratio of order sizes in a day, an order
pattern P2={5%, 15%, 80%} is also considered.

4.1 Planning Auction for Today's Orders

The capacity of the system depends on the schedule of orders. In this system
a schedule with minimum setup times is the most efficient schedule since the
processing times of all products are the same. All today's orders are scheduled
before the operation of the day starts and thus the auction for today's orders is named
planning auction. The auction procedure is given below, where the item for auction
could be one single order or a set of orders to be determined later.

Planning Auction:

Step 1: (Co) Set orders into items based on the specified rules.

Item A: A single order

Item B: A set of orders with same kind and type (no setup required)

Item C: A set of Item B with same kind (short setup time required)

Step 2: (Co) Select one item by the specified selection policy. Then the characteristics of the item are announced to cells.

Policy 1: Randomly select Item A

Policy 2: In the decreasing order of total processing time of Item B

Policy 3: In the decreasing order of total processing time of Item C

Step 3: (Cell) Assume to process the item after the last item assigned to the cell. Calculate the setup time and completion time of the item. If the completion time is later than T, the item will be delayed to the shipping time and thus the bid is "not available". If "available", the bids are "setup time" and "present load (=completion time of the last order except the item)".

Step 4: (Co) Select cells with shortest setup time and then select a cell with the lightest present load among the selected cells, i. e., the earliest completion time. If more than one cell remains, select one randomly. The item is awarded to the selected cell. Go to *Step 2* if items for auction remain. Otherwise, stop.

4.2 Efficiency of Planning Auction and System Capacity

To investigate the efficiency of the planning auction, preliminary experiments are performed for selection policies of items. The results for one set of orders are shown in Fig. 3. From the figure the effectiveness of the policy 3 is obvious, and Policy 3 is adopted in the planning auction in this study.

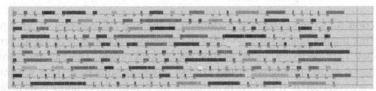

Fig. 3 (a). Policy 1: Item A, Random

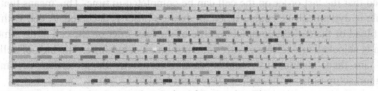

Fig. 3 (b). Policy 2: Item B, Decreasing Order of Processing Time

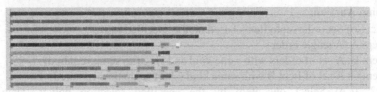

Fig. 3 (c). Policy 3: Item C, Decreasing Order of Processing Time

The capacity of the system can be defined as the maximum number of orders to be processed in one day without any delay. Increasing the number of orders, the system utilization in 8 hours operation and the number of tardy orders which delayed to the shipping are evaluated by running 10 simulations for each number of orders. The averaged results for each number of orders are given in Table 1. Based on the results, the maximum capacity of the system is considered to be around 1300.

Table 1. System Performance for given Number of Orders

Number of Orders	Utilization (%)	Number of Delayed Orders
1000	68.07	0
1100	74.41	0
1200	79.20	0
1300	86.89	6.9
1400	91.69	49.5
1500	92.53	111.1

4.3   Auction for Express Orders

The auction for express orders is performed at the time of reception of an express order. This implies that *Steps 1* and *2* of the planning auction will be set to Item A and Policy 1, respectively, in the auction for express orders. The bids provided by cells depend on the timing when the express orders are proessed. Two scheduling patterns are considered. If the orders including the express order under consideration cannot be completed in time by any cell, the order will not be accepted.

Pattern 1: Express orders are processed after the order with minimum setup time, provided that the last order on the cell can be completed in time. This means that the schedule is dynamically changed when an express order is accepted. A cell with the lightest load or the earliest completion time of the last order on the cell at the time of auction is selected among those with same minimum setup time. The bids of cells in *Step 3* are then "availability (can or cannot complete the all orders in time)", "minimum setup time on the cell" and "present load"

Pattern 2: Express orders are processed after completing the last order assigned to the selected cell. This means the schedule for today's order is fixed. The cell is selected by the lightest load rule. The bids of cells in *Step 3* are then "availability" and "completion time of last order assigned by the time auction".

The effectiveness of the pattern is investigated under the condition that today's orders generated will require 7 hours to process on the average. Typical schedules for these patterns are shown in Fig. 4. It is easily observed that more orders are scheduled when the schedule is dynamically changed inserting the express orders in the schedule of today's orders. Number of express orders generated for 6 hours (= T2- T0) is increased from 80 to 140 and the system utilization and the number of tardy orders are obtained by simulation. The results are shown in Fig. 5 and Pattern 1 shows better performance with 130 to 140 acceptable express orders with less than one tardy orders and higher utilization than that of Pattern 2.

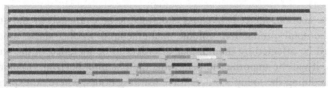

Fig. 4 (a). Schedule of Today's Orders

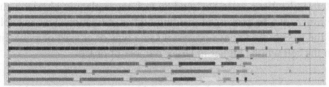

Fig. 4 (b). Schedule of Express Orders with Pattern 1

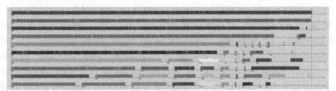

Fig. 4 (c). Schedule of Express orders with Pattern 2

4.4   Reverse Auction for Advanced Future Orders

If cells complete all assigned orders before the end time of the day, orders with future shipping dates can be processed. This will be preferable not only to improve the utilization of the system but also to absorb the daily variation of the production volume incurred by the fluctuation in the number of ordinary orders. The auction for such future orders is quite different from the planning auction and auction for express order. The auction is initiated by a cell which has a slack time and thus the cell becomes the coordinator and the future orders are the participants. Since the relation between cell and order are reversed from the planning auction, the auction for future orders is named a reverse auction in this study.

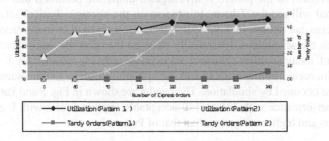

Fig. 5. Effects of Number of Express Orders and Scheduling Patterns

In the reverse auction, the effectiveness is defined to be evaluated by the number of orders or the total production volume manufactured in the slack time. These measures will be affected by the number of orders to be included in the auction. In other words, it will be important to determine the planning horizon. Simulations are run after scheduling the today's orders for 7 working hours, where no express orders are considered. The numbers of future orders processed in the slack time for cases with the planning horizons of one day and two days were 158 and 165, respectively, and the system utilizations were 86.2 and 86.6. Longer planning horizon shows that more future orders can be processed yielding higher utilization. This is explained by the fact that the possibility to have orders of same type or at least of same kind to the last order on the cell will be higher in larger number of orders.

5   Conclusions

This paper considers a cell manufacturing system of assembling electronic devises. In addition to a large number of orders to process in a day, express orders are also to be accepted as many as possible. To cope with these requirements, auction based scheduling procedures are proposed as a dynamic and flexible planning and scheduling system. Planning auction is presented for scheduling orders before the daily operation starts. By simulation studies, it was shown that the auction should be made as a group of orders with a same kind in the decreasing order of total group-wise processing time. For express orders, an auction is performed when it is received. High performance will be attained by a scheduling such that orders are processed just after an order of the same type or at lest in the same kind is completed. A reverse auction is proposed for scheduling future orders to be processed in slack times of cells. The experiments showed that higher performance will be attained when longer planning horizon is set for future orders.

To implement these procedures in a system, the period to receive the express orders, the time to start reverse auction and other parameters are to be determined, but they are left for further studies..

References

1. Cover Story, "Need to avoid vulnerability in Cell Manufacturing", *Nikkei Monodukuri*, Nikkei BP, July, 2004. (In Japanese).

Sizing of Heijunka-controlled Production Systems with Unreliable Production Processes

Christian R. Lippolt, Kai Furmans
Institut für Fördertechnik und Logistiksysteme (IFL),
Universität Karlsruhe (TH)
Kaiserstraße 12, D 76128 Karlsruhe, Germany
WWW home page: http://www.ifl.uni-karlsruhe.de

Heijunka is the notion to level a production system by removing ups and downs in volume caused by batch processing and customer order fluctuation in order to reach a mixed model production system with a constant flow of parts. We show how to implement lean production principles in systems with unreliable production processes. Process unreliabilities occur because tool machines may have small overall equipment effectiveness. Our present results were derived during performed implementation projects, where supermarket-pull-systems had to be dimensioned. In particular, the calculation of required inventory levels is presented which uses analytical mathematical models on the basis of discrete time queuing systems. By considering variable capacities we essentially extend the content of reference [1]. The application of our model is demonstrated by an example.

1 Introduction

Production unreliability is a frequent problem when lean production systems have to be installed. The problems occur because unreliability leads to variability in processing times and consumption, which must be compensated by inventory buffers. Production orders for the relevant process, which would guarantee appropriate refill of the process exit buffer supplying goods for the next process step are behind schedule and the next step is starved. This effect is more noticeable with increasing process utilization.

In cases where all processes are highly reliable with low variability, the standard Toyota formulas can be used for sizing the buffers. Otherwise the relevant literature suggests concentrating first on the process itself (point kaizen) prior to implementing kanban cycles. Unreliable processes are causing constraints. Special tool machines often have an overall equipment effectiveness (OEE) lower than 70%. OEE

Please use the following format when citing this chapter:

Lippolt, C.R. and Furmans, K., 2008, in IFIP International Federation for Information Processing, Volume 257, Lean Business Systems and Beyond, Tomasz Koch, ed.; (Boston: Springer), pp. 11–19.

comprehensively indicates the relative productivity of a piece of equipment compared to its theoretical performance. Low reliability may be caused by technological complexity, which is not under control. Therefore it is the question whether lean production can only be implemented and the production be levelled if all production processes are highly reliable or if it is possible to begin with levelling before making improvements. [2] dealt with the problem of determining the number of circulating kanbans for a manufacturing system with machine breakdowns utilizing perturbation analysis. In order to find the optimal number he estimated gradients and preformed stochastic approximations.

We approach the problem by developing a method for the calculation of buffer sizes. A path towards an implementation of kanban cycles and levelled production for cases where the production processes are unreliable is shown by calculating the required inventory levels which are necessary to guarantee a certain service level. The following sections provide insights into the impacts of variability in production systems and into production levelling and present the derived model and its assumption as well as the analytical method to compute the required inventory levels. We finish the text with an illustrative example.

2   Basic concepts

2.1   The effect of variability on Lean Manufacturing

Lean Manufacturing is a management philosophy focusing on reduction of the seven types of waste (over-production, waiting time, transportation, processing, inventory, motion and scrap) in manufacturing or any type of business [3]. [4] note that is possible to achieve the same throughput either with long cycle times and large work or short cycle times and small work in process. The difference between both cases is variability. It exists in all production systems and affects significantly production throughput, delivery, quantity, costs and customer satisfaction [5]. The most common causes of variability in manufacturing environments according [4] are: natural variability (including minor fluctuations in process time due to differences in operators, machines, and material), random outages, setups, operator availability, rework and scrap. [6] distinguish between process and flow variability. After [4] both kinds of variability in production systems will be buffered by some combination of inventory, capacity and time and we can conclude that variability is the root cause for waste. Because in a perfect balanced system no buffering is needed, increasing variability always degrades the performance of production systems [4].

2.2   Production levelling strategy

The basis of a lean or just-in-time production is to level the work flow for optimizing the manufacturing line [7]. Customer orders may arrive relatively constantly in the long run but they appear to be inconstant and unpredictable in short intervals. The aim of levelling is the reduction of the customer order variability by analysis of the orders in a given time span resulting in a pattern which fits into a smaller time scheme. It creates a constant flow of parts in a mixed model production and reduces or eliminates the need for spare capacity or stocks to cope with peaks of demand. [8] distinguishes two phases of levelling: I. Of the total production volume, II. Of the product mix. Phase I specifies both kind and quantity of product variants (model types) which are to be produced in an individual manufacturing shift. The computation starts with the monthly order of each product variant. The quantity of a given levelling horizon per variant is divided by the number of available manufacturing shifts. Thus the levelled outputs per shift of each variant and the cycle times for all products are found. The aim of the continuous improvement is to produce every-part every-day or better every-shift [9]. Because in today's production systems the number of variants can be very high, [10] suggests to level in a first step only the large-volume variants (high runners), which are to be produced following the average demand in a given time interval (every-part-every-interval, EPEI). The length of the EPEI is an indicator for the capability of the production process. Its determination is described in detail in [9].

The many small-volume products (low runners) are scheduled upon need in a reserved period of the day. If a production order for a low runner cannot be fulfilled completely within a reserved time block, then it is scheduled into the next cycle [11]. The reduction of flow variability by smoothing the orders leads to a decoupling of production and demand which must be compensated by an inventory buffer for finished goods. A short levelling horizon facilitates the implementation and minimizes the required inventory buffer for finished goods, however the desired levelling effect is lost, if the period is chosen too short. The optimal level depends on the fluctuation of the customer orders and the price of finished goods.

In phase II the production sequence of the individual orders per shift is determined, which leads to a finer levelling of the product mix. Numerous relevant algorithms exist in the literature [e.g. 8, 12]. The final result of levelling is a production sequence with a continuous flow adjusted to the customer demand and leading to an even utilization of the production stages.

3 Buffer sizing model for unreliable systems

3.1 System Model and Control Policy

A manufacturing structure, where each process has only one predecessor and one successor [12] is the one with the lowest possible complexity. The complexity increases with the number of the possible preceding and following processes. Evidently an even utilization of all resources is much more difficult in a system with high material flow complexity. To improve transparency and to reduce system variability, lean manufacturing tools introduce and steadily improve flow production. The flow production method arranges the production processes complying with the material flow of the products. The parts flow after each production process to the subsequent process without buffering and are processed immediately. There is no over production, because each stage produces exactly what the next stage needs at a given time. Abandoning of buffers results in short throughput times and low work-in-process inventory levels. To realise pure flow production, the production times must be balanced perfectly. This is often only a vision but nevertheless the aim of the continuous improvement process. A useful tool to improve flow is value-stream design initiated by [8]. One important design principle is to arrange directly connected production processes in a flow and manage the flow between the sections by continuous flow with pull control loops [8].

Each stage consists of a manufacturing process, which is a sub-part of the production system, and an output buffer (supermarket). The manufacturing process contains parts that are currently being processed in the stage (either waiting for, or receiving service at the different machines), referred to as the work-in-process (WIP) of the stage. The output buffer contains the finished parts of the stage, referred to as the finished good inventory of the stage.

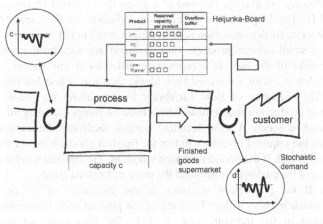

Fig. 1. Scheme of a Kanban cycle: Single stage Heijunka-controlled production

The coordination between the stages is achieved by a pull mechanism. Each material withdrawal generates a production order for the previous process with the goal of filling up the gap as soon as possible. As information medium between consumers and the previous production process in practice a kanban is used.

There is a flow of parts moving from upstream to downstream stages, and a flow of demands is going from downstream to upstream stages. Fig. 1 illustrates a single stage production unit as a segment of the whole process chain. The customers request parts in each period n according to a stochastic density function d. The kanbans attached to the requested products move to the Heijunka Board and are loaded into the corresponding hole to create a production order. For each product a certain capacity of the overall capacity is reserved according to the average demand. If the amount of kanbans for a given product is less than the reserved capacity, the kanban is put in the next empty hole for the product. Otherwise, the kanban is put in the overflow box. The overflow box contains backorders that will be produced as soon as the demand during one period is lower than the capacity. The peaks of the stochastic demand are thus cut and the production is levelled. If the production process with capacity c is unreliable, a stochastic maximum production output C_n of the stage exists. Because of machine breakdowns and other unexpected difficulties the real output may deviate from the planned output. For modelling the unreliability of the relevant process, its temporal losses of capacity are evaluated retrospectively and the probable daily distribution of working capacity c_i is calculated and is assumed to be identically each day. On the basis of this distribution the process exit buffer (supermarket) is filled with parts in a way that the following process is always supplied.

Reserved capacity which can not be filled remains empty in order to avoid producing of goods, which are not requested. The amount of consumed parts in one period is equivalent to the stochastic demand of the stage given in form of a kanban to the pervious stage.

3.2   Mathematical model formulation

A methodology for sizing the buffers (supermarkets) by using the $G|G|1$-queueing system on discrete time is developed. The number of items in the supermarket (buffer) results from the superposition of two stochastic processes: Filling up by the (limited) production with capacity C_n and emptying by selling the quantity D_n. The inventory level X_n changes in each interval with:

$$X_n = Q_n - C_n.$$

W_n, the number of kanbans (cards) on the Heijunka board is given by:

$$W_{n+1} = \max\{ (W_n + X_n) ; 0 \} \tag{1}$$

The number of items in the supermarket-buffer is the difference between the number of kanbans in the system and the last value of W_n. Equation (1) is equivalent to Lindley's equation for queuing systems in discrete time. The production capacity corresponds with the arrival vector, the demand rate with the service time vector. Methods of [15] can be used to determine the numbers of items in the supermarket and of kanbans on the Heijunka board. [15] determine waiting time and idle time distributions of a $G|G|1$-queue where the inter-arrival time A is distributed by a_i and the service time S is distributed by s_i . The inter-arrival time between two customer orders specifies the time period with decreasing workload, which corresponds to the production capacity in our model. The service time of an arriving customer order increases the workload, which is equivalent to the sold quantity, because this quantity must be reproduced.

The algorithms of [15], which are based on a Wiener-Hopf factorization using ladder height distributions, can be used to solve equation (1). Therefore, the same methods which are used to compute the distribution of the waiting time, can be used to compute the distribution of the number of waiting orders at the end of a period (allocation of the overflow box), which is equivalent to the number of kanbans on the Heijunka board. This results in a vector $\vec{w}$, where w_i is the probability that the number of waiting orders in the overflow box is exactly i. Additionally, the idle capacity distribution can be computed by the algorithm of [15], because it is equivalent to the idle time distribution.

We assume that the replenishment time is one period (EPEI = 1). Then the probability distribution $\vec{h}$ of the number of items not yet replaced in the finished goods stock, which is equivalent to the allocation of the Heijunka board at the end of a period, is given by

$$\vec{h} = \vec{d} \otimes \vec{w} \qquad\qquad (2)$$

In order to reach the desired alpha service level SLα, the base stock of finished goods and hence the number of required kanbans at the considered production stage k is the absolute value of the smallest integer k, where the relation

$$SL_\alpha \geq \sum_{i=-\infty}^{k} h_i \qquad\qquad (3)$$

is satisfied. The number of waiting production orders at the end of a period is equivalent to the amount of kanbans in the overflow box. For each kanban in the overflow box, there must be one part in the finished goods supermarket to fulfil the customer order. The allocation probability of the supermarket sj depends on the constant maximal overall inventory I (WIP cap), which is the sum of items in the supermarket and amount of kanbans on the Heijunka board. Thus the allocation of the supermarket at the end of a period is

$$s_{I-j} = h_j \qquad 0 \leq j \leq I \qquad\qquad (4)$$

If the EPEI is longer than one period, we suggest to add for each additional period the amount of one maximal request per period extra in the supermarket to guarantee the desired service level.

Further, we conclude that the capacity will be completely used, if the number of items not yet replaced in the finished goods stock, given by h, is at least the available capacity; Otherwise, exactly the capacity will be used to fill up the items in the finished goods supermarket. The production vector is denoted by q and represents the amount of required material in one period. Therefore q is the demand vector to the preceding production level. We obtain

$$q_i = c_i \cdot \sum_{j=i}^{\infty} h_j + h_i \cdot \sum_{j=i}^{c^{max}} c_j \qquad for\ c^{min} \leq i \leq c^{max} \qquad (5)$$

To explain the usage of the modelled production system and the G|G|1-queue in discrete time we give an example in the next section.

3.3   Explicatory application

The required amount of kanbans in the kanban cycle to ensure a given service level has to be calculated. At first, the data for the calculation has to be provided. The demand function can be determined easily by taking the customer orders or forecasted demands. The effective production capacity is the difference between total capacity and the sum of all breakdown times of one shift or day. Often only the mean length of a downtime of a machine (MTTR) and the mean time between two successive down times (MTBF) are used to describe the availability A of a machine (A = MTBF/(MTTR + MTBF)). But the performance of a production system is heavily depending on the higher moments of the distribution. It is Important, whether the breakdowns are frequent and short-lived, or seldom and long-lasting. First of all, the cause of the output-gap has to be determined and classified as e.g. breakdowns or changeover. The effective production capacity needed to get a discrete density function can be determined as an excerpt from the shift-book and displayed as illustrated in Fig. 2.

With the algorithms from [15] the allocation of the Heijunka Board, the overflow-box and the demand function of the process are calculated. Table 1 illustrates the performance of the calculation from data input to result. The result is the service level with a given amount of kanbans, which is taken from the record.

Fig. 2. Example of a histogram with shift-output

Table 1. Illustration of the computational steps of the model

Demand distribution		Production capacity		Number of kanbans	allocation of Overflow-Box	Heijunka-Board	Servicelevel SL	Effektive Production	
0	0%	0	0,0%	0	37,8%	0,0%	0,0%	0	0,0%
1	17%	1	0,0%	1	13,2%	6,5%	6,5%	1	6,5%
2	17%	2	0,0%	2	12,2%	8,4%	14,9%	2	8,4%
3	17%	3	30,0%	3	9,6%	10,5%	25,5%	3	32,7%
4	17%	4	40,0%	4	6,8%	12,1%	37,5%	4	33,8%
5	17%	5	30,0%	5	5,2%	13,0%	50,6%	5	19,3%
6	17%	6	0,0%	6	3,9%	14,2%	64,8%	6	0,0%
7	0%	7	0,0%	7	2,9%	8,4%	73,2%	7	0,0%
8	0%	8	0,0%	8	2,2%	6,7%	80,0%	8	0,0%
9	0%	9	0,0%	9	1,6%	5,1%	85,0%		
10	0%	10	0,0%	10	1,2%	3,7%	88,8%		
				11	0,9%	2,8%	91,6%		
				12	0,7%	2,1%	93,7%		
				13	0,5%	1,6%	95,3%		
				14	0,4%	1,2%	96,5%		
				15	0,3%	0,9%	97,3%		
				16	0,2%	0,7%	98,0%		
				17	0,2%	0,5%	98,5%		
				18	0,1%	0,4%	98,9%		
				19	0,1%	0,3%	99,1%		
				20	0,1%	0,2%	99,3%		

4   Summary and outlook

Our result is a new analytical calculating method for the required inventory levels in the buffers (supermarkets) of a manufacturing system and is applicable when unreliable machines are involved. For that purpose, the manufacturing system is treated as a multi-stage production system. The application of standard formulas for lean production systems is limited because they require reliable processes. The benefit of the new approach is that the buffers can be sized without performing laborious and time consuming simulations, which were used so far.

Uncertainty of the results may be due to inevitable limitations set by assumptions: The availability of raw material has to be assumed to be 100%, the distribution of daily demand has to be independent and identical, and the demand pattern cannot be modelled. Hopefully further research will relieve these restrictions.

References

1. Furmans, K. (2005): Models of Heijunka-levelled Kanban-Systems. In: C.T. Papadopoulos (Ed.): 5th International Conference on Analysis of Manufacturing Systems - Production and Management 2005, Zakynthos Island, Greece, pp. 243-248. Publishing Ziti, Thessaloniki, Greece, http://www.icsd.aegean.gr/aic2005/Papers/Furmans.pdf.

2. Yan, H. (1995): The optimal number of kanbans in a manufacturing system with general machine breakdowns and stochastic demands, Internat. Journal of Operations & Production Management, Vol. 15, Nr. 9, pp. 89-103.

3. Ohno, T. (1988): The Toyota Production System: beyond large scale production, Productivity Press, Portland, OR, Cambridge, Mass.

4. Hopp, W. J., Spearman, M. L.(1996): Factory Physics, Foundation of Manufacturing Management. Irwin/McGraw-Hill, Boston, Mass., 2nd edition 2000, 668 p.

5. Adams, M., Schroer, B. J., Gunter, L. (2001): Impact of process variability on lean manufacturing systems. Proceedings of the Huntsville Simulation Conference, 2001, Huntsville, AL.

6. Koch, T., Kornicki, L. (2003): Minimizing variability in manufacturing systems in the context of lean manufacturing implementation. Modern trends in manufacturing. 2nd Internat. CAMT Conference. Wrocław, Poland.

7. Liker, J. K. (2004): The Toyota way: 14 management principles from the world's greatest manufacturer. McGraw-Hill, New York. 350 p.

8. Monden. Y. (1983): Toyota Production System, practical approach to production management. Industrial Engineering and Managment Press, Institute of Industrial Engineers, Norscross, GA. USA.

9. Rother, M., Shook, J. (1999): Learning to see: Value-Stream Mapping to Create Value and Eliminate Muda, Lean Enterprise Institute (LEI), Brookline, Mass., 112 p.; ISBN: 0966784308.

10. Takeda, H. (1996): Das System der Mixed Production, flexibel, rationell, kundenorientiert. Verlag Moderne Industrie, Landsberg, Deutschland.

11. Smalley, A. (2004): Creating level pull: a lean production-system improvement guide for production-control, operations, and engineering professionals. Lean-Management-Institut (LMI), Aachen, Deutschland. ISBN: 0-9743225-0-4 (englisch); 0-9763152-4-6 (deutsch). c..110 p.

12. Miltenburg, J., Sinnamon, G. (1989): Scheduling mixed-model multi-level just-in-time production systems. Internat. Journal of Production Research 27, pp.1487-1509.

13. Lödding, H. (2004): Verfahren der Fertigungssteuerung: Grundlagen, Beschreibung, Konfiguration. Buch der VDI-Reihe, Springer, Heidelberg, Berlin. 540 p.

14. Günther, H.-O., Tempelmeier, H. (2005): Produktion und Logistik (6. Auflage; Erstauflage 1995), Springer-Lehrbuch. Springer, Heidelberg.

15. Grassmann, J. L., Jain, W. K. (1989): Numerical solutions of the waiting time distribution and idle time distribution of the arithmetic GI|G|1 queue, Operations Research 37 (1989), No 1, pp. 141-150.

A New Approach for Finite Capacity Planning in MRP Environment

Hong-bum Na[1], Hyoung-Gon Lee[1], and Jinwoo Park[1]
1 Dept. of Industrial Engeering / Automation & Systems Research Inst.
Seoul National University
San 56-1, SinRim-Dong, GwanAk-Gu, Seoul, 151-744, Korea
WWW home page: http://mailab.snu.ac.kr

Abstract. MRP (Material Requirement Planning) process generates a production plan which guarantees an exact quantity of right materials on needed time but it sometimes causes capacity problems in the shop floor because of its ignorance on capacity constraints. This paper presents a new planning method which involves the capacity planning during the MRP process. This planning method starts from generating resource-based data structure and grouping resources which can act as a bottleneck. Explosion of resources and adjustment of production schedules in accordance with the time horizon and the critical resources follow the former step.

1 Introduction

MRP (Material Requirement Planning) process is one of the key components in current manufacturing planning systems. The primary role of MRP is to generate a production plan so that we have the exact quantity of right materials at right place on time. The process of MRP is well defined and gives us exact timing information on purchasing or producing materials but it has some drawbacks. One of the most serious drawbacks would be its ignorance on capacity constraints. The MRP system performs part explosion process with fixed lead time on the assumption that resource capacity is infinite. Therefore the generated production plan may exceed the production capacity and the plan would become infeasible.

In order to solve the infinite capacity problems with regard to original MRP process, there have been many efforts for the past several decades mostly by industrial practitioners. Established studies aimed to integrate MRP and capacity planning in a closed loop planning system to make MRP more practical. In spite of these enormous efforts the problem has not been largely conquered yet, in the sense that we cannot get the solution in a reasonably short time to be of practical value. And the problem is still left to the hands of high-caliber consultants.

Please use the following format when citing this chapter:

Na, H.-b., Lee, H.-G. and Park, J., 2008, in IFIP International Federation for Information Processing, Volume 257, Lean Business Systems and Beyond, Tomasz Koch, ed.; (Boston: Springer), pp. 21–27.

In a dynamic market environment, production orders tend to include high variety of product mixes and therefore production resources on shop floor level should be shared as much as possible to increase the utilization of resources. However, it can cause serious and complicated capacity problems also. This study aims to mitigate such problem by approaching the problem from a different perspective. Proposed approach starts by building a new resource view extracted from the basic MRP information (i.e. bills of material, routing) and then use scheduling algorithms by considering the capacities of resources and taking advantage of information obtained by this new data structure.

This paper is organized as follows. Section 2 presents a literature review about solution approaches to the finite capacity MRP problem. Section 3 introduces some basic steps which organize the finite capacity MRP process. In section 4, the framework of finite capacity MRP process is presented. Section 5 summarizes the work.

2   Literature review

Studies designed to solve finite capacity MRP can be mainly divided into two types: to solve the capacity-sensitive lot sizing problem mathematically and to adjust the production plans generated by infinite capacity MRP.

Capacity-sensitive lot sizing has been focused by extensive research. With capacity-sensitive lot sizing the capacity load is taken into account in the lot size computation. An early effort to model this problem was done by Billington et al. (1983) who formulated a capacity-constrained MRP system as a mixed-integer program (MIP). They used product structure compression techniques to reduce the size of the MIP and still maintain optimality. Tadrif et al. (1993) proposed a computationally fast procedure, which they labeled as MRP-C. They started with a capacity aggregated LP formulation, which was then solved via a greedy heuristic. The limitations to their model are: (1) it does not contain lot sizing constraints, (2) has the same lead time structure as the earlier models. Nagendra et al. (2001) also began with an LP formulation with different lead time model and lot sizing rules. They designed a concurrent procedure of finite capacity planning and lot sizing called MRP progressive capacity analyzer (PCA) and it outperformed other methods used in practice according to their reports. However, this result needs to be proved under dynamic production environments since these type of algorithms tend to show nervous behavior.

It is not easy to generalize the adjustment approaches since many diverse methods are possible to solve and prevent capacity problems, e.g. moving production orders between time buckets, changing routings, etc. An early proposal, schedule-based MRP (Hastings et al. 1982) used a form of forward loading to schedule the jobs on the available capacity. This guarantees feasible start and finish dates for the production orders. Sum and Hill (1993) describe a method that not only adjusts lot sizes to minimize set-ups but also determines the start and finish times of production orders while considering capacity constraints. Their algorithm iteratively splits or combines production orders to minimize set-up and inventory cost. Tall and

Wortmann (1997) suggest that the capacity problems be resolved at the material planning stage itself through an integrated approach to MRP and finite capacity planning, but the performance of their model is not presented.

Another attempt basically distinctive from other research to solve finite capacity MRP is to suggest a unified database schema of BOM and routing (Tatsiopoulos, 1996). This paper examines the far-reaching consequences of unifying BOM and routings on the basic functions of production planning and control. Our proposed method may be viewed as one ramification of adjustment approaches.

3   Basic steps

In our approach, we divide the capacity adjustment process into three steps: 1) the structured resource formations step, 2) the resources grouping step, 3) schedule adjustment step. The structured resource step and the resource grouping step are preliminaries to involve the capacity constraints into the MRP and scheduled adjustment step is actual planning process to generate a production plan.

3.1   The structured resource formations step

The structured resource formations step is a basic step for capacity adjustment process by simplifying and integrating the production master data. In this step, the information contained in the BOM (Bills of Materials), routing and production orders are converted into a tree structured data before the part explosion process. The new data structure is called the Process oriented Inverted BOM (PI-BOM).

The PI-BOM is the main structure for implementing capacity planning. The PI-BOM contains the information about processing time of certain resources to produce corresponding parts so that the requirements to meet the customer order quantity could be calculated into a resource usage. So total orders which should be planned in the planning period converts into the total amount of using resources in this step.

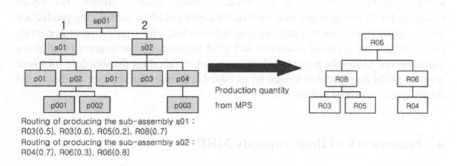

Routing of producing the sub-assembly s01 :
R03(0.5), R03(0.6), R05(0.2), R08(0.7)
Routing of producing the sub-assembly s02 :
R04(0.7), R06(0.3), R06(0.8)

Fig. 1. Converting production master data into the PI-BOM

Figure. 1 shows an example of the conversion from a standard type of production master data into the PI-BOM. The PI-BOM contains only the key information needed for shop floor scheduling and has much simpler structure than ordinary engineering or manufacturing BOM.

3.2 The resources grouping step

Some resources have a problem of capacity overload because the production resources are not evenly used in the production shop floor. These resources trigger the capacity problem which affects the whole manufacturing process. This capacity overflow leads to a failure for meeting the customer order while keeping the due date. Especially the high-mix production environment requires high level of the resource sharing and therefore the capacity overload can occur on many resources. Resources which frequently face the capacity overload problem are considered to be critical resources of whole production process.

In the resources grouping step, we gather the resources into a resource group that can act as a number of critical resources by searching for interconnections and usage frequency of the resources from historical data or analyzed result of the PI-BOM. The critical resources are the resources that may cause bottlenecks in the production sequence and bring about capacity problems. Thus, critical resources are the main target to be involved for schedule adjustment. The critical resources and PI-BOM which is mentioned on former section are the basic tools to cope with the problems of overloaded production capacities.

3.3 Schedule adjustment step

In schedule adjustment step, we trace and use the information contained in the PI-BOM. We rearrange the exploded resource requirements in accordance with the time horizon and the critical resources, and then adjust the excess capacities in the planning period. First, adjusting procedure starts with the backward scheduling, the most simple inventory reduction process. Then further adjustments are made by moving orders which contain overloaded critical resource groups. We adjust resources levels and generate new material requirement plans considering production orders, capacity constraints, and pegging information. The pegging records contain part numbers, the types of resources and most importantly, the sources of all gross requirements. Using the pegging information, we could adjust the schedule for lower level PI-BOM items, which in turn let us adjust schedules for upper-level items, and finally to the customer orders.

4   Framework of finite capacity MRP

The proposed finite capacity MRP process starts from generating PI-BOM and ends with creating the plan of material requirements. Figure.2. shows the framework of finite capacity MRP process.

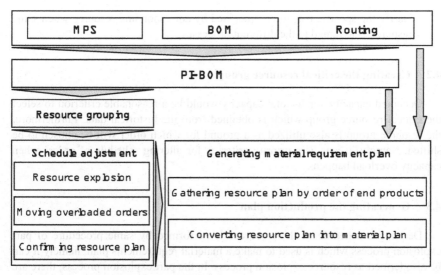

Fig. 2. The framework of finite capacity MRP

4.1 Generating the PI-BOM

To generate the PI-BOM, the information of Material BOM and Routing is essential. We can abstract the sub-assemblies and parts which build final items from the Material BOM. From the Routing information, we can determine the resource name and the processing time that are needed to produce sub-assemblies and parts. Therefore the records of PI-BOM contain the customer order (pegging information), parent resource, child resource, processing time and the level of process as main attributes. Conducting the part explosion and resource allocation at the same time, this data structure yields a feasible production plan by checking the capacity availability and adjusting the lead time when capacity overflow occurs.

The main attributes to build a finite capacity production plan are as follows:

- customer order(pegging information) : Information regarding the ownership of the order needs to be traced for the reason that the requirement plan from the same order has to be treated by group when capacity overflow occurs and scheduling adjustment follows.
- parent resource : Instead of parent item defined in Material BOM, it defines resource corresponding to the later process producing an item. This attribute is needed to examine the precedence of utilizing resources.
- child resource : Contrary to the parent resource concept, this object prescribes resource applied in the process that precedes each resource.
- processing time : It indicates the processing time that has to be processed by the given resource set. The sum of processing time determines the quantity used in specific resource for each period.
- level : It checks the locations which are occupied by current resources among the whole process for the production of end items. Also, especially, it can

clarify the specific part to be processed by corresponding resource when same resource is assigned to the different processes.

4.2   Creating the critical resource group

Occupied capacity versus total capacity would be a reasonable criterion to select the critical resource group which is obtained from the historical data. Furthermore, the resource group is also utilized as a ground for which order will be chosen to be shifted. Namely, it acts as a priority criterion for altering schedule of orders when capacity overload happens.

4.3   Generating the production plan

Deriving a schedule of the resources is performed by same procedure of part explosion process which is used to make a material requirements plan, namely it can be also termed as resource explosion process. In the part explosion process, there are 4 types of records; Gross requirements, Scheduled receipts, Projected available balance and Planned order releases. These attributes should be converted into a resource-related terms for the resource explosion procedure. The types of records for resource explosion process are as follows.

- Capacity requirements from Gross requirements – resource usage time according to the actual order quantity
- Scheduled capacity from Scheduled receipts – utilizing reserved resource in advance (previously summed for capacity computation)
- Projected allowance from Projected available balance – anticipated by available capacity for the end of the given period
- Planned usage from Planned order release – final   processing time corresponding to the actual order

Resource explosion proceeds iteratively until it produces total usage time for every lower level resource analogous to part explosion process.

The first step of adjusting schedule is a backward scheduling figuring out the resource on which the capacity overload occurs after the explosion process is conducted. For the reason that a single occurrence of schedule adjustment leads to alteration of every production schedule involving individual orders, all the orders involved in the resource with capacity overload should be traced. Furthermore, every production schedule prior to the resource tackled by capacity overload has to be moved forward.

Finally, the result of resource explosion considering the schedule adjustment is converted into requirement plan of material. This period-to-period conversion is done by deciding appropriate resource, referring to customer order and PI-BOM, is to be used for producing proper part. As a result, the same shape of time-phased requirement plan of production order is computed as the standard MRP process.

5   Conclusion

In this study, we presented more convenient planning method which considers the capacity problem. To involve the capacity issues into the MRP process, three basic steps were suggested : 1) The structured resource formations step, 2) The resources grouping step, 3) Schedule adjustment step. Records of standard MRP process were converted into a PI-BOM in the structured resource formations step. The records of the PI-BOM consist of the usage of resources and pegging information. In the resources grouping step, resources that occurs capacity problem were grouped into critical resource groups. Finally, the resources were exploded and adjusted to generate a plan of material requirements which satisfies the resource constraints.

Finite capacity MRP based on PI-BOM can improve the performance of manufacturing planning and control system based on standard MRP system. Computational burden for scheduling algorithms may be reduced by taking into consideration of the upper level requirements of production orders up to final assembly schedules of the final products. Work is continuing with implement and further refinement of procedures. Experimental results will be compared with the current MRP and capacity planning methods.

References

1. Billington, P. J., McClain, J. O. and Thomas, L. J., 1983, Mathematical programming approaches to capacity-constrained MRP systems. *Management Science*, 29, 1126-1141.

2. Hastings, Nicholas A.J., Marshall, Peter and Willis, Robert J., 1982, Schedule Based M.R.P. : An integrated Approach to Production Scheduling and Material Requirements Planning. *Journal of The Operational Research Society*, 33, 1021-1029.

3. Nagendra, P.B. and DAS, S. K., 2001, Finite capacity scheduling method for MRP with lot size restrictions. *International Journal of Production Research*, 39, 1603-1623.

4. Sum, C. C. and Hill, A. V., 1993, A new framework for manufacturing planning and control systems. *Decision Sciences*, 24, 739-760

5. Tatsiopoulos, I. P., 1996, On the unification of bills of materials and routings. *Computers in Industry*, 31, 293-304.

6. Tall, Martin and Wortmann, Johan C., 1997, Integrating MRP and finite capacity planning. *Production Planning & Control*, 8, 245-254.

7. Tardif, V., Spearman, M., Coullard, C. and Hopp, W. A., 1993, Framework for capacitated MRP. Working Paper, Northwestern University.

Preemptive Jobs Scheduling on Parallel Machines with Setup Times and Renewable Resources

Tomasz Śliwiński, Eugeniusz Toczyłowski
Warsaw University of Technology,
Institute of Control & Computation Engineering,
00-665 Warsaw, Poland

Abstract. A two-stage algorithm for scheduling preemptive jobs on parallel machines with minimum makespan criterion and requirements for limited renewable resources and existence of sequence dependent setup times is investigated. In the first stage of the algorithm a set of best elementary feasible plans is obtained through column generation. For the second stage we compare genetic algorithms for sequencing elementary plans, where various approximate criterions for calculation minimum makespan are used.

1 Introduction

Problem of scheduling jobs on parallel machines with the presence of renewable resource constraints and setup times is of considerable importance in many process industries such as chemical, pharmaceutical, food, etc.

Machines working in parallel constitute a cell where simultaneous processing of different jobs (production of different item types) is possible. Set of jobs K is to be processed by the set of heterogenous machines L working in parallel. The jobs can be divided in time and space, i.e. each job can be split and processed on many machines, it can also be interrupted at any time and later resumed on the same or different machine. The machine cannot process more then one job at the time.

Machines are not fully independent - we consider the case where there is a common renewable resource shared between the machines. Examples of such a resources are workers or tools needed for production and available in a limited number. We consider a general case, when the amount of the resource allocated for processing a job depends on that job and on the machine.

The change of the job processed on a given machine entails the setup/changeover to occur. Its duration depends on the previous and the following jobs and on the machine.

Please use the following format when citing this chapter:

Śliwiński T. and Toczylowski E., 2008, in IFIP International Federation for Information Processing, Volume 257, Lean Business Systems and Beyond, Tomasz Koch, ed.; (Boston: Springer), pp. 29–39.

The goal is to minimize the total length of the schedule (makespan) preserving all the required constraints.

2 Two-phase approach

The difficulty of the problem is related to the presence of resource constraints and setup times in a single model. The problem of scheduling jobs on a single machine with changeovers is NP-hard. Increasing the number of machines and adding common renewable resource constraints makes it even more difficult to solve. Some heuristics for such problems were presented in [1, 2, 3, 5, 6]. The approximate two-phase algorithm presented in this paper extends the structural approach proposed by Toczyłowski [7, 8].

Modern production systems are designed to minimize setup times, which then represent not more than a few percent of the total production time. This justifies the two-phase approach where in the first phase only production planning with resource availability problem is considered and changeovers are left aside for detailed scheduling performed in the second phase.

In the presented approach production planning can be seen as an asynchronous, multistage decision process, where decision horizon is divided into many elementary stages. Each of them spans a different period of time when the state of the process, i.e. assignment of jobs to machines and resource allocation, is constant. The single stage will be called elementary production plan. The special structure of the problem makes it possible to decompose it to subproblems in which resource constraints only for one elementary production plan are taken into consideration. This approach based on the Danzig-Wolf decomposition and called column generation technique greatly simplifies and accelerates the optimization process. The result of this phase is the set of elementary production plans used later as the starting point for detailed scheduling.

Unfortunately, first phase column generation algorithm that creates optimal set of elementary production plans does not take into account neither the setup times between consecutive plans nor even the detailed schedules. Moreover, the sequence of the plans is fully random with respect to the setup times. This is why the second phase is needed. There are two problems that can be formulated in this phase. One is to sequence elementary plans by minimizing the setup times/costs, and the other is to calculate the detailed schedule based on the sequenced plans. Sometimes, the two above problems are not distinguishable, which means that detailed schedules are needed during sequencing to produce reliable results. Of course this approach greatly increases the complexity of the problem, so in most cases only an approximate measure of the objective is used during sequencing whereas the detailed scheduling is performed as the final step.

3 Production planning

Let us introduce the following notation.

Indices

k – job $(k \in K)$

l – machine $(l \in L)$

β – elementary production plan $(\beta \in B)$

Inputs

p_{lk} – processing time of the entire job k on machine l

α_{lk} – amount of renewable resource allocated for job k on machine l

W – renewable resource available

Decision variables

y_β – duration of β

v_{lk}^β – binary variable equal 1 if and only if job k is processed on machine l in elementary production plan β

Set of elementary production plans minimizing the makespan can be obtained by solving the following problem:

$$\min \sum_{\beta \in B} y_\beta \tag{1}$$

$$\sum_{\beta \in B} \left(\sum_{l \in L} \frac{1}{p_{lk}} v_{lk}^\beta \right) y_\beta = 1, \quad k \in K \tag{2}$$

$$\sum_{k \in K} v_{lk}^\beta \leq 1, \quad l \in L, \beta \in B \tag{3}$$

$$\sum_{l \in L} \sum_{k \in K} \alpha_{lk} v_{lk}^\beta \leq W, \quad \beta \in B \tag{4}$$

$$v_{lk}^\beta \in \{0, 1\}, \quad l \in L, k \in K, \beta \in B \tag{5}$$

$$y_\beta \geq 0, \quad \beta \in B \tag{6}$$

Constraints (2) ensure, that each job will be completed. Constraints (3) and (4) apply to only one elementary plan. First of them prevent processing more than one task on a single processor. Second, ensure that the renewable resource constraints are not violated.

The problem (1)–(6) is a difficult quadratic programming problem with number of variables growing exponentially with its size. Its structure, however, makes it possible to solve it effectively by applying Danzig-Wolfe decomposition and thus the column generation method. This kind of decomposition can be used due to the existence of two groups of the constraints. First group (2) binds all the variables y_β present in the objective function. Second group (3)–(4) applies to only one column of the constraints matrix (2).

3.1 Master problem

Applying Danzig-Wolfe decomposition to problem (1)–(6) one gets the following master problem:

$$\min \sum_{\beta \in B} y_\beta \tag{7}$$

$$s.t. \sum_{\beta \in B} (\sum_{l \in L} \frac{1}{p_{lk}} v_{lk}^{\beta}) y_{\beta} = 1, \quad k \in K \tag{8}$$

$$y_{\beta} \geq 0, \quad \beta \in B \tag{9}$$

One should notice, that in contrary to the original problem, v_{lk}^{β} are not variables but constant parameters of linear constraints (8). Constraints matrix must include all the columns corresponding to all feasible combinations of these parameters, thus, the number of variables y_{β} can be enormous. However, not all columns have to be hold in the computer memory, instead, they can be handled implicitly with the column generation scheme. We only need to identify the best column during the pricing and to generate selected column for pivoting.

3.2   Pricing problem

New column generated during the pricing problem should minimize the reduced cost of the corresponding variable y_{β}. For the problem (7)–(9) the reduced cost is given by the formula

$$y_{0\beta} = 1 - \sum_{k \in K} (\sum_{l \in L} \frac{1}{p_{lk}} v_{lk}^{\beta}) \pi_k = 1 - \sum_{k \in K} \sum_{l \in L} (\frac{\pi_k}{p_{lk}}) v_{lk}^{\beta},$$

where π is a vector of dual variables of the current basic solution corresponding to constraints (8). The column generated during pricing defines assignment of jobs to machines and thus one elementary production plan. Feasibility of that plan can be ensured by additional constraints

$$\sum_{k \in K} v_{lk}^{\beta} \leq 1, \quad l \in L \tag{11}$$

$$\sum_{l \in L} \sum_{k \in K} \alpha_{lk} v_{lk}^{\beta} \leq W \tag{12}$$

$$v_{lk}^{\beta} \in \{0,1\}, \quad l \in L, k \in K \tag{13}$$

The pricing problem can be extended with any suitable constraints that apply to single elementary plan, for example, one can define maximum number of machines (L_{max}) that can process given job $\sum_{l \in L} v_{lk}^{\beta} \leq L_{max}$

4   Detailed scheduling

Detailed scheduling can be seen as two overlapping problems. One is sequencing of elementary production plans and the other is detailed scheduling based on the given sequence. In our work we decided to separate sequencing and detailed scheduling by applying approximate sequence quality measures during sequencing. In a perfect case optimal sequence in the sense of the applied measure should result in the optimal final schedule. Unfortunately, there is no simple way of constructing a measure, that ensures optimal final detailed schedule and is computationally efficient. That is why we decided to apply approximate sequence quality measures resulting in reasonable good final schedules.

For the given sequence of elementary production plans the quality measure can be evaluated with one of the three methods differing in computational effort: (i) total changeover time, (ii) critical path method, and (iii) critical path method with job reallocation. Measures (ii) and (iii) can be used to determine relatively accurate final schedules.

Total changeover time. Processing a job on a single machine in one elementary production plan will be later called *operation*. In the system with one processor finding the optimal sequence of elementary plans corresponds to minimizing the total changeover time. But in general, in the systems with multiple parallel machines the shortest total changeover time doesn't guarantee the best detailed schedule. The reason for that is the need for full time access to the common resource and the resulting synchronization between schedules on different machines and in different elementary plans.

The experiments showed the total changeover time can be considered as a very good quality measure of the elementary plans sequence. Computational efficiency is its most important property.

Critical path method. Hindi and Toczyłowski [4] developed an approach where detailed schedule for a given sequence of elementary plans can be found using critical path method. The idea is to build a task graph taking into account precedence relationships between operations and changeovers. The task graph is constructed in a way that prevents overlapping of the neighboring elementary plans which would result in the violation of the resource constraint. Its structure is defined by precedence relations for all operations according to the sequence of the elementary plans they belong to. The simplest way of establishing a consistent and sufficient set of precedence relationships is to consider as followers for each operation the set of operations, one for each machine, that follow it soonest.

Precedence relations for sample sequence of elementary plans are shown in Fig.1. If one associates the processing times with the nodes and changeover times with the horizontal edges, the resulting graph is a potential task graph. Hence, the minimum makespan (critical path) and the earliest starting times of each operation can be easily determined by finding the longest path.

Critical path method can be used as an approximate quality measure for sequencing. It is more accurate then total changeover time and still very effective computationally. The major drawback of this method is poor density of the resulting schedule – machines have to wait for all operations of the previous elementary plan to complete. Toczyłowski [9] proposed significant improvement to this method by allowing shifting of operations between elementary plans.

Critical path method with job reallocation. In this approach we are allowed to shift small portions of the job between elementary plans the given job was assigned to, thus reducing idle time of the processors. An efficient way to achieve this is to construct an LP model corresponding to the task graph with variable duration of operations. Unfortunately, this approach doesn't take into account the possibility of removing empty operations, i.e. operations with resulting duration of 0. In such a case, an approximate approach is suggested. All empty operations together with corresponding changeovers are removed and the new LP model is constructed. This procedure is repeated as long as one can find at least one empty operation in the results of the LP model. Let us introduce the following notation:

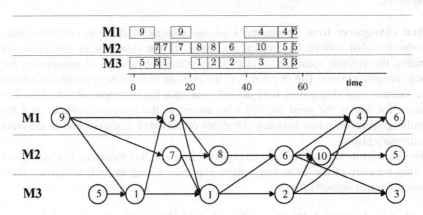

Fig. 1. Sequence of elementary production plans and the corresponding precedence graph

O — set of all operations if the precedence graph ($n \in O$)
O^k — set of all operations job k consists of
l_n — machine where the operation n is processed
k_n — job the operation n belongs to
p_n — processing time of the whole job k_n on machine l_n ($p_n = p_{l_n k_n}$)
x_n — portion of job k_n corresponding to operation n
s_n — moment when the operation n starts
e_n — moment when the operation n ends
F^n — the set of followers of n in the precedence graph
f^n — direct follower of operation n on the same machine
B — set of operations without followers
c_{nm} — changeover time between two consecutive operations n and m on the same machine

Now we can formulate LP problem corresponding to the critical path method with job reallocation.

$$\min T \tag{14}$$
$$e_n = s_n + x_n p_n, \quad n \in O \tag{15}$$
$$e_n \leq s_m, \quad n \in O, m \in F^n \tag{16}$$
$$e_n \leq c_{nf^n} + s_{f^n}, \quad n \notin B \tag{17}$$
$$e_n \leq T, \quad n \in B \tag{18}$$
$$\sum_{n \in O^k} x_n = 1, \quad k \in K \tag{19}$$
$$0 \leq x_n \leq 1, \quad n \in O \tag{20}$$

The objective (14) expresses the makespan. Constraints (15) and (16) ensure correct precedence relations between operations in the consecutive elementary plans. (17) inserts changeovers to the schedule and (19) ensures that each job in the resulting schedule will be completed.

5 Sequencing of elementary production plans

The problem of sequencing elementary production plans is of permutational nature. For each sequence one can compute some quality measure. Finding optimal sequence equals finding permutation minimizing this measure.

In our work we decided to use genetic algorithm as a basic approach to the elementary plans sequencing problem. The major drawback of this method is the need for a large number of objective computations during the optimization process. As the result, genetic algorithms are best suited for applications where the objective value can be obtained relatively easy. We also decided to use this approach because genetic algorithms do not need special knowledge about the problem, what in this case is of great importance. Simpler problem of scheduling jobs on a single machine with total changeover time as the quality measure can be modeled as the traveling salesman problem. However, when critical path method with or without job reallocation is used as the quality measure, the problem considered here lays far beyond the TSP problem.

Basic scheme of the genetic algorithm applied in our experiments is following. First, a set of the random feasible solutions (sequences) is generated. Then they are evaluated with one of the quality measures. Basing on the resulting values, some of the solutions are selected for mutation and crossover. Changed or totally new solutions are evaluated again and the procedure repeats.

An example of sequencing and detailed scheduling is shown in Figure 2. For the production plan from Figure 1 the optimal sequence of elementary plans was computed using the genetic algorithm. The sequence is optimal (suboptimal) according to the final detailed schedule. That means the detailed schedule had to be computed for all sequences that were constructed by the genetic algorithm. The optimal sequence is shown in Fig. 2a. The detailed schedule for the given sequence computed using the critical path method is shown in Fig. 2b. The final detailed schedule computed using the critical path method with job reallocation is shown in Fig. 2c.

6 Computational experiments

Computational experiments were carried out for the first and for the second phase of the presented algorithm. All tests were based on the randomly generated problems. The generation procedure worked as follows. First, processing times p_{lk} and required resources α_{lk} were generated as random numbers uniformly distributed in the intervals, respectively, [10, 30] and [6, 10]. Next, the amount of the common renewable resource was determined in such a way that on average only 75% of machines could operate. For problems where there are fewer jobs than machines, this resource constraint was set to the level, where only 75% of jobs were processed at the same time. Finally, for each machine – previous job – following job combination changeover times were generated as random numbers uniformly distributed in the interval [1.2, 2.0], which represent 6 to 10 percent of the average processing time p_{lk}. All computations were performed on a PC with the Pentium 1.7 GHz, employing the CPLEX 9.1 package.

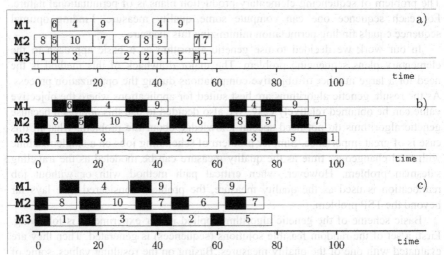

Fig. 2. The sequence minimizing critical path with job reallocation: a) the sequence, b) detailed schedule for the given sequence computed using critical path method, c) detailed schedule computed using critical path method with job reallocation

A series of tests were performed to evaluate the computational efficiency of the first phase. We tested solution times for different numbers of jobs and machines and different levels of common resource available.

The results presented in Tab. 1 are the average times for 10 random problems with freely available common resource. In Tab. 2 are shown results for problems with active common resource constraint. The index states for the number of tests (among 10) for which the timeout of 200 seconds occurred.

We also performed computational tests for the second phase of the algorithm. The purpose of the experiments was to compare sequencing algorithm using two approximate quality measures (total changeover time and critical path method) and one exact quality measure (critical path method with job reallocation). The resulting values are the average for 10 random problems with 10 machines, 40 jobs and active common resource constraint. We used following parameters for the genetic algorithm: mutation probability 0.06, crossover probability 0.5, population size 50.

Table 1. Solution times in the first phase for problems with freely available common resource

number of machines	number of jobs			
	10	20	30	40
10	0.0	0.2	0.3	0.6
20	0.0	0.3	0.8	1.5
30	0.0	0.4	0.7	2.1
40	0.1	0.4	0.7	2.7

Table 2. Solution times in the first phase for problems with restricted common resource

number of machines	number of jobs			
	10	20	30	40
10	0.2	1.6	2.2	5.1
20	0.8	5.3	8.6	17.0
30	1.0	9.7	20.2	41.3
40	0.8	^{9}82.3	53.5	^{2}61.7

In the first experiment the convergence of the sequencing algorithm was tested. The results presented in Fig. 3 were determined as if the sequencing algorithm stopped after a given number of seconds and for the best sequence found so far final detailed schedule was computed using critical path method with job reallocation. This explains why plots corresponding to approximate measures are not monotonic.

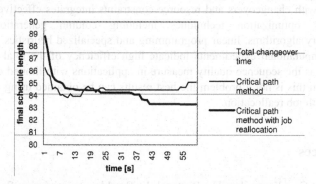

Fig. 3. Convergence of the sequencing algorithm in time for different sequence quality measures

In the second experiment the convergence of the sequencing algorithm was tested as a function of the number of objective computations. The tests were carried out up to 5000 objective computations. The test problems are exactly the same as in the previous experiment. The results are shown in Fig. 4.

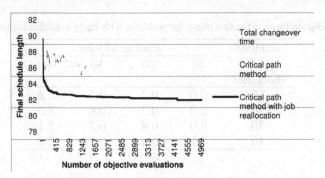

Fig. 4. Convergence of the sequencing algorithm as the function of objective computations for different sequence quality measures

One can notice the algorithm employing the exact quality measure, i.e. critical path method with job reallocation, performed much better than algorithms with approximate quality measures. This was achieved, however, in the expense of the computing time – the algorithm with the approximate quality measure ended after a few seconds while the algorithm with the exact measure needed over half an hour to complete.

7 Concluding remarks

Presented here structural algorithm for preemptive scheduling of jobs on parallel machines with changeovers and resource constraints integrates effectively different elementary optimization techniques including column generation method, evolutionary algorithms, linear programming and specialized heuristics. The results of the computational experiments indicate high efficiency of the total changeover time used as the sequence quality measure in applications with limited computation time. When this is not a problem the best results can be obtained using critical path method with job reallocation.

References

1. Dobson G., Karmarkar U., Rummel J.: Batching to minimize flow times on parallel heterogeneous machines. Mgmt Sci. 35 (1989) 607-613.

2. Figielska E.: Preemptive scheduling with changeovers: using column generation technique and genetic algorithm. Computers & Industrial Engineering 37 (1999) 81-84.

3. Figielska E., Toczyłowski E.: Algorytm szeregowania podzielnych operacji na równoległych procesorach przy ograniczeniach zasobów zużywalnych

i odnawialnych. Optymalizacja w zagadnieniach kombinatorycznych, Wyd. WSM (1997) 18-31.

4. Hindi K. S., Toczyłowski E.: Detailed Scheduling of Batch Production in a Cell with Parallel Facilities and Common Renewable Resources. Computers and Industrial Engineering 28 (1995) 839-850.

5. Oliff M.D.: Disaggregate planning for parallel processors. IIE Trans 19 (1987) 215-219.

6. So K.: Some heuristics for scheduling jobs on parallel machines with setups. Mgmt Sci. 36 (1990) 467-475.

7. Toczyłowski E.: Niektóre metody strukturalne optymalizacji do sterowania w dyskretnych systemach wytwarzania. WNT (1989).

8. Toczyłowski E.: Algorithms for preemptive scheduling of independent tasks in the presence of general renewable and consumable resources. Zeszyty Nauk. AGH, Automatyka 59 (1991) 163-172.

9. Toczyłowski E.: Preemptive Scheduling of independent Tasks in the Presence of Setup Times and Renewable Resources. 17th International Symposium on Mathematical Programming ISMP'2000, 7-11 August 2000, Atlanta, USA.

Dynamic Production Management Architecture Considering Preparative Operation

Akira Tsumaya[1], Minoru Koike[2], Hidefumi Wakamatsu[1], Eiji Arai[1]
1   Osaka University, Graduate School of Engineering,
Yamadaoka 2-1, Suita, Osaka 565-0871, Japan,
WWW homepage: http://www6.mapse.eng.osaka-u.ac.jp/index-eng.html
2   Collage of Industrial Technology,
Nishi-konyo 1-27-1, Amagasaki, Hyogo 661-0047, Japan,

Abstract. Automated factories have become complicated and need higher flexibility to satisfy various requirements today. In this environment, many concepts of autonomous & distributed production systems have been proposed for a dynamic production management recently. In this paper, the preparative operations are discussed, that is focused on the decision of production process order with consideration of set-up time, and a dynamic production management architecture considering such preparative operations is proposed. First, the decision rule of the processing order by using production process information and real-time production system information is introduced. Then, we also pay attention to the combination and timing of processing sequences on both machining cells and parts in order to propose the timing rule and the set-up time rule referring to the real status of that are applied to be dynamic scheduling. Finally, real-time production-scheduling system using the proposed rules is developed, applied to a case study, and it is shown that the proposed system has the feasibility of the flexible correspondence against the disturbance.

1   Introduction

It is required for the production system to recognize a variety of turbulences, to make the action plan, and to modify the production plan promptly. It is difficult from both cost and time viewpoint to manage the whole system intensively in today's enlarged and complicated production systems. Therefore, the concept of autonomous & distributed production systems has been proposed in recent years. Numerous intelligent and autonomous production systems, which are focused on product facilities and constructed intelligent system using network structure, have been proposed so far. By using the network system, each production facility can

Please use the following format when citing this chapter:

Tsumaya, A., Koike, M., Wakamatsu, H. and Arai, E., 2008, in IFIP International Federation for Information Processing, Volume 257, Lean Business Systems and Beyond, Tomasz Koch, ed.; (Boston: Springer), pp. 41–48.

understand production status and can respond to the status. These methods are suitable to adopt an automated lot production factory [1-6]. However, most of such production systems work under the assumption that the production process in the factory is restricted to the result of process planning done beforehand while the distributed production system composed of some/many autonomous flexible machine cells does not need to fix the process beforehand. We think that higher flexibility can be realized with some degree of freedom in the order of production process. Integrated architecture that unites the process planning and production scheduling system is needed there.

On the other hand, in the lot production system, the production lot size is an important factor for productivity. A size is becoming smaller in recent years because a small lot size production is suitable in order to reduce the work-in-process inventory and to realize the higher flexibility. However, a small lot size has the disadvantage that the total set-up time is increased, and reducing set-up time is an important issue for introducing the small lot size. To solve this problem, in the process-planning phase, a lot based on group technology are widely introduced with the aim of reducing set-up time. However on production phase contains with various disturbances, it is still remained problem.

In this paper, a dynamic production management architecture considering preparative operations is proposed. We paid attention to two kinds of the preparative operations, that is focused on the decision of production process order and consideration of set-up time.

2   Dynamic decision method of processing order

The discrete production processes are usually expressed by arrow diagram. Generally, the only one optimum process that is not contradicted to arrow diagram is decided in the process-planning phase, and the master production schedule is constructed by using the decided process. However, the appropriate processing order may be possible depending on the real-time situation of the production system such as delay of one of a process or trouble of a machining cell. So, we assume that dynamic selection of appropriate processing order is useful for shortening the production tact time, and we also introduce the decision method of the processing order by using production process information and real-time production system information.

It is assumed here that the best one is selected as a dispatching rule from all candidates those can be done as next process. That is, the process that minimizes the following P_{ij} is selected.

$$P_{ij} = \left(V_i/a_{ij} + W_{ij}\right)/\left(\overline{V_j}/\overline{a_j} + \overline{W_j}\right)$$

Here a_{ij} is a processing ability for job j on machining cell i. V_j is a volume of job j. W_{ij} is a sum of the waiting and set-up time of job j on machining cell i. $\overline{a_j}$ is a mean value of processing ability for job j. $\overline{V_j}$ is a mean volume of job j. $\overline{W_j}$ is mean value of waiting and set-up time of job j. This expression formula can be considered to be a relative SPT (Shortest Processing Time First) rule.

3   Consideration of set-up time

In this section, we focused on the combination and timing of processing sequences referring to the real status of that is applied to the dynamic scheduling. For example, if the machining cell processes the same processing continuously, there are no need to change the neither machining tools nor jigs, so the tool exchange time is not needed. The on-line set-up that stops machine is classified into two types. One is the on-line set-up time without part (WOP set-up time) that can be done only with information of next processing part/product such as setting tool, setting jig, etc. The other is the on-line set-up that needs together with part (WP set-up) under the condition of finishing transportation process in order to deliver the part/product such as setting part/product, the positioning, etc. We further classified WOP set-up into three; the process depend on shapes of the part/product, the process depend on processing type of the part/product, and the process that cannot be skipped. WP set-up is also further classified according to at what condition the operation can be omitted. Table 1 shows such classification of the set-up operation.

Table 1. Classification of set-up time

Type of on-line set-up time	Sub categories of set-up operation	Set-up operation
On-line set-up without part/product (WOP set-up)	Depends on figure type	Setting jig(s), Remove Jig(s)
	Depends on processing type	Setting tool, Remove tool
	Can not skipped operation	Cleaning
On-line set-up with part/product (WP set-up)	Two continued processes are done by same machining cell with no change for attach	Setting part/product, Remove part/product
	Can not skipped operation	Position Setting

Then, we proposed timing rule and set-up time rule in selection and allocation, and adopted these classified set-up time to estimate the total processing time including the set-up time on each machine. If the shape type or the processing type of the continuous two processes on one machine is the same, WOP set-up time that depends on such type is skipped. WP type set-up can execute under satisfying following two conditions.

-       Processing part/product has already delivered to the machine.
-       WOP type set-up has been already finished.

Therefore, WP type set-up start time becomes later than transportation finishing time and WOP set-up finishing time. Figure 1 is an example of allocation process of the next process. On this case, machine 3, which is the fastest process finishing time of the next process, is selected to allocate as the next process.

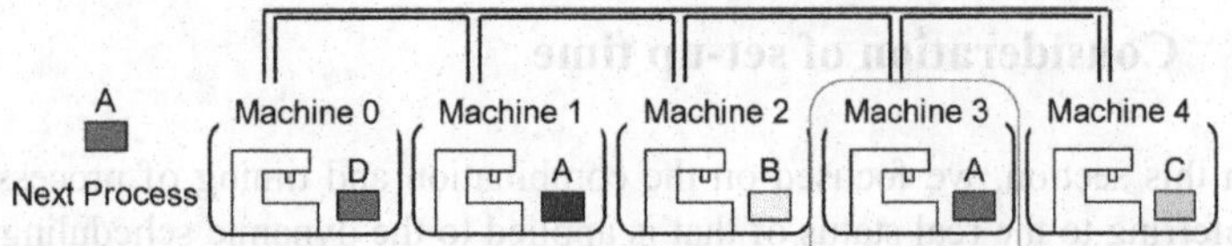

	A Next Process	Machine 0	Machine 1	Machine 2	Machine 3	Machine 4
		D	A	B	A	C
Process finishing time		10:00	10:15	10:00	10:05	10:00
Transportation time		0min.	9min.	12min.	15min.	18min.
Transportation finishing time		10:00	10:09	10:12	10:15	10:18
WOP set-up time (figure)		0min.	6min.	8min.	0min.	8min.
WOP set-up time (processing)		6min.	0min.	5min.	0min.	6min.
WOP set-up time (need)		3min.	2min.	2min.	3min.	3min.
WOP set-up finishing time		10:09	10:23	10:25	10:08	10:17
WP set-up start time		10:09	10:23	10:25	10:15	10:18
WP set-up time (setting part)		0min.	6min.	7min.	6min.	6min.
WP set-up time (need)		3min.	3min.	2min.	2min.	2min.
Processing time		35min.	30min.	25min.	20min.	20min.
Process finishing time		10:47	11:02	10:58	10:43	10:46

Fig. 1. A decision example of allocation process

4   Concept of parts & packets unification system

Recognizing the real-time status of both machining cells and parts/products are required for realizing the proposed approach. RFID technology is recently widely utilized and available from a practical viewpoint of cost, tip size and memory size Thus, we introduced parts &packets unification system architecture [7, 8] here. The concept of a dynamic production scheduling system using parts and packets unified architecture is shown in Fig. 2. The read/write type IC tag is attached in the parts, and ID number and the present status are written in it. The IC tag attached on a unit transmits the real-time information of ID number, current position, and status through the network system whenever it passes through the gate provided in the factory.

The production planning system, by comparing with real-time information on each part with the master schedule, can detect the gap between the master schedule and the actual state. According to the gap, re-scheduling is performed.

Using this kind of architecture, the system can grasp real-time status of all facilities and parts/products.

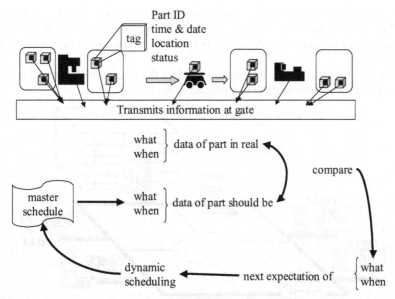

Fig. 2. The concept of dynamic production scheduling system using parts & packets unified architecture

5 Dynamic production scheduling system and application

In this section, we explain a pilot system of production process in a factory, and show some results of case studies. The components of the system are shown in Fig. 3. This virtual factory example has following preconditions. Facilities of this factory are five machining cells, two AGVs, and storage. The initial value of machining ability on each machining cell is set up previously. Each part/product carried out from storage and made several jobs to be the complete product. It is assumed that the conveyance capability of two AGV is equal, and it moves in the orbit with one way.

The scheduling system decides the allocation of the part to the cell according to the following procedures.

(1) A previous notice of the processing end time is notified from the processing cell to the scheduler at defined time before the finish processing.
(2) When the scheduler receives the notice, it sends part/product, which is almost finished on current job, a requirement of sending its next job information.
(3) Part/ product sends required information to the scheduler.
(4) The scheduler sends each processing cells the part/product 's shape and next processing type, and required calculation result of the set-up time and the processing time if the cell undertake the job. The scheduler also sends each AGV the part/product 's current position and finishing time of current process, and required calculation result of transportation finishing time on each machining cells.

(5) Each machining cells sends required information to the scheduler; those are WOP set-up time, WP set-up time, and processing time. Each AGV sends required information, which are transportation-finishing time to each cells, to the scheduler.

(6) The scheduler uses these information to adopt the relative SPT scheduling rule, and decides allocation of the part/product to the cell.

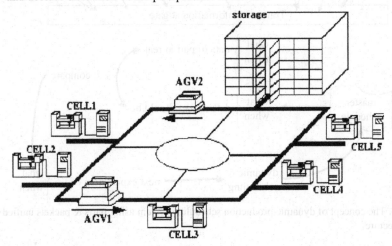

Fig. 3. The component of the system in a factory

Some virtual simulation was performed using the system. First, we compare proposed set-up time with constant set-up time. The Gantt chart of the simulation is shown in Fig. 4. As these results, the system introducing the proposed set-up time rules worked effectively to shorten the total production time. We also compare proposed dispatching rule with normal SPT dispatching rule. Figure 5 shows the Gantt chart of each simulation. These results suggest proposed dispatching rule is useful under each lot's processing status is recognized. Furthermore, we found the proposed dispatching rule becoming the most effective under the environment where the general-purpose machine tool exists together to a special purpose machine tool.

6   Conclusion

A real-time production scheduling architecture considering preparative operations is proposed. Decision method of production process order by using process order information and real-time production system information is introduced. Moreover, set-up time is analyzed in detail considering with the processing order for each machining cell, and proposed sequence timing and set-up time rules. Using the proposed rules, a pilot system is developed and applied to the case study. Although proposed production management architecture can realize local optimization of production schedule, not total optimization, the system worked effectively to shorten the total production time. The results also shows the proposed system has the feasibility of the flexible correspondence against the disturbances.

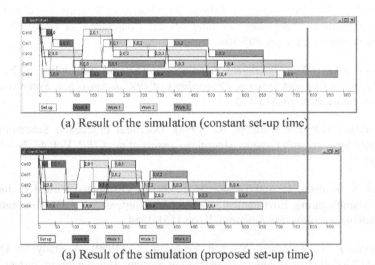

(a) Result of the simulation (constant set-up time)

(a) Result of the simulation (proposed set-up time)

Fig. 4. The Gantt chart of the simulation (considering set-up time)

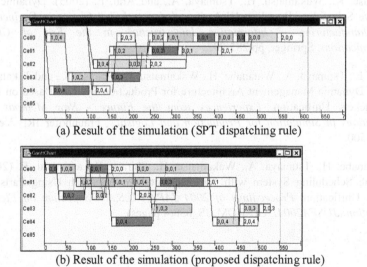

(a) Result of the simulation (SPT dispatching rule)

(b) Result of the simulation (proposed dispatching rule)

Fig. 5. The Gantt chart of the simulation (considering dispatching rule)

48   Akira Tsumaya, Minoru Koike, Hidefumi Wakamatsu, Eiji Arai

References

1. Ueda, K. (1992). An Approach to Bionic Manufacturing Systems Based on DNA-Type Information, *Proceedings of International Conference on Object-Oriented Manufacturing Systems*, pp. 305-308.

2. Ranky, P.G. (1992). Intelligent Planning and Dynamic Scheduling of Flexible Manufacturing Cell and Systems, *Proceedings of 1992 Japan-U.S.A. Symposium on Flexible Automation*, pp. 415-422.

3. Wiendahl, H.P. and Garlichs, R. (1994). Decentral Production Scheduling of Assembly Systems with Genetic Algorithm, *Annals of the CIRP*, Vol. 43, No. 1, pp. 389-396.

4. Fujii. S., Kaihara. T., and Tanaka, M. (1999). A Distributed Virtual Factory in Agile Manufacturing Environment, *Proc. 15th Conference of the International Foundation for Production Research*, II, pp.1551-1554.

5. Sugimura, N., Tanimizu, Y., and Yoshioka, T. (1999). A Study on Object Oriented Modeling of Holonic Manufacturing System, *Manufacturing System*, Vol. 27, No. 3, pp. 253-258.

6. Shirase, K., Wakamatsu, H., Tsumaya, A., and Arai, E. (2005). Dynamic Co-operative Scheduling Based on HLA, *Knowledge and Skill Chains in Engineering and Manufacturing – Information Infrastructure in the Era of Global Communications*, Springer, pp.285-292.

7. Arai, E., Tsumaya, A., Watanabe, H., Wakamatsu, H., Shirase, K., and Takata, M. (2004). Dynamic Management Architecture for Production Systems Based on Parts and Packets Unification, *Experiences from the Future - New Methods and Applications in Simulation for Production and Logistics*, Fraunhofer IRB Verlag, pp.491-500.

8. Watanabe, H., Tsumaya, A., Wakamatsu, H., Shirase, K., and Arai, E. (2004). Dynamic Scheduling System with Variable Lot Size Approach Using Parts and Packets Unification, *Proceedings of 2004 JAPAN-U.S.A. Symposium on Flexible Automation (JUSFA2004)*, CD-ROM, JS_038(4 pages).

Planning and Balancing of Disassembly Systems

Gert Zülch and Rainer Schwarz
ifab-Institute of Human and Industrial Engineering, University of Karlsruhe
Kaiserstrasse 12, D-76131 Karlsruhe, Germany,
WWW homepage: http://www.ifab.uni-karlsruhe.de

Abstract. Legislative changes triggered by the exhaustion of natural resources have increased the importance of disassembly as a form of recycling. The implementation of computer-supported procedures in recycling has become indispensable. Time management data was used to develop a tool for the economic planning of disassembly processes, allowing for load balancing of disassembly systems with division of work.

1 Motivation for Disassembly Planning

The European Union has defined binding guidelines for the prevention and disposal of waste, which must be implemented by the member states into national legislation within a limited period of time. As a result, several new laws have been passed in Germany in the last few years requiring manufacturers and importers to take back the devices they produce at the end of their lifecycle and to re-integrate them into the material cycle.

The expected increase in the return of used products will force manufacturers to optimize the disassembly of used products in order to re-integrate the involved raw materials into the production cycle as secondary raw materials or secondary products or to dispose of materials in an appropriate manner [1]. When recycling used products the objective is always to disassemble the reusable parts without damaging them. Thus, new approaches are necessary to solve impending organizational problems and a demand for new tools is at hand. In addition to their applications in the field of disassembly, these tools can also be beneficial in the service area, especially for the maintenance of products.

The proportion of manual and (semi-)automated disassembly systems is also of substantial importance in the service area for the maintenance of products [2, 3]. In the future, the disassembly of used products will take on an even more industrial

Please use the following format when citing this chapter:

Zülch, G. and Schwarz R., 2008, in IFIP International Federation for Information Processing, Volume 257, Lean Business Systems and Beyond, Tomasz Koch, ed.; (Boston: Springer), pp. 49–56.

character, whereby the economical design and control of disassembly processes will be of primary importance.

2 Disassembly Planning Procedure with Load Balancing

2.1 Tasks of Disassembly Planning

The objective of disassembly planning is to create an organizational, staff and - techniques foundation for the ergonomic and economic separation of used products into their constituent parts. In addition to defining the disassembly tasks, the planning of a disassembly system comprises creating a suitable sequence and materials plan. This includes the structuring of used products, the creation of disassembly work plans, the definition of the separation procedures, the disassembly depth, the number of needed workplaces, the selection of equipment, the flow of materials system and many more(cf. [4], pp. 245-253).

Disassembly is by no means a mere reversal of the assembly. In contrast to assembly, in which e.g. all parts are defined geometrically and are in the same qualitative state, disassembly must also take into consideration the fact that each used product has been subject to a diversity of influences throughout its lifecycle (corrosion, wear, deformation etc.) and is thus in a different state when it comes to recycling. Therefore, stochastic influences, which make planned disassembly sequences unpredictable, must be taken into account during the planning of disassembly processes (e.g. the selection of separation procedures) and the determination of disassembly operation times [1]. This lends great significance to time management evaluations (cf. [5], pp. 147-156].

2.2 Scope of Investigations

In the field of recycling, the application of computer-supported procedures has become an indispensable necessity. A computer-aided procedure supporting the planning of disassembly systems has been developed at the ifab-Institute of Human and Industrial Engineering at the University of Karlsruhe within the context of a project supported by the German Research Association (DFG - Deutsche Forschungsgemeinschaft).

The developed software tool TANJA (German abbreviation for "Disassembly Planning with Object-oriented Load Balancing") serves to support the planning of economically feasible disassembly processes while also taking the given organizational, personnel and technical conditions into account.

During the development of the procedure, analyses and data gathering (concerning work organization, equipment, applied separation procedures, time data capturing etc.) were carried out in several disassembly enterprises. Time building blocks were created using registered data and MTM standard data for manual disassembly operations (e.g. remove screw connection, apply separation sander etc.) in order to determine the disassembly operation times. The workers' specific, technical disassembly knowledge (work process knowledge) was documented through questioning (interviews) and video analyses and was implemented in a help system along with examples of good practice.

2.3 Characteristics of the Software Tool TANJA

The software tool TANJA makes it possible to digitally represent operations and resources in a disassembly system, to develop various planning solutions and to compare these to each other. The primary objective during the development of this computer-supported planning tool was to provide disassembly enterprises with a practical assistance for the planning of disassembly systems. The procedure allows the user:

- to structure disassembly processes through disassembly precedence diagrams,
- to assign individual disassembly operations to decoupled work systems,
- to balance the load of the disassembly system based on a pre-determined cycle time or a given number of disassembly stations or workers,
- to carry out an ergonomic assessment of the physical stress to the workers resulting from manual activities,
- to digitally represent the planned disassembly system as well as
- to compare the developed planning solutions based on assessment criteria selected by the user and supported by the software tool.

2.4 Structural Design of TANJA

The planning procedure TANJA was conceived for PC implementation. *Microsoft Windows XP* was chosen as the operating system and the object-oriented programming language *Microsoft Visual Basic.net* was selected as the development environment. This computer platform allows for a broad spectrum of implementation in industrial disassembly systems. In order to ensure easy use and acceptance, the procedure's functionalities were modelled after prevalent *Microsoft Office* Software packages (e.g. cut & copy, drag & drop, menu structure design etc.).

In TANJA time building blocks developed according to MTM are used for the time management analysis of disassembly operations. For this, data material from earlier research work was taken and supplemented with data collected in disassembly enterprises [6, 7, and 8]. These time building blocks were then used to specify operation times for individual disassembly operations and to allocate them to individual work stations in disassembly systems with division of labour while also taking disassembly-specific influencing factors (corrosion, separation procedures etc.) into account.

The load balancing to be carried out is dependent upon a predetermined cycle time or the number of work stations defined or available in the disassembly workshop. A further module was developed for the description of workplaces, the selection of equipment, buffers, conveyors, collection bins for disassembled parts etc. Further modules for the description of workplaces, the execution of worker stress analyses as well as a help system with examples of good practice were also implemented in TANJA.

In order to plan a disassembly system, the individual disassembly tasks should be illustrated in an appropriate manner. Modelling, in particular as disassembly precedence diagrams, is particularly well suited for designing possible disassembly operations. In disassembly precedence diagrams nodes and arcs are used to describe the sequence restrictions between the individual disassembly operations in a sort of network. The nodes contain detailed descriptions of the disassembly operations, whereas the arcs define the predecessor-successor relationships between the individual disassembly operations.

With regards to the disassembly of used products, in particular the availability of product data is a specific problem. From experience, disassembly enterprises rarely possess drawings or CAD-data with detailed information, regarding e.g. components, the type of connections between the individual components or about the materials used. The determination of the individual disassembly operations is thus usually carried out through test disassembly runs.

The main steps in the structural planning of a disassembly system are in principle analogous to those in assembly planning [9]. Like in assembly planning, the planning of a disassembly system consists of several consecutive phases: determining the - work process principle (e.g. line disassembly), allocating the individual disassembly operations to work systems (pre- disassembly, main and final disassembly) and by carrying out a load balancing. A module was developed for TANJA which can allocate the disassembly operations illustrated in a disassembly precedence diagram to individual disassembly work systems. The selection of these work systems is comparable to the definition of pre-, main and final disassemblies. The classification of the complete disassembly into independent work systems allows the individual disassembly operations to be decoupled, meaning they can be executed in part independently of one another.

2.5   Planning Disassembly Systems with Division of Labour

Using the developed software tool TANJA the planning of disassembly systems is carried out in three main steps: Development of the disassembly precedence diagram for a specific product, load balancing of the whole disassembly system and configuration of the layout.

The integration of the time study of the individual disassembly operations into the structure planning is highly advantageous. This was achieved by entering all information relevant to the disassembly contained in the respective nodes of the disassembly precedence diagram developed in the first planning step into the TANJA module ANGELA (German abbreviation for "Planning Tool for Time Study of Manual Disassembly"). Specifically, these are the disassembly operations along with their operation times as well as disassembly operation costs, detailed work plans, tools, materials used etc. This makes a shift of the individual nodes within the pre-, main and final disassembly areas possible without losing information about the details of the individual operation. In this manner all standard disassembly separation procedures necessary for the disassembly of a component can be planned. If ANGELA cannot describe a separation procedure, the planner can then enter an additional time allowance into the system that he deems necessary to cover the disassembly time of the non-defined disassembly operation. In the work plan integrated in ANGELA, all the individual work operations, the tools used and any special features of the disassembly are described in text form.

Once the cycle time and the number of work stations have been defined, the load of the disassembly system is balanced automatically, providing results such as e.g. the utilization of the individual work stations. The user can change the automatically generated assignment of disassembly operation to workplaces manually, should he deem this to be necessary.

Dependent upon the selected number of pre-, main and final disassembly areas, the workplaces are automatically grouped in the layout configuration by the planning tool. The complete disassembly system can be visualized by depositing a hall floor plan and supplementing it with symbols (e.g. objects, tools etc.) provided by TANJA. In this manner several planning solutions can be developed and then compared and assessed using assessment criteria contained in TANJA (short lead times, number of workers, activities etc.). They can be weighted by the planner based on an additive preference function.

3   Practical implications

The planning procedure has been tested and verified in a disassembly workshop for motorcycles. The task was to plan a motorcycle disassembly with the goal of recovering all reusable parts and components (motor, carburettor, electronic elements etc.) and to break the non-reusable material down into the purest fractions possible.

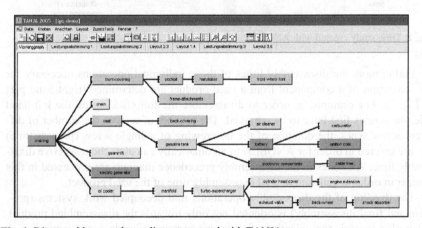

Fig. 1. Disassembly precedence diagram created with TANJA

For this project, several motorcycles of the same model were regarded. The disassembly work was carried out by skilled labourers. First, a test disassembly of a motorcycle was carried out according to the normally applied procedures within the company, whereby the disassembly operation times were recorded and the separation procedures, tools, aids, auxiliary activities etc. were documented. Subsequently, a disassembly precedence diagram was generated using drawings of the motorcycle and based on the results of the test disassembly (see Fig. 1). Finally, the disassembly system was re-planned using TANJA.

Next, the data necessary for the disassembly operations for the individual components was entered into the nodes of the disassembly precedence diagram (see Fig. 2). The degree of detail was thereby defined by the planner.

Figure 2 shows some content from the node for the example of the motorcycle front cladding. In addition to general information about the used product and the disassembly components, the disassembly purpose, such as reuse or recycling, is defined since completely differing time building blocks are used for the respective purposes (left-hand part of Fig. 2). The times allocated for recycling are longer than those allocated for reuse since recycling demands a higher degree of purity of the separated material, thus requiring more attention during the disassembly.

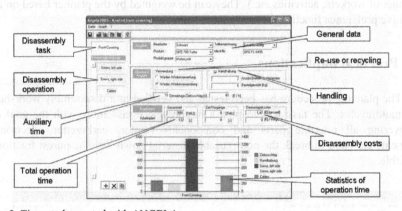

Fig. 2. Time study created with ANGELA

Furthermore the disassembly times of those individual operations necessary for the separation of a component from a used product are determined (right-hand part of Fig. 2). For example, in order to disassemble the full cladding on the left-hand side, the screws first have to be removed. The number of screws, the number of different screw types, the duration of the unscrewing of a single screw (process time) etc. are entered in order for ANGELA to automatically calculate the respective disassembly time. All nodes in the disassembly precedence diagram are processed in this manner in order to generate to total disassembly time of the used product.

The division of the disassembly operations into decoupled work systems (pre-, main and final disassembly) is oriented not only towards the disassembled product, rather also towards the objective of removing certain, valuable components, which are intended for sale as secondary products. In the project case this is due to a typically large demand, from the old product as soon as possible. These components are primarily premium plastic cladding elements, the tank, any electrical components (ignition coil, dynamo etc.) as well as the muffler.

The load balancing was carried out based on the conditions of the existing workshop. It resulted in three work systems with a total of five workplaces (cf. Fig. 3).

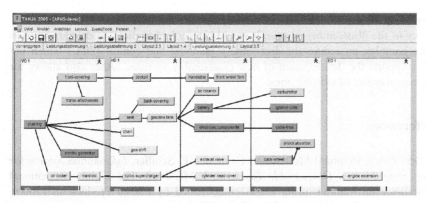

Fig. 3. Disassembly load balancing created with TANJA

The realignment of disassembly operation sequences, the implementation of alternative separation techniques, the provision of additional tools at various spots around the motorcycle and the resulting significant reduction of throughput times etc. brought about a reduction of the total disassembly time of 40% compared with the conventional procedure.

4 Aspects of Future Research

TANJA is a new procedure which uses time study to make load balancing in disassembly systems possible. With TANJA individual workplaces, disassembly group work systems or disassembly lines can be planned and assessed.

During the research project it was confirmed that disassembly enterprises are in great need of an adequate planning procedure and a time study of disassembly processes. Furthermore, it is imperative for these enterprises not only to plan the disassembly operations to be executed which are characterized by stochastically occurring situations, rather also to control the running operations.

Due to the unpredictability of disassembly operations a procedure for controlling disassembly systems must be able to react quickly to unscheduled activities and disturbances and to intervene in the running system state with appropriate control measures. The following starting points can be defined for the development of such a procedure:

- Planning of order sequences in the disassembly system for used product variants (batch-wise for single products or a total mix of models),
- Simulation of order sequences with stochastic operation times and interruptions,
- Alignment of the disassembly depth dependent upon the disassembly system utilization,
- Varying assignment of disassembly operations to work systems,
- Flexible selection of disassembly procedures, dependent upon the system load,
- Dispatching of different used products to one disassembly line.

A complex planning and control tool which is aligned with the demands of the disassembly by means of proven disassembly operation times can ensure an efficient flow of operations within the disassembly system and thus also the economic efficiency of the disassembly system. It would hereby be beneficial to develop an even more complex procedure for disassembly planning and control (DPC) which not only supports the development of new disassembly systems, rather also allows for the improvement of existing ones.

References

1. Gert Zülch, Reinhard Müller, and Emmerich F. Schiller, *Information System for Supporting Manual Disassembly Tasks*, in: ICME 2000, The Eighth International Conference on Manufacturing Engineering, edited by Causal Productions (2000), Compact disk, file:///D|/HTML/ME00S104.HTM.

2. Gert Zülch and Jörg W. Fischer, *Increasing the Flexibility of Working Times and Personnel Control in an Industrial Repair Work System*, (Espoo, Sim-Serv, 2004) http://www.sim-serv.com/white_papers.php (August 13, 2004).

3. Gert Zülch and Joachim Greinke, *Simulation-aided Reconfiguration of an Industrial Service System for the Repair of Electrical Tools* (Espoo, Sim-Serv, 2004), http://www.sim-serv.com/white_papers.php (November 05, 2004).

4. Gert Zülch, Emmerich F. Schiller, and Milko Schneck, *Adaptive Dynamic Process Plans - A Basis for a Disassembly Information System*, in: ECO-Performance '96, edited by Rainer Züst, Gabriel Caduff, and Michael Frei (Zürich, Verlag Industrielle Organisation, 1996), pp. 245-253.

5. Jörg Fischer, Patricia Stock, and Gert Zülch, *Simulation of Disassembly and Reassembly Processes with Beta-distributed Operation Times*, in: Integrating Human Aspects in Production Management, edited by Gert Zülch, Harinder S. Jagdev, and Patricia Stock (New York, Springer, 2005), pp. 147-156.

6. Olaf Mönig and Rainer Schwarz, *Zeitermittlung für die manuelle Demontage*, in: Aktuell, das Info-Magazin der Deutschen MTM-Vereinigung, 2(2002), (Hamburg, 2002), pp. 14-15.

7. Gert Zülch and Rainer Schwarz, *Demontagesystemplanung an einem Beispiel aus der Elektroindustrie*, in: Good Practice. Ergonomie und Arbeitsgestaltung, edited by Kurt Landau (Stuttgart, ergonomia Verlag, 2003), pp. 347-362.

8. Gert Zülch, Reinhard Müller, and Emmerich F. Schiller, *A Disassembly Information System*, in: Life Cycle Networks, edited by Frank-Lothar Krause and Günther Seliger (London, Weinheim, New York et al., Chapman & Hall, 1997), pp. 400-412.

9. Wolfgang-Jürgen Braun, *Beitrag zur Festlegung von Arbeitsteilung in manuellen Arbeitssystemen* (Aachen, Shaker, 1995), p. 26.

Demand Planning & Control – Handling Multiple Perspectives Through a Holistic Approach to Hierarchical Planning

Peter Nielsen and Kenn Steger-Jensen

Aalborg University, Department of Production, Fibigerstraede 16, 9220
Aalborg, Denmark,
Centre of Supply Chain Integration, WWW home page:
http://www.misg.aau.dk

Abstract. Hierarchical Demand Planning (HDP) is an intricate part of most companies today. HDP is based on the assumption of independence among variables, and this allows for simple and easy aggregation and separation of plans and data. However, the most commonly used arguments for grouping and subsequent aggregating is shared traits contrary to the assumption of independency. One of the predominant issues is the conflicting objectives on different decision levels. An example of this is found in hierarchical forecasting of demand. When forecasting on e.g. a product family level to establish capacity requirements, the objective is usually to achieve a Mean Error (ME) of zero. This conflicts with forecasting for Demand Planning (DP) purposes on SKU level, where minimization of the Standard Deviation of Error (SDE) might be more important. In this paper these issues are addressed through a simple example of hierarchical forecasting and use of a Goal Programming (GP) approach to satisfy both objectives. It is found that some general guidelines for handling multiple objectives within HDP can be inferred from this, leading the way for a holistic demand planning framework.

1   Introduction

Companies today find themselves facing: Short Product Life Cycles, complex products, supply networks as well as rising demands for profitability. As a result the Demand Planning and Control (DPC) situation is highly complex and dynamic. This sets new standards for companies' ability to; share information internally and in their supply network, quickly arrive at an "optimal" plan, execute the plan and take corrective measures as necessity dictates. Due to the varying nature of manufacturing companies with regards to products and competitive priorities, the DPC processes and objectives vary greatly between companies and planning areas. Typically manufacturing companies have a need to plan on several levels, i.e. a planning

Please use the following format when citing this chapter:

Nielsen, P. and Steger-Jensen, K., 2008, in IFIP International Federation for Information Processing, Volume 257, Lean Business Systems and Beyond, Tomasz Koch, ed.; (Boston: Springer), pp. 57–65.

hierarchy is present. Several different approaches to handle this have been presented, and the most important among them is the Hierarchical Demand Planning Approach (HDPA) [1, 2, 8]. However the HDPA has some weakness, among these the problem of feasibility and optimality of plans. Furthermore, several planning objectives exist and these need not be coherent. One approach to handling these issues of conflicting objectives would be a holistic demand planning framework where goals for satisfying a number of the objectives were achieved.

2   Literature review

A literature review of HDPA, hierarchical forecasting and Goal Programming (GP) was conducted.

A descriptive HDPA was first presented by Hax and Meal [8] to give an easy planning algorithm that would yield plans for several planning levels through a number of steps, starting with an aggregate plan. In many situations, the hierarchical planning (HPA) paradigm has been and continues to be a suitable and satisfactory framework for structuring the management tasks (e.g. planning and controlling). Bitran et al. [1], Bitran and Hax [3], Hax and Golovin [7] and Hax and Meal [8] are the major pioneers in the development of HPA models. The success of the HDPA has been so widespread that certain authors recommend the approach for almost any medium-to-large scale situation [13, 15]. Today, HDP is widely implemented in companies and supported by major ERP-system providers such as Oracle and SAP. However the issue of feasibility of the plans has not been completely addressed. The issues of feasibility and optimally of plans on different planning levels are negated by the assumption of independence between e.g. products with different product families. However, in reality dependencies exist, often due to the modularity of products, which gives a need for a new approach. The main reason for using the HDPA is that it delivers a plan with a minimum of processing; feasibility and optimality are however not guaranteed. A main issue is how (within a simple framework) to handle multiple planning objectives on multiple planning levels. Hax and Meal [8] use an absolute priorities approach and suggests optimizing for one objective (cost minimization) on an aggregate level and then to use this as a constraint on lower planning levels. There is of course ongoing discussions about which decisions are found at each level, which will be dealt with later, and this can depend on the type of manufacturing being conducted (e.g. Hendry and Kingsman [9]) and the degree of decentralization, but the general approach to sequential decision division is followed. In the original Hax-Meal system it is possible to obtain a feasible solution to the aggregate problem that will not permit any feasible solution to the subsequent family and individual-item scheduling problem, because of the aggregation at the production planning stage. Bitran et al. [2] suggest aggregating products with similar production costs, inventory costs and seasonal demand to product types. But an applicable definition of "similar" is lacking. Furthermore, the grouping of products based on similar attributes wills inevitable conflict with the main assumption of the HDPA, i.e. independency of demand.

Hierarchical forecasting can be conducted in a number of ways, some methods concern forecasting on an aggregate level and on a lower level and then use a combination of methods arrive at a better lower level forecast [5, 14]. This however defeats on the major advantages associated with using aggregate data namely it is simpler, quicker and exhibits good qualities regarding variance. When focusing on fitting forecasts to a demand pattern, the regression techniques used ensure that ME=0 and the noise is n.i.d. In practice many companies use simple times series techniques either due to the cost of using more complex techniques or due to limited capabilities within the company. These techniques do not always achieve a ME equal to zero. Firstly, many companies only forecast on aggregate data (e.g. product family demand data) and use simple distribution keys to arrive at lower level forecasts, which often is the approach supported by ERP and APS vendors. Secondly, a ME of zero on aggregate forecasts does not explicitly correspond to a low SDE on the disaggregate level when independency between product demands is present. This conflicts with the needs for data performance in the HDPA. I.e. the issue is how to balance an objective of ME=0 on an aggregate forecast and still get as low a SDE on a lower level as possible since both are used as input to the HDP process.

Goal Programming (GP) [4, 10, 11] is an approach to multiple objective scenarios in which each of the objectives has a target or goal. Its distinguished feature is that the objectives can be started as minimizing deviations from pre-specified goals. GP differs from other optimization methods through the distinguishing between hard and soft constraints. Soft constraints are particularly well suited to address the real life situations encountered as in DP. The search strategies used are related to those used when solving mixed integer programming (MIP) problems via branch-and-bound procedures. In most MIP problems, constraints represent limitations or requirements, which must be met. The solution to a MIP problem does not allow a constraint to be violated. Thus, a way of modeling soft constraints is needed. Basically, there are two approaches to integer GP, which are called non-preemptive and preemptive. Non-preemptive is based on a weighted GP approach, where the goals are of roughly comparable importance, and the preemptive is based on a hierarchy of priority levels of the goals. Here, the weighted GP using mixed-integer variables (G-MILP) as in MIP will be used, since it is suitable for representing decision problems of the type encountered here.

3   Goal programming applied to hierarchical forecasting using simple times series

In this section, forecasting an example of the problems inherent in both neglecting the existence of diverging objectives and the dependency when utilizing the HDPA.

A product family of three products was used to exemplify the issue. For all three products 25 periods of demand existed. The three products have respectively: a constant demand (Product I), a linearly decreasing (Product II) and a linearly increasing trend (Product III). All had a stationary demand of 150 units/periods and a random element that is n.i.i.d. with mean zero and variance σ^2 of 10^2. Demand for product II decreases with the same rate as demand for product III increases – a typical occurrence when a new product is taking over from an old product. This is an important issue when grouping items for aggregation purposes.

To use a simple approach the demand data was aggregated and four simple time series forecasting methods were used on the data. These were: the naive, simple moving average using six periods of data, exponential smoothing using an α of 0.3 and exponential smoothing with trend were the smoothing constants using Holt-Winters' approach [13]. A six month moving average of demand for the individual products relative to the product family demand was used to find the distribution keys giving individual product forecasts. In the researchers experience with both medium and large sized companies this is a typical approach to get a SKU level forecast. The results with regards to ME, SDE and MAPE are shown in table 1.

Table 1. The table shows respectively, the forecast on aggregated data, three disaggregated forecasts for Products I-III and an average of the performance of the disaggregated forecasts performance. Values marked with bold are used in the subsequent optimization.

	Naive (j=1)		Moving Average (j=2)		Exponential smoothing (j=3)		Exponential smoothing with trend (j=4)	
	ME	SDE	ME	SDE	ME	SDE	ME	SDE
Aggregate Forecast	**0,3**	21,0	**-0,7**	19,4	**0,7**	17,7	**0,9**	21,2
Product I	-0,1	**11,0**	-1,1	**9,6**	-0,6	**9,4**	-0,6	**9,9**
Product II	8,0	**13,2**	7,5	**14,1**	7,7	**13,6**	7,9	**14,3**
Product III	-6,7	**10,1**	-7,1	**9,0**	-7,4	**8,8**	-6,4	**9,7**

The approach to use distribution keys when dependency exists between sales of some products giving, as one would expect, a constant undershoot and overshoot of forecast on the disaggregated level. This of course runs contrary to good DP procedures. However, in a practical environment a constant over-/undershoot of forecast might not be nearly as costly as a high SDE, since the latter is used to establish service level – yet again it is recognized that the service level typically assumes noise to be n.i.d. with a mean of zero. Firstly, this is only relevant when the variance of the noise is small compared to the numerical deviation from ME equaling zero. Secondly, in a practical application shifts in demand patterns will typically result in some deviations from this assumption, due to e.g. sales discount.
It is recognized that some companies uses more complex forecasting techniques than those presented above. These would almost all use some form of regression approach to achieve ME=0. However, this would only enhance the problem described, since no explicated relationship exists between ME and SDE when trend is present on the product level. And since multiple conflicting objectives exist on different planning levels some method to create a balance between these objectives is needed.

The next step was to use GP to balance performance on both planning levels, i.e. minimize SDE on SKU level and solving ME≈0 on the aggregate level.

The following variables are needed:

x_j =   Binary decision variable to decide whether to use a given aggregate forecast j indicates the forecast type (e.g. naïve $j = 1$)

w_k =   Weight of goal k

d_{j+} =   Deviation variable, ME > 0, for aggregate forecast j on aggregate level

d_{j-} =   Deviation variable, ME < 0, for aggregate forecast j on aggregate level

d_{ji+} =   Deviation variable indicating deviation from lowest SDE (SDE$_{min,i}$) for product i using forecast j on aggregate data

ME_j =   ME of aggregate forecast using forecast type j

SDE_{ji} =   SDE of product i using forecast type j on aggregate level

The decision variable d_{ji-} needs not be defined since SDE$_{min,i}$ is by definition the minimum. The decision variables x_j are binary since the interest is only to use one time series forecast. The problem is then formulated with objective is to minimize the deviation from an ME = 0 on aggregate level, while minimizing the deviation from the lowest SDE for products i. Equal weights of goals is used in this example, so the normalization constraint is not strictly necessary:

$$\text{Minimize:} \quad w_k \sum_j d_{j+} + w_k \sum_i \sum_j d_{ji+}$$

S.t.
$$\sum_k w_k = 1$$
$$ME_j \cdot x_j - d_{j+} + d_{j-} = 0$$
$$\sum_j x_j = 1$$
$$\left(SDE_{ji} - SDE_{min,i}\right) \cdot x_j - d_{ji+} = 0$$
$$x_j, d_{j+}, d_{j-}, d_{ji+} \geq 0$$

It can easily be seen that this is a weighted G-MILP problem. Furthermore, d_{j+}, d_{j-} and d_{ji+} are zero for $x_j = 0$, thereby ensuring that only one aggregate forecast is used. Conducting the optimization yields the results as seen in table 2.

Table 2. Resulting decision and deviation variables values for optimum, with equal weights to ME=0 and sum of SDE.

Decision variable		Naïve (1)	Moving Average (2)	Exponential smoothing (3)	Exp.smoothing with trend (4)
		x_1	x_2	x_3	x_4
Deviation variables		0	0	1	0
	d_{j+}	0	0	0,654	0
	d_{j-}	0	0	0	0
	d_{ji+}	j = 1	j = 2	j = 3	j = 4
Product I	i =1	0	0	0	0
Product II	i=2	0	0	0,392	0
Product III	i=3	0	0	0	0

Another approach could be to assign a particular weight to one of the d_{ji^+} variables. This would be prudent if e.g. one product was significantly more expensive than the two others. The weights will be addressed in the discussion paragraph.

The binary constraint can be relaxed to achieve a linear combination of forecasts, this however requires a dynamic recalculation of forecast error for the linear combination forecasts as well as the introduction of three new deviation variables. The need for a dynamic recalculation of the forecast error SDE makes the problem non-linear. If only ME=0 was used as the goal, the problem would be a simple LP problem, there would however be a risk of multiple solutions with widely diverging SDE_i values. Moreover, the deviation from $ME_{ji} = 0$ might be included in a number of situations, see following paragraph.

4   Discussion

The way that DP is handled varies greatly depending on the assumed perspective. Otto and Kotzab [12] argue that six perspectives on SCM exist: System Dynamics, Operations Research (OR/IT), Logistics, Marketing, Organization and Strategy. The metrics and consequent criteria for success naturally depend on the assumed perspective. More critically however, is that the criteria for success often seem to conflict – e.g. from the System Dynamics' perspective; capacity utilization and from Logistics perspective; inventory levels. This issue is particular important in connections with HDP.

A number of inferences can be reached from the use of GP to find the optimal forecast on aggregate data, when simple distribution keys are used and the data on the disaggregate level is interdependent. Firstly, the approach is not perfect, but it is simple and cost effective and will fit well into most companies DPC processes. Secondly, it is apparent that the ability to balance these diverging goals is a needed extension of the HDPA. This goes not only for reaching an optimal and feasible plan on more than one planning level, but also for the information to be used to achieve this plan. The simple approach presented here addresses this through balancing the need for a given forecasting performance on aggregate level with the need for a given performance on a disaggregate level. As seen in the GP approach to balance different types of forecast errors in hierarchical forecasting some guidelines for how to weight the error types in a DP hierarchy must be established. As a starting point the critical planning areas must be identified, e.g. to match capacity internally or up-stream in the supply chain (focus on $ME_{aggregate}$) or to find critical products (focus on $ME_{products}$ and/or $SDE_{products}$). ME=0+ (bias to overshoot) would be a problem if capacity is scarce, ME=0- (bias to undershoot) is a problem when capacity is expensive – since too much capacity would be reserved compared to the average needs. If capacity is not an issue compared to say the price of the products being produced, the SDE of the individual products should be weighted higher. When a balance has been achieved between the relative importance of matching capacity on an aggregate level precisely compared to achieving suitable forecasts for inventory management, the next step is to weight the relative importance of the products within a given product family. Two dimensions typically need to be addressed, respectively the relative price and volume of the products [6]. However, dimensions such as customer size and criticality of products/components might be more important in some DPC situations. Assuming price and volume are critical some guidelines for weights are shown below.

		Price	
		Low	High
Volume	Low	The product is not important and should either not be included in the weighting or weighted very low.	SDE of the products should be minimized and should have a high priority. If the ME of the forecasts is high compared to the SDE this should also be sought minimized.
	High	Deviations from $ME_{product}=0$ should be minimized. SDE should be weighted lightly unless there are constraints on e.g. inventory capacity, the product lifecycle is short or the product is critical.	Include both ME and SDE in the deviation variables on the disaggregate level; ME because of volume and SDE due to value. Both should be weighted high.

These weights could be quantitatively established using a simple spreadsheet by taking the combined relative volume and price and use these and then normalize these so that the weights between aggregate and disaggregate levels match.

The presented method can with some work be utilized in the hierarchical forecasting procedures treated in e.g. Fliedner [5] so that forecasts on both aggregated and disaggregated data are used to arrive at forecasts for both the aggregate and disaggregate level. The goal would still be to balance the deviation from ME equal to zero and minimize SDE on the disaggregate level. However, solving this problem would entail using non-linear optimization techniques. Furthermore, it is not immediately apparent whether this would be a convex problem.

5   Conclusion and further research

Based on the example it is concluded that it is possible to achieve a balance between aggregate and disaggregate forecasts in a hierarchy of forecasts. This is done by using distribution keys on an aggregate forecast and then through GP finding the aggregate forecast that best matches the objective of ME equaling zero on the aggregate level and has a minimum SDE on the disaggregate level. The paper addresses the important issue of being conscious of the limitations in the hierarchical demand planning approach. Moreover, it presents a simple holistic way of dealing with this tradeoff using G-MILP.

However, further research should take another approach to this issue. Basically the HDPA is flawed in its conception of independence between objects and objectives. Products are typically not independent with regards to sales within a product family, product families are typically not independent of each other and so on. The conclusion is that it is necessary to rethink the methods behind the data used within the HDPA through a new paradigm. The way forward must be to use a data structure and planning methods that include and utilize these interdependencies. One approach that seems to be probable to yield results would be multivariate analysis methods using folded distributions of sales data, which includes the covariance between e.g. product families. If such a method could be developed, then the assumption of independence within the HDPA could be relaxed, yielding a method that more closely mimics the reality of Manufacturing Planning and Control.

References:

1. Bitran, G. R., E. A. Haas, and A. C. Hax, Hierarchical Production Planning: A Single Stage System, *Operations Research*, 29, pp. 717–743, 1981.

2. Bitran, G. R., E. A. Haas, and A. C. Hax, Hierarchical Production Planning: A Two Stage Approach, *Operations Research*, 30, pp. 232–251, 1982.

3. Bitran, G. R. and A. C. Hax, On the design of hierarchical production planning and inventory control systems, *Bulletin of the Operations Research Society of America*, 23, 1975.

4. Chankong, V., and Y. Y. Haimes, "Multiobjective decision making: theory and methodology", North-holland series in System Science and Engineering; 8, Elsevier Science, 1983.

5. Fliedner, G., Hierarchical forecasting: issues and use guidelines, *Industrial Management & Data Systems*, 101, pp. 5–12, 2001.

6. Flores, B. E., and D. C. Whybark, Multiple Criteria ABC Analysis, *International Journal of Operations & Production Management*, 6, pp. 38–46, 1986.

7. Hax A. C. and J. J. Golovin, Hierarchical production planning systems, *Studies in Operations Management*, North-Holland, 1978.

8. Hax, A. C., and H. C. Meal, Hierarchical Integration of Production Planning and Scheduling, in *Logistics*, edited by M. A. Geisler, vol. 1 of *Studies in the Management Sciences*, North-Holland/American Elsevier, 1975.

9. Hendry, L. C. and B. G. Kingsman, Production Planning Systems and Their Applicability to Make-to-Order Companies, *European Journal of Operational Research*, 6, pp. 1-15, 1989.

10. Ignizio, J. P., *Goal Programming and Extensions*, Lexington Books, 1976.

11. Lee, S. M., *Goal Programming for Decision Analysis*, First edition, Auerbach Publishers Inc., 1972.

12. Otto, A., and H. Kotzab, Does supply chain management really pay? Six perspectives to measure the performance of managing a supply chain, *European Journal of Operational Research*, 144, pp. 306–320, 2003.

13. Silver, E. A., D. F. Pyke, and R. Peterson, *Inventory Management and Production Planning and Scheduling*, third ed., John Wiley & Sons, 1998.

14. Theil, H., *Applied Economic Forecasting*, vol. 4 of *Studies in Mathematical and Managerial Economics*, North-Holland Publishing Company, 1966.

15. Vollmann, T., W. Berry, and D. Whybark, *Manufacturing Planning and Control Systems*, fourth ed., Irwin/McGraw-Hill, 1997.

Review of an ERP System Supporting Lean Manufacturing

Kenn Steger-Jensen* and Hans-Henrik Hvolby
Centre of Supply Chain Integration
Department of Production, Aalborg University, Denmark.

Abstract This paper presents a case study and discusses the issues of implementing Lean manufacturing within a global organisation and the adoption of it in an Erp-system. It discusses and presents how the modelling and design of the manufacturing planning and control task can be done, and how it is implemented within the Erp system, to support the daily operation in the case company. The Erp system used by the organisation is Oracle E-business suite, but not the whole suite. Regarding adoption of Lean manufacturing, the Erp-systems' capabilities of supporting manufacturing planning and control Mpc in a Lean environment are in focus.

1 Introduction

A common misconception about Lean is that it does not mix well with information technology systems. But, as Lean spreads beyond the relatively stable manufacturing environment it originally was designed to support, companies realise that information technology can play a vital role. Information technology systems, such as Erp, can be used successfully to support Lean transformations, especially for manufacturers who have highly variable demand for a large number of low volume products, and who operate in mixed-mode manufacturing environments.

While Erp systems once had a reputation for not supporting Lean initiatives, times have changed completely. There are Erp systems that do support Lean. However, manufacturers should examine the capabilities of their Erp systems closely to examine whether they can support their Lean initiative adequately.

The paper is a contribution to Mpc issues related to capabilities of Erp systems and IT-technologies within a Lean environment, and it is structured as follows: In section 2, the demand-driven Lean requirements to Mpc are discussed. In section 3, the case company is presented. In section 4, modelling and design of the Mpc task within the Erp system is presented and the case results are discussed. Finally, conclusion and further research are outlined in section 6.

Please use the following format when citing this chapter:

Steger-Jensen, K. and Hvolby, H.-H., 2008, in IFIP International Federation for Information Processing, Volume 257, Lean Business Systems and Beyond, Tomasz Koch, ed.; (Boston: Springer), pp. 67–74.

2   Demand-driven Lean Requirement to Mpc

The growing competition and truly relentless pressures to increase customer satisfaction have forced manufacturers to become more demand-driven. This has triggered a dramatic shift in the focus of Lean planning processes away from production and inventory and towards a much more demand-driven approach.

The typical approaches for Lean used by most companies today do not provide an optimal return on investment for companies. The missing link between Lean goals and successful projects that produce the intended result is a strategy for Lean. Many companies start off with a tactical approach, rather than a strategic one. This is a key factor in the high percentage of failed programs within Lean; less than 20% of companies are successful with Lean [1].

Reduce non value-added manufacturing and supply chain costs	66%
Implement continuous culture and methods	52%
Implement manufacturing and supply chain flexibility	38%
Customer demand driven maunfacturing	29%
Focus on Customer value-adding activities	27%
Reduce inventory and assest required to produc and deliver poduct	27%
Improve product quality	20%

Fig. 1. Best-in-class Strategic Actions of Lean [2]

As shown in Figure 1, a recent survey show that 66% of best-in-class companies point out cost reduction in manufacturing and the supply chain as the key target for their Lean initiative. The other actions are operational, cultural and quality focused. The lesson learned is that Lean in practice is viewed as a cost-reduction strategy, not as a market domination one, by the majority of companies. Companies should primarily focus on Lean as a growth-enabler rather than a cost reducer, and a change in perspective is required.

A proper Erp system can help overcome the challenges of applying Lean to the demand-driven manufacturers face. The combination of real-time data collection and monitoring; the ability to map highly variable customer demand to a smooth manufacturing plan along with various operational capabilities such as real-time pull requirements and backflushing transactions has actually placed Erp systems in the centre of the new Lean evolution.

The key point is that the Erp system is a tool to handle the increasing manufacturing design activities, daily operation activities and transactions, and it is an important tool to increase innovation and reduce delivery time, as a result of moving beyond the relatively stable manufacturing environment to a more demand-driven approach with highly variable, low volume demand.

This paper focuses on the Erp system's capability to support the Mpc issues for demand-driven manufacturing, which Mto belongs to in general.

The following issues are of special interest in the following case study:

- Overcome the difficulty of calculating Heijunka schedules (Uniform Plant Loading), having an increased number of products with low volume. Demand smoothing is important as the production lines are designed based on an average daily mix.
- To implement dynamic line balancing and customer order scheduling to improve flexibility.
- Implement smaller levelling periods and more frequent adjustment of Kanban loop and sizes, as customers require shorter delivery time.

Furthermore, the order management is more complex, since the interface to the manufacturing system is demand-driven with highly variable, low volume demand, which also increases the complexity of the supplier network and inventory control.

3   Case Company's Goals and Issues

The company's competitive advantages and priorities were (and still are) product innovation, flexibility and delivery in the described order. To increase and support the competitive priorities and contents, responsiveness to the changing customer demand needs to be improved.

The company has good experience with Lean manufacturing on the shop floor level. The products involve a high amount of engineering skills and are among the most reliable products on the marked. There are some seasonal fluctuations in sales, primarily on the professional markets.

An analysis shows that the primary issues to the responsiveness are 1) the approach to Mpc and 2) the reduced use of the Erp system. Also the new product development process was an issue, as the Erp system was not used in this activity.

In general, the Erp system was not used to integrate and to streamline the business processes nor the information flows, as the Erp system was decoupled from the order management and down to the shop floor control. All information flow from order entry to manufacturing release was handled with spreadsheets, email and other sub systems and has to be entered manually into the Erp system. The Erp system was more or less only used for costing and accounting and to coordinate and deliver due dates and availability information for downstream purposes in the supply chain.

Order Management was not able to use the planning and control functionality within the Erp system due to lack of master data setup. Because of the demand fluctuation, a lot of manual re-planning was necessary. Due to the Mto approach the order management process was quite complex and difficult to handle without using facilities in the Erp-system such as planning and demand time fences, available-to-promise, capable-to-promise, scheduling rules, etc. This made the order management process slow and time-consuming and caused increased backlogs and backorders. As a consequence the competitive priority, delivery, was very low and it was difficult to fulfill the delivery goals.

The master data was organised for manufacturing, assembly and shop floor activities in general, but maintained in another system not integrated with the Erp system.

Therefore Mpc was primarily made within spreadsheets, since the setup and modelling of master data within the Erp system was insufficient. Finally the employee knowledge on the Erp system's capability for Mpc was insufficient as well.

The company's production system is based on the demand flow technology principles of Costanza [3]. The lead-time is between 80 minutes and approx. 50 hours per unit, with short changeover time. The production layout is line flow-based and split into two groups: four feeder lines and one main line, which is used for whole product mixes. All material supplies are controlled through Kanban. The in process Kanban on the main line contains one unit.

An analysis of the Erp system showed that it was capable of supporting a Lean manufacturing environment and should be used for this puspose.

4   Modelling and Design of the Mpc and Control Task

The new Mpc concept is presented in figure 2. The customer order de-coupling point is at the raw material inventory, and the manufacturing is split into two planning areas. One planning area is the material supply to the feeder lines and main line, based on Kanban, and the other one is the lines. All items are controlled through two bin Kanban systems. The pull sequence of external Kanbans (items from suppliers delivered to inventory) are controlled by 5 Kanban cards and items from inventory to row in-process and the lines are controlled by 2 Kanban bins, which means that only the size of the Kanbans needs to be calculated.

The Kanban systems design is based on a simulation of the flow within the Erp system. Internal Kanbans are used on three different types of items. A-items are physically big and of high price. 4 different sizes of Kanban bins are used for B-items. The size of the item is the decision variable for using a specific Kanban bin size. C-items are e.g. bolts and nots which are small and cheap compared to the final product costs.

By using Kanban on all items the material requirements are planned when generating the Kanban Plan, which can be done based on a forecast schedule or Mps. This gives the opportunity to level both supplies and the production rate at the same time, and more specific to balance the capacity requirements on line operation level and material and inventory requirements for specific items. Only the production layout and the in-process-Kanban size of one is preserved, all other master data is redesigned. Items, Bom's, and routings have all revision control and audit on data, which ensures that the right master data and information is used. All master data is defined and maintained in the Erp system. The manufacturing engineering instruc-tion is maintained in another application and linked as an attachment to the standard operations in the Erp system. The Mpc master data setup is presented in figure 3.

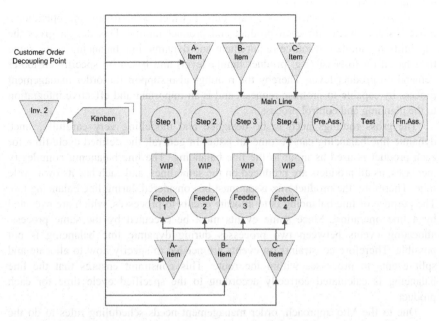

Fig. 2. The Mpc concept contains two planning areas: the lines and the supply from inventory to the lines, respectively

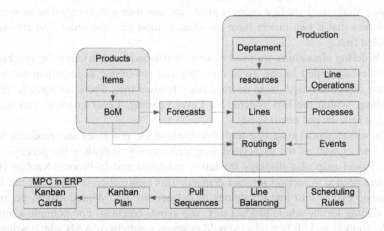

Fig. 3. The master data design setup and relationship in the Erp system

The Bom and related routing is designed to support both sales configuration and production on shop floor level at the same time. The Bom design supports order management, since it is now possible to make available-to-promise requests. It is also now possible to forecast both on products and product families and to derive the forecast on Stock Keeping Units, based on aggregated forecast and time series models. Most of all, the redesign of the master data gives an opportunity to do dynamic Kanban calculations.

The routing is designed as a gross routing, which contains all line operations, processes and events for each product and product family. This design gives the capability to simulate resource requirement and dynamic line balancing at the same time based on forecast (e.g. product family level) and based on specific customer demand on product level. Thereby the routings also support the order management process by capable-to-promise requests and is an important and effective integration to the planning and control process.

The gross routings need to be designed and modelling very carefully, since dynamic line balancing can become an issue. In general, the defined cycle time for each product is used as input to the line balancing. The line balancing complexity increases, as all products are produced on the same lines, and each has its own cycle time. Therefore, the product mix issue must be considered during line balancing too. The purpose of line balancing is to allocate events to processes, which are executed by a line operation. Since some events must be executed by the same process, allocating events between two processes during dynamic line balancing is not possible. Therefore constraints on events are needed to specify how to allocate and split events to processes within the route. This constraint ensures that the line balancing is calculated correctly according to the specified cycle time for each product.

Due to the Mto approach, order management needs scheduling rules to do the order planning effectively. Sequencing rules consist of a combination of one or more sequencing criteria and one scheduling algorithm. Sequencing criteria are used to determine the scheduling priority of sales orders.

The criteria used are first order request date, and then order entry date as second. This means that if two orders have the same request date the order first entered is scheduled first.

Scheduling algorithms are used to smooth demand by restricting the number of assemblies scheduled in any given day. Demand smoothing is important since the lines are designed based on an average daily product mix. There are three levels of smoothing, within the Erp system: No Level Loading, Level Loading, and Mixed Model, where the last one is used.

The mixed model map is a tool that displays the processes and products for a given line as well as the associated weighted times to complete the process. The mixed model map also displays the labor, machines and In-Process-Kanban (Ipk) resources needed to support forecast demand. This information is used to decide how to regroup events into line operations to balance the line. Mixed Model performs level loading for the whole product mix, and avoids batching. For example a mix of 100 A products and 50 B products could generate a pattern of AAB which would be repeated 50 times to schedule the total demand. This provides the most consistent pace through the main line, and will cause the least disruptions to the supply chain, and the fastest way to produce a whole mix.

This is a preferred method of demand smoothing, since it will minimize the gap between the design mix and the actual demands. This method is useful if customers are somewhat flexible in their delivery dates, and set-up times are insignificant. The other two methods can be summarized as follows.

With a *daily rate level*, a demand ratio is calculated, based on the mix of demand over the time horizon. This ratio is multiplied by the amount of available capacity each day to determine how much of each item will be scheduled on a given day. Items are then prioritised based on the sequencing criteria.

With *no level loading*, the system performs no demand smoothing. Orders are scheduled solely based on the sequencing criteria and the line capacity. This method is useful when customers are not flexible regarding delivery dates. For example: a customer is running a Jit facility that needs delivery exactly at the requested date. But scheduling without level loading may create a mix of products that is very different from the mix line design. If products vary significantly in build time, set-up time, or the parts used, it will cause either large imbalances to the line, or shortages of material in Kanbans.

As an example: Assume Product A takes 2 hours to assemble at one operation, and product B only takes 1 hour. The line is designed to make 4 A's and 8 B's every day (the line runs 16 hours each day). But today, customer orders are received for 8 A's and 4 B's. This new mix requires 20 hours to assemble at the operation, and then there is not enough capacity to produce the requested mix without using overtime.

The Mpc environment reduces maintenance of the master data in general. Figure 4 presents the Mpc production setup in the Erp system. The new Mpc approach has, combined with the improved use of the Erp-system, increased the speed of innovation, flexibility, manufacturing plan and control quality as well as delivery performance. The company has obtained some of the fundamental means to support fulfilment of the ultimate goal. The purpose of the case study has been to demonstrate the value of using Erp systems within a Lean manufacturing environment.

Single source of data by using the Erp system for handling the information flow and the master data has reduced the manual load and increased responsiveness.

The case company has more than the one manufacturing location where the same Erp system is used. As the Erp system is able to handle more than one organisation it is now possible to deliver and transfers a full package of master data setup and Mpc to another manufacturing site without redesign.

5 Conclusion and Further Research

The paper demonstrates the value of using Erp-systems within a Lean manufacturing environment. Based on the case study, the company has increased both its innovation skills of speed and flexibility, as well as its manufacturing plan quality and delivery performance.

Further development of methods and techniques for dynamic line balancing is needed, since the balance between material flow and resource activities is too restricted compared to what is needed. The main issue is that balanced and stabile material flow on e.g. the main manufacturing line does not by default give a balanced and stabile material flow upstream and visa versa.

This is in practice an issue for low volume and highly variable demand.

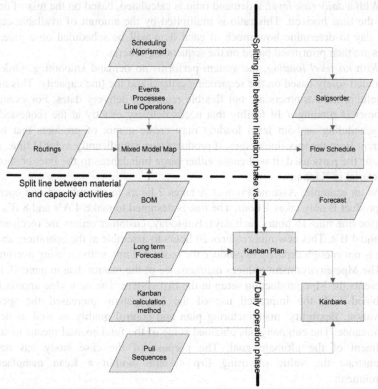

Fig. 4. Mpc production setup in the Erp system. It contains two splitting lines, one between material and capacity activities and one between initiation vs. daily operation phase activities

References

1. Kilpatrick, Jerry D and Osborne, Robert; The R(E)volution of Lean, Business Breakthroughs Inc, 2006.

2. Biddle, Jane, "The Lean Benchmark Report: Closing the Reality Gap", March 2006. Aberdeen*Group*. 20 March 2006, www.aberdeen.com.

3. Costanza, J. R; The quantum leap in speed to market, third ed., John Costanza Institute of Technology, Inc., Isbn: 0-9628182-1-6, 1996.

Orders Loading and Release in Flow Shops including Outsourcing Networks

Tatsiopoulos, I.P.*, A. Batsis, A. and G. Papadopoulos

* Professor in Industrial Management, National Technical University of Athens, 15780 Zografos, Athens, Greece, Tel:+3010 7723572, Fax: +3010 7723571

Abstract. Purpose of this paper is to analyse and compare the behavior of workload control models in flow shops of both the MTO (Make-To-Order) and MTS (Make-To-Stock) classes. A simulation model has been built, where a manufacturing cell is loaded through an input control mechanism with shop orders coming from a "pool". The "pool" itself is fed with planned orders coming from an MRP system. The MRP system releases production orders every planned period and the input control mechanism decides for the actual release of work orders. Conclusions are drawn for the performance of the system with or without an MRP system and with or without the input control mechanism in MTO and MTS environments. Compared to the pure flow shop routing, any set of stations might be excluded from the routing or *replaced by subcontractors belonging to an outsourcing network* of the manufacturing company. Thus, the general flow shop may still show routing variety with respect to routing lengths, though there is one flow direction with *outsourcing interruptions*.

1 Introduction and problem definition

The *Orders Release* function includes those activities, which must take place before an order defined by a planning system, can be released to an execution system. These activities are necessary to control the flow of information and orders passing from the planning system to the execution system and to ensure that the orders released have a reasonable chance of being completed by the time and in the quantity wanted. According to the above definition, *Orders Release*, at least in *push* production planning and control systems of the MRP II type (Manufacturing Resources Planning), forms the link between the production planning system and the shop floor control (SFC) system.

Please use the following format when citing this chapter:

Tatsiopoulos, I.P., Batsis, A. and Papadopoulos, G., 2008, in IFIP International Federation for Information Processing, Volume 257, Lean Business Systems and Beyond, Tomasz Koch, ed.; (Boston: Springer), pp. 75–92.

Most of the order release models found in the research literature refer to job shops and make-to-order (MTO) manufacturing under the terms of *input/output control* or *workload control*. Research effort in the area of workload control for flow shops and make-to-stock (MTS) manufacturing driven by push MRP (Material Requirements Planning) systems is rather limited. The much discussed alternative family of *pull* production control systems of the CONWIP type (Hopp and Spearman, 2000) is not addressed or compared in the present study.

Out of the Hayes and Wheelwright (1979) well-known taxonomy of production systems, we select as our flow shop perspective the *disconnected line flow*, where product batches are produced on a limited number of identifiable routings (i.e. paths through the plant) and inventories can build up between work centres. In this *general flow shop* environment - as opposed to the *pure flow shop*, where each job has exactly the same routing - a movement between any combination of two workstations may occur, but the flow will always have the same direction. Compared to the pure flow shop routing, any set of stations might be excluded from the routing *and replaced by subcontractors belonging to an outsourcing network* of the manufacturing company. Thus, the general flow shop may still show routing variety with respect to routing lengths, though there is one flow direction with *outsourcing interruptions*. In industrial practice, the following two manufacturing settings are characteristic of the general flow shop type:

a) *Sequenced operations* through functionally organized departments. Many manufacturing companies produce a wide range of products through a more or less well-defined production process. The product flows from one department to another in a single direction. Sometimes the resulting schedules, lead times, and work-in-process inventories exhibit the worst characteristics of those of the true job shop, in spite of the opportunities for a more thoroughly organized scheduling system, which this form of production organization makes possible (McGee and Boodman, 1967).

b) *Manufacturing cells*. In this case, a uniform range of similar products flows through the manufacturing cell. Here, too much effort has been devoted on detailed scheduling algorithms within SFC systems, while there is a scarcity of publications on shop orders release loading and release as a link between the MRP system and the SFC system.

Flow shops may belong to either the MTO (Make-To-Order) or the MTS (Make-To-Stock) types of manufacturing systems. In both cases the focus of shop orders loading and releasing should be shifted from balancing the workload of individual work centres into balancing the flow through flow shops (*balance flow not capacity*, Goldratt, 1982). Within this setting, SFC is organized to enhance the ability of the system to maintain an uninterrupted flow of materials. The orders release and detailed assignment activities frequently take place at the same time. The order in which the jobs are to be processed is determined not on the shop floor but in the shop orders loading and release phase.

Section 2 of this paper presents a literature review and state of the art of the orders release and workload control field. Section 3 describes a new concept for workload conrol in flow shops based on Goldratt's ideas about balancing flow instead of capacity, Section 4 includes extensive simulation experiments and Section 5 concudes the research work.

2   Literature review and state of the art

Observing the Orders Release function in the industrial practice, it can be seen that not all jobs (production orders, shop orders or work orders) are released to the shop immediately after it becomes theretically possible to do so. Rather they are retained in a   "suspence file", thus being nothing more than a notation in a scheduling book which takes the form of a *"job pool"* (Irastorza and Dean, 1974). Utilisation of this job pool can reduce the level of work-in-process and allow more control over the flow of jobs through the shop. This is in fact equivalent to cleaning up the shop floor by not allowing excess jobs to move into the shop. The literature on orders release is sparce in comparison to the literature on detailed scheduling and sequencing. However, the articles that have been written indicate that effective orders release is a prerequisite to the development of a good SFC system.

Under the job pool concept the shop consists of a pool of jobs not yet released to the floor plus distinct work centres with a queue of jobs in front of each. Loading consists of the release into the shop of a subset of the pool every scheduling period. The scheduling period can be a shift, a day, a week, etc.

The key to the successful use of the job pool is the availability of a good mechanism to select those jobs from the pool that should be moved to the factory floor. This mechanism is in fact the *Input/Output Control (IOC)* methodology. The idea of Input/Output Control was first mentioned by White (1970) and further supported by Plossl and Welch (1979) some years later. Since then, many authors (Bertrand and Wortmann 1981, Tatsiopoulos and Kingsman 1984, Wiendahl 1987, Bechte 1988, Wein 1988, Glassey and Resende 1988, Kingsman et al 1989, Bertrand et al 1990) have studied the subject.The method calculates planned input, planned output, planned queue and deviations at each work centre, in order to decide on the release of shop orders. Variations to the Input/Output Control concept appear in the literature under the name *workload control, work backlog control* and *load-oriented orders release.*These concepts are mainly developed for job shop environments and the pure job shop model has been used for evaluation. Different approaches have been proposed, which all aim at keeping work backlogs at a low and stable level.

(a) The workload control concept developed at the IFA in Hannover (Wiendahl, 1995), estimates the input from jobs upstream to the direct backlog (queue) of a workstation. The estimated direct backlogs workloads are subjected to norms.

(b) The workload control concepts developed in Eindhoven (Bertrand et al, 1990) and Lancaster (Kingsman et al, 1989) avoid estimating the input to the direct backlogs. They aggregate the direct and the indirect workload of a workstation by adding them and subject this *aggregate workload (or backlog)* to a norm.

Effort in the area of flow shops or manufacturing cells is limited. Bertrand and Van Ooijen (1996), Tatsiopoulos and Prastacos [16], Enns (1995), and Oosterman et al (2000) are among the authors that have studied the application of input control methodology in a flow shop type of production system.

The main objective of this paper is to study and compare the behaviour of workload control in various forms of flow shops, i.e. the MTO (Make To Order) flow shop without using an MRP system and the MTS (Make To Stock) flow shop using an MRP system. A new balancing flow principle is developed for controlling the input of work into the flow shop, which is called B-LOB (Backlog Line-Of-Balance). Furthermore, the paper tries to investigate the influence of an MRP system to the pool of unreleased orders by means of a releasing mechanism between the MRP system and the flow shop. Conclusions are drawn for the performance of the system with or without an MRP system and with or without the input control mechanism in MTO and MTS environments.

3 Workload control in flow shops

The input/output control or workload control method obviously needs to know input and output of work centres at the very moment they happen. However, input information is considered reliable only for gateway work centres. On the contrary, the timing of work input to the following downstream work centres is highly unpredictable.

To solve this problem an aggregate input/output approach can be used (Kingsman et al, 1989) relying on the aggregate released backlog instead of actual queues. The *aggregate released backlog* of a work centre is defined as the sum of all released work on the shop floor for this particular work centre, regardless of where it resides, either in the centre's actual queue or in the queue of any other previous (upstream) work centre.

The main advantage of the aggregate released backlog as a planning tool is that all the operations of a job to be released join the released backlogs of the corresponding work centres in the job sequence simultaneously at the job release time and stay there until the job is processed and leaves the work centre. This means that input to the aggregate released backlog can be easily controlled for all the work centres, gateway or downstream they maybe, since there is no need to forecast uncertain operation transit and arrival times.

The mathematical expressions for the Released Backlog, the Input/Output relationship and the Released Backlog Length are as follows:

$$RB(J,T) = \sum_{R} \sum_{F} W(I,F(J),T)$$

$$RB(J,T) = RB(J,0) + \sum_{t=1}^{T} R(J,t) - \sum_{t=1}^{T} C(J,t)$$

$$RB(J,T) = RB(J,T-1) + R(J,T) - C(J,T)$$

$$RBL(J,T) = RB(J,T) / C(J,T) \text{ where,}$$

RB(J,T)	= Released Backlog of work centre J at period T.
W(I,F(J),T)	= Work content of operation of job I to be carried out in the future at work centre J, where job I resides at time T in the queue of wok centre F.
F	= Number of work centres in the shop.
R	= Released jobs to the shop floor.

R(J,T)   = Amount of work that is released during period T for work centre J.

RBL(J,T)   = Released Backlog Length of work centre J at period T.

C(J,T)   = Planned capacity of work centre J at period T.

RB(J,0)   = Initial Released Backlog of work centre J.

The queue Q(J,T) of work centre J is only a part of its Released Backlog RB(J). The rest will be called the Indirect Released Backlog IRB(J,T) of work centre J at period T.

$$RB(J,T) = Q(J,T) + IBR(J,T) = \sum_I W(I,J(J),T) + \sum_I \sum_{L \neq J} W(I,L(J),T)$$

where,

W(I,J(J),T)   = Work content of operation of job I to be carried out at work centre J, where job I presently resides in the queue of work centre J.

W(I,L(J),T)   = Work content of operation of job I to be carried out in the future at work centre J, where job I presently resides in the queue of work centre L.

L   = All the work centres apart from work centre J.

The Released Backlog Length RBL(J,T) is equal to the sum of the Indirect Released Backlog Length IRBL(J,T) and the Queue Length QL(J,T).

$$RBL(J,T) = QL(J,T) + IRBL(J,T)$$

The behaviour of the relation between the Indirect Released Backlog Length and the Queue Length within their sum, which is the Released Backlog Length, has to be carefully analysed. On the nature of this relation depends the ability of the planner to control the average queue lengths through aggregate Input/Output Control of the released backlogs of all the work centres. In the case of the flow shop, where a distinct main material and order flow can be found, a Mean Position MP(J) can be defined for all the work centres belonging to the main flow:

$$MP(J) = \sum_I P(I,J)/N \quad \text{where,}$$

MP(J)   = Mean position of work centre J. It is the mean number of work centres passed through before a job getting to work centre J.

P(I,J)   = Position of work centre J in the job sequence of job I.

N   = total number of jobs passing through work centre J over a long time period.

Assuming that the main flow is well balanced, i.e. the same mean waiting time and queue length applies for all the work centres across the path, the following conditions will hold:

a)   *Input rate to work centre J = Output rate from work centre J.*

$$\sum_I \sum_{L \neq J} W(I,L(J))/C(J)) * P \quad = \sum_I W(I,J(J)/C(J)$$

P_{LJ} = The probability of work flowing from work centre L to work centre J.

Assuming that $\sum_L P_{LJ} \cong P_{J-1J} \cong 1$ then

$$\sum_I W(I,J-1(J))/C(J) = \sum_I W(I,J(J))/C(J)$$

where J-1 is the work centre previous to J in the main flow of work in the flow shop.

b)   Output rate from work centre J-1 = Input rate to work centre J.

$$\sum_I W(I, J-1(J-1))/C(J-1) = \sum_I W(I, J-1(J))/C(J) = \sum_I W(I, J(J))/C(J)$$

Working the same way across the chain of work centres in the main flow upstream to the first work centre, we get:

$$\sum_I \sum_{L \neq J} W(I, L(L))/C(L) = \sum_I \sum_{L \neq J} W(I, L(J))/C(J) \Rightarrow \sum_{L \neq J} QL(L) = IRBL(J) \Rightarrow$$

$$\sum_{L \neq J} QL(L) + QL(J) = RBL(J) \Rightarrow MQL * MP(J) = RBL(J)$$

where, MQL is the common mean queue length over all the work centres.

Therefore, the released backlog length of a work centre is equal to the product of the mean position of the work centre in the main flow and the mean queue length. The indirect released backlog length of work centre J is equal to the sum of the queue lengths of all the previous work centres a job has to pass before it is processed at work centre J.

The concept of discrete orders release (not time-phased) using the Input/ Output Control (IOC) methodology in flowshops including outsourcing networks is described below:

Whole partner factories performing a single manufacturing operation or a sequence of operations are considered as black box capacity units. The role of the "order pool" is played by the unreleased Production Orders (PPOs) file.

- At the supply chain release level a workload control method has been developed, which is directed rather to the balance of production flow through the supply chain rather than the balance of capacities. This method is characterised by two main principles: Production orders are allowed to remain unreleased for up to a maximum of a few time periods to form a backlog of unreleased orders (pool), with the maximum delay added to the manufacturing time to obtain the lead time.

- Production orders are released periodically in such a way that each partner or indoor work centre and all its downstream partners.work centres are provided with a balanced inflow of work so that their mean released backlogs lengths (actual queue plus released work residing in the upstream partners/work centres) do not exceed their maximum limits.

To solve this problem an aggregate input/output approach can be used relying on the aggregate released backlog instead of actual queues. The *aggregate released backlog* of a subcontracting partner is defined as the sum of all released work for this particular partner, regardless of where it resides, either in the partner's actual queue or in the queue of any other previous (upstream) partner.

The main advantage of the aggregate released backlog as a planning tool is that all the operations of a production order to be released join the released backlogs of the corresponding partners in the order sequence simultaneously at the order release time and stay there until the order is processed and leaves the partner. This means that input to the aggregate released backlog can be easily controlled for all the partners.

The basic tool of our approach for making input control interactive decisions is the backlog length chart (Figure 1). A basic concept of this tool is the *Backlog Line-of-Balance* (B-LOB). This concept has its origin in the Line-of-Balance (LOB) technique of production control in batch production (Bestwick and Lockyer, 1982). In our case the LOB concept has been combined with the Input/Output Control (IOC) concept and produced the B-LOB technique which is suitable for applying IOC in flow shops. The characteristics of this graphical tool are:

(a) The bars represent backlog lengths of partners/work centres, i.e. relationships between backlogs and capacities. The backlog lengths are multiples of the backlogs and capacities. They change with the capacity even if the backlogs remain the same.

(b) The chart is not time-phased. The backlog lengths of all the partners are depicted at the same time period. On the contrary the classical load reports show time-phased capacity requirements of just one work centre at a time, so that the overall load situation cannot be grasped at a glance.

(c) All the operations of a production order are loaded simultaneously at the time period of order entry, so that the inaccurate loading due to the uncertainty of interoperation transit time is avoided.

(d) The released backlogs of downstream partners/work centres are multiples of the released backlog of the gateway partner/work centre. In the case of flow shops this is analoguous to the position of the work centre in the sequence of operations forming a "line-of-balance" for the ideally balanced shop (thick line profile in Figure 3).

(e) Norms of maximum and minimum backlog lengths are depicted on the chart. Actual performance can then be drawn on the chart, the difference between plan and performance becoming obvious. It is very useful when progressing because it is immediately obvious when corrective action needs to be taken.

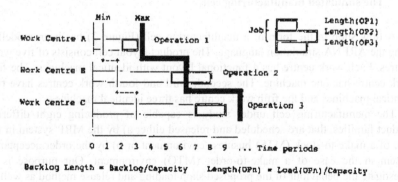

Fig. 1. Backlog length chart and Line-Of-Balance

At the moment of an order release to the cell, there is a contribution to the total workload for each work centre, which the order will visit. The respective amount of work (set-up and process time), after the completion of an operation, is deducted from the total workload, the released backlog of work of the respective work centre. Every moment we know the total amount of workload, the released backlog, which resides in every work centre of the cell, and by controlling the levels of the released backlogs in each work centre, with predetermined norms, we ensure that the total backlog and the flow or work through the cell is smooth and controlled. Assumed is that the master plan (overall LOB-norm) is fixed by one central point in the manufacturing network, which the prime contractor who has direct contact to the customers. At the moment of an order release to the manufacturing network, there is a contribution to the aggregate released backlog of each partner/work centre, that the order will visit. After operation completion, the amount of work (set-up and process time) is deducted from the released backlog of the respective work centre. Every moment we know the released backlog of every partner/work centre, and by controlling the levels of the released backlogs in each partner/work centre, with the predetermined norms of the line-of-balance, we ensure that the backlog and the flow of work through the shop is smooth and controlled.

By means of the above methodology we can also control the operation lead times and the total manufacturing lead times, moreover to compute and apply more reliable delivery times for customer orders. Knowing the capacity of a partner/work centre, in standard labour hours per day, and the predetermined backlog of work for a certain work centre we can compute the mean lead time for the work orders. The mean lead time is equal to the ratio of the backlog of work and the output of work (capacity).

4   The Simulation Model

4.1   The simulated manufacturing cell

A flow shop in the form of a manufacturing cell (Figure 2) has been modelled using the ARENA simulation language. The product layout cell consists of five work centres. Each work centre has a functional layout with identical machines. The first work centre has one machine. The second, third and fourth work centres have two identical machines and the fifth work centre has three identical machines.

The manufacturing cell under study is capable of producing eight different product families, that are scheduled and released either a) by the MRP system in the case of a make-to-stock (MTS) business environment or b) by the order acceptance system in the case of a make-to-order (MTO) environment. Our purpose is to investigate the behaviour of the proposed shop loading and release method as well as the influence of the pool concept to the two different environments.

Each product family can have a number of similar products. The products that belong to the same family have physical (material, dimensions, weight) and functional (routing, set-up time, operation time) similarities. The natural flow of parts in the system is from work centre 1 to work centre 5 (Figure 2). Following the principle of a flow shop, an order is allowed to skip a work centre, however it is not allowed to flow inversely nor to revisit a work centre (backtracking).

The part routings for each family are given in Table 1 together with the five different product mixes that are examined in this study.

Table 1. Number of families, part routings and product mix

Family	Routing	Product Mix				
		A1	A2	A3	A4	A5
1	1-2-3-4-5	0.125	0.050	0	0	0
2	1-2-3-5	0.125	0.050	0	0	0
3	1-2-4-5	0.125	0.050	0	0	0
4	1-3-4-5	0.125	0.125	0.2	0.125	0.05
5	2-3-4-5	0.125	0.125	0.2	0.125	0.05
6	1-3-5	0.125	0.200	0.2	0.250	0.30
7	2-3-5	0.125	0.200	0.2	0.250	0.30
8	2-4-5	0.125	0.200	0.2	0.250	0.30
	Sum	1.000	1.000	1.0	1.000	1.00

The orders arrive under a Poisson distribution; in other words the time between arrivals follows the exponential distribution with a mean of 1.4 hours. This value is chosen as a result of initial pilot runs that produce a 90% average utilisation of the system. A new order that arrives to the system is assigned a number of attributes: the family number, the standard operation and set-up times, the order size, the standard MRP lead time, the due date and the earliest release date.

The family number for a newly arrived order is extracted from a discrete probability distribution according to a predetermined product mix. The product mix is the probability for a newly arrived order to belong in one of the eight possible families.

According to the different product mixes there are five different types of experiments. There is the ability to give zero probability for any family. Thus we force the cell to produce fewer families of products and by the appropriate selection to have a cell with less than five work centres (see Table 1).

The operation processing times follow a uniform distribution. The earliest release date is the next planned order release period. The MRP system plans orders on a weekly planning period. Every week (40 simulated hours) shop orders are planned by the MRP system and loaded into the pool. The pool is then responsible to release orders according to the current *Aggregate Workload* of the manufacturing cell. The objective of the releasing mechanism is to control and balance the released workload according to predetermined norms following the B-LOB principle.

Calculation of order due dates is based on the *Total Manufacturing Lead Time*, which is the sum of the time spent in the pool (*Pool Delay Allowance*) and the time spent in the manufacturing cell (*Throughput Time*). For every planned MRP order that enters the pool, the *Operation Lengths* (*OPLs*, see Figure 3) of all order operations are calculated. An OPL is the sum of the run and set-up times of the operation. Each order that enters the pool contributes to the *Work Centre Pool*

Lengths (WCPLs), which are the sum of all OPLs for their respective work centres. The WCPLs are updated every period that the pool is loaded by planned MRP orders or releases orders to the cell. The Max (WCPLj), where j is a work centre of the order's routing, is defined as the Pool Delay Allowance for that order (Figure 3). The *Throughput Time* of an order equals to the sum of the total run and set-up times for all operations (*Job Cycle Time*) plus a *Queue Allowance Factor*. The queue allowance factor equals to the product of the average queue length (in hours) times the number of operations of the order. The average queue length is set to eight simulated hours and represents the operation lead- time for every work centre.

The goal is to keep the average lead times (total manufacturing lead time and throughput time) under control through the predetermined norms concerning the Pool Delay Allowance and the Queue Allowance Factor. An order with five operations, for example, will have an estimated throughput time equal to 40 hours plus the job cycle time. Thus the calculated total manufacturing lead time of an order is based on the time that the order spends in the pool waiting for its release plus the time that the order spends into the manufacturing cell being processed and waiting in work centre queues.

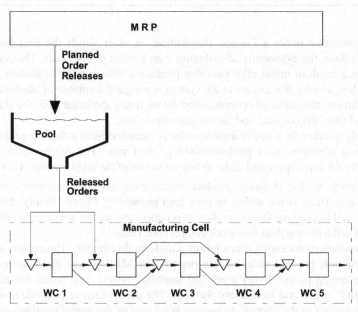

Fig. 2. Layout status of the manufacturing cell

Input Control Mechanism

The input control mechanism is also constructed according to the aggregate workload principle. It is based on the released backlog lengths for every work centre. For an order to be released into the cell, all the work centre released backlog lengths must be within minimum and maximum predetermined norm. The goal is to keep the average backlog lengths, which are the average operation lead times, balanced.

The pool is responsible to control work centre backlogs by releasing orders in the cell or delaying them in the pool according to the norms of released backlog lengths.

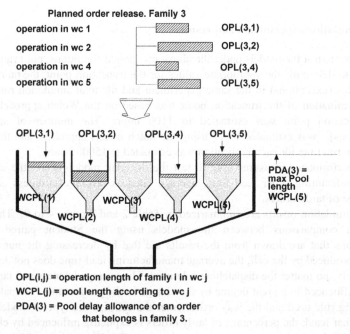

Fig. 3. Pool delay allowance of a shop order

Dispatching rules

In this study two dispatching rules used within the manufacturing cell are examined. The FIFO (First-In-First-Out) rule that supports the natural flow of the orders through the system, and the EDD (Earliest Due Date) rule that places the orders in the queues according to the earliest due date that has been calculated by the input control mechanism. There is also a dispatching principle that schedules the MRP planned orders to join the pool. This dispatching principle organises the position of the orders according to the minimum number of operations in each order.

Types of models examined.

There are three different types of models that are examined in this study. The manufacturing cell environment is the same for all model types. Model type I include an MRP system and an input control mechanism. Model type II includes only an input control mechanism, and model type III includes only an MRP system that releases orders to the cell without an input control mechanism. We can say that model types I and III represent a make-to-stock production environment (MTS) and model type II a make-to-order production environment (MTO).

We name the five different product mixes used in this study from A1 to A5 (Table 1). A classification system is used that helps recognition of the different types of models examined. Thus the code I/EDD/A1 represents models type I, who uses the EDD dispatching rule and the A1 products mix probability distribution. This codification of 3*2*5 parameters leads to 30 different types of simulation experiments.

4.2   Simulation experiments and results

In order to test the models under the above mentioned conditions, pilot runs were executed to determine the appropriate values for the truncation point, the number of the samples (executions) in the same experiment and the total simulation run time. The determination of the truncation point was based on the Welch approach [17]. The truncation point was estimated to 1100 hours. The number of samples (replications), was estimated to 17 using the batch means approach, and the total simulation run time for each replication was estimated to 15000 hours.

The performance measures used to test the different models were: the average total manufacturing order lead time, average lateness, average tardiness and the percentage of tardy orders.

The simulation results are summarized in Table 2 and Figures 4 to 9. They are based on comparisons between the models using the Student paired t-test. Conclusions that are drawn from the results are that by decreasing the number of families produced by the cell, the average manufacturing lead-time does not decrease respectively, no matter the dispatching rule used. The average lateness and tardiness are not influenced in a great degree by the change in the product mix, no matter the dispatching rule used and the way orders enter the cell, i.e. the type of model used. On the other hand, the percentage of tardy orders is explicitly influenced by changes in the product's mix structure.

Using the EDD dispatching rule, the percentage of tardy orders is significantly decreased independently of the product mix and the type of model used. The average manufacturing lead time is greatly reduced using the EDD dispatching rule instead of FIFO rule, which stands the same for a model that has an MRP system but does not use an input control mechanism. Generally with the use of EDD dispatching rule the average tardiness of the orders is reduced independently from the model type examined. In the case of model types I and II the values of average lateness are not influenced by the dispatching rule used and are approximately the same for both rules. This is not the case for model type III, where FIFO rule gives better results.

The way that orders enter the cell (model type used) influences the average manufacturing lead-time. When the pool is periodically loaded by a bulk of planned orders released from the MRP system, the result is the increase of manufacturing lead times and tardy orders. Using the pool the average tardiness is dramatically reduced independently of the model type.

In the case of MTS production environment, the use of the pool gives better results concerning the average lateness. In an MTS production system we have the accumulation of end product inventories, so that the input control mechanism is the preferred system according to the determination of order due date and due date dependability. There is not a great difference between the model types III (MTS environments) concerning the average order tardiness and I.

Table 2.
Experiment results.

Experiment Code	Lead time	Lateness	Tardiness	% Tardy	Experiment Code	Lead time	Lateness	Tardiness	% Tardy
I/FIFO/A1	97.9	-16.8	1.06	18	II/EDD/A1	40.2	-13.9	7.11E-02	3.38
I/FIFO/A2	85.8	-11.9	1.88	28.6	II/EDD/A2	29.9	-13.9	0.231	7.81
I/FIFO/A3	120	-21.8	1.53	24.5	II/EDD/A3	80.5	-16.9	0.228	8.46
I/FIFO/A4	80	-10.1	2.21	32.9	II/EDD/A4	26.4	-13.8	0.318	8.95
I/FIFO/A5	75.2	-6.47	3.06	42.4	II/EDD/A5	21.5	-15	0.417	8.56
I/EDD/A1	98.4	-15	0.175	5.05	III/FIFO/A1	89.7	-219	2.58	4.16
I/EDD/A2	83	-11.2	0.526	14.3	III/FIFO/A2	83.7	-205	3.14	4.52
I/EDD/A3	107	-18	0.171	5.29	III/FIFO/A3	114	-176	10.5	11.1
I/EDD/A4	77.1	-9.7	0.706	18.4	III/FIFO/A4	78.9	-196	2.89	4.46
I/EDD/A5	72.5	-6.38	1.49	32.4	III/FIFO/A5	74.7	-187	3.05	4.46
II/FIFO/A1	40.9	-12.8	0.514	12.4	III/EDD/A1	69.3	-240	0	0
II/FIFO/A2	31.1	-12.7	0.764	15.2	III/EDD/A2	64.2	-225	2.53E-02	0.206
II/FIFO/A3	78.2	-16.6	0.878	23.3	III/EDD/A3	71.8	-217	2.00E-02	0.165
II/FIFO/A4	27.6	-12.7	0.789	14.8	III/EDD/A4	59.4	-215	1.28E-02	.0951
II/FIFO/A5	22.6	-14	0.701	10.9	III/EDD/A5	57	-205	0.126	0.573

Using an input control mechanism it is not necessary to use different and complex dispatching rules in the waiting queues. It is more convenient to let the orders flow through the production system according with the way they are released from the pool. Some times a dispatching rule different from the FIFO rule, which supports the natural flow of orders through the system, may produce worse results.

Finally comparing the model types III, and I, that use the MPR planning system, we conclude that the input control mechanism did not increase the performance of the system concerning the average lead-time. In the case of the FIFO rule this difference is not significant. Consecutively in the case of EDD rule the difference is very significant. We can find the same results in Baker (1984) and Melnyk and Ragatz (1989).

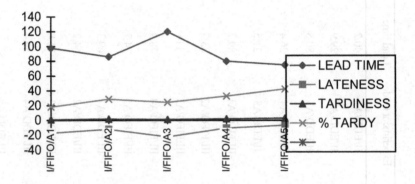

Fig. 4. Models type I, with FIFO for the five product mix distributions.

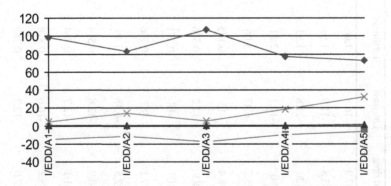

Fig. 5. Models type I with EDD for the product mix distributions.

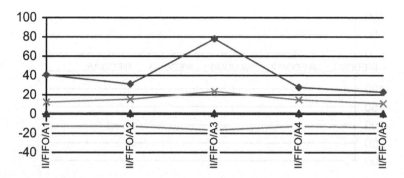

Fig. 6. Models type II with FIFO for the five product mix distributions.

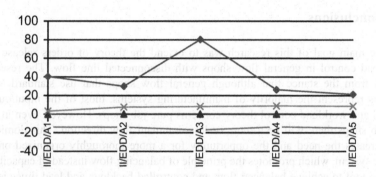

Fig. 7. Models type II with EDD for the five product mix distributions.

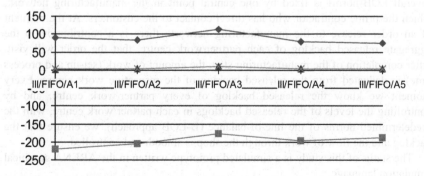

Fig. 8. Models type III with FIFO for the five product mix distributions.

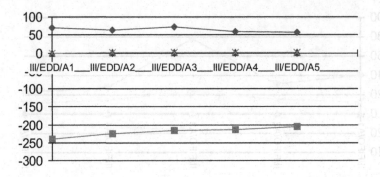

Fig. 9. Models type III with EDD for the five product mix distributions.

5   Conclusions

The main goal of this research was to extend the theory of orders release and workload control in general flow shops with disconnected line flow. The research started from the stance that although general flow shops that use standard MRP systems represent the majority of manufacturing systems, most of the input/output control and workload control theory concerns pure job shops. However, even in real life job shops there will be a more or less dominant flow direction. This dominant flow creates the need and the opportunity for a more thoroughly organized orders release system, which promotes the principle of balancing flow instead of capacity.

The tool to achieve balanced flow and controlled backlogs and lead times is the B-LOB technique and chart (Backlog Line of Balance). Our results are expected to be useful for those interested in including an orders release mechanism between the MRP system and the shop floor control system. Assumed is that the master plan (overall LOB-norm) is fixed by one central point in the manufacturing network, which the prime contractor who has direct contact to the customers. At the moment of an order release to the manufacturing network, there is a contribution to the aggregate released backlog of each partner/work centre, that the order will visit. After completion of the manufacturing step, the amount of work (set-up and process time) is deducted from the released backlog of the respective work centre. Every moment we know the released backlog of every partner/work centre, and by controlling the levels of the released backlogs in each partner/work centre, with the predetermined norms of the line-of-balance (B-LOB approach), we ensure that the backlog and the flow of work through the shop is smooth and controlled.

The status of this study is a simulated prototype written in the ARENA graphical simulation language.

References

1. Baker, K.R., 1984, "The Effects of Input Control In a Simple Scheduling Model", Journal of Operations Management, Vol. 4, No. 2, pp. 99-112.

2. Bechte, W., 1988, "Theory and Practice of Load-oriented Manufacturing Control", International Journal of Production Research, Vol. 26, No. 3, pp. 375-395.

3. Bechte, W., 1994, "Load-oriented Manufacturing Control, Just-In-Time Production for Job Shops", Production Planning and Control, Vol.5, No.3, pp. 292-307.

4. Bergamaschi et al., 1997, "Order Review and Release Strategies in a Job Shop Environment: A Review and Classification", Int. Journal of Production Research, Vol. 35, No.2, 339-420.

5. Bertrand, J.W.M. and J.C. Wortmann, 1981, "Production Control and Information Systems for Component Manufacturing Shops", Elsevier, Amsterdam.

6. Bertrand, J.W.M., Wortmann, J.C. and Wijngaard J., 1990, "Production Control. A Structural and Design Oriented Approach", Elsevier, Amsterdam.

7. Bertrand, J.W.M. and H.P.G. Van Ooijen, 1991, "Flow Rate Flexibility in Complex Production Departments", International Journal of Production Research, Vol. 29, No. 4, pp. 713-724.

8. Bertrand, J.W.M. and H.P.G. van Ooijen, 1996, "Integrating material coordination and capacity load smoothing in multi-product multi-phase production systems", Intern. J. of Prod. Econ. (46-47) 1-3, pp. 1-12.

9. Bestwick, P.F. and K. Lockyer, 1982, "Quantitative Production Management", Pitman Publishing, Mass.

10. Enns, S.T., 1995, "An integrated system for controlling shop loading and work flows", Int. Journal of Production Research, Vol.33, No. 0, pp. 2801-2820.

11. Glassey and Resende, 1998, "Closed-loop Job Release Control for VLSI Circuit Manufacturing", IEEE Transactions on Semiconductor Manufacturing, 1, 1, 36-46.

12. Henry, L.C. and B.G. Kingsman, 1991, "Job Release: Part of a Hierarchical System to manage manufacturing lead times in make-to-order companies", J. Opl. Res. Soc., 42, pp. 871-883.

13. Hopp, W.J. and M.L. Spearman, 2000, "Factory Physics", McGraw Hill, Boston.

14. Irastorza, J.C. and R.H. Deane, 1974, "A Loading and Balancing Methodology for Job Shop Control", AIIE Transactions, Vol. 6, No. 4, pp. 302-307.

15. Kingsman, B.G., Tatsiopoulos, I.P. and L.C. Hendry, 1989, "A Structural Methodology for Managing Manufacturing Lead Times In Make-to-Order Companies", European Journal of Operational Research, Vol. 40, pp. 196-209.

16. Kingsman, B., 2000, «Modelling Input-Output workload control for dynamic capacity planning in production planning systems», Int. J. of Production Economics, 68 (1), pp 73-93.

17. Land, M.J. and Gaalman G.J., 1996, "Workload Control Concepts in Job Shops: A Critical Assessment", Int. Journal of Production Economics, Vol. 46-47, pp. 535-548.

18. Melnyk, S.A. and G.L. Ragatz, 1989, "Order Review/Release: Research Issues and Perspectives", International Journal of Production Research, Vol. 27, No. 7, pp. 1081-1096.

19. Oosterman, B., Land, M., Gaalman, G., 2000, «The Influence of Shop Characteristics on Workload Control», Int. J. of Production Economics, 68 (1), pp. 107-119.

20. Plossl, G. and Wight, O., 1973, Capacity Planning and Control, Production and Inventory Management, 3rd Qtr., pp. 31-67.

21. Plossl, G.W. and W.E. Welch, 1979, "Decision Systems for Inventory Management and Production Planning", Reston Publ. Co.

22. Tatsiopoulos, I.P. and B.G. Kingsman, 1983, "Lead Time Management", European Journal of Operational Research, Vol. 14, pp. 351-358.

23. Tatsiopoulos, I.P, 1986, "Some Aspects of the Input/Output Methods for Managing Work-in-process Inventories", Engineering Costs and Production Economics, No. 15, pp. 235.

24. Tatsiopoulos. I.P., 1993, "Simplified production management software for the small manufacturing firm", Production Planning and Control, 15, 25-40.

25. Wein, 1988, Scheduling Semiconuctor in Wafer Fabrication, IEEE Transactions on Semiconductor Manufacturing, 1, 3, 115-130.

26. Welch, P.D., 1983, "The Statistical Analysis of Simulation Results", in the "Computer Performance Modelling Handbook", S.S. Lavenberg, ed., pp. 268-232, Academic Press, NY.

27. Wiendhal, H.P., 1995, "Load Oriented Manuacturing Control", Springer Verlag, Berlin.

28. Wight, O.W., 1970, "Input/Output Control: a Real Handle on Lead -Time", Production & Inventory Management, Vol. 11, 3rd Quarter.

A Service Oriented Architecture to Support Industrial Information Systems

F. Biennier, A. Legait

PRISMa – INSA de Lyon – 69621 Villeurbanne Cédex France

Abstract. In order to fulfill economical constraints, enterprises are more and more involved in collaborative organizations. To develop such co-industry frameworks, a particular attention has to be paid on enterprises organisation and on the common information system. To provide the required agility level involved by such lean collaborative organizations, one may use a Service Oriented Architecture to support the information system infrastructure. Despite of its intrinsic flexibility and openness (given by a rather "free" service orchestration), such architecture may lack of inter-operability, mostly as far as industrial information systems are concerned. In this paper we propose an architecture to couple both management and production processes in a common service oriented approach so that different levels of inter-operability can be supported.

1 Introduction

Due to the economical context involving more and more customization and "service oriented products", enterprises have to adapt their organizational strategy: while focusing on their core business, outsourcing or collaborative strategies must be set to fit the market requirements (i.e. getting a critical size and being able to provide a high service level to the consumer). These organizational trends enhance the enterprise's agility, i.e. the ability to answer to structural changes quickly (client requests, technological or activity changes, supplier management...) [4, 7] and to reduce waste (leading to lean manufacturing organization) [12]. These organizations make a heavy use of information and communication technologies leading to increase the call for IT inter-operability: their performance level is related to an efficient information sharing system so that deviation risks are reduced [2]. Moreover, the efficiency involves also to take into account lean manufacturing [9] constraints while organizing the enterprise so that service and the associated processes should be strongly coupled. **Consequently, this context requires both an**

Please use the following format when citing this chapter:

Biennier, F. and Legait, A., 2008, in IFIP International Federation for Information Processing, Volume 257, Lean Business Systems and Beyond, Tomasz Koch, ed.; (Boston: Springer), pp. 93–100.

agile Information System and an agile organization to allow « on-demand » re-configuration.

While traditional information systems focus on the management and business sides, a particular attention must be paid on the production (or industrial) side to support efficiently co-production constraints. This leads to take into account several inter-operability constraints:

- "Organizational" inter-operability means that enterprises must share a same goal and have compatible management strategies
- "Industrial" inter-operability means that enterprises must share information on production processes and on product information
- "Technical" inter-operability means that the different components of the information systems can share and exchange pieces of information
- Semantic inter-operability means that the different systems can understand in a similar way a same piece of information.

After introducing the context, we'll focus on the architecture we propose to integrate "workshop information systems" into the enterprise global information system.

2   Context

Due to the high diversity of the IT support systems according to both a technological point of view (several languages, DBMS, information internal organisation…) and to the supported functions (ERP are devoted to management and planning functions while PLM manages technical data and MES are in charge of production monitoring… [10]) the enterprise information system is complex. To bring more flexibility, the Service Oriented Architecture paradigm consists in orchestrating conveniently "services", i.e. components. Based on a common referential, such an architecture is used to interconnect the different IS components, i.e. ERP, CRM, SCM… systems. Thanks to a service repository service consumers can locate dynamically the service they need before executing it remotely thanks to a service request/ service result mechanism (using the SOAP protocol). Despite of its intrinsic openness, this orchestration mechanism leads to a formal workflow structure of the business and management processes.

Workflow based approaches can be fruitfully used to support both business processes and production processes description [5] but these "on demand" made tools may increase the information system complexity and inconsistency. ICT tools supporting the production process execution (as MES, Profinet CBA…) are based both on web technologies (including web services) and a workflow based model to support the production process description [10]. Consequently, as they are supported by similar technologies, both service and production views can be coupled at a technological level. This involves adding new connections to the enterprise information system as shown figure 2 to set an industrial information system. Moreover, integrating the production process in the common orchestration involves also managing its maturity level to identify the exact process organization to use (ad-hoc or formal workflow) and its impact on the workshop management system. This involves a full re-design of the SOA orchestration principle.

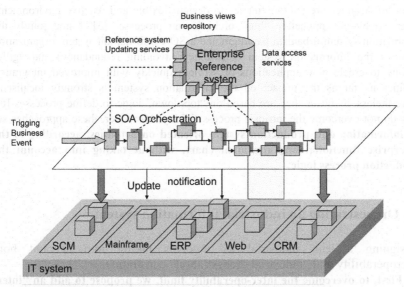

Fig. 1. Using the SOA paradigm to federate the enterprise information system

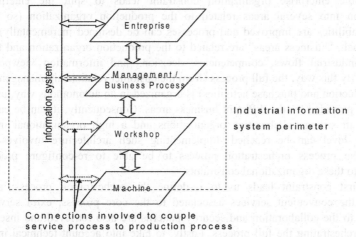

Fig. 2. Industrial information system

Nevertheless, using the SOA paradigm is not enough to bring the required agility level to the IS. As the global IS is a complex system, one must re-organize it in order to get a simplified structure, easier to manipulate and to control evolutions. To solve these problems, the information system urbanization approach [8] splits the information system into sub-systems related to different business areas [1]. Coupled to a Service Oriented Architecture (SOA) this urbanism approach also splits the information system into different levels, separating activities from the information system and from the technical infrastructure. Thus, the introduction of the Service Oriented Architecture (SOA) enables to design flexible and reactive environments federated by an applicative "bus" orchestrating processes [3]. Using jointly the information system urbanism paradigm and a SOA information system organization improve the information system consistency (avoiding redundancy) and agility (ability to create new applications or services quickly with improved integration abilities as far as the impact on the information system is strongly localised). Nevertheless, as far as they are based on "top-down" logic to define processes [6], they do not overcome the intrinsic process rigidity. Moreover, these approaches **set an information and production system oriented on activities, according to the enterprise functional organizational chart, without taking into account the production process logic.**

3   Orchestrating an industrial information system

Designing a lean industrial IS involves taking into account both interoperability and "industrial orchestration" constraints.

First, to overcome the inter-operability limit, we propose to add an "inter-operable" organization constraint so that both service and production processes can be strongly related while designing the industrial information system. This inter-operable enterprise organization constraint leads to split the enterprise organization into several areas related to the production organization (so that evolution abilities are improved and processes can be designed incrementally). In this approach, "business areas" are related to the production organization and they integrate industrial flows, competencies, decisions and information viewpoints (figure 3). By this way, the full process (from the customer relationship management to the production and purchase activities) is organized in an autonomous way, using "services" provided by the different business areas. Consequently, it can be easily integrated in strong collaborative organizations and a high organizational inter-operability level can be reached. Implementing such architecture involves re-defining the process orchestration process to be able to re-configure process according to these organizational constraints.

This first constraint leads us to re-define the orchestration process: after searching the convenient services associated to the core process, extra services associated to the collaboration and security patterns are also retrieved and inserted while re-orchestrating the full process. Lastly, to take into account technical inter-operability, we propose to integrate standard to manage information exchange: dedicated services are used to format information into XML or B2MML formats. By this way a rather open and agile architecture can be built.

Then taking into account industrial constraints involves adapting the orchestration constraints to take into account the physical process own constraints:

1.   Depending on the product, different maturity levels must be taken into account: from a basic production order leading to a rather informal

production process specification, well defined, automated and optimised processes can also be modelled into a formal workflow

2. Physical constraints (QoS, job duration, material flows) must also be taken into account while combining the convenient services set

3. Different points of view must be integrated while managing a workshop: concurrent workflow used to support production or resources management are simultaneously under execution. This involves orchestrating and scheduling conveniently services to be executed on a same resource.

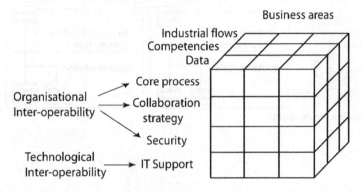

Fig. 3. Different inter-operability levels

To satisfy these requirements, we propose to split the process organisation into 2 parts. The "core" production process (called "process" in figure 4) provides a generic model including both the routing and the bills of material. This common interface is used to generate local implementation, taking into account the exact manufacturing process. The industrial interface, set between the Business/Production abstraction level and the Technical Abstraction level consists in:

1. The industrial flow interface: this area is devoted to exchange information taken from the routing and from the bill of material to define the different resources involved in the manufacturing process

2. The process maturity level: this area is used to set the process maturity level defined according to the CMMI discrete scale [11] (see figure 5): the initial level is devoted to basic production order with an informal description and is associated to a simple ad-hoc workflow. Then, level 2 is used when the manufacturing workflow can be defined formally. Level 3 and higher impacts the workshop manger so that generic models, performance indicators and dynamic tuning can be achieved.

3. Manufacturing constraints as QoS requirements, synchronisation points... are described so that the orchestration can be efficiently monitored to fulfil these requirements.

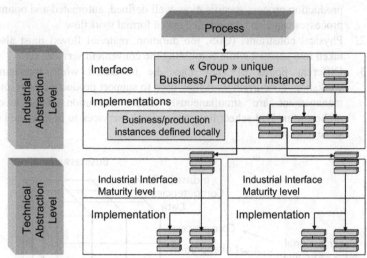

Fig. 4. Process organisation

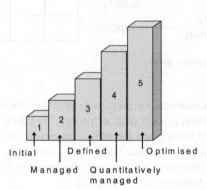

Fig. 5. CMMI discret escale

- Level 1: Initial : ad-hoc and chaotic process. Non stable manufacturing environment
- Level 2: Managed: processes are more formalised so that they can be
- Planned, performed, measured and controlled
- Level 3: Defined: processes are well characterized and understood and are described in standards, procedures, tools and methods
- Level 4: Quantitatively managed: performance indicators and dashboards are attached to the process
- Level 5: Optimising: process are continuously improved.

In order to manage both the manufacturing process and the workshop, we split the industrial orchestrator into 2 parts:

- The manufacturing orchestrator is devoted to the manufacturing process enactment and supervision (taking into account both ad-hoc and formal workflow)
- The workshop orchestrator is split among the different resources and integrates the workshop management workflow.

Building such an architecture involves organising a distributed workflow management. A continuous tuning is achieved, integrating the manufacturing industrial constraints to schedule conveniently the different tasks on the resources. Moreover, the workshop orchestrator is also used to optimise globally the workshop and consequently to orchestrate the physical flows between the resources.

4   Conclusion and further works

In this paper we present how the service oriented architecture can be used to support an agile industrial information system. Firstly set for traditional information systems, we enrich this approach to integrate inter-operability and manufacturing constraints in the orchestration process. Nevertheless, a simple "manufacturing orchestration" is not enough to manage conveniently the production processes. Taking into account the manufacturing maturity level (adapted from the CMMI discrete scale) allows the orchestrator to select the convenient workflow management systems (ad-hoc or formal workflow, connection to the workshop management process...).

Further works will focus on the different workflow integration so that a global optimization could be achieved while "orchestrating" a resource activity.

Acknowledgements

This paper presents early results from the INTER-PROD project funded by the Rhône-Alpes area council.

References

1. CIGREF 2003. "Accroitre l'agilité du système d'information". Livre blanc du CIGREF, septembre 2003.

2. DeVor R., Graves R., Mills J.J., 1997. Agile manufacturing research: accomplishments and opportunities. IIE Transactions n° 29, pp. 813-823.

3. Guergachi H, 2004. Urbanisme et architectures techniques. Séminaire Cap Gemini. 184 p.

4. Goldman S. Nagel R., Preiss K., 1995. Agile competitors and virtual organisations. New York: Van Nostrand Reinhold.

5. Huang C.Y., 2002. Distributed Manufacturing Execution Systems: a workflow perspective. Journal of Intelligent Manufacturing, 13, pp. 485-497.

6. IFAC-IFIP, 99 "GERAM: Generalized Enterprise Reference Architecture and Methodology", Version 1.6.3, IFAC-IFIP Task Force on Architecture and Methodology.

7. Lee H.L., 2004. The Triple A Supply Chain. Harvard Business Review, Octobre 2004, pp. 102-112.

8. Longepe C., 2003. The Enterprise Architecture It Project : The Urbanisation Paradigm, Kogan Page Science, ISBN:1903996384.

9. Mahoué F., 2001. The E-World as an Enabler to Lean. MSc Thesis. MIT.

10. Mc Clellan M., 1997. Applying manufacturing execution systems. St Lucie press.

11. Williams R., Wegerson P., 2002. MINI CMMI(SM) (SE/SW/IPPD/SS Ver 1.1) Staged Representation. Cooliemon.

12. Womack J.P., Jones D.T., 2003. Lean thinking, 2ème édition. Simon et Schuster, 404 p.

Development of Promise Data Structure

Jacopo Cassina[1], Maurizio Tomasella[1], Marco Taisch[1], Micheal Marquard[2],
Altug Metin[2], Andrea Matta[1]

1   Politecnico di Milano
Piazza Leonardo da Vinci, 32, 20133 Milano, Italy
2   InMediasP, Henningsdorf, Germany

Abstract. This work presents the product object model developed inside the eu-funded FP6-IST project PROMISE, which aims at closing the whole set of information loops concerning a product's life. The ultimate goals of the project are: to integrate product data from the entire life cycle via different sources, to support comprehensive analysis on this data and finally to enhance the operational businesses with the obtained insights on products. To achieve these goals, a set of hardware and software tools are being developed. This paper presents the conceptual model behind one of the components of this infrastructure, called the PDKM (Product Data and Knowledge Management) System, which is responsible for the integration and management of both product data and knowledge from all lifecycle phases, on a logically consistent basis.

1   Introduction

Within the globally scaled scenario, the "product" and its related management is becoming unavoidably a key-aspect, creating a "product centric" or "product-driven" problem. This kind of approach is represented by three main layers: PLM (Product Lifecycle Management), Product Extensions and Product Traceability.

PLM in particular has emerged as an enterprise solution. It implies that all software tools/systems/databases, such as CAD, PDM, CRM, etc., used by the various departments and suppliers throughout the product lifecycle have to be integrated such that the information managed by these systems can be shared promptly and correctly between people and applications. Nevertheless, PLM is not primarily an IT problem, but at first, it represents a strategic business orientation of the whole enterprise [Garetti 2004]. From a strategic organization point of view, the adoption of a "product centric" approach means a remodelling of all of the relations existing among the resources (people and equipment) involved into the relevant business processes specifically oriented in a "product" lifecycle direction. From an ICT point of view, this product-centric approach to product and production management, which

Please use the following format when citing this chapter:

Cassina, J., Tomasella, M., Taisch, M., Marquard, M., Metin A. and Matta, A., 2008, in IFIP International Federation for Information Processing, Volume 257, Lean Business Systems and Beyond, Tomasz Koch, ed.; (Boston: Springer), pp. 101–110.

- until now - has been executed no more than in "isolated islands" (e.g. PDM and ERP), is being integrated into a larger system, in order to provide a wider and more effective use of product and production information.

The PROMISE (PROduct lifecycle Management and Information tracking using Smart Embedded systems) project's approach to PLM aims at developing a new-generation Product Information Tracking and Flow Management system. This system will allow all actors that play a role during the lifecycle of a product (managers, designers, service and maintenance operators, recyclers, etc.) to track, manage and control product information at any phase of its lifecycle (design, manufacturing, MOL, EOL), at any time and any place in the world.

This paper describes the conceptual model behind one of the main components of this new type of PLM system, the so-called PROMISE PDKM (Product Data and Knowledge Management) system, which is devoted to the integration and management of product lifecycle data from different sources and to the creation, update and management of knowledge concerning the product, in order to improve future generations of products, starting from data on the current products collected directly from the field.

PROMISE PLM System is composed of many software and hardware systems and related infrastructures, the main are:

• The PROMISE PDKM (Product Data and Knowledge Management) system, for the management of both product data collected from the field via smart product-embedded devices, and knowledge created and updated from this data, in order to enhance e.g. the design of new products in the future.

• The PROMISE DSS (Decision Support System), which is part of the PDKM system and is devoted to support lifecycle decision making activities, thus providing the analytical basis to the whole project. This is done by defining decision strategies to be applied in the different application scenarios, as well as the related algorithms implementing these strategies.

• A set of PEIDs (Product Embedded Information Devices), i.e. RFID (Radio Frequency IDentification) active and passive tags, sensors and on-board computers, with the related embedded and backend software systems.

In the following, particular attention will be paid to the first of these systems. First, a description of it will be provided, and then the conceptual model behind the development of the same system will be presented.

2   The PROMISE PDKM

The PROMISE PDKM (Product Data and Knowledge Management) system aims at integrating and managing data from all lifecycle phases of products, in particular, from design, development, production, through use and maintenance, to recycling, and finally, to the end of life, in order to support comprehensive data analysis in business intelligence applications. The Promise Project and the PDKM are extensively explained in a previous paper of the authors. [Cassina 2006].

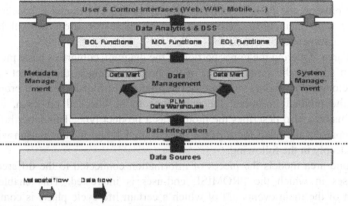

Fig. 1. Architecture overview of the PDKM system

3   Analysis of Enterprise Standards

To develop a flexible and easily compatible data model, an enterprise standards analysis has been done [Cassina 2006]. Many standards exist, each one focused on a specific area of the product lifecycle, but none including all the pieces of information needed to be managed during the whole lifecycle chain, as shown in the next figure, that represent the analyzed standards and their collocation within the product life.

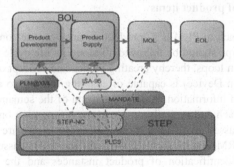

Fig. 2. Standards through Life Cycle Phases

4   Semantic model of the PDKM

The model provides a conceptual view on the PROMISE PDKM System, representing the main concepts belonging to the domain of interest, i.e. to the field of product data modelling throughout the whole product life cycle.

The model is represented in the UML 2.0 modelling language. In particular, since the focus is on the static view on the PROMISE PDKM System, only the UML Class Diagram will reported in the following.

Figure 3 represents the PDKM Semantic Object Model. The model is conceptually divided into two main areas of interest, though these two areas are well linked together by a proper set of associations.

• A first area, covering the upper portion of the diagram, comprises basic pieces of information such as the serial number of the product instance, the product type to which it belongs, the product structure of the product if needed, the main properties valid for the product instances, the conditions to be checked on them, etc. In addition, this area also describes the product as a product type. This latter however does not represent the main focus of the present model, and for this reason will not be treated deeply in the following.

• A second area models the pieces of information connected to the different life cycle phases in which the PROMISE end-user is interested. This enables the description of the main events out of which a certain life cycle phase is composed (i.e. product failures or breakdowns, replacements of components of a complex product, etc.), of the PROMISE end-user's resources involved in the scenario concerning that life cycle phase (i.e. the garage crew, the designer, the production manager, etc.), and finally the activities performed by these resources in that life cycle phase (e.g. dismantling of a car's components, maintenance of a truck, etc.). Besides this, an important portion of this area is dedicated to the representation of field data, one of the crucial elements in the PROMISE approach.

In the following, some major portions of the diagram will be discussed in details, in order to outline its most important and original features.

4.1   Identification of product items

The PROMISE approach to PLM is a "product instance-centric" one. Each instance of a certain product type should be followed all along its life cycle in order to close the desired information loops, thereby creating value. The concept of PEID (Product Embedded Information Device) is capable of enabling the link to all these product items and their related information. A central portion of the semantic model should thus reflect this approach and properly represent the information on each product at the item level. The classes involved in these traceability issues are in particular the ID_INFO, the INFORMATION_PROVIDER and the URI classes; these classes together enable the identification of product instances and the retrieval of the information on where it is possible to find other information on the same product instances.

Many traceability systems have been developed up to now (e.g. the Dialog System developed by the Helsinki University of Technology, the WWAI-World Wide Article Information concept, the AUTO-ID proposal, etc.), and the set of classes cited above should be compatible with all of them, at least from a conceptual viewpoint. There are two types of links to additional information, URI and INFORMATION_PROVIDER objects. The central class here is the ID_INFO class, where one can find the identifier of the product item (ID attribute), the coding schema used (ID_Type attribute) and eventually other formats in which the id can be presented (Alt_Pres attribute) for some reason of clarity, use, etc. The URI class identifies the external data sources which are linked to the id, when relevant for some scope (as in the Dialog System, where URI stands for Uniform resource Identifier). The URI attribute identifies e.g. the IP address on the web where the information can be retrieved, while the INFORMATION_PROVIDER class contains information that can be used to control the request for information from a traceability system. This includes e.g. the inter-enterprise communication systems which, as usual in traceability systems, take care of identifying the information providers (also possible with the URI information sources).

4.2   Description of product structures

In order for the model to be capable of modelling both "atomic" products (i.e. "one-piece" products) and complex products, some classes should be devoted to representing different kinds of product structure, following the specific needs of each application case. A first example of these classes is given by the PHYSICAL_PRODUCT class, which states the product type, the lot to which it belongs, the "birth date" of the product, the "end date" in case the product has reached the end of its life, and finally the product structure "as produced", with the specification of the identifier of all the instances of the components/subassemblies belonging to this structure. Another important class is the AS_DESIGNED_PRODUCT class, which describes on the contrary the product "as designed" structure, with all the needed information, such as CAD data, BoMs (Bill of Materials), cost information, and all the other pieces of information which are typically stored and managed by PDM (Product Data Management) systems.

4.3   Properties and Conditions

Another important feature of the proposed model is the capability of modelling properties which must be valid for some specific product type and/or product item. This is made possible by the PROPERTY class, which can also be used to describe the properties related to some important resources involved in the PLM application case of interest. This class was originally inspired by ISA-95.

The CONDITION class aims at expressing some either atomic or complex kind of condition which must be checked in some product life cycle scenario. E.g. it can be important to check if the current reading of some sensor attached to the product is over a pre-defined threshold, and eventually to start the needed activities in order to perform the needed maintenance before the product breaks up. The Condition_ID attribute univocally identifies the condition, while the Group_Identifier_ID and Reference_Group_ID attributes are used to define complex conditions, by grouping atomic conditions together. The Type_ID attribute states if a condition relates to a property of a product type/instance or to some kind of data collected on the field and concerning a specific product instance (in this case, the kind of field data must be specified, as well as the interested data source). Finally, the actions to be taken in case the condition is met/ not met must be specified (Action_When_Met and Action_When_Not_Met attributes respectively).

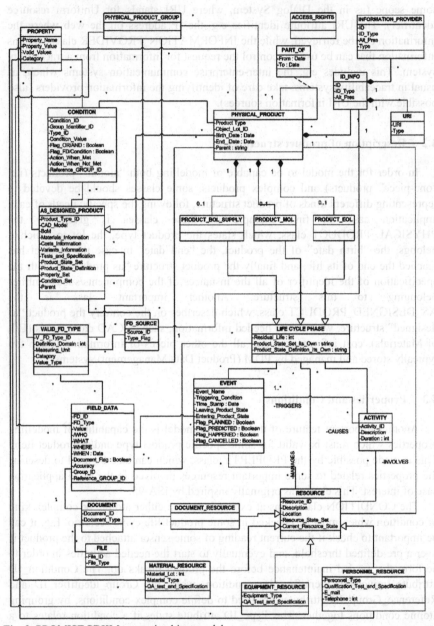

Fig. 3. PROMISE PDKM semantic object model

4.4 Life Cycle Phases

A PLM data modelling framework such as the proposed model must be also
capable of modelling the whole set of lifecycle information on the product

considered in each application case. Different applications are related to a different set of life cycle phases. The proposed model must cover these different needs. For this reason, the three classes named PRODUCT_BOL_SUPPLY, PRODUCT MOL and PRODUCT EOL were created. The names of these classes reflect the viewpoint of PROMISE on the product life cycle. The first class refers to the pieces of information related to the BOL (Beginning Of Life) phase of a product instance, from the production phase to the final delivery of the product to the customer (thus only the information concerning the design of the product is excluded from this class). The second class refers to the pieces of information related to the MOL (Middle Of Life) of a product instance, i.e. the usage phase and the maintenance phase. Finally, the third refers to the pieces of information related to the whole set of possible EOL (End Of Life) phases of a product instance (e.g. the remanufacturing phase, the recycling phase, etc.). All the pieces of information which are common to these three phases are provided by the class named LIFE_CYCLE_PHASE, which e.g. describes some important issues such as the residual life of a product component, or the set of states in which a product instance can be.

4.5   Event, Resources and Activities

Up to this point, none of the mentioned modelling elements has been intended to describe each single life cycle phase in the way the same phase is intended to be managed, i.e. none of the shown modelling elements represented the main events happening during a certain life cycle phase, the people and other kinds of resources of the company which are involved in the life cycle phase, and the activities performed during this phase. These issues are addressed by the EVENT, RESOURCE, and ACTIVITY classes. These classes of the proposed model were inspired by the production simulations, that usually uses the same concepts. Moreover there are some similar classes within STEP-PLCS and resources are structured using the same approach of ISA-95.

For instance, in a typical predictive maintenance scenario, such as those in the PROMISE project, one would like to model the event of breakdown of a component/subassembly or even of the entire product as a whole, as well as the maintenance activities and the resources, human and not human, involved in such activities. The aim could be for example to predict the point in time when the product will probably break down, to plan the related maintenance activities, and finally to record the actual time instant when the breakdown really occurs, or even to delete the breakdown event from the "list of predicted events", just because the component causing the possibility of product breakdown has been replaced by a new one, which eliminates the main cause of breakdown. The repair activities at the garage of the maintenance provider should also be first described and then properly managed in accordance with the corporate strategy of the company and in a PLM vision. So the availability of resources like free hours of the garage crew to be possibly allocated, or even the availability of the needed materials and equipments to perform the maintenance activities should be checked, and eventually, such as in some PROMISE application scenarios, the maintenance activities should be economically planned and managed.

For these purposes, the RESOURCE, ACTIVITY and EVENT classes with a certain set of attributes have been added to the model. In addition, three associations, one for each pair of these classes, have been added to state that an event triggers an activity, which involves some resources, which in turn manage the event as an important part of a specific life cycle phase. The attributes state that an event is something related to a specific time instant, while an activity generally concerns a time interval and is thus associated to a duration in terms of time. An activity has at least two events associated with it: the event "ACTIVITY STARTS" and the event "ACTIVITY ENDS". The event is triggered by some kind of condition and causes in general the shift of the product state from some "STATE A" to another "STATE B". Again, one should have the possibility, as written above, to mark with a proper flag if the event is a planned event, or if it is a predicted event, or again if the event has already happened, or has been cancelled because it cannot happen anymore (refer to the Flag attributes in the EVENT class). In addition, an activity can cause an event, such as the maintenance activity can cause the "REPLACEMENT OF COMPONENT XYZ PERFORMED", with a consequent update of the product's residual life that, if no more under the minimum threshold, causes the "PRODUCT BREAKDOWN" event to be cancelled, such as in the example above. Finally, the resources can be human beings (PERSONNEL_RESOURCE class), equipments (EQUIPMENT_RESOURCE class), materials (MATERIAL_RESOURCE class) and documents (DOCUMENT_RESOURCE class). Some of the information related to these resources is given as attributes, and some other kind of information is specified as objects of the PROPERTY class. Some important examples can be the maintenance crew as objects (e.g. one for each person) of the PERSONNEL_RESOURCE class, the tools for performing the maintenance activities as objects of the EQUIPMENT_RESOURCE class, the spare parts needed as objects of the MATERIAL_RESOURCE class and finally the product user manual, the maintenance manual or the CAD model of the product layout as objects of the DOCUMENT_RESOURCE class.

Moreover, for each resource a set of possible states is defined, and the current state is recorded. This is required for example in cases where the information on the availability of the garage all along a certain time period can be very important to plan the maintenance activities at the garage, such as in the PROMISE application scenario concerning the predictive maintenance performed over an entire fleet of trucks. Thus, two states such as AVAILABLE and NOT AVAILABLE can be defined as exhaustive and mutually exclusive states, and the setting of the product state of the garage to one or the other of these values can be used to understand if a given time interval can be assigned to the maintenance of a specific product item or not.

In addition, there also exists an association between the RESOURCE class and the PHYSICAL_PRODUCT class, to state that it sometimes can be possible that the object of the PLM system which is a resource for one company, e.g. a truck used for the delivery of the products produced by the company, may be a product item for another company, e.g. it can be part of a fleet of trucks on which the truck builder/dealer performs predictive maintenance. Such a scenario is up to now not so realistic, but anyway it is interesting to notice that the boundary between an object as a resource and an object as a product itself, as implied by the PROMISE vision, is not so well defined and even not so thick as one would think.

4.6 Field Data

Another central class of the diagram is the FIELD_DATA class, which enables the overall PROMISE approach to PLM by collecting data from the field, thus also enabling the improvement of product performance and in general the creation of economic value from PLM activities.

Field data can be of different types (VALID_FD_TYPE class), and is collected by means of sources like e.g. sensors (FD_SOURCE class). It might be organized in documents (DOCUMENT class) with attached physical files (FILE class).

In the following, a brief overview of the most important attributes of the FIELD_DATA class is reported. The FD_ID attribute univocally identifies each field data record, while the FD_Type attribute states the type of field data (e.g. that it is a temperature of a certain sensor). The Document_Flag attribute says if the field data as an attached document related to it, while the Value and Accuracy attributes should be self explaining. The /WHO attribute says "who" is responsible for the field data measurement, i.e. which is the source of the field data. This information can be also derived from the corresponding object of the FD_SOURCE class linked to the same FIELD_DATA object. The WHAT attribute explains in details what the field data stands for, i.e. the meaning of the data itself, while the WHERE attribute states the location where the measurement was carried out (if needed). The WHEN attribute then represents the timestamp indicating the m oment in time when the measurement was carried out. Finally, the Reference_GROUP_ID and the Group_ID attributes are used when there s the need of grouping some records of the same field data type together, e.g. because of the need of clustering in some way the data before analysing it.

5 Conclusions

This work led to the development of a semantic model for a PDKM, which will be able to interoperate within different systems and store all kinds of product life cycle data. This model was also tested using different application scenarios within the PROMISE consortium.

At the present time the development of the technical model starting from the semantic model is ongoing and a first prototype has been developed in collaboration with InMediaSp and SAP, partners of the PROMISE Project. The model will be also improved with the results from the use of this prototype.

Finally, the semantic model will also be used for standardization efforts; at first it will be proposed to other standardization institutions, like for example the PLCS community, to be merged inside these standards.

Acknowledgement

This work has been partly funded by the European Commission through the FP6-IST Project entitled PROMISE: PROduct lifecycle Management and Information tracking using Smart Embedded systems (No. IST-2004-507100). The authors wish to acknowledge the Commission for their support. We also wish to acknowledge our gratitude and appreciation to all the PROMISE project partners for their contribution during the development of various ideas and concepts presented in this paper.

References

1. Cassina J., Taisch M., Terzi S.; "Towards an Intelligent Extended Product"; IFIP APMS 2005.

2. Cassina J., Tomasella M., Marquard M., Metin A., Matta A., Taisch M.; "Development of the semantic object model for a PDKM System"; ICE 2006: pg.383-390.

3. Garetti M. Terzi S., Product Lifecycle Management: definition, trends and open issues, Proceedings at III International Conference On Advances In Production Engineering, 17 - 19 June 2004, Warsaw, Poland.

4. ISO9000, International Standard Organisation (ISO), 2000, International Standard ISO 9000:2000 Quality Management Systems - Fundamentals and vocabulary.

5. Jansen-Vullers J., A. van Dorp, B. Beulens, 2003, Managing traceability information in manufacture, 2003, International Journal Of Information Management 23 : 395-413.

6. Kärkkäinen J., G. Holmström, J. Främling, G. Artto, 2003, Intelligent products – A step towards a more effective project delivery chain, Computers in Industry 50 : 141-151.

7. Morel G., H. Panetto, A. Zaremba, G. Mayer, 2004, Manufacturing enterprise control and management system engineering rationales and open issues, IFAC Annual Reviews in Control, 27 : 199-209.

8. McFarlane D., J. Sarma, G. Chirn, J. Wong, A. Ashton, 2003, Auto-ID systrems and intelligent manufacturing control, Journal of Engineering Applications of Artificial Intelligence, 16 : 365 – 376.

9. Promise Project Deliverable 9.1 and 9.2 www.promise.no

10. Van Moll J.H., 2002, The importance of Life Cycle Modelling to the development and testing of complex products, TestNet Najaarsevenement, Nieuwegein.

Streamlining Asset Maintenance throughout Analysis of its Usage Data

Hong-Bae Jun, Maurice Ruibal, Dimitris Kiritsis, and Paul Xirouchakis
EPFL (STI-IPR-LICP), Staion 9, ME B1,
CH-1015 Lausanne, Switzerland
WWW home page: http://licpwww.epfl.ch

Abstract. Recently, with the advent of emerging technologies such as radio frequency identification (RFID), various sensors, and wireless tele-communication, we can have the visibility of asset status information over the whole asset lifecycle. It gives us new challenging issues for improving the efficiency of asset operations. One of the most challenging problems is the predictive maintenance that makes a prognosis of the asset status via a remote monitoring, predicts the asset's abnormality, and executes suitable maintenance actions such as repair and replacement. In this study, we will develop a prognostic decision algorithm to take suitable maintenance actions by analyzing the degradation status of an asset. To evaluate the proposed approach, we carry out a case study for a heavy machinery.

1 Introduction

In general, asset maintenance is defined as all technical and managerial actions taken during usage period to maintain or restore the required functionality of an asset. Maintenance has mainly three types: breakdown maintenance (corrective maintenance), preventive maintenance, and predictive maintenance. Among them, the predictive maintenance focuses on the prediction of degradation process of the asset, which is based on the assumption that most abnormalities do not occur instantaneously, and usually there are some kinds of degradation process from normal states to abnormalities [1]. Hence, unlike breakdown maintenance and preventive maintenance, the predictive maintenance concentrates on degradation monitoring and prognostics rather than fault detection and diagnostics of components. It enables us to identify and solve problems in advance before asset damage occurs. Until now, it is difficult to achieve effectiveness of maintenance operations because there is no information visibility during asset usage period. Although there are recommendations concerning maintenance strategy from vendors or manufacturers, they are neither practical nor cost-effective because they are too

---

Please use the following format when citing this chapter:

Jun, H.-B., Ruibal, M., Kiritsis, D. and Xirouchakis, P., 2008, in IFIP International Federation for Information Processing, Volume 257, Lean Business Systems and Beyond, Tomasz Koch, ed.; (Boston: Springer), pp. 111–119.

generic. However, recently, with emerging technologies such as radio frequency identification (RFID), various sensors, micro-electro-mechanical system (MEMS), and wireless tele-communication, asset embedded information devices such as RFID tags are expected to be rapidly used for gathering and monitoring the status data of assets during their usage period. Under the new environment, an asset embedded information device can log the asset history related to distributing route, usage conditions, failure, maintenance or service events, and so on. Therefore, using this information gives us new challenging issues for improving the efficiency of asset maintenance operations. We can make a prognosis of asset status, predict asset's abnormality, and execute proactive maintenance, upgrade or decommission, i.e. do predictive maintenance.

To implement a predictive maintenance approach, it is required to resolve several research issues related to data gathering, analyzing, decision, and actions. Among them, in this study, we focus on the analyzing and decision making levels. For this, we will develop an algorithm that can analyze the degradation status and determine the prognostic maintenance strategy. If a degradation status can be measured and detected in a real time way, then predictive maintenance activities can be performed before a worse degradation or failure occurs. In other words, maintenance interval can be optimized through predictive maintenance. It means that we can reduce non-necessary maintenance cost. Hence, it is important to develop a proactive decision algorithm for predicting the time of product's abnormality; and executing the appropriate maintenance actions. It will minimize the overall maintenance cost. To evaluate the proposed approach, we carry out a case study for a heavy machinery.

The rest of the paper is organized as follows: In section 2, we look into relevant previous research. In section 3, we address a predictive maintenance algorithm. In section 4, we introduce a case study.

2　Previous Research

There have been several research works about predictive maintenance. For example, Fu *et al.* [1] proposed a predictive maintenance framework for hydroelectric generating unit. They presented three key elements for the predictive maintenance such as monitoring and forecasting, diagnosis and prognosis, and decision-making. In addition, Bansal *et al.* [2] described a real-time predictive maintenance system for machine systems. The aim of the proposed system is to localize and detect abnormal electrical conditions in order to predict mechanical abnormalities that indicate, or may lead to the failure of a motor. They used a neural network approach to predict parameters of a machine. On the other hand, the predictive maintenance has been highlighted with the concept of e-maintenance and the product identification technology. For example, Koç and Lee [3] addressed the concept of web-enabled predictive maintenance in an intelligent e-maintenance system which is implemented via Internet and showed its system elements. Lee [4] introduced a new methodology of predictive maintenance, called machinery dynamics and data fusion through remote machinery monitoring. They also presented an example of a remote wireless application currently in use for monitoring machinery in industrial plants. In addition, recently, Djurdjanovic *et al.* [5] proposed the framework of watchdog agent for predictive condition-based maintenance by realizing multi-sensor assessment and prediction of machine or process performance. The concept of watchdog agent based its degradation assessment on the readings from multiple sensors that measure critical properties of the process or machinery under a networked and tether-free environment. Although there have been some relevant research works so far, they have some limitations from the following viewpoints. First, there is a lack of research to address the issue of combining information technologies with the predictive maintenance. Another limitation is that the predictive maintenance is still an undeveloped area and its approaches are unreliable. Hence, the current approaches have the limitation in detailed methods or validated predictive models.

3   Predictive Maintenance Approach

To cope with the previous limitations, in this study, we develop a prognostic decision algorithm to select the best maintenance strategy throughout the analysis of asset usage data. The following are notations used in this study.

Notations

T_D	Designed life time
T_M	Asset operation time
T^*	Remaining life time
T'	Theoretical remaining life time, $T' = T_D - T_M$
ε	Arbitrary small number empirically determined by companies

The following is the detailed procedure for a predictive maintenance approach.

Predictive maintenance algorithm

Step 1. Collect status data of an asset

In this step, using an embedded information device, we gather product status data. Here, the embedded information device plays a role in sensing and gathering the asset status data, and transmitting them to a relevant information system. Depending on the type of the asset, various kinds of embedded information devices can be used, e.g. RFID tag, on-board computer, and so on.

Step 2. Estimate remaining life time of the asset at a certain time T

With gathered data, we can estimate the remaining life time of the asset. For this, a prediction model for calculating the remaining life time of the asset should be developed considering the asset's characteristics.

Step 3. Check asset status

With estimated remaining life time, check whether the asset can last as long as it was originally intended to. If $T^* \leq T' - \varepsilon$, do predictive maintenance. Here, T will be the best time to take maintenance actions. Else if $T^* \geq T' + \varepsilon$, then take no actions, or adjust the severity of mission profile for the use of more intensive applications, or inform design department that the asset is overdimensioned designed. Otherwise, let the asset be without taking any maintenance actions.

Step 4. Decide suitable maintenance strategy
    1. Generate possible maintenance strategies considering what to do, when to do, how to do, and where to do.
    2. For each strategy, build up a maintenance cost model
    3. Calculate the maintenance cost for each maintenance strategy
    4. Compare them and select the best one

Step 5. Implement the selected maintenance strategy
Following the selected maintenance strategy, take suitable maintenance actions.

4   Case study

To evaluate our approach, we carry out a case study for a heavy machinery of *AAA* company in France. The *AAA* company uses an embedded information device (*on-board computer*) with sensors in a structural part of the heavy machinery to gather its usage data. With gathered data, we analyze the degradation of the structural part; predict remaining life time, and decide the best cost effective maintenance operation, which are described below in detail. The following are notations used in the case study.

Notations

a	Crack length coefficient (depending on the crack geometry)
a_i	Crack length coefficient at a certain measurement time
a_f	Critical crack length coefficient
$\dot{a}$	Crack growth rate
C	Empirical parameter
C_B	Logistics cost of borrowed machinery (transport to customer)
C_C	Cost of compensation for customer
C_D	Disassembly cost
C_{L_i}	Labor cost for repair or replace, i=1, 2 (1: repair, 2: replace)
C_{P_i}	Part cost for repair or replace, i=1, 2 (1: repair, 2: replace)
C_{P_3}	New part or component cost
C_T	Transportation cost for delivering a failed machine to a dealer or transporting a maintenance engineer to a customer site
c_R	Repair consumable hourly cost
F	The number of stress cycles
h_R	Hourly labor cost
i_R	Hourly immobilization cost

K	Stress Intensity Factor (K_{max} : Maximum stress intensity, K_{min} : Minimum stress intensity)
m	Empirical parameter
R_i	Remaining life time factor, i=1, 2 (1: repair, 2: replace)
r_R	Daily borrowed machinery cost rate
t_1	Duration of repair maintenance operation (hour)
t_1'	Duration of repair maintenance operation (day)
t_2	Duration of replace maintenance operation (hour)
t_2'	Duration of replace maintenance operation (day)
w_i	Warranty coverage parameter, i=1, 2 (1: repair, 2: replace)
α	Percent of disassembly
β	Correction factor to the crack geometry and loading conditions
σ	Stress of cyclic load (σ_{max} : Maximum stress, σ_{min} : Minimum stress)
ΔN	Remaining number of cycles
γ_i	Empirical correction parameter, $i = 1, 2$

Step 1. Collect usage status data of the heavy machinery at T

We can gather machine operating time (T_M), stress levels ($\Delta\sigma$) of a structural part, the number of stress cycles (F), and crack propagation data ($a, \dot{a}$) from an embedded information device with sensors.

Step 2. Estimate remaining life time of the structural part of the heavy machinery at a certain time T. The following is a detailed procedure as to how to estimate the remaining life time of the structural part.

1. Find mission profile parameters ($\Delta\sigma, F$)

Considering the future usage of the structural part, select suitable $\Delta\sigma$ and F in the user model.

2. Calculate stress intensity factor (ΔK)

With the following equation, we calculate stress intensity factor. Here β can be empirically determined from previous experience.

$$\Delta K = K_{max} - K_{min} = \beta \cdot \Delta\sigma \cdot \sqrt{\pi \cdot a} \text{ where } K_{max} = \beta \cdot \sigma_{max} \cdot \sqrt{\pi \cdot a} \text{ and}$$
$$K_{min} = \beta \cdot \sigma_{min} \cdot \sqrt{\pi \cdot a}$$

3. Select suitable C and m at Paris-Erdogan model [6] (eq. (1))

Using fracture mechanics theory [6], we can know the relation between crack propagation speed ($\dot{a}$) and stress intensity factor (K). The law relating crack propagation speed $\dot{a}$ to ΔK is derived from experimental results. The most widely accepted one for several materials is the Paris-Erdogan model.

$$\dot{a} \cong \frac{da}{dN} = C(\Delta K)^m \tag{1}$$

where C and m are empirical parameters determined by the fitting equation (1) to the fatigue data. Factors which affect crack propagation can be grouped into the following categories: material microstructure, processing, load spectrum, environment and geometry of a component. In this study, we will only consider load spectrum, component geometry, and working environment for the crack propagation modeling and remaining life time prediction.

4. Calculate the remaining life time (T^*)

Using the following equation, we can calculate the remaining life time of the structural part.

$$T^* = \frac{\Delta N}{F} \text{ where } \Delta N = \int_{a_i}^{a_f} \frac{1}{C \cdot (\Delta K)^m} \, da = \int_{a_i}^{a_f} \frac{1}{C \cdot (\beta \cdot \Delta \sigma)^m \cdot (\pi \cdot a)^{m-2}} \, da$$

Step 3. Check the status of the structural part

Let us take a simple example. If we get $T^* = 7500$ under $T_D = 11000$, $T_M = 2294$, and $\varepsilon = 48$, then, since $T^* \leq T' - \varepsilon$, we can conclude 'do predictive maintenance operation'. Here, $T (= T_M)$ is the best time to take the maintenance operation.

Step 4. Decide suitable maintenance strategy

Figure 1 shows the possible maintenance strategies depending on the variation of maintenance policy, amount of disassembly, and maintenance location. First, we should decide what to do: repair or replace. Here, repair indicates maintenance operations that all original components of the structural part remain and new material is added. On the other hand, replace means the operation that substitution of some components of the structural part with possibly new material being added. Second, we should decide how to perform the selected maintenance operation with respect to disassembly: no, partial, and total disassembly. Finally, we should decide where to do maintenance operation: on site or at dealer site. Depending on them, we can generate 14 maintenance strategies as depicted in Figure 1.

In this study, to show a simple example of our approach, we consider a failure of a component of the structural part: a damaged component L. The following equations are two maintenance cost models, A, B (see dotted lines in Figure 1).

A: Repair cost function

$$w_1 \cdot R_1 \cdot \gamma_1 (C_{L_1} + C_{P_1} + C_C + C_T) = (\frac{T_D - T_M}{T_D})(1 - \frac{T^*}{T_D - T_M}) \cdot \gamma_1 \cdot$$

$$((h_R t_1 + \alpha C_D) + (C_R t_1) + (C_B + r_R t_1' + i_R t_1) + C_T)$$

B: Replace cost function

$$w_2 \cdot R_2 \cdot \gamma_2 (C_{L_2} + C_{P_2} + C_C + C_T) = (1 - \frac{T_D - T_M}{T_D})(\frac{T^*}{T_D - T_M})$$

$$((h_R \cdot t_2 + \alpha C_D) + (C_{P_3} + C_R \cdot t_2) + (C_B + r_R t_2' + i_R t_2) + C_T)$$

In the repair and replace functions, the warranty coverage (w_i) is an important factor since it is an element which indicates to the manufacturer of the system what it will cost him in order to maintain a machine still covered by warranty. Furthermore, the remaining life time factor (R_i) is also important to decide the repair or replace option. As the remaining life time factor becomes increasing and the warranty coverage becomes reduced, the repair option is more preferable to the replace option. To take it into account, we consider w_1, w_2, R_1, R_2 in the functions. The labor cost contains the direct labor costs of maintenance personnel during repair/replace operation period and indirect labor costs considering the percentage of disassembly. The compensation cost indicates the cost related to the compensation given to the customer while his machine is in repair/replace, e.g. cost related to lending him another machine. In addition, γ_1 and γ_2 should be empirically determined by companies. Here, γ_1 and γ_2 were estimated from relevant failure reports of the C company that contain real repair and replacement costs. The values of other parameters could be obtained from the company. The following are calculations of repair cost and replace cost.

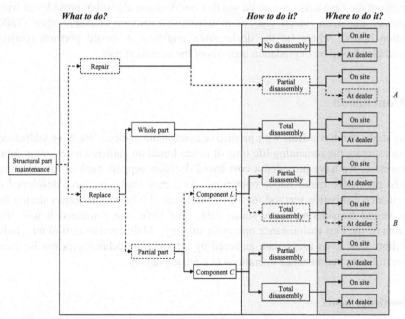

Fig. 1. Maintenance strategies for the structural part

A: Repair cost

$$(\frac{11000-2294}{11000})(1-\frac{7500}{11000}) \cdot 0.40979 \cdot$$
$$((100 \cdot 3 + 0.1 \cdot 200) + (30 \cdot 3) + (1000 + 500 \cdot 1) + 1000) = 300.30$$

where $T_D = 11000$, $T_M = 2294$, $t_1 = 3$, $t_1' = 1$, $\alpha = 10\%$, $\gamma_1 = 0.40979$, $C_D = 200\$$, $C_R = 30$, $C_B = 1000$, $C_T = 1000$, $h_R = 100$, $r_R = 500$ and $i_R = 0$.

B: Replace cost

$$(1 - \frac{11000 - 2294}{11000})(\frac{7500}{11000}) \cdot 1.11276 \cdot$$

$$((100 \cdot 8 + 1 \cdot 200) + (3000 + 30 \cdot 8) + (1000 + 500 \cdot 1) + 1000) = 1066.42$$

where $\alpha = 100\%$, $\gamma_1 = 1.11276$, $t_2 = 8$, $t_2' = 1$, $C_{P_3} = 3000$, $C_R = 30$, $C_B = 1000$, and $r_R = 500$. As you can see, the repair cost for the damaged component L is cheaper than that of replace option. Hence, repairing the component with partial disassembly at the dealer site is preferable to replacing the whole component.

Step 5. Implement the selected maintenance strategy
Since the repair option is more economic than the replace option, we take repair maintenance operation in the dealer site at 7500 operation hours.
Throughout the case study, we could see that our decision algorithm provides us with a practical guide on which type of maintenance operation (repair), when (7500 operation hours), where (at the dealer site), and how it should perform (partial disassembly) based on degradation analysis of the structural part.

5 Conclusion

In this study, we have dealt with predictive asset maintenance. We have addressed how to estimate the remaining life time of assets based on gathered asset status data. Furthermore, we have provided a cost based decision support method for selecting the best predictive maintenance operation. As a case study, we have developed a performance estimation method for a structural part of a heavy machinery during its usage period considering usage status data. We have also combined it with the selection of the best maintenance operation strategy. Main contribution of our study is to show how asset usage data gathered by information technologies can be used for streamlining maintenance operations in a proactive way.

Acknowledgements

The work reported in this paper was based on the PROMISE project that is currently under development (www.promise.no). Therefore, we wish to express our deep gratitude to all PROMISE partners. Specially thanks to Cecile Corcelle.

Reference

1. C. Fu, L. Ye, Y. Liu, R. Yu, B. Iung, Y. Cheng, and Y. Zeng, Predictive maintenance in intelligent-control-maintenance-management system for hydroelectroic generating unit, *IEEE Transactions on energy conversion*, 19(1), 179-186 (2004).

2. D. Bansal, D. J. Evans, and B. Jones, A real-time predictive maintenance system for machine systems, *International Journal of Machine Tools and Manufacture*, 44, 759-766 (2004).

3. M. Koç and J. Lee, A system framework for next-generation E-maintenance systems, *Transaction of Chinese Mechanical Engineer*, 12 (2001).

4. L. D. Lee, Using wireless technology and the Internet for predictive maintenance, *Hydrocarbon processing*, 80(5), 77-96 (2001).

5. D. Djurdjanovic, J. Lee, and J. Ni, Watchdog Agent-an infotronics-based prognostics approach for product performance degradation assessment and prediction, *Advanced Engineering Informatics*, 17, 109-125 (2003).

6. N. E. Dowling, *Mechanical behavior of materials* (Prentice hall, 1999).

Development of an Information-interoperable Environment Based on Open Technologies for Lean Production Systems

Toshiaki Kimura[1], Hirohisa Tezuka[2] and Yuichi Kanda[3]
[1] Japan Society for the Promotion of Machine Industry,
1-1-12, Hachiman-cho, Higashikurume-city, Tokyo, 203-0042 Japan
WWW homepage: http://www.tri.jspmi.or.jp/english/index.html
[2] Nippon Telegraph and Telephone Corp.,
3-9-11, Midori-cho, Musashino-city, Tokyo, 180-8585 Japan
WWW homepage: http://www.ntt.co.jp/index_e.html
3 Toyo University,
2100 Kujirai, Kawagoe-city, Saitama, 350-8585 Japan
WWW homepage: http://www.eng.toyo.ac.jp/eng/index.html

Abstract. Lean production systems require an information-interoperable environment that can process diverse factory information for all workers to do KAIZEN activities. Moreover, the information-interoperable environment should be connected to an inter-enterprise collaboration environment. For those reasons, an Information-Interoperable Environment (IIE) that can connect device-level information and Manufacturing Execution System (MES)-level information was developed using Open Robot (or Resource) interface with the Network (ORiN). Moreover, CaoSQL2FDML for changing the IIE's information to Factory Data Markup Language (FDML) information was developed for inter-enterprise collaboration. This paper describes development of IIE including CaoSQL2FDML, prototype system development, and results of the system's operational testing.

1 Introduction

Rapid and flexible production is sought through the use of information-interoperable production functions such as supply chain, manufacturing planning, manufacturing execution, and device controls for adapting to increasingly diverse product demands and shortening product life-cycles. A production culture is necessary to carry out various tasks through cooperation among workers for lean production. Moreover, an environment in which all workers can do KAIZEN activities using diverse information from factories is important.

Please use the following format when citing this chapter:

Kimura, T., Tezuka, H. and Kanda, Y., 2008, in IFIP International Federation for Information Processing, Volume 257, Lean Business Systems and Beyond, Tomasz Koch, ed.; (Boston: Springer), pp. 121–128.

However, many *de facto* standards for information systems depend on the device industry, even though multi-devices such as machine tools and robots exist in factories. Therefore, information acquisition at factories from the device-level for KAIZEN activities is difficult. Development of an information-interoperable environment for factories that considers the relation between the device-level and the MES-level is increasingly important. In addition, a mechanism to connect the information-interoperable environment and inter-enterprise collaboration systems is required.

For that purpose, Open Robot (or Resource) interface with the Network (ORiN) [1] was developed as an open technology by the ORiN Forum for robots. Today, however, development of gateway systems between ORiN and other standards such as OPC [2], CC-Link [3], Profibus [4], and DeviceNet [5] are active in the ORiN Forum. Therefore, an Information-Interoperable Environment (IIE) [6] that can connect device-level information and MES-level information has been developed using ORiN. Moreover, CaoSQL2FDML, which is useful for changing the IIE's information to Factory Data Markup Language (FDML) [7] information, has been developed for inter-enterprise collaboration. The FDML is also an open resource that is useful for Application Service Provider (ASP) services. The present report describes developments of IIE, CaoSQL2FDML, a prototype system based on these technologies, and system evaluation.

2   Development of IIE

2.1   Requirements of information-interoperable environment

An information-interoperable environment that can handle diverse information from factories for all workers to do KAIZEN activities is necessary for lean production systems. Figure 1 presents requirements of the information-interoperable environment. The bottom of Fig. 1, *Manufacturing systems*, shows that the reference architecture of a manufacturing system should be the target of KAIZEN activities. The top of Fig. 1, *Activities*, shows that functions of Information Communication Technology (ICT) tools should be used for KAIZEN activities based on Plan, Do, Check, Action (P • D • C • A) cycles of Total Quality Management (TQM). Acquiring information from classes of various functions in the reference architecture of a manufacturing system is necessary for lean production systems, as shown in the bottom of Fig. 1. Especially, an information-interoperable environment is required that can acquire information from heterogeneous machinery at the device-level, and which relates to MES-level information. Moreover, use of information from the information-interoperable environment is required along with an easy and flexible programming environment of application systems depending on purposes of KAIZEN activities of lean production systems.

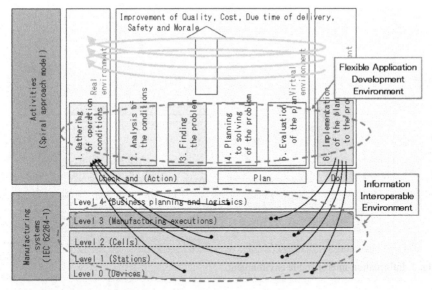

Fig. 1. Requirements of information-interoperable environment

2.2   IIE for factories

Two standard interfaces are provided by ORiN: an application interface for application system programs and a provider interface for resources such as devices and databases. In its kernel, ORiN has a device model called Controller Access Object (CAO). The IIE was developed using CaoSQL, which is middleware for ORiN's application systems to manage access control of information from devices and to record a history of variables of devices that are connected with the CAO.

The CaoSQL has a CaoSQLController class for discriminating among different devices; it also has a CaoSQLItem class for defining various types of information from devices. Information corresponding to CAO that is connected to multi-vendor machine tools, robots and Programmable Logic Controllers (PLCs) can be selected for KAIZEN activities of lean production systems and can be defined in CaoSQLItem objects and CaoSQLController objects. Moreover, MES-level information is definable in CaoSQLItem objects in connection with device-level information, as shown in Fig. 2.

Using the IIE with a web server, remote monitoring of device-level information and MES-level information through web applications can be customized easily by the user. Along with accumulation of data available from the device-level and MES-level database histories, other application systems such as an operation management system can be created using a computer spreadsheet program (e.g., Excel; Microsoft Corp.), thereby granting users even greater freedom in their computing environments. Users can entrust IIE with information gathered from the device-level and MES-level. Software development costs can be reduced because users can thereby concentrate on development of application systems.

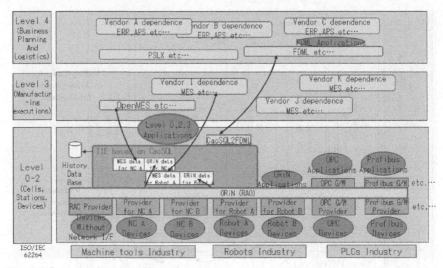

Fig. 2. Information-interoperable environment

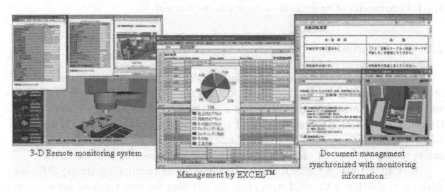

Fig. 3. Examples of application systems

Figure 3 depicts examples of application systems using the IIE. The left side of Fig. 3 shows a three-dimensional (3-D) remote monitoring system that can indicate the status of a manufacturing system through multimedia consisting of 3-D models, text, and still images together with MES-level information. With the accumulation of data available from the device-level and MES-level database histories, other application systems, such as an operation management system, can be created using a computer spreadsheet program (e.g., Excel; Microsoft Corp.), giving users even greater freedom in their computing environments, as shown in the middle panel of Fig. 3. The right panel of Fig. 3 shows a document management system that works with the 3-D remote monitoring system.

2.3   IIE for Inter-enterprise collaboration environment

For inter-enterprise collaboration and for changing the IIE's information to FDML information, CaoSQL2FDML was developed. It can also send FDML information to the Factory Data Center (FDC) as a commercial Application Service Provider (ASP) service. Using the FDC, secure information and application-sharing services can be provided for inter-enterprise collaboration. This section provides an overview of FDML, and FDC.

The FDML is a *de facto* standard for describing information from the point of production. The FDML was proposed by the Manufacturing Science and Technology Center (MSTC) in Japan. Moreover, the FDML is based on eXtensible Markup Language (XML) technologies, which can facilitate description of information about a wide range of information such as device-level information, MES-level information, and business planning information. The FDML can manage information from devices that are dispersed in the factory by adding a time stamp to the information. Furthermore, FDML is widely and flexibly applicable to users' application systems through addition of logical information such as data names, data types, and maximum/minimum values to physical information. Table 1 shows that FDML has tags of XML such as InfoTag for describing sources of information, and DefinitionTag for describing the relation between physical information and logical information.

The FDC is an internet server that is used through access with FDML; it has some functions such as those of a hosting server, database, ASP, and a security function by Virtual Private Network (VPN). In addition, FDC is used for remote maintenance for multi-vendor manufacturing systems through inter-enterprise collaboration of device vendors and inter-enterprise collaboration in obtaining joint orders through access from multi-point users.

Table 1. FDML Tags

Content of FDML	Description
<?xml version=" 1.0" encoding=" Shift_JIS" >	XML Declaration
<FDML version=" 1.02" >	FDML start tag
<Info></Info>	Field machine information
<Definition></Definition>	Correlation with physical channels and logical channels
<Condition></Condition>	Condition to send FDML
<Data></Data>	Time-series field data
</FDML>	FDML end tag

2.4   Integration of both IIE for factories and Inter-enterprise collaboration

Finally, CaoSQL2FDML was developed. It is a method for connection of the IIE and the FDC as one inter-enterprise collaboration environment. No information of whole IIE for factories is necessary with inter-enterprise collaboration. Therefore, information from the CaoSQLController class and CaoSQLItem class that is selected for inter-enterprise collaboration can be converted to FDML format and can be sent to FDC using CaoSQL2FDML. Figure 4 shows a conversion method of CaoSQL2FDML. Using this method, data names, data types, and maximum/minimum values of the CaoSQLController class and CaoSQLItem class of CaoSQL of the IIE are mapped to the Definition class of the FDML. In addition, values of the CaoSQLItem class are mapped to the Data class of the FDML.

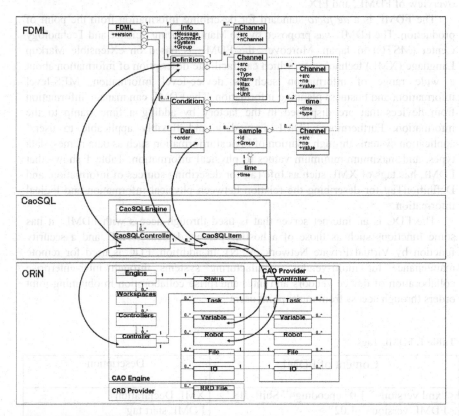

Fig. 4. Class chart mapping between CaoSQL and FDML

3   Development of a prototype system based on the IIE

A prototype system was developed based on the IIE and the CaoSQL2FDML. Evaluations of the prototype system were performed. Targets of the prototype system are a turning center and a multi-vendor manufacturing system line consisting of one transfer robot and two machine tools at Japan Society for the Promotion of Machine Industry (JSPMI, Higashikurume-city, Tokyo). The prototype system is integrated with the FDC server at NTT Corp. (Musashino-city, Tokyo), with a monitoring client at Tokyo Big Sight Inc. (Koto ward, Tokyo) using the internet, as shown in

Fig. 5. Evaluations of remote monitoring from the client to the IIE were done directly. Evaluations of remote monitoring from the client to the FDC were also done using CaoSQL2FDML, considering inter-enterprise collaboration. Moreover, identity was evaluated using these monitoring results.

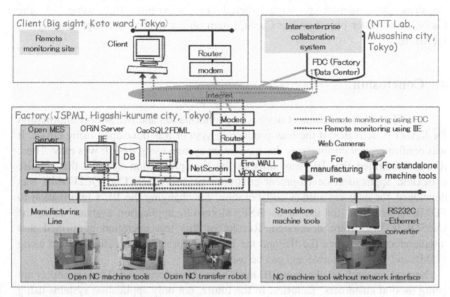

Fig. 5. Configuration of the prototype system

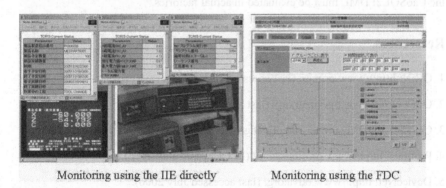

Monitoring using the IIE directly   Monitoring using the FDC

Fig. 6. Test operation of the environment

The prototype system was exhibited at the 2005 International Robot Exhibition held in November 2005 at Tokyo Big Sight Inc. The client computer was able to stably monitor the prototype system at the JSPMI during the entire exhibition (4 days, 7 h/day), both using FDC and not using FDC. Moreover, the similarity of information using FDC and information not using FDC was confirmed. Figure 6 shows an example of the indicator screen for monitoring electrical consumption of the turning center at JSPMI on the client in the test operation. Results of this test operation confirmed that interconnection between the IIE and inter-enterprise collaboration system using FDML and FDC was possible and that the system can be used stably.

Moreover, it was confirmed that modification of the application system was easy. For example, in the case of application software of monitoring, target machines and variables for monitoring were altered by re-writing the name of the CaoSQLController object and/or CaoSQLItem object written in Script language in HTML file.

4   Conclusion

The IIE, which can connect device-level information and MES-level information for KAIZEN activates of the lean production system was developed using ORiN. It was confirmed that customizing the application system using the IIE was easy. Then, it was confirmed that IIE was suitable for lean production systems that require a flexible application development environment. Moreover, CaoSQL2FDML was developed for inter-enterprises collaboration, for changing the IIE's information to FDML information for use at an ASP. Moreover, application systems using the CaoSQL2FDML were developed. Results of this test operation confirmed that interconnection between the IIE and the inter-enterprise collaboration system using FDML and FDC is possible and can be used stably.

Several research results from IIE have been commercialized. These products are being used at customers' factories. In the future, not only application systems using IIE for factories but also application systems of inter-enterprise collaboration using the CaoSQL2FDML must be evaluated in actual factories.

References

1. ORiN: http://www.orin.jp/ (last accessed July 2006).

2. OPC: http://www.opcjapan.org/ (last accessed July 2006).

3. CC-Link: http://www.cc-link.org/eng/t_html/top.html (last accessed July 2006).

4. Profibus: http://www.profibus.com/ (last accessed July 2006).

5. DeviceNet: http://www.odva.org/ (last accessed July 2006).

6. T. Kimura and Y. Kanda, Development of an information-interoperable environment between device-level information and MES-level information, Proc. of APMS2005 (Advances in Production Management Systems), (2005).

7. H. Tezuka, Y. Nanjo, N. Katafuchi, Y. Nakamura, S. Iwaki, T. Machino, and K. Shimokura, Sensor and Robot Collaboration based on a Network Robot Platform, Proc. of Workshop on Network Robot System at International Conference on Robotics and Automation, (2005).

The Operations Excellence Audit Sheet

Erlend Alfnes, Heidi Dreyer, and Jan Ola Strandhagen
Department of Production and Quality Engineering, Norwegian
University of Science and Technology, NTNU, Norway
WWW homepage: http://www.produksjonslogistikk.no

Abstract. This paper presents an Operations Excellence (OE) audit sheet that enables companies to get a quick assessment of their operations performance. The sheet is based on well known assessment schemes within lean manufacturing developed by Godson, Kobayashi, and Schonberger. These three schemes are combined and enhanced in the audit sheet, which defines 15 areas of operations excellence. The audit sheet is a powerful tool to assess the current state and to plan the future state of enterprise operations. It has been successfully applied in several enterprise reengineering projects to provide decision-makers with sufficient input to identify improvement targets and revise the current operations strategy. The use of the audit sheet is demonstrated in two case examples from Norwegian industry, and some insights are given regarding the sheet's applicability for different types of manufacturing processes.

1 Introduction

Searching for and learning from "best practices" has been a topic for both industry and academia for decades. A lot of effort has been put into identifying "best practices" to support companies achieve superior performance. However, the piece-mal application of best practices which are common in many enterprises - limited to specific parts or functional areas and with conflicting objectives - often lead to inefficiencies and disappointing results [6].

Assessment schemes such as the Baldrige award, the European Foundation for Quality Management, and other business excellence approaches [3] are powerful tools to achieve coherence between strategy and best practice programs. However, in the area of manufacturing operations, such tools are rather few and limited to the assessment of lean performance. The purpose of this paper is to analyse the most well-known assessment schemes within lean manufacturing, and to propose a more generic Operations Excellence (OE) audit scheme that enables enterprises to get a quick assessment of their manufacturing operations performance.

Please use the following format when citing this chapter:

Alfnes, E., Dreyer, H. and Strandhagen, J.O., 2008, in IFIP International Federation for Information Processing, Volume 257, Lean Business Systems and Beyond, Tomasz Koch, ed.; (Boston: Springer), pp. 129–141.

The paper is structured as follows. First, the link to the lean paradigm and how this influences the generality of the OE audit sheet is discussed. Next, three lean assessments schemes are analysed and a set of key factors to assess operations excellence is proposed. Subsequently, the use of the OE audit sheet is demonstrated in two case examples. Finally, the paper is concluded with some insights about the sheet's applicability for different types of manufacturing processes.

2   Point of departure – lean manufacturing

The OE audit sheet aims to be a generic and neutral tool to assess operations excellence for all types of manufacturing. However, the audit sheet is based on tools developed within the lean paradigm, tools that equalise operations excellence and lean performance. The major reason for this limited, and rather biased point of departure, is the significant role of lean concepts for improving and describing manufacturing operations.

The lean manufacturing approach developed at Toyota provides a set of concepts, methods, and techniques that are more detailed and interrelated than any other approach available, and has led to significant improvements during the last two decades. To quote Godson [4] "A revolution in operations has occurred over the last fifteen years as a result of world competition and the implementation of best practices. This revolution is largely based on the Toyota Production System (TPS), and the concepts from this system have spread from Toyota to the rest of the world". Lean concepts (such as 5S, SMED, TPM, and so on) are therefore essential building blocks for enterprises that aims to develop best-in-class operations. (See Bicheno [2]for a comprehensive overview of lean concepts and techniques).

Lean concepts were developed for repetitive manufacturing of automobiles. The lean vision of excellent operations therefore refers to the type of repetitive operations found in batch or line production. The lean vision of operation excellence can be described by the following quotation from Kobayashi [5].

"In the level five factory .... the entire factory has become a single line with zero internal inventory. The plant uses quick changeover technology and runs a fully mixed production schedule, leading to ultimate adaptability".

This vision of the excellent enterprise, as a single line that can produce a mixed set of products, is clearly most suited for batch or line type of operations. Lean manufacturing requires standardised work and minimum variation, and is most suited for standard products with minor customizations, or customisation that involves choosing from a set of predefined options, and for markets with relatively stable demand. (See Suri [11] for a discussion about the suitability of lean concepts for high variety operations). All lean concepts is therefore not applicable for job shop type of operations (which typically compete on customisation and high level of craft work), or continuous processing type of operations (which typically compete on efficiency and resource utilisation).

The audit sheet aims to provide a generic definition of operations excellence. However, the lean roots of the audit sheet make the 15 areas most suitable to describe excellence for batch or line type of operations. For other types of operations, it might be necessary to add other areas of excellence, and it might not be possible to achieve the defined excellence objectives in all 15 areas. Furthermore, no enterprise can be excellent in every dimension, trade-offs has to be made. The audit sheet is therefore a useful tool to assess the gap between operations capability and operations strategy, and to prioritize the targets for improvements.

3   Critical areas for operations excellence

The OE audit sheet is based on the well-known assessment schemes developed by Godson [4], Kobayashi [5], and Schonberger [7] for lean manufacturing. The major areas of excellence and the related factors/principles in these three approaches are presented below.

3.1   A comparison of audit schemes for manufacturing excellence

Godson has developed the Rapid Plant Assessment (RPA) tool to assess the state of an operation based on a brief plant tour. The RPA tool focuses on visual cues and key data generally available, and enables visitors and managers to assess the operations performance of the plant. The two other schemes are not only assessment tools, but are also guides for implementing lean manufacturing. Kobayashi's scheme is classic Japanese, concentrating on shop floor management. Schonberger's goes wider in bringing in customers, benchmarking and perhaps a more western view of employees. As a generalisation, Godson's scheme covers the major aspects of plant floor operations, but lacks the assessment of "borderline" factors (such as order management performance) that may have dramatic influence on manufacturing performance. The strongest aspects of Kobayashi's scheme are related to management at the workplace and waste or muda. The strongest aspects of Schonberger's scheme are the links with the customer, on worker involvement in continuous improvement, on design, and simplicity of process.

The OE audit sheet and the related factors/principles in each of the three evaluation schemes are given in Table 1. For each scheme, the number of the principle is shown in brackets. The detailed rating systems are not given, and the reader is referred to the original schemes for details.

Table 1 shows the major areas in the proposed audit sheet and the related factors/principles in Godson's, Kobayashi's, and Schonberger's schemes. Godson's RPA tool is the most modern and coherent of these schemes. However, Kobayashi, and Schonberger propose some crucial areas of excellence that should be added:

- Both Kobayashi and Schonberger propose technology and quick changeover as two important keys to operations excellence. Leading process technology provides efficiency and processing capability. Quick changeover enables enterprises to produce small series of products and still maintain a high level of equipment utilisation.
- Kobyashi proposes information technology (micro processors) as a key to operations excellence. The use of information technology in manufacturing can

enable real time execution and shop floor control, and is another important area of operations excellence.

- Order management is an integrated part of manufacturing operations and an important area of excellence in many enterprises (especially the make-to-order type). This view is partly supported by Schonberger, who proposes efficient transactions and reporting as a key to operations excellence.

Table 1. The audit sheet and related areas in three other assessment schemes

	ALFNES	GODSON	KOBAYASHI	SCHONBERGER
1	Customer Satisfaction	Customer Satisfaction (1)	Mgment of objectives (2) Effiency control (17)	Team up with customers (1) Use customer information (2), Align measures with customers wants (13) Promote every improv. (16)
2	Leading technology	-	Leading technology (20) Zero Monitoring (7)	Seek simple, flexible, movable equipment (15)
3	Safety, environment, cleanliness, & order	Safety, environment, cleanliness, & order (2)	Cleaning and organising (1)	-
4	Visual Management Deployment	Visual Management Deployment (3)	-	-
5	Manufacturing planning and control system	Scheduling system (4)	Production scheduling (16)	Operate close to customers' rate of use or demand (7)
6	Order management	-	-	Cut internal transactions and reporting (12)
7	Information system	-	Using micro processors (18)	-
8	Layout, product flow, space, material movement	Product flow, space, material movement (5)	Coupled manufacturing (8)	(part) "..organise by product family" (1)
9	Inventory & WIP Levels	Inventory & WIP Levels (6)	Reducing inventory and WIP (4)	Cut flow time and changeover (6)
10	Teamwork, skill level, & motivation	Teamwork, skill level, & motivation (7)	Small group activities (3) Work. empowerment (14) Kaizen (6) Cross func. work (15) Conserv energy/matr. (19)	Continual improvment (3), Frontliners invol. in strategy & change (4), Train everbody for new roles (8), Expand reward variety (9), Teams records (11),
11	Equipment & tooling state & maintenance	Equipment & tooling state & maintenance (8)	Maintenance (9)	Improve present capacity before new equipment (14)
12	Quick changeover	-	Quick changeover technology (5)	Cut flow time and changeover (6)
13	Value chain integration	Supply chain integration (10)	Developing suppliers (12)	Cut to best components, operators, suppliers (5)
14	Commonality of work and components	Mgmt. of complexity and variability (9)	Work floor time policies (10)	Cut to best components, operators, suppliers (5)
15	Quality System Deployment	Quality System Deployment (11)	Quality assurance (11) Waste elimination (13)	Reduce variation and mishaps (10)

In the OE audit sheet proposed in this paper, four areas of excellence have been added to Godsons original scheme. In addition, most of Godson's areas of excellence has been altered both in scope and depth to provide a more neutral and generic tool. The most radical changes are carried out in:

- Godson's area no. 9 "Management of complexity and variability" which is rather diffuse. This area of excellence is therefore simplified and limited to

"Commonality of work and components", which is a key lean success factor according to Spear and Bowen [10].

- Manufacturing planning and control, where "pull" control systems are defined as a characteristic of operations excellence in the original schemes. This is not necessarily true. Excellence is achieved (regardless of system type) when the manufacturing planning and control system enables an enterprise to efficiently satisfy customer demand. What should be regarded as the proper type of system depends on the particular manufacturing environment.

3.2   A definition of each area of excellence

This section provides a definition of each area of excellence in the OE audit sheet. For a more extensive description that also includes the major factors to assess within each area, see Alfnes [1]. The list aims to be generic and cover all important areas of operations excellence for a manufacturing enterprise, but of course it still does not include everything. A first practical exercise is therefore to evaluate the list, ensuring people understand it all, and add to it other areas that are needed for a particular enterprise.

1 Customer satisfaction: *From no measurement and understanding of customer satisfaction to fully displayed ratings and interactive, cross-functional involvement at all levels.*
In the best enterprises, customer information and understanding is mutually shared by marketing and operations. Workers in such enterprises clearly know who their customers are – both internal and external – and make customer satisfaction their primary goal. Customers are served individually and rapidly, and experiences that their need for personalisation, high quality, and efficient deliveries are satisfied.

2 Leading technology: *From low awareness to full awareness and utilisation of leading technology to provide a competitive advantage*
In the best enterprises, the use of leading manufacturing technology provides a competitive leverage. Manufacturing technology is the set of skills, know-how, and devices that a particular enterprise has acquired during the development of manufacturing processes and enhancement activities. Technology does not improve simply by the introduction of new equipment. In the best enterprises, manufacturing technology enables the enterprise to do the right things exceptionally well (low costs, high quality, quick response etc.), and all investments and improvements are in line with the overall operations strategy.

3 Safety, environment, cleanliness and order: *From untidy to 100% organised, 100% of the time*
In a clean and orderly enterprise, parts are easy to find, inventory is easy to estimate, and products move safely and efficiently. Everything is labelled and everything is in place. The facility is safe, clean, orderly and well lit. The air quality is good and the noise levels are low.

4 Visual management deployment: *From informal, infrequent, and fragmented, to 100% updated and 100% visualised information about objectives, status and performance.*
The best enterprises are able to gain all operating information and control without having to go off the shop floor. Tools that provide visual cues and directions are readily apparent to guide workers to appropriate locations and tasks. Organisational boundaries are clearly labelled, and interaction between operations areas is supported by visual tools such as Kanban. The status of the total operations can be viewed from a central control room, a status board or a computer screen.

5 Manufacturing planning and control system: *From poor delivery performance often with high inventory, to excellent performance in delivery, quality, cost, and schedules being achieved 100% of the time*
The best enterprises use a MPC system that integrates and simplifies planning and control at long, intermediate, and short term level. Most enterprises have some form of long term and intermediate term planning system. However, the best enterprises have adapted the MPC system to their particular resource and demand situation, and they also uses efficient execution systems to control final assembly, sub-assemblies, components and supply. Regardless of the system type (pull systems, push systems, or push-pull systems, [11], the best manufacturing execution systems are easy and effortless to use. Furthermore, they provide rapid and smooth flows through predetermined or flexible routings, and enables enterprises to satisfy demand with sufficient utilisation rates.

6 Order management: *From functionally oriented, manual, and cumbersome, to customer-oriented, responsive, and automated order management*
The order management cycle typically consist of 10 steps, some of which may overlap: order planning, order generation, cost estimating and pricing, order receipt and entry, order selection and prioritisation, scheduling, fulfilment, billings, returns and claims, and post sales service [8]. The best enterprises have reorganised and streamlined their order management, and are able to provide a single point of contact and immediate response to customers. All types of work that does not require human judgement or intuition are automated by information technology.

7 Information system: *From low awareness of the potential of IT to 100% computer integrated and enabled manufacturing.*
The best enterprises use information systems that integrate equipment and sub-systems, are user-friendly, and easy to adapt to new requirements. IT is used to automate all tasks that do not need human intervention, and to support all types of routine decisions-making in operations. In other, less successful enterprises, manufacturing based computer systems are very complex and difficult to change. Furthermore, sub-systems are added over time, and, as a result, systems cannot communicate well with another.

8 Layout, product flow, space use & material movement means: *From functional to 100% interconnected and flow-oriented layout*

The best enterprises have interconnected and rapid flows through operations. Space is used efficiently. Materials and products are moved only once, over as short distance as possible, in efficient containers. Production materials are stored at each operations area, not in separate inventory storage areas. Tools and set-up equipment are kept near the machines. The enterprise is laid out in product-oriented operations areas or lines, rather than in "shops" dedicated to a particular type of machines. The flow follows unidirectional and predetermined routes between operations areas, and is controlled by planning boards, replenishment boards, or inventory levels.

9 Levels of inventory and work-in-progress: *From no recognition of the waste of overproduction to mixed model production with low inventory and high customer service.*
Internal operations seldom require high inventories, so the observable number of any component part is a good measure of operations performance. The best enterprises have minimum work-in-process and can respond instantly to the many demands of the customers. If necessary, the enterprise can run fully mixed custom orders without slowing down, and freely adjust its mix in response to the needs of the customers. Such enterprises have no overproduction and only produce what the customers want.

10 Team work, skill levels and motivation: *From strict hierarchy to a highly empowered, flexible and team based organisation*
In the best enterprises, people consistently focus on the enterprise's goals for productivity and quality, and knows their jobs well. Workers are not only caretakers of equipment, but craftspeople involved in improving the overall process. The work-organisation is segmented in closed-loop, collocated, multifunctional, cross-trained teams responsible for a product-focused operations area, and empowered to make necessary decisions. The flexibility is further enhanced through education, training programmes, and job rotation that enables the enterprise to deploy its employ to any position at will.

11 Condition and maintenance of equipment and tools: *From no maintenance, or expert maintenance, to full participative TPM*
In the best enterprises, equipment is clean and well maintained, and the total equipment efficiency is greater than 90 percent. A thorough program for participative maintenance control is used to repair vital equipment before it breaks down.

12 Quick changeover: *From belief that the way to reduce total set up time is via increased batch size to full SMED*
The best enterprises have developed their quick changeover technology to the point where it is economically viable to have very frequent changeovers. This enables the enterprise to produce small volumes of a large variety of goods while still maintaining the competitive advantages of single-product mass production. According to Kobayashi [5], it is possible to shorten changeover time to less than 10 minutes in almost any enterprise. The Single Minute Exchange Of Die (SMED) methodology developed by Shingo [9], or investments in flexible equipment can

contribute to reduce set-up times. The best enterprises are capable of Single Minute (or less) Exchange of Die and one piece flow.

13 Value chain integration: *From adversarial, guarded to full partnership with information sharing and value chain co-operation.*
The best enterprises keep costs low and quality high by working closely with a relatively small numbers of dedicated and supportive partners. The best partnerships aim at zero receiving inspection, and delivery directly to the point of use. Packaging and part orientation are designed to reduce waste. Delivery is based on Kanban or Vendor Managed Inventory. Communication and information transfer is based on EDI or XML. Both sides work toward schedule stability, the customer to not change his mind at the last moment, the supplier to provide reliable delivery. Order management operations are streamlined and automated.

14 Commonality of routines, equipment and components: *From complex, varied, and unspecified, to simple and 100% standardised operations.*
In the best enterprises, every activity is simplified, specified, and standardised in order to reduce variability and complexity. Every operator follow a well defined sequence of steps for a particular job, and it is instantly clear when they deviate from specification. By commonality in designs, materials, sizes, capacities, machines, tooling, and operating procedures, the best enterprises are able to standardise the jobs so they can be performed efficiently by multiple operators, and to use the same types of parts in the manufacture of different products. The result is repetitiveness and economic of scales, less quality errors, and flexibility to handle variable demand.

15 Quality system deployment: *From supervisors being responsible for inspections to total quality management based on process control, prevention, operator responsibility and failsafing*
The best enterprises are always striving to improve quality and productivity. Employees are proud of their quality programme, and the commitment to continuous improvement is highly visible. Procedures and measurements are developed for processes and products. Workers are organised in quality improvement teams, and use problems solving tools and techniques to improve operations. Statistical quality control methods are being used. The final inspection is done automatically, and the abnormality rate (including scrap, rework, and special adjustments) is less than 0.1 percent, despite a stringent final inspection.

4   How to use the audit sheet

The OE audit sheet defines the meaning of excellence in fifteen areas that have a major impact on operations performance (costs, quality, time, precision, and so on), The purpose is to assist a team of managers and consultants to:
- Perform an audit of the state of a manufacturing enterprise.
- Judge the operations performance of a manufacturing enterprise.
- Prioritize the targets of opportunity for improvements

The rating should be based on the experiences and observations of the team members, and supported by performance measures and enterprise descriptions. The result of the audit is a short report, assessing the operations performance and suggesting improvement initiatives.

4.1   The audit sheet

The team should use the audit sheet to rate operations performance. Figure 1 shows a audit sheet populated to assess a high-volume manufacturer of aluminium components. The example enterprise (enterprise A) is described in the next section.

No	Measure↓ Score →	Poor 1	Below Average 2	Average 3	Above Average 4	Excellent 5	Best in Class 6	Scores
1	Customer Satisfaction			x				3
2	Leading technology				x			4
3	Safety, environment, cleanliness, & order				x			4
4	Visual Management Deployment				x			4
5	Manufacturing planning and control system		x					2
6	Order management		x					2
7	Information system			x				3
8	Layout, product flow, space, material movement				x			4
9	Inventory & WIP Levels		x					2
10	Teamwork, skill level, & motivation				x			4
11	Equipment & tooling state & maintenance				x			4
12	Quick changeover		x					2
13	Value chain integration		x					2
14	Commonality of work and components			x				3
15	Quality System Deployment					x		5
	Totals →	0	5	3	6	1	0	48

Fig. 1. The audit sheet – the assessment of a high-volume manufacturer of aluminium components

The OE audit sheet in Figure 1 supports management in the assessment of operations performance. Each of the 15 areas should be rated on a scale from "poor" (1) to "excellent" (5) to "best in class" (6). Best in class is meant literally. Only one enterprise in each industry, worldwide, deserves this rating. The enterprises total score on the audit sheet, and the current performance ratings gives an fairly accurate assessment of the enterprise capability. This kind of assessment is particular useful because the 15 areas highlight broad areas of strengths and weaknesses. Areas with low ratings are instantly visible opportunities for improvements and should be the first steps on a company's journey to operations excellence. The total score of all areas will fall between 15 (poor in all areas) and 90 (the best in the world in all areas), with an average score of 45. The rating should be based on the definitions of excellence that was proposed in the previous chapter.

Many companies have made considerable efforts in certain areas, however, no company is yet to be excellent in all areas. Trade-offs has to be made. The analysis carried out through the audit is an input to the overall operations strategy development, and should result in a path of improvement for a particular enterprise. Improvement initiatives should be formulated that improves capabilities in one or several of the 15 areas of excellence (5S, TPM, TQM, SMED, CIM, Visual management, and so on).

The authors have carried out a range of enterprise reengineering projects in the Norwegian manufacturing industry. The OE audit sheet has been applied in several of these projects as a tool to assess current state and to plan the future state of enterprise operations. Two of these cases are presented below.

4.2   Enterprise A - a high-volume manufacturer of aluminium components

Enterprise A is a manufacturer of aluminium components to the automotive industry. The enterprise produces 5 – 6 million units per year with a product range of approx. 100 products. The products are made-to-stock on 4 lines, and produced in batches that vary between 2000 and 12000 units. The production is highly automated and capital intensive. The current and future profile is illustrated in Figure 2.

Enterprise A has an average performance in areas such as cleanliness and order, visual management, layout and flow team work, and commonality of work, and has been extremely successful in quality deployment. Their process technology is very efficient, but dedicated to certain products, and with set-up times that range from one – four hours. The inventory levels are therefore high, and there is a potential to improve equipment utilisation.

The major objective for Enterprise A is to maximise its yield. Other important performance objectives are equipment utilisation (OEE to exceed 70%), productivity (cost per unit), and delivery precision (more than 96%).

The mapping and analysis of the enterprise resulted in a range of improvement initiatives. Improvements initiatives are carried out in area 5 (to develop an integrated MPC system), area 6 (to reengineer and streamline the order management process), and area 13 (to develop a closer collaboration and information sharing with key suppliers in the value chain). Together, these initiatives will improve equipment utilisation and inventory levels through an optimised production schedule.

4.3   Enterprise B – a manufacturer of highly customised staircases

Enterprise B is a manufacturer of wooden staircases to the European market. The enterprise produces approx. 6000 staircases per year, and each stair is constructed on individual customer specifications (make-to-order manufacturing). The product structure is relatively complex and consists of 100 – 200 customised components.

The enterprise is organised in flow shops where highly automated equipment is used in combination with labour intensive operations.

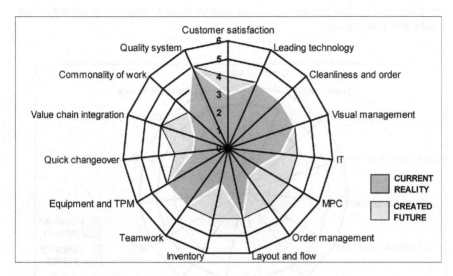

Fig. 2. Current reality for enterprise A, and planned improvements

The major objective of enterprise B is to satisfy their customers through an efficient specification-, order-, production-, and delivery-process. The products should meet customer specifications, have a competitive price and quality, and be delivered on-time. Other performance objectives are therefore delivery precision (95%) and productivity (cost per unit). The current and future profile of enterprise B is illustrated in Figure 3.

The mapping and analysis of enterprise B resulted in a range of improvement initiatives. Improvements are carried out in area 4 (visual management at the shop floor), area 5 (an integrated MPC system), area 6 (a streamlined and responsive order management and construction process), area 7 (implementation of a new ERP system and a advanced product configuration software), area 8 (a flow oriented layout), area 13 (new systems for interaction and information sharing with dealers and customers). Together, these initiatives will create an efficient specification-, order-, production-, and delivery-process, which delivers quality products on-time (area 15), and thereby radically improve customer satisfaction (area 1).

5   Conclusions

An approach for analysing enterprise operations is proposed in this paper. The purpose of this exercise is to provide sufficient knowledge to identify problems in the existing operations that could be targeted in a revised operations strategy. Operations strategy should provide the premises for any improvement initiative.

Each of the 15 areas should be rated against an ideal state. This enables the decision-maker to identify gaps between the existing state and the state that would support the overall operations strategy. The sheet should therefore be used to identify the particular profile of an enterprise, and to identify areas to improve in order to align capabilities with strategy.

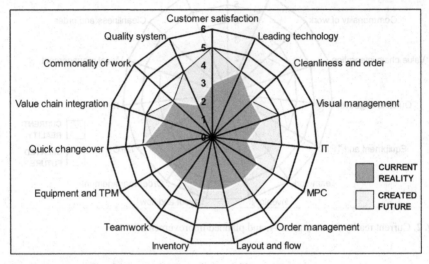

Fig. 3. Current reality for enterprise B, and planned improvements

However, no enterprise can be excellent in every dimension, trade-offs has to be made. The cases in this paper illustrates that the process-characteristics of an enterprise will influence on what should be regarded as the optimal profile. Enterprises with repetitive batch or line type of operations have a larger potential for high score in all areas. Job shop manufacturing is typically very flexible and involves a large element of craft work. This type of manufacturing is most suited for the production of one-of-a-kind-products that are customised to the customer. It could therefore be very difficult to achieve:

(7) Information system: 100% computer integrated and enabled manufacturing

(8) Layout and flow: 100% interconnected and flow-oriented layout

(9) Inventory: mixed model production with low inventory and high customer service

(14) Commonality: 100% standardised operations.

Continuous processing is typically highly automated and efficient, but not very flexible, and is best suited for standard commodity products in high volumes. It could therefore be very difficult to achieve:

(1) Customer satisfaction: fully displayed ratings and interactive, cross-functional involvement at all levels.

(9) Inventory: mixed model production with low inventory and high customer service

(12) Quick changeover: full SMED

It is also important to notice that some areas generally have a higher potential for improvement. For example, management often focus too much on shop floor activities, and underestimate the impact of poor office processes. Many manufacturing enterprises can achieve large improvements by addressing their order management process. The author's experience from several projects is that in addition to order management, the potential for improvement is especially high in (5) manufacturing planning and control, (8) layout and flow, and (9) inventory. These observations are also supported by Goodson's [4] dataset, which shows that these three areas consistently receive the lowest ratings.

References

1. Alfnes, E. (2005). *Enterprise reengineering: A strategic framework and methodology.* Faculty of Engineering Science and Technology, Department of Production and Quality Engineering. Trondheim, Norwegian University of Science and Technology, NTNU. Doctoral thesis, 2005:153.

2. Bicheno, J. (2000) *The lean toolbox.* PICSIE Books, Buckingham.

3. Fagerhaug, T. (1999) *A new improvement oriented method and model for self-assessment for business excellence.* Dr. thesis no. 127, NTNU report 99018.

4. Goodson, R.E. (2002) *Read a plant: fast.* Harvard Business Review, May, pp. 105-113.

5. Kobayashi, I. (1990) *Twenty keys to workplace improvement.* Productivity Press, Cambridge.

6. Rummler, G.A., Brache, A.P. (1995) *Improving performance: How to manage the white space on the organisation chart,* Jossey-Bass Publishers, San Fransico.

7. Schonberger, R. J. (1996) *World Class Manufacturing: The next decade, building power, strength and value.* The Free Press, New York.

8. Shapiro, B., Rangan, K., Sviokla, J. (1992) *Staple yourself to an order.* Harvard Business Review, July-August, pp. 113-122.

9. Shingo, S. (1985) *A revolution in manufacturing: the SMED system,* Productivity Press, Cambridge, Mass.

10. Spear, S., Bowen, H.K. (1999) *Decoding the DNA of the Toyota Production System.* Harvard Business Review. September-October, pp.97-106.

11. Suri, R. (2002) *Quick response Manufacturing: A competitive strategy for the 21st Century.* Proceedings of the 2002 POLCA Implementation workshop.

Comparing Performance Measures for the Trade Off of Flow Time and Throughput in Complex Manufacturing Systems

M. Macchi

Politecnico di Milano, Dipartimento di Ingegneria Gestionale
Piazza Leonardo da Vinci 32, 20133 Milano, Italy
WWW home page: http://www.dig.polimi.it

Abstract. Management of the trade off of logistic performances has always been a key issue in industry. The trade off results from the contrasting business objectives defined at strategic management level and is part of the subsequent decisions taken at shop floor level. Therein, performance measures influence decisions. These are, in general, operational measures and might be more or less aware of the trade off fixed at strategic level. The present paper aims to demonstrate how awareness may change in a production context where both flow time and throughput assumes a strategic importance. The demonstration is achieved by means of 2 case studies: the first one is simulated from scratch in laboratory, the second one is a simulation from a real industrial setting.

1 Introduction

Performance measurement of the trade off of logistic performances is clearly not a novelty. If one looks over literature, in the industrial engineering and operations management arena, 2 approaches for performance measurement can be identified. A typical approach is to define a cockpit of measures (throughput, flow time, ...) [3]. A relatively new approach is to define some indicators of logistic efficiency, proposed to characterise the trade off of logistic performances in a synthetic measure, instead of a cockpit. Also these indicators are derived from basic measures (throughput, flow time, ...) [2,7]. In this paper, the 2 approaches are compared to show the different decisions that they may lead to. The decisions are also evaluated with respect to defined strategic objectives, to deduce if the performance measures permit to be aware of them. The performance measures are, firstly, selected after a state of the art analysis (par. 2). Their theoretical and experimental comparison is shown (par. 3, 4). Concluding remarks are eventually pointed out for future works (par. 5).

Please use the following format when citing this chapter:

Macchi, M., 2008, in IFIP International Federation for Information Processing, Volume 257, Lean Business Systems and Beyond, Tomasz Koch, ed.; (Boston: Springer), pp. 143–150.

2   State of the art

A cockpit of performance measures is the typical approach to support decisions concerned with the trade off. This approach can be interpreted as a natural follow up of theoretical backgrounds of the Little's law. According to this approach, a decision at operational level can be reached after a concurrent analysis of throughput and flow time. The trade off of these measures can be shown in typical diagrams, such as flow time – throughput diagram. This diagram is referred to a production system or some of its subsystems and clearly leads a decision maker to a concurrent analysis of the 2 measures. Hence, decisions are somewhat aware of the trade off. Other alternative measures can be introduced in the cockpit. OEE [5,6] is well known. It is adopted, in TPM, for reducing efficiency losses at equipments of the production system. Its metric is correlated to the system throughput. Besides, even if the improvement in OEE is expected to bring benefit in flow time, OEE does not really count for it. OEE is then usually adopted aside other measures, such as flow time itself, and analysed concurrently with them to take into account the trade off. E metric [1] is a slight modification of OEE: similar notes can be pointed out to its concern. OTE [4], instead, complements OEE, by directly measuring an efficiency ratio of the achieved system throughput with respect to the maximum achievable throughput (achievable by its bottleneck resources). OTE still lacks of consideration of the flow time efficiency. Again, it requires other measures so that the decision is aware of the trade off. The second approach is to measure system performances by means of synthetic indicators of logistic efficiency. 2 indicators may be cited. The first one is the manufacturing performance P [2], the second one is OFE (Overall Fab Efficiency [7]). These are intended to measure, in a unique model, the efficiency of flow time and throughput. P metric is detailed in next par. 3. OFE is built as a product of 3 factors. The production efficiency (pe) is the factor that measures the trade off, normalised according to a reference situation, the so called "Practical Worst Case", defined as a production line, whose stations are single machines and balanced, with exponential distribution of processing times and CONWIP control.

3   Theoretical comparison

This section compares how decision is reached using the flow time – throughput and P – throughput diagrams. Attention is paid to one of the main decision making problem faced when solving the trade off: to decide the best operating point of the production system, if there is need to improve its efficiency (by increased utilisation or, equivalently, throughput) or to improve its responsiveness (by reduced utilisation, leading to a reduced flow time). Decision is supposed constrained by 2 objectives fixed at strategic level, and constraining the operational level. The first constraint is "max flow time". This cannot be overcome being it not acceptable for the operations strategy. It can be, e.g., the case of a MTO (make to order) operations strategy when order delivery time overcoming "max flow time" is not competitive in the market. The second constraint ("min throughput") may regard, e.g., the Break Even Point of a production system. These 2 constraints are included in the flow time – throughput and P – throughput diagrams, to create awareness of the strategic objectives.

3.1   Flow time – throughput diagram

Next figure 1 shows an example of flow time – throughput diagram with strategic constraints. According to such a diagram, a decision maker should decide to operate the system at an operating point over 21 orders / shop calendar day, so the Break Even Point is guaranteed. He/she should not exceed 26, otherwise the achieved flow time would not be competitive in the market. On the other hand, the diagram does not provide any criterion to decide if there is a best operating point in between.

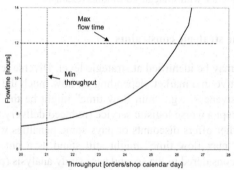

Fig. 1. Flow time – throughput diagram with strategic constraints (example)

3.2   P – throughput diagram

P metric is product of 2 efficiencies, flow time and throughput efficiency, calculated with respect to reference measures. Hence, $P = \eta_\varphi * \varepsilon_\delta$, where: $\eta_\varphi = \varphi_{ref} / \varphi$; $\varepsilon_\delta = \delta / \delta_{ref}$. φ_{ref} is normally fixed at the minimum achievable flow time (sum of all processing times required in process plans). δ_{ref} is normally fixed as the maximum achievable throughput (achievable by the bottleneck resources of the system). Next figure 2 shows an example of P – throughput diagram with strategic constraints. The representation of the strategic constraints is obtained by fixing acceptable thresholds such as a minimum throughput ($\delta = \delta_{min}$) or a maximum flow time ($\varphi = \varphi_{max}$). According to such a diagram, the operating point should be again between 21 and 26 orders / shop calendar day. The decision maker is then aware of the strategic objectives, similarly as with the flow time – throughput diagram. On the other hand, this diagram provides a new criterion to decide the best operating point in between: optimum point of P is reached at a throughput of about 22 orders / shop calendar day. Moreover, P is close to optimum in the range between 21 and 22. This was not fixed in the flow time – throughput diagram.

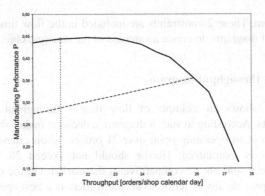

Fig. 2. P – throughput diagram with strategic constraints (example)

3.3   Remarks on the strategic constraints

Other constraints may be identified at strategic level. Diverse levels of flow time may be, e.g., competitive in a market, depending on how much the client is sensible to the system responsiveness: e.g., "min flow time" might be the level over which a client is eager to accept a worse logistic service (reduced delivery time), but only in the case that the supplier offers discounts or pays some penalties with respect to the full cost; whilst the "max flow time" might still stand as a not acceptable level. A similar situation is considered in the second case study analysis (par. 4.2).

4   Experimental comparison

2 case studies were simulated in ARENA tool for experimental comparison. The simulation results were then used to build flow time – throughput and P – throughput diagrams. The simulation results are reported in next subsections: the first case study is used to compare decisions resulting from flow time – throughput and P – throughput diagrams; the second case study integrates strategic / economic issues, a comparison on how decision changes is then done by adopting the P – throughput diagram (with strategic constraint) and a Gross margin – throughput diagram.

4.1   Case study 1 – job shop system

The first case study (fig. 3) is a job shop with 3 shops (WS1, WS2, WS3). Each WS is a set of parallel machines (with equivalent processing capabilities). The order mix is fixed for type (P1, P2, P3, P4) and percentage (30%, 35 %, 25 % and 10%). Unit processing and set up times are fixed as well. Inter-arrival times at the job shop are exponentially distributed and a FIFO dispatching rule is used at each machine. Other issues (transport, failures, buffer spaces, ...) are neglected.

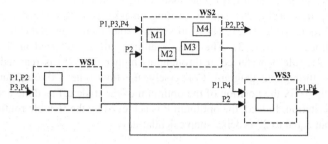

Fig. 3. Production flows and machines in the job shop

Being all fixed, some alternatives for product routing through the WS2 machines (WS2 is the bottleneck resource) are then compared: rule 1 (routing "all products to all machines" using a random rule), rule 2 (routing "all products to all machines" using a rule for selection of the machine with "minimum queuing times") and rule 3 (with rigid product-machine allocations, i.e. M1 and M2 allocated to products with high work loads – M1 allocated to P1, M2 to P2 –, M3 to products with low work loads – P3, P4 –, M4 to all products, to provide a degree of routing flexibility –). The simulation results are shown in the following P – throughput and flow time – throughput diagrams (fig. 4).

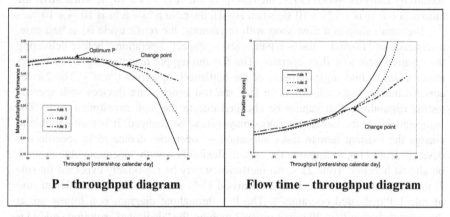

Fig. 4. Selecting the best operating point in case of alternative routing rules

According to the P - throughput diagram, rule 2 is preferred at lower throughputs, rule 3 outperforms other rules at higher throughputs. In fact, at lower throughputs, rule 2 outperforms rule 1 thanks to its routing criterion ("minimum queuing time") instead of random routing. Rule 3 is, any how, the worst one, since it suffers from waiting times subsequent to the constraints in product routings created by the rigid product-machine allocations: an order may risk to wait much of the times being its dedicated resource busy, the worst flow time then results which, finally, reduces the P performance. A change point comes out at higher levels (close to 25 orders / shop calendar day). The losses of the flow time efficiency are now due to the set up times (plus the induced waiting times) much more registered with the flexible solutions (rule 1, 2). These losses are smoothed with dedicated product-machine allocations (rule 3). The same ranking (rule 2 preferred at throughputs lower than 25, rule 3 preferred at throughputs higher than 25) is reached with the flow time – throughput diagram. Conversely, the flow time – throughput diagram does not help to fix the position of the optimum of the trade off as done accordingly with the P criterion. Indeed, the optimum P is achieved by the flexible routing rule 2, at throughput equal to 22 orders / shop calendar day.

4.2   Case study 2 – flow shop with re-entrant flows

The case study concerns repairing of radar components of air planes' fleets. The turn time (time to receive a radar component, test, complete repairs and return it to the fleet operator) is a strategic objective, to avoid the risk of lengthy AOG (aircraft on the ground). This requires high responsiveness from the repair shop. The quick response is rewarded: a constant premium price is rewarded by the fleet operator, if the flow time is lower than a threshold ("min flow time"). Otherwise, the premium price is reduced by a penalty cost, with an almost linear penalty cost function: if the flow time increases ft % over the "min flow time", the premium price is reduced at a p %. Different ratio p % ÷ ft % have been experimented in simulation for sensitivity analysis. When LOW, the ratio p % ÷ ft % is 5 % ÷ 10 %; when MID, the ratio p % ÷ ft % is 7,7 % ÷ 10 %; when HIGH, the ratio p % ÷ ft % is 10 % ÷ 10 %.

The repair shop is a flow shop with re-entrants: the repair cycle is, at best case, a sequence of "inspect – test – repair – test – inspect" operations, before delivering the repaired item to a fleet operator. The P – throughput diagram (fig. 5) compares then 2 rules to find improvements of the bottleneck operation ("test"). The 2 rules concern human tasks allocation. In fact, the test benches are devices with specific testing capabilities that cannot be changed due to the high investment costs. The competencies of the human operators may instead be changed. It is then possible to change the existent human tasks allocation – "operators dedicated to specific test devices" (rule 1) –, to improve the system flexibility – with "operators able to work on all test benches" (rule 2) –. An inefficiency may be reasonably expected for rule 2: the unit testing time was in fact estimated 15 % shorter in the most efficient case of rule 1 ("dedicated operators"). The P – throughput diagram is a follow up: at throughputs higher than 30 repair orders / months, the "dedicated" solution (rule 1) is preferred thanks to its efficient unit testing time; at lower throughputs, the "flexible" solution for the product routings (rule 2) wins over the advantages of the testing efficiency and should be chosen. The best operating point, according to optimisation of P, is again achieved at low throughputs (between 25 and 26 repair orders / month) by the "flexible" solution (rule 2). This may not correspond to the economic optimum if penalty costs are taken into account beside P.

Indeed, the gross margin diagram (see again fig. 5) leads to the same optimum as with P only in the case of MID p % ÷ ft %. The penalty cost is too high in the HIGH case: if the throughput is incremented over the "min flow time", the increase in repair volumes is not sufficient to counterbalance the penalty cost resulting from worse flow time efficiency, hence the gross margin is reduced. In this case, then, the economic optimum corresponds exactly to the "min flow time" point, where major gains result from achieving premium price whilst avoiding penalty cost. The LOW case is the opposite situation: if the throughput is incremented over the "min flow time", the increase in repair volumes brings more benefit than reduction in unit gross margin due to the penalty cost resulting from worse flow time; so the gross margin is augmented. The economic optimum, in such a case, is reached by pushing production as maximum as possible according to capacity constraints.

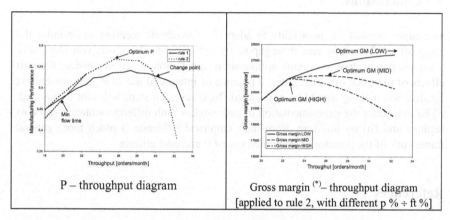

| P – throughput diagram | Gross margin (*)– throughput diagram [applied to rule 2, with different p % ÷ ft %] |

Fig. 5. Selecting the best operating point in case of alternative rules for human tasks allocation; (*) Gross Margin = [(premium price - penalty cost - other variable costs) * throughput * working days per year] (Note 1. premium price fixed at a fictitious level of 100, Note 2: other variable costs constant at different throughputs).

Thereafter, comparing with P, it can be concluded that P is a sufficient criterion to identify the best operating point when the strategic setting is in a specific situation. In the case study, being "min flow time" fixed, P can be used to optimise the trade off only when the stipulated contracts maintain a ratio p % ÷ ft % around 7,7 % ÷ 10 %, after a more detailed sensitivity analysis, it was established that P would also be sufficient in a range between 7,5 % ÷ 10 % and 8 % ÷ 10 %. In other cases: (i) better to push production to the maximum capacity, when ratio is lower than 7,5 % ÷ 10 %, using rule 1 ("dedicated operators"); (ii) better to work at minimum throughput, correspondent to the "min flow time", when ratio is higher than 8 % ÷ 10 %.

4.3   Remarks on the strategic constraints

The second case study helps to point out another constraint that may exist beside those already issued: the repair demand clearly depends on how many contracts are stipulated, so from a decision strictly related with strategic level. This repair demand might, however, lead to throughput requirements which are not consistent with either the P (logistic) or Gross Margin (economic) optimum. E.g., an high repair demand would be good in case of ratio lower than 7,5 % ÷ 10 %: it favours the economic optimisation. In other cases, it is not good. A reconciliation with the strategic level should then be planned. In the case study, 2 situations are now under consideration to reconcile: (i) to outsource the excess of repair demand, so to make only the optimum throughput; (ii) to re-negotiate contracts, to reduce the penalty cost (lower than 7,5 % ÷ 10 %).

5   Conclusions

The paper showed the possibility to adopt P as synthetic measure to optimise the trade off of flow time and throughput. Its optimisation, however, considers only a logistic perspective, economic optimisation may be integrated to consider the cost effects of the trade off. Thereafter, a practice of integrated use of P and cost criteria for decision making should be envisioned. Next research steps will aim to this end: (i) by extending the experimentation in case studies with different strategic and cost settings and (ii) by building, from their empirical evidence, a much more general framework of the practice of integrated use of P and cost criteria.

References

1. De Ron, A. J. and Rooda, J. E. Equipment Effectiveness: OEE revisited. IEEE Transaction on Semiconductor Manufacturing, vol. 18, no. 1, 190-196, 2005.

2. De Ron, A. J. and Rooda, J. E. Fab Performance. IEEE Transaction on Semiconductor Manufacturing, vol. 18, no. 3, 399-405, 2005.

3. Hopp, W. and Spearman, M.L. Factory physics: foundation of manufacturing management. McGraw-Hill, Boston, 2000.

4. Huang, S. H., Dismukes, J. P., Shi, J., Su, Q., Razzak, M. A., Bodhale R. and Robinson, D.E. Manufacturing productivity improvement using effectiveness metrics and simulation analysis. International Journal of Production Research, vol.41, no.3, 513–527, 2003.

5. Nakajima, S. Introduction to TPM Total Productive Maintenance. Productivity Press, Cambridge, Massachusetts, Norwalk, Connecticut, 1988.

6. SEMI. Standard for definition and measurement of equipment productivity, SEMI E79-0200. Semiconductor Equipment and Material International, Mt. View, California, 2000.

7. SEMI. Provisional guideline for definition and calculation of overall factory efficiency (OFE) and other associated factory-level productivity metrics. Technical Report SEMI E124, International SEMATECH, Inc, 2003.

A Method for Measuring Operational and Financial Performance of a Production Value Stream

Tomasz Sobczyk[1], Tomasz Koch[1]
1   Institute for Production Engineering and Automation,
Wroclaw University of Technology,
ul. Wybrzeze Wyspianskiego 27, 50-370 Wroclaw, Poland
WWW home page: http://www.pwr.wroc.pl/

Abstract. The paper explains the conceptual framework of so called costs, effects and resources map that is intended to support performance analyses of the production value stream. Its purpose is to enhance manufacturing decision taking processes by providing relevant information related to production flows. The tool consists of five modules: production system model (value stream map), cost module, financial statement and inventory valuation module, resources analyses module, and operational metrics module. The tool has been equipped with appropriate metrics that enable analyses of production system dynamics. In the last section of the paper example application of the tool in the production environment has been explained.

1   Introduction

Lean production (also known as the Toyota Production System) triggered a global transformation in virtually every industry over the last decade and became the foundation of dozens of books [1]. According to Womack, Jones and Ross, lean production is a means for rapidly developing world-class manufacturing skills without massive capital investments [2]. Many companies try to imitate the Toyota Way developing their production systems based on lean assumptions. However, numerous operational initiatives are often rejected as traditional cost accounting systems do not provide relevant and timely information to support them. Great amount of publicity has been generated by the writings of many authors criticizing current management accounting practices and their lack of relevance to today's business imperatives. Some authors advocate that many accounting textbooks teach the managers to put aside understanding the concrete particulars of how the business organizes work and focus exclusively on abstract quantitative generalizations about financial results [3]. According to Johnson managers too often manipulate processes

Please use the following format when citing this chapter:

Sobczyk, T. and Koch, T., 2008, in IFIP International Federation for Information Processing, Volume 257, Lean Business Systems and Beyond, Tomasz Koch, ed.; (Boston: Springer), pp. 151–163.

to achieve accounting results, instead of monitoring well-run processes and occasionally checking accounting results [4]. Other authors suggest that cost cutting exercises are too often ritual activity which gives the appearance of something happening rather than the probably much needed but less comfortable rethink of some underlying causes of cost [5]. Some other argue that cost improvements not only come from reducing direct expenditures but also from properly managing indirect costs. According to Miller and, most production managers understand what drives direct labor and material costs but are much less aware of what drives overhead costs [6].

Value stream costing proposed by Maskell and Baggaley is one of the methods that can be successfully applied for measuring performance of a lean production system [7]. Although perfectly tailored for lean production organizations, it can be of little use by companies that are in an early stage of a lean journey . The authors articulate this by stressing the need for numerous "lean assumptions" that must be in place before the method can be effectively used [7, p. 140]. In the paper alternative method for measuring performance of a production system will be presented. The objective is to present a way of measuring system's performance regardless of the company's "lean maturity". The method is also intended to serve as a tool for monitoring current performance, estimation of gains envisioned by future state blueprints and individual improvement initiatives as well as assessment of value stream performance over time.

2   Conceptual framework of the tool

Production value stream's costs, effects and resources map (called hereafter value stream cost map) is a model used for measuring the performance of the selected manufacturing area modeled by means of the value stream map. The idea behind the model assumes the integration of a value stream map with a set of appropriate modules that aim at explicit description of the production system's state over time. The concept has been graphically presented in Figure 1.

The core of the model is given by the production value stream map (see 1 in Fig. 1). A Value Stream Mapping tool derives from Toyota's standard method for portraying material and information flows and was adapted by Rother and Shook into value stream maps [8]. According to Womack and Jones, the mapping process clearly reveals the potential for a major leap in performance if a relatively small number of flow and process improvements can be conducted and then sustained [9]. To measure the performance of any given value stream over time, four integrated modules have been proposed:

1. Cost module (or positioned cost pools module), in which each cost category is broken down into cost pools and any given cost pool is positioned along appropriate processes; the cost module enables assignment of costs to production entities (see 2 in Fig. 1);
2. Financial statement and inventory valuation module (see 3 in Fig. 1);
3. Resources analyses module (see 4 in Fig. 1);
4. Additional metrics module (see 5 in Fig. 1).

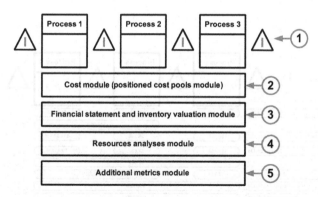

Fig. 1. Building blocks of the value stream cost map

Developed model represents a performance measurement platform that can be used for assessing any given production system in financial and operational terms. The model can support the analyses of:
1. State of the production system over time;
2. Financial consequences of changes presented on a value stream future state map along with establishing a set of necessary conditions required to implement operational ideas envisioned by a future state blueprint;
3. Individual improvement initiatives and investments (creation of financial scenarios based on different operational assumptions);
4. Value stream process costs and their root causes.

2.1   Cost pools and cost objects. Assigning costs to cost objects.

It has been assumed that in the model processes visualized by process boxes will form basic cost objects. Assignment of costs onto cost objects is a three-stage process that consists of the following steps:
1. Grouping cost into cost categories;
2. Braking cost categories into cost pools;
3. Assigning cost pools to a single process or group of processes.

It has been proposed that depending on the needs any cost category can be created. Cost categories must than be allocated to the processes (cost objects) using pre-defined cost pools. Three types of cost pools have been defined: single process cost pool, group of processes cost pool, and value stream cost pool. The example configuration of cost categories and their value stream assignment has been shown in Figure 2.

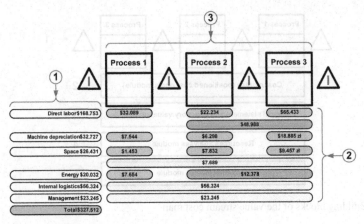

Fig. 2. Cost categories decomposed into cost pools. Assignment of cost pools into cost objects

Figure 2 shows six different cost categories (1). Costs within each category have been decomposed and assigned to the value stream processes (3) via cost pools (2). This enables for the following observations and conclusions:

1. How much costs is being used by the value stream and how much each category is worth;
2. How much costs is assigned to each process (or group of processes) in the value stream (for example it can be seen that process No. 1 requires as much as $32.098 of the direct labor costs);
3. For creation of what cost is each of the value stream processes responsible.

This form of visualization is aimed at achieving production value stream cost identification and tracking. In addition, costs of shared resources can be visualized as value stream cost map is being created. This is true for both costs (resources) shared within sub-streams within any given value stream as well as costs (resources) shared by different value streams within the same company.

2.1.1 Resources shared within different value streams

Since a part of a value stream may be shared among different value streams within single production entity (what can not be seen on the value stream map), it is important to include this information on the value stream cost map. The way this information can be contained on the map has been visualized in Figure 3.
Shaded cost pools on the cost map indicate that the processes share the resources (people, machines, space, etc.) with other value streams. In order to asses the level of sharing cost allocation must be performed. It is suggested that for this purpose single cost drivers are used or the calculations with use of activity-based costing method is performed [10]. It can be seen from Figure 3 that part of labor, machine and energy costs assigned to process No. 1 is shared with the value stream referred to as S2. On the other hand, value stream non-direct costs are the part of total overhead factory costs and are shared with two other value streams referred to as S2 and S3.

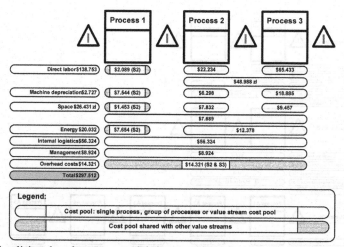

Fig. 3. Visualizing shared resources and their costs using value stream cost map

2.1.2 Resources shared within different value stream sub-streams

In the case a value stream consists of different sub-streams, value stream cost map shall contain cost information about each of them. The example of the cost map consisting of three parallel streams has been shown in Figure 4.

The figure presents example cost structure assigned to the main stream (A) and two sub-streams (B and C). The following are the general rules for the design of a cost map consisting of additional sub-streams (see Figure 4 for reference).

1. The main stream and sub-streams shall be identified (see respectively A, B and C on Figure 4);
2. All sub-streams ought to be located above main stream of the production value stream;
3. Processes belonging to sub-streams shall be assigned their own cost pools (1 and 2 respectively). It is suggested however, that the same cost categories as in the case of the main stream are used;
4. Cost pools of shared resources should be shaded (see also point 2.3);
5. Those cost pools that are shared both within main stream and sub-streams should be dotted. It is suggested that one writes down which processes or sub-stream any given cost pool is shared with. For example:
   a. Cost of energy is a shared cost of the main stream and all other sub-streams;
   b. Labor cost is a cost shared between processes A3 and C2 (see 3 and 3' in Fig. 4);
6. Costs that are shared within the value stream and other company value streams should be plotted in vertical lines (see 7 in Fig. 4);

7. One ought to calculate summary costs of each sub-stream (see 8, 9 and 10 in Figure 4) as well as total costs of the entire value stream (see 11 in Figure 4).

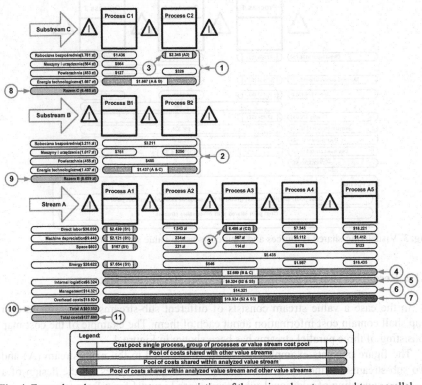

Fig. 4. Example value stream cost map consisting of the main value stream and two parallel sub-streams

2.2   Financial statement and inventory valuation module

Financial results are calculated using throughput costing methodology to prevent overproduction. This implies that all costs except from material costs are regarded period costs. What is more, in valuing the inventory only material costs are taken into consideration. Figure 5 presents the value stream cost map linked with financial statement and inventory valuation module.

Selected positions are related to:

1. Value of inventory at the end of the analyzed period (see 1, 2 and 3 in Fig. 5);
2. Income reported at the end of the analyzed period (see 4 in Fig. 5);
3. Cost of goods sold throughout the analyzed period (see 5 in Fig. 5);
4. Value stream costs incurred in the analyzed period (the sum of all cost pools);
5. Amount of revenue gained in the period.

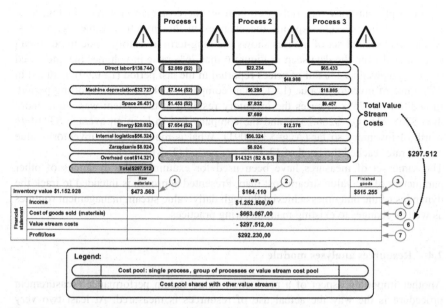

Fig. 5. Inventory valuation and profit calculation using value stream cost map

2.3 System dynamics analyses

The static nature of the value stream map and dynamic nature of the production system calls for measuring the state of the production entity over the time. The analyses of system's dynamics will be explained on the example of the analyses related to inventory value. This type of analyses is twofold and aims at establishing the following:

1. What is the value of inventory in the value stream and what had been the reasons behind the raise (or fall) of inventory value against previous reported period;
2. How current inventory relates to the overall, long-term trends.

Figure 6 presents the example of how the dynamics of inventory value can be tackled using value stream cost map.

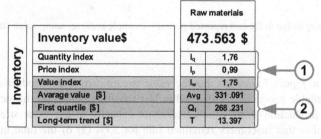

	Raw materials
Inventory value$	**473.563 $**
Quantity index I_q	1,76
Price index I_p	0,99
Value index I_w	1,75
Avarage value [$] Avg	331.091
First quartile [$] Q_1	268.231
Long-term trend [$] T	13.397

Fig. 6. Chosen parameters used for the analyses of system dynamics with use of value stream cost map

Figure 6 presents raw materials section from the cost map presented in Figure 5. First set of indexes (1) explains the changes in the inventory value against last period. The second set of metrics shows the long-term inventory value trend. It can be deducted from the data seen in Figure 6 that 76% raise in volumes manufactured (I_q=1,76) as well as 1% fall of prices reported in the last period (I_p=0,99), resulted in 75% raise of inventory value (I_v=1,75) as compared with previous reporting period. In addition, in 75% of cases the inventory residing in the system was worth more than \$268.231 (Q_1=\$268.231), and the company had to keep on average \$331,091 worth of inventory so far (Avg=\$331,091). What is more, average inventory value growth rate reached the level of 13.397\$ per period (T=\$13.397).

The same set of measures have been used for examining the dynamics of other parameters of the value stream cost map. Presented approach is intended to track the dynamics of the outcomes achieved through daily value stream management routines as well as changes to existing manufacturing practices.

2.4   Resources analyses module

Another important aspect of a production value stream performance measurement procedure is the way the actual use of resources is measured. At least two very important "lean" aspects should be taken into consideration:
1.   Production equipment usage;
2.   The use of human resources.

2.4.1 Production equipment usage

The method for measuring machinery usage has been graphically presented in Figure 7.

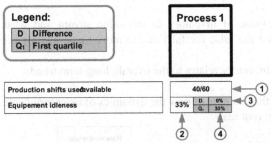

Fig. 7. Machinery usage in the last reported period – example analyses using value stream cost map

The data in Figure 7 suggests that the value stream carried out production on 40 out of 60 available production shifts within last reporting period (at the same time, 60 available production shifts equals maximum capacity of the value stream) (1). The data implies that machinery remained idle for 33% (2) of the time in the last period. Compared to the previous reporting period, no changes had been noticed in that matter (3). However 75% of cases, production equipment stayed non-productive for not less than 33% (4).

In addition to the usage of the machinery, it is important to consider the use of human resources as well as associated labor costs and its productivity.

2.4.2 Human resources usage

Given that human resources are active does not necessarily imply that they are productive. Hence, there is a need to distinguish between different types of human activities carried out and the amount of time they require. The basis for comparison is the time devoted to production which can be divided into categories shown in Figure 8.

Each category that impacts the use of resources in a given process (1) has been assigned percentage of time out of total available time used by the process in the analyzed period (2). In addition, each category has been equipped with appropriate indexes similar to those presented on Figure 6 to measure the dynamics of changes as improvement initiatives take place (3).

Given the example from Figure 1 one can arrive at the following conclusions:
1. 40% of time the resources were used for actual production 8.3% of which was overproduction.
2. Even though production volume was higher than required, customer satisfaction reached only 95% (the value stream produced more than expected however not the part numbers that were needed) (4).

It important to realize that the time used for production was close to 40% what suggests that the rest of it was wasted (see relevant categories in Fig. 8). It also implies that one should search for causes of wasted human effort that is the effect of existing production practices.

If connected to the cost module, the tool enables the following:
1. Analyses of the cost of waste related to any activity within value stream;
2. Analyses of the potential gains due to waste elimination.

These two enablers will be explained in more detail in point 3.

2.5   Additional metrics module

Depending on the production type, metrics used by the company/corporation, or individual needs of the user, the cost map may be supplemented by additional set of operational and financial indexes. In addition, the dynamics of the parameters can be measured by means of proposed set of indexes explained in point 2.4.

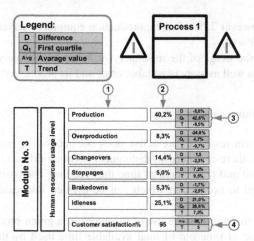

Fig. 8. Categories of activities performed by human resources employed in the production value stream – notation of the value stream cost map

3   Application of the tool

The application of the cost map will be explained on the example of the company manufacturing metal nets used in coal mines. The data was gathered on the basis of six-month project. Four complementary ways of use have been graphically presented in Figure 9.

As it can be seen in Figure 9, the model is based on the production current state value stream map (1). The tool can be used for the following analyses:
1. value stream current state operational and financial performance measurement (1);
2. monitoring operational and financial performance of the value stream over time (2);
3. operational and financial assessment of the future state blueprint;
4. operational and financial assessment of the individual improvement initiatives (both technical and organizational) (4).

The application of the latter issue will be explained in more detail in the following section of the paper. It has been assumed that the reference for the following analyses will be the cost map designed in May 2006.

3.1   Operational and financial assessment of the individual improvement initiatives

Modernization of the existing fabrication cell became the study with use of value stream cost map methodology. Improvement ideas became the subject to further assessment. Proposed changes were related to reduced cycle times and improved use of production resources. It had been assumed that additional investment ($ 1.320 for fixtures and $5.000 for employee training) would be required. Achieved results in form of the value stream cost map are presented in Figure 10.

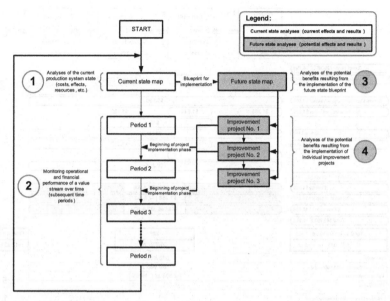

Fig. 9. Four complementary ways of using value stream cost map methodology

Expected changes to map's analytical positions have been colored. According to data in Figure 10 proposed organizational and technical changes lead to the following considerations:
1. The same production volume might be manufactured using half of the resources available (1); this in turn leads to 50% reduction in direct labor costs (2);
2. Increase in productive use (3) and at the same reduction in non-productive use of resources (4);
3. 10% reduction in value stream costs and 64% profitability increase (5);
Similarly to the future state financial considerations it is possible to propose many different scenarios based on different assumptions. What is more, the model can be used for assessing the impact of operational changes that may not have any influence on bottom-line results. In this case such a scenario may be rejected.

4   Summary and conclusions

The platform for measuring performance of a production value stream called value stream cost map has been presented. In the research work, value stream mapping method has been linked to the cost analyses module and integrated with:
1. financial statement and inventory valuation module (based on throughput costing methodology);

2. resources analyses module;
3. operational metrics module.

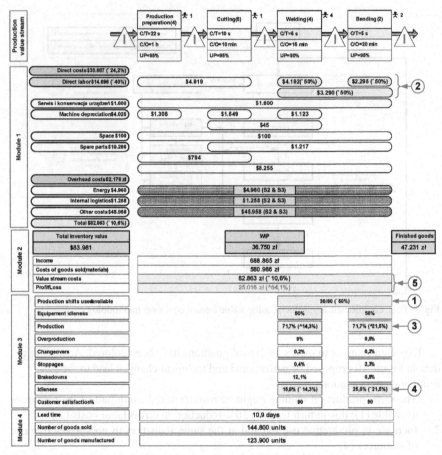

Fig. 10. Assessment and validation of the improvement project with use of value stream cost map

Graphical structure of the model supports analyses of the state of a production value stream with parallel focus on resources usage, costs, profits, value of inventory, and other important operational and financial parameters. The potential users of the model are manufacturing engineers and production managers who look for appropriate tool to support their strategic and daily operational decisions.

The model is an alternative solution for the existing performance measurement systems (particularly traditional cost accounting and management systems). It has been proved that it can be successfully applied by the production facility. The major distinction to value stream costing proposal is that the value stream cost map:

1. Does provide alternative method for measuring profitability and resources usage as well as the costs of individual processes and the entire value stream;

2. Utilizes existing inventory valuation method based on throughput approach;
3. Does not require the resources (costs) to be dedicated process costs (it visualizes costs of shared resources);
4. Can be used by any company regardless of the maturity in Lean Manufacturing implementation;
5. Provides graphical representation of the value stream's operational and financial data – usually on one piece of paper;
6. Supports analyses of complex value streams with many fabrication sub-streams;
7. Enables the analyses of the dynamics of any given production value stream.

The method can be used by any company regardless of its size, country of origin or production profile as long as the production system can be modeled by means of the value stream map.

References:

1. Liker, J., K., The Toyota Way: 14 Management Principles from the World's Greatest Manufacturer, McGraw-Hill 2004.

2. Womack, J., P., Jones, D., T., Ross, D., The Machine That Changed the World. Who's ahead in the Global Auto Wars and why: Japan's Revolutionary Leap from Mass Production to Lean Production And What Industry Everywhere can Learn from, Simon & Schuster Inc., p. 256.

3. Johnson, T.H.; Broms, A., Profit Beyond Measure : Extraordinary Results through Attention to Work and People, Free Press, November 2000, p. 58.

4. Johnson, T.H., 1992, Relevance Regained: From Top-Down Control to Bottom-Up Empowerment, Free Press, January 2002, p. 26.

5. Slack, N., 1992, The Manufacturing Advantage: Achieving Competitive Manufacturing Operations, Management Books 2000 (April 1992), p. 99.

6. Miller, J.G.; Vollmann, T.E., The Hidden Factory, Harvard Business Review, September-October 1985, p.143.

7. Maskell, B., H., Baggaley, B., Practical Lean Accounting. A Proven System for Measuring and Managing the Lean Enterprise, Productivity Press Inc. 2003.

8. Rother, M., Shook, J., Learning to See, Ver. 1.3, The Lean Enterprise Institute, 2003.

9. Womack, J.P.; Jones, D.T., Lean Thinking. Banish Waste and Create Wealth in Your Corporation, The Free Press 2003, p. 316.

10. Sobczyk, T., Koch, T., Cost Management Framework for a Value Stream, International Conference on Changeable, Agile, Reconfigurable and Virtual Production.

Reference Models for Mass Customisation Production of High Fashionable Products: Application to the Shoe Manufacturing Domain

Yves Ducq, Bruno Vallespir
LAPS/GRAI University Bordeaux 1 – ENSEIRB – UMR CNRS 5131
351, cours de la libération   33405 TALENCE CEDEX - FRANCE
tel.: +33 5 4000 2408   fax: +33 5 4000 6644

Abstract. In order to face the competitors with low cost of human resources, one solution consists for industrial enterprises to evolve from mass production to mass customisation. In this kind of system, the product is customised for each customer in order to answer his requirements at the best . In this frame, several European shoe enterprises have decided to evolve towards mass customisation in order to offer customised shoes with an industrial way of working. In order to help them in this task and to derive research results, a European project has been set up: the Euroshoe project ("Development of the processes and implementation of management tools for the Extended User Oriented Shoe Enterprise" - *GRD1 – 2000 - 25761*). The objective of this paper is to present how the enterprise modelling techniques were used in the project in order to identify the existing running of shoe companies and to define reference models for the future running of these mass customisation manufacturing systems.

1   Introduction

If the 20th century was the one of mass production, the strong competition in a global market has modified the way companies will do business in the 21st century. In order to face the competitors with low cost of human resources, one solution consists for industrial enterprises to evolve from mass production to mass customisation [1]. The term took its root since the publication of the book *Mass Customisation* [2] and another book *Agile Product Development for Mass Customisation* [3]. In this kind of system, the product is customised for each customer in order to answer his requirements at the best. In comparison to classical One of a Kind Production system, mass customisation implies to have for each product a design phase combined with mass production. This leads to high-mix

Please use the following format when citing this chapter:

Ducq, Y. and Vallespir, B., 2008, in IFIP International Federation for Information Processing, Volume 257, Lean Business Systems and Beyond, Tomasz Koch, ed.; (Boston: Springer), pp. 165–173.

system with lean organisation which aims to minimize costs and lead time. The purpose is to have performances close to mass production ones with more adapted services.

In this frame, several European shoe enterprises have decided to evolve towards mass customisation in order to offer customised shoes with an industrial way of working. In order to help them in this task and to derive research results, a European project has been set up: the Euroshoe project ("Development of the processes and implementation of management tools for the Extended User Oriented Shoe Enterprise" - *GRD1 – 2000 - 25761*).

The objectives of this project, including thirty three partners, were to imagine, to specify, to develop and to implement techniques (machines, software, ...) and organisations required for a shoes mass customisation system, from the scan of the feet, the product configuration, the design of adapted last, sole, uppers, to the final assembling of the shoe and its distribution to the final customer using express mail. The total lead time targeted is two weeks maximum.

The objective of this paper is to present how the enterprise modelling techniques were used in the project in order to identify the existing running of shoe companies and to define reference models for the future running of these mass customisation manufacturing systems. The methods used were mainly IDEFØ and GRAI.

Another challenge of these reference models is to be generic enough to be reusable for other kinds of mass customisation systems as fashion clothes.

So, after a slight presentation of the Euroshoe project, the paper will present first how the six enterprise models were built with the selected enterprise modelling methods. Then, all these models were combined in order to build an equivalent AS IS model. The interest of this equivalent AS IS was to have a synthetic view of common existing practices in this domain.

Then, based on the equivalent AS IS models, a first diagnosis was elaborated and will be presented in the second part of the paper. This diagnosis highlighted the strong points and the points to improve in such systems. This diagnosis was derived and extended for each system in order to advice each company on points to improve in their current system.

In a third time, the paper will present the TO BE models, i.e. the models of the future system for a typical mass customisation system for shoe manufacturing.

2   The EUROSHOE Project

EUROShoe [4] is a research project aiming at a dramatic renovation of the concept of the shoe as a product and of its production, based on the transformation of the first from a mass produced good towards a mass customised one. This product evolution goes in parallel with a transformation of footwear companies into extended and agile enterprises capable of handling the complexity that such a change in the nature of the product implies and of mastering the new challenges deriving from a direct involvement of the consumer in the design and manufacturing process of the shoe he is going to buy. Such a radical change in the product nature forces a complete revision of the processes that support the various phases of the product life cycle (design, production, sale and distribution, use, dismissal and recycling) in a systemic view that is developed within the EUROShoe project according to the model of the product – processes matrix leading to a research effort that encompasses the development, for each of them, of all the relevant critical technologies. This total and global rethinking of the footwear business needs large resources and the EUROShoE project is therefore an ambitious and large research initiative involving all the actors of the value added chain.

The approach is, on one side, looking at the *"shoe system"* and on the other side developing the necessary methodologies and technologies needed at every step of the value added chain.

The project originates from the statement that there is a trend that indicates a growing demand for a certain level of customisation in the products or services the consumers are buying. This trend is certainly similar to what exists for products like cars, garments or services of various kinds.

The challenge of the EURO ShoE project is precisely to manufacture customised / custom made shoes (so shoes that can guarantee a much higher level of individual satisfaction) at a price that is affordable for the great majority of the consumers.

Having a such research wide scope, several results are expected. The main project outputs can be summarised as follows:

- a *detailed survey* of the specific aspects of the demand for customised shoes,
- a *reference model* of the business and operational processes of the shoes companies,
- a *set software tools and procedures* to select, configure, integrate ERP/PDM/CAD/CAM,
- a *fully implemented ERP/PDM/CAD/CAM environment* for a testbed,
- a new generation of foot *feature capturing devices* and camera based foot *scanners,*
- a *knowledge based CAD/CAM software* for the design of customised shoes,
- a variety of *new design versatile and multi purpose shoe machines and systems,* and
- a *physical and virtual (web based) sale environment* for the selection of customised shoes.

The second output will be especially detailed in the following part of this paper.

3   The reference models: from AS IS towards TO BE models

The methodology set up to develop generic TO BE models is presented figure 1. In order to understand the running of shoe manufacturing companies in Europe, six different enterprises were modelled. These six companies were located in different countries, with different sizes (from 50 to 2000 employees), different cultures, different organisations (single or in supply chain). So, even if the GRAI Methodology [5] includes five kinds of models and views, according to the project objectives, it was applied in order to model each company from only three points of view: functional, physical, and decisional.

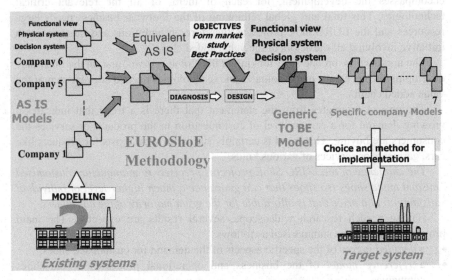

Fig. 1. The EUROShoE methodology to develop reference TOBE models

Based on the six models, an equivalent (generic) AS IS model was developed in order to synthesise the practices. Then, based on the diagnosis about the equivalent AS IS and on the objectives of shoe industry for mass customisation identified from the market study, a vision was defined and then Generic TO BE model was elaborated. Finally, the generic TO BE was instantiated for the six specific companies and one scholar case study.

3.1 Equivalent AS IS Model

The objective of equivalent AS IS model was to describe a synthesis of the mechanisms and operation logics which cover all the functions of the extended enterprises [6].

In fact, each of the six enterprise models was scrutinised in order to detect common ways of running and to create a consistent overview and detailed knowledge about shoes manufacturing.

So, the equivalent AS IS model was build from several points of view: the functional view, the physical system which adds value to the product and the decisional system which controls the physical system. This AS IS model covers the various functions of enterprise, from the merchandising to the distribution. However, it was mainly detailed for the design and the manufacturing functions because the mass customisation system required a very high integration between these two parts of the enterprise.

The equivalent AS IS models from functional and decisional points of view are presented figure 2 and figure 3.

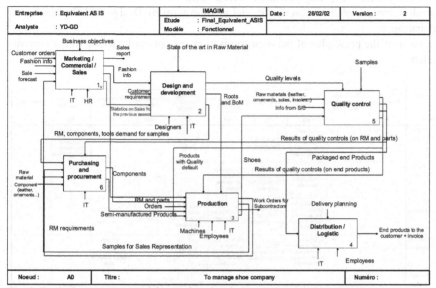

Fig. 2. Equivalent AS IS Model for the functional view at the global level (A0)

The functional view was performed using actigram formalisms [7]. Six main functions have been selected in order to limit the domain of study for the existing systems. The links between functions are shown as well as required resources (mechanisms) to perform the functions.

In order to limit the length of this paper, only this diagram is presented but each function was detailed. Moreover, the equivalent AS IS of physical system was also performed and detailed for each activity: to design shoes (to generate new ideas, selection or design of last, selection or design of sole, design or modifications of uppers, production and test of prototype and industrialisation), and to manufacture shoes (to manufacture uppers, to assemble, to finish and to deliver). Finally, the equivalent AS IS model was performed from a decisional point of view using GRAI Grid as shown figure 3 and GRAI nets. In this GRAI Grid, the functions are almost the same than for the functional view and the central functions are the decomposition of the production function: to manage products, to manage resources, to manage production planning. This equivalent GRAI Grid includes most of the points to improve in the shoe manufacturing companies:

• few long term decisions,
• a lot of decisions with a period of six months, corresponding to the period of a collection, which are not reconsidered during this collection (horizon=period),
• decisions with coordination problems (several objectives in conflicts…),

- no decision concerning the management of final customer satisfaction: the shoe companies have relationships with retailers but not with final customer which leads to a lack of knowledge about the customers' expectation and a lack of returns,
- few anticipation of quality problems at long term, and
- no decision on modification of a model at short term by Design and Development department.

So, most of the principles of mass customisation are not implemented in the current systems.

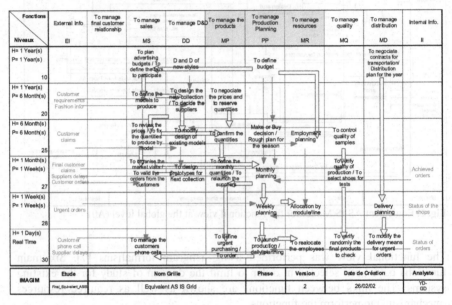

Fig. 3. Equivalent AS IS Model for the decisional system: equivalent GRAI Grid

3.2 The TO BE Models

The first base for these models was of course the experience gained during AS IS modelling, equivalent AS IS and diagnosis elaboration. The second base was the vision of experts [8] of shoe manufacturing, mainly consultants in charge of shoe manufacturing improvement.

This vision explained how this kind of system should operate, according to the new technologies available for shoe design and manufacturing and the expectation for each of the six companies for the future.

The generic TO BE model includes functional modelling as shown figure 4.

In comparison to the model of figure 2, it was decided to combine marketing function with CRM (Customer Relationship Management) because CRM aims to better know the customers and to improve their satisfaction.

The sale function is now independent because it involves more activities as the scan of the feet and the product configuration as well as customer data collection.

Purchasing and procurement include a quality control function which enables the final company (which performs the final assembling) to select the leather and materials. Quality control is also integrated to the production in order to have a quality deployment all along the production process. Of course, all these six activities are detailed.

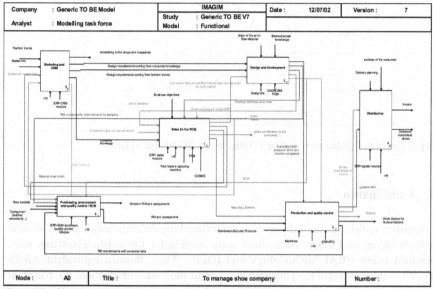

Fig. 4. The functional TO BE model at the global level (A0)

In a second time, process modelling was performed including sales, design, manufacturing and distribution activities. Each of these four activities was detailed at several levels in order to have a very deep and detailed view of each elementary activity in order to specify future machines and software functionalities to design, sale, configure and manufacture shoes.

This TO BE model also includes decisional modelling for the whole enterprise, including manufacturing (figure 5) and then design.

The functions of the GRAI Grid are adapted to the functional view of figure 4. The main change is to consider that the shoe production control is not aligned on a six month collection but that the collections are continuous. So, it is possible to have long term decisions as a business planning with a horizon of three years. The number of decision levels is limited to five: one strategic, two tactical and two operational. The management of resources is improved in order to forecast and adapt the required capacity to the various collections (at least, four a year).

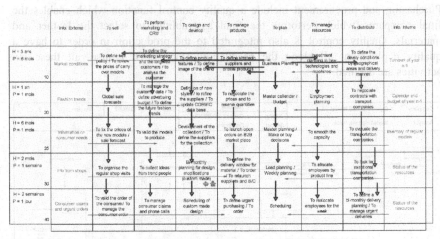

Fig. 5. Decisional global view for the TO BE Model: TO BE GRAI Grid

4   Conclusion

Enterprise modelling was fully used to understand the different mechanisms of shoe manufacturing in Europe. More than sixty models for the existing systems were obtained using GRAI Methodology and IDEF0. Then, thirteen equivalent AS IS models were elaborated to synthesise the current shoe mass production. So, based on the diagnosis of these models and the vision of experts, enterprise modelling was used to describe the future of shoe systems. Thirty five TO BE models (8 functional views, 20 process views, 2 GRAI Grids for the whole enterprise and for design activity control and 5 GRAI nets) were defined. These enterprise models were used to specify functionalities of machines and software (ERP and CAD) for shoe mass customisation system.

The following of this work was the instantiation of the TO BE model for the scholar shoe manufacturing system of Caslano (Italy). In the future, these TO BE models will be instantiated to the six companies and will be generalised for other mass productions of good and services.

References

1. Huang, G.Q., Simpson, T.W. and Pine II, B.J. The power of product platforms in mass customisation" Int. J. Mass Customisation Vol. 1, No 1, pp 1-13.

2. Pine, II B.J. Mass Customisation: The new frontier in Business Competition, Boston MA, Harward Business School Press, 1993.

3. Anderson, D.M. and Pine II B,J. Agile Product development for Mass Customisation, Chicago IL: Irwin Publisher.

4. Euroshoe Project – Annex 1: Description of work - GRD1 – 2000 – 25761 – October 2000.

5. G. Doumeingts, B. Vallespir, D. Chen. – Decisional modelling GRAI grid. – in *International handbook on information systems*, P. Bernus, K. Mertins & G. Schmidt ed., Berlin : Springer, 1998.

6. Y. Ducq, G. Doumeingts, F. Wagner, Top level overview on existing structures, processes and mechanism of the footwear industry - EUROSHOE Project – Deliverable D2.1.1 - October 2002.

7. CAM.I, Architecture manual: ICAM definition method IDEF0 - CAM. I doc n°DR-80-ATPC-01, April 1980.

8. Y. Ducq, G. Doumeingts, S. Dulio, Summary of the requirements for the TO BE Model, - EUROSHOE Project – Deliverable D2.2.1 - October 2002.

Lean Manufacturing Systems Optimisation
Supported by Metamodelling

Milan Gregor[1], Andrej Štefánik[1], Juraj Hromada[2]

[1] University of Žilina, Faculty of Mechanical Engineering, Department of
Industrial Engineering, http://fstroj.utc.sk/kpi/
Univezitná 1, 010 26 Žilina, Slovak Republic
[2] SLCP Consulting, Internátna 18, 010 08 Žilina, Slovak Republic

Abstract. This paper presents metamodelling method as a practical approach
to the statistical summarisation of simulation results. Metamodels enable to
reduce memory requirements by experiments and, on the other side, they can
be use as fast support tools for the manufacturing systems control. The chosen
metamodelling approach was applied in various projects. Given example
shows practically how can be metamodel developed and verified using simple
Conwip production systems.

1 Introduction

The current and future markets require production systems with high flexibility,
effectiveness and reliability. To achieve such targets the designers and planners of
production systems have to utilize advanced technologies, like modelling,
simulation, digital factory, etc.

The design of future manufacturing systems is very complex and complicated
task, solving estimation of manufacturing system performance, layout planning,
integration of other processes, control system, suppliers integration, etc.

Discrete event simulation, supported by 3D animation and virtual reality is used
as a very powerful tool for estimation and evaluation of future manufacturing system
behaviour and performance. Simulation enables to test designed manufacturing
system by given, virtual experimental conditions.

Current top simulation systems are very expensive for developing countries,
what slow downs the spread of this very powerful method in their industries.

Simulation, as the experimental method, is time consuming and expensive. Any
change of manufacturing systems conditions requires new simulations and
evaluations of their results.

The simulation is not able to solve automatically all production problems. It does
not offer directly explanation of behaviour of the analysed system and the analyst

Please use the following format when citing this chapter:

Gregor, M., Štefánik A. and Hromada, J., 2008, in IFIP International Federation for Information
Processing, Volume 257, Lean Business Systems and Beyond, Tomasz Koch, ed.; (Boston: Springer),
pp. 175–183.

needs certain experience to be able to interpret achieved results. The trail and error method is often used by experiments. Even if experiments design and planning increases probability of optimum finding, common current simulation systems don't offer direct single run optimisation approach. Optimisation systems are complicated, not user friendly and usually very expensive.

Modelling of large systems, hierarchical models of entire enterprises require high computing power which is multiplied by utilisation of 3D animation with virtual reality features. It is difficult to interpret the comprehensive tables with statistical results, even for experienced analysts. Optimisation in this case is only theoretical desire of analysts.

Metamodelling offers practical approach to the statistical summarisation of simulation results. It enables a given extrapolations in the framework of simulated conditions borders. Metamodells enable to reduce memory requirements by experiments and, on the other side, they can be used as fast support tools for the approximate manufacturing systems control. The fastens is often required by decision making process in advanced manufacturing systems.

2   Metamodel

The simulation searches answers to the question: Which results will be achieved by a given combinations of changed input factors? In this case goes on the analysis and definition of input – output relationships. The simulation model represents simplification of real manufacturing system. Even when the real system was simplified by simulation it is still very pretentious and time consuming to conduct all simulation experiments by changed and validated conditions. In search of further simplification possibilities, metamodelling was developed. The complicated simulation model and experimenting with them are replaced by validated metamodels. This was enabled by the approach which is very similar to hierarchical modelling (see following figure).

As it is possible to see from the figure, this approach goes from chaos of reality to organised simulation model followed by modelled input – output relationships of simulation model represented by regressive model.

Kleijnen (1979a) defined metamodell, going out of description of real system behaviour whereas real system was characterised by set of parameters entitled as reactive vector Yc (c = 1,2, ..., w). The reactive vector is influenced by real system inputs, so called input factors Xj (j=1,2,.....,s).

The problem of a large parameters number is possible to simplify into system with simple response Y (it is followed only response of one parameter on the given combination of input factors) whereas the system of multiple responses can be evaluated as a set of systems with a simple response.

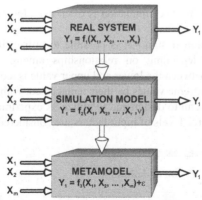

Fig.1. Metamodelling principles

The relationship between response variable Y and its inputs X_j can be represented as:

$$Y = f_1(X_1, X_2, ..., X_s)$$ (1)

The simulation model is then real system abstraction whereas analyst evaluates only chosen subset of input variables $(X_j / j = 1, 2, ..., r)$, where r is significantly lower as unknown s (we neglect all, from the point of view of solved problem unsignificant input factors).

Simulation response Y′ is then defined as a function f_2 of this subset of input variables and random number vector v representing effect of eliminated inputs (allowed failure is the difference between responses of real system and simulation model):

$$Y' = f_2(X_1, X_2, ..., X_r, v)$$ (2)

The metamodel represents further abstraction, in which analyst evaluates only chosen subset of input simulation variables $(X_j / j = 1, 2, ..., m, m \leq r)$ and describes the system as :

$$Y'' = f_3(X_1, X_2, ..., X_m) + \varepsilon$$ (3)

whereas ε represents a given error, with awaited value of zero. Such relationship is possible to describe mathematically by regressive model. The description of input – output relationships of simulation model is then entitled as metamodel.

The obtained regression model goes out from simulation results instead of real data. It means that analyst disposes with more input/output combinations for regression analysis what brings larger span for input variable.

3   Steps of Metamodel Development

The development of metamodel usually requires steps shown in the following steps:

Problem definition - the Industrial Engineer has to clearly define the problem, its borders and limitations. He has to define the targets and the way the metamodel will be used. The controllable variables have to be known or estimated depending from the fact that the modelled system is real or conceptual. Besides this input variables should be analysed and required output variables defined.

The framework of input variables definition - often it is difficult to define given input variables ranges and their limitations. It is usefull to utilize experts experience and evaluations. The simulation is often used for determination of given ranges of input variables.

The experiments plan design - it is possible to utilize full factorial or partial factorial experiments, depending on relationships among input variables. For example – if the range between the lower and upper value is too wide it is possible to eliminate the effect of extreme values by their replacement with their average values. In this case it is more useful to design and to utilize 3k experiments plan than 2k (the experiments in which three levels of input factors are considered).

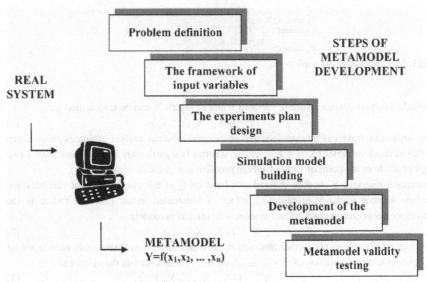

Fig. 2. Steps of metamodel development

Simulation model building - the designed simulation model has to be tested and validated so that it will precisely represent the analysed problem. Only such model can be used for simulation experiments.

Metamodel development - the metamodels are usually designed in several stages. At first the set of simulation experiments has to be conducted according to factorial experiments design. The factorial experiments plan increases effectiveness of this step. The simulation realised in accordance with the experiments plan brings outputs dependable from input variables and designed model input/output relationships. The simulation results create the bases of data.

As the next stage of regression analysis, typically, it is realised the identification of the most significant input variables. Based on this data, required metamodel is developed, for forecasting of dependent variables.

Metamodel validity testing - this step validates the precise of developed metamodel by the forecasting of dependent variable. One way of validation is the comparison of forecasted outputs from metamodel with the simulation results. The input variables satisfying the model limitations should be used for appropriate metamodel evaluation.

4   Simulation Model of Production Management

To be able to show the principles of metamodelling we have chosen simple manufacturing system.

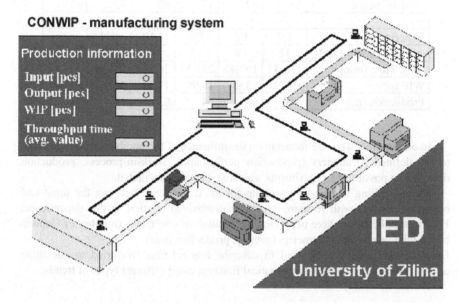

Fig. 3. The Manufacturing System Structure

The simulation model of this manufacturing system was developed in the software ARENA. The metamodel of manufactuirng system was developed, based on simulation results. Using this model we were testing different kind of production systems (Kanban, Conwip, DBR, LOC and MRP).

The difference between Kanban and Conwip was, that the control circuit in Conwip is built between the first and the last workplace, let us say between the first and the last storage. It can be used only in the case of production system with the synchronized production line that means production times at each workplace are like the same.

The number of Conwip cards directly determinates the level of work-in-process in the system. In same cases the manufacturing system applies to immediately change the number of Conwip cards. The managerial staff being responsible for these changes, have to bear in mind, that the number of Conwip cards influences not only work-in-process but also the others output parameters as are production performance, utilization of workplaces, etc. It is not possible easily forecast system response for these changes using standard tools. But there is possibility to simulate these changes in the computer with the various setting of the model parameters and to look how system is responding to them.

Table 1. Summarization of the simulation result

Experiment	E1	E2	E3	E4	E5	E6
No. of Conwip Cards	1	2	3	4	5	8
Avg. Time (min)	61,04	61,27	62,06	64,11	75,87	118,91
WIP (pc)	0,99	1,99	2,99	3,99	4,99	7,99
Production (pc)	16	32	47	60	63	63

Experiment	E7	E8	E9	E10	E11
No. of Conwip Cards	11	14	17	20	23
Avg. Time (min)	158,47	197,42	233,13	268,01	299,26
WIP (pc)	10,99	13,99	16,99	19,99	22,99
Production (pc)	64	64	64	63	64

In our analysis we were focusing on the influence of the number of Conwip cards to the defined parameters (production performance, work-in-process, production time). From possible 23 experiments we chose 11 being simulated.

Metamodelling is based on looking for the dependence between the input and output parameters with focusing on the mathematical relation of this dependence. For the simplicity we were observing the relation of one factor (number of Conwip cards) with one output parameters (average production time).

Using regress analysis we tried to describe this relation. We tried to substitute achieved behavior with the mathematical function using different types of trends.

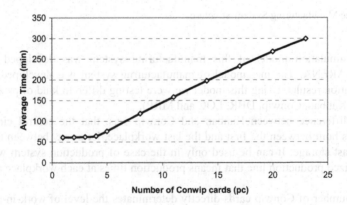

Fig. 4. Relation between the number of Conwip cards and average production time

R^2 reflects error rate being creating by the substitution of obtain value with the value from the trend equation. R^2 was calculated as follow:

$$R^2 = 1 - \frac{SSE}{SST}, \qquad 0 \le R^2 \le 1,$$

where $SSE = \sum(Y_i - \overline{Y}_i)^2$ and $SST = \sum(Y_i^2) - \dfrac{(\sum Y_i)^2}{n}$.

Next figure shows comparison of several trends and the origin value. It is clear that the trends with $R^2 \rightarrow 1$ give better results.

Table 2. Results of regress analysis

Type of trend	Trend function	R^2
linear	$y = 11{,}734x + 30{,}209$	0,9899
logarithmic	$y = 79{,}865\ln(x) - 6{,}099$	0,8097
exponential	$y = 53{,}637e^{0{,}0825 \cdot x}$	0,9642
polynomial II.	$y = 0{,}0767x^2 + 9{,}9704x + 35{,}993$	0,9913
polynomial III.	$y = -0{,}0277x^3 + 1{,}0712x^2 + 0{,}5603x + 54{,}248$	0,9973
polynomial IV.	$y = 0{,}0028x^4 - 0{,}1603x^3 + 3{,}0816x^2 - 10{,}028x + 68{,}259$	0,9994
polynomial V.	$y = -0{,}0002x^5 + 0{,}014x^4 - 0{,}399x^3 + 5{,}189x^2 - 17{,}241x + 75{,}134$	0,9997

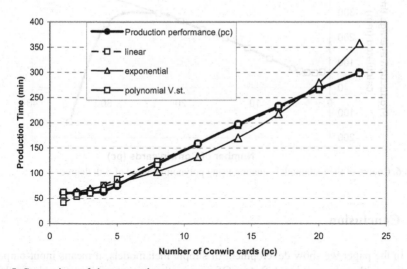

Fig. 5. Comparison of chosen trends course

Predefined equation gives possibility to very quickly and without using simulation find out average production time for given number of Conwip cards. For example assuming the number of Conwip cards to 14, based on polynomial equation of the 5-th degree, we can calculate the average production time to 197.4519 min. Comparison calculating value with the simulation result shows insignificant difference (0.0319min). We made comparison of the control value (being not used by developing metamodel) to verify the quality of metamodel. The results of the verification are in the following table:

Table 3. Verification of the metamodel

Comparison of average production time	Number of Conwip cards						
	6	7	10	12	15	19	22
Simulation	89,52	104,62	145,84	173,09	210,14	256,89	290,20
Metamodelling	89,20	102,69	145,28	172,31	209,45	255,71	288,28

The problem started by using value over the interval being used by development of metamodel. If we assumed using of 30 Conwip cards, the average time from calculation is 254.3195 min and from simulation is 365.63 min. This difference is really important and as it is shown in the next figure. It is not appropriate to used polynomial equation of the 5-degree as a substitution of simulation for these values.

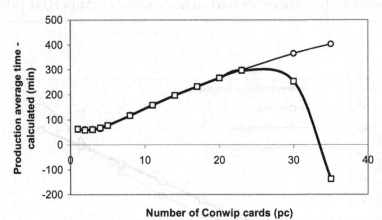

Number of Conwip cards (pc)

Fig. 6. Course of the metamodel equation using polynomial trend of 5-th degree

5   Conclusion

In the paper we show development of simple metamodels, it means input-output relation with only one input factor. Of course, there is possibility to enlarge this approach to developing metamodel of two input parameters (for examples number of Conwip cards and various types of the bottleneck solution) and one output parameter (for example average production time). The main advantages of the metamodels are simply and fast forecasting behaviour of the systems with given condition (it is not necessary to change the model at first) and easy and simplicity of their using. The main disadvantage is the sophistication of metamodel development.

References

1. CHATURVEDI, M. - GOLHAR, D. Y.: Simulation modelling and analysis of a just in time production system. Production Planning nad Control, 1992,Vol.3, No.1, pp.81-92

2.GREGOR, M. - KOŠTURIAK, J. - HROMADA, J. - BALCERČÍK, V.. How the Simulation Helps to Improve Manufacturing Systems. In proceedings of the Second World Congress on Intelligent Manufacturing Processes and Systems. Budapest 1997. pp. 110 - 115.

3. ŠTEFÁNIK, A. – GREGOR, M.: Quick and Appropriate Changes with Support of Modelling and Computer Simulation. In: Inżynieria Produkcji 2005, ATH Bielsko-Biala 2005, Poland, ISSN 1644-0315, pp.153-158

Integration of Factory Planning and ERP/MES Systems: Adaptive Simulation Models

Kai Mertins, Markus Rabe, Pavel Gocev

Fraunhofer Instiut Produktionsanalgen Konstruktionstechnik (IPK)

Pascalstrasse 8-9, 10587 Berlin, Germany

Abstract. The purpose of this paper is to demonstrate the approach of a scalable, flexible and adaptive simulation model used in factory planning on the basis of existing ERP and MES data. The dynamic simulation model was developed to validate and verify the changes of the production yield during factory planning and restructuring in the shop floor. This includes machinery relocation and ramp-up, new product phase-in, product portfolio changes and new product qualification processes. The objective is to enable an industrial engineer without simulation knowledge and experience to perform the simulations. Moreover, the model facilitates an analysis of the results for different scenarios, using the actual data from the ERP and MES systems.

1 Introduction

Projects that aim to restructure complex production systems concurrently with ongoing system operation are always constrained by customer demand and agreed delivery dates.

Usually restructuring projects are characterised by continuous delays and changes of already planned project activities, which cause modifications of production strategies on a daily basis. The suggestions and modifications can be proved by modelling and simulation of operative activities of the production system and the restructuring actions. The updates of the operating parameters on a daily base trigger the use of simulation models again to simulate the current situation. The daily update of the parameters can be provided by direct insertion of data from an MES system.

In general the data describing the future factory concepts are not contained in company ERP/MES systems due to the early planning phase, uncertainty, or reduced experience of system engineers. This information is usually dispersed in various MS-Office documents containing contradictions and maintained by different people. Usually an additional interface is needed in order to enable the user (analyst) to

Mertins, K., Rabe, M. and Gocev, P., 2008, in IFIP International Federation for Information Processing, Volume 257, Lean Business Systems and Beyond, Tomasz Koch, ed.; (Boston: Springer), pp. 185–193.

integrate such data without the engagement of a simulation expert and without changing the existing data in the ERP/MES system.

This paper describes a method for the application of a flexible and adaptive simulation model that has already been proved in practice. The factory planning data and data from ERP-/MES systems are integrated in one simulation model that supports the factory planning in the execution of the following activities:

- implementation of new production organisation or layout changes,
- planning of machine relocation and start-up within the shop floor,
- developing of ramp-up plans for new products or product variants,
- scheduling of machine qualifications considering therewith reduced production capability.

The adaptability of the model was proved on manufacturing systems for complex products produced in small series with considerable work content, like railway wagons and gas turbines. The challenge was to support the phases of factory planning and realisation of restructuring. The necessity of planning in short terms (days or weeks) regarding long process times (days) determined the integration of the actual Work-In-Progress (WIP), because a daily manual update was not justifiable due to complexity and the time needed.

2   Related Work

Usually simulation models utilise databases extracted from the company's ERP system. Bolmsjö and Randel [10] developed a database driven factory simulation model that utilises the ERP data in order to test the master plan and to find the bottlenecks. The VIVACE project [11] developed a data-driven simulation for a supply chain where the model does not consider the planning and scheduling of orders. For standardisation purposes the National Institute for Standards and Technology (NIST) developed a shop data model and specified the interfaces with the simulation model [12]. The architecture for a generic data driven simulator [13] utilises a simulation model that deploys data from a neutral shop data file. Sivakumar [14] connects ERP/MES data to optimise scheduling integrating the shop-floor data, and allowing the user to enter manually non-system data. Fraunhofer IPA developed a method for web-based configuration and simulation of production systems [15] concerning only the conceptual phase of new production systems. An interface with the operating shop floor is obviously not available. Weiger and Werner [16] developed a simulation model based on data from the ERP system, including a simple scheduling logic. The differences between the performance of a simulation system and the real production system are smoothed when some parameters exceed a user-defined value. The results from the simulation are used for real production system order scheduling by an independent scheduler. Jensen and Hotz [17] developed a method for data consolidation from distributed systems using XML-based [18] interfaces. The NIST [19] gives an overview of a mechanism to transfer data between a database and XML files used for simulation model generation.

Concerning the optimisation of an existing production system or scheduling and searching for bottlenecks, many related works suggest the integration of data from the ERP system. An analysis of the future production system (for factory planning purposes) under consideration of the current shop floor operations is not supported.

3 Model Architecture

The manufacturing system was modelled with the simulation software ARENA® (Rockwell Software) [20], using the data that defines products, production capabilities and production schedules. These data serve as a basis for simulation and preparation of the results in an output database for evaluation purposes (Figure 1).

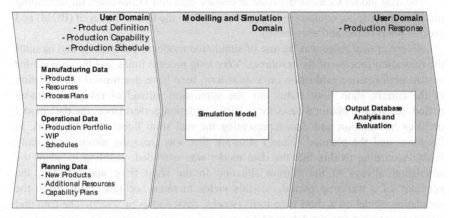

Fig. 1. Simulation Model Architecture

The functions of the model architecture have to enable the user without modelling and simulation proficiency to perform simulations. Due to the nature of the factory planning process the user has to be able to insert new products, new machines and new orders into the model and change the parameters without performing any changes on the simulation model. These requirements can be satisfied only by simulation model architecture with the following features:

- Data consistency - integration of data from ERP/MES systems with continuous changing planning data,
- Flexibility - consideration of new or alternative data or even change (extend or reduce) of already integrated data (from ERP and MES),
- Adaptability - development of simulation scenarios and conduction of a simulation by users without significant simulation experience,
- Customisable - analysis of the results and evaluation of the production system performance defined by the user.

3.1   Data Model

The data required for the simulation and analysis was extracted from the company ERP/MES systems. Utilising structures that are described in the ISA-95 standard [21] the data was transferred in a MS-Access® database for two reasons. Firstly, the planning information and project data for the future production systems and new production portfolios that also have to be considered into the data model are usually dispersed in various MS-Office® documents within the company, or are provided by the partners (e.g. machine vendors). Secondly, the low level of XML knowledge proficiency of ordinary industrial engineers and project (factory planning) managers made it seem critical to use an XML-based interface between ERP/MES and the simulation model.

The data model includes the most necessary data and information for describing production portfolio, equipment list, product model - the Bill-of-Material (BOM) and process plans (basic and alternative).

A very critical issue was the use of simulation model to accompany and monitor the relocation process of the resources. Very long process times and the demand for system performance evaluation on a short-term base have determined the inclusion of the current shop floor status into the simulation instead of using a warm-up period. In order to obtain a basis for a daily simulation performance, the data model includes information and data representing the real shop floor situation (Work In Progress) and the planned (future) situation that was changing almost on a daily basis. According to this fact the data model was extended, enabling to adapt the simulation always to the current situation in the shop floor and avoiding the necessity of a warm-up period. All this yields to more accurate results from the simulation model on a short time basis (weeks, days and even hours). The data that were incorporated into the data model comprise:

- Current resource status.
- Capability plans of the resources related to the shift plan, qualification plan, ramp-up phase, start-up phase and relocation plan.
- Work in Progress (WIP) describing the current status of the materials in the shop floor considering the orders seizing the machines (also number of items already produced within each order) and the status of the waiting orders in the buffer or in front of the machines.

The addition or deletion of some production system elements (products, equipment or orders) or even change of their parameters can be performed without update of the simulation model through entering/deleting of some database records or change of the values. This approach enables the user without modelling and simulation experience to maintain the updates coming from the factory planning process on a daily basis.

3.2   Simulation Model

The requirements for a simulation as a support for factory planning that integrates data from ERP/MES systems resulted in the simulation model presented in figure 2.

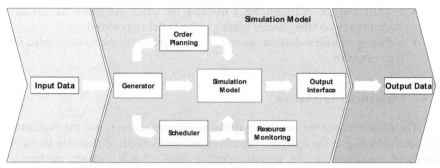

Fig. 2. Simulation Model Components

The generator module is responsible for data integration into the simulation model and initialisation of resources and products with their components. The values of the data are stored as one or two-dimensional array variables.

The production portfolio is processed by the order-planning module that generates production orders for the consisting components of each product from the portfolio. The production orders are further dispatched under consideration of the delivery dates and throughput times deduced from the process plan.

The scheduler module monitors the resources' utilisation and production orders' status and assigns each production order to the basic or the alternative process plan. Alternative resources are assigned in accordance with the waiting times in the queue, due date and machines' status. More accurate results for the production system performance on a short basis were achieved through an interface, which prepares the planned production orders for the MES and receives (from the MES) the scheduled and fine-planned orders as an input for the simulation.

Each production order is presented in the model as an "order entity" and carries information about one product. The process plan related to that product determines the machines where the order will be processed on and the times needed.

The production response information like start/end time, product type, resource and quantity are saved as array variables and stored in the output database.

3.3   Equipment Capability and Status

The production capability as an examined characteristic of the production system has a big impact on the simulation model. Very critical for the process of factory planning, estimation of relocation and evaluation plans for the resources and satisfaction of the customer demands was to model, simulate and evaluate all possible statuses of the resources considered with the analysis.

For that reason, in addition to the usual resource statuses like idle, inactive, busy and set-up, other necessary statuses like: rework, failed; in relocation, ramp-up, start-up; qualification and maintenance were modelled.

A module for monitoring and assignment of the resource-status within the simulation model controls the resource status and performs:

- changing the status of the resource according to the capability plan,

- rescheduling the order seizing a machine for which relocation has already started or rescheduling orders waiting in the buffer respectively,
- gathering statistical data for the resources and preparing the values needed for the evaluation.

3.4   Evaluation and Analysis

The adaptability of the simulation model architecture extends into the evaluation model. According to the analysis' objectives and user's needs, different granularity levels of evaluation can be selected (product item – batch – order, machine – production line – area – site, daily – weekly – monthly – quarterly). The user can change the granularity level in order to provide the most suitable evaluation and support analysts by taking decisions with strategic and operative importance.

The most important recorded data within the output database comprises: customer order number, production order number, product name, production operation ID, machine or production line ID and start-time and end-time for queuing, setting-up and processing on the designated machine. The module for monitoring and assignment of the resource status tracks and controls each resource and records the history data during the simulation. A participative modelling approach (simulation expert and user) leaded to various queries for the evaluation of the database. The queries were developed to enable the analysis of the production system and to present the results as diagrams and report tables needed for strategic decision taking, comprising:

- throughput time of each order or aggregated per product,
- utilisation and status of the resources (weekly, monthly or quarterly),
- adherence to delivery dates (per product, or production order, or customer),
- waiting or queuing times (per product or machine),
- demand on additional capabilities (machines and personnel),
- delays due to the rework,
- inventory levels.

The results are stored as MS Office® files that are suitable for easy comparison of various scenarios or for benchmarking of different products, resources or even production lines.

4   Model Application

The model architecture (figure 3) has been used in applications for layout planning of a gas turbine production system and a railway wagon production and assembly system. It is considered to be applicable to other types of small series production with minor customisation and adaptation efforts. However, care has to be taken for modelling the specific business process, and for using suitable reference models.

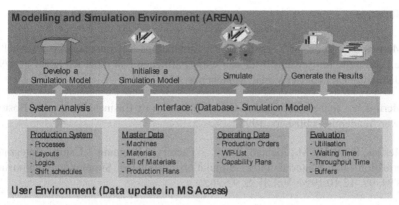

Fig. 3. Simulation Model Architecture

The scope of the model application was to plan the needed capacities during machine relocations within the shop floor under consideration of qualification plans and delivery dates. The emerging tasks to be solved and supported through simulation were development and estimation of: required equipment capabilities, machine-relocation plans, qualification plans and layout concept.

This approach enables the user without further support from modelling and simulation expert to analyse the existing system, to prove new layouts, capabilities, production portfolios and alternative production plans under consideration of actual changes and states on a daily basis.

5   Conclusions and Further Developments

A scalable, flexible and adaptable simulation model was developed, integrating ERP/MES and WIP that can be updated and extended by the user. This approach offers an exploration of different scenarios and consideration of the factory planning uncertainties about new products or new equipment. Analysis and evaluation of system performance using the user-defined queries and macros give an additional flexibility.

A supplementary aspect is further development of the interoperability with MES conforming to ISA-95. Furthermore XML interfaces can be developed through the implementation of transactions described by B2MML (Business to Management Mark-up Language) as a part of the ISA-95 standard or BOD (Business Object Documents) specified with the OAGIS® 9.0 schema [22].

Reference

1. Mertins, K.; Rabe, M.; Friedland, R.: Simulations-Referenzmodelle erschließen neue Potentiale. In: Zeitschrift für den wirtschaftlichen Fabrikbetrieb (ZWF), 10/96, 91. Jahrgang. Carl Hanser Verlag München, s. 479 – 481.

2. Mertins,K.; Jochem,R.: Quality-Oriented Design of Business Processes. Boston: Kluwer Academic Publishers, 1998.

3. Mertins, K.; Rabe, M.; Jochem, R.:   Factory Planning Using Integrated Information and Material Flow Simulation. European Simulation Symposium ESS'94, 09.-12.10.1994, Vol. II, S. 92-96.

4. Mertins, K.; Rabe, M.; Könner, S.: Reference Models for Simulation in the Plannung of Factories. IMACS Symposium on Systems Analysis and Simulation, Berlin 1995, S. 655-658.

5. Mertins, K.; Rabe, M.: Reference Models of Fraunhofer DZ-SIMPROLOG.In: Bernusm P.; Mertins, K.; Schmidt, G. (Hrsg.): Handbook on Architectures of Information Systems. Springer-Verlag, Berlin, Heidelberg, New York 1998, pp. 639-649.

6. Mertins, K.: 24.07.1987 Bandung, Indonesien The Role of Simulation in Design of Manufacturing System, Seminar & Kursus Singkat, Flexible Manufacturing System & Flexible Manufacturing Cell.

7. Mertins, K.; Rabe, M.; Könner, S.:02.-03.03.1995Magdeburg Integration von Fabriksimulation und CAD. Fachtagung "Integration von Bild, Modell und Text. Otto-von-Guericke-Universität Magdeburg.

8. Mertins, K.:14.02.2002 Tokyo Modelling and Simulation Environments for Design and Planning of Globally Distributed Enterprises – The European Module.MISSION Open Day, Tokyo.

9. Mertins, K.; Rabe, M.; Jäkel, F.-W.3.-5.07.2002Porto, Portugal Distributed Modeling and Simulation of Supply Chains.18th International Conference on CAD/CAM, Robotics and Factories of the Future.

10. Bolmsjö, G., Randell L. (2001) 'Database Driven Factory Simulation: A Proof-Of-Concept Demonstrator', Winter Simulation Conference 2001, pp. 977-983.

11. Cao, B., Farr, R., Byrne, M., Tannock, J. (2005) 'Data-driven Simulation of the Extended Enterprise', 18th International Conference on Production Research.

12. McLean, Lee T., Shao, G., Riddick F. (2005), 'Shop Data Model and Interface Specification', www.mel.nist.gov/msidlibrary/doc/nistir7198.pdf.

13. McLean, C., Lee T., Riddick F., Jones A. (2002) 'An Architecture for a Generic Data-Driven Machine Shop Simulator', Winter Simulation Conference, 2002, pp.1108-1116.

14. Sivakumar, A.I. (1999) 'Optimization of Cycle Time and Utilization in Semiconductor Test Manufacturing Using Simulation Based, On-Line, Near-Real-Time Scheduling System', Winter Simulation Conference 1999, pp. 727-735.

15. Sihn, W., Graupner, T.-D., Kuhlmann, T., Richter, H., (2002) 'Internetbasierte Konfiguration und Simulation von Produktionssystemen', Simulation und Visualisierung 2002. pp.225-235.

16. Weigert G., Werner S., Kellner M. (2002), ‚Fertigungsplanung durch prozessbegleitende Simulation', 10. ASIM-Fachtagung, pp. 42-51.

17. Jensen S., Hotz I. (2006), Mit standardisierten Datenstrukturen zur integrativen Simulation', Simulation und Visualisierung 2006, pp. 89-103.

18. www.w3c.org

19. Luo Y., Lee T. Y. (2005) 'Data Exchange for Machine Shop Simulation', Proceedings of the 2005 Winter Simulation Conference, pp. 1446-1452.

20. www.arenasimulation.com

21. www.isa.org

22. www.openapplications.org

Using Simulation-Generated Operating Characteristics Curves for Manufacturing Improvement

Jan Olhager and Fredrik Persson
Linköping University,
Department of Production Economics,
SE-581 83 Linköping, SWEDEN
WWW home page: http://www.ipe.liu.se

Abstract. Improving manufacturing operations is an initiative that all manufacturing firms need to engage in to stay competitive. The needs and ways to improve differ between companies. A thorough understanding of the operating characteristics is required for successful improvement of manufacturing operations. By modeling the plant or manufacturing system in a simulation model and create operating characteristics curves, it is possible to investigate trade-offs and improvement potentials that otherwise would be impossible to quantify by other means of analysis. This paper describes how to manage such an approach by using a simulation model of a manufacturing plant to derive operating characteristic curves. The paper also describes how these operating characteristic curves can be used to improve plant performance.

1 Introduction

In order to stay competitive any manufacturing firm needs to continuously improve their manufacturing operations. The operating characteristics, that describe how different variables such as lead times, lot sizes, capacities etc are interrelated, differ between companies with respect to specific manufacturing conditions. However, a thorough understanding of these is required for successful improvement of manufacturing operations. By introducing simulation modelling, it is possible to create operating characteristics curves that otherwise would be impossible to quantify by other means of analysis. This task is increasingly more difficult with the number of products, the number of resources, the number of routings, and capacity constraints. Different parameters interact and may have direct and indirect effects, which are difficult to predict. For example, multiple products create different queuing situations at resources with constrained capacity, with respect to the

Please use the following format when citing this chapter:

Olhager, J. and Persson, F., 2008, in IFIP International Federation for Information Processing, Volume 257, Lean Business Systems and Beyond, Tomasz Koch, ed.; (Boston: Springer), pp. 195–204.

routings, setup times, processing times, order quantities, etc. Knowledge concerning these interactions is important for understanding how to best improve manufacturing operations towards a specific goal. In order to illustrate these interactions, a simulation model of a production system in a manufacturing plant can be developed. The construction of operating characteristics (OC) curves or performance curves can then be used for decision support concerning improvement initiatives in the manufacturing system. Han and McGinnis (1989) use OC curves to analyze the effect of buffer space, flow control rules, and processing time variation on the relationship between throughput and flow time. Nazzal et al. (2006) use a simulation model to create dependency curves between cycle time and production volume for certain technology choices.

This paper describes how to manage such an approach by using a simulation model of a manufacturing plant to derive different types of OC curves. The paper also describes how these operating characteristic curves can be used to improve the performance of the plant.

2   Operating Characteristics Curves

Operating characteristics (OC) curves are curves displaying the relationship between two or more variables. The factors of interest can be related to market factors such as demand volume and variability, system factors such as setup and processing times, control parameters such as lot size and planned lead times, and output variables such as capacity utilization, queuing times, and costs of various kinds. The relationships illustrated through OC curves are such that the specific shape most typically will differ between different manufacturing systems, wherefore it is important to establish the specific relationships for each system, for example as a basis for improving the manufacturing operations. Another characteristic of OC curves is that the relationship is not fundamentally mathematical, i.e. that one of the variables can be calculated from the other. Of course, the OC curve can be displayed in such cases, but it would most likely be more useful to use the mathematical relationship, when analyzing manufacturing improvement initiatives.

Figure 1 displays a basic form of an OC curve. This figure illustrates the relationships among two variables; in this case capacity utilization and lead time. The specific curve will depend upon the distribution of orders arriving to the system and the distribution of the processing times. For simple systems queuing theory formulas can be developed for this relationship. However, for more complex systems, these relationships are non-trivial and specific to the manufacturing system. So if a firm wants to have an illustration of the relationships for a specific plant, simulation offers a way to derive the specific OC curve.

In Figure 2 variability is added as a third variable. Variability can be induced by market demand or by internal system imbalances. If three variables are to be included in one graph, one of these needs to be treated as a factor leading to different curves. This means that the third variable is treated as a discrete (non-continuous) variable.

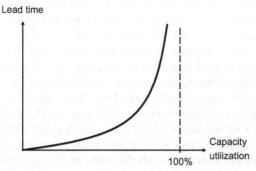

Fig. 1. An operating characteristics curve displaying the relationship between two variables; lead time and capacity utilization

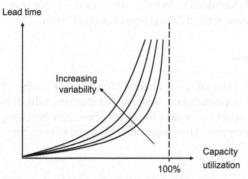

Fig. 2. An operating characteristics curve displaying the relationship among three variables; lead time and capacity utilization for different levels of variability

The shape of the curve illustrating the relationship between the two (or three) variables is of interest. For example, if the relationship is linear or non-linear, convex or concave, or if other shapes are present. Especially, many relationships between variables change when moving from a slack capacity situation to one with tight capacity.

3 Simulation Model

Simulation can be used as a technique for analyzing manufacturing systems that are too difficult or too costly to analyze in any other way. Simulation modeling offers a highly flexible tool that provides assistance in solving a variety of different problems and to find 'cause and effect' relationships. Simulation modeling can also be used in order to find relationships between two or more variables in a manufacturing system.

This paper uses the term simulation in a rather narrow sense. What is really meant is discrete event – continuous time simulation, where time is treated as a continuous variable and events occur at discrete instances in time. These kinds of models are stochastic, dynamic, and discrete in nature depicting the modelled system (Persson, 2003). Discrete event simulation has found an application in the field of operations research as a tool to improve, analyse, and visualise different characteristics of manufacturing systems and supply networks. The simulation results are often used as predictions or for what-if questions (Law and Kelton, 1991).

When generating operating characteristic curves to analyze manufacturing or supply chain systems, the parameters can be divided into three groups; (i) input factors, describing the market environment and the system characteristics, (ii) control parameters, describing the active choices for planning and control of the system given the input parameters, and (iii) output variables, describing the performance outcomes and statistics concerned with the status of the system. In the simulation model used here, input factors, control parameters, and output variables are concerned with the characteristics of a production and inventory control system. The simulation software used in most parts of this paper is PICSIM (Production and Inventory Control Simulator); initially developed by Jönsson (1983), and most recently used and described in Olhager and Persson (2006).

3.1   Input Factors

Input factors are external and internal factors that define the manufacturing environment, such as product mix, demand distributions, bills of material, capacities, processing times, setup times and routings. These can be changed or affected by decisions of the company. The change process is however typically associated with time and cost.

3.2   Control Parameters

The parameters that define the control system in the simulation model are called control parameters and are used as inputs to each simulation run together with the input factors. Each item must be given an order quantity (or lot sizing technique in combination with setup ordering and inventory holding costs), a lead time (potentially including safety lead time), and a safety stock. Safety stocks or safety lead times can be used to cover for uncertainties in demand or lead time. The simulator allows for using a reorder point system, material requirements planning (MRP), and cyclic production scheduling.

3.3   Output Variables

Outputs of the simulation model include performance measures as well as production statistics. The basic performance measures include customer service and total inventory levels (raw materials, work in process and finished goods inventory). These are traditionally assumed to be conflicting since low inventory is typically associated with poor customer service, and high customer service requires large inventory. In the simulation model, customer service is calculated as the fill rate for finished goods inventory; a fill rate of 100 % is equal to no shortages. Costs for handling backorders, and setup and ordering costs can be added to the inventory holding costs to provide for the cost performance. The production statistics include actual lead times per item, average queue times and capacity utilisation rates per work centre, and inventory turnover rates for raw materials, work-in-process, and finished goods.

4 Generating Operating Characteristic Curves

Operating characteristics curves can be generated through simulation results or from data collected in a manufacturing system. However, simulation offers many advantages over observing and collecting data from a system. OC curves can be generated that are difficult, or even impossible, to get from a real system. Simulation offers the opportunity to extend the analysis beyond what is currently done or is realisable in the physical system, as well as simulating scenarios related to different improvement initiatives. Even though simulation typically is performed as discrete-event systems with discrete variables, OC curves illustrate a continuous relationship such that the curve has to be fitted to the simulation output data.

4.1 Types of Operating Characteristic Curves

In general, there are three basic types of OC curves: (i) an input factor vs. an output variable, (ii) a control parameter vs. an output variable, and (iii) an output variable vs. another output variable. Thus, the y-axis is always related to an output variable. If the analysis is expanded to three variables (cf. Figure 2), the third variable (not on the x- or y-axis) has to be an input factor or a control parameter, since this one has to have discrete choices, and cannot thus be an output variable which cannot be controlled to have discrete steps.

Input factors and control parameters are inputs to the simulation model and can thus be changed in a controlled manner. Thus, it is possible to create equidistant steps along the x-axis. Also, it is possible to perform multiple simulation runs with different seed numbers to the random number generator at each x-value, whereupon confidence bounds can be calculated. Although the OC curve typically is a single curve, it is valuable to know if the curve is exhibits a strong relationship with little variance or if the relationship is heavily influenced by any stochastic behaviour of the system. Thus, when generating the first and second OC curve type, the x-axis factor or parameter can be controlled and upper and lower bounds with respect to confidence levels can be generated. In the third type two output variables are analysed. These cannot be controlled in terms of equidistant steps with multiple seeds for creating confidence levels. The type of chart for this case is a scatter diagram plotting the two output variables relative one another, with subsequent curve fitting. Here, joint confidence regions can be established. If the shape of the OC curve is non-linear, the curve can be segmented and approximated as piece-wise linear, around which confidence regions can be calculated.

In figure 3, 4 and 5, the three types of OC curves with respect to the type of variable are illustrated.

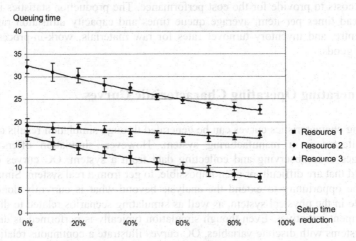

Fig. 3. Operating characteristics curve, type 1, illustrating the impact of setup time reduction (input factor) on queuing times (output variable) at three different manufacturing resources

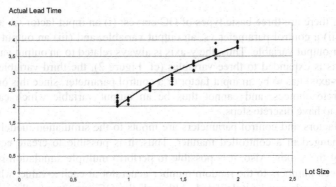

Fig. 4. Operating characteristics curve, type 2, illustrating the impact of lot size (control parameter) on actual lead times (output variable)

These curves show that input factors and control parameters can be controlled in a simulation setting, whereas output variables cannot. The three examples above are taken from three different simulation projects wherefore they differ somewhat in terms of result presentation design.

4.2   Simulation Procedure to Generate Operating Characteristic Curves

The simulation procedure to create operating characteristic curves is to first identify the variables that are of interest to study, secondly to determine the experimental plan to set the boundaries of the variable values. First, the input factors, control parameters and output variables must be determined. The improvement initiatives are typically related to input factors such as setup times, quality factors and bottleneck capacity or to control parameters such as lot size, planned lead time and planned buffer sizes. The output variables are typically the performance indicators of the system behavior.

Fig. 5. Operating characteristics curve, type 3, illustrating the relationship between actual finished goods inventory (output variable) and customer service (output variable).

The controllable variable must be sampled for values that span the area of interest for the output variables and the number of observations in that area must allow for a resolution in the operating characteristic curve that includes all interesting aspects of the relationship between variables. For each observation of the influence of the controllable variable value on the other variables, a number of replications are simulated. This will allow for analysis of variances and not only mean values. The number of observations and replications can only be determined by studying the simulation model and running a few test experiments.

For the first two types of OC curves, the input factor or control parameter are controllable and are subject to the experimental design procedure described above. The third type of OC curves, however, do not need dedicated simulation runs but can be based on output data from the other simulation runs. The tighter the scatter diagrams between two output variables irrespective of the changes in input factors or control parameters, the stronger the relationship between these two output variables. If the scatter diagram seem to display two or more curves, then backtracking is necessary to identify the source of this diversity.

There are two approaches for using OC curves when analyzing specific improvement initiatives. One approach is to study the direct impact of a change in an input factor or a control parameter on a performance indicator (output variable), such that the factor that is to be improved is depicted on the x-axis or as a curve indicator. The other approach is to define different scenarios involving improvements in one or more areas. Based on these scenarios the relationships among various variables are studied in OC curves. The first approach is used by Han and McGinnis (1989), and

Persson and Olhager (2002), and the scenario approach is used by Nazzal et al. (2006).

However, introducing simulation modeling in the process of generating operating characteristic curves will add uncertainty to the outcome and recommendation given by a decision maker. The process of generating these graphs is divided into three steps, (i) obtaining basic factor data from the real system, (ii) creating the simulation model and making sure it is a valid representation of the system, and (iii) running the simulation model to get output data so that the operating characteristic curves can be constructed. Each step can introduce errors into the final result and the data collection, simulation modeling, and simulation experimentation must be done in such a way that risk of introducing errors is minimized.

5   Using Operating Characteristic Curves for Improving Operations

Questions like "what if..." can easily be answered with a simulation analysis and providing decision makers with a set of operating characteristics curves is one way of shoving what would happen if some decisions were to be undertaken. Using simulation we can also extend the analysis beyond what is currently realisable in the system and allow the imagination of the decision maker to flow freely.

Simulation generated operating characteristics curves also introduces the possibility to test extreme scenarios, to test the boundaries of the system. How far is it possible to stress a certain parameter or factor? When will the system start behaving poorly? How can the system cope with extreme circumstances?

Operating characteristics curves also allow for the analysis of how control parameters and input factors affect output variables in terms of the sign (decreasing or increasing behaviours), the magnitude (amplifications of relationships), and the shape (linear or non-linear, convex or concave).

The use of OC curves is at least twofold; there is a learning aspect (which indirectly can lead to the improvement of manufacturing operations) and a decision support aspect.

5.1   Learning

Learning about a certain system and how the system behaves under different scenarios can indirectly lead to manufacturing improvements. Curves that map relationships between input factors and control parameters can be used to increase the understanding of system behavior both concerning a specific system and in more general terms. This understanding will implicitly lead to better informed decisions on how to improve the system.

5.2   Decision Support

Operating characteristics curves can be used as a decision support system. It is a simple task to choose the best or most suitable system from a set of scenarios using the operating characteristics curves as decision variable. Both the magnitude and the robustness of a solution can be studied and based on such an analysis, a decision can be made.

Operating characteristics curves can also be constructed with a certain aim with the analysis; cf. e.g. Nazzal et al. (2006). In this case it is important to have a fairly good idea about the relationships between studied parameters and variables. It is easy to miss the interesting part of a relationship if the analysis does not allow the parameters and variables to take on their extreme values.

As part of a decision support system, operating characteristics curves can be used to study the potential effects of a change initiative. What are the benefits of reducing setup times? Is it worth pursuing a setup time reduction and what is the cost limit for that? Operating characteristics curves can also be used to investigate how e.g. the demand variability influences the rest of the system. In this case, operating characteristics curves can be used to capture the effects of increasing (or decreasing) demand variability, or as a support tool to tweak the system so that it can counteract any increase in variability.

Improving planning and control is another issue within the decision support. The planning and control system can be optimised so that the best setting among control parameters such as lot sizes, lead times and safety mechanisms are found. The operating characteristics curves are developed for this certain manufacturing and supply chain system environment and the results can be implemented directly.

One example of an OC curve involving one input factor (quality), one control parameter (lead time), and one output variable (total cost) can be found in Persson and Olhager (2002). In figure 6, the relationship between quality levels, lead times and total operating cost is depicted. Persson and Olhager (2002) modelled a real supply chain and used the simulation model to generate a set of graphs to capture the relationships among variables. Different lead times were introduced as different scenarios where the supply chain configuration was altered. The quality levels were introduced as different levels in a set of quality control functions. This input factor (lead time, related to a specific supply chain design) and control parameter (quality level) provided observations on the output variable of total operating cost.

As part of the study by Persson and Olhager (2002), the relationships between lead times, quality levels, and total cost could be quantified. It also permitted an analysis of the behaviour of the relationships as being non-linear. As lead times increase and quality levels get worse, the total cost increases in a non-linear way.

6 Concluding Remarks

In this paper we have demonstrated how to derive operating characteristics curves using simulation, and how these can be used to gain knowledge about a particular manufacturing system to guide the choice of improvement initiatives. OC curves can be used for learning about the system behavior, as well as for decision support concerning specific situations. An important aspect of using simulation for the construction of OC curves is that the analysis can be extended beyond what is currently realisable in the physical system; thus testing for more far-reaching improvement initiatives.

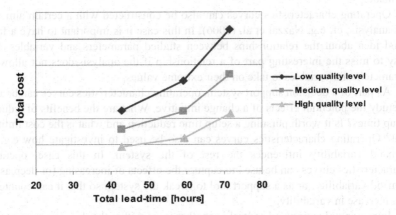

Fig. 6. The relationship between quality levels, lead times and total operating cost (Persson and Olhager, 2002)

References

1. Han, M-H., and McGinnis, L. 1989, Shop operating characteristic curves for shop control, International Journal of Production Research, 27(11), 1843-1853.

2. Jönsson, H., 1983, Simulation studies of hierarchical systems in production and inventory control, Ph.D. dissertation, Linköping Studies in Science and Technology, No.91.

3. Law, A. M., and Kelton, W. D. (1991) Simulation Modeling & Analysis, 2nd Ed., McGraw-Hill, New York.

4. Nazzal, D., Mollaghasemi, M., and Anderson, D. 2006, A simulation-based evaluation of the cost of cycle time reduction in Agere Systems wafer fabrication facility – a case study, International Journal of Production Economics, 100, 300-313.

5. Olhager, J. and Persson, F., 2006, Simulating production and inventory control systems: a learning approach to operational excellence, Production Planning and Control, 17(2), 113-127.

6. Persson, F., 2003, Discrete Event Simulation of Supply Chains – Modelling, Validation and Analysis, Doctoral Thesis, Department of Production Economics, Linköping Institute of Technology, Linköping.

7. Persson, F and Olhager, J., 2002, Performance simulation of supply chain designs, International Journal of Production Economics, 77(3), 231-245.

Experimental Exploration of Decision Making in Production-inventory System

Felicjan Rydzak [1], Agata Sawicka [2]

1 Centre for Advanced Manufacturing Technologies, Wroclaw University
of Technology, ul. Lukasiewicza 5, 50-371 Wroclaw, Poland
Phone: +48 71 3204184 / Fax: +48 71 3280670

2 Faculty of Science and Engineering, Agder University College
NO-4876 Grimstad, Norway
Phone: + 47 37 25 33 58 / Fax: + 47 37 25 30 01

Abstract. Despite availability of advanced decision aids, manufacturing managers should master basic control tasks within production systems. Still, there is substantial evidence that even highly educated and experienced practitioners mismanage even very simple production-inventory systems. We report an experimental study investigating strategies in a simple production-inventory control task. The study was conducted using an interactive computer simulator. Consistent with previous observations, the subjects failed to execute a satisfactory control in the first trial. Most, however, learned to manage the system as they gained experience. Application of single subject experimental design with think-aloud protocol and debriefing interviews allowed to identify strategies followed by the subjects. The paper reports on the key results of the study, discussing its implications for the production management research and practice.

1 Introduction

Production-inventory control is fundamental for effective management of both manufacturing process and manufacturing supply chain. Regardless of the complexity of the relationships within the production-supply environment, the main challenge is unchanged – i.e., to have the right number of right products at the right place and time. This is difficult because of the inherent delays in the flow of materials, information and money, as well as ever changing and unpredictable demand [1, 2].

Over the last two decades various strategies and approaches have been proposed to improve decision making along a whole supply chain as well as at a particular echelon. One line of research advocates development of robust control algorithms to optimize the use of available information and consequently improve the inventory

Please use the following format when citing this chapter:

Rydzak, F. and Sawicka, A., 2008, in IFIP International Federation for Information Processing, Volume 257, Lean Business Systems and Beyond, Tomasz Koch, ed.; (Boston: Springer), pp. 205–213.

management. Towill [1] and White [3], for instance, applied control theory and more sophisticated control algorithms, such as proportional, derivative and integral (PID), to reduce inventory level by 80% – a result especially desired in just-in-time (JIT) or material requirements planning (MRP) techniques. The latest research investigates possibility of fuzzy logic control application [4]. However, better control algorithms are very often too sophisticated to be successfully incorporated into managerial practice.

Another line of research focuses on decision making processes in production-supply systems. Production management games have been developed – with a pioneering Beer Game created by Jay W. Forrester at MIT in the beginning of 1960s – to create virtual production management laboratories. These laboratories have been used often as training aids [5, 6]. However, they have also been applied in research. Experimental results show that most people fail to control even overtly simplistic systems [7-11]. Forrester [12] and Sterman [8] suggest that people instead of developing a good understanding of the system rely on an anchoring and adjustment heuristic – a rule that starts with a salient reference point (anchor) and adjusts it to reach a final value; the problems occur because the adjustments are insufficient.

This paper reports on findings from an experimental study on decision-making in a simulation-based environment called INVENT. The study investigated strategies applied in a production-inventory control task. Consistent with previous findings [7, 10], we observed that people have difficulties in controlling a very simplified production-inventory system – one echelon of the whole supply chain. While most subjects initially used an erroneous anchoring and adjustment heuristic, many successfully improved the rule after a period of hands-on experience in managing the system. In decade when companies compete through their supply chains [13] improving people's ability to effectively manage production-inventory systems becomes increasingly important. Our results suggest that applications like INVENT may be a valuable aid in various training programmes for both students and practitioners of industrial management.

The paper is organized as follows: The next section discusses the design and methodology of the experiment. Following, we present the key findings. Finally, conclusions are drawn indicating limitations, implications and contributions of the research.

2 Design and methodology

The experimental study was conducted using a simulation-based production game called INVENT. The game was developed based on a System Dynamics model [2]. The structure of the model is presented in **Fig. 1**. The model consists of three sectors: *Production and Inventory*, *Customer Orders*, and *Costs*. In the System Dynamics notation rectangle boxes represent accumulations within the system – in our case they are stocks of elements in production (*Production in Progress*), stock of ready products (*Inventory*) and costs incurred during a period of an experiment (*Cumulative Costs*). Values of the accumulations within the system are changed by flows (arrows with valves) representing the movement of materials, information and cost; for instance, *Planned Production* indicates information impulse that starts production process, *Shipment Rate* indicates shipment of finished products to the customers. Additional variables specify certain parameters of the model, e.g. production lead time (*Manufacturing Time*) equal to 4 weeks. Usually System Dynamics models include also decision functions specifying the way in which the material flows are controlled. However, in this case that part of the model was replaced by the direct decisions of the experiment subjects.

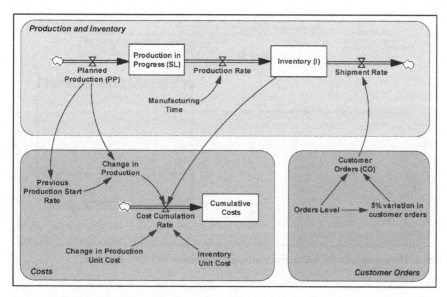

Fig. 1. The System Dynamics model structure of a simple production-inventory system used in the interactive learning environment INVENT

For the INVENT game, four different decision-making interfaces were designed. All four interfaces contained a spreadsheet like report on the problem variables and provided complete information about the current and past results. They differed in how explicitly they exposed the inherent manufacturing delay. The example shown in **Fig. 2** presented the delay in the most explicit way by providing an animated diagram of the production-inventory system.

The study was designed as a single subject experiment [14] and involved 15 students attending MSc course in Management and Manufacturing Engineering at Wroclaw University of Technology. Because of the applied design, each subject attended the experiment individually.

The subjects took on the role of a production manager of one of the divisions of the ABC Manufacturing Co. At the start of the experiment each subject read the instructions. The subjects were asked to set weekly production so to minimize costs of operations. To accomplish this goal the inventory level should be maintained at the minimal level ('zero inventory') but simultaneously order losses should be avoided. Subjects were informed of the starting value of customer order and that they should expect the orders to follow a random walk with +/-5% fluctuations and to have a one-time, step increase within the first 10 of the 32 simulated weeks.

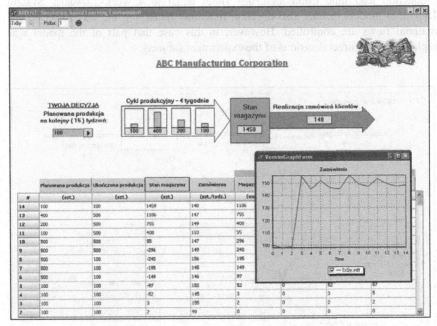

Fig. 2. The example of the interactive learning environment INVENT interface

Before playing INVENT subjects filled in a prior-test knowledge questionnaire. Next, they played INVENT three times. Each decision and all results were saved in a computer log. During conducting the task the subjects were encouraged to comment on their decisions ('think-aloud protocol'). After each trial an interview was conducted to elicit self-evaluation of the performance. At the end of the experiment each subject filled in the post-test questionnaire and evaluated the whole task.

3   Findings

The anchoring and adjustment heuristic proposed by Sterman [8] assumes that, when controlling inventories, the subjects anchor their decisions (Ot) in the imminent expected losses (ExpLt) and adjust for the inventory (I) and supply line (SL) discrepancies:

$$O_t = MAX[0, ExpL_t + (I^* - I_t) + (SL^* - SL_t)] \tag{1}$$

where t indicates the current point in time and * indicates the desired values.

Based on regression analysis, Sterman suggests that poor inventory control may be attributed to the subjects' fixation on the initial inventory level and their failure to account fully for the supply line [8, see pp.334-335].

To evaluate performance of our subjects, we compared their results with Sterman's anchoring and adjustment rule. Table 1 presents an overview of the subjects' inventories together with a reference inventory achieved when the anchoring and adjustment heuristic (1) is followed correctly. In Sterman's experiment, mismanagement following the demand increase led to inventory fluctuations [8, see Fig. 4, p. 330]. In our experiment we also observe such fluctuations, especially in the 1st trial (see Table 1). However, to determine whether the subjects indeed misapplied the anchoring and adjustment heuristic proposed by Sterman other data need to be also examined.

Table 1. Inventory levels – overview of the experimental results. Grey, bold line tracks the inventory level simulated using Steraman's anchoring and adjustment heuristic. Black colour is used to mark inventories of the individual subjects

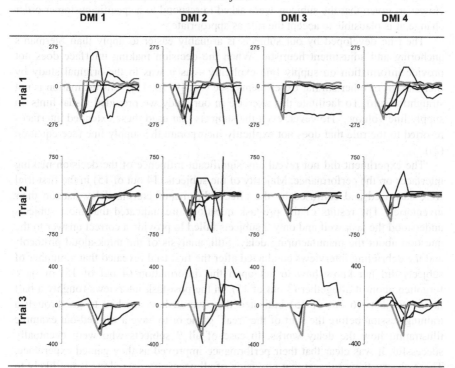

When comparing the cumulative costs, many of our subjects outperformed the heuristic – their cumulative costs were lower than those generated when the heuristic-based decisions were simulated. Further analysis of the think-aloud protocols suggested that most successful subjects did not follow the anchoring and adjustment heuristic as proposed by Sterman [8].

During the first trial only one subject controlled the system completely all the time. His decision rule was anchored in the imminent expected losses (represented by the current customer order level, CO) but it did not involve explicit adjustments for inventory or supply line. The subjects adjusted rather for the losses expected over the next 4 weeks (i.e., duration of the manufacturing delay) and the rule applied may be formulated as follows:

$$O_t = MAX[0, CO_t + \sum_{i=1..4} (ExpCO_i - PP_i)] \tag{2}$$

where ExpCO indicates the expected level of customer orders and PP indicates planned production.

Most subjects (9 out of 10), who managed to stabilize the inventory over the three trials, developed a similar decision rule.[1]

While the anchoring and adjustment heuristic proposed by Sterman [8] (see equation (1)) is robust for any type of customer order fluctuations, the decision rule followed by our subjects (see equation (2)) is robust only for the one-time step increase in the customer orders. As such, it could be deemed as suboptimal. However, given that the subjects were asked to respond to a specific customer order change, it is plausible to accept the rule as appropriate.

The rule developed by our subjects is arguably easier to apply than Sterman's anchoring and adjustment heuristic. When the decision making interface does not provide information on supply line explicitly – as it was in the original study by Sterman [8] or other similar experiments (see e.g., [9, 10, 15]) – its estimation is not straightforward. To facilitate this exercise in our study we provided visual hints on supply line volume.[2] However, even the subjects that used these extended interfaces resorted to the rule that does not explicitly incorporate the supply line (see equation (2)).

The experiment did not reveal any significant influence of the decision making interfaces on the performance. Majority of the subjects (14 out of 15) in the first trial were surprised and confused by the effects the manufacturing delay had on their inventories. The results of the pre-task questionnaire indicated that most subjects understood the task well and only 2 subjects failed to provide a correct answer to the question about the manufacturing delay. Still, analysis of the think-aloud protocols and the debriefing interviews conducted after the first trial revealed that a number of subjects did not know how to act upon this information (4 out of 15) or have forgotten about it altogether (3 out of 15). In the post-task interviews roughly a half of the subjects (6 out of 15) indicated they would have wished to go through a training session before the start of the "real" game or to have a worked-out example illustrating how the delay works. In case of all 9 subjects who were eventually successful, it was clear that their performance improved as they gained experience. These observations suggest that provision of all necessary data alone is not likely to be sufficient for people to control effectively a production-inventory system. A hands-on-experience has a vital role in building the true understanding of the system and in developing the ability to control it.

---

[1] The one subject who controlled INVENT successfully while not following the described decision rule misunderstood the instructions, and tried to achieve a zero inventory level only at the end of the trial rather than as soon as possible.

[2] The most explicit presentation of the supply line was the interface presented in **Fig. 2**.

4   Conclusion

The System Dynamics model used in the experiment focused mainly on the dynamics resulting from production delay. It considered only one echelon of a supply chain and did not include such constraints as production capacity or raw materials availability. To facilitate development of decision rules, the applied model of costs assumed equal unit costs of inventory and change in production. Despite such simplified environment, we managed to observe problems common to more complex supply chain systems. Since any simplification of the experimental environment facilitates analysis of decision making processes, this finding is positive [16, 17].

Rather than group design, we used a single subjects approach collecting only a small number of observations. Consequently, we cannot make any generalizations based on our results. However, we were able to gain a unique insight into individual decision making, unattainable in the group design. The value of such deeper insight is illustrated well by our observation that although the subjects' performance trails are similar to those observed earlier, our data suggest that the subjects relied on different anchoring and adjustment heuristic than this defined by Sterman [8]. This suggests that the single-subject design may be more suitable for investigations aiming to uncover decision rules.

In the current study we have not managed to observe any clear effects of different decision making interfaces on the subjects' performance. This may be due to the limited number of observations we gathered per interface – each interface type was used by only 3 to 4 subjects. Further studies are necessary to explore whether there are certain elements of the decision making interface that may facilitate the production-inventory task.

Still, even with the current, imperfect decision-making interfaces, we observed that many of our subjects developed successful decision rules in the course of the three trials. These results suggest that a hands-on experience is important for learning successful management of inventory-production systems. Indeed, many subjects emphasized that they had fully understood the task and the system only after a period of practice. Hence, it seems advisable to advocate for INVENT-like games to become an integral part of the manufacturing training programmes both at the university and professional levels.

Acknowledgements

The study reported in this paper has been initiated by Dr. Agata Sawicka as a part of a greater research project sponsored by the Research Council of Norway (grant no. 160789/V30). It has been carried out at two research institutions – Agder University College, Norway, and Technical University of Wroclaw, Poland; support of the research leaders at both institutions – Professor Jose J. Gonzalez and Professor Edward Chlebus, respectively, is gratefully acknowledged. We also thank Dr. Piotr Magnuszewski and Piotr Obrąpalski, MSc, for their help in development of the INVENT simulation environment.

Reference:

1. Towill, D.R., *Dynamic analysis of an inventory and order based production control system*. International Journal of Production Research, 1982. **20**(6): p. 671-687.

2. Sterman, J.D., *Business Dynamics. Systems thinking and modeling for a complex world*. 2000: McGraw-Hill.

3. White, A.S., *Management of inventory using control theory*. International Journal of Technology Management, 1999. **17**(7/8): p. 847-860.

4. Ge, Y., et al. *Controller Design for the System Dynamics Model of a UK Supermarket Supply Chain*. in *6th World Multi-conference on Systemics, Cybernetics and Informatics*. 2002. Orlando, USA.

5. Rauch-Geelhaar, C., K. Jenke, and C.M. Thurnes, *Gaming in industrial management - quality and competence in advanced training*. Production Planning & Control, 2003. **14**(2): p. 155.

6. Hofstede, G.J., et al., *A chain game for distributed trading and negotiation*. Production Planning & Control, 2003. **14**(2): p. 111.

7. Sterman, J.D., *Testing behavioral simulation models by direct experiment*. Management Science, 1987. **33**(2): p. 1572-1592.

8. Sterman, J.D., *Modeling managerial behavior: Misperceptions of feedback in a dynamic decisin making experiment*. Management Science, 1989. **35**(3): p. 321.

9. Croson, R. and K. Donohue, *Behavioral Causes of the Bullwhip Effect and the Observed Value of Inventory Information*. Management Science, 2006. **52**(3): p. 323-336.

10. Diehl, E. and J.D. Sterman, *Effects of Feedback Complexity on Dynamic Decision Making*. Organizational Behavior and Human Decision Processes, 1995. **62**(2): p. 198-215.

11. Hieber, R. and I. Hartel, *Impacts of SCM order strategies evaluated by simulation-based 'Beer Game' approach: the model, concept, and initial experiences*. Production Planning & Control, 2003. **14**(2): p. 122.

12. Forrester, J.W., *Industrial Dynamics*. 1961, Cambridge, MA: The M.I.T. Press.

13. Hill, T., *Manufacturing Strategy – Text and Cases*. 2 ed. 2000, Houndsmills, Hampshire: Palgrave.

14. Barlow, D.H. and M. Hersen, *Single Case Experimental Designs: Strategies for Studying Behavior Change*. 2nd ed. 1984, New York: Pergamon Press.

15. Wu, D.Y. and E. Katok, *Learning, communication, and the bullwhip effect.* Journal of Operations Management, in press.

16. Edwards, W., *Conservatism in human information processing*, in *Judgment under Uncertainty: Heuristics and Biases*, D. Kahneman, P. Slovic, and A. Tversky, Editors. 1982, Cambridge University Press: Cambridge, UK.

17. Moxnes, E., *Misperceptions of basic dynamics: the case of renewable resource management.* System Dynamics Review, 2004. **20**: p. 139-162.

Building a Reference Model for the PLM Processes in Engineering and Contracting Sector

Prof. Mario Tucci[1], Ing. Romeo Bandinelli[1] and Ing. Diego Carli[2]

1 Dipartimento di Energetica "Sergio Stecco"
Università degli Studi di Firenze
2 Technip Italy S.p.A.

Abstract. The management of the processes related to proposal, design, construction, start-up, operation and decommissioning of industrial plants, in few words the whole Plant Lifecycle, are usually performed each by means of a specialised information tool, because of the peculiarities of the Engineering and Contracting (E&C) sector. The E&C Companies are aware of the need to move towards an integration of such tools, under the umbrella of the PLM (Product Lifecycle Management) new acronym. As in other sectors, like the manufacturing industry, such convergence happens in two different ways: a) the modular offer of a single software vendor, usually a market leader, who tries to establish a proprietary data warehouse of all the lifecycle information; b) an agreement of different players on some standard for the representation of such information, in order to develop IT tools which are able to access and exchange meaningful information. Whichever approach will emerge as a winner, the authors think that it would be useful to define a Reference Model for the Plant Lifecycle processes, proposing an ontology for their business and technical objects, their relationships and management. Such reference model, developed in a standard modelling language, could be of great help both in developing new integrated PLM solutions, and to enable stand-alone packages to establish an effective integrations based on the data and information.

1 Introduction

The management of the processes related to proposal, design, construction, start-up, operation and decommissioning of industrial plants, in few words the whole Plant Lifecycle, are usually performed each by means of a specialised information tool, because of the peculiarities of the Engineering and Contracting (E&C) sector. The E&C Companies were born in the 50' in order to answer the demand to high complexity big plants that required an effort of integration of multidisciplinary activities, fulfilling time, cost and quality needs. This way, by their nature, EPC

Please use the following format when citing this chapter:

Tucci, M., Bandinelli, R. and Carli, D., 2008, in IFIP International Federation for Information Processing, Volume 257, Lean Business Systems and Beyond, Tomasz Koch, ed.; (Boston: Springer), pp. 215–222.

Projects are typically complex, multidisciplinary and costly, and involve a major investment by Owner Companies. As a result, the individual activities that include their design and construction work processes are themselves highly variable from project to project. Moreover, the multidisciplinary characteristics of EPC Projects force E&C employees to use several and different tools in order to develop all the necessary documents.

The E&C Companies are aware of the need to move towards an integration of such tools, under the umbrella of the PLM (Product Lifecycle Management) new acronym. As in other sectors, like the manufacturing industry, such convergence happens in two different ways: a) the modular offer of a single software vendor, usually a market leader, who tries to establish a proprietary data warehouse of all the lifecycle information; b) an agreement of different players on some standard for the representation of such information, in order to develop IT tools which are able to access and exchange meaningful information.

Whichever approach will emerge as a winner, the authors think that it would be useful to define a Reference Model for the Plant Lifecycle processes, proposing an ontology for their business and technical objects, their relationships and management. Such reference model, developed in a standard modeling language, could be of great help both in developing new integrated PLM solutions, and to enable stand-alone packages to establish an effective integrations based on the data and information.

1.1 Known Results

In literature there are many works regarding standardization of project management processes and some top down modeling of complex project at least for some part of the all process, i.e. finance and cost control [8] or product development. At the same time, several European project have tried to develop software integrations in order to manage or coordinate extended enterprises [9][10], facilitate project collaboration and provide advanced features to manage concurrent engineering.

Even if these works are correlated to E&C sector, in authors opinion none of them has been able to include all the features and peculiarities of this area. Moreover, even if in some projects the objective is closer to authors' vision, the methodology developed in order to achieve it is not winning.

2   The E&C processes

In order to give a better comprehension of the processes to model, it's useful to briefly present the E&C main processes as related to the first part of the Plan Lifecycle, with some forward view to the second part of it, that is the operation, maintenance and decommissioning of the plant.

2.1 Description of the Plant Lifecycle processes

The Plant Lifecycle is usually divided in three main phases[1], which become four, taking into account the decommissioning of the plant.

The Front End Engineering Design involves the owner/operator (O/O) of the plant, who chooses a technology or a process, usually licensed by *Technology Licensor*. The latter sells the rights to use his know how and technology, usually providing a *process package*, that an *engineering company*, hired by the O/O, uses to define the basic process parameters, described in the FEED documents.

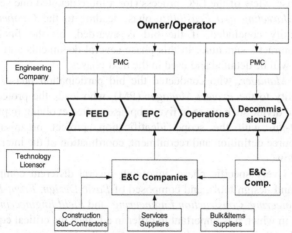

Fig. 1. The chain of participants in a Process Plant Project

Basing on the FEED documents, the O/O put out an international bid concerning the design and construction of the plant, with the help of the *Project Management Consultant* (PMC), who possibly implements the FEED with preliminary *Piping & Instrumentation Diagrams*. The E&C Companies, able to compete by themselves as *Main Contractor* or in joint venture with others, after preliminary study which leads to the *bid-no bid decision*, enters the *Engineering, Procurement and Construction* (EPC) fist phase[2], participating to the bid and, according to the rules, presenting a technical and commercial proposal with preliminary design, times, costs, subcontractors and suppliers.

The E&C Company, winning the bid, takes the role of EPC Contractor and starts the execution phase[3]. The information flows of the Plant Lifecycle first two phases are the focus of our research which we want to manage with a new reference model.

A the end of the construction, during the commissioning activities, the EPC Contractor proves the O/O or the PMC that the plant performs as stated in the contract in order to get the acceptance certificate. Usually the hand over of the plant and of all the related materials, is immediately after the final acceptance; the O/O sometimes requires the EPC Contractor a first period of operation in order to reduce the risks of poor or unreliable plant performance. When the EPC Contractoris also the provider of the main critical equipments, he may be requested to operate the plant, delivering to the owner only the service (as in facilities plants), or to provide the maintenance under a *Global Service Agreement.*

The *decommissioning* of the plant, may be considered "symmetrical" to the construction and it can often be played by an E&C Company. In special cases of chemical plants, when the decontamination of the sole is the main issue, a specialized E&C must be involved.

2.2   The EPC process

In a very concise view of the EPC process (for a more detailed one see [3] and [4]), we have a *Marketing and Feasibility* phase leading to the *Competitive Bid Participation*, luckily concluded, if the bid is awarded, by the final details' negotiation and contract's signature. In this phase several documents and drawings are produced, that will be detailed and used in the next phases.

The *Proposal Manager*, who conducted the bid participation phase, transfers project responsibility to the *Project Manager* (PM), who leads the project till the hand over. We can divide such phase in five subphases, often evolving in parallel:

- *Project Start-up*, with the scope identification, project organisation and planning, resource definition and recruitment, coordination of the interfaces and information flow.
- *Engineering*, a very specific phase, involving several different competencies, technologies and design tools, and composed of *Basic Design, Front-End, Item and Bulk Engineering, Construction Engineering* and *Field Engineering.*
- *Procurement*, in which it is important to order in advance the critical equipments from selected and qualified vendors, and to find the local providers for bulk materials. The purchase activities are followed by the material management which consists in expediting vendors' work, carrying out periodical inspection and organizing shipment on the site..
- *Construction*, which comprises the *Planning* of construction activities and their execution, possibly under the responsibility of a *Construction Manager,* and using local civil and mechanical subcontractors.
- *Close-out*, with the *Precommissioning, Commisioning/Start-up,* and the issue of the *Provisional* and *Final Acceptance Certificate.*

2.3   Why EPC projects is not only Project Management.

Even if Project Management (PM) activities, and consequently, PM techniques and software tools, are the core of the EPC process, there are several reasons to have a broader view of this subject, which we try to list hereafter:

a.   PM is just the glue of a lot of different technical activities ranging from materials management, from cost to progress control, from quality to risk management, from integration and coordination actions to problem solving techniques.

b.   EPC process is just one phase, even if very important, in the plant lifecycle, and, as the *Product Lifecycle Management* (PLM) paradigm teaches, it's worthwhile, that is more effective and efficient, to manage all the lifecycle of the product, from the idea to the use and decommissioning, with integrated software tools, based on common model for the representation of the product (in our instance the plant) and all the processes to design, produce, operate, maintain and dismiss it.

c.   Even if PLM could be the right paradigm and we could imagine to utilizing PLM software suites and tools, the structure of E&C market is quite different from the manufacturing industry, where the PLM was developed. One of the reasons is the relationship among the players, as showed in Figure 1, where the strong player is the O/O, who often drives the E&C adoption of software standards, as the final delivery of a digital model of the plant is usually considered part of the scope of work. The O/O actually uses such digital model in his software tools for maintenance management and related tasks, as revamping and decommissioning.

d.   PM tools usually integrated in ERP solutions are considered incapable of managing a complex EPC project, whilst the specialized PM packages normally used by E&C companies are provided by vendors who don't have the power to impose their PM centric view to the vendors of the other tools used in EPC projects.

A review of the IT systems' architectures used by main Italian E&C Companies [6] showed the great number of different software packages used in the EPC process, and the variety of solutions adopted. These software families can be classified as *Electronic Document Management Systems, Project Management, Computer Aided Design/Engineering, Plat Data Warehouse, Material Management Systems, ERP, e-Procurement Systems, Construction Management Systems*.

In many cases more than a dozen of packages are used, each for a different aspect or phase of the EPC process (see Fig. 2), never covering all the activities, and such tools are rarely integrated. Even when integration exists, it's more common that exportation files are generated, converted and adapted to the data model of the destination package, and finally imported into it.

This solution creates several problems, as opposed to actual data centered integration:

a.   The creation of conversion software to interface each package to all the others with which it has to establish and information flow.

b.   The upgrading of these interfaces, every time a new major release of software packages is delivered.

c.   The frequent generation of export files, and their importation in the destination package, possibly loosing the changes made in this last one.

d.   Being this task heavy and error prone, the consequence is a poor real time updating of the information .

e.   If a software vendor, as strong as the CAD producers in this sector, tries to provide the interfaces to the main software packages out of his scope, he has to develop and maintain a plethora of modules or functionality, leading to a costly and low effective solution.

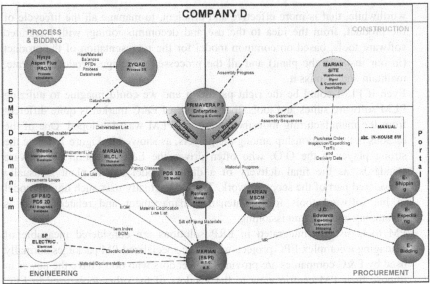

Fig. 2. One of the IT systems' architecture mapped in [6]

3 Our proposal

As a matter of fact, the coexistence and the use of several software and tools is a necessity of E&C companies. Therefore, the development of an integrated software cannot be the only way to solve the above problems. Authors' idea is to develop a *Reference Model* for the Plant Lifecycle processes, starting from EPC process, proposing an ontology for their business and technical objects, their relationships and management.

The use of this reference model will permit to define a standard for the exchange of the information and for object coding, that could be used by all the commercial tools, in order to guarantee the interoperability among the software, and the exchange of information across different documents.

The Italian E&C Companies are attempting to develop highly integrated systems for the engineering area, using tools with data-centric structure. This means bringing together the information required by several users in centralized databases for every design tool. In addition, the aim is to make the information contained in the individual databases accessible, thanks to a Plant Data Warehouse (PDW). A PDW makes it possible to move from one application to another, while maintaining a good quality of the information.

Even if some software houses are working is this direction, together with their customers, no important results have been achieved so far. Author's opinion is that, in order to solve this impasse, a creation of a consortium of several software houses and E&C companies is necessary to define and approve a reference model, and consequently a standard for EPC processes, data and documents.

In order to achieve this long view result, some first step has been carried out by the authors.

At the beginning[7], the EPC phases were analyzed and modeled. Then the use of UML as a formalism permitted to describe processes in an object oriented view, focusing on the exchange of information among documents along the whole project life.

Starting from this vision, several diagrams describing the phases of an EPC project were drawn. First the user cases diagrams were developed, then all the packages diagrams were described, splitting them into: roles, elements, phases and documents. Then timing diagrams were drawn, dividing them into sequential and state diagrams.

Hereafter a part of the document diagram is reported in order to demonstrate the approach.

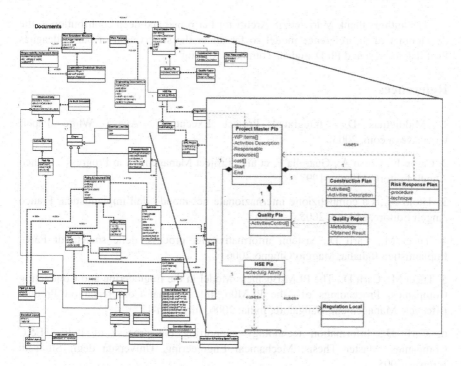

Fig. 3. The document diagram

At the moment a validation phase is ongoing, checking the applicability of such reference model to Italian E&C companies and the first results are positive, as the modeling started from the review in [6]. Obviously we do not expect a perfect match of our reference model to the way the single company works, or even to the single project manager inside the same company. But such diversity is often due to the habits of a PM and it is not justified but actual needs. The sharing of a common reference model is always an opportunity to reengineering the processes to converge to the best practices. This standardisation of practices is a problem recognised by the companies who are not able to force their PMs, as a formalised approach supported by software tools is still missing. The companies could benefit by our proposal in this area as well

In parallel the reference model is being submitted to the review of a main software vendors of this sector.

If the first two phases will have positive outcomes, the next step should be the creation of a consortium among the above actors, in order to develop a complete reference model. With such standard the software vendors would be able to develop compliant software tools, both starting from scratch or creating interface models only to this objects.

Acknowledgments

The authors thank Marialetizia Arcuri for her broad and deep contribution to the developmet of the reference model so far under the supervision of our colleagues Prof. Paolo Nesi and Ph.D student Tommaso Martini .

References

1. Middlemas D., "Integrated Project Execution", Aveva White Paper, www.aveva.com, 2003.

2. Caron F., Corso A., Guarella F. et al., "Project Management in Progress", Franco Angeli Editore, Milano, 1997.

3. Titolo M., La competizione internazionale nel mondo dell'impiantistica, Franco Angeli Editore, Milano, 2005.

4. Tucci M., Carli D., Sistemi informativi nei processi delle società di E&C, Impiantistica Italiana, Maggio/Giugno 2006.

5. Tucci M., Carli D., The PLM Business Model in the Engineering and Contracting Companies, Proceedings of the PLM06, International Conference on Product Lifecycle Management, Bangalore, India, 2006, July 10th-12th.

6. Carli D., Information technology supporting the process of Italian E&C Companies, Master Thesis, Mechanical Engineering, Università degli Studi di Firenze, 2005.

7. Arcuri M., Modello di riferimento per le fasi di gestione dei progetti di una società di Engineering & Contracting, Master Thesis, Informatic Engineering, Università degli Studi di Firenze, 2005.

8. Mosca R., Revetria R., and Forgia C., Top Down Modeling and Monte Carlo Simulation for Financial & Cost Control in Complex Projects, Proceeding of Modelling, Identification, and Control, 2005.

9. Whales project, website: http://whales.gformula.com/, last access June 2006.

10. Ecolead project, website: http://virtual.vtt.fi/virtual/ecolead/, last access June 2006.

Integration in Manufacturing Systems

Professor Krzysztof Santarek, PhD, DSc
Warsaw University of Technology, Faculty of Production Engineering,
Institute for Production Systems Organisation, 85 Narbutta Str.,
02-524 Warsaw, Poland, k.santarek@wip.pw.edu.pl

Abstract. Co-ordination of activities within an organization can be performed in a different way. One of them is system integration. In the paper a typology and features of manufacturing systems integration concepts will be discussed. Efficiency and effectiveness assessment of net-worked integrated systems for innovation development and transfer needs special approach. A concept of a new method will be introduced. The method is based on a process approach, benchmarking and involves elements of the Business Excellence Model. It can be used to conduct ex ante and ex post assessments and as a self assessment tool.

1 Introduction

Co-ordination of complex tasks (processes), divided between several executors (employees, organizational units) is one of basic organizational problems. An appearance of this problem was a direct consequence of the principle of work division and specialization of workers which is dated back to the first industrial revolution and is attributed to Adam Smith. Efficient and effective operation of an organization needs better co-ordination and co-operation of their elements and activities.

The importance of co-ordination is growing when products and processes are becoming more complex, organization itself, number of its workplaces and processes, external supply and distribution chains are growing too.

It is assumed that system integration is one of basic tools of co-ordination. The concept of integration means connection, joining, relationships or interdependency of elements and activities of a particular manufacturing system. It exists several ideas, approaches and means of a manufacturing systems integration. The search for more effective and efficient way of manufacturing systems integration is still an essential problem for many organizations. Some tendencies like SME's sector expansion, virtualization of enterprises, globalization of economy, popularity of outsourcing and lean manufacturing, development of supply and distribution chains are bringing about a growth of inter-organizational integration. Inter-organizational

Please use the following format when citing this chapter:

Santarek, K., 2008, in IFIP International Federation for Information Processing, Volume 257, Lean Business Systems and Beyond, Tomasz Koch, ed.; (Boston: Springer), pp. 223–230.

integration is usually considered in a context of linking supply, manufacturing and distribution processes. Organizations more and more often are establishing complex networks dedicated to a joint R&D projects conducting products development, their manufacturing and in some cases also product distribution, marketing and selling. Integration in this case can include all or some parts of a product life cycle.

2   Manufacturing system decomposition

Contemporary manufacturing systems represent complex sets of machines and technological equipment, people, control and communication devices coupled by numerous functional, technical, informational and organizational links, performing complex processes, accompanying with material, energy and information flow. Identification, design, improvements and management of these systems are extremely difficult. In a praxis it is necessary to decompose a manufacturing system into simpler elements (sub-systems) and to use suitable models for describing them.

As prof. S.Chajtman pointed out, every manufacturing system can be decomposed and fully described using only four criteria [2]. According to his concept a manufacturing system will be treated as:
- systematized set of every processes connected with material, energy and infor-mation flow and transformation, which results represent a certain value for internal or external customer,
- systematized set of distinguished system elements – assets participated in a manufacturing system operation,
- hierachically ordered set of organizational units – elements of a manufacturing system,
- a sequence of a manufacturing system life cycle stages.

A necessary condition in order to correctly describe (identify) or design of a manufacturing system is to use at least first three criteria. Every model of a manufacturing system build according to the certain decomposition criteria will represent a specific structure, containing separate system elements and relations between them.

An original and a basic view of a manufacturing system is a structure of its all processes, their division into specific groups and relations between them. A process is a completely closed, logically and timely sequence of activities which are required to work-on process-oriented business object [1]. A general typology of processes executed in a manufacturing systems distinguish usually:
- basic, supporting and information and control (management) processes [2],
- value-added and non value-added processes (or activities).

Another example of process typology are sets (libraries) of reference models of processes, which were originally developed for process-reengineering and today are used as support in process management [3].

According to the second criterion of a manufacturing system decomposition following basic groups of a manufacturing system elements (assets) are distinguished:
- people (staff)   - machines, tools, equipment

- materials, semi-finished products, products   - financial resources,
- information and knowledge.

Relations between them developed at the same time are specific, depending upon particular system elements.

According to third criterion a division of a manufacturing system into hierarchically ordered organizational units (production departments, functional units), produced using certain criteria are distinguished. An example can be an organizational structure (chart), layout plan, etc.

A fourth criterion of a manufacturing system decomposition will display a dynamics of a system change. Some from above mentioned changes will concern a manufacturing system as a whole as well as its specific elements (subsystems). From this perspective a manufacturing system and product life cycle can be distinguished.

Using all four criteria of a manufacturing system decomposition several (and different) manufacturing system models can be developed as a mean of manufacturing system identification. Specific models of manufacturing systems are not a subject of this paper. Concepts of manufacturing systems integration can be now derived directly from criteria of manufacturing systems decomposition.

3 Concepts of manufacturing systems integration

Co-ordination of activities within an organization can be achieved in different ways. One of them is integration (fig.1).

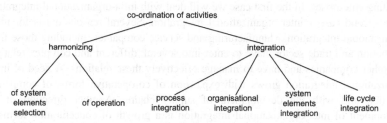

Fig. 1. Basic approaches to co-ordination of activities.

The primary kind of integration is process integration. Its results in making and in delivering products or services which fulfill client needs. Process integration gives prominence to the flow of activities in time and space. A key meaning is assigned to the integration of activities corresponding to the execution of certain production orders:

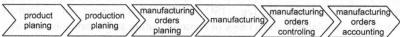

Execution of production orders requires performing not only basic (manufacturing) processes but also supporting processes (which assist and create proper conditions for performing basic processes) but also management processes, connected with production orders co-ordination, their planning, controlling, motivating of people, etc.

Process integration should take into consideration relations between:

- basic manufacturing processes,
- supportive manufacturing processes,
- information and control (management) processes.

Process improvement and integration are key issues in process and project management, reengineering, lean manufacturing, total quality management.

Another category is integration of workplaces (manufacturing cells, organizational units). Relations between them results from a sequence of executed by them activities which are elements of given processes. In order to control them following activities are necessary: work division, work station grouping into some larger organizational units, building an organizational hierarchy, delegation of responsibility, establishing of communication links, etc.

This kind of integration is developed when certain approach to the development of a manufacturing system structure as well as of its management is applied. Functional integration is a specific case of an integration. It is based on the involvement into manufacturing system (or an organizational unit) all necessary processes and functions connected with performing some tasks and acceptance of a certain criterion of manufa-cturing tasks (operations) and work stations (machines) grouping.

The necessity of integration concern in equal level staff (employees), manufacturing (organizational) units, processes and subsystems of an enterprise as well as other co-operating enterprises. In the first case we will deal with intra-organizational integration, in the second case – inter-organizational integration. Several reasons exists for inter-organizational integration. Manufacturing and service companies, including those from distribution and trade sector, have to enter into several, different and complex relations with other companies and have to manage effectively these relations. A need of inter-organizational integration grows with expansion of co-operative forms of company's operation and with the development of supply chains. Another direction of the development of inter-organizational integration is a growth of concentration forms of co-operation (eg. holdings), company's mergers and fusions, horizontal integration, etc. In every case co-operation of enterprises or their selected parts (plants, organizational units) depends to a large extent from effective and efficient co-ordination of their co-operation.

Among external factors being conducive to a development of inter-organizational integration it can enumerate: liberalization of trade, globalization of entrepreneurial activities, a growth and standardization of quality requirements, dissemination of common quality standards (eg. ISO 9000), development of information infrastructure, availability and a range of communication and information services.

Integration in manufacturing systems can concern also system elements (resources). Great importance is played by technical and social integration. Technical integration means physical (mechanical, electrical, etc.) joining of system elements: machines and other technical equipment (transport, storage, etc.). A growth of technical integration goes usually hand with hand with an increase of system automation. Technical integration can concern: equipment, information and data.

Equipment integration consists in a technical adjustment of technical resources, which make possible their co-operation, in particular flow of materials, energy and information streams, accompanying executed manufacturing processes. Within manufacturing systems it will concern eg. machines, transport and storage equipment, which enables an automatic transfer of loads between them.

Data integration means a possibility of using the same data in different subsystems of an enterprise, which makes necessary standardization and achievement of full conformity of its structure. Information integration means however methods and tools of data flow and control in production planning and control systems, manufacturing orders supervision, inventory, quality and costs control. At present IT is a main approach to technical integration of manufacturing systems. A manufacturing system in which all main functions are integrated on a basis of IT is called computer integrated manufacturing (CIM).

Apart from the above discussed functional and technical integration it can also distin-guish social integration. It has several dimensions: management integration, integration of functional teams of employees and organizational units, integration of users, etc. Management integration involve decision makers responsible individually or in groups for strategy at certain areas of a company, employees responsible for co-ordination and operational decisions eg. within PPC systems. Integration of functional teams of employees include workers linked in connection with completing jointly tasks, eg. inter-disciplinary teams of designers, task force group members, executors of complex project, etc. This form of integration is produced eg. within a concept of a process and project management and in general is connected with a team work. Information of users involve people using the same technology, treated as a specific social environment, eg. users of CAD system, operators of CNC machines, etc. Technical and social integration build together an integrated manufacturing environment.

The fourth direction of an integration of manufacturing system concern its life cycle. The significance of the integration of the manufacturing system life cycle is growing when manufacturing system should be adopted continuously to the growing and changing market conditions and match competitiveness requirements. Reduction of a lead time of innovation implementation, manufacturing costs reduction, quality improvement, global scientific and engineering progress need effective and efficient co-ordination of all performers and of all phases of process of the development and implementation of product, process and organizational innovation. Integration in this specific case will concern a cycle of new product development, a manufacturing system design and development or its modernization, adopting an existing system to changed external conditions. Integration of a product life cycle can involve following sequence of activities:

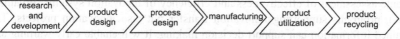

research and development › product design › process design › manufacturing › product utilization › product recycling

Integration of a manufacturing system life cycle will involve however:

| market needs identification | feasibility study | manufacturing system design | building of a manufacturing system | use of a manufacturing system | upgrading of a manufacturing system | liquidation of a manufacturing system |

First three directions of a manufacturing system integration are linked closely each other by common:

- activities / operations which are elements of a manufacturing process, resulted as an output in products and services fulfilling certain customer needs,
- work places (stations, organizational units) at which they are performed,
- teams of workers conducted jointly certain activities at their work places.

Moreover work places are linked by a sequence of operations, common service conducted by a group of workers performing maintenance activities, 5S practices, acting within quality circles, etc. Links between workers result from a joint operation of the same sequence of tasks being part of some process, which deliver certain value to internal or external customers and which need to communicate each other within certain formal or informal groups.

4 A method of an assessment of networked organizations supporting innovation transfer

A development and a transfer of innovations is an example of activity (process) which is often conducted within complex networks of organizations including several partners. Some examples of them are: centers of advanced technologies, centers of excellence, technology platforms, industrial clusters, regional innovation networks, industrial parks and many others. One of several problems affecting substantially the efficiency and effectiveness of innovation development and transfer within those structures is a way how activities performed by all involved partners are coordinated and integrated. Outputs of activities conducted within this structures are directed towards customers, which could be the next (subsequent) partner in this structure, building a link in an innovation process.

Therefore an assessment of these structures should involve also an efficiency and an effectiveness of the integration of all participants of an innovation process and realized by them activities (processes) which will be assumed is equivalent to the product, process or organization (manufacturing system) life cycle. The developed method enables not only an assessment of results of the innovation process (using certain criteria) but also an identification and an assessment of main (key) processes (and activities or operations as their elements) affecting significantly how innovation system operates and on results it generates. A characteristic feature of the method is an integration of an assessment of innovation system goals and its results (outputs) as well as of innovation processes (activities) divided into two stages: research and development (R&D) and transfer of innovation. This approach enables ex post and ex ante assessment of effectiveness and efficiency of innovation systems (organizations), programs supporting innovation transfer but also innovation projects. The obtained information can support decision making. It will enable early warning and it will support implementation of certain improvements with the aim of achievement better future results (outputs).

Main attributes of the proposed method are following:
- it is linked to an organization strategy and / or R&D program,
- it enables a decomposition of strategic goals of an organization and/or programs into operative tasks and an assessment of their contribution in achieving strategic goals,
- it is directed towards an improvement of existing structure and/or its operation of the organization and/or program,
- it enables a self-assessment and an identification and dissemination of best practices,
- it enables relative and dynamic assessment (trend analysis, early warning),
- it is based on a reference model of innovation processes and organizations,
- it is highly flexible, it uses a diverse set of criteria, measures and processes, it can easily be adapted to different particular innovation systems, programs or projects,
- it uses a benchmarking, productivity measures and is based on process approach for innovation management and in particular on Business Excellence Model.

For the purpose of an assessment a following model of innovation transfer has been applied, Fig.2.

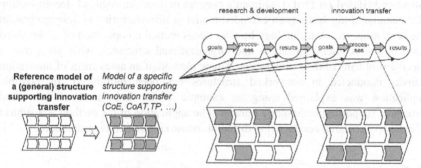

Fig. 2. A model of innovation transfer used as a basis for its assessment (simplified)

A process of an assessment includes following steps:
1. development of a model of an innovation system (program, project) to be assessed using a reference model
2. identification of goals, activities, resources and appropriate assessment measures,
3. identification of key success factors and best practices,
4. R&D assessment
    4.1. R&D goals assessment
    4.2. R&D activities assessment
    4.3. R&D results assessment
5. innovation transfer assessment
    5.1. a preliminary assessment and a selection of innovation solutions to be implemented
    5.2. feasibility study of the innovation transfer
    5.3. an assessment of innovation transfer activities
    5.4. an assessment of economic effectiveness of results of the innovation transfer

6. analysis of assessment results, formulation of improvement suggestions and correction activities
7. implementing improvement suggestions and correction activities.

In every step the intended level of defined goals, achieved results as well as key success factors (best practices) are identified and assessed. Process (activities) assessment include process results as well as way they were obtained. A modified pattern of Business Excellens Model has been adopted.

The developed method of an assessment of innovation transfer conducted within networked structures can be used as a tool supporting the management of:
-     innovative enterprises (incl. virtual),
-     programs supporting technology transfer,
-     innovative projects.

5   Concluding remarks

In the paper the integration as a tool for co-ordination of activities has been introduced. Based on Prof. Chajtman's concept of four dimensional decomposition of a manufacturing systems an extended model of manufacturing system integration has been proposed. A technology transfer needs mutual co-operation of all involved partners and is often realized in inter-organizational structures, what gives rise to specific problems of their integration. A new method of an assessment of innovation transfer conducted in networked structures has been introduced. Its possible application was explained using an example of an assessment of networked structures supporting technology transfer. The application of the method is a subject of extensive research conducted in different industrial research environments.

References

1. Becker J., Kugeler M., Rosemann M. (eds.), Process Management. A Guide for the Design of Business Processes, Springer-Verlag, Berlin, Heidelberg 2003.

2. Chajtman S., Information systems and processes (in Polish), PWE, Warsaw 1986.

3. Kasprzak T. (ed.), Reference models in business process management (in Polish), Difin, Warsaw 2005.

4. Santarek K., Kosieradzka A., Rafalski R., Networked structures of enterprises (in Polish), Warsaw University of Technology Publishing. Warsaw 2005.

This research was partially supported by the Ministry of Science and Informatisation within a project coordinated by the Institute of Exploitation Engineering, research grant no PW-004/01/2004/3/UW-2005.

Which Manufacturing Logistics Decisions are Supported by Operational Research? A Literature Survey

Marco Semini[1], Hakon Fauske[2], and Jan Ola Strandhagen[2]

1 Norwegian University of Science, Dept. of Production & Quality
Engineering, NTNU Valgrinda
N-7491 Trondheim, Norway

2 SINTEF Technology and Society, Logistics
S.P. Andersensvei 5
N-7465 – Trondheim, Norway

Abstract. This paper presents a literature survey of operational research applications to manufacturing logistics decision-making. A total of 80 applications published in *Interfaces* were reviewed in order to identify the decisions supported, their horizon, and their system boundary. The references to the papers reporting on these applications are included in the paper. Most OR applications were found in short-term production planning and scheduling, plant location and physical distribution system design, production system design, and master planning. Other areas, such as supplier selection and business process design, had few or no applications. While the survey sample does not allow generalizations, the unequal distribution of applications suggests that there is a rather clearly defined set of decision areas that are regularly supported by operational research. Findings also suggest that not only operational, but also certain strategic decisions, such as plant location, plant capacity and equipment capacity, are supported by OR. Finally, a lack of applications crossing organisational boundaries has been identified.

1 Introduction

Manufacturing logistics deals with the design, planning and control of material flows and related information flows in manufacturing companies and their supply chains. It includes strategic, tactical and operational tasks, with scopes ranging from a single piece of equipment all the way to global supply chains encompassing several independent actors.

Operational research (OR) is concerned with the development and use of quantitative models to support managerial decision-making. It is an umbrella term, covering a wide variety of models and techniques. A number of these, including

Please use the following format when citing this chapter:

Semini, M., Fauske, H. and Strandhagen, J.O., 2008, in IFIP International Federation for Information Processing, Volume 257, Lean Business Systems and Beyond, Tomasz Koch, ed.; (Boston: Springer), pp. 231–238.

mathematical programming and optimisation, simulation, inventory theory and queuing theory, have been applied frequently to manufacturing logistics decisions, such as network design, production planning and scheduling, and inventory management.

However, OR is based on a number of assumptions limiting its use to a specific kind of situations. In particular, it assumes that the problem situation has been clearly defined and is well structured, that it can be sufficiently well insulated from its wider system, and that it is of a technical nature devoid of politics [1]. Recognizing these limitations, the question arises of where the line is drawn between problem situations that are analyzed by OR, and those that fall outside its scope [2].

The purpose of the survey presented in this paper is to shed some light on this question by reviewing literature reporting on OR applications to manufacturing logistics. All papers published by the journal Interfaces between 1995 and 2004 were surveyed and those describing OR applications in manufacturing logistics selected. The survey's results inform researchers and practitioners about the areas in which OR applications are reported and provide insight about historical trends and future directions for further development. The present paper can also be used in practice and education as a reference to papers reporting on OR applications.

A number of surveys have been carried out previously on the use of OR in industry [3, 4]. However, recent surveys are mainly concerned with the popularity of different OR techniques, paying little attention to application areas. The lack of recent investigations on OR application areas emphasizes the need for such work.

The remainder of this paper is organised as follows: First, scope and decision areas of manufacturing logistics are presented. Next, the methodological approach is discussed, followed by a presentation and analysis of survey findings. Finally, some conclusions are outlined and future research opportunities suggested.

2 Manufacturing logistics

Manufacturing logistics deals with the design, planning and control of material flows and related information flows in manufacturing companies and their supply chains. It includes strategic, tactical and operational tasks, with scopes ranging from a single piece of equipment all the way to global supply chains consisting of several independent actors. Wu et al [5] suggest a taxonomy that characterizes research areas and directions in manufacturing logistics.

Manufacturing logistics encompasses aspects of several overlapping fields, including operations and production management, logistics and supply chain management, and advanced planning. As a consequence, there are several different approaches to structure manufacturing logistics decisions. Chan [6], for example, places the manufacturing planning and control system at the heart of manufacturing logistics. In this paper, a slightly adapted version of the Supply Chain Planning Matrix as defined by Fleischmann et al [7] is employed. 15 decision areas are distinguished and roughly arranged along "decision horizon" and "supply chain process" (Figure 1). The long-term decision areas are shown in a single box to illustrate the comprehensive character of such tasks. Note further that the importance and detailed role of each decision area in the matrix varies between enterprises. The matrix is simply one way of organising the decisions constituting the field of manufacturing logistics.

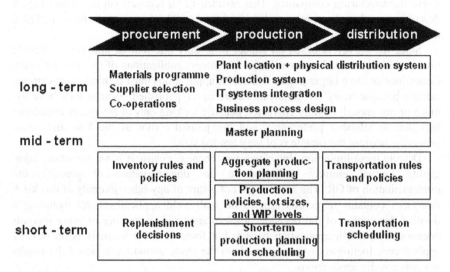

Fig. 1. Manufacturing logistics decision areas (based on Fleischmann et al [7])

In addition to decision horizon and supply chain process, manufacturing logistics decisions can also be arranged along their system boundary (spatial scope). The system boundary separates the system and its environment; the environment may be affected by the decision, but it lies outside its direct control.   Wu et al [5] distinguishes the following levels:

- Production Unit – This can be a single piece of equipment, a work station, or a physical grouping of several work stations and equipment such as a manufacturing line or area, a job shop, or a flexible manufacturing cell.
- Production Facility – In a facility, several production units are gathered under one roof and integrated by a certain means, such as vertically by corporate organisation, or horizontally by products.
- Enterprise – This level defines the boundaries of the corporation. An enterprise consists of one or several plants and also includes other aspects of the business, such as design, engineering, marketing and sales.
- Supply Chain – At the broadest level, several independent corporations cooperate to deliver end products. A typical supply chain consists of suppliers, carriers, manufacturers, distributors and warehouses.

3   Methodology

The papers included in this study were published by the journal *Interfaces* between 1995 and 2004. *Interfaces* is issued by the institute of operations research and the management sciences (INFORMS) and entirely dedicated to the documentation of practice and implementation of OR. Between 1995 and 2004, *Interfaces* published over 500 papers, which were studied one-by-one in order to select those reporting on OR applications that supported manufacturing logistics decision-making in real-world manufacturing companies. This resulted in 60 relevant papers. Some papers describe several applications, resulting in a total of 80 relevant applications included in the analysis.

Since the survey is based on papers from only one journal and from a limited time period, results hold primarily for *Interfaces*' publications of the past 10 years. Generalisations to a larger population of OR applications must be made with extreme caution because many OR applications are never published because they have too much or not enough novelty character, because looking only at *Interfaces* introduces bias due to editorial preferences and the journal's root in the US, and, more generally, because the sample is of very limited size.

Despite these limitation, *Interfaces* was chosen because it is an important, high-quality journal entirely dedicated to the documentation of practice and implementation of OR. The authors are not aware of any other journals of this kind. *Interfaces* contains numerous articles on real-world applications, all including a detailed description of the decision problem analyzed. A number of other journals occasionally publish application papers, but focus in these journals is on novelty applications. Inclusion of these journals in the study would have biased the results towards novelty applications.

Finally, note that a questionnaire-based survey of companies or practitioners would constitute a useful supplement to the literature survey. The former overcomes most of the limitations of the latter. However, company/practitioner surveys have their limitations as well, including difficulty in acquiring a representative sample, low response rates, problems related to question wording, and incorrectly completed questionnaires. Thus, the present literature survey can constitute one component in a more comprehensive study employing several different research strategies in order to increase validity of results.

4   Survey findings and analysis

4.1   Decision areas

This survey examined application papers to find out which manufacturing logistics decisions are reported to be supported by quantitative OR techniques. An important finding is the number of applications in each of the specific decision areas introduced in Section 2 (Table 1). It shows that most frequently addressed area is short-term production planning and scheduling (23 applications), followed by plant location and physical distribution system (15 applications), production system (11 applications), and master planning (9 applications). These four areas account for almost 75% of all applications, leaving relatively few applications to other areas. Six applications concerned inventory rules and policies, five are related to the development/testing of production rules and policies, such as lot sizes and WIP levels (for example number and size of KANBAN cards). All other areas had three or fewer applications.

Tabel 1. Number of applications in each decision area of manufacturing logistics

Decision area	Number
Short-term production planning and scheduling	23
Plant location and physical distribution system	15
Production system	11
Master planning	9
Inventory rules and policies	6
Production policies, lot sizes and WIP levels	6
Aggregate production planning	3
Transportation rules and policies	2
Transportation scheduling	2
Materials programme	1
Supplier selection	1
Replenishment decisions	1
Co-operations	0
IT systems integration	0
Business process design	0

While the sample in this study - as mentioned earlier - does not allow generalizations, the unequal distribution suggests that there is a rather clearly defined set of decision areas that are regularly supported by OR. In other decision contexts, different approaches seem to be preferred, such as "soft", qualitative approaches and management accounting. Simple quantitative spreadsheet calculations are also very common in many areas, but such analyses do not normally find their way into research literature. A lack of papers on business process design was not only identified in the present study, but also in a second survey by the authors, which concentrated on applications of one particular OR technique, namely simulation [8]. The findings contradict common claims that business process design is a typical application area of simulation [9].It may well be so that human and organisational aspects are too predominant to warrant an OR-based analysis approach in this and related areas. In conclusion, while many problem areas lie outside the traditional scope of OR implementations, some areas have clearly benefited from such endeavors.

4.2   Decision horizon

In the survey, 21 of the decisions supported are of a relatively long-term (strategic) character, 33 are classified as mid-term (tactical), and 26 as short-term (operational). While OR has traditionally been applied mainly in operational decision-making [10], this finding indicates that certain specific long-term decisions, such as plant and equipment capacities, are also analyzed using OR. It rejects claims that OR is not suitable for strategic, one-of-a-kind decisions because of their qualitative character and inherent uncertainties [2]. Strategic OR usage has been investigated by numerous authors, including [10].

4.3   System boundary (spatial scope)

The spatial scope of the applications in the survey is distributed with 2 applications at supply chain level; 35 at enterprise level; 31 at facility level; and 12 at production unit level. Thus, only two applications cross organisational boundaries, considering supply chains consisting of several independent actors. Similar findings have also been reported in other survey papers [8, 11]. This is surprising in view of recent years' focus on supply chain management. A possible explanation is that concepts such as supply chain management and global optimization are still relatively new. Only recently, larger parts of supply chains have been analyzed in a holistic way. The novelty character of supply chain simulations may increase the reluctance of industry to reveal the benefits obtained from such studies. Another possible explanation is that logistics decision problems that cross organisational boundaries are characterized by differing strategies and interests, lack of trust and openness, and lacking IT-integration. As a consequence, they may not be easily analysed using quantitative OR techniques. These findings and the explanation are in line with theoretical work on the suitability and limitations of OR; such work emphasizes that in order for OR to be an appropriate approach, high consensus between stakeholders is imperative [2, 12, 13].

5   Conclusions and further research

This paper has presented a literature survey of operational research (OR) applications to manufacturing logistics. The purpose of the survey was to shed light on the question of which manufacturing logistics decisions are supported by OR. Its findings hold primarily for publications in *Interfaces* from 1995 to 2004, since this constituted the sampling frame in the study. Generalizations should therefore be made with extreme caution. Nevertheless, the survey provides evidence for several conclusions:

- Most OR applications were found in short-term production planning and scheduling, plant location and physical distribution system, production system, and master planning. This indicates that these areas have frequently been analyzed by OR. Other areas, such as business process design, have received little attention; this supports the claim that the scope of OR is limited to specific decision areas; decisions outside these areas can be analyzed using other, "softer" approaches and, amongst others, management accounting.
- Several applications have supported decisions related to plant location, plant capacity, and equipment capacity. This indicates that some long-term strategic decisions are analyzed by OR, in spite of claims that OR is not suitable in such situations.

- Despite recent years' focus on supply chain management, there have been very few OR applications to supply chains consisting of several independent actors, such as supplier-manufacturer or manufacturer-distributor. This supports theoretical research emphasizing that in order for OR to be an appropriate approach, high consensus between stakeholders is imperative.

This study contributes to a more detailed understanding of the line between decisions analyzed by OR, and those that fall outside its scope. Further research is required to investigate the decision contexts supported by OR. An industry survey could be carried out in order to support or falsify the present study's findings. In addition, empirical and conceptual investigation of the link between decision areas and different OR techniques, such as optimisation or simulation, can provide useful insights for researchers and practitioners.

References

1. H.G. Daellenbach and D.C. McNickle, *Management Science – Decision Making through Systems Thinking* (Palgrave, 2005).

2. J. Rosenhead and J. Mingers, in: Rational Analysis for a Problematic World revisited – Problem Structuring Methods for Complexity, Uncertainty and Conflict, edited by J. Rosenhead and J. Mingers (Wiley, Chichester, 2001).

3. C.L. Morgan, A Survey of MS/OR Surveys, *Interfaces 19*(6), 1989.

4. I. Munro and J. Mingers, The use of multimethodology in practice – results of a survey of practitioners. *Journal of the operational research society* **53**, 369 – 378 (2002).

5. S.D. Wu, R.O. Roundy, R.H. Storer and L.A. Martin-VegaWu, *Manufacturing logistics research: taxonomy and directions* (1997). http://www.lehigh.edu /~sdw1/nsfws.pdf

6. J.W.K. Chan, Competitive strategies and manufacturing logistics – an empirical study of Hong Kong manufacturers, *Int. J. of Physical Distribution & Logistics management* **35**(1), 20-43 (2005).

7. B. Fleischmann, H. Meyr and M. Wagner, in: H. Stadtler and C. Kilger, *Supply Chain Management and Advanced Planning* (3rd edition, Springer, Berlin et al, 2005).

8. M. Semini, H. Fauske and J.O.Strandhagen, Applications of discrete-event simulation to support manufacturing logistics decision-making: a survey. Forthcoming in the *Proceedings of the 2006 Winter Simulation Conference*, (2006).

9. J. Banks, J.S. Carson, B.L. Nelson, *Discrete-event simulation. 2nd edition* (Prentice-Hall, Upper Saddle River, 1996).

10. H. Akkermans and W. Bertrand, On the usability of quantitative modelling in operations strategy decision making, *International journal of operations and production management* **17**(10), (1997).

11. A. Neely, Production/operations management: Research process and content during the 1980s. *International Journal of Operations and Production Management* **13**(1), 1993.

12. A.G. Hopwood, in: Topics in Management Accounting, edited by J. Arnold, B. Carsberg and R. Scapens (Philip Allen, Deddington, 1980).

13. M.C. Jackson and P. Keys, Towards a system of systems methodologies, *Journal of the operational research society* **35** (1984).

Appendix

Plant location and physical distribution system: Tyagi et al (34.5); LeBlanc et al (34.2); 2 x Keefer et al (33.2); 2 x Gupta et al (32.4); Keefer et al (32.4); Sery et al (31.3); Linton et al (30.6); Karabakal et al (30.4); Köksalan et al (29.2); Camm et al (27.1); Taube-Netto (26.1); Arntzen et al (25.1); Yoshizaki et al (26.6).

Materials programme: D'Alessandro et al (30.6).

Production System: Srinivasan et al (33.4); Patchong et al (33.1); Gupta et al (32.4); Liberoupoulus et al (32.3); Leachman (32.1); Pfeil et al (30.1); Bermon et al (29.5); Rajaram et al (29.1); Burman et al (28.1); Watson (27.6); Keefer (27.4).

Supplier selection: Wagner et al (26.6)

Master planning: Tyagi et al (34.5); 2 x Gupta et al (32.4); Keefer (32.4); Brown et al (31.6); Schuster et al (28.5); Taube-Netto et al (26.1); Leachman et al (26.1); Arntzen et al (25.1)

Aggregated production planning: Lee et al (32.6); Gazmuri et al (31.4); Taube-Netto et al (26.1)

Inventory rules and policies:; 2 x Bangash et al (34.5); Kapuscinski et al (34.3); Billington et al (34.1); Cohen et al (29.4) Lee et al (25.5)

Production policies, lot sizes and WIP rules: Srinivasan et al (33.4); Denton et al (33.2); Leachman et al (32.1); Tayur (30.5); Vandaele et al (30.1); Rajaram et al (29.1)

Transportation rules and policies: Martin (28.4); Adenso-Diaz et al (28.2)

Replenishments decisions: Katok et al (31.6)

Transportation scheduling: Sesh et al (29.5); Bausch et al (25.2)

Short term production planning and scheduling: Dawande et al (34.3); Keefer (32.5); Gupta et al (32.4); Brown et al (32.3); Leachman et al (32.1); Brown et al (31.6); Katok et al (31.1); Lyon et al (31.1); Olson et al (30.5); Katok et al (30.2); Moss et al (30.2); Vandaele et al (30.1); Bermon et al (29.5); Sesh et al (29,5); Mollaghasemi (28.5) Brinkley et al (28.1); Portougal (27.6); Demeester et al (26.2); Leachman et al (26.1); Taube-Netto et al (26.1); Bowers et al (25.4); Flanders et al (25.2); Sinha et al (25.1).

The Selected Problems of Lean Manufacturing Implementation in Mexican SMEs

Mariusz Bednarek[1], Luis Fernando Niño Luna[2]

1 Warsaw Technical University, Warsaw, Poland

2 Politechnical University of San Luis Potosí, Mexico

Abstract. This paper presents the results of investigation of selected problems concerning Lean Manufacturing Implementation at SMEs in México. The analysis is a result of survey conducted in a sample of 24 manufacturing enterprises and it has been supported by some Mexican governmental information sources as well as additional studies which have been conducted before. The paper presents also a preliminary proposal of a methodology of implementation of lean manufacturing and the model of lean manufacturing appropriate in Mexican industrial plants conditions.

The findings of this research are the following: a)The most important problems related to Mexican manufacturing SMEs, b) The problems related to the implantation of lean manufacturing in Mexican SMEs

The limitations presented in this research are the following:

a)The Lean Manufacturing is the concept developed in Toyota and it seems difficult to implement it in Mexican SMEs because of different organizational and social culture of Mexican enterprises and labour.

b)The concepts related to lean manufacturing have been frequently misunderstood in Mexican enterprises because of poor employees training and educational program.

The future research will concentrate on the development of a methodology of implementation of Lean Manufacturing in Mexican industrial plants .This methodology is expected to be a key to the successful implementation of lean manufacturing in Mexican SMEs. This paper does not have any practical implications. Any practical observations can be develop after a practical validation of a proposed methodology in practical industrial conditions.

The main value of the paper is the presentation of:

-current practical problems related to the lean manufacturing concepts application in Mexican SMEs

-a proposal of a lean manufacturing implementation methodology appropriate to Mexican industry. It should be mentioned that this kind of methodology does not exist in México yet.

Please use the following format when citing this chapter:

Bednark, M. and Niño Luna, L.F., 2008, in IFIP International Federation for Information Processing, Volume 257, Lean Business Systems and Beyond, Tomasz Koch, ed.; (Boston: Springer), pp. 239–247.

1 Introduction

According to INEGI (National Institute of Statistics, Geography and Informatics) [3] the institution that is in charge of recollecting, processing and publicizing all statistical and geographical information generated in Mexico, the distribution of different types of enterprises in Mexico is as shown in table 1.

Table 1. Distribution of Enterprises in Mexico by Size

Enterprise size	Number of enterprises	Enterprises percent	Number of employees	Employees percent
Micro	2,673,257	95.43	5,315,309	39.09
Small	95,773	3.42	1,939,169	14.26
Medium	22,631	0.81	1,872,146	13.77
Large	9,719	0.35	4,470,137	32.88
TOTAL	2,801,374	100	13,596,761	100.00

According to the same source, in the case of industry, enterprises employing 10 to 250 people belong to the first three categories. These enterprises generate 65.5% of incomes gained by all industrial companies in Mexico.

In manufacturing industries there are 379,341 enterprises, of which:

- 99.6% are medium and small companies
- 0.4% are large companies.

Manufacturing companies are generating 21.1% of total Mexican exports.

As a part of the integral Mexican policy of the enterprises' development to help micro, small and medium companies, these will be assisted by technical training and relevant information that would provide impulses to their activities.

The Mexican "National Development Plan 2001-2006" [5] includes the documents called "Enterprise Development Program"(EDP) submitted by the Secretary of Economy.

The introductory part of the Enterprise Development Program tells that the SMEs would benefit by a support making them suppliers of large companies in the locations, where those are predominant.

The most important activity for the Government of Mexico [3] supporting the competitiveness of SMEs consists of providing the institutional support which gives legal assurance of establishment, promotion, development and maintenance of the enterprises, especially the micro, small and medium ones.

This new policy of enterprise development is going to increase the creative potential of the employees and of the technological innovation of the small and medium enterprises. The Mexican government wants to:

- create national financial support net for SME enterprises by creation of flexible productive units with high potential to develop and to improve their management and to adapt quickly the new technologies to their needs
- increase governmental attention paid to SMEs
- create the Intersecretarial Commission of Industrial Policy (ICIP) that will reinforce the coordination of the government programs which support the development of SME's in Mexico, and evaluate and report the impact of these programs on the national economy
- promote aggressively the support programs through governments of Mexican states.

In spite of ambitious plans of the Mexican government related to the development of Mexican SMEs one can notice that their competitiveness is based mainly on cheap workforce. According to the present research carried out on a sample of SMEs operating in central Mexico they face a wide range of problems that create low efficiency (63–65%) in their management and manufacturing processes.

In order to improve the level of competitiveness of Mexican SMEs the authors suggest developing and implementing in Mexican SMEs the concept of Lean Manufacturing.

2   Most important problems related to Mexican Manufacturing SMEs

The Mexican small and medium size enterprises live a problematic situation really hard, they have a lot of problems, which inhibits their development, and some of them are shown in this paragraph.

Enterprises Development Program establishes the following factors as the most frequent problems identified in Mexican companies [5,6]:
1. High costs associated with regulations and legal topics. (Source: Federal Commission for Regulatory Improvement. Program of Regulatory Improvement 2000 – 2006)
2. Limitations in training and development of human resources (Source: National Financial. Mexican enterprise in front of modernization challenge. 1999)
3. Exiguous information systems, ignorance of the markets and commercialism problems. (Source: Microbussines National Survey '98)
4. Lack of links with the instruments for the development and technology innovation (Source: National Council of Science and Technology. Special Program of Science and Technology 2001 – 2006)
5. Difficult accesses to get financial support with opportunity adequate to its needs and in competitive conditions. (Source: Bank of México, Survey of Credit Market 2000 – 2001

Points two and four can be considered directly related to the topic of this paper.

Intersecretarial Commission of Industrial Policy (ICIP) has identified some problems for Mexican SME's too, in year 2002, the Secretary of Economy with Inter-American Development Bank, University of Bologna in Argentina and National Institute of Statistics, Geography and Informatics developed the first study that integrated a group of more than 1,000 Mexican SME's, which answered a survey designed to determine its strengths, tendencies, problems and opportunities (The sample was considerate statistically representative of the total of Mexican SME's). Some problems identified in this report, related directly with the paper are presented as follows:

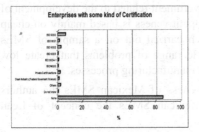

Fig. 1. Enterprises vs. quality system certification

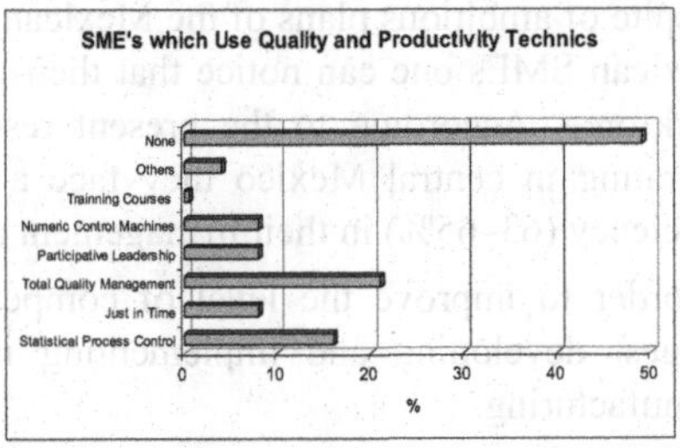

Fig. 2. Enterprises using quality or productivity techniques

The figures 1 and 2 show some important aspects to be considered:
  a) Lean manufacturing is not specified in this list of techniques, so it must be included in "Others" that represent only 4% of companies.
  b) Just in time as a system very similar to lean manufacturing is used by approximately 9% of the SME's in México.
  c) According to these results, 21% of Mexican SME's are using Total Quality Management. If less than 10% of enterprises are certified ISO 9000, can the other 11% of enterprises work in a TQM environment? This is a result of the lack of knowledge that the enterprises have about real concepts applied in modern productivity techniques.

3 Problems related to the implementation of Lean Manufacturing in Mexican SME's

Talking about lean manufacturing and in order to analyze the problematic situation in operative level, a survey was applied by the authors in October and November of 2005.The survey was sent to 300 enterprises and 96 manufacturing enterprises answered.

From the enterprises which answered the survey, 33 of them mentioned they have implanted lean manufacturing. But, at this point it is necessary to review the concept of lean manufacturing system that every enterprise uses, because some of them have different perceptions about what lean manufacturing really means.Five levels were established with the different perceptions that Mexican SMEs used more frequently related to lean manufacturing. These were used to identify the level of enterprises knowledge about final objectives of lean manufacturing.

Level I. Misunderstanding of the concept.
Level II. Use of several tools to get down costs and/or improve the enterprise's productivity
Level III. Waste elimination
Level IV. Lead time reduction on production and delivery
Level V. Improvement on process flexibility to target the client's and market's requirements.

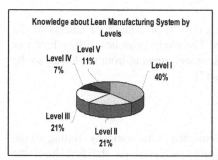

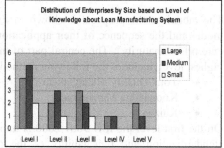

Fig. 3. Knowledge of Lean Manufacturing System. The levels of different perceptions of Lean Manufacturing concepts

Fig. 4. Distribution of Enterprises by its size based on level of knowledge of Lean Manufacturing concepts

In the same survey the respondents were also asked about the time of implementation of Lean Manufacturing in the company. The data below relate to enterprises in which the implementation of Lean Manufacturing is between the third and the fifth level.

- 38% of the enterprises are just planning the implementation of Lean Manufacturing in the nearest - but not clearly defined - future.
- 45% of the companies started implementation two years ago and still continues it.
- 17% started the implementation of Lean Manufacturing this year.

The analyzed companies were also asked about the most difficult impediments in the implementation of Lean Manufacturing. The most frequent problems mentioned by the respondents include:

- difficulties in changing corporate culture;
- insufficient knowledge of the implemented tools and methods;
- focusing on individual, short-term objectives not considering the development of the enterprise as a whole;
- resistance of the employees;
- using models not adjusted to the specific character of Mexican enterprises;

- lack of adequate implementation plans;
- lack of adequate training;
- lack of resources necessary for project implementation;
- no engagement of the board of directors and managers in project implementation.

Lack of Lean Manufacturing models and implementation methods adjusted to the specific character of Mexican enterprises, corporate culture and Mexican employees was considered one of the most vital problems. The model and a general outline of its implementation is presented below.

4   The model of Lean Manufacturing

The model of the proposal is shown in Figure 5. It presents the elements of the model and the sequence of their application. The model consists of four levels of enterprise "maturity". The central part of the model, running from the lowest to the highest level, includes the following methods [2]:

- Total Quality Management
- Knowledge Management
- Kaizen

On the first level the ISO 9001:2000 is implemented in the company. Basing on the standardization and repeatability of the quality achieved on the first level the following processes can be implemented (level 2):

- Business Process Reengineering (BPR)
- Group Technology (TG)
- Theory of Constraints (TOC)

As a consequence, flexible processes, the real base for planning and flattening of company structure are created. Improvement of service processes (level 3), such as maintenance and set up of machines and equipment will constitute the base for creation of production system (level 4) eliminating waste, producing the exact amount of goods that is needed at the right time, what will enable to achieve high quality and to optimize costs.

Implementation of the methods in the sequence shown in Figure 5 will support the company in achieving the last, fourth level, the Lean Manufacturing.

The methods of TQM, Kaizen and Knowledge Management presented in Figure 5 constitute the "core of the system" linking all levels in the company. It is the graphic presentation of the following assumptions of the model:

- Each level of the model generates knowledge that should be analyzed and adopted to the company by Knowledge Management rules
- On each level of its development the company applies rules of team work, management based on the theory of systems, the managers become coaches and leaders and quality improvement stimulates to action and integrates all company employees

The company operates on the basis of continuous improvement of all processes with participation of all its employees.

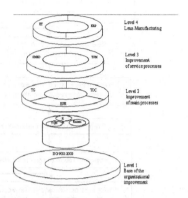

Fig. 5. The proposal of the model of Lean Manufacturing [2]

Implementation of the methods presented in Figure 5 has iterative character. That means a company that has already achieved a certain level of development, can apply methods from the lower levels of maturity. It may have complimentary character, connected with e.g. implementation of additional ISO procedures in the company.

Implementation of the Lean model may begin with the implementation of any of its elements and it will depend on the company's maturity level before starting the program of changes. The only limitation there will be compliance with the suggested by the model sequence of implementation of the methods.

5 The proposal for model implementation

Figure 6 presents a diagram for implementation of the model of Lean Manufacturing. It starts from enterprise analysis and assessment based on the three following elements [2]:

- Internal efficiency of the management and production system
- Assessment of customers point of view
- Human resources management efficiency.

The analysis is carried out by an auditing team in order to identify:

- Relations between inefficiencies in the company and their negative effects on company's performance
- Characteristics of the company manufacturing cells which activities directly or indirectly lead to the inefficiencies.

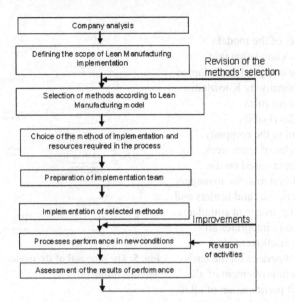

Fig. 6. The diagram of implementation of the Lean Manufacturing model [2]

In order to define the scope of Lean Manufacturing implementation it is advised:

- To keep to the sequence of methods suggested in the model
- To consider resources that the company can assign for implementation activities
- To consider education and work experience of employees.

Implementation of selected Lean Manufacturing methods is a difficult and complex process because:

- It is constantly being revised according to achieved business results
- It is constantly being improved, because of implementation of, in particular:
  - o Total Quality Management(TQM)
  - o Kaizen.

6 Conclusions

1. Implementation of the model can be used to restructure the enterprise thus starting a period of stable and balanced development. This can also lead to the improvement of economic parameters of performance. It has also enhanced competitive position of the enterprise on Mexican market.

2. Pilot implementation of the model has evidenced, that subject to the situation, and based on the results of analysis of the situation, there is a need to select specific methods in order to restructure the enterprise effectively and efficiently. The set of these methods has to be selected on the case-by-case basis, without resentments to create one uniformly applicable model.

3. Efficiency of implementation of the model depends upon:
   - people working in the enterprise;
   - features of the enterprise;
   - all surrounding restructuring program.

One of the main issues is related to education level, norms and values, attitudes and goals of employees. These elements impact upon cause-result effects of implemented changes, reduce resistance to change, and find means to adapt to new conditions. The other relates to knowledge and dedication of managers, that if on adequate levels, may guarantee success of restructuring. Finally, an important element depends upon methods of human-resource management, and in particular, whether or not these management practices are innovative and positively motivating employees.

References

1. M. Bednarek, Study of New Competences Required by Professional Employees by Mexican Enterprises (Politechnical University of San Luis Potosi, Mexico, 2004).

2. M. Bednarek and F. Nino Luna, The Proposal of the Lean Manufacturing for Mexican SMEs' (HAAMAHA, San Diego, USA, 2005).

3. F. Moctezuma, A Model for Implementing Manufacturing Integral Systems in Small and Medium Size Mexican Companies, Doctoral Dissertation (Orgmasz Institute, Poland, 2002).

4. Observatorio PYME, Statistical information about the situation of SMEs in Mexico (2003) http://www.cipi.gob.mx/html/observatorio.html, Secretary of Economy.

5. Plan National de Desarrollo 2001-2006 (National Development Plan 2001-2006), Document published in Presidential Internet System, http://pnd.presidencia.gob.mx/ (14-02-2005).

6. Programa de Desarrollo Empresarial 2001-2006 (Enterprises Development Program 2001-2006), (Secretary of Economy, Mexico) www.cipi.gob.mx.

Experiences with Lean Management

Jan Frick
University of Stavanger 4036 Stavanger, Norway
http://www.uis.no

Abstract. The International Manufacturing Strategy Survey (IMSS) have collected data in 1992, 1996, 2000, and 2006. The paper does longitudinell studies on these data focussing on data relevant for Lean Management. We see that there has been an adoption of the Just in Time and Lean issues, but that there is still a way to go.

1 Introduction

Lean Management emerged (Jones, 1990) as a "new" paradigm to provide competitiveness for companies. The term was new from studies in automobile industries, but most of the ideas were much older even if they here became presented in a new context.

The International Manufacturing Strategy Survey (IMSS) (Lindberg, Hörte, International Manufacturing Strategy Survey, & Institute for Management of Innovation and Technology, 1994; Lindberg, Voss, & Blackmon, 1998) became a team with partners in more than 20 countries that have gathered data in industrial companies in 1992, 1996, 2000, and 2005. The normal is one partner organization per country and there are partners in all continents except Africa. This makes the dataset unique in the sense that it both have subsets of data from more than 20 years and that it contains data from many parts of the industrialized world. Most of the partner organizations have used the data for journal papers, conferences, thesis, and student tasks. ((Acur, Gertsen, Sun, & Frick, 2003; Crowe, Brennan, Coughlan, & Dromgoole, 2003; Evensen, 2002; Gertsen, Sun, Riis, & IPS - Integrated Production Systems, 1994; Klingan, 2000; Laugen & Frick, 2002; Nyvoll, 2004; Skåle, 2000; Sun, 1996)) But most of these analysis have been based on only one set of the data.

This paper base the analysis on relevance for Lean issues. These data is present in all sets and countries, and these topics have been focused on in the industry in this period due to relations to popular conference issues. (Womack, Roos, & Jones, 1991; Østebø, 2000) The Østebø thesis also shows that these issues are relevant for industries far from the automobile or general manufacting. In this case it was used for drilling wells for the offshore petroleum industry.

Please use the following format when citing this chapter:

Frick, J., 2008, in IFIP International Federation for Information Processing, Volume 257, Lean Business Systems and Beyond, Tomasz Koch, ed.; (Boston: Springer), pp. 249–256.

The IMSS datasets contain much more data than we utilize here, but these were useful as a reference regarding the lean management. Regarding the reliability of the IMSS, we know that data collection took place in various circumstances and therefore does contain uncertainty, but we hope by selection to keep it as reliable as possible.

2   Analysis and results

The analysis of the IMSS datasets in this paper are based on simple statistics used on the longitudinal datasets. (Hedeker & Gibbons, 2005) We have to remember that we have different companies (with few exceptions) in each dataset and the countries participating change from set to set. (Sun & Hansen, 1992) This adds some considerations that are discussed in another paper. (Frick, 2006)

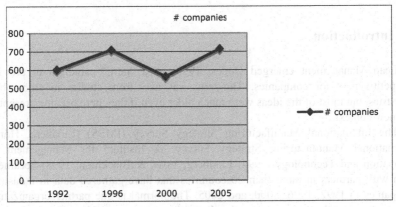

Fig. 1. The number of companies in each of the IMSS data collections

Figure 1 shows that the number of companies included in IMSS is different each time, but the differences are small when it comes to our discussion of cost numbers. The number of countries varies also with the highest number included in 1996, but for all four dataset the majority of companies and countries are European with some addition from Australia, Asia, and North and South America.

Figure 2 shows the trend of overhead cost as percentage of total cost. We see a clear decline over the period for the world. This was surprising since local cases have shown an increase in overhead due to increased automation even if the attention on lean management seems to have increased.

Figure 3 shows an increase in the use of preventive maintenance measured as a percentage of all maintenance cost. The use of preventive maintenance double from 1996 to 2000 and seems to be stable before and after this change.

It is interesting that the pattern shown in figure 4 hold an earlier improvement compared with figure 3. Figure 4 charts the percent of end-product deliveries done by JIT. There seems to be an adoption process where deliveries have as a general rule changed into a JIT concept before a similar change in the way to organize maintenance.

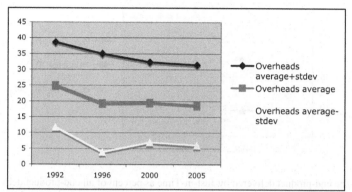

Fig. 2. The overhead as percent of total cost. It is showed as average and average plus and minus standard deviation. We see a clear declining trend

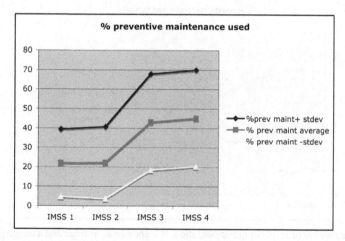

Fig. 3. The preventive maintenance as percent of all maintenance. It is showed as average and average plus and minus standard deviation

We see a similar development in the earliest three datasets in figure 5. Figure 5 shows the number of organizational levels in the company. Here we have the expected decline from IMSS 1 to IMSS 3. But, with IMSS 4 we see a change in the trend. Instead of a continued decrease in the number of organizational levels, we find an increase both in the average and in the standard deviation. We have no explanation for this change. (Sun, 1993).

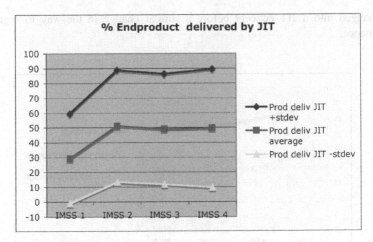

Fig. 4. The end-product delivered by Just-in-Time as percent of all end-product deliveries. It is showed as average and average plus and minus standard deviation

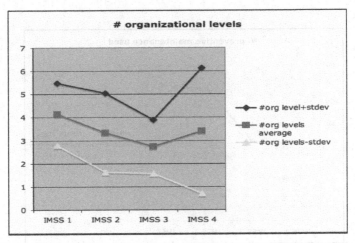

Fig. 5. The number of levels in the organization. It is showed as average and average plus and minus standard deviation

Figure 6 shows the percentage of deliveries that are late. Even if there is a slight decrease, an average of one in ten is still a high number and when we add the standard deviation one in four is not good.

Figure 7 shows the action program for Lean Management in 2005. All the IMSS questionnaires ask about many action programs. The basic idea is to document the connection from strategies to improvement action to change in performance. (Lindberg, Voss, & Blackmon, 1998) This question asks on a scale 1-5 if there have been use of lean management as an action program in the last 3 years, and if there are plans for utilizing lean management in the next 3 years. We see a slight increase.

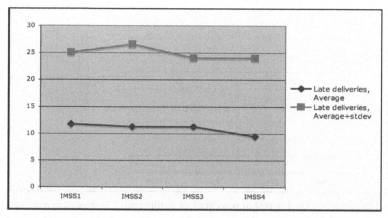

Fig. 6. The end-product delivered late as percent of all end-product deliveries. It is showed as average and average plus standard deviation

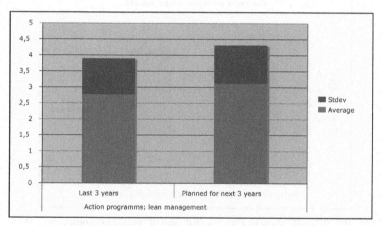

Fig. 7. The Action program for Lean Management as a 1-5 scale. It is showed as average and average plus standard deviation. The figure shows answers for last 3 years and if it is planned for next 3 years. We see a slight increase

In figure 8 we see the preventive quality cost as percentage of total quality cost. We see a slight increase here from 1996 to 2000, and it is interesting that this is in parallel with the increase of preventive maintenance as seen in figure 3.

At last in figure 9 we see two status parameters both measured as percentage of total cost. This is the "scrap and rework cost" and the "customer complaints cost". Both is high when we look for lean performance.

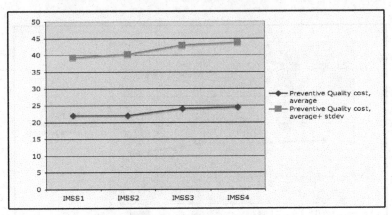

Fig. 8. The preventive Quality cost as percent of all quality cost. It is showed as average and average plus standard deviation

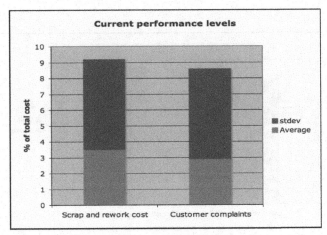

Fig. 9. The 2005 status of "scrap and rework cost" and of "customers complaints". Both measured as percentage of total cost

3   Conclusion

We see that several issues related to lean management have made a way into companies from 1992 to 2005. We also see from the action program and the status charts that emphasis on lean management are increasing and that there are still large possibilities for improvements.

References

1. Acur, N., Gertsen, F., Sun, H., & Frick, J. (2003). The formalisation of manufacturing strategy and its influence on the relationship between competitive objectives, improvement goals, and action plans. *International Journal of Operations & Production Management,* 23(10), 1114-1141.

2. Crowe, D., Brennan, L., Coughlan, P., & Dromgoole, T. (2003). *International Manufacturing Strategy Survey, Irish Report.* Dublin: University of Dublin, Trinity College.

3. Svensen, Ø. (2002). Lean produksjon- *En sammenligning mellom Japan og Europa.* Unpublished Bachelor, Stavanger University College, Stavanger.

4. Frick, J. (2006). *Trends in cost structure based on the international manufacturing strategy survey logitudinal data.* Paper presented at the Euroma 2006, moving up the value chain, Glascow.

5. Gertsen, F., Sun, H., Riis, J. O., & IPS - Integrated Production Systems. (1994). *Compare your company with the world's best Danish report of the International Manufacturing Strategy Survey (IMSS).* Aalborg: Department of Production.

6. Hedeker, D., & Gibbons, R. D. (2005). *Applied longitudinal data analysis.* Hoboken, N.J.: Wiley-Interscience.

7. Klingan, E. (2000). *Strategiske forskjeller mellom Argentinske og Brasilianske metallprodusenter.* Unpublished Bachelor, Stavanger University College, Stavanger.

8. Laugen, B. T., & Frick, J. (2002, 4 Juni 2002). *Linking of strategy and supply chain management: change management or opportunity driven development.* Paper presented at the Euroma 2002, København.

9. Lindberg, P., Hörte, S.-Å., International Manufacturing Strategy Survey, & Institute for Management of Innovation and Technology. (1994). *Produktion jorden runt : strategier i 600 företag från 20 länder.* Göteborg: Chalmers tekniska högsk. IMIT.

10. Lindberg, P., Voss, C., & Blackmon, K. L. (1998). *International manufacturing strategies : context, content and change.* Boston: Kluwer.

11. Nyvoll, E. T. (2004). *En sammenligning av Brasil og Nord-Europa når det gjelser organisasjonsmessige faktorer.* Unpublished Bachelor, Stavanger University College, Stavanger.

12. Skåle, V. (2000). *IMSS, Opplæring i Tyskland og Canada.* Unpublished Bachelor, Stavanger University College, Stavanger.

13. Sun, H. (1996). *Benchmarks for world-class benchmarking : a Norwegian report of international manufacturing strategy survey (IMSS)*. Stavanger: [H*gskolen i Stavanger].

14. Sun, H., & Hansen, P. H. K. (1992). *Research Metodology in an empirical study of technological-organizational development and market dynamics*. Paper presented at the Methods for Integration in Manufacturing, Proceedings of the 6th IPS research seminar, Fuglsøe.

15. Womack, J. P., Roos, D., & Jones, D. T. (1991). *The machine that changed the world : [the story of lean production]*. New York, N.Y.: HarperPerennial.

16. Østebø, M. H. (2000). *Er anvendelse av "Lean Enterprise" relevant for bore - og brønnoperasjoner?* Unpublished Master, Stavanger University College, Stavanger.

Implementing Lean Manufacturing in High-mix Production Environment

Remigiusz Horbal[1], Robert Kagan[1], Tomasz Koch[1]

1 Center for Advanced Manufacturing Technologies (CAMT), Institute of
Production Engineering and Automation, Wroclaw University of
Technology
ul. Lukasiewicza 5, 50-370 Wroclaw, Poland
WWW home page: www.pwr.wroc.pl, www.lean.org.pl

Abstract. Lean Manufacturing concept is well described in the literature in the context of low-mix high-volume production. There are numerous case studies proving outstanding benefits of implementation Lean principles. Nowadays enterprises have to face the problem of high variety of products and dynamically changing demand. Lean tools and methods known from repetitive production do not always fit to high-mix environment. It causes problems with proper design of one-piece-flow production cells and material flow based on pull system. The purpose of the paper is to present a case study of implementing Lean concept in the enterprise producing high-mix of industrial fittings.

1 Introduction

The chosen enterprise is a leader on the Polish marketplace in industrial fittings producing over 1000 of types of valves used in the processes of liquid and gas flows regulation. The production is made to orders. Demand is irregular and seasonal. Additional obstacle is the fact that products are differentiated in the very first steps of production process. The process typically consists of casting, machining, assembly, testing, cleaning, special treatment and painting. The paper focuses on assembly department reorganization based on Lean approach.

At the very first stage of the project Value Stream Mapping tool [1] has been used to elaborate the current and future state value stream map. Future state map allowed estimating the potential influence of planned reorganization of assembly system on the rest of the production operations and identifying the improvement areas. Based on the future state map the goal for assembly system reorganization has been defined to increase productivity by 20% with the same resources.

Please use the following format when citing this chapter:

Horbal, R., Kagan, R. and Koch, T., 2008, in IFIP International Federation for Information Processing, Volume 257, Lean Business Systems and Beyond, Tomasz Koch, ed.; (Boston: Springer), pp. 257–267.

During the first observations it was noticed that assembly operators' work content contains significant amount of non value adding activities such as e.g. waiting for parts, reaching for parts and tools, moving within the workplace. It was decided that elimination of non value adding steps from work content is crucial to achieve the determined goal of the project. To fulfill that following lean tools were identified to apply:

T1. One-piece-flow to reduce WIP level within workplace and shorten lead time.
T2. Standardized work to reduce variability of assembly cycle time for given product type.
T3. Proper material presentation at the workplace to reduce reaching for parts and unnecessary movement of operators.
T4. Milk run material delivery system to reduce the level of inventories at the workplaces and prevent operators from leaving workplaces to bring the parts.
T5. Pull based material flow system from machining to assembly to reduce shortages of parts for assembly.

The tools mentioned above were originally suited to low-mix, repetitive production. Their application to the described project required necessary adaptations to specific, high-mix production conditions. All the listed tools T1-T5 could be considered as a combination of conceptual layer (general concept) and technical layer (technical solution). The assumption was made that the general concept may be applied to any type of production but technical solution has to be changed and adapted to specific conditions of high-mix production. The Table 1 presents both conceptual and technical layers of all the mentioned tools T1-T5.

For the case study described in this paper the tools T3-T5 had to be adapted for hig-mix production conditions. Section 2 contains the description of standardized work and material presentation and section 3 milk-run deliveries and pull system suitable for high-mix production.

2   Implementing one-piece-flow assembly cells

The first steps on the way to achieve the goals defined on the Future State Value Stream Map and to create a lean assembly system following elements were designed:
• a suitable placement of equipment and assembly workstations,
• appropriate flow routes of parts and subassemblies
• pull system.
The goal was to convert the logic of both information and material flows from the Future State Map into technical specification of the assembly system layout while finding the minimum amount of equipment, materials and people needed to build high-mix of orders. Here very useful lean manufacturing techniques were applied: continuous flow and the method of equipment arrangement into assembly cells. Mentioned tools are described in [2] and [3].

Table 1. Conceptual and technical layer of selected lean tools

Tool	Conceptual layer	Technical layer for repetitive production	Problems
T1. One piece flow	Moving and processing products in one piece batches	Product workcell with balanced operators' work content (every operator in workcell has almost the same cycle time)	Balancing of operators' work according to different work content for different product types
T2. Standardized work	Defining detailed standards and procedures for all operator's work elements	Formal instruction in graphic form (usually one page A4) placed on the workplace	Standardized work varies according to different product types
T3. Material presentation	Providing materials directly to operators' fingertips	Flow racks with components placed near to operator's fingertips	High variety of different components for different product types.
T4. Milk run deliveries	Regular and frequent deliveries of small amount of materials according to defined routine	Material handler provides frequently variety of components in small quantities directly to workcell flow racks based on kanban signals. During one course several workcells are served.	Set of components for production changes several times during the shift and components could not be replenished according to typical kanban cards
T5. Pull system	Material flow driven by signals from next process instead of MRP production schedule	Components are stored in the supermarket in predefined quantities and replenished according to actual consumption	Replenishment pull system generates large inventories for high-mix production

According to observations made on the shop floor there were a lot of different components, materials and subassemblies stored on the floor around workplaces. It was also noticed that operators spent a significant amount of their time bringing parts from storeroom to the workplaces, searching for materials, reaching for parts and tools. Moreover the production was performed by operators in batches e.g. for 4 hours production. Additional problem observed in high-mix production realised within one workplace was high mix of different component types stored around a workstation.

The idea of organising assembly system in assembly cells was based on assumption that any transport activity as well as any interruption of material continuous flow is waste. The assembly cell arranges assembly equipment and personnel in process sequence and includes all the operations necessary to complete a product or a major assembly sequence. When operations are arranged into cells, operators can produce and transfer parts one piece at the time (one-piece-flow) with improved safety and reduced effort.

There was also assumed that all components and materials should be properly presented to assembly operators and delivered on time and directly to the operators' fingertips. To do that the containers with parts and assemblies should be placed on flow racks in point of use within cell.

Figure 1 shows a 3D computer model of proposed and implemented assembly worksation including the flow rack for material presentation. Implementation of such a one-piece-flow solution, where one operator can perform all necessary assembly steps from beginning to the end effected in 50% reduction of needed production space. Also the efficiency of assembly department was increased by 33% in average (depend on type of product).

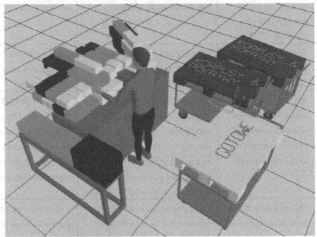

Fig. 1. An example of the designed assembly workstation

2.1   Standardized work and flexible material presentation

An important lean tool supporting one-piece-flow production is a standardized work. The standardized work instruction defines in details all work elements performed by operator on assembly station and has usually a graphical, very visual form. A challenge here was to prepare such an instruction for high-mix production workstation in spite of different product types and assembly processes.

To create such a standardized work instruction all types of assembly processes performed on assembly stations were caught on video tape and analyzed. The analysis showed that only 40% of all operations performed by assembly operators were value-adding operations. The goal here was to define a detailed assembly procedure including only necessary steps to produce one selected product. The effect of those analyses were 25 standardized work instruction cards for 30 different product types assembled on designed workcell. Their implementation caused 10% improvement on product quality. Figure 2 presents an example of standardized work instruction card.

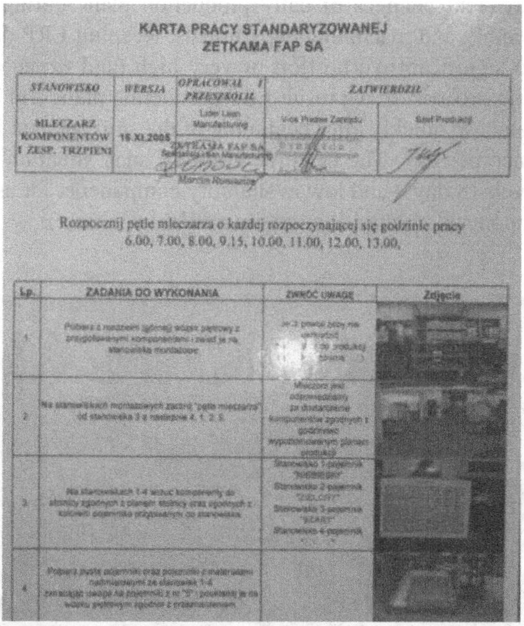

Fig. 2. Standardized work instruction card on workstation

Effective and quick assembly process within the workcell required an effective material delivery system to the operators' fingertips. As already mentioned very important element of this system is, a proper equipment for material presentation – a flow rack at parts' point of use. The main goal here is to design such a flow rack which ensures that all parts and assemblies are available for operators without any unnecessary movement and reaching. However, to reach this goal in high-mix production performed on one versatile assembly cell was a real challenge. In described case special analyses were performed and a suitable flow rack designed where all parts are in the best ergonomic location for operator. Because of many different product types produced on the workstation it is needed that parts are delivered to the flow rack in kits prepared for one or two hours of production and placed in dedicated slides on the rack. The rack is able to hold the material for 3 hours of production. Colour coded bins for parts facilitates delivery process managed by material handlers. Figure 3 presents an example of flow rack for assembly station.

3 Implementing pull system

The pull system was identified as a crucial tool to decrease the level of inventories and improve the availability of the components for assembly. The components are produced by machining department and provided to the warehousing area between machining and assembly departments. The problems to manage these components were typical for companies using ERP systems. Changing customer demand caused frequent changes of daily production plans during the production shift both for assembly and machining departments. Keeping ERP database updated real time required significant work effort or very high (and expensive) automation level of data mining process. In the result ERP production plans and inventory levels recorded in the database quickly after beginning of the shift became invalid and then were corrected once per day. The negative effect of such situation was reasonably high inventory levels (8 days) and low availability components for assembly process (only 35% of components produced internally available on time).

Fig. 3. Flow rack for material presentation within assembly cell

Numerous case studies proves that implementation of leveled pull system allows to avoid frequent changes in production plans and to control inventories on lower level while improving components availability [4][5][6][7]. From the other side all the cited papers concern repeatable production with limited product variants. Considered company produced about 1000 different types of product for individual custormes. The pull system was planned to improve material flow from machining to assembly for two main components: bodies and covers in approx. 230 types.

The typical supermarket pull system is shown in the fig. 4. Customer and supplier processes may be the different production processes in the same facility. Supermarket holds every type of components produced by supplier in predefined quantity.

Customer process has always all the types of components available in the supermarket. Supplier process does not use ERP plan to schedule production of components but replenishes what was taken by customer process from the supermarket. In the result supplier process is insensitive for any invalid data in ERP database. Supermarket pull system allows providing right components to the customer process on time with reasonably low level of inventories if the components are delivered only in few types and consumption of components is stable.

In the case of considered company typical supermarket pull system was inefficient because demand was not stable and high variety of components was demanded by assembly process. To find proper solution the customer demand was analyzed for every type of components. All the components were divided into three categories: A. High-runners, B. Medium-runners and C. Low-runners. Below in table 2 the characteristics of all the categories have been described.

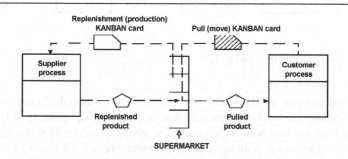

Fig. 4. Flow Typical supermarket (replenishment) pull system [1]

Table 2. Division of the components into ABC categories according to customer demand

A. High-runners	Components for products ordered by most of the customers in large volumes. The consumption by assembly department repeatable. Average daily demand for assembly more then 15 pcs. Components consumed in assembly process irregularly, usually once per week.
B. Medium-runners	Components for products often ordered by the customers. The average daily consumption lower then for high-runners, among 5-15 pcs. Components consumed by assembly process once per 2-3 weeks.
C. Low-runners	Components ordered rarely or in very low volumes as part of bigger orders for high- and medium-runners. Components consumed by assembly process once per several moths.

ABC analysis showed that the components defined as high-runners are parts for the products which are ordered by final customers regularly but produced irregularly, usually once per week in big batches of 500 pieces or more. It was decided to implement leveled production plan for high-runner products and to produce them every day in small batches, e.g. 100 pcs every day instead of 500 once per week. In the result these components became to be consumed by assembly in the similar way like components in the repeatable production process. The inventories on hand required for these components were dramatically decreased (in above example from 500 to 100 of pcs).

Medium runners were divided into 2 groups:

- B1. Components consumed by assembly regularly but rarely,
- B2. Components consumed irregularly in small volumes.

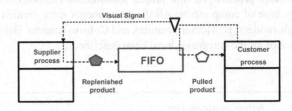

Fig. 5. The sequential (FIFO) pull system

The components of B1 group were designated to assembly once per week (leveled schedule in weekly batches). It was decided that components of B1 group would be hold together with high-runners (A group) in supermarket and controlled by typical supermarket pull system. For components of B2 and C groups the sequential pull system were designed. The main idea of the sequential pull system is shown in the fig.4. In this system customer process does not receive any ERP plan but produces the products according to the component FIFO queue set in order by supplier process.

Finally the mixed pull system was installed (see in fig.5). This system contained supermarket pull system for high-runners and medium-runners of B1 group and sequential (FIFO) pull system for low-runners and medium-runners of B2 group.

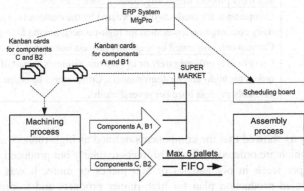

Fig. 6. Mixed pull system

In the result most of the components (A and B1) are produced based on replenishment signals and became insensitive for incorrect data of ERP systems. Additionally thanks to leveled production the frequency of changes of production plan for assembly department was reduced. The rest of components (B2 and C) are produced by the machining department according to ERP plan, but then their flow is controlled by FIFO queue (first-in-first-out). The main effort of maintaining ERP system has to be focused on C and B2 components which constitute less then 40% of production volume.

The result of implementing mixed pull system was improvement the availability of components on time from 35 to 95% while reducing inventories.

Pull system is usually implemented together with milk-run delivery routes of material handlers. The overall idea of milk-run deliveries is shown in the fig. 6. Material handler regularly, e.g. every hour, drives his tuger along the standardized route (a milk-run route) and provides components for hourly production to all the workcells placed along the milk-run route. While providing components to the workcells he collects the kanban cards (or empty boxes) which provide information what kind of components and in what quantity need to be provided to the particular workcell during the next milk-run. Milk-run deliveries are efficient method to keep inventories on the shop floor on very low level and to increase material handler productivity. This scheme works perfectly for repetitive production, where the same types of components are used for longer period.

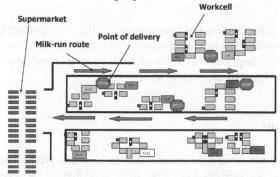

Fig. 7. Milk-run deliveries of components to production workcells

After implementing leveled production in small batches of variety of products in the considered company, every hour the different type of product is produced and different set of components is required. That is why kanban cards can not be used to provide material handlers with the information what components deliver to the workcells during the next milk-run. To resolve this problem the final product kanban cards were implemented instead of components kanban cards. This method is shown in the fig. 7. Material handler during each milk run delivers components to the workcells for 2 hours of production and takes final product kanban cards for the next 2 hours from scheduling board. Then he provides these cards to the component supermarket. Product kanban card holds information about the whole set of components required to assembly the given final product. Thanks to this information material handler knows what components pick up for the next milk run.

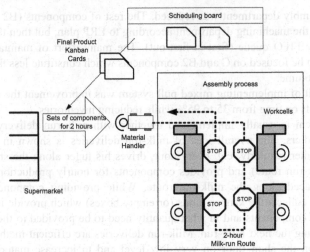

Fig. 8. Final product kanban cards provide information on what set of components provide to the workcells during the next milk-run

During the next milk-run the set of components together with product kanban card is provided to the workcell. After implementing milk-run delivery system the level of inventories on the shopfloor was reduced to 2 hours and the space required for production was reduced by approx. 50%.

4   Conclusions

The lean concept can be applied successfully in high-mix production environment however the lean management tools have to be modified on the level of technical solution for high-mix constraints. The proposed lean tools such as flexible parts presentation, milk-run deliveries and mixed pull system allowed to improve productivity of assembly department in the analyzed enterprise by 33% and to reduce space required for assembly by 50%. In table 3 the required adaptations are briefly described.

Table 3. Adaptations of selected lean tools for high-mix production

Tool	Technical layer for repetitive production	Technical layer for high-mix production
T3. Material presentation	Flow racks with components placed near to operator's fingertips.	Flexible material presentation Assignment of components to the flow racks shelves changes during production shift according to different product types.
T4. Milk run deliveries	Material handler provides frequently variety of components in small quantities directly to workcell flow racks based on kanban signals. During one course several workcells are served.	Sequential milk run deliveries Kanban signals provide information about necessity of components delivery but not the type of component required. The type of needed components is obtained from next 4-hour production schedule.
T5. Pull system	Components are stored in the supermarket in predefined quantities and replenished according to actual consumption.	Mixed pull system Components divided into ABC categories according to pace of consumption. Different types of pull system applied to different categories, e.g. replenishment pull system for high-runners, sequential pull system for low-runners.

References

1. Rother M., Shook J.: Learning to see – value stream mapping to create value and eliminate muda. The Lean Enterprise Institute. Brooklin Massachusetts, 1999.

2. Rother, M., Harris, R., Creating Continuous Flow, The Lean Enterprise Institute. Brooklin Massachusetts 2001.

3. Harris, R., Harris, Ch., Wilson, E., Making Materials Flow, The Lean Enterprise Institute. Brooklin Massachusetts 2003.

4. Shingo, S., A study of Toyota Production System, Productivity Press, Oregon USA, 1989.

5. Wójcik, K., Sawicz, P., Implementing pull system and continuous flow in the company Inter Mind, Proceedings V Lean Manufacturing Conference, Wroclaw Centre for Technology Transfer WCTT, Wroclaw 2005.

6. Szostak, J., Bielewski, A., Delco Remy Poland – Implementing continuous flow, Proceedings IV Lean Manufacturing Conference, Wroclaw Centre for Technology Transfer WCTT, Wroclaw 2004.

7. Horbal, R., Koch, T.: From supplier to production line – lean approach for purchased material flow. Systems 2005 vol. 10 no 1 with Appendix pp. 81-88, Wroclaw 2005.

Implementing Lean Management in the Romanian Industry

Paul Marinescu[1], Sorin George Toma[2]

1   University of Bucharest, Faculty of Administration and Business,
4-12 Regina Elisabeta, Bucharest, Romania
WWW home page:http://www.unibuc.ro/ro/fac_fad.ro

2   Academy of Economic Studies Bucharest, Faculty of Commerce,
13-15 Mihai Eminescu, Bucharest, Romania
WWW home page: http://www.comert.ase.ro

Abstract

Category of paper - Research paper combined with a case study

Purpose - To demonstrate that lean management could be successfully applied in an enterprise from an Eastern European country like Romania. To propose solutions in order to improve the current management practices in the Romanian industry and to increase productivity in order to deal with global competition. To implement the customer-supplier logic within a Romanian manufacturing enterprise.

Design/methodology/approach - The main objectives of the paper were achieved by using quantitative and qualitative research methods. A survey, based on a questionnaire applied to the firm's employees, was conducted and the work processes during a product cycle were observed by the two authors. Focus-groups were also organized within the Romanian enterprise.

Findings - Findings are related to the business environment and economical changes in Romania. Due to the implementation of lean management in the Romanian enterprise, waste decreased in a significant manner, work productivity increased and work area decreased. Also, by using lean production and management, emphasis is put on inter-functional effectiveness, process efficiency and system flexibility. Training (for instance "5S" training) and team work play a key role in implementing a customer-supplier logic (or internal client or customer-in) within the Romanian enterprise.

Research limitations - There are little statistical methods applied in the Romanian industry. That is why future research should focus on the performance measurement and the indicators used in the management of the processes in a manufacturing enterprise.

Practical implications - Romanian government, private and public enterprises could use the findings in order to rethink some of theirs management strategies and practices. Changes should be made within manufacturing enterprises in order to gain a flexible and organizational structure.

Originality/value - The paper shows that the lean paradigm leads to a management-by-process organization. On the other hand, the paper demonstrates that lean management could be successfully applied in a Romanian manufacturing enterprise. Suggestions are made

---

Please use the following format when citing this chapter:

Marinescu, P. and Toma, S.G., 2008, in IFIP International Federation for Information Processing, Volume 257, Lean Business Systems and Beyond, Tomasz Koch, ed.; (Boston: Springer), pp. 269–276.

regarding the solutions needed for improving the current managerial practices in the Romanian industry.

Keywords Lean thinking, lean manufacturing

1   Introduction

Originated at Toyota, the principles of lean management are applied in today's companies around the world because of their positive impact on company performance. Lean management shows a way to obtain more products with fewer resources while providing customers exactly what they want. The key factor behind the development of lean management is the elimination of waste (muda in Japanese). In order to deal with global competition, companies should adopt the lean paradigm, a flexible, adaptive and responsive paradigm.

The purpose of this paper is to demonstrate that lean management could be successfully applied in any Romanian manufacturing enterprise. The case study presented as an example is TOPEX, one of the leading Romanian manufacturers of communications solutions, which has introduced lean production in its plant. Changes required by lean production lead to a management-by-process organization. This assertion is based on a study of how TOPEX obtained outstanding performances through implementing lean management principles. The main objectives of the paper were achieved by using both quantitative and qualitative research methods. Finally, the authors made several suggestions regarding some possible solutions for improving the current managerial practices in the Romanian industry.

2   From lean manufacturing to lean management and lean thinking

The post-World War era brought the first pioneers of lean manufacturing. In Japan, a country with few natural resources, E. Toyoda, T. Ohno and S. Shingo created and implemented the Toyota Production System [5]. Focused on the elimination of all non-manufacturing wastes (for example, inventory, quality defects, transportation), the system established and developed a lean manufacturing philosophy in response to the poor use of human, financial, and material resources. Lean thinking became the generic term to describe the universal application of the lean manufacturing philosophy.

The Japanese lean manufacturing emphasizes the importance of small batch sizes and just-in-time (JIT) delivery. By contrast, the traditional American production system puts on the first place the batch-and-queue concept. As Emiliani recently pointed out, the level of American awareness of lean manufacturing remained low until the 1980's. Twenty years ago, Mather [3] anticipated the emergence of lean manufacturing in USA. Based on the JIT production method, he stressed on the importance of producing the right products for the right markets at the right time and traced six ways to prepare the future factory (box 1).

Box 1
In 1988, Mather asserted that there are six ways to prepare for a factory with a future:
1. "simplify the environment to cope better with complexity;
2. institute simpler, more effective control systems;
3. spend more time on future if you want to have a future;
4. give your people the right training now- before it's too late;
5. redefine your organizational structure to make smart decisions and get fast results;
6. pave the way for important changes in responsibility and accountability".
Source: [3, pp. 216-220]

As a multi-dimensional approach, lean production encompasses "a wide variety of management practices, including, JIT, quality systems, work teams, cellular manufacturing, supplier management, etc. in an integrated system" [6]. Lean management is designed to identify and eliminate all forms of waste in the process of producing goods and services. Many companies from different countries and various fields of activity obtain significant gains by implementing the lean management principles.

Lean management and lean thinking are strongly linked. According to the lean thinking, the business has to be managed starting from the customer definition of value. The customer is the only one who determines whether or not a product/service satisfies his/her needs. In the 1990's, Womack [7] presented the following key concepts of lean thinking:

- Value. Value represents the product/service's capability provided to a customer at the right time, at an appropriate price.
- Value stream. Value stream comprises all activities required to bring a product/service from order to the hands of the customer.
- Flow. All the activities needed to the completion of a product/service have to be organized in a continuous flow.
- Pull. The pull system enables the production of what is really needed, only when the customer (internal or external) requests it.
- Perfection. In order to strive for perfection, companies are aware that the elimination of all forms of waste is endless. In other words, there will always be wastes to be eliminated in a company.

Although these lean concepts have been predominantly applied in the manufacturing enterprises, during the last decades, they have proven to be universally successful at improving companies performance.

3 Implementing lean management in Romania. Case study

Lean management is rather a new concept in Romania. In 2003, the University of Gent (Belgium) and the Romanian National Council of Private SMEs started a two-year project, called "Enhancement of the productivity in the productive SMEs by applying the lean manufacturing method". In 2005, some of the participants at the project created the "Association of Romanian Lean Experts" [8], in order to continue the know-how transfer in the field of lean production. TOPEX has been one of the ten Romanian SMEs selected to implement lean manufacturing and management.

Founded in 1990 by ten engineers experienced in telecommunications, TOPEX is a private Romanian company [9]. In the last fifteen years, TOPEX has become one of the most important Romanian manufacturers of communications solutions for small to large companies as well as for telecommunications operators and service providers. Partners of TOPEX are Siemens, Cisco System, Alcatel and Telemobil. Its main activity is directed to the design and production of telecommunication equipment, but TOPEX also considered the training and after-sale service as an integral part of the solutions it provides. The company has 122 employees and 8 departments (Production, Marketing, Sales, Finance, Service, Human Resources, Quality Assurance, and Research & Development). Most employees are part of the Production Department (29 employees) and of the R&D Department (29 employees). All products are designed within the R&D Department. More than 70 % of the output is exported in 34 countries from Europe (Germany, France, Spain, United Kingdom, Italy etc.), Asia, Africa and USA through a wide network of local and international distributors.

The Production Department is structured as follows: Planting Workshop (11 employees), Control Workshop (12 employees), Mechanical Workshop (4 employees), Packaging (2 employees). In the production activity (Figure 1), the main unit is the card. The card is made of electronic components, imported from Europe and USA, and is assembled on a Printed Circuit Board (PCB), imported from Asia. Within this department, the employees use:

- One ASSEMBLEON "pick and place" robot (Holland), making equipments according to the European Directives on the environmental protection and consumer safety, purchased in 2006.
- One FRITSCH robot (Germany), purchased in 2000.
- One SMD gluing stove with 5 areas, VIP 70 (USA), purchased in 2006.

For the purpose of using the robots, the employees have been sent to training at the producers of such.

Three TOPEX engineers participated in lean manufacturing and management trainings. Since 2005, they have successfully implemented the lean management principles at TOPEX. According to the lean thinking, the TOPEX slogan became: "To serve the internal customer as if it was the final one".

In order to understand and apply lean manufacturing, all employees were trained by the three engineers (main themes were: 5 S, total productive maintenance, Kaizen, lean management etc.). The implementation of lean manufacturing and management started with an analysis of the company's results and of the customers' needs. Grounded on such analysis and on the role of the cards in each of the equipments designed, the management established the following objectives:

- The increase of the work productivity by 30 %.
- The decrease of lead time by 40 %.
- The decrease of the production time by 20%.

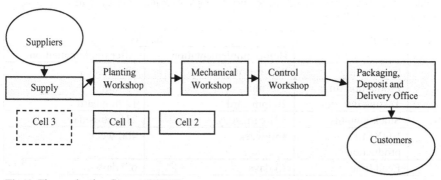

Fig. 1. The production flow at TOPEX

Changes required by lean production lead to a management-by-process organization at TOPEX. According to lean manufacturing, 2 work cells have been designed in the Production Department, each of them with 2 employees (Figure 2). The time needed in order to implement a work cell was of 1 ½ hour. Proceedings and working instructions were created for the each work cell and for each employee.

Cell 1 in the Planting Workshop	Cell 2 in the Control Workshop
First employee:	First employee:
• Placing labels	• Assembling card front side
• Scanning the card series	• Assembling card modules
• Updating Excel file with specific information	• Applying labels
	• Packing
Second employee:	Second employee:
• Cut pins	• Card testing
• Cards movement	

Fig. 2. The two work cells of the Production Department at TOPEX

Automatically, the working tasks within a cell have been balanced, and by this the inactive periods were eliminated. Even if the tasks are modified, each cell member is subordinated to only one workshop supervisor. Each employee performs quality control in his/her own workplace. The damaged parts are placed into distinct boxes and then are re-tested individually by the employees.

TOPEX obtained outstanding performances through implementing lean management principles (Table 1). Regarding the VOXELL equipments produced, the results were quite impressive: productivity and efficiency were way up and the employees became enthusiastic and eager to learn more.

Table 1. The results obtained before and after the implementation of lean manufacturing and management at TOPEX

Item	Criteria	Results	
		Before implementation	After implementation
1.	Card testing	22 cards/day	32 cards/day
2.	Production time	315 min	75 min
3.	Testing duration	20 min/card	12 min/card
4.	Stock quantity	321 cards/day	215 cards/day
5.	VOXELL production	150/week	400/week
6.	Lead time	13 days	6.7 days

A total time economy of approximately 28,000 minutes per year was obtained or, in other words, an additional production of 3,500 cards each year. The work productivity increased with up to 45%. In the future, another work cell will appear.

The authors carried out a research at TOPEX. The research was grounded on:

> ➤ quantitative methods (questionnaire);
> ➤ qualitative methods (focus-group).

The questionnaire was applied in the Production Department, on 27 employees. The questionnaire comprises 21 questions, referring to: the need of implementing lean manufacturing and management, the means in which it was implemented, the results obtained after the implementation, the modality of noticing the manufacturing errors, the type of organizational culture in the company, the leadership style, the decision making process, the evaluation of the implementation (stocks, work processes, maintenance, relationship with the suppliers and customers, quality, planning and control of the processes, visual management).

Throughout several visits at TOPEX, the authors identified the production processes, the main flows and the intra and inter departmental relations, by means of direct observation. Also, the authors set out two focus-groups with 5 employees and 3 managers from the Production and Quality Assurance Departments. The focus-groups were aimed towards the following themes: the need of applying lean manufacturing and implementing lean management principles, the role of lean trainings and working in teams, the importance of the customer-supplier logic consequent to the implementation of lean manufacturing, the employee's motivation.

The findings of our research are the following:

- All TOPEX employees are aware of the importance of the implementation of lean manufacturing and management. The employees' involvement has significantly increased.
- The implementation of lean management has lead to a better correlation between production and market demand, to the establishment of flexible work cells, to the reduction of the manufacturing errors and of the waiting times between the production phases, to job enrichment and improvement of the working conditions, to an increase of the processes efficiency and of the inter-functional effectiveness.

- The company's performances after the implementation of lean are manifested in the increase of the turnover and of the work productivity, and of the decrease of costs.
- The leadership style combines consultation and participation.
- The organizational culture is characterized by team work and discipline.
- The employees are motivated by the diversity of the tasks, by professional development (5S training, mentoring) and by means of wages and bonuses.
- The implementation of a lean strategy is necessary for the purpose of eliminating waste.
- Team work and trainings play a key role in order to implement are a customer-supplier logic (or internal client or customer-in) within the company.
- The complexity of the customers' activities (fix and mobile telephony, Internet providers, aeronautics, post services etc) has imposed a rapid adaptation to their needs, by means of flexible production.
- Only 40% of the production process is statistical controlled and 35% of the production flow is realized without intermediary stocks.
- The contracts are concluded with the suppliers for an average duration of 20 months because 30% of them have implemented total quality management systems.

From the research it results that the implementation of lean in all the phases of the production process is needed. TOPEX has evolved to a management-by-process company. In the near future, the application of lean will continue at TOPEX in relation with the suppliers for the purpose of reducing the raw materials and materials stocks.

4 Conclusions

The aim of this paper is to contribute to the subject of lean management. The case study described demonstrates that lean management could be successfully applied in any Romanian manufacturing enterprise. Once rare outside the factory, lean tools are increasingly applied in the private and public enterprises from different fields of activity. In this respect, Romanian government, private and public enterprises could use the findings of our paper in order to rethink some of theirs management strategies and practices.

In Romania, lean manufacturing and management has been implemented in a relatively small number of companies and that is why campaigns should be initiated in order to promote the advantages of lean. The participation of specialists from countries with tradition (Japan, USA etc) in implementing lean management in the Romanian industry should contribute to the development of a national network of lean experts and organizations.

Thoughtfully implemented in Romania, lean will lead to excellence and to a collaborative and creative environment. In a globalized world, Romanian companies should understand that lean improvements give stakeholders what they need, and managers the possibility to keep their business running side by side with the competitors.

References

1. Arnheiter, E. D. and Maleyeff, J., The integration of lean management and Six Sigma, The TQM Magazine, Vol. 17 No. 1, 2005, pp. 5-18.

2. Emiliani, M. L., Origins of lean management in America. The role of Connecticut businesses, Journal of Management History, Vol. 12 No.2, 2006, pp. 1678-184.

3. Mather, H., Competitive Manufacturing, Prentice Hall, Englewood Cliffs, New Jersey, 1988.

4. Jones, D. T., Building a Lean Management System, Production Systems Conference, Stuttgart, 14 June 2004, www.leanuk.org.

5. Ohno, T., Toyota Production System, Productivity Press, Portland, OR, 1988

6. Shah, R. and Ward, P. T., Lean manufacturing: context, practice bundles, and performance, Journal of Operations Management, 21 (2003), pp.129-149.

7. Womack, J. and Jones, D. T., Lean Thinking, Simon&Schuster, New York, 1996.

8. The Association of Romanian Lean Experts, www.lean.ro.

9. TOPEX, www.topex.ro.

Lean Transformation of Multinational Concerns

Rikke V. Matthiesen[1], John Johansen[1]

1 Aalborg Universitet, Center for Industriel Produktion (CIP)
Fibigerstræde 16, 9220 Aalborg Ø, Denmark
WWW home page: http://www.cip.aau.dk/

Abstract. Competitive pressure demands that companies constantly strive to catch up to world class manufacturing performance and practice. Continuous change is a mode of competition for many companies [1]. This is a departure from the punctuated equilibrium model of change in which change is event triggered. This paper reports on exploratory studies from a multinational company adopting centrally managed pilot projects as a transformation mechanism for continuous change towards a lean business system and an organizational culture of continuous improvements (CI).

1 Introduction

Today companies may be in need of a swift transformation process. Here the global company faces the special challenge of transforming several sites simultaneously. Between such sites learning and knowledge sharing would be a means of obtaining an effective transformation process. This requires sameness in methods and tools and an effective means for this is centralized coordination of implementation.

In the literature one finds important discussions on the transformation process which overlap and supplement each other but do not match or subsume one another. In the first research on lean manufacturing [2] distinguished lean manufacturers by their performance regarding human effort, space, investment, and engineering hours. More recent work, e.g. [3, 4], uses constructs in terms of lists of practices to distinguish the lean operations. But recently there has been an increased focus on the missing correlation between working with lean practices and staying a healthy business. As opposed to practice lists and result orientation[5] and [6] emphasize a process oriented approach in building up process and continuous improvement capabilities respectively. [6] suggests doing improvements for the sake of improvements so as to build up quality awareness in the workforce. Building culture by such practicing of new ways of identifying and solving problems is in line with the view of organizational culture as learned responses to problems the organization

Please use the following format when citing this chapter:

Matthiessen, R.V. and Johansen, J., 2008, in IFIP International Federation for Information Processing, Volume 257, Lean Business Systems and Beyond, Tomasz Koch, ed.; (Boston: Springer), pp. 277–284.

has encountered in the past [7]. [6, 8] emphasize the importance of policy deployment to direct continuous improvement efforts and numerous authors stress the importance of management attention and role modelling during transition periods.

2   Approach

The present research is based on experiences from a multinational company with more than 50 factories involved in a corporate-wide transformation.

The company is family owned and one Denmark's largest industrial companies with 18.000 employees globally. It is organized in three business units supplying components and control devices to OEM customers. The company has a financial goal for 2008 of reaching a turnover of €3.200 million from the current €2.200 million and of increasing its EBIT margin from 5,5% to 10% so as to catch up with industry peers who are achieving 10%+.

The company has a history of undertaking larger rationalization activities and has initiated efforts to develop and adopt its own lean business system. The programme was launched in 2003. The aim of the production programme is to cover all larger production areas with pilot projects in order to improve lead time and productivity in the short term and obtain a lean flow and a CI culture in the long term. Changes primarily take place on shop floor; they involve common lean tools and are lead by corporate change agents. The pilot projects should work as training grounds for local project members and management who are responsible for the continued sustaining, evolving, and cascading of implemented changes so as to drive a transformation of the entire production organization.

The programme is organized with two senior consultants who are in charge of its execution. They also consult factories on tactical issues regarding their efforts to become lean. Corporate change agents are mainly recruited from within the company and are expected to stay with the programme for 2-3 years. The pilot projects follow a standardised schedule but the focus of each project is adapted to the particular business needs in the area. Between these pilot projects, the corporate project leaders exchange experiences and tools. So far this sharing has resulted in decisions regarding demands for management support, mandatory tools implementation and project management elements, awareness of stress symptoms, teambuilding events, and greater emphasis on high productivity targets and layout changes.

2.1   Research Method

The aim of this study is to identify key themes and hypotheses relevant to the transformation process initiated through pilot projects, driven by a corporate staff of experts. An inductive and exploratory qualitative approach was adopted as a research approach. The focus area is twofold: 1) Management reflections, plans and actions regarding a transformation, 2) The dynamics arising during and after pilot projects.

Interviews are chosen as the primary data. As a starting point for the interviews, a list of themes relevant to a transformation process was developed from researchers in the field of organizational change. During the interviews probing questions were asked based on observations of shop floor practices as well as experiences from one of the researchers 1½ years of employment within the change programme.

2.2   Case Descriptions

Four factories have been selected for this initial exploratory research. They are all located in Denmark, and three of them are part of the same division. Factories vary in size and number of shifts, see Table 1, but their processes are quite similar. Three of the four factories are organized with operational team managers; factory beta stands out as supervisors in this factory report directly to the plant manager.

Table 1. Comparison of factories

Factory:		Alfa	Beta	Gamma	Delta
Location		By HQ	City	By HQ	By HQ
# blue collar workers		100	200	230	90
# shifts		1-3 shifts	2-5 shifts	2-3 shifts	2 shifts
Projects	W03	C Machine area.			
carried out	S04	L Assembly area.	C Mach.	C Ass.	
(L) local	W04		L Mach.		C Ass.
(C) corporate	S05	L Ass.	C Ass.		
↓	W05			C Ass.	L Ass.
	S06		2L Ass,+ Mach.		
Production area coverage		80%	50→60%	40%	70→100%
Supervisors involved		4/4 (2 newly hired)	4/7	2/5	2/4
Operations team managers involved		2/2 (2 newly hired)	0/0	2/2	2/3
# of interviews		16	15	14	16

All four factories have or have had change agent(s) employed with direct report to the plant manager. These change agents participated as team member in the centrally managed pilot projects in the respective factories. In factories alfa, beta, and delta, the change agents had subsequently been responsible for locally managed project(s) more or less copying the centrally managed project. A factor common for the locally managed projects though was that they resulted in less significant changes and they spent more time on involving employees and utilizing their ideas as a means of reducing resistance and increasing buy in.

The factories have been subject to corporate projects in different stages of the roll out and have despite similarities also taken different routes from there. Factory alfa and beta have in addition to pilot projects been focusing on broader issues such as flow across the plant. Both factories experienced projects resulting in employee and supervisor resistance or dissatisfaction, and in both factories plant managers had been quite involved in discussing the future state picture. It appeared that they saw an improved flow as the means for convincing employees, winning them over, and changing behaviour and mindset. Factory delta focused on projects covering whole value streams one by one. Projects would be used as a platform for improving further towards a more cost efficient and lean operation. In factory gamma the organization had been swamped in ramping up a new production. Therefore focus on lean had been reduced during a period following the first corporate project. Now, however, the company is working with team building and employee mindset which is seen as the platform to build better performance on.

Comparing these three tactics, factory delta stands out as not focusing so intensely on mindset changes but primarily on improving performance and thus having a very clear vision of the future state. Several factors could help explain this. The factory had experienced less frustrating projects, and has fewer shifts and more middle managers. The organization also has a good track record of increasing performance and a general sense of sufficiency in CI capabilities.

All interviews from the beta case have been transcribed. These transcriptions along with impressions from the other cases were used to form the initial analyses frameworks. Seventy percent of interviews conducted in cases alfa, gamma, and delta have been reviewed in order to test and expand the frameworks.

3   Analysis

3.1   Six Expressed Opinions about Change Goals

The interviews showed that the organizations were not engaged in a broad practicing of the new tools outside the pilot area as a means of reaping improvement potentials, building up capabilities, and increasing improvement awareness across the organization. The most obvious transformation mechanism triggered by the pilot projects was that of cascading change by copying the pilot project approach locally. But a CI culture is not built up during a pilot project. Building a culture requires that the implemented systems are used as a platform for ongoing experimentation with new behaviours [5, 6]. In regard to using pilot projects as such platforms, the interviews left the impression though, that only few interviewees considered the organization to be in the middle of a transformation and that many only focused on equipment problems in relation to CI. This signifies that the projects build up only a low transformation drive towards a new culture and it points to the relevance of investigating this transformation drive and the mechanisms affecting it.

This section presents 6 categories of statements about change and the future state found in the interviews. From these categories a framework of transformation drive is sketched out. This is applied in an analysis of the levels of the transformation drive within various organizational functions. From this the main trends for each function are identified and deviations are analysed.

Interviews were scrutinized for statements about the changes, about future state perspectives, and about opportunities for improvement. It appeared that 6 groupings were necessary to distinguish between the most significant differences. In the following each of these 6 groupings are described.

1. Project thinking: Interviewees expressed a view that other things were on the agenda now. They did not express that the project was a step on a journey or anticipate that they would be responsible for or participate in significant changes – except for maybe copying the project to other areas.

2. Transformation: Interviewees expressed that they had specific and multiple goals regarding culture, capabilities and performance and they were actively trying to achieve those. [9] quotes authors for seeing transformative change as episodic and abrupt, but in this case the opposite is found to apply as managers need to show that changes have not finished together with the project.

3. Slave of the system: Interviewees talked about the surrounding system as limiting their internal performance. In the following such views are listed according to declining degree of strength: Actively opposing implemented tools, seeing more resources as only means for solving problems, denying opportunities to improve should exist within the system, being passive or helpless, expressing that change only happens occasionally but generally the best we can do is to do our best.

4. Mastering the system: As opposed to (3) some interviewees saw the technical system from outside in. They expressed the view that the rate at which we usually tackle our technical problems in the system is sufficient.

5. Changing people: Some interviewees saw employees as part of the system. They were slowly pushing so as to develop some mindset or behaviour aspect. In a less active version they were hoping for a better behaviour among colleagues.

6. Desiring a more involving and lively process: Some interviewees expressed that the change process should get higher focus. They were wishing for more dialogue and involvement so as to shape the future state together in a more creative process bringing more topics into the debate.

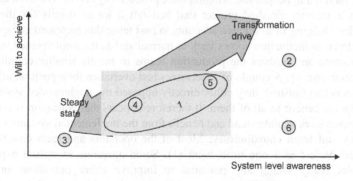

Fig. 1. A tentative transformation drive framework of future state perspectives

Each grouping expresses some desire for progress but their perceived support of the transformation varies. Two dimensions distinguishing the underlying values were tentatively chosen to form a framework to range the groupings according to the transformation drive they expressed: One dimension relates to desire for speed of change, willingness to work for change, and ability to make it happen which is categorized as 'Will to achieve change'. The other dimension is named 'System level awareness' and refers to Boulding's 1956 classification and the systems perspective taken: What constitutes the system to improve, and what capacity does the system contain for action. Applying a higher level systems perspective aids in identifying improvement levers effectively and constructively. Using these dimensions the six groupings of statements can be arranged according to their transformation drive as displayed in Fig. 1. The axes may not be entirely independent but the model should illustrate that moving from the bottom left to the top right represents an increasing transformation drive.

3.2   Trends and Deviations Related to Organizational Functions

The individual interviews were analysed according to this framework of transformation drive. To some extent views within organizational functions or levels were alike – more so than opinions expressed within the same factory or project. Common education, work experience, and job requirements build occupational cultures [10] but also the individual project role, e.g. a supervisor would have, would be similar across projects. Still there were deviations from the main trend within each organizational function or level. Analysing these deviations triggered some insights into the mechanisms that affect transformation drive in relation to the pilot projects. In the following arrows (←↑→↓) are used to indicate the directions interviewees appear to have moved in the transformation drive framework.

Supervisors: Most of the supervisors viewed the project as a project (1) and many took on the slow development view (5) with increased focus on cross training →. Only three supervisors accounted for a transformation process – two of these in past tense. These two had both been involved in projects that had built up frustration among employees and they therefore had been deeply involved in changing mindsets, motivating people and bringing back productivity levels. The third account was from a recently finished project that had left a lot of details for the local organization. Judging from the two accounts in past tense this increased engagement throttles down as motivation comes back to normal and as the implemented systems become routine and enables the production teams to handle smaller coordination tasks on their own ↑↓. A couple of supervisors had overtaken their position after the pilot projects had finished; they either directly opposed the implemented systems or did not see the benefit in all of them. It therefore appears that education is required for new supervisors to understand and benefit from the implemented systems ←.

Operators and team coordinators: Most of the operators and team coordinators viewed the project as a one time event (1). Some operators expressed a passive attitude not really seeing any potential to improve either operations or their conditions as operators (3). This was especially so on assembly lines where operators had gotten a considerable larger workload as a result of the project. In these assembly areas operators felt that interesting parts of their jobs had been taken away and that they now worked more like robots while team coordinators were given all the tasks that had previously been a welcome break or a challenge to deal with←↓. Especially in areas where the team coordinator had a strong coordinating role, some team coordinators were hoping for their operator colleagues to take more responsibility (5)→↑. In the two machining areas, team coordinators had been appointed reluctantly. They gave examples of how they on some aspects opposed the implemented systems as a means of insisting on not coordinating their own colleagues←. Some operators and team coordinators had seen the project as a step towards a different culture and were hoping for a more lively approach to improvements and learning (6) – some wanted more time or latitude from management and others were hoping for their colleagues to take a greater interest in learning and developing the area. Interest in a more lively development seems to be very individual, but in general a positive experience with prior involvement in some improvement activities appeared to underlie this desire → while group dynamics appeared to affect it negatively. The issues described above signify a potential for utilizing operator and team coordinator viewpoints for improvements of the system.

Support functions: Most support personnel expressed project thinking (1). Some engineers were involved in the daily operations utilizing the new systems but the projects they worked on did not relate to lean or to the productivity improvement project as such. Planners were generally absorbed with daily operations and thus had little opportunity to work with lean tools. However, exceptions in both directions were found. It appeared that participation in the projects did bring about increased 'System level awareness'→. While operations personnel that had not been involved in the projects tended to have their tasks staying on the task lists for too long and thus affected transformation drive negatively in the entire pilot organisation ↓.

Change agents: They expressed the transformation view (2) – more than project participants involved with daily operations→↑. They were quite involved with discussions about the future state and seemed to be important sparring partners for supervisors and plant managers.

Managers: Plant managers were all aiming at a transformation (6), and the transformation appeared to take up a relatively large part of their agenda →↑. Two newly hired operations team managers from external companies expressed a desire for a more energetic change process. Only two operations team managers expressed the project view (1). They were both worked in areas that had been substantially transformed during projects and now performed at a new level. The implemented systems formed a solid platform to maintain this level and the managers expressed greater confidence in the organizations capacity to accomplish improvements ↑.

Overall primarily change agents, managers, and some team coordinators appear to be moving towards a larger transformation drive. With supervisors and support personnel, the movement in the framework is primarily horizontal towards increased systems awareness. But in some cases especially with operators, movements are in the direction away from transformation drive.

4 Summary

The pilot project organization, form and content is successful in leveraging performance and practices. Though as a transformation mechanism the approach is not unproblematic. The pilot projects favour management, change agents and to some degree the new team coordinator role. Post pilot transformation focus is on copying projects as a means of building new behaviours via the copied systems and on building project management skills. It is not evident that this is a strong transformation mechanism since corporate managed projects already have demonstrated that as a platform for learning and developing a new culture the pilot project is not a strong concept. Two years after a pilot project, focus is still limited to technical problems. And the pilot projects have built up only a temporary transformation drive among supervisors on the one hand while they have built up resistance or passivity among operators on the other hand. This group is generally not activated in the development of a new culture and where they potentially could be, this has not been supported and made use of. Comparing organizations, it is found that existing organizational culture has a strong influence on pilot project outcomes. But where locally managed projects have adjusted to better fit local organizational culture, dynamics within the corporate programme have increased the focus on mechanistic efficiency. This is problematic since an effective corporate organization is allowed a stronger position and thus maintains the focus on projects as the primary transformation mechanism.

References

1. S.L. Brown and K.M. Eisenhardt, The Art of Continuous Change: Linking Complexity Theory and Time-paced Evolution in Relentlessly Shifting Organizations, Administrative Science Quarterly 42, 1-34 (1997).

2. J.P. Womack, D.T. Jones, and D. Roos, The Machine that Changed the World (Harper Perennial, 1990)

3. C. Karlsson and P. Åhlström, Assessing changes towards lean production, International Journal of Operations and Production Management 16(2), 24-41 (1996).

4. R. Shah and P.T. Ward, Lean manufacturing: context, practice bundles, and performance, Journal of Operations Management 21, 129-149 (2003).

5. S. Spear and H.K. Bowen, Decoding the DNA of the Toyota Production System, Harvard Business Review 77(5), 97-106 (1999).

6. M. Imai, Kaizen (The KAIZEN Institute Ltd., Skive, 1986)

7. E.H. Schein, Coming to a New Awareness of Organizational Culture, Sloan Management Review 25(2), 3-16 (1984).

8. J. Bessant and S. Caffyn, High Involvement innovation through continuous improvement, International Journal of Technology Management 14(1), 7-28 (1997).

9. D.C. Dunphy and D.A. Stace, Transformational and Coercive Strategies for Planned Organizational Change: Beyond the O.D. Model, Organizational Studies 9(3), 317-334 (1988).

10. E.H. Schein, Three Cultures of Management: The Key to Organizational Learning, Sloan Management Review 38(1), 9-20 (1996).

Orchestrating Lean Implementation

Jens Ove Riis[1], Hans Mikkelsen[1], and Jesper Rank Andersen[2]

1 Center for Industrial Production, Aalborg University, Fibigerstraede 16,
DK-9220 Aalborg, Denmark
http://www.cip.aau.dk

2 KnowIT ApS, Østervold 23, 2. sal, DK-8900 Randers, Denmark

Abstract. The notion of Lean Manufacturing is not merely confined to a set of well defined techniques, but represents a broad approach to managing a company. Working with lean entails many aspects, such as production planning and control, production engineering, product development, supply chain, and organizational issues. To become effective, many functional areas and departments must be involved. At the same time companies are embedded in a dynamic environment. The aim of the paper is to propose a comprehensive approach to better implementation of lean initiatives, based on two empirical studies. The paper will discuss how a concerted effort can be staged taking into account the interdependencies among individual improvement initiatives. The notion of orchestration will be introduced, and several means for orchestration will be presented. Critical behavioral issues for lean implementation will be discussed.

1 Lean implementation requires a concerted organizational effort

The notion of Lean Manufacturing is not merely confined to a set of well defined techniques, but represents a broad approach to managing an enterprise [1]. Lean draws on a number of more specific focal areas, such as Just-in-Time, Total Quality Management, Business Process Reengineering, Reduction of Waste, Flow Manufacturing. Thus, working with lean entails many aspects, such as production planning and control, production engineering, quality management, product development, supply chain, and organizational issues. To become effective, many functional areas and departments must be involved.

In many respects lean implementation seems to be no different from other management development efforts, for example introduction of computer integrated manufacturing technologies and business process reengineering. Empirical studies indicate that only a fraction of all initiatives, although technical successful, ever manage to deliver the desired competitive improvement [2]. Kaplan & Norton [3]

Please use the following format when citing this chapter:

Riis, J.O., Mikkelsen, H. and Andersen, J.R., 2008, in IFIP International Federation for Information Processing, Volume 257, Lean Business Systems and Beyond, Tomasz Koch, ed.; (Boston: Springer), pp. 285–293.

claims that only one out of ten companies ever succeeds in implementing strategies to the extent that intended results are achieved. This points to the importance of addressing the organizational issues related to lean implementation.

The paper will draw on the results of a study of how companies manage a portfolio of internal development initiatives [4]. It involved more than 30 companies from different industries and covered a variety of themes, including lean implementation. Also, a study of five Danish companies' work with agile portfolio management will be included [5].

The next section will place lean implementation in an organizational context. Then the notion of orchestration will be introduced to cope with internal and external dynamics. Managing interdependencies among development initiatives is key and will be discussed in a subsequent section leading to a discussion of means of forming and orchestrating a campaign and a program of internal development activities. At the end behavioral issues will be discussed.

2   The myriad of development initiatives

The empirical studies suggest the proposition that at any point in time in a company there are many internal development initiatives in progress competing for attention. For good reasons each functional area, e.g. sales and marketing, product development, production engineering, logistics, purchase, human relation, or IT-systems, is expected to propose activities that can improve the overall company performance. For example, production and logistics may want to improve quality, but have to rely on cooperation with product development and purchase; or the HR-section may want to launch a large-scale competence development program, but will depend on active involvement of the whole organization. In addition, top management often has its own agenda with respect to attending to the public image and shareholders' opinion which also may give rise to internal development initiatives.

Figure 1 illustrates the wide spread of internal development activities from large renewal programs involving almost all departments and functions to local improvement initiatives.

A general pattern emerged rather quickly, namely that companies experienced the greatest difficulties in managing internal development initiatives in an area in-between major strategic initiatives and local initiatives carried out solely in organizational units (sections and departments). The explanation offered goes as follows: The large company-wide effort usually attracts sufficient top management attention, and initiatives originating in one department usually are well managed by department and section heads.

In addition to characterize development initiatives according to their width in terms of the number of departments involved, they may also be characterized according to the depth of the change implied, spanning from large turn-around programs, strategic business developments, to continuous improvement tasks and cost reduction efforts.

Although some of the lean techniques appear easy to understand, the implementation of their derived results implies a drastic change in the way of thinking and behavior on part of both operators and management.

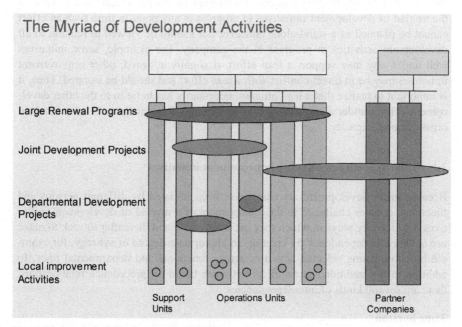

Fig. 1. The myriad of development activities

3   Orchestration

The empirical studies point to the increased turbulent environment that companies experience, indicating that the environment significantly determines the appropriate actions for management. Not only does a company experience short-term dynamics; but its strategic situation may also change over time, and consequently this calls for a regular shift in management focus. In periods, unforeseeable changes in the environment call for a capability to rapidly adjust implementation plans.

To acknowledge this complex and dynamic management situation we shall introduce the notion of orchestration to indicate that management of development initiatives is about harmonizing the activities of many interested parties into a concerted effort being able to continuously shifting the balance between actors and focal areas. The metaphor of managing the development of a company like conducting an orchestra or a band may capture important characteristics. For example to create a uniform mode of expression from different instruments; to let the theme shift from one group of instruments to another; to allow for individual interpretation and sometimes improvisation, yet maintaining the overall theme and mood of the piece; to change the tempo and expressions during the piece; and to create an impression of a whole through a sequence of movements.

Implementing lean thinking requires a concerted effort to initiate and realize a broad organizational development process. Not only is it necessary to coordinate the various activities directly associated with implementation of lean. But in view of the myriad of development initiatives in progress at any point in time such an effort cannot be planned as a stand-alone endeavor but should be viewed in relation to all development activities in progress in the company. For example, some initiatives well under way may support a lean effort, if slightly adjusted; other improvement initiatives may be in direct conflict with a lean effort and should be stopped. Thus, it is important to realize that a lean program necessarily has to tie in to the other development efforts undertaken; they are all competing for management attention and organizational capacity.

3.1   Interdependencies among improvement initiatives

Because many development activities have been initiated by different persons and functions, a major challenge to the management of a myriad of development initiatives is to identify ways in which they are interrelated and thereafter to seek to make use of this interdependency by creating an appropriate degree of synergy, for example by coordinating selected activities across functional and departmental lines. In addition to the traditional network of activities based on precedence relationships, there are several kinds of interdependencies.

Time horizon
The proposed development activities, as well as activities already in progress, may be characterized according to the built-in time horizon.
·   Short-term activities (0-2 years), for example a productivity increase project, a market penetration effort, or a quality improvement program
·   Medium-term activities (2-5 years); for example development of a new product and corresponding production system, introduction of new manufacturing process technology
·   Long-term activities (beyond 5 years); for example exploration of new business opportunities, implementing a global manufacturing strategy
Different criteria and performance measures apply to each time horizon, and it is very difficult, if meaningful at all, to project initiatives on to the same scale. However, a table indicating all development and improvement activities may inspire management to realize if there is a proper balance, and if short-term activities can be related to long-term activities, and vice versa.

Interdependencies across disciplines and functions
A large development effort, such as lean implementation, requires a contribution from several disciplines and functions. If these areas are viewed as parallel streams of activities, it is possible to identify interdependencies. For example, production engineering may make it possible to reduce the batch size drastically; organizing in production groups may provide a basis for decentralized planning, etc.

Business processes
In recent years, process thinking has brought new perspectives to the study of operations management. Key business processes as well as supporting processes are identified. Moreover, in several companies two or more parallel business processes have been identified, each pertaining to a specific product group or group of customers. Such a picture may support identification of needs for improvements as well as establishment of a coherent program for a concerted effort.

3.2   Forming and managing interrelated development activities

The traditional portfolio management has been used in product development to ensure an appropriate mixture of mature and novel products [6]. Also in financial management the portfolio theory has been used to seek a combination of development projects [7]. Several methods have been developed especially with the use of Management Science techniques to select among competing proposed development projects a portfolio that maximizes the expected revenue within a given budget.

However, internal development activities do not necessarily have the same types of interdependencies as do product development projects. Furthermore, turbulent internal and external conditions require that a company should be able to adopt a broader approach in order to capture the many interdependencies among internal development initiatives and to manage their dynamic nature.

Two examples from the empirical studies illustrate ways of managing interdependencies:

(1) A software company needed to change its process of delivering software from a Big Bang roll-out plan to more frequent releases, because of constant changing conditions and demands in the environment. They applied a new rolling wave plan combined with time boxes, and adopted elements from the concept of the learning organization.
(2) Three small manufacturing companies from different industries have adopted measures concerning the ability to act quickly. Their primary agent is visible management, e.g. managers walking and talking around and weekly information to all employees about the latest customer contacts and market situation.

We propose that implementing lean through an orchestrated effort be carried out by first analyzing interdependencies among internal development initiatives pertaining to lean implementation. It would encompass new proposed initiatives as well as activities already in progress. Second, they should be formed (composed, shaped, scoped) into either a campaign or a program. We see a campaign as a short-term effort of coordinated decentralized initiatives, typically running for two years, guided by a vision and slogan. A program represents a broader, well-structured set of development projects addressing both short-term and long-term goals.

Third, the campaign or program should be implemented by adopting an organizational learning approach, allowing for experimentation and adjustments called for by external and internal changes.

The case studies of Danish companies point to several means of orchestrating a campaign or a program adopting several ideas from the growing interest in agile project management [8].

Develop a vision

Many authors recommend that an overall vision be developed, e.g. [9], [1], [10]. Not only does a manufacturing vision serve as a link to corporate strategy, but it will motivate all persons involved in lean implementation by providing a shared, overall picture of where the company is heading, why, and with which results. Furthermore, a manufacturing vision will spur and focus creativity and will help explain: "What is in it for me?"

Dispatch only a few development initiatives at a time

The observed practice and thinking of management from the empirical studies showed that many managers deliberately overload the organization and initiate new development projects with no regard to the available capacity of the organization. Not only does this lead to stress in the organization and long through-put times for the projects, but management risks to loose overview of the large number of ongoing development initiatives.

Some companies were able to cut the number of development projects to one half, partly by discontinuing dying projects starving for management attention. In other companies a program was formed, but only a few development projects were selected, and furthermore only the first phases of these projects were actually dispatched. This allowed management to adjust the course within a short horizon and thus obtained a high degree of flexibility in view of the dynamic environment.

Visualizing

In a turbulent environment it is difficult to specify clearly the desired end-result. It is just like walking on the beach looking for a beautiful stone; first when you see a number of stones, it is possible to determine the beautiful ones. A way of coping with the many interdependencies among development initiatives is continuously to visualize the individual expected results as a basis for discussing how they eventually may contribute to the overall vision. Prototyping is such a means used in product development and software development. We propose that prototyping should be applied also for internal development.

Adopt a Time-Box planning principle

Traditional project planning is concerned with the time duration until a given activity is completed. In the face of the dynamic environment, software development managers have successfully adopted a Time-Box principle, characterized by frequent deliveries. At the end of the period, all parallel projects are discussed and coordinated. Typically, this leads to adjustments in direction and scope for the individual projects.

The management behavior will change

Adopting a more agile approach to orchestrate internal development initiatives will imply a change in the management behavior towards conceptual planning, coaching through interacting, and discussing issues, rather than detailed program and project planning.

4   Behavioral aspects

According to recent experiences of several Danish companies engaged in implementing lean the greatest challenge to ensure a successful implementation and realization of its potential lies in managing organizational changes. Following an organizational learning approach these experiences may be formulated into a set of recommendations:

Enable people to identify value for customers
To deliver value is the primary principle in lean thinking. Understanding the situation of the customers and end-users guides the assessment of which activities have value.

Enable people to identify waste
It is not sufficient to talk about reducing waste; each person should be told how to identify waste. For example, a short training course on the shop floor with built-in exercises enabled operators to see many different types of waste; and they started to propose ways of reducing waste.

Enable people to see a business process
Often the ERP system prescribes an in-process inventory inserted between two subsequent processes. In consequence operators miss the opportunity to get to know who is the sender and who is the receiver of goods and information in a business process. In one company, for spare parts produced in high volume managers chose to eliminate all in-process inventory along the production process; they even painted the boxes red and told the operators to contact the sender and receiver to discuss daily planning problems – with the result that the through-put time was reduced to one fourth.

Hasten slowly
Often, management is eager to rapidly implement planned changes in order to realize the identified potential benefit. Yet, the organizational changes are significant, for example new working habits, skills and attitudes have to be developed. This is more likely to be successful, if done at a pace in which the operators do not feel forced to adopt new qualifications and working modes. Therefore, a preparation phase should be inserted during which operators are trained and motivated, for example by use of games, exercises and simulations.
An organizational learning approach will favour making experiments. Among other things this will allow for anchoring the intended change, will create ownership and will lead to innovative proposed solutions from operators and middle management. This will also stimulate a continuous effort beyond a program or campaign to strive for lean.

5   Summary

The empirical studies of more than 30 Danish companies have suggested that at any point in time there are many internal development initiatives in progress. Therefore, implementation of lean, encompassing itself a blend of different development activities, will need to be tied in with ongoing initiatives and new proposals competing with for management attention and funding.

The complex environment and operations of modern companies call for means for developing a coherent picture of internal development activities. It was argued that being able to address the interdependencies among such activities is key to successful company development. A new approach was introduced, called orchestration, using the metaphor from conducting an orchestra or a band. Identifying and working with the interdependencies among the individual internal development activity was shown to form the basis for orchestration. Several dimensions of such interdependencies were offered.

Implementing lean through an orchestrated effort could be carried out as a program or a campaign, indicating that a concerted effort should be organized for a 2-3 year period. However, experience from the Danish companies indicated that the program should be planned and managed as an organizational learning process allowing for experimentation and adjustments called for by external and internal changes. Several means for orchestration were discussed. Also behavioral issues were identified and discussed.

The paper has pointed to a new direction for managing a multitude of simultaneous development activities in a complex and dynamic environment by introducing and exploring the notion of orchestration, suggesting agile project management methods be used for lean implementation.

References

1. Womack, J. P., and Jones, D. T. (1996) Lean Thinking, USA-Simon & Schuster.

2. Voss, C. A. (1988) Success and failure in advanced manufacturing technology, International Journal of Technology Management, No. 3.

3. Kaplan, Robert S. & Norton, David P. (2001) The Strategy-Focused Organization, Harvard Business School Press.

4. Mikkelsen, Hans (2005) Managing the myriad of projects (in Danish), Børsens Forlag.

5. Andersen, J.R., Riis, J.O. & Mikkelsen, H. (2005) Agile Project Portfolio Management – A contribution to Company Development Competence, Proceedings of the ICAM 2005 International Conference on Agile Manufacturing, Helsinki, Finland.

6. Cooper, R.G. (2005) Lean, Rapid, and Profitable New Product Development, Product Development Institute.

7. Sharpe, William F. (2000) Portfolio theory and capital markets, McGraw-Hill, New York.

8. Highsmith, Jim (2004) Agile Project Management, Addison-Wesley.

9. Kotter, John P (1996) Leading Change, Harvard Business School Press.

10. Riis, Jens O & Johansen, John (2003) Developing a manufacturing vision, International Journal of Production Planning & Control, Vol. 14, No. 4.

Set-up Reduction for Lean Cells and Multi-Machine Situations

Dirk Van Goubergen

Ghent University, Department of Industrial Management,
Technologiepark 903, B-9052 Zwijnaarde, Belgium
WWW home page: http:// tw18v.ugent.be

Abstract. Set-up reduction is a key requirement nowadays for many lean implementations. Current set-up reduction methodologies, most of them based on Shingo's SMED, focus merely on simple one machine-one person situations, where as many value streams contain long multi-stage machine lines (e.g., in food industry) or multi-machine cells (e.g., in metal industry). In these situations, using SMED is not enough, one needs to look at reducing and optimizing all set-up activities across all available persons and machines. This paper presents a comprehensive approach for these situations (MMSUR) that yields very good results and that is easy to apply with any improvement team of operators. A real life case study will be used to illustrate the approach and the results.

1 Introduction

These last years many companies have embarked on a journey implementing Lean as their major business strategy for improving competitiveness. Due to these lean implementations, set-up reduction - reducing the downtime between producing the last product A and good products B on a machine or a line - has become even more important than before. This freed-up capacity can be used for producing more (on bottlenecks that are not meeting takt time) or for more flexibility [1].

First of all it is clear that set-ups are one of the main root causes of several out of the 7 classical types of waste: overproduction, inventory and waiting [2].

While implementing flow using value stream mapping, one is often confronted with these high inventories and long lead times due to long set-ups on upstream shared resources and in downstream mixed model pacemaker loops. Here is the concept of the interval (or EPEI= Every Part Every Interval) critical. The more often products of a product family can be scheduled (i.e. the smaller the interval), the smaller the lot sizes that can be produced, the shorter the production lead times and the lower the inventories (finished goods and WIP). A procedure is shown in [3] on how to

Please use the following format when citing this chapter:

Van Goubergen, D., 2008, in IFIP International Federation for Information Processing, Volume 257,
Lean Business Systems and Beyond, Tomasz Koch, ed.; (Boston: Springer), pp. 295–303.

determine the future state EPEI for a mixed model cell by setting targets for set-up reduction.

2   Existing set-up reduction methodologies

2.1   Taxonomy of set-ups

In order to identify different types of set-ups and to characterize these situations in an unambiguous way, we propose following taxonomy. Two variables can be identified: the number of machines (X) and the number of persons (Y) that are performing the set-up on these machines. Hence every set-up can be characterized by a pair (X, Y).

2.2   Existing approaches for set-up reduction and their limitations.

Most existing publications on set-up reduction are based on the SMED system [4]. The main goal is to minimize what needs to be performed during the downtime. This is done in three steps [1]:
- SMED step 1: identifying what can be done while the machine is running (mostly organizational and method improvements)
- SMED step 2: moving set-up activities out of the downtime by technical solutions
- SMED step 3: minimizing and streamlining all remaining set-up activities

This approach is very straightforward and yields very good results in (1,1) and (N,1) situations. However in multi-person and multi-machine situations (1,M) and (N,M), a broader view is needed. It is not enough to apply SMED to each individual machine or person. There can be interaction between machines and between people. These situations are very common when dealing with long machine lines (present in many types of industry) and in lean mixed model cells involving multiple machines. Especially in these last ones, the lean principle of separating people and machines, results often in one person being responsible for several machines. Also there can be a varying number of operators in these cells (flexing in or out) in order to match the capacity with the demand (according to takt time). Existing literature does not deal with these situations.

3   An overall approach for multi-machine situations MMSUR

3.1   Introduction

Our proposed approach, named MMSUR - Multi Machine Set-Up Reduction - still uses the SMED system as the basic technique for looking at individual changeover activities as they are performed by an operator on a machine. But we need to take a look at the broader picture in order to have a better approach for identifying where to start in a multi machine situation and how to make the best use of the available operators in order to obtain the optimal set-up reduction of the whole cell or line.

We want to minimize the overall downtime of the cell or of the machine line. Note that we assume here that first a target for set-up reduction has been established before the start of the project (e.g., based on an EPEI calculation).

3.2   Steps of MMSUR

Figure 1 depicts an overview of the different steps of our methodology (13 steps). A key tool is the 'Multi-Activity Diagram'. This old industrial engineering tool (examples and background information can be found in [5]) is used in two ways (*Step 1*):

- The Machine Multi-Activity Diagram: A column is assigned to every machine/process step in a consecutive (logical) order. All activities are drawn as a block in the column of the machine on which they are performed, at the correct vertical position along the time axis. The Multi-Activity shows the overall downtime of the machine line as well as the waiting time of every machine (when no one is performing a set-up activity on this machine)
- The Person Multi-Activity Diagram shows who is doing what and when. All activities are blocks and every column corresponds with a person.

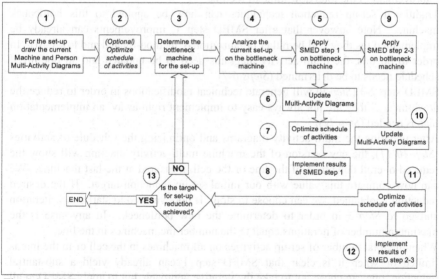

Fig. 1. MMSUR - Set-up reduction methodology for multi-machine situations

We will provide now additional information on the less self explanatory steps:
Step 2: The Multi-Activity Diagrams that were created in *Step 1* illustrate the current way of performing the set-up, before applying any set-up reduction techniques. However, this does not necessarily represent the optimal way of doing the set-up (given the current activities and available persons). At this point we can consider rescheduling and/or re-assigning the activities (blocks in the Multi-Activity Diagram) to the available persons by shifting the corresponding blocks (without

knowing all the details of the activities that occur inside every block). Hence, downtime may be reduced and/or work balance might be improved (more details on how to optimize the schedule will be given in Section 3.3). This step however is optional and will only be executed if there is clear evidence that a substantial downtime reduction can be achieved. If not, then it is better to immediately proceed to the next step in order to reduce set-up activities first, especially if it is clear that some quick wins can be achieved. An optimization of the activity schedule will follow afterwards on the improved situation.

Step 3: A lot of set-ups of multi-stage machine lines are rather complex because several workstations are involved with many (sometimes long) activities and because of the relationships between these activities on the different machines and between the different persons. Hence, it is in most cases advisable to deal with the set-up problem in small steps instead of tackling the whole problem at once. Therefore the approach that we propose in this Section is iterative. Set-up reduction techniques can be applied in an iterative way. In every iteration we identify in this step the bottleneck machine with regard to the set-up. This is the machine on which the most work needs to be performed. The activities performed on this machine are very likely to be part of the 'critical path' of the changeover. A reduction of the set-up time on this bottleneck will result in the best ratio effectiveness/effort for the improvement of the total downtime of the line.

Traditional set-up reduction techniques can now be applied to this bottleneck machine. Note however that after SMED step 1, improvements can already be implemented (as they will be rather organizational, method-related and low cost). In order to do this, the multi-activity diagrams need to be updated and an optimized schedule needs to be determined (*Steps 6-7*).

SMED step 2-3 (*Step 9*) will generate technical modifications in order to reduce the downtime; as they are not always easy to implement right away, an implementation plan is needed (*Step 12*).

After updating the multi-activity diagrams and optimizing the schedule of activities (*Step 10-11*), the new version of the machine multi-activity diagram will show the reduced overall downtime of the line or the cell, measured at the last machine. We can now compare this value with our initial set-up reduction target. If the desired reduction is obtained, we can choose to stop. If not, we need to start a new iteration and go to *Step 3* in order to determine the new bottleneck. In any case is the maximum number of iterations equal to the number the machines in the line.

When the total number of set-up activities on all machines in the cell or in the line is limited or when it is clear that SMED step 1 can already yield a substantial reduction, one can chose not to take the iterative approach, but to apply SMED to all machines at the same time. In that case it is not necessary to identify the set-up bottleneck; one needs to update the multi-activity diagrams only once.

3.3   Optimizing the schedule of activities in a qualitative, diagrammatic way

The machine multi-activity diagram shows the downtime of the cell or the line, with blocks indicating all activities that need to be performed. The primary objective is to

schedule these blocks resulting in a minimal downtime; however we can identify secondary objectives:
- we want a balanced workload across all operators
- if there is slack (waiting time for an operator), it is preferable to have this grouped at the end of the changeover, so that this person can be used for another task
- we want to minimize the movements of the operators

There are some constraints such as a labor constraint (max. number of operators available) and sequence constraints among activities (precedence, concurrence, etc.). These have to be identified first, but in practice it suffices to have operators on the improvement team that are knowledgeable about the set-up activities.

Starting with a blank machine and person multi-activity template on a wall, the team can come up with a schedule (using post-it notes or paper pieces) as follows:
- locate the bottleneck machine with regard to the set-up and try to schedule all activities on this machine with leaving as little slack as possible, then schedule the other activities on the critical path (if applicable).
- Put the scheduled activities on the person multi-activity diagram
- Schedule the remaining activities on the machine multi-activity diagram taking into account all constraints; put them afterwards on the person multi-activity diagram to check the balance of the workload.
- The labor constraint and the movement constraint can be checked visually on the machine multi-activity diagram:
  o When drawing a horizontal line at any time point, no more blocks can be crossed than corresponding to the number of available persons
  o Connecting the blocks assigned to the same person results in a line; the more zigzagging (and less vertical), the more movement.
- Repeat the last two steps until an acceptable and feasible solution has been found.

4 Case application

4.1 Problem Description

In this Section we will describe the use and the results of our proposed methodology on a case study in food industry in Europe. This plant had a long machine line for manufacturing a product family of snack products. The process started with raw material and at the end of the line the packaged finished product came out. From a Value Stream Mapping point of view, this line was nothing more than a series of process boxes connected with FIFO lanes. A lean implementation in this situation should focus on two efforts: increasing the reliability of the line and increasing the flexibility (or decreasing the interval – EPEI). The main focus of this project was on the flexibility part, as initially the line produced all 6 flavors in one week (EPEI= 1 week) but marketing was planning on introducing additional flavors, adding up to 11 in total. The objective was to keep the interval one week.

Additionally, the market for this product family was growing fast, so any additional freed up capacity through downtime reduction was also important. The engineering department was, at the time of this project, working on building a second line.

Initially the set-up took about 2,5 hours and was conducted by 13 operators. With an hourly cost of all personnel of 500 €/hr and a net profit loss due to lost production of 2520 €/hr (due to the growing demand), it is straightforward to determine the total yearly cost of this downtime: 1,6 million € for 5 set-ups a week and 3,2 million € after introducing the new flavors.

The line consist of following machines/workstations: 22 baking ovens (in parallel), a vibrating conveyor, a (wet) coating machine, a drying oven, a cooling conveyor, a transport conveyor, a multi head weighing unit and a packaging machine. Hence this is a (8,13) set-up.

An improvement team was established, composed of operators, technical people and the production area manager. Engineering people were involved during the improvement process when needed.

4.2   Application of MMSUR – the results

As explained in the previous section, the first step is to make the machine multi-activity diagram of the set-up of the line. This way the bottleneck, being the machine that needs to be studied first, can be determined. In this case however, there was no standardized work method for the different operators, so it was not possible to draw the initial diagrams. We chose to study all machines at the same time based on a changeover recorded on video. All activities were drawn on the multi-activity diagrams and SMED step 1 was executed, resulting in a 60% downtime reduction. The remaining changeover time was 60 minutes, only using 11 operators. Figure 2 and 3 show the machine and person multi-activity diagrams before and after SMED step 1.

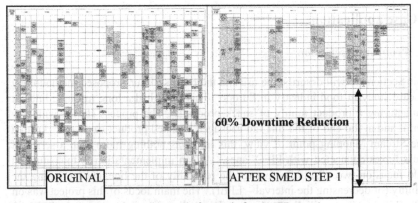

Fig. 2. Machine multi-activity diagram before and after SMED step 1

The new set-up method was immediately introduced and after a short learning period, the effective set-up time was a little more than 1 hour. In the meanwhile

MMSUR Step 9 (see Figure 1) was performed. The improvement team looked for technical SMED step 2-3 solutions, both multi-activity diagrams were updated again and all blocks were rescheduled (MMSUR Step 10-11) resulting in a set-up time of about 30 minutes (an overall reduction of 80% compared to the starting situation). Additionally the number of people needed for this set-up method was reduced to only 7 persons. An initial estimate of the cost of the technical proposals showed that it was only a fraction of the yearly downtime cost-reduction that could be obtained. Figure 4 depicts both multi-activity diagrams for this new situation

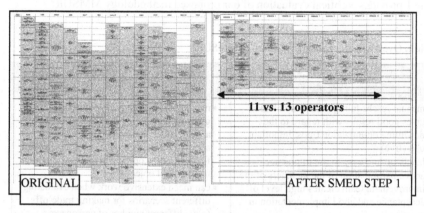

Fig. 3. Person multi-activity diagram before and after SMED step 1

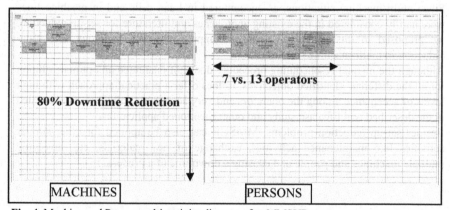

Fig. 4. Machine and Person multi-activity diagram after MMSUR.

4.3   Other applications of MMSUR

Besides the described case study, our methodology was also applied in other cases (on different multi machine situations in different types of industry). Some results:
-    steel plant continuous caster (3,8): 72 to 30 minutes (60% reduction)

- steel galvanizing line (2,4): 450 to 100 minutes (78%)
- ice cream processing line (5,2) : 80 to 10 minutes (88%)
- lighting assembly cell (6,3): 390 to 25 minutes (ù)
- food extrusion line (7,2): 171 to 40 minutes (78%)

5 Critical evaluation of MMSUR and conclusion

Table 1 provides a critical evaluation of our proposed methodology MMSUR.

Table 1. Overview of a critical evaluation of MMSUR

Strong points	Weak points
• manual rescheduling of activity blocks gives good results with regard to the downtime optimization (most important objective) • hands-on and easy to use in practice • active participation of the members of the improvement team creates high level of acceptance and good implementation in practice • can handle large problems	• manual rescheduling of activity blocks gives no certainty about the optimality of all objectives, it is only qualitative approach; a mathematical model is needed for finding the optimal solution with regard to all objectives • can mean extensive work when evaluating different scenarios for making trade-offs (e.g., different number of persons vs. downtime)

Since multi-machine situations, as encountered in Lean cells and in machine lines were hardly considered in the existing approaches and literature for set-up reduction, we proposed in this paper MMSUR, a comprehensive methodology for set-up reduction in multi-machine situations.

Although the manual rescheduling procedure does not guarantee an optimal solution for all the different identified objectives, it does offer a practical approach with high levels of acceptance among the operators and very acceptable solutions, as illustrated in the described real life case study and other mentioned applications.

Besides set-up reduction problems, MMSUR can also be applied for other similar activities like maintenance activities, exchange of raw materials, etc. involving multiple machines and people and causing a downtime of a process.

References

1. Van Goubergen, D. and H. Van Landeghem, Rules for integrating fast changeover capabilities into new equipment design. *International Journal of Robotics and Computer Integrated Manufacturing*, 18: p. 205-214 (2002).

2. Prasad, B., A structured methodology to implement judiciously the right JIT tactics. *Production Planning and Control*, 6(6): p. 564-577 (1995).

3. Duggan, K., *Creating Mixed Model Value Streams*. (Productivity Press, New York, NY (USA) 2002).

4. Shingo, S., *A revolution in Manufacturing: the SMED system*. (Productivity Press, Cambridge, MA 1985).

5. Kanawaty, G., *Introduction to Work Study*. (International Labour Office, Geneva, 1992).

Lean and Self Directed Teamwork - Differences, Difficulties and Future Developments – A Case Study

Ina Goller[1], Manfred Kehr[2], and Christoph Lindinger[1]

1 PTA Praxis fuer teamorientierte Arbeitsgestaltung GmbH Office Zurich, Switzerland
WWW home page: http://www.pta-zuerich.com
2 Parker Hannifin GmbH Division Ermeto, Bielefeld, Germany
WWW home page: http://www.parker.com

Abstract. A value stream oriented organisational structure following the Lean philosophy, often is seen as contradictory to the concept of self directed teamwork (SDT). Whereas SDT is broadly defined by the takeover of responsibilities for a certain range of management tasks by a team within defined boundaries Lean is defined as an approach of continuous improvement for process design and development with an advanced toolbox and clear standards. The following case study describes two manufacturing companies that implemented SDT during the 90's before they decided to implement Lean strategies on the shop-floor level. Both companies used different approaches. In both cases the "new" Lean philosophy caused reasonable friction with the existing team structure. In this study we will describe the perceived differences and difficulties as well as the similarities between the two concepts. As a conclusion a way to integrate the two concepts will be considered.

1 Introduction

A growing number of production systems claim to be the only solution for a successful continuous improvement process with convincing results. In practice, even the Lean philosophy stands for a great variety of "homemade" systems only sharing some basic assumptions. The focus of all improvement activities is considered to be the value stream.

In recent years a majority of globally acting manufacturing companies have implemented such a system. Some put all their activities under the roof of TPM [1, 2]. Others use the EFQM model [3] as their guideline or the Six Sigma approach [4] while another group of companies name their production system in one or the other way Lean, mostly based on the ideas of the Toyota Production System [5]. Most of

Please use the following format when citing this chapter:

Goller, I., Kehr, M. and Lindinger, C., 2008, in IFIP International Federation for Information Processing, Volume 257, Lean Business Systems and Beyond, Tomasz Koch, ed.; (Boston: Springer), pp. 305–313.

them share a holistic point of view. They do not only want to contribute to an improvement of selected processes, but also claim to be part of the culture of a company. In the public mind still each of them is seen as a tool for one focused intention.

The concept of Self Directed Teamwork (SDT) [6] experienced a strong renaissance during the 90s after the publication of Womack, Jones and Ross [7] not only in the automobile industry. It was often seen as the European answer to the Japanese KAIZEN [8] philosophy and all of its spin-offs. In the northern part of Europe SDT received a growing attention as an effective organisational tool to increase productivity [9]. Although both concepts (Lean and SDT) are related to the same principle objectives they have often been seen as antagonists.

2   Contents of the case study

The paper investigates some frequently found opinions about the assumed and existing differences between the Lean and the SDT concept at two manufacturing sites of two different companies of the metal industry. Both companies gained experiences with both concepts for some time. The presented findings are based on expert interviews with managers of the two companies (Lean managers (N=3), line managers (N=5)) and expert consultants of the Lean and SDT concept (N=4).

The interviews were done either on telephone or face-to-face and took approximately 1,5 hours. There was a written guideline focusing on the following topics:

- Definition of Lean and SDT in the company
- Perceived shortcomings
- Perceived differences as well as similarities of the two concepts
- Possibility of integrating the two concepts

The question about the concept definition were asked in order to assure that our definition of SDT and Lean will fit to the concepts valid in the company.

The results will be described in three passages following the two main issues:

- Differences and difficulties of the two concepts
- Similarities of the two concepts and conclusions

3   Definitions

3.1   Self Directed Teamwork (SDT)

Since the 1980's the organisational concept SDT is perceived as a major means to improve flexibility of an organisation. It promises substantial success for manufacturing industry through an increase of productivity and reduced labour costs. In order to register a successful implementation of SDT a certain framework must be given including the set-up of a team-orientated factory layout (e.g. manufacturing cells).

In this paper, SDT is understood as semi-autonomous teamwork [6]. In this context a team is defined as a group of people who combine different skills on a common purpose or goal with restricted managerial supervision. Such a team organises itself, plans and controls the processes and tasks within a framework that was previously defined by the management.

Interacting with the outside world, the team is represented by a team speaker who usually has been elected by all members of the team. This team speaker is thereby often equal in status to the other team members and a productive worker himself. In this context, the team speaker should in no case carry out all non-manufacturing tasks alone. Recent developments like the star model [9] allocate those tasks among a defined number of team members (stars) who take care of essential responsibilities.

It also takes a longer time for a team to become able to work fully semiautonomous-ly. The concept cannot be deployed as a means for rapid results but it has proved to be a promising instrument for reaching long-term success [6].

3.2 Lean Concepts

Lean has its origins in the Toyota Production System developed by Taichii Ohno [10]. The elimination of waste due to restricted resources was at that time one of the driving principles. The customer and the fulfilment of his needs began to play a crucial role in the further steps of its development. Womack and Jones [11] outlined the basic components of a modern Lean system:

1   Specify value from the standpoint of the customer,
2   Identify the value stream for each product family,
3   Make the product flow,
4   Allow the customer to pull production forward and
5   Work toward perfection in your offering.

The value stream defines the Lean Enterprise [12]. The main objectives of the Lean Enterprise are to correctly identify and specify value to the ultimate customer in all its products and services. Waste is any activity, which the customer is not willing to pay for since it adds no value to the product or service and often at times, is consuming resources. Waste exists in all parts of the business – front office to the factory. This effort results in redefining the current value stream to one of value adding activities and what is called sustaining activities. Sustaining steps are defined as, non-value-added activities performed for one of two reasons: it is required by law or regulation or because it contributes to business effectiveness.

The Lean approach defines the tools and principles that determine how all aspects of a business operate from sales through distribution. In order to be successful, one must follow a rigid process. Depending on 'easy goals', savings can be realized in several months and have an immediate impact. However, one must be committed for the long run as some change efforts can take as long as 2 years an more.

4 The two companies

4.1 The motion control parts manufacturer

The first company looked at in this case study is a European Division of a North American corporation that manufactures products for the motion control process at three different locations in Europe. The European headquarter is stationed in Germany and employs around 700 employees. Since 1996 the company introduced SDT during an implementation process of 4 years with striking success. In the German plant, around 80 teams were installed not only in the production department but also in administration and other service departments.

Dedicated facilitators for the transition process were selected within the company that have been formerly working in different departments and turned back to their line alignments after a certain period of time.

2002 the mother company decided to aim the corporation to the Lean culture for all the divisions throughout the globe. Each division had to name a Lean manager. Depending on the size of the company a certain number of Lean leaders who are acting as supporters for line management were nominated. The general managers of each divisions act as sponsors. A measurement system called 'The Lean journey' which allows each division to rate its status quo regarding Lean was introduced. Today both concepts are alive, but Lean is seen as the dominant model.

4.2 The packaging material manufacturer

The second company also belongs to a North American corporation. It manufactures packaging materials for different market sectors at its site in Southern Germany with around 1.300 employees. The first attempt to establish self-directed teamwork started 1994 in selected areas in the production department with little success. Nevertheless the concept was rolled out throughout the entire production department.

Constant struggle with the concept due to disputes over the role of the team speaker was one of the reasons for management to decide in the year 2000 to readjust the model. Until then the team speaker was elected by all team members but never fully accepted by the middle management. The team speaker was replaced by a team leader function. A project team introduced further adjustments of the SDT concept that was implemented with the help of an experienced facilitator.

At the same time the corporation initiated the global roll out of its Lean model under the headline 'Continuous Improvement'. The approach was launched with a clear statement to use Lean and Six Sigma together as a concept for maximizing opportunities by improving the company's competitiveness and efficiency.

In the very beginning, the new concept was only applied for projects limited to process improvements with considerable cost reduction effects. Only trained experts were participating at those projects. Shop-floor teams had nearly no exposure to the new concept. The corporation invested a considerable sum for trainings of the selected experts in Lean and Six Sigma techniques. SDT and Lean seemed to belong to two different worlds. Today there are attempts to integrate both concepts, because more and more projects tackle value stream processes, where shop-floor workers are directly touched and involved.

5   Differences and Difficulties between the two concepts

There are undoubtedly differences and incompatibilities between SDT and the Lean philosophy. Because Lean is focusing on the value stream, experts state that it looks merely at the process and not at the people. This results in a frequently observed opinion that Lean is a neutral and technical approach (hard facts concept) whereas SDT with its clear focus on people is perceived as strictly people oriented (soft facts concept). Therefore a lot of people in both companies don't see connections, because in their eyes SDT only seems to cover actions regarding the quality of collaboration while Lean is strictly perceived as a toolbox for process improvements.

Most of the perceived differences and difficulties are arising out of the different focus. While Lean can only be implemented in a top-down manner (the commitment and involvement of the top management is a given), SDT can only be implemented with a combination of both top-down and bottom-up approaches. Agreement processes are essential to all implementation steps and need a defined scope of action. Voluntariness of the team members seems to be inevitable for SDT whereas Lean can more or less be ordered. Lean has to deal with the human factor only when the concept encounters significant reluctant behaviour endangering the success of the implementation process. This difference is caused by the methodologies used in the two concepts. Every step you take in Lean is formalized. The SDT model in contrast is using the empowered employee to come up with the best solution in a given situation. If a team finds a good solution it will be implemented as a standard mostly for the individual team alone and is based on agreements.

Empowered employees are also important for Lean, but here they act in a different setting. The basic idea is that the process is designed in such a simple and reliable manner that a single employee can control each possible deviation. The decision process is insofar reduced to a selection process of different options. The decision making process differs between clearly defined boundaries for every step (Lean) and a more fuzzy approach (SDT).

For both companies this had its impact on the selection process for the facilitators and trainers. For the SDT concept the social competency of a facilitator are of major importance as well as training abilities and communication competencies. The Lean leaders receive in contrary their vast amount of training in tools and techniques. Only a short part deals with soft factors. Accordingly the selection process took place.

Another difference deals with the communication and information structures. Both systems rely on the same communication channels – e.g. team meetings and visualisation boards. The team meetings have a clear structure in both systems. In SDT team members are encouraged to bring forward their own topics additional to the standard agenda. Lean is working on given standards alone and will not allow contributions, which do not belong to the focussed topic.

This shows another fundamental difference. Lean is perceived as a way to reduce complexity because everybody is focused on one problem only. SDT is in contrast focusing on the problems of the employees whenever they bring them forward. It therefore leads to sometimes even more complexity. As a result of this, Lean is often perceived as the more pragmatic approach. But on the other hand in both companies have been areas were the SDT model was implemented prior to Lean. The degree of reluctant behaviour towards the Lean tools was significantly lower then in other areas where the concept was introduced without existing SDT. There seems to be no short cut for dealing with complexity.

Table 1. The perceived differences of the two concepts: an overview

Lean	SDT
▪ Hard facts concept	▪ Soft facts concept
▪ Focus on value stream and process	▪ Focus on people
▪ Goal: process improvement	▪ Goal: improvement of collaboration
▪ Top-down implementation	▪ Mix of top-down / bottom-up implementation
▪ Can be ordered from top-down	▪ Needs voluntariness of team members
▪ Formalized system, uses standardized methods	▪ Uses the employee for finding the best solution
▪ Pragmatic, result driven system	▪ Behavioral, agreement driven system

It is most interesting that the further involved into Lean a company gets, the less these differences are emphasized. It seems clear that the further you go into the Lean journey the more you have to rely on concepts and ideas out of the SDT concept like empowering people and enforcing ownership. And obviously the degree of a deeper understanding of what both concepts are all about increases, which make their appearance more and more alike.

6   Similarities of the two concepts and conclusions

As all expert interviews and observations in the two companies indicate, there are a lot of similarities between the two concepts as well. First of all the overall objective seems to be the same: establishing a continuous improvement process for the company. Both SDT and Lean refer to this as the primary goal. Standard working procedures are also demanded by both concepts. The way in which they are accomplished however is indeed completely different (as described in chapter 5).

Although Lean is often stated as the easier way to improve a company and hence the concept that is able to reduce complexity all experts are in agreement that there still remains the need to think. Both concepts have a holistic understanding of improvement and therefore are in the end intellectually challenging. The development of individuals is an inevitable precondition.

This leads to another similarity: the need for extended training. Lean as well as SDT is relying on empowered employees who are needed to make sensible, useful and correct decisions. The training needs are significant for the supervisory level too. Lean offers only in the beginning a more efficient support for weak managers because of its standardised procedures and measurements. When the quick wins are achieved the going gets tougher and all the competencies that are related to leadership are again in desperate need.

Both systems require a major cultural change for a company and cannot be easily implemented in a year or two. Both concepts are vulnerable to outside interferences through unexpected growth or downsizing processes. Since both concepts need a lot of care and are time consuming they will degenerate if not enough energy is delivered to sustain the assistance and support for the vital elements of the concepts. Therefore only with a long-term commitment of the top management the organisational change process is possible in the long run.

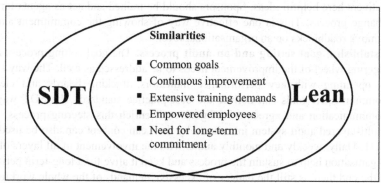

Fig. 1. Where both concepts meet

There is one basic statement all experts agree upon: if Lean would not exist it had to be invented as the perfect extension of SDT. Lean without SDT can run successfully up to a certain degree. After first steps into the improvement cycle however the management tends to find out they cannot improve the processes anymore. The lack of competencies in social and communication skills hinders the management, the Lean leaders and the employees similarly. Suddenly not everything can be clarified with a simple, ready-made standard – everybody who is involved has to make a contribution. This needs more commitment and ownership than Lean alone can create.

Integration of the two concepts is more complicated as it seems in the beginning. In the two considered companies this attempt could not be fully executed because a variety of clashes and misunderstandings happened. The conclusion of the experts suggests that one has to be absolutely clear about what to take from which concept and how to implement it. Nevertheless there are defined elements that are in need regardless of the main focus of the improvement a company is opting for:

1. **Enhance empowerment on all levels of the workforce**. Competency frameworks for every team as in SDT should be implemented but also simple problem solving tools from Lean.
2. **Define rules and consequences applying to everybody in the company**. The most important will be: you are either part of the party or you will have to find another company to work for. If employees will violate this ground rule one has to act accordingly.
3. **Train middle management not only in problem solving tools but also in all aspects of leadership**. SDT here gives a good clue which competencies are needed to help the employees developing. Continuous training and also a more forceful selection of supervisors have to take place.
4. **Establish a coaching process for all levels of the organisation.** Coaching will gain more and more importance for both concepts. It is an essential tool for SDT regarding the supervisory level and inevitable to sustain Lean after advanced levels of the process have been reached.
5. **Make sure that the top management stays involved.** The Lean philosophy delivers here helpful ideas. Sponsors should be trained and act as agents for the change process. This is one effective way of showing the commitment and to remove roadblocks on an organisational level.
6. **Establish a goal setting and an audit process.** The goal setting process as a steering wheel of the improvement needs to be addressed as well. The way Lean is operating with key performance indicators, tracking boards and clearly communicated goals can deliver the best practice standard. The SDT way of communication and agreement of goals will enrich this steering process. The multi-layered audit system introduced by the Lean concept can also be used for SDT. Daily, weekly and monthly audits with the involvement of all layers of the organisation help to sustain the process and keep it alive for a long-term period.

In the end there is still the danger of excessive demands of the whole workforce, employees and management alike. Being able to keep to small steps, integrating the concept into the world of the company and throwing a party if success is seen, seem to be still the only remedies for that.

References

1. Y. Takahashi, T. Osada, TPM: Total Productive Maintenance (Asian Productivity Organization, Tokyo, 1990).

2. Productivity Press Development Team, TPM: Collected Practices and Cases (Productivity Press, University Park, 2005).

3. K. J. Zink, TQM als integratives Managementkonzept (Hanser, München, 2004).

4. M. Harry, Richard Schroeder, Six Sigma (Campus, Frankfurt a.M., 2000).

5. J. K. Liker, The Toyota Way: 14 Management Principles from the World's Greatest Manufacturer (McGraw-Hill, New York, 2004).

6. Hurtz, A. in: Werkstattmanagement – Organisation und Informatik, edited by E. Scherer., P. Schönsleben and E. Ulich (vdf Hochschulverlag AG, Zürich), pp. 115-129.

7. J. P. Womack, D. T. Jones and D. Ross, The Machine that changed the world (Harper Collins Publisher, New York, 1990).

8. M. Imai, KAIZEN-The Key to Japan's Competitive Success (McGraw-Hill, New York, 1986).

9. I.Goller, T.Bronnsack, Von den Besten lernen, REFA Nachrichten. Heft 3, 34-38 (2006).

10. T. Ohno, Toyota Production System (Productivity Press, University Park, 1995).

11. J. P. Womack and D. T. Jones, Lean Thinking: Banish Waste and Create Wealth in Your Corporation (Simon & Schuster, New York, 1996).

12. W.A. Levinson, R. Rerick, Lean Enterprise: A Synergistic Approach to Minimizing Waste (ASQ Quality Press, Milwaukee, 2002).

PART TWO

Bridging Production Process with Sales and Distribution

Gathering Production Processes of Services and Goods: Towards the Mixed Enterprise

ALIX Thècle, VALLESPIR Bruno
LAPS/GRAI University Bordeaux 1 – ENSEIRB – UMR CNRS 5131
351, cours de la liberation 33405 TALENCE CEDEX FRANCE
tel.: +33 5 4000 6532 fax: +33 5 4000 6644

Abstract. In 2003, the French government advised manufacturing enterprises to associate service to the product they manufacture in order to keep competitive and profitable. This service orientation represents a huge challenge that impacts organisation, management, and control of industrial firms but also people's focus and skills which must be less technology oriented but rather customer oriented. Here we focus on the organisation required to propose products and services at the same time. In this objective, this paper recalls the differences and similarities between goods and services characteristics, processes and problematic to provide in fine a functional and control grids of an enterprise able to propose to its customers a combined (good+service) offer or a simple one.

1 Introduction

In 2003, a French governmental report invited manufacturing firms to associate peripheral services to the products they deliver to gain in competitiveness and to be profitable [1]. As SMEs are aligned from a competitive point of view as regard to technologies or know how mastered, a way of positioning manufacturers on durable bases is to direct their offers to meet customers' interests. This means to complement the product oriented added value with a customer oriented added value proposing to their customers offers made up with tangible goods and additional services [2].
The consequences of this new positioning are twofold:

- for manufacturing firms because they are obliged to extend their abilities or to develop alliances with services providers,
- for services providers that are obliged to mass customize their offer to face a new concurrency.

The objective of this paper is to analyze the implications of this trend for manufacturing firms willing to extend their offer internally and then become mixed enterprises. So, after a slight reminder of the characteristics of goods and services,

Please use the following format when citing this chapter:

Alix, T. and Vallespir, B., 2008, in IFIP International Federation for Information Processing, Volume 257, Lean Business Systems and Beyond, Tomasz Koch, ed.; (Boston: Springer), pp. 317–325.

the paper will detail the production and "servuction" processes to underline the elements that are taken into account in each one separately. The goal is to demonstrate that as goods and services, the processes to create them are neither exclusive and can be combined in a provuction process. The problematic proper to each industry are developed in a fourth part in order to be taken into account during the design study of a mix enterprise. It emerges a functional and control grid of a provuction system that underline the main function to manage in such a case.

2   Contrast between services and goods characteristics

Services are most of the time defined in contrast with goods using attributes that do not concern these latest [3], [4]. Even if the delineation is less and less obvious [5], [6], the four main attributes used to characterise services are intangibility, heterogeneity perishability and inseparability.

Intangibility refers to service immateriality. However, since a need of service can results in a set of materials that make it tangible for a physical distribution, or that a set of material respond to a need rendering a service, materials and services can be twin vision of a same object and components of a whole whose dominant is service oriented. In this case, we use the term of *'product'* for the couple (*material, service*) and *'basic service'* for the delivered service. Then a service can exist as such (intangible pure service that can not be stored) or supported by a product [7], [8].

The customer implication in pure service delivery system confers to services an attribute of heterogeneity which is mainly explained by the presence of human factor that influences the quality of result and prevents service standardization [9]. However, because an expected result is defined, the human factor only implies a customer particularization, as it exists in manufacturing production. A standard process can be defined that could allow to homogenize pure services.

Another strong characteristic of services is that they are perishable and can not be stored because of their intangibility [10]. This characteristic loses its meaning since basic services are stored in a product and that basic services such as training can be stored in systems, knowledge, persons.... Moreover, if the concept of perishability is associated to the concept of obsolescence, materials are also perishable.

Inseparability constitutes the last strong attribute of the services. It results in the simultaneous contribution of the customer and the producer during service set up. As some parts of the processes are automated because of the search for profitability, service delivery system is more and more disconnected from the customer whose presence is not mandatory since the beginning of the service design. Conversely and even if it implies heavy constraints related to the productivity, customers are more and more implied in the design phase of goods.

As we can see, the four properties above-mentioned do not make possible to radically distinguish goods from services that can have the same attributes under time and space scale constraints. The narrowness of the border between them led to the conclusion that there can be a common base to create them.

3   Contrast between services and goods processes

The service delivery system corresponds to the systematic and coherent organization of all the physical and human elements coming from the customer/enterprise interface that are necessary for service delivery according to predetermined commercial characteristics and quality levels of appreciation [11], (see figure 1). The three elements required to deliver a pure intangible service are the customers, the contact people and the physical support.

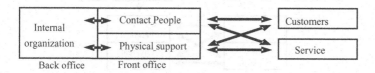

Fig. 1. Service delivery system

The production process integrates all the processes that are necessary for the transformation of materials using technical and human resources (see figure 2). Then the three elements required to deliver goods are technical human resources, technical operative resources and raw materials.

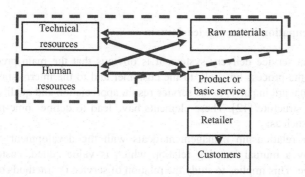

Fig. 2. Production process

The main difference is the place of the customer. Considered as an actor in the service delivery system, he is out of the production process. The justification comes from the idea that the customer is mandatory to define the service he needs and that he creates and consumes the service during the same period of time. However as seen before, a part of the service process can be automated in back office for profitability raisons and personalized to the customer in front office. This way of doing is coherent regarding the current manufacturing process for which the customers can intervene to personalize the product he wants to buy before its end.

The practical similarities lead us to propose a common provuction process that can be instantiated to the provision of personalized goods and/or services that can be automated for a part of their realization (figure 3).

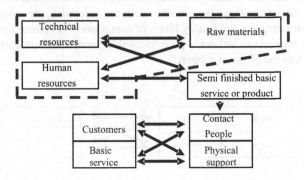

Fig. 3. Provuction process

4   Contrast between services and goods problematic

The preoccupations in the service domain and in the production domain are quite different. This implies that the focus is not put on the same things and that even if some issues are common, they can have different meanings according to the context.

4.1   Preoccupation in the service domain

Regarding the service delivery system, it is obvious that the main preoccupations will refer to the process by itself, to the customer and to the interrelations between the persons that are in party, to the service result, appreciation and quality, and to the system offer structure [12]. These elements have lead to define some management problematic such as:

- Customer relationship management deals with the development of customer loyalty by a mutual learning relation which is value added, customized and interactive. This implies to study the relation of service i.e. methods of exchange, communication protocols for the before and after sales, consumer behavior of purchase, customer forms of participation …
- Quality management because since the customer is co producer of the service, the level of quality of a service depends on:
  - The different implications and interrelations: customer, contact people, other customers,
  - The result of the service,
  - The operations fluidity, exchange facilities between individuals.

  Contextual and subjective, the customer feelings (influenced by his personal needs, prior experience, environment…) act on its perception of the quality of the service and on its decision of service purchase.

- Load and capacity management because as service are subject to demand fluctuations, it is then very difficult to anticipate the quantity and the type of service to be returned. A challenge is to determine the right service to provide (sub problematic of quality) to the right customer (sub problematic of customer relationship management) in the right place (sub problematic of (e-)distribution) at the right price (sub problematic of price fixing and by extension of yield management).

4.2   Preoccupation in the production domain

Regarding the production domain, the main preoccupations refer to the process management by itself, to the resource management (human or technical), to the product management (raw material, semi finished or finished) and to the synchronization between the products and the resources. Other elements such as distribution, sales... are also managed but the focus depth can be different regarding the enterprise objectives. As in service delivery the customer relationship management and the quality management seems to be key functions of management but have different representation:
- the customer relationship is most of the time only managed before the sales and consists in a marketing action to identify the product to manufacture.
- the quality criterion depend mostly on a functional schedule of conditions, even if an evolution can be noted to take all these elements into account because of competitiveness growth.

5   Generic model of a mix enterprise

This part assumes that as a mixed enterprise will propose goods and services, its models must gather the particularities of each output separately. Then, the functional model and control grid proposed are based on the provuction process presented before and on the management functions that can not be bypassed when a good or a service is provided. The formalism used is the GRAI formalism [13].

5.1   Basic components of the provuction system

The provuction process presented before permits to define the basic components of the mix enterprise. Are distinguished:
- technical resources: material elements physical support for the transformation activity,
- products which can split up into raw materials (inputs for production process) and semi finished / finished products or services (output of provuction process),
- human resources which can be split into human resources with technical competencies that intervene in back office on the product realisation and human resources with commercial competencies that intervene in front office to personalize the output of the process,

- the customer: individual recipient of the combined offer.

According to the type of production considered at a given moment, each component will be globally (or not) taken into account to manage the process.

5.2   Strategic functions to manage

The latest developments lead us to integrate among the strategic functions to manage: "provuction" management, commercial/marketing and quality management functions. Two others functions need to be taken into account to help deciders to manage a mix enterprise: Finally, service orientation represents a huge challenge that impacts organisation, management, and control of industrial firms but also people's focus and skills which must be less technology oriented but rather customer oriented. distribution management and innovation management functions. Figure 4 represents the functional grid of a provuction system.

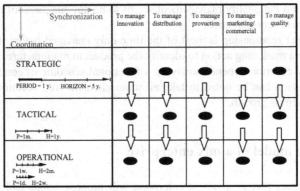

Fig. 4. Functional grid of a provuction system

Provuction function. The "provuction" function gathers the two functions of production and service delivery necessary for the management of the respective processes. The goal of this function is to synchronize the basic components above-mentioned. The management of the provuction can be apprehended from a temporal and functional point of view:

- the temporal decomposition allows to define the strategic level (which activity portfolio?), the tactical level (which component organisation as regard to commercial forecasts) and the operational level (which execution modalities for the activities),
- the functional decomposition that implies the management of products, human resources, technical resources and customers. The goal is to ensure the availability of these components per time units, sort of macro planning that needs to be refined at the operational level according to customer availability. A synchronisation function is then necessary to coordinate customers, resources, and products flows.

Such a classification implies a hierarchy of representations. Each decisional level is characterised by a couple (horizon, period) and by a level of detail of the information taken into account. Figure 5 presents the detail of the provuction control system. It summarizes the decisional structure of the system considered.

Commercial/marketing function. Service costing and price fixing is a problem of huge importance in the domain of service because as they are for a part intangible, their value is influenced by customers feeling of quality (§4.1). Furthermore, in the particular case of activities diversification such as it is for manufacturing firm, studies have shown that whatever the type of service, only 31% of firms sell them [14]. A strategic plan must be held to determine the best coupling (product/service) taking account of the marketing and commercial strategy that lies on the global strategy of the firm. Then the marketing function must define the global offer and fix its price taking account of the service and product process cost and of the customer perception of the offer value. At a tactical and operational level, the function will have to manage customers thanks to a relational approach and to set up loyalty programs. The commercial function must determine on the long term how to maximize the profits of the firm optimizing on the medium and short term the resource utilisation regarding their capacity.

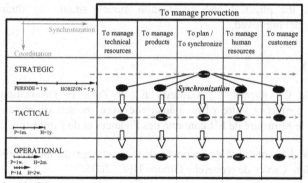

Fig. 5. Control grid of the provuction system

Quality function. Quality is the main loyalty indicator, the main asset considering the concurrency and the essential axis to ensure the growth and profitability of firms. As a consequence it must be manage at each decisional level. A problem comes from the difficulty to define quantitative metrics representative of the service quality and productivity [15]. At a strategic level, procedures to check process quality should be defined and at the operational level metrics can be used to demonstrate the quality of the tangible part of the offer whereas measures that will solicit customers or contact people could be defined for the other part.

Innovation function. Innovation recovers all the creative processes that are used to enhance or introduce new goods, services or processes in firms. Tool for differentiation its articulation regarding the global strategy of the firm and the commercial/marketing strategy will allow to anticipate the further developments of firms, investments in term of technical or human resources and technologies or competencies to master.

Distribution function. Service delivery or good provision requires to determine when, where and how to distribute. The TIC widespread in the service domain imply that the commercial/marketing strategy of the mix enterprise takes time and space parameters into account and focus on physic and electronic delivery. A strong correlation exists between the information system, the customer relationship and the distribution functions that need to be managed on the short, medium and long term.

5 Conclusion

The economic delineation that exists between goods and services looses its interest regarding the provision of a combined offer and the set up of processes to perform it. Then, erasing the existing border between goods and services, we have proposed a provuction process that allows providing personalised goods as well as standardized services. The decisional structure of an enterprise able to propose such an offer and to support such a process is also presented. In order to define the complete model of such a firm, the physical and information models should be studied and the decisional model improved.

References

1. Lagaronne C., Ramus V., Gallardo E., et Zaeh F. Orientation service – Entreprises : renforcez votre offre industrielle avec du service, note de synthèse rédigée pour le Ministère de L'Economie des Finances et de l'Industrie, 2003.

2. Malleret V. La rentabilité des services dans les entreprises industrielles : enquête sur un postulat, Cahier de recherche Groupe HEC, 2005.

3. Rathmell J.M. What is meant by services, *Journal of marketing*, October, 1986.

4. Gummesson E. Evert Gummesson : Stockholm University, in services marketing self-portraits : introspections, reflections and glimpses from the experts, 2000.

5. Judd R.C. The case for redifining services, *Journal of marketing*, 28(1), 1964.

6. Vargo S.L., and Lusch R.L. Evolving of a new dominant logic for marketing, Journal of Marketing, 68 (january),2004.

7. Gronroos C. Service management and marketing: a customer relationship management approach, West Sussex, UK :Wiley, 2000.

8. Alix T., Vallespir B. Product and complementary service: looking for the right pair, Proceedding of the IEEE SSMC conference, Troyes, 2006.

9. Malaval P. L'essentiel du marketing B to B, *Editions Publi-Union*, Paris, 1999.

10. Vargo S.L., and Lusch R.L. The four service marketing myths: remants of a good-based manufacturing model, Journal of Service Research, 6(4), 2004.

11. Eiglier P., Langeard E. Servuction, le marketing des services, Mc Graw Hill, Paris, 1987.

12. Tannery F. Le management stratégique des services : synthèse bibliographique et repérage des questions génériques, *Finance Contrôle Stratégie*, 4(2), 2000.

13. Doumeingts G., Vallespir B. and Chen D. Decisional modeling GRAI grid in International Handbook on Information Systems, eds Springer, Berlin, 1988.

14. Baglin G., Malleret V. Le développement d'offres de services dans les PMI", cahier de recherche du Groupe HEC, CR 800/2004.

15. Norman R. and Ramirez R. From value chain to value constellation: designing interactive strategy, Harvard Business review, 71, july-august, 1993.

A Lifecycle Simulation Framework for Production Systems

Masaru Nakano[1] , Shigetoshi Noritake[1] , Toshio Ohashi[2] ,

1   Toyota Central R&D Laboratories., Inc., Nagakute, Aichi, 480-1192,
Japan
URL: http://www.tytlabs.co.jp/eindex.html
2   Toyota Motor Corporation, Toyota, Aichi, 471-8571, Japan
URL: http://www.toyota.co.jp/en/

Abstract. The prediction of market behavior is helpful for a manufacturing enterprise to build efficient production systems, but unfortunately these predictions are usually not very reliable. Subsequently, development of more flexible production systems is important to adapt to changing markets but basically cause a higher cost than less flexible ones. This paper proposes a lifecycle simulation framework for production systems by combining the two topics. The simulation structure has several template libraries consisting of many scenarios or patterns of market behaviors, product lineups, production lines, and reconfiguration policies. The framework is initially described for a factory, and afterwards expanded for a global production network.

1   Introduction

A modern manufacturing enterprise producing and selling consumer products has a complex business architecture, integrating many processes from marketing research to the product and production development process to supply chain and sales management (Kubota, Sato and Nakano [1]). The entire enterprise has a more complicated decision making process related to production system design in need of constant improvement to stay competitive in the world. Prediction of market behavior is very helpful to build efficient production systems, but unfortunately, demand forecasting is not overly reliable. Development of more flexible production systems is important to adapt to turbulent, fast-changing markets and basically requires higher costs than less flexible ones. Many studies have been done for either market analysis or the flexibility, adaptability and changeability of production systems. Studies integrating both the market demands and the flexibility provided by the production system are required to design production systems for the future. These

Please use the following format when citing this chapter:

Nakano, M., Noritake, S. and Ohashi, T., 2008, in IFIP International Federation for Information Processing, Volume 257, Lean Business Systems and Beyond, Tomasz Koch, ed.; (Boston: Springer), pp. 327–335.

topics are very related to the studies on lifecycle-oriented design or the flexibility for production systems (See [2], [3], [4]).

The literature regarding manufacturing flexibility was classified by Toni and Tochia [2]. While they provided many references for the process and volume flexibility in production, no studies are introduced for the flexibility related to a change in the product itself. Autich and Barbian [3] proposed a project management technique for lifecycle oriented design by evaluating the flexibility. Burkner et. al. [5] evaluated the flexibility for volume changes from the view of risk by simulation in combination with market scenario analysis. This paper discusses the flexibility for not only product volume but also changes in the product itself from the view of production system lifecycle and proposes a framework for lifecycle simulation.

2   Lifecycle Oriented Design for Production Systems

There are two ways how production systems can strategically adjust to market changes: product engineering and sales, or production engineering as shown in Figure 1. The production engineering and management may be considered on a factory level (In-factory), a supply chain level including multiple factories (Cross-factory), or an enterprise level (Outsource). The cross-factory and outsource levels have more flexibility than the in-factory level.

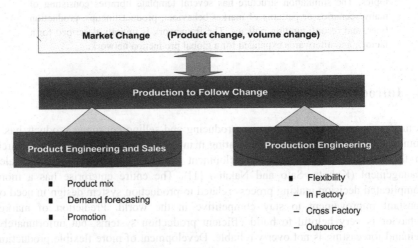

Fig. 1. Production Flexibility and Market Change

The lifecycle-oriented design has engineering processes from product ramp-up to end of life stages as shown in Figure 2. The flexibility for production has two main phases of the reconfiguration: The first phase is the investment during production preparation and start-up phase, and the second phase is the efficiency improvements during regular production. Lifecycle simulation should be used only after the start-up phase is completed because the start-up phase is too complex and has too much manually involvement to be simulated. Large changes in the number of product features, production volume or product mix may require a similar engineering process as with the start-up stage. However, if the revisions to the original production plan are relatively small, the stages can be simulated by providing basic patterns of revisions.

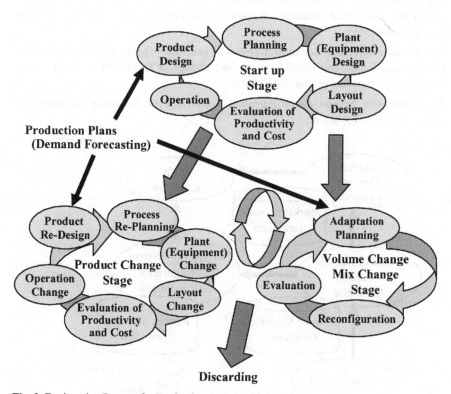

Fig. 2. Engineering Process for Production System Lifecycle

3   Lifecycle Oriented Simulation

A lifecycle simulation structure is proposed for a single factory as shown in Figure 3. The program modules can be computed using an iterative routine with the orders as shown by the arrows in Figure 3 or alternatively using a distributed architecture as explained in Nakano, et al. [7]. The templates and the program modules are explained as follows:

The *Product Scenario Templates* specify the timing and change rates in features to be launched for product change.

The *Factory Scenario Templates* define the limit of changes in demand or the number and complexity of product features for small changes. Reconfiguration patterns are also provided for large changes. Reuse patterns of machines, process planning, and machine configuration are included in the detailed case.

The *Market Scenario Templates* provides market demands as time series. These are generated using historic data or market prediction simulation.

The *Initial settings* navigate the user to initially set decision variables such as the initial production volume. Initial production lines and the sets of the efficiency curves are also typical decision variables used to optimize the production systems during the lifecycle.

The *Product Lifecycle Scenario Generator* generate triggers which happen at a predetermined time and initialize a product change, a specification change, or a change in the expected production volume.

The *Production System Reconfiguration Scenario Cost Estimator* estimates the cost of the reconfiguration.

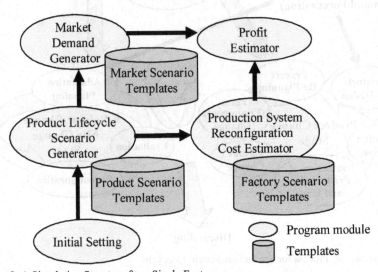

Fig. 3. A Simulation Structure for a Single Factory

The *Market Demand Generator* generates the market demands as a time series with fluctuations based on a selected scenario template as defined by the Market Scenario Template. A Monte Carlo simulation generates many market fluctuation scenarios with many different variations.

The *Profit Estimator* calculates the lifecycle cost of the production, and estimates the profit obtained from the sales at the factory level. The outcome is a distribution of the EBIT (earnings before interest and tax). The simulation period includes a few changes for each product model. If an accurate simulation is required, a production system simulator (for example, see [8]) can be employed as a part of the estimator.

4   Usage of the Lifecycle Oriented Simulation

4.1   Aim of Simulation

The following questions can be answered with the use of the lifecycle oriented simulation:
1) How much does the flexibility of a machine or a structure of a production system affect the lifecycle cost and profit? The information provides a guideline to develop or reuse machines and production systems.
2) How far can market fluctuation be allowed while still guarantee a profit? The information can provide the goal of product planning and sales promotion.
3) Which strategy is the best for a reconfiguration?

4.2   Reconfiguration Cost Calculation

A reconfiguration may be necessary to adapt to a large change in demand beyond the limit of the flexibility of the production system or to a product change. The following three methods are considered to calculate the reconfiguration cost.

a)   Experience based functional with flexibility relations
    The efficiency of a production line is related through a curve to the production volume. A reconfiguration scenario for volume changes is made by jumping from one curve to another depending on the details of the changes as shown in Figure 5. The volume flexibility influences the timing of reconfiguration. The more flexible a production line is, the less often a reconfiguration is expected. If the change cost is estimated based on experience, the total lifecycle cost can be evaluated. The timing of reconfiguration can also be used to adapt for product changes. The reconfiguration cost is calculated according to the extent of product change. The more flexible a production line is, the more initial investment and the less change cost can be expected in the case of automated processing lines. Figure 6 shows these relations.

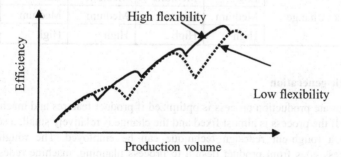

Fig. 4. Production Volume and Efficiencies for Different Flexibilities

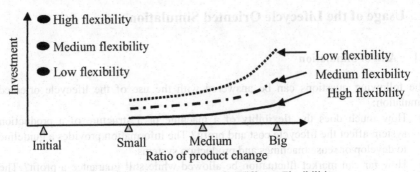

Fig. 5. Product Change and Required Investment for Different Flexibilities

b) Experience based table with flexibility relations

A table can be prepared based on experience to determine the reconfiguration cost by summing up the change costs of machines and the costs for relocating workers. A very simple example is shown in Table 1. An initial investment cost for different flexibility is evaluated in the same way as the reconfiguration cost.

Table 1. A Simple Example of Reconfiguration Cost for Different Flexibilities

		Production Flexibility		
		Low	Medium	High
Volume Change	Low	Low	Low	Low
	Medium	High	Medium	Low
	High	High	High	High
Mix Change	Low	Low	Low	Low
	Medium	High	Medium	Low
	High	High	High	Medium
Product Change	Low	Medium	Medium	Low
	Medium	High	Medium	Medium
	High	High	High	High

c) Automatic generation

An appropriate production process is optimized if product features and machines are provided. If the process is almost fixed and the change is relatively small, a semi-automatic or a rough-cut redesign technique can be employed. The rough-cut redesign process goes from product design to process planning, machine redesign, and layout redesign, to evaluation of the productivity and cost. Additional templates such as production processes and machines are also needed. See Okuda et al. [6] for a related study.

4.3   How to use the Simulation for a Simple Example

This section shows the steps to use the simulation for simple examples. Assume a simple example consisting of a product and a production line with a related efficiency curve. The initial production demand and the production efficiency to meet the demand are given. Choose some demand curves in the Templates of Market Demand, samples of which are shown in Figure 7.

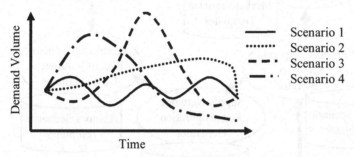

Fig. 6. Sample Demand Curves

For example, assume each of the four curves has 25% possibility. When the volume in demand exceeds the predetermined extent, the Production System Scenario Generator invests to increase the production capacity, as for example a duplicate of the line. The production flexibility for reconfiguration is shown in Table 1. Select from three levels in flexibility to be used as a decision variable. The redesign process is periodically initiated through a product change in the product model cycles. The Profit Estimator calculates the lifecycle cost by averaging the results from multiple replicas of simulation with different demand scenarios under the selected possibilities. The risk can be estimated in terms of value at risk (VAR).

5   Extension of the Framework to Evaluate Global Supply Networks

A global production network with multiple factories has more flexibility and adaptability than a single production line. If different factories have different efficiency curves due to different characteristics such as automation rates or possible mixture rates, you can select appropriate production lines at appropriate locations to adapt to the volume or product change. The idea is extended to integrate a lifecycle simulation with a supply network simulation including outsourcing. If a business component is not a core source, you can outsource it to a supplier in order to optimize the flexibility and adaptability in the supply network. The topic can also be extended to optimize a product lineup to maximize profits. Therefore this research topic is not only related to production system design but also enterprise design in terms of mid-term lifecycle management. Therefore, this paper proposes a technical framework of modeling, evaluating and planning a production system lifecycle model in the manufacturing enterprise. Figure 8 shows the extension of the simulation model for a global supply chain model.

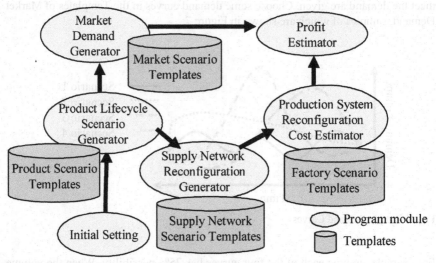

Fig. 7. A Simulation Structure for a Global Network

The following new modules are added to the simulation of a single factory to extend the model to a global supply chain simulation:

The *Supply Network Scenario Templates* includes various supply network configurations. Economies of scale can be considered for outsourcing, merging, collaboration, and vertical or horizontal integration.

The *Supply Network Reconfiguration Generator* selects appropriate production systems in appropriate factories in a globally distributed network, decomposes the estimated production volumes to the appropriate production systems, and reconfigures the supply network with a scenario tree where each node in the tree represents a possible plan of the supply network configuration.

6   Conclusion

The paper proposes a framework for lifecycle simulation for production systems and shows the extension of the production system simulation to entire supply networks. The study was done in the international collaboration project LicoPro between EU and Japan. While simple experiments are studied in the project (see [5], [6]), this paper describes the basic idea for further discussion. The authors believe that the discussion of the leanness in production management with a viewpoint of the lifecycle of entire production systems within this paper will stimulate the interests of researchers in the academic society.

Acknowledgments

The study was supported by the IMS program under Ministry of Economy, Trade and Industry of Japan.

References

1. F. Kubota, S. Sato, M. Nakano, Enterprise Modeling and Simulation Integrating Manufacturing System Design and Supply Chain, IEEE Int. Conf. on System, Man, and Cybernetics, pp.511-515 (1999).

2. A. De Toni and S. Tonchia, Manufacturing flexibility: a literature review, Int. J. of Production Research, Vol.36, No.6, pp.1587-1617 (1998).

3. J. C. Autich and P. Barbian, Production Projects – Designing and Operating Life-cycle-Oriented and Flexibility-Optimized Production Systems as a Project, Int. J. of Production Research, Vol.42, No.17, pp.3589-3601 (2004).

4. G. Schuh, C. Schleyer and F. Zohm, Planning Methodology for Lifecycle-Oriented, Flexible Production Systems, The 1st Conf. on Changeable, Agile Reconfigurable and Virtual Production (CARV) (2005).

5. S. Burkner, M. Schmitt, J. Roscher and M. Friese, Methods for Flexibility Evaluation in the Automotive Industry, The CARV (2005).

6. T. Okuda, K. Ohashi, H. Matsuoka, S. Noritake, H. Nagase, M. Nakayama, K. Furusawa, T. Muraki, S. Chino, S. Fujita, K. Wada, Y. Sano, M. Nakano, H. Kubota, M. Anan, T. Ohashi, F. Kimura, Lifecycle-Oriented Design of Flexible and Agile production System (LicoPro), IMS Int. Forum2004, pp.626-633 (2004).

7. M. Nakano, F. Kubota, Y. Inamori and K. Mitsuyuki., Method and Tool to Visualize and Analyze Business Processes, Knowledge and Skill Chains in Engineering and Manufacturing, edited by E. Arai (Springer), pp.177-184 (2004).

8. M. Nakano, N. Sugiura, M. Tanaka, and T. Kuno, ROPSII: Agent-Oriented Manufacturing Simulator on the Basis of Robot Simulator, Proc. of JAPAN-U.S.A. Symposium on Flexible Automation, pp.201-208 (1994).

From Order to Delivery: An Integrated Process Approach for Customer Satisfaction

Gilles Neubert, Andréa Wattky Crestan, and Abdelaziz Bouras
University of Lyon2, PRISMA laboratory IUT Lumière,
160 bd de l'université, 69676 Bron, France

Abstract. Today, companies are evolving towards business process oriented organization. This approach relies on integration and collaboration between interdependent activities that must be redesign and managed to increase the performance of the global system. After some consideration about integration, collaboration and business process re-design, this paper will present a case study that concerns the reorganization of the European commercial assistantship, the logistics and transport office as well as the production planning of a world-leading chemical company, for better customer satisfaction.

Key words: Business Process Reengineering, Collaboration, Integration,

1 Introduction

Business environment has changed in the past decades and is more complex and unforeseeable than ever. In this new century companies are led to believe that the most valuable characteristic of an organization is its ability to adapt to the dynamic environment in which they operate. To be successful, each company needs to work as a team where all the functional areas of the business are properly integrated. These last years, much attention has been focused on the management methodology of supply chain management (SCM), which integrates business processes from suppliers to customers and manages various tasks, such as sales, manufacturing, logistics, and finance. Integration and business process management look like the new issue in the problem of designing and operating modern industrial systems. As identify by Lindsay et al. (2003), much of the literature produced by the business process management and reengineering (BPM/R) community suggests that implementing process orientated structures will help organizations to be more responsive to an increasingly changing environment.

Please use the following format when citing this chapter:

Neubert, G., Crestan, A.W. and Bouras, A., 2008, in IFIP International Federation for Information Processing, Volume 257, Lean Business Systems and Beyond, Tomasz Koch, ed.; (Boston: Springer), pp. 337–345.

The transition of the company organization for more integration between company functions and services has had as consequence the emergence of BPR. It means the reorganization of the company organization in order to transform it from a vertical silo organization, with independent functions and services, into a horizontal organization that is based on transverse processes (Kramer and Tyler, 1995).

This paper aims at describing a large scale Business Process Reengineering that encompasses the European Sales department, the Logistics department, and the Operations Planning department of a major actor of the chemical industry. The objective was a better description of the global process from the customer order to the customer delivery in order to improve its efficiency and increase the "On Time In Full" (OTIF) Key Performance Indicator.

The next section will address the concept of integration and coordination that support business process approach, when section 3 will describe a case study of business process redesign to increase customer satisfaction while reducing the company's organization complexity. Section 4 will conclude this paper.

2   Business Process Approach

BPR supposes the interdependency of company services and functions and looks for reaching significant improvement in critical performance measures (Mentzer, 1999). Literature witnesses this phenomenon and several books confirm this tendency (Hammer and Champy, 1993), (Stevens, 1989), (Davenport, 1993). BPR is a process approach that concerns internal modifications of the company organization in order to attain better integration and internal collaboration within the organization.

2.1   Integration

The concept of integration can be approached through different perspectives (functional, business process, Information System, etc.), but in all cases, it aims at shifting from local management to system management. From literature, it emerges that integration can support business processes at two different levels (Romano, 2003):

1. intra-company integration, aiming to overcome the functional silos boundaries, and relating to activities to manage and re-design the business processes across the individual members of the supply network.
2. inter-companies integration, aiming to overcome the individual company boundaries, and relating both to a initial extent of integration, or "inter-companies dyadic integration", and to an advanced extent of integration, or "overall supply network integration".

2.2   Coordination

As described by Danese et al. (2004), how to achieve efficient and effective coordination among the various activities in business processes within companies is one of the issues most thoroughly investigated by organizational researchers. Coordination is particularly problematic when considering supply networks, as the scope of business processes overcomes the individual company's boundaries. In this case, the complexity of coupling different companies within supply networks combines with the complexity arising from how within-firm elements (e.g. divisions and departments) are linked together. As proposed by Lambert et al. (1998) and developed by Choi and Hong (2002), managers simultaneously face three different forms of structural complexity in supply networks: vertical, horizontal and spatial. Vertical complexity refers to the number of levels in the whole system (i.e. the number of tiers), horizontal complexity refers to the number of different entities in the same level of the supply network (e.g. number of suppliers in each tier), and spatial complexity refers to the average distance between operating locations. Thus, managing business processes across supply networks is a very complex task that requires managers to properly activate coordination mechanisms to adapt, align and synchronize activities carried out by the different and interdependent members of the network (Danese et al., 2004).

Starting from a broad definition of coordination, "the act of working together harmoniously", Malone and Crowston (1990) proposed several components of coordination : there must be one or more actors, performing some activities which are directed toward some goals, the word "harmoniously," referring to the fact that activities are not independent. They defined these goal-relevant relationships between the activities as interdependencies and they proposed a definition of coordination as "the act of managing interdependencies between activities performed to achieve a goal ».

Their work (Malone and Crowston 1994) and other previous works such as the work from Thompson (1967), lead to the definition of some standard types of interdependencies. Frayret et al (2004) proposed a summary of the main types of interdependence. First, the most commonly cited type of interdependence concerns organizational resources sharing. It is related to the concept of pooled interdependence (Thompson 1967), in which each part of a system renders a discrete contribution to the whole, while each part is supported by the whole. Another type of interdependence concerns the producer–consumer relationship (Malone and Crowston 1994), or sequential interdependence (Thompson 1967). This type links two manufacturing activities for which the output of one is the input of the other. Another type of interdependence called reciprocal relationships concerns activities whose outputs are the reciprocal inputs of the other activity. Next, intensive interdependence is related to the intrinsic sophistication of activity embeddedness (Grandori 1997). In distributed manufacturing, this type of interdependence occurs when the activities distributed among centers are highly connected in terms of time requirement, reciprocity, output/input transfer, or input usability.

2.3   Customer satisfaction and Business process Design

According to Davenport (1993), a process « is simply a structured set of activities designed to produce a specified output for a particular customer or market ». A process thus consists in multi-actor activities, which are carried out through time and space; the links between these activities and the activities them-selves may belong to different functions, different production site or even to different organizations. In that sense, following Malone and Crowston definition, it is a set of linked activities, and, managing a process consists in managing interdependencies between activities performed to achieve a goal.

By restructuring their processes, companies pursue the objective of releasing financial resources, reduce costs, lighten the company management, and improve global performance (Palvia, 1995), (Lacity and Hirschheim, 1993), (Rittenberg and Covaleski, 2001).

Looking at Customer satisfaction as the goal, managing the process to reach this goal consists in managing the interdependency between activities that contribute to this goal. Business processes can be described at different levels of detail depending on the abstraction put into analyzing the organization, which depends in turn on the purpose of the analysis. In the case of Business process Reengineering, the goal is not only to better manage the actual activities interdependency, but also to redesign this set of activities, their contains, to simplify the flow of information and to reduce the complexity of the entire process.

As modeling the processes from scratch is a hard task, the SCOR-model (Supply Chain Operations Reference-model) was used because it describes with standard component (Processes, Activities, Best practice, Performance Indicators,..) an ideal process state, which can be reached or adapted through an "as is" process analysis and reorganization of that process. Hence, the company attains, regarding to its own strategy and constraints, the "to be" process thanks to a comparison and analysis of its actual processes with the processes proposed by SCOR.

3   Process and organization redesigning: case study

With research and production centers in France, USA, China and Japan, a world-leading manufacturer of products containing fourteen different rare earths, Rhodia Electronics & Catalysis' (REC) is quite complex. Many products are produced in small a quantity, which has an important impact on the production process flow. Insufficient inventory and inadequate supply may thus have direct consequences on delivery delays and thus on customer satisfaction.

The objective of REC's process simplifying concerned the European commercial assistantship, the logistics and transport office as well as the production planning and scheduling office, which were considered as essential for the company's competitive advantage. Within this context, the supply chain process redesigning of the company's production site was seen as the means to clarify and to improve the process from order processing to product delivery.

3.1   As Is situation

As noticed earlier, BPR and the SCOR-model suppose the description and analysis of actual processes in order to understand them and transform them into redesigned processes with better performance. REC's initial organization was complex (Figure 1) and needed more integration within the company. The process reengineering efforts concerned all activities, from the customer order down to the customer delivery. Those include order acknowledgement and processing, charge capacity evaluation, transport planning and scheduling, order tracing, packaging, shipping and invoicing.

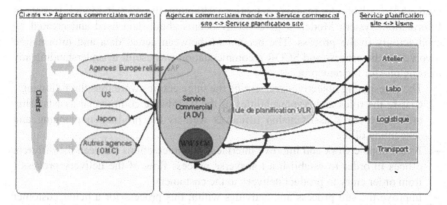

Fig. 1. « As is » company organization

Three different entities of the company were concerned:
- The worldwide commercial assistantship offices, in direct contact with customers: customer support, salesmen support, order registration, commercial forecasts, invoicing and claim follow-up, etc.
- The production site's commercial assistantship office, in contact with the worldwide offices as well as the production planning and scheduling office: assistantship office interfaces, order entry for assistantship offices that are not linked to the site's information system, order follow-up, product allotment management, business unit support, data base maintenance, etc.
- Manufacturing plant (production, product analyzing office, and logistics and transport office), organized through workshops and in contact with the production planning and scheduling office: interfaces with planning and scheduling office, sub-contracting management, information system data base maintenance, product and rare earth requirement coordination, etc.

The company's objective was to move the organization from the three distinct entities (European Sales department, logistics department and the operations planning department) to two integrated entities: 1) Sales Management, and a so called 2) Product coordination department in order to better coordinate sales, production planning, and distribution.

Analyzing the difference between the "as is" situation and the flow proposed by SCOR enables to find differences in the sequence of activities, or missing of some activities or execution of one activity by another actor or department. This gives good indication on the needed reorganization of the activities or on the understanding of the barriers in the process structure, its fluidity bottlenecks and their impact on the performance.

3.2   Process redesigning objectives

A deeper analysis has then being done to verify that all the needed information is used and available to manage activities. Although the SCOR-Model is not an Information System Model, it gives many details about data used and created by each activity in the process. The benchmark between actual data and information involved in the process and SCOR recommendation was useful in understanding any missing one for the new process.

The redesigning objectives concerning the three entities were thus the following:
−   Clarify the roles and responsibilities of the worldwide commercial assistantship office, the site's assistantship office as well as the production planning and scheduling office
−   Avoid double work and improve interfaces and interactions between the different offices in order to establish a transverse process flow of the delivery process (from order entry to product delivery to the customer)
−   Improve the sub-process and activities within this process for a better customer service

The initiative for process redesigning consisted in the establishment of a unique assistantship office, located at the production site, by regrouping the different European offices. After the reorganizing effort from the initial three entities only two of them were left (Figure 2):

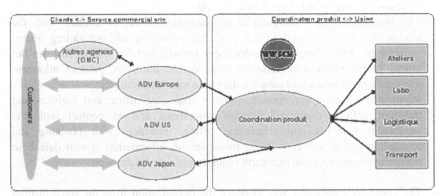

Fig. 2 . « To be » company organization

−   One commercial assistantship office (and only a limited number of worldwide offices) in direct interaction with customers: salesmen support, quoting request answering, order processing, unique interface for the customer concerning complex payment regulation, consignment stock management, data management for order forecasts, customer dossiers, price lists, etc.

- The product coordination office in interaction with the manufacturing plant: consolidation of logistics and transport office with the production planning and scheduling office in order to create an office, called product coordination office, production scheduling management and industrial plant tests, allotment management, customer returns, follow-up of performance indicators (overall equipment efficiency, delivery performance on time in full, etc.).

3.3   Process redesigning results

The process redesigning effort allowed the company to simplify its organization by reducing the number of entities and services. The company's supply chain has thus become clearer and more efficient because on one hand, it is more customer oriented (assistantship office consistence and permanence vis-à-vis the customer, production location closeness through the product coordination), and on the other hand there is a facilitated access to training for the commercial assistants (thanks to their company location proximity). Moreover, money-saving benefits have been registered through the regrouping of different offices and allowed the company to reduce the charges of the former assistantship offices and to have them under control.

4   Conclusions

The project was carried out through the following steps: 1) Macro cartography of the existing activities in the "as is" process, 2) analysis of the "as is" process and sub processes through the SCOR-model standardized sequence of activities, 3) comparison of each activity in the processes with the help of company and SCOR inputs, outputs, information used and created to identify the main differences between the existing situation and the SCOR ideal process.

Thanks to the new process organization, the new commercial assistantship office and the logistics and transport office, which were linked in an important manner creating for the customer a certain confusion about the company reactivity and responsiveness, were separated. This also helped to clarify the roles of every actor and to allow the customer to dispose of one unique point of contact within the company. As for the logistic and transport office regrouping with the production planning and scheduling office, it allowed evolving towards an integrated and complete order management.

The process redesigning of the concerned offices has also consequences on employment because the different jobs has to be reassigned. The existing staff was therefore reorganized according to the required competencies for the new process organization. In case of gaps between detained and requires competency, certain actors were assigned to other jobs and new actors hired.

However, a company should not embark on such a process reengineering analysis without having profoundly thought about the reasons and the possible obstacles concerning this company and process reorganization. Using SCOR and

BPR for the process optimization, one needs to simplify and base the process configuration on two levels: the material flow and the information/work flow. Process reorganization needs to be made in light of people, process and technology. Not only the tactical and strategic processes need to be optimized, but also the individual user's motivation and the technology they use to operate. Without all three molded into a final methodology, continuous improvement cannot take place.

References

1. Aguilar-Saven R.S., " Business process modelling: Review and framework", Int. J. Production Economics 90 (2004) pp 129–149.

2. Choi T.Y., Hong Y., "Unveiling the structure of supply networks: case studies in Honda, Acura, DaimlerChrysler". Journal of Operations Management 20 (5), 2002, 469–493.

3. Danese P., Romano P., Vinelli A., "Managing business processes across supply networks: the role of coordination mechanisms", Journal of Purchasing & Supply Management 10 (2004) 165–177.

4. Davenport T.H., "Process Innovation: Reengineering Work Through Information Technology", Harvard Business School Press, Boston, 1993.

5. Frayret J.M., D'Amours S., Montreuil B., "Coordination and control in distributed and agent-based manufacturing systems", Production Planning&Control, Vol. 15, No. 1, January 2004, 42–54.

6. Grandori A., "An organizational assessment of interfirm coordination modes", Organization Studies 18 (6), 1997, 897–925.

7. Hammer M., Champy J., "Reengineering the corporation: A manifesto for business revolution", Harper Collins, New York, 1993.

8. Kramer R.M., Tyler T.R., "Trust in Organizations: Frontiers of Theory and Research", Sage Publications, Berkeley, CA, 1995.

9. Lacity M.C., Hirschheim R., "The Information Systems Outsourcing Bandwagon", Sloan Management Review, 1993, 73-86.

10. Lambert D. M., Cooper M. C., Pagh J. D., "Supply Chain Management: Implementation Issues and Research Opportunities", International Journal of Logistics Management 9 (2), (1998), 1–19.

11. Lambert D.M., García-Dastugue S.J., Croxton K.L. "An evaluation of process-oriented Supply Chain Management Frameworks" Journal of Business Logistics, Vol. 26 (1), 2005, 25-51.

12. Lindsay A., Downs D., Lunn K., "Business processes—attempts to find a definition" Information and Software Technology 45 (2003) 1015–1019.

13. Malone T. W., Crowston K., "What is Coordination Theory and How Can It Help Design Cooperative Work Systems", in Proceedings of the Conference on Computer Supported Cooperative Work, Los Angeles, California, October, 1990, 15p.

14. Mentzer M.S., "Two heads are better than one if your company spans the globe", Academy of Management Executive, no 13, p. 89-90, 1999.

15. Plavia P.C., "A dialectic view of information systems outsourcing : Pros and cons", Information & Management, no. 29, 1995, 265-275.

16. Rittenberg L., Covaleski M.A., Internalization versus externalization of the internal audit function: an examination of professional and organizational imperatives, Accounting, Organizations and Society, no. 26, 2001, 617-641.

17. Romano P., "Co-ordination and integration mechanisms to manage logistics processes across supply networks" Journal of Purchasing & Supply Management 9 (2003) 119–134.

18. Shena H., Wallb B., Zarembab M., Chena Y., Browne J., "Integration of business modelling methods for enterprise information system analysis and user requirements gathering", Computers in Industry 54 (2004) pp 307–323.

19. Stevens G., "Integrating the supply chain", Physical Distribution & Materials Management, no. 19 8, p.3-8, 1998.

20. Thompson J.D., "Organizations in Action », USA: McGraw-Hill, 1967.

Lean Information Processing in the Specification Process

– Using operational data to enable real mass customization

Carsten Svensson

Enterprise Integration, Inc., 5971 Kings Towne Village Parkway,
Alexandria, Virginia, USA

Abstract: To improve the overall efficiency, from a supply chain perspective, manufactures are focusing their activities around a limited number of core-processes. Consequently the internal processing degree is reduced. When the degree of internal processing is reduced, the organizational balance between manufacturing processes and cross-organizational integration processes shifts, and this is reflected in the cost drivers. The reality is that while the cost of direct manufacturing is reduced, business processes becomes major cost drivers. This is a radical shift from conventional industry where the cost drivers typically were associated with the transformation of material. This paper will argue that focusing on production optimization have become less important to the end-manufacturer because the industrial paradigm have change. Instead the ability to orchestra the manufacturing of customized products presents a significant potential for efficiency improvement. In acknowledgement of this trend manufacturing concepts such as lean are successfully being applied to administrative processes such as the product specification process.

1 Introduction

Manufactures of end products have, in regions with high wages and limited access to raw material, evolved in to assembly plants, development centers and administrative offices. In most cases, the company names are still the same the products better than ever, and the majority of the population is still employed. So what happened? Instead of transforming material the companies and people are transforming information.

This paper will focus on the information transformation associated with the vision of manufacturing products adapted to the individual customer, at the cost of a mass produced product, also called mass customization.

A typically example of the change from manufacturing to a knowledge economy is Denmark. A large portion of the industrial production is heavy machinery such as

Please use the following format when citing this chapter:

Svensson, C., 2008, in IFIP International Federation for Information Processing, Volume 257, Lean Business Systems and Beyond, Tomasz Koch, ed.; (Boston: Springer), pp. 347–354.

wind turbines, cement factories, printing presses, powder processing plants, homogenizers etc. these products are typically highly specialized and customized. These manufactures have often started out as machine shops with a good idea and have over time evolved into world leaders within their respective niche fields. As the products have become more complex these manufactures focused their production to a point where they only manufacture a few key components were as the majority of generic components are bought from large supplier networks.The background for this trend is that in order to remain competitive manufacturers have through the last 20 years been going through a focusing process [16]. The internal degree of processing have been reduced leaving only a limited core activities in house [15] as a result the ability to control and coordination supply chains have become the core functions of the company, but it is a core function with low visibility. End-manufacturers are currently realizing that the ability to process information may become the single most important process, as specialized suppliers carry out the majority of the physical processing, and consequently lean projects in the conventional sense are not meaning full. However lean information processes are of value as they address the main processes of modern corporations.

2   The Deficiencies of Push- and Pull Production

For the end-manufacturer specializing in BTO (Build To Order) products, the transition from being a manufacturer mastering a production process to being a supply network manager and distributor of information is challenging both with regards to operations and organization, because a new set of product data and production data have to be generated for every product. Consequently many manufacturers have been looking to the concept of mass customization. With regards to mass customization there has been a tendency to focus on the market value of customization (e.g.[1],[4],[6],[12],[13]&[14]) rather than the need demanding operational preconditions [19]. Especially "build to order" manufacturers have underestimated the need for operational skills and believed that mass customization would be a short cut to a larger market rather than a manufacturing strategy much more complex than mass production or craft manufacturing. Consequently delivering the customized product has proven to be a problem for manufacturers of customized goods, in relation to cost and time [19].

In conventional mass production the finished goods inventory absorb the variations in the market demand; thereby it is possible to enable a high utilization of the production system. However the inventory or lack thereof is the soft spot of this production from, and as it will later be demonstrated customized products have the potential to compete, because with the combination of iterative configuration and an integration of planning and selling it is possible to ensure a high utilization of the production system without an inventory of finished goods.

In systems where the value of the products are high relative to the production system or where the products are customized, a pull system can be applied to compensate for the variations in demand and product-structure, consequently the production system must be flexible, to address these challenges.

In a BTO production, which per definition is a pull system, the order specification process (figure 1) can be a major cost driver [8]. To realize the vision of mass customization the BTO unique cost associated with specifying the product will have to be kept at a minimum, and to improve the efficiency, lean administrative processes supported by technology can be applied. Customization might create unique value for the customer resulting in a strong competitive position, but often customized products are disqualified from the market by the basic product attributes cost, quality and delivery time. A large portion of this cost is associated with the engineering and administration of the specification process which will have to bed done of each individual product compared to mass production where the specification cost is distributed over all the products of a production run.

Fig. 1. A generic example of the specification process (Based on Barfod & Hvolby[3])

This situation is very different from mass production, because variations are most often absorbed by the production system .The result is often a low utilization of the productions system. Observation from seven profitable manufacturers indicates that a utilization of the production system less than 50 % is not uncommon, thereby paralyzing the competitiveness compared to mass production. And in addition manufactures are compensating for long delivery times by to carry and inventory of less used and expensive components [14] leading to an annual inventory overturn (value) of less than two. The background for the low utilization the production system in a build to order context, can be found in the insufficient distribution of workload. Bottleneck machines are often overloaded but because this information is not available when new products are being customized in the sales situation, no action is taken to sell configurations that are not utilizing overloaded equipment or choosing modules in inventory over modules that have to be ordered, despite there will be no functional difference in the customers perception of the product.

To avoid these BTO compensation models information management tools can be applied to manage the customization process based on customer value, thereby creating a production situation more similar, in transparency, to the one of a mass production manufacturer, by enabling a higher utilization of inventory and production system, without sacrificing throughput time and cost.

In the order specification phase the manufacturer is giving the customer a promise without knowing the precise workload on the machines and which components are in stock. Consequently the actual delivery time and cost is unknown. Decisions are often based on experience and intuition instead of operational data. To reach an acceptable level of efficiency this craft based approach must be replaced with decisions based on facts, and this can only be done through and industrialization process, where data is structured, and formatted for reuse.

One of the major reasons that the production - and inventory systems are not used to it fullest is the lack of valid information since precise data have never been so critical as with customized products [5]. Lack of valid data has proven to be a problem for manufacturers of customized products [10], and without accurate data efficient production, not to mention mass customization, is not feasible.

3 Tools Supporting Mass Customization

However the tools to realize the full potential of mass customization are available. Configurators have proven to be capable of handling constraints determined by structural and business rules, and Advanced Planning Systems (APS) have demonstrated the capability to optimize manufacturing and inventory management for fixed product structures, however APS and configurators are currently trapped in sales- and planning stove pips.

Since the days of Henry Ford information systems have had a tendency to be build as vertical stovepipes based on organizational boarders, and this is also true for the specification process. Currently state of the art offers integrated solutions within an area e.g. structural design where we have seen how configurators have revolutionized the structural adaptation, APS systems have provided production planners with tools that will enable them to optimize production and lean projects have the potential to revolutionize business processes by overcoming the barriers of data silos allowing a process orientated cross organizational integration to the direct benefit of the customer. But these improvements will only fulfill their full potential when they are integrated, and data can travel freely between them. In this paper will be looking at configurators and planning systems as mass customization enabling technologies. From a lean perspective these technologies plays a critical role in delivering value to the customer. The customer perceived value when it comes to mass customization is primary the improved functionality relative the cost and delivery trade of. By applying the methods suggested, the balance will be tipped towards lower cost and shorter delivery times to a point where cost is not only comparable to mass produced products but lower, and delivery time is acceptable, and can become a parameter that is a function of cost. This goes beyond what Pine [13] setup as the initial vision. The key to realizing this potential will be through the dynamic utilization of inventory as well as production capacity allowed through the integration of advanced planning systems and product configurators.

The use of configurators has improved the efficiency of the specification process radically [9].

The typically consequences of installing configurators are [2],[7]:

- Reduced adaptation time
- Increased customer satisfaction
- Increased uniformity in solutions
- Fewer technical problems
- Improved enquiry to order ration
- Engineering focus on long term development
- Better opportunity for accurate planning

By using a configurator the customer can improve the structural design through an iterative decision process. By switching modules the customer can easily work on perfecting the solution, thereby getting the best possible solution, for the customer that is. The price calculation is based on the exploded BOM, where each unit used is priced. After the configuration is locked the order is entered in to the back office system. The configurator is a static representation of the knowledge in the operational system. By holding this knowledge in a configurator, it is easily accessible. Being a static representation, the configurator holds no knowledge regarding the dynamics of the operational system, thereby providing insufficient knowledge regarding the materialization process.

The price calculation of most configurators is based on the exploded BOM (bill of material), where each unit used is priced using a list price thereby the actual not representing the actual manufacturing cost, but most often a best case scenario. This pricing model is totally inadequate for mass customization build to order product, because a BOM do not reflect the manufacturing context at the time of production, so ensuring profitability is at best a gamble.

If we look at the current state of the art specification processes, the sales process is completed and the configuration is locked the order is entered in to the back office system. Leading software companies (SAP R/3 APO, Oracle business suite) have solutions that can provide a delivery date estimation based on an ATP (available to promise)[11]. The problem of this approach is the assumption that the production system is a stable system with fixed through put times and production cost. This is far from the case especially in "build to order" production where the workload is constantly shifting. Especially, if the number of units is low, the fluctuations will constantly be altering the cost and throughput times. Giving an ATP is a step in the right direction, but it is a one way communication thereby leaving little room for optimization, and no information about the actual cost of the product. But it is not possible to consider production data as variables equal to the modules of a customized product.

The key to eliminating the stove pipes is a performance based approach to product configuration. Instead of conventional configuration where the customer chooses a set of modules, the customer defines a performance criteria. For a homogenizer that might be volume/hr. max/min temp., and desired pressure. These requirements then constrains the solution space initially. Within the constraint solution space the customer chooses to optimize based on criteria's such as delivery time, cost, potential for upgrades etc.

Basically this method is a iterative compared to the conventional waterfall approach. By pulling the information from the APS system into the configuration it will be possible to calculate the lowest production cost and delivery time based on workload and current inventory under the constraints of customers performance requirements and the structural solution space.

In the approach illustrated in figure 2, the first step is that the combination of modules that meet the customers functional requirements is calculated. An initial subset of product structures are the submitted to the planning system based on lowest estimated/average cost and delivery time. These product structures are then submitted to the planning system where actual cost and delivery time is calculated, and within these product structures, structures that contains components manufactured on bottleneck machines are the modules are replaced with components manufactured on non-bottleneck machines. Components that are not in inventory are replaced with components in inventory (with a cost similar to the original component and purchasing cost if the delivery is optimized based on cost) additionally components with a high inventory overturn can be replaced with components with a low inventory overturn to keep a current inventory etc..

Then the configuration is presented to the customer and the customer can then chooses an alternative modules for each selected module and the customer can select among valid alternatives and the consequences will be recalculated.

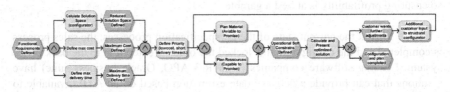

Fig. 2. An example of the iterative process of configuration and planning that allows optimized utilization of inventory and capacity.

By having direct access to the tradeoffs that are made in the customization process it will be possible to optimize the utilization of inventory and production. This can be achieved if the data from the planning system can be integrated in the configurator, thereby the customer and manufacturer can find a solution that is mutual beneficial. The customer will get lower prices as the manufacturer can improve inventory turnover and utilization of the production system. An application of the production data in the sales situation can be an optimization of the configuration against delivery time.

By prioritizing the utilization of existing inventory over purchases and utilization of available production equipment over bottleneck machines, it is possible to configure a solution that is optimized from both a manufacturer and customer perspective, and potentially the cost can be significantly lower than conventional

BTO production where inventories rapidly become obsolete and the distribution of work load is poor, and this is enabled by integrating sales data with operational data over the organizational boundaries.

The reason why this is optimization is possible is that the configuration is based on functional requirements rather than the conventional approach of using the product structure, so instead of focusing on components used, it would focus on what the customer is going to use the product for as described in [17],[18].

4 Conclusion

In the modern manufacturing organization information have become the key to profitability. Integrated digital order processing significant potential, currently the majority of order realization processes are still manually operated or only supported by stovepipe legacy systems. This is probably related to complexity and our historical inability to align cross-functional software solutions with business processes. This paper demonstrates how cross-functional business processes may be aligned with product specification systems in a cross organization environment by integrating planning systems and configuration systems thereby providing an end-to-end integrated and an automated solution to the built to order challenge. As an outcome the potential market for customized products will expand, through a reduction in administrative and manufacturing cost. Ideally the IT-infrastructure would be laid out to accommodate this type of operation, unfortunately there is often a disconnect between the actual task and the IT landscape. This paper suggests that the current scope of IT-systems is often misaligned with the implications of lean business processes and consequently the true potential of mass customization is not realized. This paper has described how mass customization potentially has an efficiency potential that goes beyond what Pine [13] setup as the initial vision. The key to realizing this potential will be through the dynamic utilization of inventory as well as production capacity allowed through the integration of advanced planning systems and product configurators.

References

1. Agrawal, M., Kumaresh, T.V and Mercer, G. A. (2001). The false promise of mass customization; The McKinsey quarterly, 3, 62-71.

2. Bonehill E. and Slee-Smith P. (1998). Product configurators. Responsiveness in manufacturing. IEE. 213.

3. Barfod, Ari and Hvolby, Hans-Henrik (1994): Administrative Rationalisation by Applying Activity Chains". Issues of Integration in Manufacturing, 9th IPS Research Seminar, Department of Production, Aalborg University, April.

4. Boynton, A.C. Victor, B. and Pine, B.J. (1993). New competitive strategies: challenges to organization and information technology, IBM systems Journal, 32, 1993.

5. Eastwood, M. A. (1996). Implementing mass customization. Computers in industry, 20, 171-174.

6. Gilmore, J. H. and Pine II, J.B. (1997). The four faces of mass customization, Harvard Business Review, 75(1), 91-102.

7. Horneys, D. (1993). A better way to "build to order". Machine design, august 13.

8. Hvam, L. Have, U. (1998). Re-engineering the specification process. Business process management journal, 4(1).

9. Hvam L., Riis J., Malis, M. and Hansen B. (2000). A procedure for building product models. Proceedings, PM (Product models) Linköbing.

10. Hvolby, H.H. and Barfod A. (1998). Design of integration in manufacturing. Proceedings of the 13'th IPS Research Seminar, Denmark..

11. Knolmayer G., Mertens P. and Zeier A.. (2002) Supply Chain Management Based on SAP Systems, Order Management in Manufacturing Companies, Springer.

12. Kotha Suresh. (1995). Mass customization: implementing the emerging paradigm for competitive advantage. strategic management journal, 16, 21-42.

13. Pine II, J.B. (1993). Mass customization, the new frontier in business competition, Harvard business school press, Boston.

14. Pine, J. Victor B. Boynton A. (1993) Making Mass customization work. *Harvard Business review, 108-119.*

15. Prahalad, C.K.and Hamel G. (1990). The core competence of the corporation. Harvard Business Review, may- june. 79-91.

16. Skinner, W. (1974) The focused factory. Harvard Business Review. may-june. 113-121.

17. Svensson, C. (2002) Experiences from implementing a low cost configurator,The 5th International SMESME Conference. Danbury .

18. Svensson, C. and Jensen, T. (2003) Mass Customization for Competitive Advantage, edited by Mitchell M. Tseng and Frank T. Piller, to be published by Springer.

19. Zipkin, Paul. (2001). The limits of mass customization. MIT Sloan management review, spring, 81 -88.

PART THREE

Value Chains

Exploring Competitive Advantage through Lean Implementation in the Aerospace Supply Chain

Valerie Crute, Allan Wickham, Richard Johns and Andrew Graves
UK Lean Aerospace Initiative, School of Management
University of Bath, Bath, United Kingdom

Abstract. This research paper provides an initial exploration of the factors influencing whether lower tier suppliers gain a competitive advantage through their implementation of Lean manufacturing, and highlights the implications for the aerospace industry and for the SMEs. The research findings indicated that the SMEs regarded Lean as a necessity to meet the growing demands of their customers and to remain profitable in an increasingly competitive environment. The study concludes that while Lean initiatives have lead to numerous benefits for the SMEs, the assumption can not be made that Lean initiatives directly provide sustainable competitive advantage, as this is dependent on a number of complex and interdependent issues.

1 Introduction

Many UK aerospace companies are in the process of adopting the lean manufacturing philosophy, developed in the automotive industry by Toyota (1,2). As Lee and Oakes (3) suggest, at the forefront of Lean implementation are the prime aerospace manufacturers whose increasing dependence on outsourcing places significant pressure on the smaller component manufacturers to undergo significant change. Lee and Oakes state, *"[as] large companies concentrate on their core activities, the development of alliances and partnerships becomes a key strategic issue and smaller firms struggle to compete on cost, quality and delivery, to maintain a place within a supply chain"* (p.197). Many lower-tier suppliers are now attempting to implement Lean practices in their operations (4). Suppliers recognise that they must either develop the capabilities that customers seek or face the possibilities of acquisition or exit from the industry, through diversification or closure. For many SMEs Lean implementation has become 'a survival issue as well as an improvement issue' (4). However, while Lean implementation has been shown to provide operational benefits, it is difficult to track the financial benefits associated

Please use the following format when citing this chapter:

Crute, V., Wickham, A., Johns, R. and Graves, A., 2008, in IFIP International Federation for Information Processing, Volume 257, Lean Business Systems and Beyond, Tomasz Koch, ed.; (Boston: Springer), pp. 357–364.

with these improvements (5) and to identify whether such benefits have provided competitive advantage.

The term 'strategic competitive advantage' emerged in 1985, when Porter identified types of strategies the firm can implement to gain competitive advantage. He went on to describe that when these advantages are resistant to erosion by competitors' efforts then firms achieve sustainable competitive advantage (6). This concept of sustained competitive advantage was then further defined by Barney (7), "*a firm is said to have a sustained competitive advantage when it is implementing a value creating strategy not simultaneously being implemented by any current or potential competitors and when these other firms are unable to duplicate the benefits of this strategy*" (p102). Barney (7,8) argues that the sustainability of competitive advantage depends upon the possibility of duplication by current or future competitors, that is competitive advantage is only sustained if it continues to exist after all the efforts to duplicate the advantage have ceased.

However, creating more value than your competitors is not enough unless this difference is recognised by the customer within the marketplace. Coyne (9) reflected this when he stated that "*For a producer to enjoy competitive advantage in a product/market segment, the difference or differences between him and his competitors must be felt in the marketplace: that is they must be reflected in some product or delivery attribute that is a key buying criterion for the market*" (p.55). Inherent in this definition is the idea that the customer ultimately defines the value of the product.

Collis and Montgomery (10) noted that the Lean manufacturing principles of Japanese automobile companies were based on organisational resources embedded in the culture, routines, and processes of a company and as such, they considered Lean to be a source of competitive advantage. However, this may not be the case for SMEs and little attention has been directed to the question "Does Lean implementation give small aerospace suppliers sustainable competitive advantage?"

2 Methodology:

This research paper provides an initial exploration of the factors influencing whether lower tier suppliers gain a competitive advantage through their implementation of Lean manufacturing, and highlights the implications for the aerospace industry and for the SMEs. The exploratory case study method was chosen due to the lack of current research in the area (11).

A "purposive" or "judgemental" sampling method (11,12) was used to identify cases where lean practices had been implemented, operational benefits had been gained and the research could examine the companies' perspective on competitive advantage. Qualitative semi-structured interviews were completed within three Small Medium Enterprises resulting in an exploratory multi-case study. A number of procedures carried out during data collection ensured the reliability of the findings including the production of an interview protocol ensured repeatability of the research (11). In each of the case studies interviews were completed with the General Manager, Production Manager and Production Engineer or Cell Leader. The interviews focused on the motivation for Lean implementation; identifying any benefits gained; and the companies' assessment of competive advantage gained through Lean implementation.

The three companies involved in the study were:

- Company A - a supplier of highly technical insulations to the aerospace industry, engineering lightweight high temperature thermal insulation systems for various applications.
- Company B - produces high quality and well-priced products to service the aerospace industry, providing expert solutions to machining requirements.
- Company C - a modern machine shop producing high precision components and assemblies to the aerospace industry. The company has both manufacturing and engineering capabilities.

This qualitative method is powerful in that it is often used to generate hypotheses and to identify variables to use in quantitative approaches (13). Future studies can subsequently use a quantitative or positivistic method to test the hypotheses that the exploratory multi-case study proposes.

3   Findings and discussion:

3.1   Motivation for implementing Lean

The primary motivation for implementing Lean initiatives amongst all the companies interviewed was to gain improvements in Quality, Cost, and Delivery metrics, and the SMEs interviewed regarded Lean as a necessity to meet the growing demands of their customers and to remain profitable in an increasingly competitive environment. Interestingly, all the SMEs interviewed had decided to undergo Lean improvements as part of their own initiative without any coercion or external pressures from customers. There was no assistance or collaborative participation from customers. This suggests that the Lean initiatives undertaken in each company were appropriate to the strategic intent of the business rather than a tactical response to customer demands. It was also clear from the interviews that none of the companies had explicitly linked Lean implementation with gaining competitive advantage and gaining competitive advantage was not a motivating factor for any of the companies at the start of their implementation process.

Hamel and Prahalad (14) favour a strategic approach to change. They highlight that business change is inevitable and that the real issue is whether this change will happen in a crisis atmosphere or with consideration and foresight. They advocate change that is made not to mimic competitors but to fit opportunities in the future environment. In this respect, Lean implementation within SMEs within this study was an appropriate strategy for dealing with the change of competitive environment within the aerospace industry.

3.2   Benefits of Lean implementation

The companies reported the following tangible benefits of Lean implementation to their organizations (Table 1).

Table 1. Reported tangible benefits of Lean implementation to the organisation

Tangible Benefits	Company A	Company B	Company C
Financial	Increased profitability	Decreased stockholdings. Improved cash flow. Increased profitability.	Increased profitability
Operational	33% reduction in focus part manufacturing time. Less effort finding equipment. Improved scheduling of work.	Monitor progress of orders.	Increased people productivity. Reduced set-up times. Production up from 60,000 to 140, 000 parts per month.

The research identified similar benefits from Lean implementation to other organisations within the supply chain including reduced manufacturing times, and reduced changeover times. However as Slack *et al.,* (15) point out, the firm must understand what factors of performance the customer values and strive to satisfy them. They highlight that the performance objectives of the firm's operations are dependent upon the competitive factors that define the customer's requirements. The companies in this study identified cost and delivery performance as being of particular importance to their customers and linked the benefits of lean implementation to the achievement of their quality, cost and delivery (QCD) performance objectives in the following way (Table 2):

Table 2. Reported contribution of Lean activities to QCD Performance Objectives

Performance Objectives	Company A	Company B	Company C
Quality		The system highlights areas to improve.	
Cost	Operational efficiency allows price reductions.	Higher throughput reduces costs.	Price reductions in face of increasing material and labour costs.
Delivery Performance	Delivery expectations exceeded due to reduction in manufacturing times.	Visibility has improved scheduling, improving reliability of supply.	Improvements in on-time delivery, from 15% to approximately 85%.

The companies also reported less tangible benefits including improved training of staff, clearer communication of business objectives, knowledge transfer, improved morale and a perceived culture change to embrace continuous improvement. Collis and Montgomery (10) consider cultural change to be the most significant of these factors, facilitating the competitive revitalisation and the

future competitiveness of the firm and the findings in this study echo findings in
the automotive sector.

4   Competitive advantage through Lean implementation

While it was possible to identify operational and cultural benefits, a more complex
picture emerged on whether these benefits lead to competitive advantage. It is clear
from the results that Lean had created capability gaps among competitors. For
example, Company A in particular saw that the implementation of Lean had
improved the company image and helped with networking. These improvements may
enhance the company's capability to brand their products or services. Urde (16)
recognised that competency at creating a brand image can be a source of competitive
advantage. Lean also enables the firms to exceed the delivery expectations of
customers leading to customer satisfaction. Good service, leading to customer
satisfaction is a core competence that leads to competitive advantage (17,18).

Evidence from the interviews suggests that Lean affects the culture of the firm.
Collis and Montgomery (10) saw that the Lean manufacturing principles of Japanese
automobile companies were based on organisational resources embedded in the
culture, routines, and processes of a company and as such, they saw Lean as a source
of competitive advantage.   The interviewed firms described Lean as creating a
learning curve, suggesting that competitors may always be behind the improvements
of the first movers. In addition, the companies interviewed had implemented Lean in
a quiet period in the industry, and firms implementing Lean in the future may find it
more difficult due to an increasing conflict between running their day-to-day
operations and making continuous improvements.

Hamel and Prahalad (14) recognised that to remain competitive for the future,
companies need to continually adapt. Lean and its philosophy of continuous
improvement would be one way to achieve the continual development and flexibility
of core competencies required by the firm. Prahalad and Hamel (19) propose that an
organisation's capacity to improve existing skills and learn new ones is the most
defensible competitive advantage of all. Therefore, continuous improvement is a
dynamic capability, which provides the basis for achieving and sustaining a
competitive edge in an uncertain and rapidly changing environment (20).

All of the companies interviewed highlighted that maintaining the advantage of
path dependency is dependent upon the other resources of the company. The Toyota
Production System philosophy or the Toyota DNA is described by Drickhamer (21)
as "*a tight coupling of doing work and learning to do work better*" (p. 26). The Lean
approach does require a long-term commitment that is difficult for many
organisations to maintain, especially with constantly rotating managerial ranks (21).
Therefore, the sustainability of Lean as a source of competitiveness requires that the
firm's make available adequate resources to maintain the momentum of its
continuous improvement programmes.

Several of the interviewees highlighted that the benefits of Lean did not
necessarily lead to competitive advantage. Interview responses suggested that the
benefits of Lean only lead to increased competitiveness if they were perceived as

favourable attributes by the customer, that is if they contribute to customer value and therefore customer satisfaction. Coyne (9) also refers to this link between business advantage and competitive advantage. For example, he argues that having lower costs will result in significantly higher margins, but describes that this business advantage only leads to competitive advantage if the producer recycles the additional profits into delivery attributes or product attributes that will be valued within the marketplace. Therefore, the benefits of Lean only lead to increased competitiveness if they are perceived as favourable attributes by the customer, that is if they contribute to customer value and therefore customer satisfaction. As in previous research (4), there was suspicion among the SMEs that some customers used Lean initiatives to reduce their suppliers operating margins, rather than to reduce waste from across the value stream. Several interviewees suggested that their customers lacked the required understanding of Lean, or were more concerned with forcing cost reductions. In addition, some customers encouraged suppliers to hold stock for them. Johns, Crute, and Graves (4) regard this as having a negative affect upon the supplier's profitability and therefore the practice is not conducive to Lean thinking. The poor practices of the customers may be due to the behavioural legacies rooted in mass production, which affect efforts to rapidly introduce change into the aerospace supply chain (22). Traditionally, there has been little inter-firm collaboration in Western business models and Lean conflicts with many preconceptions such as economies of scale. It is the attitudes of some customer organisations that may therefore prevent Lean from becoming a source of competitive advantage for some SMEs.

There was also some evidence in this study that respondents saw the Lean implementation as an 'order-qualifier' rather than 'order-winner'. Hill (23) describes order-winning factors as those things that directly and significantly contribute to winning business; they are the customer's key buying criteria. They are an important determinant of a competitor's stance, as rising performance in one of these areas will either result in more business or improve the chances of gaining new business (15). These factors therefore contribute to competitive advantage, enabling the firm to sustain profits above those of their rivals. Qualifying factors are the threshold requirements of any aspect that are necessary just for the organisation to be considered by the customer, and to therefore remain in business within the industry (Hill, 23). Any improvement upon the threshold level of a qualifying factor will not win the company further business and therefore will not gain competitive benefit (15). Some interviewees expressed the concern that Lean is becoming increasingly seen as an order-qualifier and therefore a pre-requisite for entry into the industry rather than order winner.

5 Conclusions

This study suggests that the SMEs considered Lean initiatives as an appropriate strategy for dealing with changes of the competitive environment in the aerospace industry, rather than as a tactical response to customer demands. It was also apparent that Lean gives SMEs similar benefits to other organisations within the supply chain.

Benefits included improvements in cash flow and profitability, reduced manufacturing times, reduced changeover times, improved training of staff, communication of business objectives, knowledge transfer and improved morale. Although it is clear that these benefits give business advantage in terms of improvements in QCD, it is harder to determine whether these business advantages lead to competitive advantage.

The study concludes that while Lean initiatives have lead to numerous benefits for the SMEs, the assumption can not be made that Lean initiatives directly provide sustainable competitive advantage, as this is dependent on a number of complex and interdependent issues. Further research will clearly be needed to assess the extent to which these results can be generalised to other SMEs in the sector. Likewise future areas for research are suggested which can further clarify the relationship between operational improvement and competitive advantage.

References

1. Womack J.P, Jones D.T, Roos, D. The Machine that Changed the World. New York: Rawson Associates (1990).

2. Womack, J. P. and Jones, D. T. *Lean Thinking: Banish waste and create wealth in your organisation*. Simon and Schuster: New York (1996).

3. Lee, G. L., and Oakes, I. K. "Templates for change with supply chain rationalisation." *International Journal of Operations and Production Management.* 16(2): 197-209 (1996).

4. Johns, R., Crute, V. and Graves, A. "Lean Supply: Cost Reduction or Waste Reduction?" *The Society of British Aerospace Companies*, October (2002).

5. Standard, C. and Davis, D. "Lean thinking for Competitive advantage" *SAE International* [online] (2000). Available from http://www.sae.org/topics/Leandec00.htm [accessed 11/06/2006].

6. Porter, M. E. 1985. Competitive Advantage: Creating and Sustaining Superior Performance. The Free Press: New York (1985).

7. Barney, J. B. "Firm resources and sustained competitive advantage." Journal of Management. 17(1): 99-120 (1991).

8. Barney, J. B. Gaining and Sustaining Competitive Advantage. Addison Wesley: Harlow (1997).

9. Coyne, K. "Sustainable Competitive Advantage: What it is, what it isn't." *Business Horizons 29* (January-February): 54-61 (1986).

10. Collis, D. J., and Montgomery, C. A. "Competing on Resources: Strategy in the 1990s." *Harvard Business Review*. July- August: 118-128 (1995).

11. Yin, R. K. *Case Study Research Design and Methods* 3rd edition (2003).

12. Saunders, M., Lewis, P., and Thornhill, *A. Research Methods for Business Students*. Pitman Publishing: London (1997).

13. Malhotra, N. K. and Birks, D. F. *Marketing Research: An Applied Approach*. Prentice Hall: Harlow, Essex (2002).

14. Hamel, G., and Prahalad, C. K. "Competing for the Future" *Harvard Business Review* (July-August 1994): 122-128.

15. Slack, N., Chambers, S., Harland, C., Harrison, A. and Johnston, R. *Operations Management*. 2nd Edition. Financial Times Prentice Hall: Harlow (1998).

16. Urde, M. "Brand Orientation: A mindset for building brands into strategic resources." *Journal of Marketing Management*. 15(1-3): 117-134 (1999).

17. Katayama, H. and Bennett, D. "Lean production in a changing competitive world: a Japanese perspective." *International Journal of Operations and Production Management*. 16(2): 8-23 (1996).

18. Mariotti, J. "Great Service: The Ultimate Competitive Advantage." Industry Week.com (1997). [online]. Available from http://www.industryweek.com/columns/asp/ ColumnId=302 [accessed 11/02/2006].

19. Prahalad, C. and Hamel, G. "The Core Competence of the Corporation." Harvard Business Review, 68 (May-June): 79-91 (1990).

20. Bessant, J., and Francis, D. "Developing strategic continuous improvement capability." International Journal of Operations and Production Management. 19(11): 1106-1119 (1999).

21. Drickhammer, D. "Lean Manufacturing: The 3rd Generation" *Industry Week* March 2004: 25-30 (2004).

22. Michaels, L. M. J.. "The making of a Lean aerospace supply chain." Supply Chain Management: An international Journal. 4(3): 135-145 (1999).

23. Hill, T. Operations Management: strategic context and managerial analysis. London: MacMillan Press (1993).

Intercultural Communication Management and Lean Global Supply Chains
- a conceptual approach -

Prof. Dr.-Ing. Bernd Hamacher
Faculty of Engineering & Computer Science
University of Applied Sciences Osnabrueck
D-49009 Osnabrueck, Germany

Abstract. With the development of global value chains misunderstandings due to different cultural habits and rules are a relevant issue. Studies show that lack of intercultural competence results in enormous losses and frictions in negotiations, sales and customer relationships. Despite the merits of training seminars general training will not be sufficient to solve the challenges of intercultural management. What we also need is a different perception of Information Management Systems, which not only provide proper information transfer, but also contextual awareness on cultural differences and ambiguities. The discussion of requirements and consequences of cultural issues on the design of proper communication management is subject of this paper. It will be a conceptual approach exploring findings from psychology, sociology, organisational-anthropology and communication-management, but the paper will also describe appropriate developments in Knowledge-Management Systems.

1 Introduction

Supply chain management usually is understood as planning, executing, and designing across multiple supply chain partners to deliver products of the right design, in the right quantity, at the right place, at the right time. This means integration of manufacturing and logistics along the chain, the integration of the product design, the proper cooperation management between partners and the optimization of the interfaces between customers and suppliers. Lean supply chain management in this context usually means application of lean manufacturing principles, especially the elimination of waste, on the whole chain comprising several layers of tiers. A lean supply chain also means an optimized chain where a seaming less material flow is governed by a reverse material flow (Fig. 1)

Please use the following format when citing this chapter:

Hamacher, B., 2008, in IFIP International Federation for Information Processing, Volume 257, Lean Business Systems and Beyond, Tomasz Koch, ed.; (Boston: Springer), pp. 365–372.

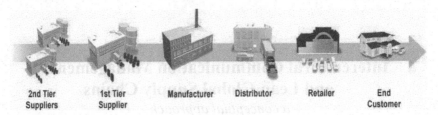

Fig. 1. A typical SCM model

But despite the achievements of information and communication technology the information management concept behind these kinds of the SCM-models are not adequate to map the requirements of global supply chains. This is not a matter of standards, interfaces and IT-performance, but a more fundamental problem that the model of human communication is not adequate. Most of the information management models consider information as a thing, which can be transferred from one place to another. This might work in very simplified situations, where information management just consist of the processing of well defined part-numbers, quantities and delivery addresses. But communication in developed global supply chains cannot be reduced to exchange of part-numbers. But if we talk about complex negotiations, conflict resolution and the set-up of business relationships we have to consider global supply chains as complex socio-technical systems, which must be managed and equipped according to the needs of heterogeneous people involved. Therefore the main two hypotheses of this paper are:

- The metaphor of communication as a transfer process is no longer adequate and should be replaced by a constructivistic concept of human interaction in SCM-systems.
- The role of misunderstandings and emotions rooted in different values, beliefs and cultural procedures must be explicitly captured in SCM-systems.

The inappropriateness of conventional Information-Management-Systems in multi-cultural environments is not new, but could be compensated by the old Tayloristic principles of simplification and standardization in many cases and for a long time. As long as Information-Management in supply-chains could be handled as transfer of simple and clear defined information between different actors, the deficits of this approach became not so evident. As long as it is possible to drill users to adhere to predefined definitions and procedures, the danger of misunderstanding is tolerable. So lean communication management could be misunderstood as well defined information transfer. But with the shift from Information-Management to Knowledge-Management this approach becomes inappropriate, as it is literally impossible to capitalize all business requirements in simple, predefined processes. Especially in a global environments, where data and symbols may have different meanings, may cause different emotions and may conflict with different values, it is a hopeless attempt to specify standardized glossaries for every piece of information, as the cultural meaning is often hidden from outside. Cultural behaviour is to a wide extend unconsciously for the actor and invisible to the spectator and this is the crucial point for proper communication management and main reason for misunderstanding.

2   The autopoietic model of communication and learning

Proper Information supply is considered as a key element in global supply chain management. But despite the improvements in ICT, this challenge is far away from being solved. Practitioner complain about weak performance of current information systems and users state tha information come often too late, are fragmented or lost in black holes in the process. Is that technically so difficult to model and support a thorough information process? May be. But it is claimed here that not the technology is really the bottleneck. The bottleneck is more likely that we have a wrong model of communication in mind, when we talk about business communication. As we believe that technology can solve the problem we refer to a model of technical communication rather to an adequate model of human communication. Indeed in most articles on communication, the communication model of Shannon/Weaver is employed even to model human communication. This model was introduced 1949 by C. Shannon and W. Weaver on the attempt to construct a mathematical theory for technical communication and signal processing [1] and can be summarized as a transfer process encoding a message to a signal by a transmitter and decoding the signal back to the original message using a receiver. Moreover the model pinpoints the role of noise and redundancy in the transmission process, the necessity that transmitter and receiver are using the same medium, that receiver and transmitter are tuned and that on both sides there is an inventory of same symbols, same meanings and same references from symbols to meanings. This requires standardization on both sides and we know from the ISO/OSI architectures on telecommunication, that reference models and standardization have successfully enabled worldwide telecommunication facilities.

Although this model has been proven to be useful in technical communication it has severe shortcomings to explain human communication, especially the difference between information and communication. With regard to information two conflicting metaphors exists: The metaphor of information as a quantity, like water in the water pipe, but there is a second metaphor, that of information as choice - a choice made by an information provider, and a forced choice made by an information receiver. Actually, the second metaphor implies that the information sent isn't necessarily equal to the information received, because any choice implies a comparison with a list of possibilities, i.e. a list of possible meanings. Many authors in information theory insist that information has an essence and exists independent from reception. According to Stonier information exists as material reality independently of human perception: *"Information exists. It does not need to be perceived to exist. It does not need to be understood to exist. It requires no intelligence to interpret it. It does not have to have meaning to exist. It exists."* [2]. On the other hand it is obvious that human beings are not forced to perceive any information provided, but have a choice to perceive or disregard offered information's. "Information isn't just information in itself; it only becomes information when it is information *to somebody*" [2]. This reference to the individual context and to recognition as an active process of the recipient makes the metaphor of information transfer, like transfer of a physical good so inadequate. According to Niklas Luhmann there are at least three reasons to reject this substance metaphor: Firstly, the substance metaphor suggests that the sender gives away something which is received by the receiver. But the sender doesn't lose anything, not even a single bit, by sending information. Secondly, it suggests that the information which has been sent is identical to the information received. Normally, this isn't true. What I wrote is not necessarily' what you read. What you said isn't necessarily what I heard. Thirdly, it suggests that communication is a two-step and thus, a one-way process; the sender sends, and the receiver receives. Again, this isn't true. Just try to phone to somebody who doesn't answer. [3]

Based on the research work of Humberto Maturana and Franscisco Varela in the 1970 a new communication paradigm evolved called Autopoiesis. According to this paradigm human beings are not open systems, but must be considered as closed systems, equipped with a personal mental system coined by socialization and learning, which makes everyone to an unique, but lonely resident in the world. In this view communication is not a process of transferring information's from one to another, but a process of mutual triggering for the selection of adequate models in an interaction. "Notions such as coding and transmission of information do not enter in the realization of a concrete autopoietic system because they do not refer to actual processes in it. (...) The notion of coding is a cognitive notion which represents the interactions of the observer, not a phenomenon operative in the observed domain." [4]. "Autopoietic machines do not have inputs or outputs. They can be perturbated by independent events and undergo internal structural changes which compensate these perturbations. What is normally perceived as interaction, seemingly based on the exchange of information, is in reality behavioral coupling of closed, mutually perturbating systems." This model of communication meanwhile is widely accepted by leading social scientists like Niklas Luhmann and Friedemann Schulz von Thun and can be considered as a new paradigm of human communication. This model has at least three practical consequences for proper information management:

1. The perception of information is not a passive, but an active process governed by the recipient. He or she has the authority to accept the information as he or she a difference to former perceptions or a meaning to accept the information. And it is the role of the source in a communication process to issue the right (or wrong) signals to trigger an adequate mental model at the recipient. In any case perception should be considered as an active process of the recipient constructing a new or revised mental model

2. Communication is to a wide extend a process to detect and settle misunderstandings. As information cannot simply be transferred to other persons, but is limited to trigger signals, the participants in a communication process should pay attention that the triggered mental model is in coherence with the sender's mental model. So in general participants of a successful

communication process provide effort and methods (i.e. counter questions) in order to the compatibility of the mutual mental models.

3. The perception of information is a learning process. According to related cognition theory, the mental models of an individual must be considered as schemes which guides behaviour and the exploration of the real world. If an object of the real world fits to the mental model representation than the validity of the model is confirmed to the owner and he will be encouraged to apply this model. This in turn means that human beings will be open for information, if they feel the necessity or a benefit to revise existing schemes or to create new mental models and add it to the asset of exiting schemes. But as there is usually a choice, there is as well uncertainty to make the right choice. The notion of uncertainty is essential for learning processes, as the learner take a risk that the new model is not adequate and will turn out to be not reliable. Therefore the process from a theoretical insight to a new behaviour, supported by a proven schema is associated with uncertainty and the individual tolerance to accept this [5]. Very interesting in this context is than learning should not only consider as a process of knowledge acquisition, but as well an enculturation process to arrive as an accepted member of group. This addresses an important driving for a cultural integrated global supply chain embedding shared ways of thinking and shared ways of common operations.

3   The role of culture and intercultural competence development

The concept of culture usually means the whole body of values, beliefs, symbols, rules and procedures characteristic for a specific group, region or nation. Geert Hofstede defines culture as "the collective mental programming of the people in an environment. Culture is not characteristic of individuals; it encompasses a number of people who were conditioned by the same education and life experience. When we speak of the culture of a group, a tribe, a geographical region, a national minority, or a nation, culture refers to the collective mental programming that these people have in common; the programming that is different from that of other groups, tribes, regions, minorities or majorities, or nations"[6]. Cultures in this sense are the commonalities what bridges the lonely island residents as outlined above and which provide identity as a group. So culture eases the interactions within a cultural group, because the members of the same culture are confident that they share the same values and beliefs, that they share common accepted procedures and that they attribute similar meanings to common symbols. There are numerous cultures in the world and scientists like Geert Hofstede introduced cultural dimensions like power distance, individualism/collectivism, masculinity/femininity and uncertainty avoidance to distinguish and describe cultural characteristics of different nations. These dimensions are very useful to understand, where the differences between countries are and where a preparation is necessary to avoid cultural misunderstandings. Cultural induced misunderstandings are an issue in global value chains and many companies place significant effort in preparation of employees to avoid cultural misunderstandings as far as possible. As there is extensive research and literature to this subject, I cannot go into details here, but will highlight three issues relevant for the design of information management in global SCM-systems:

1. In normal situations the impact of culture is not visible to members living in a culture. Members of a culture take the values, rules and procedures of a culture as granted. Therefore measures are required to allow members of cultures a view from „outside", to make the own cultural visible and to create awareness on cultural dependencies.

2. The risk of cultural misunderstandings is not rooted in the objective consequences of the misunderstanding itself, but in the possible emotional power associated with. As we know that cultural misunderstandings can cause strong emotions like shame or embarrassment, which in turn seriously influence decision or relationships, we must carefully consider this in management procedures of information. In western cultures we overestimate in general the role of rationale decision making and underestimate the role of emotions. Here the familiarisation with methodologies like Kensai-Engineering might be useful. But also the existing research on counterfactual thinking that there is a world beyond logical reasoning and decision

3. Despite the importance of cultural coining we should not overlook the individual and his personality in a communication process. Quite often you can observe that cultural stereotypes are applied to communication partners instead adequately taken in account the individual personality. This especially is important in conflict resolution situations.

The immediate consequence out of these considerations is that global supply chain management must intentionally place effort to develop intercultural competence along the chain. This in general is widely accepted and there are many programmes available in this field. Experiences show that successful programmes for intercultural management should contain three elements:

1. A cognitive element providing knowledge on foreign cultures. This addresses the rationale and factual basis of cultures.
2. An affective element providing insights on own and foreign emotional reactions. This addresses the emotional awareness on cultural differences and creates readiness to distrust own emotions in business situations.
3. A behavioral element providing training experiences in foreign interactions. This addresses the development of competences and practice in adequate foreign procedures.

Many programmes are meanwhile available addressing these elements successfully towards the development of intercultural competence. These programmes are usually based on classroom concepts where people come together in a classroom, getting lectures, videos and other materials to extend the knowledge of the target culture and doing role-games and other training exercises to achieve the right emotional awareness and competence in interaction. This way of learning bears a lot of advantages, especially by intensive supervision, close face-to-face communication and extended social communication as a group. Nevertheless these programmes are usually executed as single or repeated events prior to adventure of foreign cultures. These programmes are usually briefing measures or debriefing measures after return – during the time actually faced with other cultures they usually not occur. This is not a principal problem, it is just a question of effort. It is simply too expensive to call participants from all over the world regularly together or to send frequently trainers to all subsidiaries and construction sites of a company. To make intercultural competence development even for SMEs affordable it is therefore desirable, to provide on-the-job learning facilities to allow continuous reflection and hence a continuous improvement of the intercultural competence. The development and application of e-learning programmes is not only justified by the savings of money, but also recommended by the methodological argument that competence development is a matter of growth, which again is a function of time and continuous work. Therefore I advocate for the development of e-learning facilities for this purpose, although I admit that face-to-face meetings have unbeatable advantages. Therefore I propose to see this as complementary elements rather than alternatives.

4 Conclusion

The immediate conclusion from the findings above is that global SCM-systems requiring additional communication capabilities addressing communication as a process creating mutual understanding and acquaintance with thinking and feeling of communications partners in a supply chain. These communication Systems must be capable to support improvements in communication and understanding rather than just exchange predefined data. For an elaborate cooperation simplification seems to be a dead-end strategy. Instead richness of media, richness of communication channels and richness of communication opportunities seems to be more appropriate.

Recent developments show already tools and concepts in that direction. Especially the Business Communities [7] turned out as a very useful tool to create confidence between partners and to allow a communicative exchange between heterogeneous user groups comprising experts to novice. Exactly this is to be supported in an elaborated supply-chain especially under the heading of joint. knowledge management in a cooperative supply-chain. Another example in this direction is the internet based "METRO Business Simulation System"[8]. This system is especially designed for employees of the METRO company, to become more acquainted with the tasks and challenges of neighbored division and business sectors of METRO. Unlike conventional systems it is not rooted in predefined and standardized information units, but employs game-like facilities to support a mutual learning process of different users with different background. The usage of game-like facilities for the communication management in global supply-chains seems to me very promising and I have presented recently a framework for this [9]

Apart from adequate system support allowing rich-media and rich-concept communication it will be essential that global SCM is embedded in an adequate communication strategy and in adequate communication management. Communication management is usually seen as the task of people dealing with advertising and public relation management. This might be adequate for single companies. But for supply-chains comprising a number of different partners it is essential that the communication between the partners of a supply-chain is supported by a dedicated communication management strategy. Especially in complex supply-chain it is not sufficient to leave the design of communication between different partners up to single employees. It is the duty of each company to staff their employees with a consistent communication strategy as well as procedures and training to perform communication events successfully and coherent. This is what employees should expect.

References

1. Shannon, C.E. Weaver, W., The mathematical Theory of Communication, Urbana, Illinois (1948).

2. Qvortrup L., The Controversy over the Concept of Information. In: Cybernetics & Human Knowing, vol. 1, N. 4, (1993, S. 3-24).

3. Luhmann, N, Soziale Systeme. Grundriss einer allgemeinen Theorie Suhrkamp Verlag, Frankfurt a. M. (1984, p. 193f.).

4. Maturana, Humberto R. and Varela, Francisco J., Autopoiesis and Cognition. The Realization of the Living, Reidel Publishing Company, Dordrecht (1980).

5. Hamacher B, Theoriegestützte CIM-Gestaltung, Shaker Verlag, Aachen (1996).

6. Hofstede, G., Cultures Consequences: Comparing Values, Bahaviours, Institutions and Organizations accross Nations, Sage, California (2001).

7. Bullinger J, Baumann T., Fröschle N., Mack O., Trunzer T., Waltert J.: Business Communities. Professionelles Beziehungsmanagement von Kunden, Mitarbeitern und B2B-Partnern im Internet. Bonn (2002).

8. METRO Business Simulation http://www.metro-business-simulation.de.

9. Hamacher B., Global Value Chains, Intercultural Competence and Educational Games – Towards an integrative approach, in: Hussein B.A., Smeds R., Riis J. (eds.) Proceedings of the 10th International workshop of the IFIP WG 5.7 SIG on Experimental Interactive Learning in Industrial Management, Trondheim (2006, p 7-18).

Building Global Workflow From The Scratch

An Approach Based On Integration of Heterogenic Workflows by Mediators

Mayyad Jaber[1], Youakim Badr[1], Frederique Biennier[1]

1 INSA-Lyon, National Institute of Applied Sciences
PRISMa, Laboratory of production engineering and computer science
for manufacturing systems
7 Av. Jean Capelle, 69627 Villeurbanne – France

Abstract. In a fast changing environment, enterprises need to constantly refine their processes in order to effectively meet the requirements needed for achieving on-demand collaboration in order to win new opportunities as a result of market evolution. This paper introduces the global and common Workflow for cross-enterprises collaboration. A problem that stems from the global Workflow is the need to integrate running ad hoc processes whose descriptions unpredictably change to accommodate the business agility. Through this paper, we propose an approach based on synchronization points between processes of two or more enterprises. These points act as mediators to interface ad hoc processes without considering their definitions at the design time neither their evolution during the execution. A case study, relating to e-procurement, will illustrate the introduced concepts.

Keywords. B2B e-commerce, inter-enterprise Business Process, Workflow, ad hoc Workflow, Mediator.

1 Context

Nowadays enterprises have to deal with global competition, reduce the cost of productions, and rapidly develop new services and products. As a result, they must constantly reconsider and optimize the way they do business and adapt their information systems to support flexible Business Processes. Such dynamic process organization involves managing different process maturity levels depending on the reached structuring level (Ruiz et al. 2002). Workflow technology deals with these requirements by offering methodologies and software tools to support Business

---

Please use the following format when citing this chapter:

Jaber, M., Badr, Y. and Biennier, F., 2008, in IFIP International Federation for Information Processing, Volume 257, Lean Business Systems and Beyond, Tomasz Koch, ed.; (Boston: Springer), pp. 373–381.

Process modeling and cross-enterprises collaboration. Current Workflow products focus on two extremes: completely *unstructured processes* and highly *structured processes*. On the one hand, the groupware products that typically aim at supporting unstructured processes are completely unaware of the Business Process, where cases are handled according to a fixed definition of the tasks to be performed and their order. This kind of Business Process is characterized by a high frequency and a high level of standardization (i.e., Lotus Notes (Ginsburg et al. 1997)). On the other hand, the traditional Workflows are aware of the Business Process (i.e. Staffware, MQSeries Workflow (Aalst 2002)). In fact, they typically support highly structured Business Processes defined at the design time.

In the daily work of the real world of business collaboration between enterprises, most Business Processes are in-between the two extremes sketched above. They are known as *ad hoc Workflows* which are not based on *process templates*. These ad hoc Workflows provide the procedural backbone that can be filled in and varied upon to accommodate the requirements of individual cases. Each individual case can be modified to meet specific needs. The templates do not prescribe in detail how cases are to be handled, but allow a certain degree of flexibility(Wombacher et al. 2002).

In a fast changing environment, enterprises need to constantly refine their ad hoc processes in order to effectively meet the opportunities proposed by new market requirements and on-demand collaboration. Dealing with ad-hoc processes in an adequate way is important to improve the cross-enterprise Workflow between two or more enterprises. One of the challenging issues in ad hoc Workflows is the integration of running processes whose descriptions are modified and varied without prediction or any prior knowledge(Wombacher et al. 2002). Although the information and communication technologies facilitate the exchange of cases and information between information systems, the dynamic integration of local ad hoc Workflows into a global Workflow becomes one of the most challenging problems.

We propose in this paper a solution for the problem of ad hoc and formal Workflows integration into one coherent global Workflow maintained by different cyber-partners. We propose an approach based on Mediators between heterogeneous Workflow. The Mediator acts as an interface between distributed Workflows taking into account their dynamic definitions and their evolution during the execution.

The remainder of this paper is organized as follows. First we discuss the process of inter-enterprise Business Process orchestration together with ad hoc Workflows and the integration of heterogeneous Workflows. In section 3, we introduce the notion of Mediator and its composition as the basic item in our approach. A case study of e-procurement is illustrated about the integration of heterogeneous Workflows. Finally, we summarize the main conclusions and give an outlook on our future work (section 4).

2   Orchestration of inter-enterprise Business Processes

In the domain of B2B e-commerce, common BP can be seen as an interconnection of different enterprises local Workflows, orchestrated according to the goal to achieve (Figure 1).

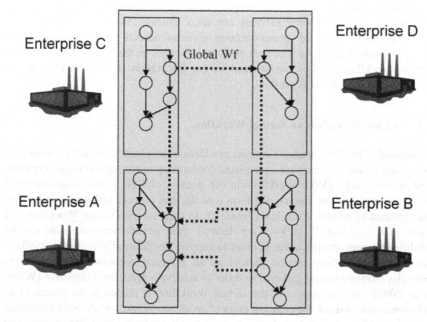

Enterprise C

Enterprise D

Enterprise A

Enterprise B

Fig. 1. Global Workflow

Common BPs are modeled as an ordered set of tasks achieved either by human or machinery actors. Consequently, they can be turned into a global Workflow oriented system(Jaber et al. 2005). In order to automate the interconnection among business entities, local Workflows should be merged so that information can be shared between partners and coordination abilities are improved.

A Workflow is a collection of activities and data that defines the paths that can be taken to complete a task within a process (Chiu et al. 2004; DiCaterino et al. 1997). A B2B Workflow based approach can be derived from traditional EDI (Electronic Data Exchange) or C-Business environment. For this purpose, Aalst (van der Aalst W. 2002) proposes multiple descriptions of shared Business Process: public and private Workflows are defined concurrently and the global consistency is achieved thanks to well-defined information exchange format (Bussler 2002). By this way collaborative business processes are defined as a set of interconnected private parts (black boxes for which only the interfaces (inputs and outputs) are known) and public parts (white boxes including precise process descriptions).

Depending on the process maturity level, different process organization can be set: either informal processes are used (in this case they can be modeled as ad hoc Workflow) or they are well defined and allow a formal Workflow implementation.

As far as inter-enterprise processes are concerned, the extended EDI based on ebXML can be used to provide an open and reactive framework to support inter-enterprise co-operation and provide heterogeneous systems interconnection abilities. According to these requirements, core components (i.e. message formats coupled to e-Business Process description) are defined as re-usable and exchangeable information units (Oasis 2001). Moreover, such e-service infrastructure can be stored in registries so that binding services can set a dynamic Workflow. Nevertheless, these approaches lack of interconnection abilities needed for the integration of heterogeneous Workflows. The next paragraph focuses on the notions of ad hoc and formal Workflows before we proceed to the integration of these heterogeneous Workflows into a global Workflow.

2.1   Ad hoc Workflow vs. formal Workflow

Traditional Workflow products support production, administrative and collaborative processes, where the cases are instantiated conforming to formal and rigid templates. The problem with global Workflow in the domain of B2B is that inter-enterprise processes could not be instantiated form a predefined process templates, rather they are modeled as ad hoc Workflow (Figure 2). In contrast with formal Workflow, the cases in the ad hoc Workflows are derived from generic templates and can be modified to meet specific needs in order to support flexibility (Dittrich et al. 1999).

An ad hoc Workflow can be viewed as an informal orchestration of different activities (sub-processes) gathered in order to achieve a predefined objective (Weber et al. 2005). Another aspect of the ad hoc Workflow is related to the nature of its sub-processes. In deed, the adjacent tasks of an ad hoc Workflow are built depending on real world models and not by using rigid templates (Ivins et al. 2004). This fact leads to a manual integration in order to connect different and distributed Workflows within a global Workflow.

Traditional Workflow overcomes the problem of interoperability when it comes to build the global Workflow based on their formal templates. In contrast, they stem from the lack of flexibility needed to deal with the frequent modifications of rules and conditions in the domain of business (Aalst 2000; Dittrich et al. 1999; Yan et al. 2001). However, in real world, both types of Workflows, i.e. ad hoc and formal Workflows coexist together and hence need to be integrated dynamically.

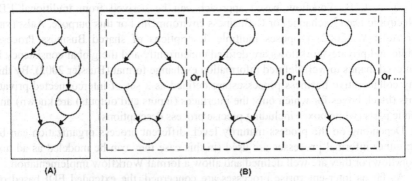

(A)   **(B)**

Fig. 2. (A) Formal Workflow – (B) Ad hoc Workflow

In the remainder of this paper, we handle the process of Distributed Workflow integration into a global Workflow.

2.2   Integration of heterogeneous Workflows

As mentioned previously, both types of Workflows, i.e. ad hoc and formal Workflows coexist together and need to be integrated without imposing the transformation of ad hoc Workflow into a formal one. In order to bring service agility and to support lean service integration, we propose to integrate the process life cycle in the service support system: first processes are designed in an exploratory way; they are implemented as ad hoc Workflows. Then, these ad hoc Workflows are integrated in a global Workflow to support efficiently the exploitation phase. Lastly, the Workflow is adapted in a re-engineering process by allowing ad hoc Workflow parts to fit the current evolution. Consequently, this lean organization support system involves to take into account both ad hoc and formal Workflows.

In this paper we propose a formal method, which permits the integration of several segments of separated Workflows regardless of theirs types. For that we propose to use a mediator between different parts of a global Workflow. The mediator grantees the interoperability between heterogeneous sub-Workflows even those which are not supported by software system.

3   The mediator

The basic aim of the mediator is to automate the process of global Workflow integration by offering standard connectors between the processes of a global Workflow.

The mediator is composed of Inbox and Outbox containers dedicated for conserving data related to processes being in treatment by an instance of the global Workflow (Figure1). In order to keep tracks of multiple instances, which might run concurrently, the mediator holds a Stack containing Process_ID, Process_Status, Process_Predecessor(s) and Process_Successor(s) for each process supervised by the global Workflow. The information gathered in the Stack is a significant resource to be analyzed and then employed as input data for the Process of Workflow reengineering.

As mentioned previously, human tasks still need to be integrated in an administrative Workflow. For that the mediator supports both types of communication ports API (Application Program Interface) and GUI (Graphical User Interface) as illustrated in figure 3.

The use of the Mediator as a connector offers a standard approach for building global formal Workflows combining both formal and ad hoc ones. On the one hand, using the mediator, global Workflows keep the flexibility needed for reconfiguring Business Process on the fly. On the other hand, the interconnection of heterogenic segments by means of formal Mediators offers a standard approach for reconfiguring and reengineering of service-based Workflows.

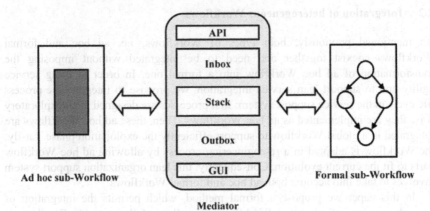

Ad hoc sub-Workflow   **Formal sub-Workflow**

Mediator

Fig. 3. The role of Mediator between an ad hoc and a formal Workflow

The mediator process consists in three steps:

- Take a request from the Inbox. This request is given either through the GUI for ad hoc Workflow or thanks to the mediator API for formal Workflow.
- Put the request in the process stack while searching the convenient Workflow segment.
- Forward the results to the outbox using either the target Workflow API for formal Workflow or the GUI for ad hoc Workflow.

In order to clarify the notions of building global Workflows by means of Mediators, a case study from the domain of B2B e-commerce is illustrated in the next paragraph.

4   Case study

As a case study we consider a global Workflow of e-procurement which depicts the treatment of a Purchase Order (PO) created by a Client in order to buy a Product directly from a Manufacturer. This Product is made up of two Raw Materials RM1 and RM2. RM1 is supplied by one Supplier S1 whereas RM2 is supplied concurrently by two suppliers S2, S3. In order to fulfill the command, an instance of a Workflow is initiated by the Manufacturer which might encompass other Workflows managed by the suppliers of the Manufacturer. With PO being validated, the next task is to verify if it can be fulfilled directly form the stock. In this case, the Manufacturer proceeds for the delivery directly. In the case where the stock level for the demanded Product does not permit the fulfillment of the PO, a fabrication process is needed. According to production capacity and the reserve of raw materials RM1 and RM2, the PO might be accepted or rejected as illustrated in figure 4.

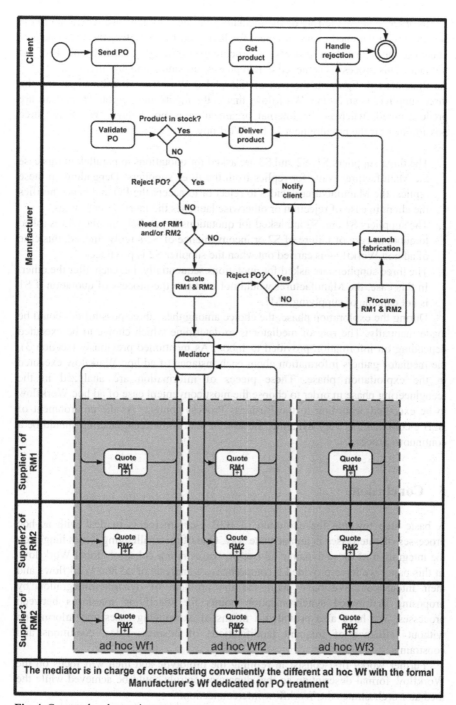

Fig. 4. Case study: electronic procurement

In order to show the role of the mediator, we focus on the case where the PO is accepted with the need of procurement for RM1 and RM2. Before the Manufacturer launches the fabrication process, a procurement process of RM1 and RM2 is initiated. This process is achieved in two phases: quotation and procurement.

As illustrated in figure 4, the part of this global Workflow distributed among the three suppliers is an ad hoc Workflow, that is the inputs and outputs of this part are predetermined, whereas the internal organization is not known. We show three possibilities for the procurement ad hoc Workflow:

1. The three suppliers S1, S2 and S3 are asked for quotations in parallel, in this case the Manufacturer waits for replies from the three suppliers. Depending on these replies, the Manufacturer decides to reject or to accept the PO and hence notifies the client in case of rejection or otherwise launches the fabrication process.
2. The suppliers S1 and S2 are asked for quotations in parallel, and then S3 is asked to quote in case of failure of S2 or inconvenience of S2's reply. Indeed, this case of ad hoc Workflow is carried out when the supplier S2 is privileged.
3. The three suppliers are asked for quotations sequentially, i.e. each after the other. In this case, the Manufacturer would not continue the process of quotation if S1 is not capable of supplying RM1.

During the exploration phase, the choice among these three possibilities could be made manually. The role of mediator is to determine which choice to be executed depending on information provided to Inbox. As mentioned previously (section 3), the mediator gathers information about each instance of ad hoc Workflow executed in the exploitation phase. These pieces of information are analyzed in the reengineering phase in order to choose the most convenient case of ad hoc Workflow to be executed according to the Business Process context. As the environment of B2B e-commerce is very dynamic, the task of Workflow reengineering should be a continuous process.

5 Conclusion

A basic step towards the evolution of B2B e-commerce is to deal with ad-hoc processes of enterprises in an adequate way. One of the challenging issues hinges on the integration of these dynamic ad hoc processes into a coherent global Workflow. In this paper we have provided a comprehensive analysis of ad hoc Workflows and their integration. We have addressed the problem of dynamic integration by proposing distributed synchronization points for specifying interfaces between processes. We have also provided a means of exchanging cases and information without influence of frequent modifications of business rules, conditions and constraints.

Further works first consist in refining the prototype and then will focus on the Workflow formal description so that dynamic controls could be achieved while the mediator orchestrates the Workflow interconnection.

References

1. Aalst, W. M. P. v. d. (2000). "Process-oriented architectures for electronic commerce and interorganizational workflow." Information Systems 24(8): 639-671.

2. Aalst, W. M. P. v. d. (2002). Making Work Flow: On the Application of Petri Nets to Business Process Management.

3. Bussler, C. (2002). "The application of workflow technology in semantic B2B integration." Distributed and parallel databases 12: 163-191.

4. Chiu, D. K. W., S. C. Cheung, S. Till, K. Karlapalem, Q. Li and E. Kafeza (2004). "Workflow View Driven Cross-Organizational Interoperability in a Web Service Environment." Information Technology and Management 5(3 - 4): 221-250.

5. DiCaterino, A., K. Larsen, M. Tang and W. Wang (1997). An Introduction to Workflow Management Sysytems, Center for Technology in Government.

6. Dittrich, K. and D. Tombros (1999). Workflow Management for the Virtual Enterprise Process. Villard de Lans, France, Int. Process Technology Workshop.

7. Ginsburg, M. and K. Duliba (1997). "Enterprise-Level Groupware Choices: Evaluating Lotus Notes and Intranet-Based Solutions." Computer Supported Cooperative Work (CSCW) 6(2 - 3): 201-225.

8. Ivins, W. K., W. A. Gray and J. C. Miles (2004). Managing Changes to Engineering Products Through the Co-ordination of Human and Technical Activities.

9. Jaber, M., Y. Badr, F. Biennier and J. Favrel (2005). An Integrated Open System To Support Cyber-Partnering. IFIP 5.7: The international conference on Advances in Production Management Systems, Rockville, MD, USA.

10. Oasis (2001). Business Process and Business Information analysis overview v1.0. Oasis:. 2006: 40 pages.

11. Ruiz, M., I. Ramos and M. Toro (2002). Integrating Dynamic Models for CMM-Based Software Process Improvement.

12. van der Aalst W. (2002). "Inheritance of inter-organizational workflows to enable business to business E-commerce." Electronic commerce research 2: 195-231.

13. Weber, B. and W. Wild (2005). Towards the Agile Management of Business Processes.

14. Wombacher, A. and B. Mahleko (2002). Finding Trading Partners to Establish Ad-hoc Business Processes.

15. Yan, Y., Z. Maamar and W. Weiming Shen (2001). Integration of Workflow and Agent Technology for Business Process Management. Proc. of CSCWD01, London: 420-426.

Review of After-Sales Service Concepts

Asbjørn Rolstadaas[1], Hans-Henrik Hvolby[2], Peter Falster[3]
1) Department of Production and Quality Engineering,
University of Science and Technology, Norway
2) Department of Production, Aalborg University, Denmark
3) Department of Informatics and Mathematical Modelling,
Technical University of Denmark

Abstract. For many manufacturing companies, after-sales service is an increasingly important part of the business and is more complex than manufacturing products. Unlike products it is not possible to produce services in advance and inventory these for future consumption. Instead an unpredictable event such as a machine failure triggers a need for manufacturing of parts for replacement and allocation of resources for the service. Various aspects of after-services are discussed with regards to business model, methodology, performance metrics, service portfolio and production planning and control.

1   Introduction

After-sales service processes play an integral role in many companies. Even though these processes are not the core business of engineering companies, services are increasing in importance. As products in the global market become more and more similar, supply chain management and services are becoming key differentiators between companies. High-quality service has become a necessity to retain customers for future sales.

Aftermarket business also represents significant revenue and growth potential for capital goods manufacturers. Against this background Accenture launched the "Aftermarket Monitor 2005" analysing the aftermarket capabilities of 58 leading capital goods manufacturers in the Nordics: "Nordic capital goods manufacturers do not fully use their aftermarket business as a strategically important source of revenue and profitability. Only 22 % of companies surveyed generate >30 % of their revenue in the service & parts sector; and 36% of the companies have experienced >10% growth in their after sales and service business over the last 3 years". In the AMR Research report – august 2002 it is said that services represent 25% of revenue and contribute 45% of profits.

Please use the following format when citing this chapter:

Rolstadaas, A., Hvolby, H.-H. and Falster, P., 2008, in IFIP International Federation for Information Processing, Volume 257, Lean Business Systems and Beyond, Tomasz Koch, ed.; (Boston: Springer), pp. 383–391.

According to the Promise project [1] the life cycle of a product is characterised by the following three phases:

- Beginning of Life (BOL), including Design and Production,
- Middle-of-Life (MOL), including Use, Service and Maintenance and
- End-of-Life (EOL), characterised by various scenarios such as: reuse of the product with refurbishing, reuse of components with disassembly and refurbishing, material reclamation without disassembly, material reclamation with disassembly and, finally, disposal with or without incineration.

This also relates after-sales services closely to the definition of *e-business*: "planning and execution of front-end and back-end operations in a supply chain using the Internet. The Internet redefines how operations, like product design, production, after-sales service, etc. are conducted" [4].

The focus in this paper is on Middle-of-Life, i.e. the Service and Maintenance phase. Thus, the purpose of this paper is to discuss after-sales service processes and its relationships to the total life-cycle of a product in general, and business models, methodologies, service portfolio, performance metrics and production planning and control in particular.

2   After-sales service in the supply chain

Demands for repairs and spare parts appear unexpectedly and sporadically and after-sales networks therefore operate in an unpredictable and inconsistent marketplace. The service supply chains are more complex than the manufacturing supply chain as can be seen in figure 1.

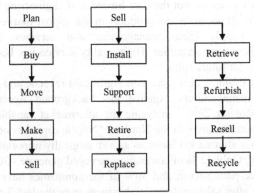

Fig. 1. Manufacturing Supply Chain (left) and Service Supply Chain (right) [6].

Wise and Baumgartner [5] document that the installed-base-to-new-unit ratio for automobiles is of 13 to 1. Furthermore, based on stagnant product demand a push downstream is seen and also a shift from manufacturing towards providing services to operate and maintain products. In other words, product sale is just a way for the provision of future services.

Wise and Baumgartner further set up nine metrics in order to provide useful insight into 1) the attractiveness of the downstream business, 2) the importance of forging strong customer relationships, and 3) the power of the distribution channel. They state that "*the old metrics (market share, cycle time, and quality levels) tend to focus solely on the product. Managing downstream businesses requires looking at new variables such as profit per installed unit, share of customer's total downstream-activity spending, and total customer return over the product life cycle*".

With after-markets becoming four to five times larger than the original equipment businesses Cohen et al. [7] also stress the importance of offering *solutions* instead of products, i.e. selling spare parts and after-sales services– conducting repairs; installing upgrades; reconditioning equipment; carrying out inspections and day-to-day maintenance; offering technical support, consulting, and training; and arranging finances – for future profits and revenues.

Especially in after-sales support of one-of-a-kind products, manufacturers are not able to store spare parts for each sold component. This often results in poor service for the customers when breakdown occur unexpectedly [7]. Basically, the problem with the market of after-sales service is their *reactionary* nature. This is why after-sales service must be more involved in *preventative maintenance scheduling* for customers.

McKinsey [8] points at that putting a price on services is more difficult than pricing products, because the benefits of services are less tangible and they often lack well-documented standard unit-production costs as a benchmark. Service costs can vary significantly by configuration, accessibility, and age of equipment, usage patterns, operating conditions, region and even individual technicians.

According to Kiritsis [1] the development of Product Embedded Information Devices (e.g. Radio Frequency Identification products) is expected to progress rapidly within advanced Product Lifecycle Management and real-time data-monitoring throughout the Product Supply Chain and explode into a multi-billion dollar market in 2006 and beyond. This technology will particularly allow producers of mass customised products to easily identify the product and its previous maintenance records and thereby improve their service.

3 Service Networks

Wise and Baumgartner [5] quotes Gartner Group for founding that a buyer of a locomotive engine ends up spending 21 times its purchase value to support its use. And Allmendinger and Lombreglia [10] suggest that any asset that costs more than 10 times its purchase value to use is clear candidate for networking.

Hartel & Burger [9] state that SMEs find it difficult to maintain their own worldwide service networks at reasonable costs and argue that companies have to build service cooperation. Therefore, they propose a *reference model* including a guideline to form inter-enterprise service collaboration, so-called *service virtual enterprise*.

A virtual enterprise can briefly be characterized as a short-term inter-enterprise cooperation where individual enterprises join core competencies in order to establish a value chain configured exactly to meet a specific customer demand. They see a service virtual enterprise consisting of three entities: 1) The service network of all potential network members, 2) the Service Virtual Enterprise (SVE) of selected member, and 3) the services as a product offered by the SVEs. The structural arrangement of these entities has been captured in the Virtual Enterprise Reference Architecture (VERA) and based on the GERAM architecture.

With focus on one-of-a-kind industry Kauer [3] defines a SVE as "*a short-term form of cooperation to fulfil services among legally independent one-of-a-kind producers, service companies, suppliers or sub-contractors in a service network of long-term duration*".

Allmendinger and Lombreglia state that it is not enough to offer services; it will have to provide *smart services*. To provide they must build intelligence into the products themselves. As they state: "*smart services are based upon actual evidence that a machine is about to fail, that a customer's supply of consumables is about to be depleted, and so on*". As an example they mention Heidelberg's printing machines. With machine communication over the Internet, relaying information about their status between the print shops and Heidelberg's regional and global technical support specialists, the company has the access and insight to optimise printing performance in customers' shops. The keyword is networking and connected products. Connected products will be able to perform the following functions: status, diagnostics, upgrades, control and automation, profiling and behaviour tracking, replenishment and commerce, location mapping and logistics.

4   Planning Processes and Managing Service Networks

In order to break a planning process into more manageable parts Franksen proposes in [19] to break the planning process into two generic steps: 1) Design of a technique (re-engineering) and 2) Operation of a technique.

The first step is one of *synthesis* in which we specify a system configuration by stating its structural properties. This step describes uniquely the inter-relationships between resources and products. Design of a technique is an open-ended problem in which we establish, heuristically, a production system in terms of its causal logic-physical and temporal relationships. The second step is one of *analysis* in which we investigate a specified system configuration in order to operate it most efficiently or economically. This decomposition is also in agreement with the concept of time-horizons in economic theory and production planning. Operation of a technique is a short-run situation where it is only possible to increase/decrease the services of certain resources such as purchase of raw material. Design of a technique is a long-run situation where it is possible to vary the structure of the production method by substitution of system configurations implying time-consuming processes. Thus, all resources and technical coefficients can be made variable.

Let's relate these generic steps with Cohen et al. [7] who say that given the complexity involved in managing service assets, companies should break the decision-making process into three planning periods. At the most immediate level of planning (days), companies should worry about repositioning decisions such as replenishment, allocation, and transhipment of resources. At the next level (weeks or months), managers should address the strategic positioning of material, human, and knowledge resources. At the furthest level of planning (years), companies must make decisions about the services strategy. The two top levels of Cohen et al. correspond to our long run situation.

In order to monitor *performance* Cohen et al. further suggest two kinds of metrics to prove useful: customer-focused and internally focused. *Customer-focused metrics* such as the waiting time for technical assistance, the waiting time for diagnosis, and the waiting time for the delivery of parts can help determine how efficiently a company creates value for its customers. *Internally focused metrics* such as fill rates and parts obsolescence costs can quantify the way companies use their service assets. In a more generalized set-up Cohen et al. [7] propose six steps for *managing service networks*:

1. **Identify which products to cover.** Support all, some, complementary, or competing products.
2. **Create a portfolio of service products.** Position service products according to response times and prices.
3. **Select business models to support service products.** Use different models for different products and life cycle stages.
4. **Modify after-sales organizational structures.** Provide visibility, incentives, and focus for services.
5. **Design and manage an after-sales services supply chain.** Decide location of resources, prioritise resource utilization, and plan for contingencies
6. **Monitor performance continuously.** Evaluate against benchmarks and customer feedback.

5   Portfolio of service products

Searching the internet illustrates quite well the companies' portfolio of after-sales services. The following sites have been studied: Nilfisk Advance [11], Niro [12], Siemens [13], ABB [14] and Heidelberg [15].

Siemens' after sales services program SIMAIN has been developed to meet the special needs of makers and marketers of electrical components, equipment, and systems as well as the requirements of machine tool makers and plant engineering companies. They provide a series of service modules: *Field- and On-line Service* performed directly at customer's site or via online connection (On-site Fault Elimination, Remote Monitoring, Management of Call desks and Helpdesks, On-call Service, Reliability Solutions), *Repair Service* is services that are performed in Siemens service centres (Repair, Calibration), *Logistics Service* is services to support and/or optimise customers service processes (Integration of logistics management systems, Management of returns, Spare parts management, Supply of instruments and tools), *Service packages* comprise service modules that are selected and combined according to individual requirements, technical synergy effects, or specific industrial processes.

ABB service guide provides a full range of lifecycle services from spare parts and equipment repair, training, migration to remote monitoring and technical support. Their services are the following: *Performance and System Services* (Asset Assessment, Consulting, Optimisation, Performance Services), *Support and Maintenance Services* (Installation & Commissioning, Maintenance & Field Services, Spare Parts & Repair, Support & Remote Services), *Retrofit and Modernization* (Environmental, Migration & Retrofits) and *Training*.

Synthesising the sites it turns out that companies offer the following categories of services as Kauer et al [3] have shown:

1   General support (basic means of communication)
2   Self support (by information available by the producer)
3   Remote support (ICT- supported interaction
4   On-site support (producer or service partner present)

Kauer et al relate the services to the phases pre-sales, sales, and after-sales as illustrated in the Service portfolio table below.

Services	Pre-sales	Sales	After-sales
1. General support	Helpdesk, contact, hotline		
		Training, upgrades	
			Spare part management
2. Self support	Product information, product news		
		Software download	
			Troubleshooting database
3. Remote support	Remote consulting		
		Remote optimisation	
			Remote diagnostic
			Remote control
4. On-site support	Process support, optimisation		
		Optimisation	
			Maintenance
			Repair

Hvam et al [16,17] describe new ways of using *configuration* systems for the targeting field services, technical support and after sales. They argue that because of lack of updates in the Customer Relationship Management system, the salesman or service technician use considerable resources to figure out the status of the product. Modularised products will change throughout their lifetime, as it is possible to change the set-up, extend the product, and exchange defective parts. Product service systems are proposed as an alternative business model in the future. Their idea is to integrate a configuration system with the product – embedded configuration - and thereby give customers a decision support system for daily maintenance of the product. Furthermore, they visualize that service contracts are configured as other products using for example a commercial tool like Array Configuration [18].

6   Business Models and Production Control

Various definitions of business models exist. According to Rappa [20] a business model is the method of doing business by which a company can sustain itself - that is, generate revenue. The business model spells-out how a company makes money by specifying where it is positioned in the value chain.

Service supply chains are described by the following characteristics: Business model seen either from the manufacture's point of view or the customer's point of view.

A business model from the customer's point of view is dependent on the service priority ranging from none to very high and who is the owner of the product (manufacturer or customer). The business models are then of the types: Disposal, Ad hoc, Warranty, Lease, Cost-plus, Performance-based and Power by the hour [7].

Business models seen from the manufacturer's point of view could be of the type as described by Allmendinger and Lombreglia [10]. They propose four business models, briefly summarized below:

1   The **embedded innovator** which is the most products centric of the models.
2   The **solutionist** who considers the single product as the dominant gateway to a business opportunity, but the scope of high-value activities associated with the product is broader.
3   The **aggregator** who connects several disparate devices within an environment to create a high-value body of data, as a single device or a single vendor of itself may not be valuable enough to create an opportunity.
4   The **synergist** who provides intelligent devices that play well with others and thereby contribute valuable data or functionality to other connected products.

Looking at the business opportunities available for a company, there are two possibilities: It may be that most of the elements of the opportunity are attached *directly* to the product's life cycle, so the company will be able to pursue the opportunity alone. Or it may be that the opportunity lies mainly in the *adjacent* activities related to their product's primary activities, so that they will have to partner with others, cf. the business models. This is left for further study.

The interplay between production control and the business model should also be considered. Choice of business model should influence the choice of control concepts depending of production form (volume/variety), industry sector (uncertainty/complexity), type of product structure (convergent/divergent) and market interaction strategies.

7 Conclusion

The paper has discussed concepts for after-sales service processes. The paradigm in service management today is shifting from Customer Relationship Management to Customer Managed Relationships for example by providing a customer visibility into the stock levels of various spares; the manufacturers can enable customers to manage their spares inventory better. Further aspects to be considered are described in the following.

Many manufacturing industries have been based on a horizontal integration of the value chain controlling suppliers and distributors. Both because of huge investment and difficulty in planning and control, a shift from vertical to horizontal integration of value chains has been seen. However, with networking and new ICT tools and architectures like Service Oriented Architectures (SOA) and Business Process Management, supply chains move to what has been called Virtual Vertical Integration. The impact of this shift on after-sales services is important to consider in the future. SOA provides a framework and architecture for interconnecting applications and software components seamlessly. This provides for more flexible loose coupling of resources than in traditional systems architectures. This is foreseen as important for effective managing the after-sales service supply chain.

It has been common practice to consider the enterprise as being hierarchical in both structure and control. However, a distributed view where organisational units communicate over intra- and internet and cooperate in both problem solving and action has evolved. A need for processes or agents to communicate directly with each other is emerging. This tendency is seen within production. A decentralized operation system for after-sales services can be built by local 'intelligent' agents who perform well defined tasks coordinated by the central control. In case of operational disturbance you should be able to detect the faults and to reduce the extent of the damage while being able to re-establish normal operation within very short time.

References

1. Kiritsis, D; Ubiquitous Product Lifecycle Management using Product Embedded Information Devices, IMS 2004.

2. Moseng, Bjørn; Promise project description, www.promise.no, Sintef Technology and Society, 2006.

3. Kauer, Martin; Burger, G and Hartel, Ingo; An Internet-based Platform for Distributed After-sales Services in the One-of-a-kind Production, in Global Engineering and Manufacturing in Enterprise Networks, Globeman (I. Karvonen et al), Vtt symposium 224, Helsinki, 9.-10.12.2002, 2003.

4. Lee, H. L and Whang, S; E-business and supply chain integration, Sgscmf-W2-2001, Nov. 2001.

5. Wise, Richard and Baumgartner, Peter; Go Downstream – The new profit imperative in manufacturing, Harvard Business Review, 133-141, September-October 1999.

6. Customer Annuity – successful companies will make customer service and after-sales support their competitive advantage, Ups, 2005.

7. Cohen, Morris A; Agrawal, Narendra and Agrawal, Vipul; Winning in the Aftermarket (HBR OnPoint Enhanced Edition), Harward Business Review OnPoint Article, May, 2006.

8. Bundschuh, R.G and Dezvane, T. M; How to make after-sales services pay off, The McKinsey Quarterly, 4, 2003.

9. Hartel, Ingo; Burger, Gerhard; Kamio, Y and Zhou, M; A Reference Model for Collaborative Service, in Global Engineering and Manufacturing in Enterprise Networks, Globeman (I. Karvonen et al), Vtt symposium 224, Helsinki, 9, 2003.

10. Allmendinger, Glen and Lombreglia, Ralph; Four Strategies for the Age of Smart Services, Harvard Business Review, 131-145, Oct. 2005.

11. Nilfisk website, www.nilfisk-advance.com/Info/AfterSalesService.aspx, last accessed 21 Jan. 2007.

12. Niro website, www.niroinc.com/html/after_sales/spare.html, last accessed 21 Jan. 2007.

13. Siemens website, www.industry.siemens.com/siemensindustrialservices/en/ solution_services/olm-ass/after-sales-service.htm, last accessed 21 Jan. 2007.

14. ABB website, www.abb.us/ServiceGuide last accessed 21 Jan. 2007.

15. Heidelberg website, www.heidelberg.com/www/html/en/content/overview1/ service/service_support_overview, last accessed 21 Jan. 2007

16. Teglgaard Christensen, Tim and Hvam, Lars; A configuration System for supportive Purposes in the middle of a product lifecycle. in "Customer Interaction and Customer Integration Series on Business Informatics and Application Systems", 2, Blecker, Th.; Friedrich, G.; Hvam, L./ Edwards, K. ISBN 3-936771-73-1 published by Gito-Verlag, Berlin, 2006.

17. Oddsson, G; Hvam, Lars and Lysgaard, Ole; Conceptualizing Embedded Configuration, conference paper "Customer interaction and Customer Integration" Imcm 22-23 June 2006 Hamburg, Germany, published as part of "Series on Business informatics and Application systems", ISBN 3-936771-73-1, Gito-Verlag, Berlin, 2006.

18. Array configuration – Version 6.2, Modellers guide. Array Technology A/S, www.arraytechnology.com, 2006.

19. Franksen, O.I; Introducing Diakoptical Simulation in Engineering Education. The Matrix and Tensor Quarterly. 1-16, Sep. 1972.

20. Rappa, M; Business Models on the web; www.digitalenterprise.org/models/models.html. Last accessed 21 Jan. 2007.

Reducing Turbulences in Industrial Supply Chains

Stanisław Strzelczak
Warsaw University of Technology, Faculty of Production Engineering,
Narbutta 85, 02-524 Warsaw, Poland

Abstract. Turbulent behavior of supply chains is drawing an increasing attention of researchers and managers in recent years. Better understanding of reasons and impacts of unsteadiness is interesting not only from the scientific point of view, but also crucial for the development of appropriate practical countermeasures. Many publications focus the bullwhip effect. Few consider other symptoms of turbulent behavior, than oscillations of material flows and stocks in supply chains or volatility of the demand. This paper takes a holistic perspective at turbulences in industrial supply chains, in terms of symptoms, effects and interdependencies. A relevant analytical framework is discussed, which employs both, qualitative and quantitative modeling. Initial results of empirical and conceptual research are presented. The final aim is to develop a well-justified methodology for simultaneous analysis of cultural phenomena and material processes. The two major streamlines of processes in supply chains were considered, i.e.: product development and production flow. The obtained and prospective results have both, scientific and practical importance.

1 Introduction

A typical global supply chain is a complex and spatially spread structure of collaborations, with many parallel cross-organizational business processes going on, including flows of materials, engineering, information, decisions, cash and finance, legal responsibilities, innovations etc. All of them go on simultaneously with social processes, i.e. interactions of organizations, groups and individuals. Not surprisingly, the high level of complexity, enhanced by the global dimension of business, easily results in unpredictable and turbulent behaviors of supply chains, reflected by both, the material and cultural phenomena. Turbulences, variances, oscillations, disturbances, disruptions, risks, perils, conflicts, tensions are just the few names, which are used to describe symptoms of volatility, vulnerability, unstableness, unpredictability and disharmony in supply chains. The opposite behavior can be named as steady, smooth, undisturbed, reliable, predictable, resilient or robust.

Please use the following format when citing this chapter:

Strzelczak, S., 2008, in IFIP International Federation for Information Processing, Volume 257, Lean Business Systems and Beyond, Tomasz Koch, ed.; (Boston: Springer), pp. 393–402.

The turbulent behavior of supply chains is usually referred to industrial and business dynamics [1,2] or the bullwhip effect [3,4], i.e. the phenomenon, where a demand flowing upstream of a supply chain exhibits a greater variance, than that at its end. The bullwhip effect has been observed in many industries, often resulting in excessive inventories, inadequate schedules, overproduction, poor customer service, tremendous inefficiencies, lost revenues and increased costs. Table 1 resumes factors usually linked to the bullwhip effect, and the typical suggested countermeasures [5]. Other suggested factors are: distortion in communication up and down supply chains, weak coordination – local decisions, long and variable lead times, delayed material and information flows, neglecting to order in an attempt to reduce stocks, overreaction to backlogs, inappropriate incentives and performance measures, free return policies. It is striking that the 3Mu concept of Toyotism (e.g. Muri means: unevenness, irregularity, variability), which extends directly to supply chains, is almost never discussed in this context, despite well-known practices of Toyota [6].

Table 1. The bullwhip effect and suggested countermeasures

Factor	Remedy
Order batching –occurs in an effort to reduce ordering costs, to take advantage of transportation economics (e.g. full truck load).	High order costs are countered with ICT: Electronic Data Interchange (EDI) and computer-aided ordering. Full truck loads are countered with third-party logistics and assorted truck loads. Random or correlated ordering is countered with regular delivery appointment. More frequent ordering result in smaller orders and smaller variance (the reduction is seen upstream, not locally; the required safety stock may increase or decrease depending on circumstances).
Demand forecasting inaccuracies: certain percents are added to the demand estimates upstream supply chain, resulting is no visibility in the true demand.	Replace the forecast-driven management and inventory replenishment by the demand-driven management (pull-flow). Collaborative forecasting, single control of replenishment or Vendor Managed Inventory (VMI) can overcome exaggerated demand forecasts. Poor demand visibility can be addressed by ICT, e.g. direct access to point of sale (POS) data. Long lead times should be reduced, where economically advantageous.
Inflated orders: rationing and shortage gaming during periods of short supply, due to the hope that possible partial shipments will be sufficient.	Proportional rationing schemes are countered by allocating unit based on past sales. Ignorance of supply chain conditions can be addressed by partnership: sharing capacity and supply information. Unrestricted ordering capability can be addressed by reducing the order size flexibility and capacity reservations (e.g. a fixed quantity for a given year; a quantity of each order is specified shortly before it is needed, assuming the sum of the order quantities does not exceed the reserved quantity).
Price fluctuations: sales incentives, trade and retail level promotions, discounts.	Minimize incentives. High-low pricing can be also replaced with every day low prices (EDLP). Special purchase contracts can be implemented in order to specify ordering at regular intervals to better synchronize delivery and purchase.

2 Existing Research

The primary issue of researching the bullwhip effect is its measurement. Fransoo and Wouters [7] discussed conceptual and practical aspects: incompleteness of data, aggregation of data, isolation of demand data for a defined chain, that is a part of a greater one. Kawagoe and Wada [8] tried to quantitatively define the bullwhip effect and discovered, that a frequency based statistical measure, such as stochastic dominance, is not appropriate to capture the bullwhip effect quantitatively, as it cannot distinguish between a case of the bullwhip effect and a counterexample. But the descriptive statistics (mean and standard deviation) work well.

The next stream of research focuses reasons of the bullwhip effect and their impacts. Kahn [9] showed that serially correlated demands ehnhance the bullwhip effect. Lee et al. [3, 4] used the same demand assumption, and a cost minimization approach to show, that a distortion in demand arises, when retailers optimize orders, and that amplification increases, as the replenishment lead-times increase. Dejonckheere et al. [10] used the control theory to evaluate the bullwhip effect. Chen et al. [11] proved that exponential smoothing forecasts by the retailer can cause the bullwhip effect, and contrasted this with the increase in variability due to the use of moving average forecasts. They considered a correlated demand process, and another one, with a linear trend. Disney et al. focused on smoothing replenishment rules that are able to reduce the bullwhip effect across a single echelon [12]. They quantified the variance of the net stock and computed the required safety stock as a function of the smoothing required. The analysis showed, that bullwhip effect can be satisfactorily managed without unduly increasing stock levels to maintain target fill rates. Moyaux et al. [13] showed by agent-based simulations, that speculation reduces price fluctuation. Papangnou et al. [14] proposed a state-space approach to analyze the simple series supply chain model with an arbitrary number of nodes and developed techniques to calculate explicitly the associated covariance matrix in parametric form, under white-noise demand profile assumption. This allows to check the effect of a parameter-set in the studied inventory policies on the bullwhip effect.

Another way to research the bullwhip effect is by modelling. Warburton presented fundamental differential delay equations to describe how the order variability increases as orders propagate along the supply chain [15]. The analytical solutions are consistent with numerical integrations and previous control theory results. Lu et al. investigated the complexity of the bullwhip effect as a phenomena, using theories of fractals and chaos [16]. They demonstrated that the bullwhip effect and the butterfly effect share the same nonlinear mechanism of amplifying self-oscillations (the ordering decisions amplify perturbations brought by errors, in the processing of demand information). Helbing and Lämmer [17] investigated stability and dynamic behavior of supply networks for different topologies, including: sequential supply chains, "supply circles", "supply ladders" and "supply hierarchies". They applied network theory models to optimize the supply chains. Makajić-Nikolić et. al. studied Petri nets' capability for modeling supply chains and developed a simple three-stage supply chain with one player at each stage: a retailer, a wholesaler and a manufacturer [18]. They used a timed hierarchical coloured Petri Net. The results were similar to those obtained through the beer game.

Carlsson and Fullér [19] used fuzzy sets theory to show, that if the members of the supply chain share information and agree on continuously improving fuzzy estimates (as the time advances) of future sales, then the bullwhip effect can be significantly reduced. Dhahri and Chabchoub [20] proposed a non-linear goal programming models to quantify the bullwhip effect in supply chain. They used preference functions, based on a statistical chronological series analysis, in order to describe: the demand, the stock level, and the order quantity.

Kelepouris et. al. used the simulation to explain how specific replenishment parameters affect: order variability amplification, product fill rates and inventory levels, across the supply chain [21]. They also studied, how demand information sharing can help reducing order oscillations and inventory levels, in upper nodes of a supply chain. A two-stage supply chain consisting of a warehouse and stores was modeled. A real demand data was used. Jakšic and Rusjan also examined the influence of different replenishment policies on the bullwhip effect [22]. Their paper demonstrates, that certain replenishment policies can in themselves be inducers of the bullwhip effect, while others inherently lower the demand variability. The main causes of increase in variability are projections of future demand expectations, which result in over-exaggerated responses to changes in demand. The authors suggest that, through appropriate selection and use of certain replenishment rules the bullwhip effect can be avoided, thus subsequently allowing supply chain management costs to be lowered. Merkuryev et al. [23] evaluated the impact of decentralized and centralized information sharing strategies combined with two inventory control policies: min-max and stock-to-demand, for a four-stage supply chain (retailer, wholesaler, distributor and manufacturer), using simulation models developed by the Arena 5.0 software package. The models with centralized information structures appeared to be superior in terms of the bullwhip effect, while stock-to-demand inventory control presented better performance than the Min-Max. No cost considerations were taken into account. Finally, Thun and Mertens [24] applied systems dynamics to research the impact of alternative reverse logistics modes on the bullwhip effect, in a closed-loop supply chain environment. Product returns can aggravate the bullwhip effect, but by planning the reverse logistics, the negative influences of the bullwhip effect can be mitigated.

Another stream of publications on the bullwhip effects presents results of the empirical research. Donohue and Croson [25] reported results of experimental studies on the behavioral causes of the bullwhip effect: decision-makers continue to exhibit the bullwhip effect even under conditions where it rationally should not occur. This suggests that cognitive limitations contribute to the bullwhip effect, even in ideal and controlled settings like the lab. Transmitting dynamic inventory information lessens the bullwhip effect, particularly at higher echelon levels. In another paper [26] the same authors used again a controlled version of the beer distribution game, as the setting for the experiment, and varied the amount and location of inventory information shared. First, they independently tested whether sharing upstream or downstream inventory information helps reduce the bullwhip behavior, and found that only downstream information sharing leads to significantly lower order oscillations throughout the supply chain. They compared the reduction in order oscillations experienced by supply chain level and found, that upstream supply chain members benefit the most from sharing downstream information.

Wu and Katok [27] also used the beer game, communication protocols and manipulated training. They found that order variability decreases significantly in a setting, in which participants start with hands-on experience, and are then allowed to formulate team strategies collaboratively. This result indicates, that while training may improve individuals' knowledge and understanding of the system, it does not improve supply chain performance, unless supply chain partners are allowed to communicate and share this knowledge. Their results also confirms that the bullwhip effect is enhanced by an insufficient coordination in a supply chain. Lurie and Swaminatham [28] examined behaviorally a two-stage supply chain: manufacturer and retailer; the manufacturer incuring setup costs and following a two point inventory (s, S) policy). They tried to explain, how information about the retailer's ordering policy and consumer demand, and performance-based incentives affect manufacturer decision making behavior. It has appeared that with or without incentives, having greater information from the retailer, improves manufacturer performance consistent with normative predictions. But they did not find any evidence for diminishing returns from information, when incentives are present.

Nienhaus et al. [29] performed a simulation research, based on the use of the beer distribution game online. It is one of the few publications, which discuss impacts of human behavior, as partner in a supply chain, on the bullwhip effect, comparing to simple agent-based strategies. The analysis proved that human behavior need to be recognized as a further factor of amplification of the bullwhip effect, as humans actually act like obstacles to the information flow in supply chains. Sterman [2] also tried to model the human behavior and proposed simulation means to analyze the cognitive process of formation and evolution of expectations of decision makers. He explained the instability and oscillations in industrial supply chains by behavior of forecasters, who systematically underestimate the growth rate of inputs. Ruël et al. [30] explicitly related personality characteristics to the supply chain performance, within experimental context of the beer game. They have shown, that differences in personality characteristics such as: risk taking, efficacy, ambiguity, and locus of control, lead to differences in performance. Low risk taking persons increase on average back order costs and lower inventory costs, while high risk taking persons are supposed to show an opposite impact on the cost structure.

The recently published book, edited by Carranza Torres and Villegas Morán [31], presents a wide overview of industrial dynamics applications to the bullwhip effect. Systemic, endogenic and structural causes of the bullwhip effect were subject of a detailed discussion. E.g. parameters like: normal inventory coverage, manufacturing cycle lead time (acquisition delay for inventories), inventory adjustment time, WIP adjustment time, time to average order rate, have strong impact on oscillations, amplifications, attenuations and phase lags of production and inventories. Following these considerations, four paradigms to mitigate and control the bullwhip effect were suggested: echelon elimination (structural complexity reduction), information transparency, time-compression, and control system.

From other publications we can derive importance of other paradigms: variety reduction (of items), variance reduction (or reliability improvement), postponement, taming constraints (bottlenecks), alignment / partnering, learning, and recently risk management and vulnerability [32]. Finally, the concepts of flexibility, adaptability, agility, sustainability, and resilience [33] are also referred to the considered problem.

3   Research Framework

The existing research on turbulent behavior of supply chains, depending on the purpose and related paradigms, typically follows the spirit of research and takes one of the two following perspectives rooted in the systems theory:

1. Process perspective: supply chain is viewed by a structure, usually network, of processes, sub-processes and operations.
2. Interdependencies perspective: supply chain is viewed as a structure of interacting organizations, resources, infrastructure and environment.

Consequently, industrial dynamics and mathematical modeling are exploited to study quantitative dynamic phenomena, while the beer game and questionnaire reviews dominated the streamline of research, which focus behavioral phenomena. Exceptionally the risk management takes another perspective of reality and considers unlikely events as atomic entities, with attributed possibilities and severities.

The operation and behaviors of supply chains can be considered at different levels of abstraction or hierarchy, and at different time perspectives: from events to long-term phenomena, that can be described by quantitative measures (e.g. "growth of variance of ...") or in a qualitative way (e.g. as "increasing mistrust"). Causal relations are crucial to understand and analyze the qualitative and quantitative phenomena, especially simultaneously, e.g. by trade-offs. This sets an issue and demand for hybrid analysis and modeling, including the means to model dynamic qualitative phenomena. Explaining causal relations empirically, or by statistical or mathematical modeling, is often risky, and sometimes not possible at all. Beliefs (of experts) are often the only (if any) available arguments to draw conclusions or verify alternative hypothesis. To meet the assumed objectives and to be consistent with the reality, the obstacle of data gathering and aggregation has also to be overcame.

Table 2. The research framework for hybrid analysis of turbulent behavior in supply chains

Stage	Means
Identification	Semi-structured questionnaires
Mapping	Development of process, structural and influence diagrams, causal networks by structured interviewing and questionnaires
Assessment (of likelihoods, impacts etc.; setting metrics)	Expert assessment (Delphi etc.) + Statistical analysis of beliefs (Pearson – correlations; Cronbach's Alpha – reliability)
Modeling	Scenarios + system dynamics (iThink) + Bayesian Belief Networks (MSBNx + Hugin Lite)
Dynamic and causal analysis	Scenarios + management games + hybrid simulations (prototype hybrid of BBN and system dynamics)
Cognitive assessment	Case studies, statistical analysis (Pearson – correlations; Cronbach's Alpha – reliability); cognitive action learning

Following these considerations a research framework has been developed. It is presented in a structured way in the table 2, reflecting the sequence of research steps. Principally diagrams are used to model the reality and phenomena (example: Fig.1). They are graphs: nodes represent variables and functions (influence, evidence etc.).

Two types of variables are possible: chance (likelihood, probability) and control (decision): one variable represents an exhaustive set of mutually exclusive events, i.e. the domain (states, levels, values, choices, options etc.; discrete or continuous). For each variable a set of likelihood or probability distributions, conditional on some variables, may be specified. Links represent relations among variables and influence functions - properties of (conditional) interdependences among variables. Influence diagrams may be applied as sequential scenarios. For a set of discrete evidence variables the evidence appears in the form of a likelihood distribution over the possible states (an evidence function or potential). A key inference task is to compute posterior probabilities, depending on the general evidence received from external sources (nodes) about the possible states/values of a subset of the variables of the network. A hybrid algebra, mixing computations (events perspective) and causal influences (conditional reasoning) drives simulations. Hierarchical networks allow work at different levels of abstraction, as well as exploit the encapsulation and inheritance concepts known from the object-oriented paradigm. Diagrams may reflect empirical results, then eventually becoming inputs to simulations.

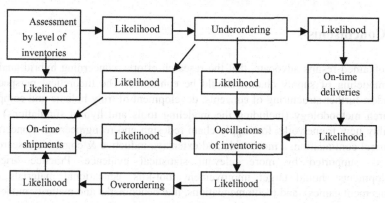

Fig. 1. An example causal diagram of supply chain qualitative and quantitative dynamics

4   Scope of the Research and the Key Findings

The research was primarily oriented to develop a well-justified methodology, that could holistically integrate qualitative and quantitative analysis and modeling of those phenomena in supply chains, that result in a turbulent behavior. Operational processes and engineering (product development) were focused. The scope of research, due to its pilot nature, was reduced to ordering and stock management policies (system dynamics), confronted with systemic solutions (performance measures, employees' assessment schemes and incentives) and behavioral qualities (trust, partnership vs. adversarial attitudes).

The empirical research was run in 44 companies (including collaborating MNEs and SMEs), operating in Central Europe, China and Japan. The first steps of the research and the inputs to the dynamic modeling were run according the framework set in the table1. Qualitative assessments were typically based on pre-defined multi-perspective and modular patterns (of behavior) and simple grading scales. Hybrid simulations were supported by management games. Several important findings, both of scientific and practical importance, were obtained, including the following:

- The impact of turbulences on supply chains performance (including the role of aligned forecasting, planning, scheduling and replenishment) is highly underestimated by practitioners; relevant reporting and modeling practices could help much to realize and understand the phenomena.
- Some factors of behavioral and non-behavioral nature, seems to play a crucial role in most practical situations, e.g. trust, attitudes toward other parties, key performance measures, which may have both, positive and negative impacts.
- Holistic consideration of material phenomena together with behaviors and cultural phenomena is crucial to avoid surprising turbulences and inefficiencies.
- Dynamic modeling of managerial and material processes by means of hybrid simulation is possible and is useful to explain the dynamics of supply chains.
- Cultures and systemic solutions can be leveraged and harmonized. In the context of global supply chains, they may be aligned, by applying the concepts and methods of business integration engineering [6].

5   Conclusions

The obtained results advocate, that the research efforts, concerning hybrid analysis and modeling of supply chains, should be continued. The theoretical perspective includes: further structuring of concepts, development of truly holistic and complete research methodology (including the modeling tools and hybrid simulations) and possibly new frameworks for supply chain redesign and reengineering. Concerning empirical continuation, a more wide and extensive inductive & cognitive research is needed, supported by more relevant statistical evidence. Practice oriented developments should target improvement tool-kits, educational materials (e.g. management games), and recommendations, like benchmarks and maturity models.

References

1. J.W. Forrester, Industrial Dynamics. A major breakthrough for decision makers, *Harvard Business Review*, Vol. 36 (1958) No. 4, pp. 37-66.

2. J.D.Sterman, Business Dynamics, McGraw-Hill, 2000.

3. H.L. Lee, V. Padmanabhan, S. Whang, The bullwhip effect in supply chains, *Sloan Management Review*, Vol. 38 (1997), No. 3, pp. 93-102.

4. L.H. Lee, V. Padmanabhan, S. Whang, Information distortion in a supply chain: The bullwhip effect, *Management Science*, Vol. 43 (1997) No. 4, pp. 546-558.

5. P.-P. Dornier, R. Ernst, M. Fender, P. Kouvelis, Global Operations and Logistics, John Wiley & Sons, 1998, pp. 216-233.

6. S. Strzelczak, Business Integration Engineering, in: edited by S.Strzelczak, Economic and Managerial Developments in Asia and Europe - Comparative Studies, Kramist Ltd.,

2003, pp. 99-118.

7. J.C.Fransoo, M.J.F. Wouters, Measuring the bullwhip effect in the supply chain, *Supply Chain Management: An International Journal*, Vol.5 (2000), No,2, pp. 78-89.

8. T. Kawagoe, S. Wada, The bullwhip effect: a counterexample, Proceedings of the IEEE International Conference on Intelligent Agent Technology, 2005, pp. 124- 127.

9. J. Kahn, Inventories and the volatility of production, American Economic Review Vol. 77 (1987), No. 4, pp. 667-679.

10. J. Dejonckheere, S.M., Disney, M.R. Lambrecht, D.R. Towill, Measuring and avoiding the bullwhip effect: A control theoretic approach, European Journal of Operational Research, Vol. 147 (2003), No. 3, pp. 567-590.

11. F. Chen et al., The impact of exponential smoothing forecasts on the bullwhip effect, Naval Research Logistics Vol. 47 (2000), No.4, pp. 269-286.

12. S.M. Disney, I. Farasyn, M.R. Lambrecht, D.R. Towill, W. van de Velde, Dampening variability by using smoothing replenishment rules, DTEW Research Report 0502, Katholieke Universiteit Leuven, 2005.

13. T. Moyaux, P. McBurney, Reduction of the Bullwhip Effect in Supply Chains through Speculation, in: Ch.Bruun (ed.), Advances in Artificial Economics - The Economy as a Complex Dynamic System, Springer, 2006, p. 77-89.

14. C. Papanagnou, G. Halikias, A State-Space Approach for Analyzing the Bullwhip Effect in Supply Chains, Proceedings of ICTA'05, London 2005, pp. 79-84.

15. R.D.H. Warburton, An Analytical Investigation of the Bullwhip Effect, *Production & Operations Management*, Vol. 13 (2004), No. 2, pp. 150–160.

16. Y. Lu, Y. Tang, X. Tang, Study on the Complexity of the Bullwhip Effect, *Journal of Electronic Science & Technology of China*, Vol.2 (2004), No.3, pp. 86-91.

17. D. Helbing, S. Lämmer, Supply and production networks: from the bullwhip effect to business cycles, in: D. Armbruster, A. S. Mikhailov, K. Kaneko (eds.), Networks of Interacting Machines: Production Organization in Complex Industrial Systems and Biological Cells, World Scientific, Singapore, 2005, pp. 33-66.

18. D. Makajić-Nikolić, B. Panić, M. Vujošević, Bullwhip Effect and Supply Chain Modelling and Analysis Using CPN Tools, in: K. Jensen (ed.): Proceedings of the Fifth Workshop and Tutorial on Practical Use of Coloured Petri Nets and the CPN Tools, Aarhus, 2004, pp. 219-234.

19. Ch. Carlsson, R.Fullér, A Fuzzy Approach to Taming the Bullwhip Effect, in: H.-J. Zimmermann et al. (eds.), Advances in Computational Intelligence and Learning: Methods and Applications, Kluwer 2002, pp. 247-262.

20. I. Dhahri, H. Chabchoub, A Nonlinear Goal Programming Models Quantifying the Bullwhip Effect in Supply Chain Based on ARIMA Parameters, Proceedings of MOPGP'04, Hammamet, 2004.

21. T. Kelepouris, P. Miliotis, K. Pramatari, The impact of replenishment parameters and information sharing on the bullwhip effect: A computational approach, Athens University, Eltrun Working Paper Series, WP 2006-011, 2006.

22. M. Jakšic, B. Rusjan, Analysis of the bullwhip effect in supply chains using the transfer function method, Working Paper, Department of Management and Organisation, Faculty of Economics, University of Ljubljana, 2005.

23. Y. Merkuryev, J. Petuhova, R. Van Landeghem, S. Vansteenkiste, Simulation-based analysis of the bullwhip effect under different information sharing strategies, Proceedings of the 14th European Simulation Symposium: Simulation in Industry - Modeling, Simulation and Optimization, A. Verbraeck, W. Krug (eds.), Dresden 2003, pp. 294-299.

24. J.-H. Thun, J.-P. Mertens, Simulating the impact of reverse logistics on the bullwhip effect in closed-loop-supply chains using system dynamics, Procedings of EurOMA 2006: Moving Up the Value Chain, Vol.1, Glasgow, 2006, pp. 265-274.

25. K. Donohue, R. Croson, Behavioral causes of the bullwhip effect and the observed value of inventory information, Management Science, Vol. 52 (2006), No. 3, pp. 323-336.

26. R. Croson, K. Donohue, Upstream versus downstream information impact on the bullwhip effect, System Dynamics Review, Vol. 21 (2005), No. 3, pp.249–260.

27. Y. Wu, E. Katok, System-wide training and communication, the impact of learning on the Bullwhip Effect: An experimental study, Working Paper, Smeal College of Business, Penn State University, 2005.

28. N.H. Lurie, J.M. Swaminatham, The Role of Demand Information and Incentives in a Two-Stage Supply Chain, Working Paper, 2006.

29. J. Nienhaus, A. Ziegenbein, P. Schoensleben, How human behaviour amplifies the bullwhip effect. A study based on the beer distribution game online, Production Planning & Control, Vol. 17 (2006), No. 6, pp. 547–557.

30. G. Ruël, D. P. van Donk, T. van der Vaart, The beer game revisited: Relating risk-taking behaviour and bullwhip effect, Procedings of EurOMA 2006: Moving Up the Value Chain, Vol.1, Glasgow, 2006, pp. 403-412.

31. O.A. Carranza Torres, F.A. Villegas Morán (editors), The Bullwhip Effect in Supply Chains, Palgrave - MacMillan, 2006.

32. H. Peck, Reconciling supply chain vulnerability, risk and supply chain management, International Journal of Logistics: Research and Applications, Vol. 9 (2006), No. 2, pp. 127-142.

33. M. Christopher, H. Peck, Building the Resilient Supply Chain, International Journal of Logistics Management, Vol. 15 (2004), No. 2, pp. 1-14.

Improving Performance of Supply Chains by Leveraged Hard Solutions and Business Cultures

Stanisław Strzelczak[1], Haifeng Huang[2]

1 Warsaw University of Technology, Faculty of Production Engineering, Narbutta 85, 02-524 Warsaw, Poland

2 Beijing University of Technology, School of Economics and Management, China Research Center for Economic Transition (CRCET), 100 Pingleyuan, Chaoyang District, 100 022 Beijing, P.R.China

Abstract. Leveraging hard solutions with business culture is an important but rarely discussed problem. The need to harmonize systems and cultures is well understood in Asia. Western researchers and managers tend to rely on reductionism and prefer to focus only those phenomena, that can be easily modeled in a quantitative manner. This paper presents initial results of an ongoing research project, which aims to develop a well-justified methodology, capable to analyze both, cultural phenomena and material processes, in supply chains. A five-dimensional hybrid model of supply chain management (SCM) practices was developed to support holistic modeling of existing or future phenomena and empirical research. The presented considerations refer to the product development and production flow processes. The obtained and expected outcomes have double, scientific and practical importance.

1 Introduction

The common meaning of culture as a complex whole, which includes values, beliefs, attitudes, assumptions, customs and habits, practices, rituals, taboos, ceremonies, traditions, communication patterns, archetypes (e.g. heroes and scoundrels), norms, morals and other capabilities and habits acquired by members of population applies also to the business context. In the organizational context, this definition can be extended by other items, like formalism, time-rigidness, reliability, trust, reasoning and learning patterns, decision-making patterns etc. Hatch [1] demonstrated, that a corporate culture is adopted, developed and disseminated by a company.

Cultures are dynamic. In case of individuals (managers and employees), they may be affected by many factors, which cannot be directly influenced by an organizational culture, like: gender, generation, personality, temperament, ambitions,

Please use the following format when citing this chapter:

Strzelczak, S. and Huang, H., 2008, in IFIP International Federation for Information Processing, Volume 257, Lean Business Systems and Beyond, Tomasz Koch, ed.; (Boston: Springer), pp. 403–412.

morale, educational background, knowledge, social attitudes, religion, life experience, historical experience etc. Business cultures may be learned, adapted, shared and transmitted. They may be conflicting, harmonizing or even synergistic. Elements of culture are interrelated. Cultural integration may be supported by cultural sensitivity and deteriorated by ethnocentrism (conscious imposition of one's viewpoint) or parochialism (lack of sensitivity born of ignorance).

Johnson [2] described a cultural web, identifying a number of elements, that can be used to describe an organizational culture:

- *Paradigm*: what the organization is about; what it does; its mission; its values.
- *Control Systems*: the processes in place to monitor what is going on.
- *Organizational Structure*: hierarchy, reporting scheme, ways of work flow etc.
- *Power Structures*: who makes decisions; how widely is power spread, what is power based on ?
- *Symbols*: logos and designs, but also symbols of power (e.g. car parking spaces)
- *Rituals and Routines*: management meetings, reports etc. (may become more habitual than necessary).
- *Stories and Myths*: build up about people and events, and convey a message about what is valued within the organization.

Recently we can observe an increasing attention paid to the organizational cultures, as important determinants for organizational success. Cultural interferences are visibly behind many stories of failing cross-border business ventures and processes. The power of cultural issues was surely enhanced by the effects of globalization. While the link between organizational culture and organizational effectiveness is still not strictly proved [3], there is no denying, that each organization has a unique social structure, and that these social structures drive much of the group and individual behavior observed in organizations. More and more authors argue, that developing a strong organizational culture is essential for success [4].

A spectacular example of corporate success rooted in organizational culture is Toyota, which for over twenty years demonstrated steady growth, outstanding business performance and superior market capitalization. Toyota does not apply peculiar materials, processes or management techniques, but its production management principles are very different from those common in USA or Western Europe. Some of them are as follows [5]:

- Base your management decisions on a long-term philosophy:, even at the expense of short-term financial goals
- Create flow to move material and information fast as well as to link processes and people together so that problems surface right away. Make flow evident throughout your organizational culture.
- Build into your culture a philosophy of stopping or slowing down to fix the problems, to enhance the productivity in the long run.
- Respect your extended network of partners and suppliers by challenging them and helping them improve. Treat them as an extension of your business.
- Become a learning organization through relentless reflection (Hansei) and continuous improvement (Kaizen).

The above statements seem to be abstract, philosophical and fuzzy, at least such is the perception by majority of Western scholars and managers, who usually love sophisticated, complex, technically faced and effortable management systems.

Actually Toyota's principles are precise and can be reflected by exact managements practices and systems, like: safety of employment, motivation system, policy deployment practices, partnership with subcontractors etc. It is worth to note, that each of them separately cannot produce impressive results, but applied as a whole, they give amazing effects. They evidently demonstrate the importance of culture of corporation for its success. It is also worth to note, that despite a commonality of the phrase 'Toyota Production System', it actually refers to the whole supply chain.

The experience of Toyota confirms, that organizational systems and cultures are interrelated. Although this statement cannot be easily proved in a strictly scientific way, according to the Western standards, there are many examples confirming that implementing lessons from Toyota without any culture consciousness result in failures (e.g. quality circles, suggestion system, pull-flow in supply chains et. al.).

An interesting difference of Asian and Western business practices is visible in the performance assessment [6]. Asians tend to take a multifaceted view of a company, oppositely to the Western analytical, piece-by-piece assessments, by many hard indicators. Internal appraisals in Asia do not include individual assessments in the Western style, which are clear and objective, but normally deteriorate the group harmony and teamwork. When put down to the departmental or individual level, they often lead to conflicts, unfair rivalry, unneeded stress and other negative effects (in Western firms, management systems are often intentionally complicated, to prove commitment to the company or just to protect jobs).

1.1 Existing Results

It is visible from the literature overview, that most attempts to research cultural impacts in business, focus the national perspective and use simply patterns of analysis. Typically, few factors are considered, mostly of behavioral nature. The existing frameworks overlap, but none of them is comprehensive. They focus nations as the dominant objects, which can be attributed by different characteristics. Alternative layers of business cultures: macro- regional, regional, organizational, departmental, group cultures, subcultures and individual cultures, are usually ignored. Other business contexts than the situational (negotiations, communications), like ventures (mergers, acquisitions, supply chains, strategic alliances) and functions (advertising, motivating, accounting) are rarely reviewed [7].

It is a common view that most difficulties of SCM stem from an uncoordinated and fragmented allocation of responsibilities of the various supply chain activities to different functional areas [8]. Many publications point cross-company, cross-borders and spatial aspects of supply chains as the additional sources of difficulty. Only few recognize cultural circumstances as a major factor of supply chain performance, despite the fashion for such concepts of SCM, like the partnership, which is entirely of cultural nature [9, 10, 11]. The most common initiatives among the SCM professionals community, like the SCOR, the VCOR, or the CPFR, focus structural and procedural aspects of SCM, while the cultural considerations are totally ignored.

The existing approaches to the cultural measurement, like the OCAI (Organizational Culture Assessment Instrument) and CVF (Competing Value Framework) [12] or the Cultural Maturity Index [13], do not support joint performance measurement and cultural measurement. The example of Toyota puts also another question, about the trade offs between the business cultures of different levels, and the elements of hard organizational systems, like: goals, strategies, decision-making patterns, structures, performance assessment patterns, information systems, policies addressing human resources, etc.

Vanpoucke et. al. [11] targeted to assess the impact of characteristics of supply chain collaboration on performance through a questionnaire research in Western Europe. Likert scales were applied to measure all phenomena, including overall satisfaction and benefits of collaboration, and similarly, characteristics of collaboration, which were evaluated from seven perspectives: attributes of collaboration, communication behavior, supplier-customer selection process, conflict resolution techniques, systems and people. The paired-sample T-test comparisons of the most and the least successful cases were reported. No causal relations were analyzed and no trade-offs were assessed.

Aryee et. al. [10] considered inter-firm trust, power and other cultural factors of supply chain performance. The research has been limited to a literature overview and conceptual considerations. No empirical results were provided.

Van de Vijver and Vos [9] researched supply chain relations by case studies of eight Dutch companies. Supporting questionnaires were built around the following headings: culture, transparency, performance, trust, problems and problem solving, risk, and learning mechanisms. Cross-case display schemes were applied to discover patterns and similarities between the interviewees. The results were not supported by any in-depth assessments or trade-off analysis.

1.2 Our Results

The possibility to explore at once both, the cultural phenomena and the material aspects of supply chains performance, by the use of available quantitative data together with the qualitative information, drawn from case studies and management expertise, has been successfully confirmed. Using case studies and Delphi, we have assessed the causal relations between trust and replenishment policies. Using hybrid simulation, based on the industrial dynamics approach and the Bayesian Belief Networks (BBN), we have assessed the trade-offs between trust levels, inventory levels and stock turbulences. Finally, using management games we have assessed the trade-offs between performance measures, trust levels, inventory levels and stock turbulences. Despite a limited scope of our research and its pilot nature, some interesting conclusions can be confirmed by the gathered information:
1. In some circumstances the cultural phenomena may be more important, than the planning and control systems, to explain turbulences within supply chains.
2. Holistic consideration of culture and hard solutions is crucial, to avoid surprising inefficiencies, as well as to exploit possible, but unpredictable synergies.
3. Cultures and hard systems should be leveraged. In the supply chain context, they should be harmonized.

2   Methodology and Scope of the Research

One of the few research projects, which considered simultaneously cultural and systemic aspects of industrial management with reference to the business performance, was the one led by JMNESG (Japan Multinational Enterprises Study Group). Since the beginning of the research, in mid 1980s, a fundamental viewpoint upon which all further studies were based, was defined as an 'organizational culture approach'. Using an originally developed analytical framework - the 'Six-group 23-Item hybrid evaluation', the JMNESG consecutively conducted case studies supported by a limited statistical analysis. Since the start of project over 650 Japanese auto and electronics transplant worldwide [14] were reviewed. The Japanese multi-national enterprises (MNE) were being compared to the non-Japanese MNE and locals.

The Six-group 23-Item hybrid reference model reflects an ideal pattern of composition of Japanese management and production systems. Its components are presented below [Table 1]. Five-grade evaluation scale was used to assess the application or adaptation of Japanese style management. The originally developed Four-perspective evaluation method [Table 2] was used to evaluate and judge the substantive content of international transfers of management systems and technologies. The method enables to examine the degree, to which a certain system has taken root in a local community or, to which various factors composing the Japanese system have been transplanted in Japanese factories overseas. Comparisons of the situation by region, by country and by industry, or between different points of time. Typically, comparisons across the world (by macro-regions), inter-industry comparisons, comparisons of strategic typologies and extractions of common patterns and models (by regions, industries etc.) were applied during the different stages of the JMNESG research.

The research methodology of JMESG although over 20 years old, remains unique. It is one of the few, that explores in a holistic and systematic way diffusion of a particular production management system and culture. However, the objectivity of such research strongly depends on the knowledge, experience and skills of the researchers; particularly on their communication skills and good understanding of local management environments (the evaluations depend on the subjective individual assessments). Nevertheless, the JMNESG research approach has enjoyed a positive perception of international research community.

The research undertaken by authors continues those by JMNESG, but targets supply chains, not factories. The items of major importance are clustered into five dimensional hybrid evaluation reference model [Table 3]. Each item is assigned a descriptive grading scale, or – alternatively – a multiple-choice checklist (due to the limited size of this paper they are not presented).

Table 1. The Six-group 23-item Hybrid Evaluation Reference Model

Group	Items
Group 1 Work organization and administration	Job classification (1); Multi-skilled employees (2); Education and training (3); Wage system (4); Promotion (5); Supervision (6)
Group 2 Production Control	Equipment (7); Maintenance (8); Quality control (9); Process management (10)
Group 3 Procurement	Local content (11); Suppliers (12); Methods (13)
Group 4 Team Sense	Small group activities (14); Information sharing (15); Sense of unity (16)
Group 5 Labor Relations	Hiring policy (17); Long-term employment (18); Harmonious labor relations (19); Grievance (20)
Group 6 Parent-subsidiary relations	Ratio of Japanese expatriates (21); Delegation of power (22); Position of local managers (23)

Table 2. Four Perspective Evaluation Method

	Human	Material
Methods (refer to the transfer of intangible elements, such as technology and know-how required in building an organization and implementing personnel administration)	G1 Work Organization and Administration All items (1-6) G4 Team Sense All items (14-16) G5 Labor Relations All items (17-20)	G2 Production Control 8 (Quality Control)9 (Maintenance) G3 Procurement 13 (Methods)
Results (concern the transfer of machinery, parts and any other visible elements of "ready-made" hardware, including the dispatch of Japanese expatriates)	G6 Parent-subsidiaries 21 (Ratio of Japanese expatriates) 23 (Position of Local Managers)	G2 Production Control 7 (Equipment) G3 Procurement 11 (Local Content) 12 (Suppliers)

Seven evaluation perspectives were assumed to assess the performance of supply chains and to leverage of cultural aspects and hard solutions of supply chain management, including: profitability, productivity, capital activity, development and growth, stability and sustainability, agility / flexibility and quality. Hard (material) and soft (cultural) aspects are considered at once.

The research has been based on the inductive approach. Empirical data was used, including the expertise extracted from managers. The supply chains (i.e. the involved companies) were researched to examine interactions and correlations of cultural phenomena and material aspects. The methodological framework of the research is presented below.

Table 3. Five-dimension Hybrid Evaluation Reference Model of SCM

Dimension	Items
Human Resources Management	(1) Job specialization (2) Employees development (3) Wages and salaries (4) Motivations (5) Promotion (6) Supervision (7) Assessments (8) Group activities
Operations management	(9) Process management (10) Quality management (11) Resources management (12) Maintenance
External integration	(13) Partnering (14) Trust (15) Autonomy (16) Information sharing (17) Policy deployment (18) Profit sharing (19) Customer value spread (20) Responsibilities spread
Organizational development	(21) Operational risks management (22) Business monitoring practices (23) Inter-organizational improvement activities
Business culture	(24) Leadership (25) Consensus role (26) Time rigidness (27) Job safety (28) Formalism (29) Business values (30) Controlling (31) Role of hierarchy (32) Time perspective (33) Communitarism

Table 4. Research Framework for Hybrid Analysis of SCM

Step	Methods	Outcomes
Modeling causal relations	Field observation Semi-structured interviewing Cognitive pre-mapping	Structured concepts Measurement scales Cause-and-effect diagrams
Empirical evaluation of impacts and trade-offs	Limited statistical analysis (Cronbach's alpha for reliability and Pearson for correlations) Delphi research Management games Bayesian-Belief Networks (BBN)	Empirically based assessments of correlations and interdependencies Influence diagrams Static charcteristics
Exploring dynamical phenomena	Hybrid simulation (hybrid algebra for symbolic and digital processing) Management games	Dynamic characteristics

The cultural phenomena and the material aspects of supply chains performance were explored at once by the use of collected quantitative data together with the qualitative information, drawn from the case studies and management expertise. Using case studies and Delphi, the causal relations between trust and replenishment policies were assessed. Using hybrid simulation, based on the industrial dynamics approach (ithink® 8.0) and the Bayesian Belief Networks (MSBN 3.0®), the trade-offs between trust levels, inventory levels and stock turbulences were assessed. Finally, using management games the trade-offs between performance measures, trust levels, inventory levels and stock turbulences were assessed.

The research presented in this paper was performed during recent three years. It was done separately and/or jointly on the basis of research grants pursued by the

Warsaw University of Technology and the Beijing University of Technology. These projects were done in twelve multi-national companies, which operate in the Central Europe and China. Demand fulfillment and product development were the two major areas of interest. The researched companies represented mostly electronic, automobile and electrical appliances sectors.

3   Results

The research was considered rather as a pilot. It was mainly aimed to gather a relevant experience and to develop a well-justified and reliable methodology, which could be later used for wider and more relevant empirical examinations, resulting in much better justified results. An expected practice-oriented site-effects were also welcomed, like tool-kits for management development and educational resources.

Although the research is still at an initial stage, and despite its limited scope and pilot nature, some interesting conclusions can be confirmed from the gathered information:

1. In some circumstances the cultural phenomena may be more important, than the planning and control systems, to explain turbulences within supply chains.
2. Holistic consideration of culture and hard solutions is crucial, to avoid surprising inefficiencies, as well as to exploit possible, but unpredictable synergies.
3. Cultures and hard systems should be leveraged. In the supply chain context, they should be harmonized.

Up to now we have focused a limited number of phenomena, including inefficiencies occurring within the supply chains, particularly those reflected by:

- delays (or long lead-times),
- shortages (or failed due dates),
- downtimes (low OEE),
- excessive stock,
- overproduction,
- oscillations and unbalanced flows,
- deteriorated quality.

The trade-offs between trust levels, inventory levels and stock turbulences were assessed and confirmed. Additionally, management games and hybrid simulations explained the trade-offs between performance measures, trust levels, inventory levels and stock turbulences in the context of different cultures.

The research incorporated practical components and extensions. An example may be the project of cultural integration done for one of the American auto-parts manufacturer operating in the Central Europe. This big globally operating company, highly integrated with many vendors and clients worldwide, has recognized that many problems at the operational level result from cultural interferences and the lack of multi-culture competencies. An example is the „bullwhip effect" in supply chains, which causes capital losses, high costs and deteriorates the competitiveness. The management of the company decided to run workshops, addressed to particular national cultures. They were focusing behavioral issues, communication patterns and specific business situations, e.g. decision making. Stereotypes and language problems were totally ignored. Cross-cultural management issues were also incorporated into functionally and process oriented improvement programs, e.g. in the proprietary corporate methodology addressing the collaborative product life-cycle management. The move up of supply chain was achieved through joint workshops, which involved all parties within the supply chain, supported by the external consultants. Substantial reduction of productivity and lead times was achieved. The whole program appeared to be very efficient and effective. The company later decided to extend it to all future structural ventures.

4 Concluding remarks

This paper briefly discussed results of research projects addressing the SCM, that jointly considered cultural phenomena and hard systems. The business impacts of multicultural environment are still poorly understood. The trade-offs between cultures and systems are not realized and the strategic potential of cultures is still commonly underestimated.

A challenging issue for the future research is the avoidance of the Heisenberg's effect, i.e. the interactions occurring between the measuring and measured, that can damage the measuring process or the measurement instruments [15]. Other problems of cross-cultural management of the global supply chains could be caused by forbidden topics, like: political correctness, taboos etc.

The following questions for the future research are still well justified:

- How to identify cultural phenomena (like habits, attitudes, values etc.)
- Systematization and structurization of concepts
- How to measure them
- How to relate casually behavioral issues to the performance effects
- How to model business impacts of behavioral phenomena, trade-offs etc.

The findings of the paper, although initial, have both, methodological and practical importance. Looking forward, the following further efforts could be continued:

- Theoretical:
  o Further structurization of concepts
  o Holistic and complete evaluation methodology (including modeling tools, cause-and-effects analysis)
  o Hybrid simulations of value-adding processes and cultural phenomena
  o New framework for supply chain organizational design
- Empirical:
  o Analyzing turbulences
  o Prove, that some common (fashionable) practices result in most circumstances in deteriorated supply chain performance
- Practice oriented:
  o Improvement tool-kits
  o Benchmarking / IFC / Best practices
  o Educational materials (management games)

References

1. M.J. Hatch, Organization Theory: Modern, Symbolic, and Postmodern Perspectives, Oxford University Press, 1997.

2. G. Johnson, Rethinking Incrementalism, *Strategic Management Journal*, Vol. 9 (1988), pp. 75-91.

3. J. Kotter, Corporate Culture and Performance, Free Press; 1992.

4. S. Strzelczak, Enhancing Competitiveness by a Multicultural Business Education, *International Management Review*, Vol. 2 (2006) No.1, pp. 68-76.

5. J.K. Liker, The Toyota Way. 14 Management Principles from the World's Greatest Manufacturer, McGraw-Hill, 2004, pp. 35-41.

6. S. Strzelczak, Business Integration Engineering, in: Economic and Managerial Developments in Asia and Europe - Comparative Studies, edited by S.Strzelczak, Kramist Ltd., 2003, pp. 99-118.

7. S. Chanchani, A. MacGregor, A Synthesis of Cultural Studies in Accounting, *Journal of Accounting Literature*, Vol. 18 (1998), No.1, pp. 1-30.

8. P.-P. Dornier, R. Ernst, M. Fender, P. Kouvelis, Global Operations and Logistics, John Wiley & Sons, 1998, pp. 216-233.

9. M. van de Vijver, B.Vos, Collaborative Relationships with Key Suppliers: An Exploratory Study of Practices in Different Industries, Proceedings of EurOMA 2006, Glasgow, 2006, pp. 1051-1059.

10. G. Aryee, R. Mason, M. Sarana, Exploring the Cultural and Trust Aspects of Business Relationships for Supply Chain Performance, Proceedings of EurOMA 2006, Glasgow, 2006, pp. 947-956.

11. E. Vanpoucke, A. Vereecke, E. Pandelaere, L. Solis, Characteristics of Supply Chain Collaboration and Their Impact on Performance, Proceedings of EurOMA 2006, Glasgow, 2006, pp. 1061-1070.

12. K. S. Cameron, R. E. Quinn, Diagnosing and Changing Organizational Culture, Prentice-Hall, 1999.

13. J. Cartwright, Cultural Transformation, Financial Times – Prentice Hall, 1999.

14. T. Abo (ed.), Hybrid Factory: The Japanese Production System in the United States, Oxford University Press, 1994, pp. 18-57.

15. S. Strzelczak, J. Strzelczak, Getting Synergy of Business Cultures in the Globalisation Era - How Asian and Western Management Cultures can Learn each from other Making Progress this Way, Proceedings of the 13th East Asia Economic Symposium, Xi'an, 2004, pp. 124-132.

Architectural Frameworks for Business Information System Analysis and Design

Jacques Trienekens[1], Hans-Henrik Hvolby[2],
Kenn Steger-Jensen[2], Peter Falster[3]
(1)Department of Social Sciences, Wageningen University, the Netherlands
(2) Department of Production, Aalborg University, Denmark
(3) Department of Informatics and Mathematical Modelling, Technical
University of Denmark

Abstract. The paper makes the first steps towards a methodology to assess frameworks for business process analysis and information system design. The assessment instrument will be designed based on key elements of architectural frameworks such as Isa, Cim-Osa and Pera. Four major frameworks will be discussed: Isa-S95, Oagis, Scor and Cpfr.

1 Introduction

In the late 1980s and early 1990s various frameworks for business analysis and information system design were developed: for example Cim-Osa [1], Pera [2] and Grai [3]. Concurrently, in the 1990s a new generation of process oriented modelling methods emerged to analyse and redesign business processes. Examples of these are Event Process Chain, the Activity Chain Model and Grai Grids. These modelling methods reflect distinct, though complementary, dimensions of business (or supply chain-) management. For example, Event Process Chain focuses on time relationships, Activity Chain Model focuses on business process flow whereas Grai Grids focus on decision structures. The models were mostly applied to single business cases, although also supply chain applications have been made [4].

These frameworks and modelling methods can be considered predecessors of reference information models that were developed in the second half of the 1990s and later. Reference models were mostly developed to be used as a basis for software development and applications. Two examples are Baan Dem and Sap. Baan Dem was developed by Baan Company in the mid 1990s to support implementations of Baan's Erp-system. Major elements of Dem were business control models, decompositions of business functions (including predefined parameter settings) and detailed process models (including roles, work instructions and links to the specific Baan transactions). The Baan Dem reference models started as a single industry

Please use the following format when citing this chapter:

Trienekens, J.H., Hvolby, H.-H., Steger-Jensen, K. and Falster, P., 2008, in IFIP International Federation for Information Processing, Volume 257, Lean Business Systems and Beyond, Tomasz Koch, ed.; (Boston: Springer), pp. 413–421.

model but moved to a multiple-domain reference model in the late 1990s. Sap also developed a reference model to support their implementation processes. Major elements of the model were process diagrams and data models. The Sap reference model is a multiple-domain model, i.e. set up for many industries [5].

In the last decade the development of (reference) frameworks to model inter-company relationships as a basis for inter-enterprise software development has emerged with examples such as Scor and Cpfr.

2 Architectural frameworks

Designing an architecture for a software system, especially for large-scale supply chain systems, is a complex process. A state-of-the-art review of the many proposals to system architectures does not show consistency in concepts.

Ieee 1471-2000 defines architecture as the fundamental organisation of a system embodied in its components, their relationships to each other, and to the environment, and the principles guiding in its design and evolution. Thus, architecture is about the manner in which the components of a specific product, system or an organisation are composed, organised and integrated and as such, an architecture determines the nature or essence of a product, system or organisation. In many contexts model and architecture are not really distinguished. Van Waes [6] states that the architecture is represented by a model and a system abstracts from an architecture (figure 1).

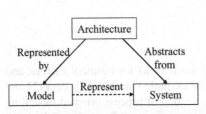

Fig. 1. Relationships between architecture, model and system [6]

Zwegers [7] and Williams [8] discuss the distinction between architecture in the art of science and architecture in model of structure meaning:

1) The structural arrangement (design) of a physical system such as the computer control system part of an overall enterprise integration system. Examples are the Nbs or Amrf reference models [9], the reference model for manufacturing planning and control [10], and the Factory Automation Model [11].

2) The structural arrangement (organisation) of the development and implementation of a project or program such as a manufacturing or enterprise integration or other enterprise development program. Examples are Cim-Osa's Open System Architecture for Computer Integrated Manufacturing [12], the Grai Integrated Methodology [13] and the Purdue Enterprise Reference Architecture [8].

These two views are unified in the following such that the first type is called reference architecture and the second type is called architectural framework (meta-architecture, i.e. architecture about architecture).

Architecture is based on a set of ontology concepts and principles. Chandrasekaran et al. [14] define ontologies as content theories about the sorts of objects, properties of objects and relations between objects that are possible in a specified domain of knowledge. Ontologies provide a clearer view on how knowledge should be structured, thereby enabling sharing of knowledge. Benjamins [15] defines an ontology as "a shared and common understanding of some domain that can be communicated across computers and people". Thus, an ontology provides a common and shared representation platform. Accordingly, ontologies may, through meta architectures and reference architectures, support the design of information systems and be the basis of the unambiguous communication between people and information systems [16]. To arrive at operational business information systems it is of immanent importance that stakeholders commit to a shared ontology and shared architecture, including communication between people involved in designing information systems.

The architecture principles applied here are decomposition, abstracting, layering, hierarchy and nesting, and reference system for orthogonal arrangement. Early work on establishing so-called architectural framework for information systems are found in Zachman's framework [17, 18].

	Data	Function	Network	People	Time	Motivation
Scope						
Enterprise model						
System model						
Technology model						
Component						
Functioning system						

Fig. 2. Zachman's framework. The dimensions people, time, and motivation were added in 1992 [17, 18]

An architectural framework is a collection of principles, methods, or tools relevant for a given domain of application [19]. Such a framework is a real or conceptual structure intended to serve as a support or guide for the building of something that expands the structure into something useful. Other examples of architectural frameworks are Cim-Osa for computer-integrated manufacturing, Geram developed by the Ifip-Ifac task force group and synthesised from other frameworks (Cim-Osa, Grai, The Purdue Enterprise reference architecture, etc.).

The concepts of architectural framework, reference model or, as we will call it, reference architecture will be discussed. Architectural frameworks found in the literature are all established within a frame of reference given by two, three or more axes (a n-dimensional co-ordinate system). Fixing those axes is the essence of these frameworks. Within the framework the architectural descriptions are positioned.

Common to most frameworks are the following three axes:
- Instantiation is the degree of particularisation from the generic level, through partial level to particular level of architectures.
- Derivation is a level of abstraction corresponding to domains of the main phases/representation of the development process (requirements, design and implementation) representing a distinct, unique perspective of the Owner, Designer, Builder.
- Generation is a decomposition according to domains of views of describing the real world's objects/variables (data model, functional model etc).

In Zachman's terminology the axis of derivation establishes the scope/enterprise model, system model and technology model. Instead of model we prefer here the term architecture. As stressed by Zachman, these representations are not merely successive levels of increasing detail but are actually different representations/ domains – different in meaning, in motivation, in use, etc. [17]. Aerts et al. [20] describe the three domains for representation by

- Business architecture which defines the business system in its environment of suppliers and customers,
- Application architecture which details the software application components and their interaction and
- Ict platform architecture which is the architecture of computers, networks, operating systems, data base management systems etc.

A reference architecture (in literature often called reference model) is defined as "a generic manner to organise and integrate system components" [7]. A reference architecture is used for comparing something to a reference. Thus, it refers to the generic and partial level of the framework. It serves as a point of departure for the design of a large number of systems in a specific application area. Thus, a reference architecture is a generic/partial (architecture) which can be used as a basis for particular architectural developments or for evaluation of particular architectures. The relation between reference architecture and (particular) architecture is therefore one of instantiation. Examples of reference architecture/models are the Osi reference model, the Nbs or Amrf models [9], and Mrpii systems [21].

An adequate reference model can reduce development costs tremendously. From an economic point of view, reference models are attractive, since they promise to accomplish two goals which are usually in conflict: higher quality and lower cost. However, the development of high quality reference models is facing severe challenges. Usually, semantics compromises the chance of re-use: The more a particular model is specialised, the higher its comfort of re-use but the lower is the chance that it fits a certain case. In order to overcome this conflict, it is required to develop concepts that allow for adapting reference models to individual needs both conveniently and safely.

3   Current Models for Information System Analysis and Design

Four different frameworks will briefly be discussed in the following:
- Supply Chain Operations Reference-model (Scor) developed and endorsed by the Supply-Chain Council
- Collaborative Planning, Forecasting, and Replenishment (Cpfr) industry initiative based on the Voluntary Inter-industry Commerce Standards Association
- Isa-S95 standards for enterprise and manufacturing integration developed by the Instrumentation, Systems and Automation (Isa) Society Consensus Committee.
- Integration Specifications developed by Open Applications Group (Oag) which is widely supported by industry and software companies (e.g. Ibm, Sap, Oracle, Boing, Ford, Automotive Industry Action Group).

Scor has been developed as the cross-industry standard for supply-chain management [22]. The Scc was organised in 1996 by Prtm and Amr Research, and initially included 69 voluntary member companies (mainly in the U.S.). At the moment more than 800 companies are members of Scc and the model is internationally broadly acknowledged. The Scor-model focuses on the processes plan, source, make, deliver and return. It provides process models on three aggregation levels, standard process descriptions, performance metrics (in the categories Delivery Reliability, Responsiveness, Flexibility, Costs and Asset Management Efficiency), and best-practice descriptions. The Scc claims to support different supply chain configurations including "pure" Make-to-Stock, Replenish-to-Order and Make-to-Order. Cpfr has developed a set of business processes, which entities in a supply chain can be used for collaboration on a number of buyer/seller functions towards overall efficiency in the supply chain. Their Xml specifications have been integrated with the broader set of Ean•Ucc Xml specifications endorsed by the Global Commerce Initiative (Gci) to ensure full coverage of the Cpfr process without creating overlapping or redundant message formats. The existing core Ean•Ucc messages for item synchronisation, party (trading partner) synchronisation, purchase order, invoice, dispatch (shipment notice) and other information have been augmented with the Cpfr product activity, forecast and other transactions [www.cpfr.org].

Isa-S95 (Iec62264) addresses the interface or exchange of data within the enterprise systems (planning, scheduling and procurement) and the production management systems (production dispatching and execution). It consists of three parts: Models and terminology, Object model attributes and Models of Manufacturing Operations. The development is based on the work by Williams [23] on the Purdue Reference Model (Prm) for Computer Integrated Manufacturing (Cim), but two other works have also a great deal of influence, which are the Isa Sp-88 "Batch Control' committee and the Mesa International Mes context model.

Oag includes a broad set of Xml schemas for sharing business information. It addresses the needs of traditional Erp integration as well as supply chain management and e-commerce. This specification provides the structure of business documents and additional meta-data, which is required as a part of the application processing.

4   Positioning Current Frameworks and Reference Architectures

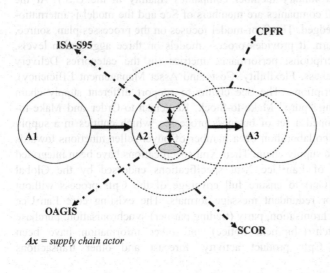

Fig. 3. Scope of four major frameworks/ reference architectures

In this section the frameworks and reference architectures described in the previous section are positioned using the basic architectural components described. Figure 3 depicts the scope of the four examples described in section 3. Scor focuses on the main company integrating demand and supply (deliver and source); Cpfr focuses on collaboration between buyer and supplier; whilst Isa and Oag focus on integration (standards) between in-company management and manufacturing layers. Figure 4 depicts domain of views of reference architectures. Scor and Isa/Oag describe the object system in terms of process, data and/or object networks and hierarchies. Cpfr focuses on how to approach the object system (e.g. collaborative forecasting) and what activities to undertake to arrive at a collaborative system. Scor also includes these two perspectives (e.g. benchmarks, best practices) whilst Isa and Oag focus less on the concrete design of systems. All four reference models pay less attention to company network and supply chain (wide) relationships, although Cpfr looks at buyer-supplier relationships and Scor at sourcing and delivering relationships. The role of people in (collaborative) processes has minor attention in all four models. Although the im-

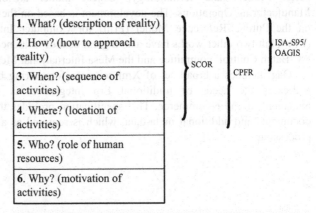

1. What? (description of reality)
2. How? (how to approach reality)
3. When? (sequence of activities)
4. Where? (location of activities)
5. Who? (role of human resources)
6. Why? (motivation of activities)

Fig. 4. Domains of views of reference architectures with different coverage areas

portance of trust and power relationships is recognised in both Scor and Cpfr, exact conditions or types of relationships in this regard are not defined. All four reference models pay no or very little attention to the companies' strategy.

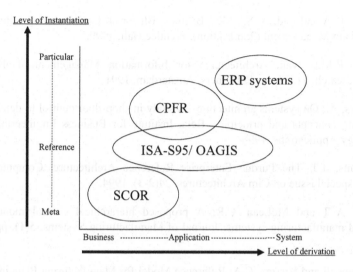

Fig. 5. Instantiation and derivation positioning of models

5   Conclusion

In this paper first steps to a method to assess information system architecture reference models have been made. We have discussed scope, coverage of different perspectives on the real-world and levels of derivation and instantiation of four current models. Future research will focus on an integrated methodology to assess these reference models. This also involves the degree to which functions are/are not supported by the models (e.g. quality control, resource management, etc.) and how well these models can be implemented in different sectors (electronics, machine and food industry) and in different dynamic business environments.

References

1. Vernadat, F; Cim-Osa – a European development for enterprise integration, Part 2: enterprise modelling. In: Enterprise integration model (C.Petrie). The MIT Press, Cambridge, MA, 1992.

2. Williams, T.J; The Purdue Enterprise Reference Architecture, Instrument Society of America, Research Triangle Park, USA, 1992.

3. Doumeingts, G; How to decentralise decisions through Grai models in production management. Computers in Industry, 6, 1985.

4. Hvolby, H.H and Trienekens, J; Models for Supply Chain Reengineering, Production Planning and Control, 2001.

5. Curran, T. A and Lad, A; SAP R/3 Business Blueprint: Understanding Enterprise Supply Chain Management (2nd Edition). Prentice Hall, 1999.

6. Waes, R.M.C. van; Architectures for Information Management. Tinbergen Institute research, 11. Thesis Publishers, Amsterdam, 1991.

7. Zwegers, A.; On systems architecting – a study in shop floor control to determine architecting concepts and principles. Beta. Institute for Business Engineering and Technology Applications, 1998.

8. Williams, T.J; The Purdue Enterprise Reference Architecture. Computers in Industry; special issue on Cim Architectures, 24(2-3), 1994.

9. Jones, A..T and McLean, C.R; A proposed hierarchical control model for automated manufacturing systems. Journal of Manufacturing Systems, 5(1), pp. 15-25, 1986.

10. Biemans, F and Vissers, C.A; Reference Model for Manufacturing Planning and Control Systems. Journal of Manufacturing Systems, 8(1), 1989.

11. Graefe, U and Thomson, V; A reference model for production control. International Journal of Computer Integrated Manufacturing; special issue on Cim Architecture, 2(2), pp. 86-93, 1989.

12. Amice Consortium, Cim-Osa, Open Systems Architecture for Cim, Springer, Berlin, 1993.

13. Doumeingts, G and Ducq, Y; Enterprise modelling techniques to improve efficiency of enterprises, Production Planning and Control, 12(2), 2001.

14. Chandrasekaran, B; Josephson, J and Richard Benjamins, V; What are Ontologies, and why do we need them?, Ieee Intelligent Systems, 20(6), 1999.

15. Benjamins, R.V; Fensel, D and Gomez Perez, A.; Knowledge Management through Ontologies, pp. 5.1-5.12, In: Proc. 2nd Int. Conf. on Practical Aspects of Knowledge Management (Pakm), Editors: U. Reimer, Basel, 1998.

16. Uschold, M., King, M., Moralee, S. and Zorgios, Y., The enterprise ontology, in: The Knowledge Engineering Review, Special issue on putting Ontologies to use, 13, Edinburgh, 1997.

17. Zachman, J.A; A framework for information systems architecture. Ibm Systems Journal, 26(3), 1987.

18. Sowa, J.F and Zachman, J.A; Extending and formalizing the framework for information systems architecture. Ibm Systems Journal, 31(3), 1992.

19. Vernadat, F.B; Enterprise modelling and integration: principles and applications, Chapman & Hall, 1996.

20. Aerts, A.T.M; Goossenaerts, J.B.M; Hammer, D.K and Wortmann, J.C; Architectures in context: on the evolution of business, application software, and Ict platform architectures, Information and Management 41, 781-794, 2004.

21. Wortmann, J.C; Muntslag, D.R and Timmermans, P.J.M; Customer-driven Manufacturing, Chapman & Hall, London, 1997.

22. SCC, Supply-Chain Operations Reference-model: Overview Version 7.0, Supply-Chain Council, 2005.

23. Williams, T.J. (ed.); Reference Model for Computer Integrated Manufacturing, International Workshop on Industrial Computer Systems, Purdue University, 1988.

The Lea®n Extended Enterprise
The Art of continuously achieving benefits through Value Adding Communities

Alexander Tsigkas[1] and Robert Freund[2]
1 Democritean University of Thrace
Department of Production Engineering and Management
Vas. Sofias 12, 67 100 Xanthi, Greece
WWW home page: http://www.duth.gr
2 University of Information, Technology and Management,
Rzeszow, Poland

Abstract. The competition of tomorrow is moving away from the level of the individual company and towards the level of supply chain. It is at this level that Lean organisations should evolve and become more flexible, self organising and self adapting entities. Today Lean implementations are based on principles with no clear scope as to how to achieve middle to long term benefits at the level of the extended enterprise. The objective is mostly based on achieving short term benefits through the implementation of mere techniques at the individual factory level. Therefore a new theory is needed to incorporate a set of practical rules. The approach for the interrelationship between theory and practice of Lean is based on systems thinking and the objectives of the learning enterprise. Lean should be practiced in conjunction with Open Innovation based upon customer-driven value creation and not merely customer-driven demand. The Lean extended enterprise should evolve towards a continuously learning organisation through customer integration in the product development and deployment cycle.

1 Introduction

Since Engineer Taiichi Ohno designed the famous Toyota Production System [1], there is a great deal of time elapsed, until Europe much later than Japan and the US has *discovered* that there is something to win, if similar techniques would be implemented in the European Industry. Under the pressure of Antagonism, companies were seeking ways to reduce operation costs in order to stay alive in a continuously globalising and antagonistic economy. The Lean approach has been adopted from an increasing number of companies in Europe slowly but steadily, now days with an accelerating pace, although some time ago many companies, some of

Please use the following format when citing this chapter:

Tsigkas, A. and Freund, R., 2008, in IFIP International Federation for Information Processing, Volume 257, Lean Business Systems and Beyond, Tomasz Koch, ed.; (Boston: Springer), pp. 423–431.

which today do not exist, have rejected the Lean approach as an approach that does not fit the European culture. What has changed today and companies have despite the cultural differences embrace the Lean way? Answer: in our view nothing – A more careful glance at the way companies implement *Lean* has very little to do with Lean. They look at practices and implement merely lean methodologies. They do not view Lean as a different way of managing a company and where the old industrial age attitude must vanish and be substituted by a completely new way of thinking, learning, measuring and acting. What they have in mind are mostly some techniques that act upon their resources in order to become more effective and efficient. Their focus, despite Lean, stays within short term cost reduction everywhere in the company with no middle or long term impact. The results have been significant in production especially in the first couple of years of implementation. However, looking at the middle to long term, benefits are really poor with little or non real improvement on the company competitiveness. It is our belief that *Lean* in conjunction with Open Innovation [2] can set the European industry off the ground if practice is based upon pure customer-driven value creation [3] and not merely customer-driven demand.

This paper looks at the presence and the future of *Lean Thinking* [4] and *Lean Practicing* in Europe and proposes ways as to how companies should be acting as to achieve the middle and long term benefits. Especially companies operating in the eastern part of Europe have the advantage to *do it right the first time* by taking a different way than their western counterparts have taken in the past and even today with the objective of steadily achieving middle and long term viability and competitiveness. The structure of the paper is the following:

- The Lean way in Europe and the US – status review
- The new Lean organisation – the theory behind the practice
- The Lea®n Supply Chain and how to sustain it

2   The Lean way in Europe and the US – status review

A report published recently from the Aberdeen Group in the US, shows that Lean Philosophy has become the mainstream [5] (Fig.1). It is stated however, that although nearly 90% of the respondents in the survey consider themselves Lean less than one-third can be considered to have mature Lean deployments. Many think of Lean as supporting only key manufacturing functions, not broader, related functions. A closer look at the data shows, that there is a wide gap between those companies that deploy some Lean techniques and those that fully embrace the Lean culture it is stated in the same report.

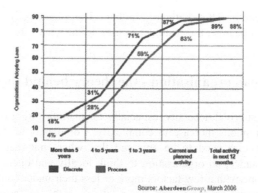

Source: AberdeenGroup, March 2006

Fig. 1. Lean philosophy has become mainstream

According to the report the Lean operational maturity characteristics are primarily focused on the use of Lean tools and techniques used in production rather than the cultural aspects of Lean. One of the reasons for this is that *culturally, many of the leadership principles espoused in* The Toyota Way *are at odds with the managerial and facilitator skills taught at traditional U.S. MBA programs* is stated in the report. One of the major drawbacks in deploying Lean is the supplier integration in the Lean program of their customers. Almost a third of respondents are challenged with integrating both other parts of the company and all its suppliers into the Lean program. Meeting customer requirements for just-in-time deliveries requires the support and cooperation of not only finance and logistics, but also the suppliers who provide the raw materials, components, and assemblies that are used early in the manufacturing process. Expansion of Lean in the supply chain is therefore an imminent factor of success. But it is a challenging issue for most of the companies in the US and Europe.

Since most of the major manufacturing companies operate today globally with globally distributed supply networks, Lean means that also the ICT infrastructure (Information and Communication Technology) should be aligned with the business strategy of the companies. ICD has prepared a white paper for reporting on a survey conducted in Europe and published in September 2005 [6]. In their report ICD are reporting that while lean manufacturing is a strategy that has been around since the 1970s, it has traditionally been a cost-cutting strategy. According to the same report commitment to lean principles, in combination with a focus on continuous product improvement and a strong commitment to innovation, are emerging as the preferred strategy for industry thought leaders.

There is a fundamental issue about adding or creating value in the whole discussion about Lean. From the Lean perspective, at least the way this has been in implemented in the US and Europe, customer value definition is literally provider-driven and scarcely user-driven. The voice of the customer is effectively echoed rather than heard. Involvement of the user or customer in the definition of what is value for him/her is mostly not an issue. Innovations in product and services are made for the customer but without him/her. The objective in the new Lean organisation should be to let the customer or user define what value is.

3   The new Lean organisation - the theory behind the practice

Going global is a survival necessity, especially for manufacturing companies, but it means also a horrendous increase in complexity. Complexity at this point implies that new competencies need to be emerged that where not there before, or not necessary. For instance, an organisation to think locally and operate locally meant that they had to cope with a few factors more or less their under control. With stable supply and operational processes and also relatively stable or foreseeable demand, companies could implement their Lean programs and have shown that remarkable results may be achieved in terms of productivity and drastic reduction of delivery times as well as WIP and finished product inventories by the mere use of lean techniques. Local suppliers could align themselves with their Just-in-Time strategies of their customers sooner or later.

However, in the global environment uncertainty in both the supply and the demand processes is increasing, the external market pressures on the organisation are changing scale and the IT infrastructure is not any more suitable to cope with so many simultaneously changing factors that were known and stable before. To continue to be Lean in this environment goes beyond the normal boundaries of the classical principles of the Lean or Toyota Production System (TPS) in our opinion, because the Lean principles, once set and institutionalised through the TPS, are not sustainable any more. To achieve sustainability of Lean in the global environment, organisations should qualify as adaptive and evolutionary systems. Moreover, the question here is not how to sustain a Lean organisation but how the organisation can sustain itself in this new environment [7], in other words to become self-sustainable. Self-sustainability is an emergent characteristic of the adaptive and evolutionary organisation. Lean self-sustained organisations must be able to produce themselves and their requisite knowledge in a changing environment. Therefore Lean adaptive and evolutionary organisations should divert from the classical perception of the Lean philosophy and modify some of its principles to fit the requirements of adaptivity and evolution that may be in certain aspect adversarial to the classical Lean ones. Furthermore Lean adaptive and evolutionary organisations should be able to continuously learn not only from within the organisation [8] but also through the direct interaction with their customers by integrating the customer or user in the value creation loop [3] and expand this knowledge in the supply chain. Especially supply chains structure also divert from the classical model of stable partnerships dominated in recent years, as a principle of Lean philosophy and will move towards more volatile and unbounded constructs. For example it is thinkable that supply chains could be formed in an ad-hoc fashion to satisfy unique requirements of a customer or a group of customers. This type of supply chain may be organised in the form of Value Adding Communities (VAC) as argued and discussed in the work of Tsigkas et. al [9, 10]. Below a summary the five principles is stated upon which Lean adaptive and evolutionary enterprises should be based:

- Enable open innovation and customer-driven value creation
- Embrace evolutionary change
- Encourage variability and tolerate errors
- Strive for dynamic equilibrium
- Nurture emergent properties

1. Enable open innovation and customer-driven value creation

The driving factor in the adaptive and evolutionary Lean organisation is the origin of value creation. The classical Lean philosophy concentrates on value-adding activities instead of value creating activities. In the Lean environment value is rather seen in a defensive way, as a production disadvantage (an operational cost position) instead of in an offensive way and a marketing advantage (a price and market share position). In the classical Lean organisation the customer (or consumer, or user) is not viewed as part of the value creation loop, reflected at the classical Value Stream Map, which is an open loop construct. In the era of mass customisation and open innovation, the customer is part of a closed loop Value Stream Map, either during the development phase, or during the production phase, until the customer completes it or issues instructions for completing it (mass customisation). Customer-driven value creation and open innovation is the prerequisite for achieving 100% customer satisfaction. In a society that scarcity of goods has been surpassed [11], differentiation can be efficiently delivered through the customer commitment and integration in the value creation loop [7]. The new Lean extended enterprise is engaged in two types of production: *heteropoiesis*, producing the other than itself (i.e. goods and services) and *autopoiesis*, producing itself (i.e. its own ability to produce). Self-sustainability is crucially dependent on the reliability of the second type of production, *autopoiesis*. Only an enterprise (as a system) that could continually produce itself, that is adapting itself to changing environmental conditions can be deemed as self-sustainable. Therefore, a new set of competences are now needed for the new Lean organisation, in order to become self-sustainable. This is an area for further research.

2. Embrace evolutionary change

It is important to view the organisation as a living system, not an engineered machine according to Taylor [12]. Taylor claims that living systems evolve through incremental changes that confer increased competitiveness in their environment. Unlike machines, they are not centrally controlled and regimented into perfect execution. Self-sustainable, self-organised enterprises are by definition adaptive organisations. According to Bergson [13], who himself was a proponent of creative evolution, *"to exist is to change, to change means to mature, and to mature is to creating oneself endlessly"*. Rephrasing Bergson and according to Zeleny [7], an organization can only exist if recreates itself. Self-sustainability is the objective. The classical lean philosophy treats the organization as a machine, like do Fordism and Taylorism through the approach of the division of labour. To embrace this new perspective, a Lean organisation should be willing to let aside the desire for increased control and begin to encourage the variability and experimentation that are essential to adaptive and evolutionary change. The classical Lean philosophy does not favour variability and experimentation is limited as fundamental issues against standardisation of products and processes. Lean and Six Sigma initiatives strive to achieve nearly zero variability in the execution of processes by design. Encouraging variability and experimentation necessarily means giving more autonomy to line organisations and individuals. If a person or group behaves in a way that increases the fitness of the organisation as a whole, that person or group should be rewarded with increasing funding or opportunities for growth within the organisation.

3.   Encourage variability and tolerate errors

An organisation that improves through variation must have a high tolerance for errors [12]. This can be achieved through redundant groups throughout value-adding operations. The goal is to allow new ideas to prove themselves while sheltering customers from the effect of ideas that do not work out. This approach is quite different from a zero-defects approach to managing operations in the Lean or Sigma Sigma philosophy. A company with no tolerance for errors at the operational level runs the risk of discovering that it has no capacity for adaptivity and evolution. If a system can be devised that tolerates variation from fixed policies in search of improvements, yet provides quick containment of variation that could cause harm, then we have the right mix for rapid evolution.

4.   Strive for dynamic equilibrium

The ability to maintain dynamic equilibrium is essential for an organisation that is thriving on change. This means that we must achieve balance through motion rather than using the status quo as the source of stability. In a business environment that demands constant change, organisations must learn to maintain their balance while moving forward at ever-increasing speeds.

5.   Nurture emergent properties

If a group of collaboration tools leads to a new level of problem solving that could not have been achieved through conventional meetings, that is an emergent property that should be recognised and harnessed for the good of the organisation [12]. Expecting, exploring and expanding on new and surprising behaviours within the organisation, is an important step toward adaptivity. It is also the step that is most likely to propel the organisation into the third level of adaptivity – namely creativity.

4   The Lea®n Supply Chain and how to sustain it

From the above it is clear that the classical Lean philosophy does not hold in any situation and especially for globally operating manufacturing companies Lean thinking should be redefined. Below there an attempt has been made to categorize manufacturing strategies according to the way of operations. The independent variable is here the way the company thinks, i.e. understands and position itself. The type of operations should be therefore aligned with the way of *thinking* and not vice versa.

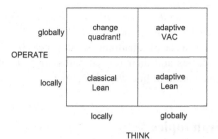

Fig. 2. Manufacturing operations strategies as a function of the thinking process

According to the above categorization there are 4 possible types of organisations:

i.   *Companies that think locally and operate locally.* This type of companies can implement the classical lean approach, because they can achieve impressive results. Most success stories have been reported from this type of organisations. Nevertheless these benefits reach fairly quickly their limits, so that it is only a matter of time, when these companies should be reconsidering moving into a different quadrant. The next logical and natural way is the way of beginning to think globally although still operating locally. It is exactly at this point where the organization should be transformed from a pure Lean to a Learning organization [8]. The adaptive lean approach is then the route to take as it has been described in the previous section for achieving sustainability of the benefits already reached. Typical representatives of this category are successful SME that wish to expand their market opportunities.

ii. *Companies that think globally and operate locally.* For companies that have already embarked on lean initiatives, by implementing classical methods of lean manufacturing, this journey is definitely a learning experience. Nevertheless, it is also an opportunity to move quickly towards an adaptive lean environment, without waiting the results of their initiatives. Learning to become more adaptive will shorten the ROI interval and accelerate the transformation of the company towards an environment that quickly adjusts to new business requirements. Typical representatives of this category are consumer goods manufacturers. Open Innovation and Mass customization is what drives these companies to sustain and expand themselves.

iii. *Companies that think globally and operate globally.* The classical Lean at that level loses its meaning. The supply chain at this level is materialized on ad-hoc basis in order to fulfill frequently individualized needs. Value Adding Communities (VAC) set up in a very flexible way is a possible solution to the problem as described by Tsigkas et. al. [9,10]. Adaptivity is seen as the way a number of companies can be fairy quickly set up a customized network to respond to specific requirements that can be one-of-a-kind. Information systems based on objects technology as agents plays a major role in this context. We see big opportunities for SME in Europe to operate in the world market by setting up specialized or even ad-hoc networks in the form of VAC for one-of a-kind activities.

iv. *Companies that think locally and operate globally*. This type of companies should redirect their strategies, since it is certainly not a wining strategy. From this perspective, the related quadrant should be abandoned as quickly as possible. New strategies and their related paths are to be defined and designed for planning and execution in line with the above.

4   Further research topics

The use of the SCOR model for the design of supply chains for the various types of organizations integrating the customer in the value creation loop is suggested. Moreover, the elaboration on the learning competences for the *autopoietic* type of production for self-sustainability of the new Lean Enterprise is a further topic.

References

1. T. Ohno, *Toyota Production System: Beyond Large Scale Production* (Productivity Press, 1981).

2. E. Von Hippel, *Democratising Innovation* (The MIT Press Cambridge, Massachusetts, London, England, 2005).

3. R. Reichwald R and F. Piller, *Interaktive Wertschöpfung* (Betriebswirtschaftlicher Verlag Dr. Th. Gabler GWV Fachverlage GmbH, Wiesbaden, 2006).

4. J. Womack and D. Jones, *Lean Thinking* (Simon & Schuster Inc, New York, 1996).

5. Aberdeen Group (April 2006), The Lean Benchmark Report: Closing the Reality Gap; http://www.aberdeen.com/summary/report/benchmark/RA_Lean_JB_2845.asp

6. ICD White paper (January 2006); http://www.easynet.nl/download/pagina/Whitepaper_enabling_lean_manufacturing.pdf

7. M. Zeleny, Autopoiesis and self-sustainability in economic Systems, *Human Systems Management*, 16, pp 256 – 262, IOS Press, (1997).

8. P. Senge, *The fifth discipline, the art and practice of the learning organisation* (Doubleday 1990, revised edition 2006).

9. A. Tsigkas, Mass Customisation through Value Adding Communities, 3rd Interdisciplinary World Congress on Mass Customisation and Personalisation, Hong Kong, September 2005.

10. A. Tsigkas, N. Karadimas and V. Loumos, Self Organising Structures of Ad-hoc Co-operations for customised products and services, 20th European Conference on Modelling and Simulation, Bonn, Germany, May 2006.

11. P. Kondylis, *Der Niedergang der bürgerlichen Denk- und Lebensform, die liberale Moderne und die massendemokratische Postmoderne* (Acta humaniora, Weinheim 1991 and for the Greek edition, Themelio, Athens, Greece, 2000).

12. D. Taylor, *Objects Technology, a Manager's Guide* (second edition, Addison-Wesley, 1998).

13. H. Bergson, *Creative Evolution* (Dover Publications, Inc. Mineola, New York, 1998).

Modelling Demand-driven Chain Networks using Multiple CODPs

C.N. Verdouw[1], A.J.M. Beulens[2], D. Bouwmeester[2], and J.H. Trienekens[3]

1 Agricultural Economics Research Institute (LEI), Wageningen UR
P.O. Box 29703, 2502 LS The Hague, The Netherlands
WWW home page: http://www.lei.wur.nl
2 Information Technology Group, Wageningen University
Hollandseweg 1, Wageningen, The Netherlands
3 Management Studies Group, Wageningen University
Hollandseweg 1, Wageningen, The Netherlands

Abstract.

Purpose – to model demand-driven chain networks on basis of multiple Customer Order Decoupling Points (CODPs). **Design/methodology/approach** – literature study and a case study in dairy industry, based on in-depth expert interviews. **Findings** – four main underlying factors of CODP diversity are addressed and modelled. **Research limitations/implications** – the proposed multiple CODP models provide the basic setup of a reference-process model for demand-driven chain networks, and should further be developed into a formalized model that incorporates detailed implementation knowledge of different industries. **Practical implications** – the research contributes to making the generic CODP concept suitable for process design of demand-driven chain networks. **Originality/value** – the paper adds to existing research on CODPs by addressing the main underlying factors of CODP diversity. Based on these dimensions, basic process models of demand-driven chain networks are proposed and applied in dairy industry. **Keywords** Customer Order Decoupling Point (CODP), Demand-driven chain networks, Dairy **Paper type** Research paper, Case study

1 Introduction

Demand-driven chain networks are often mentioned as a way to meet volatile customer demand and to involve customer impact in the execution of all chain processes. However, it is not easy to realize chain networks that are able to deliver customized products to specific customer needs and to fulfill new or adjusted customer requirements rapidly.

The main challenge of creating demand-driven chain networks is to realize rapid and customized response to customer demand. This requires a combination of efficiency to fulfil demand with minimal use of time and money, and flexibility to deal with the ever-changing amount and variety of the demand. In order to find a

Please use the following format when citing this chapter:

Verdouw, C.N., Beulens, A.J.M., Bouwmeester, D. and Trienekens, J.H., 2008, in IFIP International Federation for Information Processing, Volume 257, Lean Business Systems and Beyond, Tomasz Koch, ed.; (Boston: Springer), pp. 433–442.

balance between efficiency and flexibility, the positioning of customer order decoupling points (CODPs) plays a central role (Naylor et al. 1999). The CODP separates that part of the supply chain geared towards directly satisfying customers' orders from that part of the supply chain based on planning (Hoekstra and Romme 1992). It creates the opportunity for upstream activities to optimize independently from irregularities in market demand. Upstream the focus can be on efficient production of standardized products, while downstream the focus is on flexible strategies to deliver customized products. The strategic inventory at the decoupling point is the buffer that absorbs demand variability (Naylor et al. 1999).

The position of decoupling points is a balancing process between market, inherent product properties and process related factors (Olhager 2003). Major factors are demand volume and volatility, and the relationship between required delivery times and possible production lead times (the P/D ratio, Mather 1988).

On basis of different positions of the CODP, basic logistical configurations are proposed in literature. (Hoekstra and Romme 1992) distinguish five configurations: engineer-to-order (ETO), make-to-order (MTO), assemble-to-order (ATO), make-to-stock (MTS) and deliver from (local) stock (DFS). However, this typology is at an aggregate level. In reality companies have multiple CODPs. Main underlying factors of this diversity are the existence of different CODPs per individual product or product-market combination, per product component, per level of customer commitment (e.g. contracts versus specific call-offs), and per interface in the chain network (consumer-to-business orders and different business-to-business orders).

Taking these different dimensions of CODP diversity into account will result in many possible CODP positions and consequently in many possible chain network configurations. In responsive demand-driven chain networks, companies must be able to take part in different of these configurations concurrently in order to deliver customer or customer segment specific products. Further, they must be able to switch fast to new configurations in order to fulfill new or adjusted customer requirements rapidly. Process models are an important mean to keep this complexity manageable, whereas they enable clear and precise representation of the activities and interactions within and between all relevant configurations.

However, how to deal with the CODP diversity has received little attention in the literature so far. Several authors addressed complexity issues behind the generic CODP concept (e.g. Giesberts and Tang 1992; Trienekens 1999; Van der Vorst 2000; van Donk 2001; Wikner and Rudberg 2005), but is not yet developed it into concrete process designs.

The main objective of the paper is to model processes of demand-driven chain networks on basis of multiple CODPs. Therefore in section 2 the main dimensions of multiple CODP are modeled based on literature study. Next in section 3 these multiple CODPs are illustrated by a case study in the Dutch dairy industry based in-depth interviews with logistic and ICT experts in The Netherlands. The paper ends in section 4 with a discussion and conclusions.

2   Modeling multiple CODPs

As stated in the introduction, the widely accepted logistical typology based on different CODP positions of is on too aggregated level to be useful in process design. In this section four main underlying factors of CODP-diversity in practice (as addressed in literature, see mentioned references) are elaborated in order to make the CODP suitable for design of demand-driven chain networks. This is done by adding each dimension to a base-line model of the CODP-concept (see figure 1). At this, we define an order as an agreement between customer and supplier on the products to be delivered, the amount, price, time and place (all customer commitment information). This implies that contracts are viewed as orders. Demand forecast information is all information about future orders that is used for planning.

The distinguished dimensions are the existence of different CODPs per:

1   Product or product-market combination;
2   Product component;
3   Level of customer commitment;
4   Interface in the chain network.

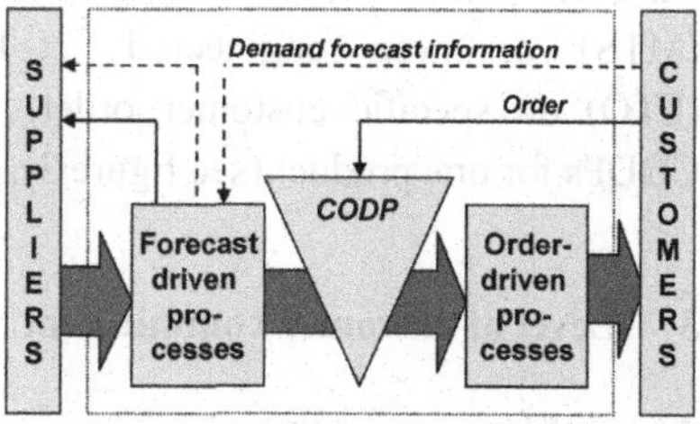

Fig. 1. Baseline CODP model

1   Product or product-market combination

Particularly in demand-driven chain networks, customers have their specific requirements to the products to be delivered. Within one company, this can result in different CODP positions for specific products or product-market combinations (figure 2). For example: companies can assemble products on customer order, while the remaining production capacity is used to make standard products on stock. Or the other way around: products with a stable baseline demand are produced on forecast, while products with a surge demand (e.g. in cases of sales promotions) are produced on customer

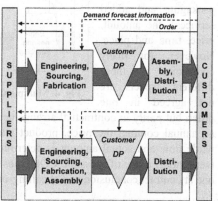

Fig. 2. Concurrent CODPs per product or product-market combination

order. In literature this is often addressed, among others by Giesberts and Van der Tang (1992), Van der Vorst (2000), Christopher and Towill (2001), Van Donk (2001), Aitken et al. (2005) and Holweg (2005).

2   Product component

The extent to what products are customized can vary much within the structure of a certain product per component (Giesberts and Tang 1992). For example: in assembly processes, often mostly standard components are used (ATO), while the components where customization adds most customer value are produced (MTS) or even engineered

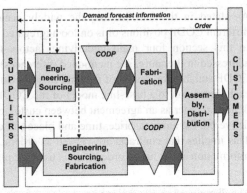

Fig. 3. Multiple CODPs per product component

(ETO) on specific customer order. This results in hybrid situations with more CODPs for one product (see figure 3).

3   Level of customer commitment

An order is an agreement between customer and supplier on the product to be delivered (including packaging and added services), the amount, price, time and place. However, for many companies these different aspects are not agreed in one

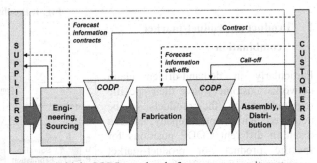

Fig. 4. Multiple CODPs per level of customer commitment

order, but partly in contractual arrangements for more transactions. For example: in an annual contract the price, product attributes and minimal amount is specified, while time and actual amount is determined by specific call-offs. This results in a (sequential) range of possible CODP positions (Wikner and Rudberg 2005), at least one at contract conclusion and at calling-off (see figure 4).

4   Interface in the chain network

In literature the CODP-concept is often applied on supply chain networks without making clear the difference between consumer orders and the varied orders in the network of collaborating chain partners. Due to this diffusion, it is suggested that there is only one CODP per chain network. However, in realty there exists a CODP for each collaboration interface (Trienekens 1999), starting with the consumer order and working backward to business -to-business orders (see figure 5).

For the design of demand-driven chain processes, these dimensions have to be modeled together in coherence. This results in many possible chain network configurations with many different positions of CODPs.

3   Dairy case

Above four basic CODP dimensions are modeled in general. In this section we illustrate these multiple CODPs by a case study in dairy. In the study, the dairy processing industry was the focal actor in the chain network, while The Netherlands was the focal country. The case study was based on structured interviews with 15 dairy logistic and ICT experts (13 managers of different dairy processing companies and retailers, 2 consultants) and additional desk research.

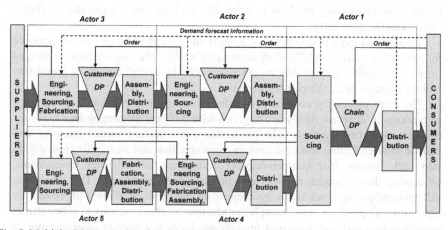

Fig. 5. Multiple CODPs per interface in the chain network

In the case study we investigated the current state in dairy industry according to market and performance requirements, network structure, processes, control systems and information technology (based on the chain framework of Van der Vorst et al. 2005, adapted from Lambert and Cooper 2000). Below we give a summarized overview of the results, focusing on the positions of multiple CODPs.

Market and performance requirements

The dairy industry is characterized by two main product categories: consumer and industrial products.

Main consumer products are fresh products (consumption milk, drinks, and desserts), cheese and butter. In the supermarkets these products belong to the basic assortment. Therefore, availability is very important. Further, shelf life is dominating the retail requirements of fresh products. In order to prevent stock outs and decay (resulting in obsolete inventory or forced markdowns), products are replenished frequently with short delivery times and high delivery reliability. Sometimes the supplier is responsible for replenishment of fresh dairy products (Vendor Managed Inventory).

Main industrial products are ingredients, mostly in the form of powders, for particularly the pharmaceutical, feed and food industry (including baby food, bakery ingredients, ice creams, cream liqueurs, food supplements and special diet food). There are two different markets of industrial ingredients: bulk delivery for the world market and specialties for specific customers, in close cooperation as per unique contracts. For bulk delivery the focus is on price and homogenous quality. For specialties the focus is on flexibility and specific quality features.

Network structure and processes

In 2005, in The Netherlands almost 11 million tons of milk were produced at about 25.000 farms (Silvis and De Bont 2006). Virtually all milk was delivered to one of the 13 dairy processing organizations, which processed the milk in a total of 55 factories. The processed milk is exported to a large extent. The Netherlands is a major exporter of dairy products to other EU member states, particular in cheese (Silvis and De Bont 2006).

Two international cooperatives –Campina and Friesland Foods– are responsible for processing more than 80% of all the country's milk. The cooperatives are obliged to take all supplied milk of their member farmers. The overall amount of production is fixed in quota by EU market regulations.

The dairy processing companies transform the supplied milk into a broad range of products in different shelf life categories with different production lead times for different customer segments. The production processes are capital intensive and include milk collection from the farmers, pasteurization and standardization, drying into milk powder (for non-perishables), refinement into different components, processing these components into end products, and packaging. The flows into different end-products are highly interdependent. By-products of one end product are input of other products. For example: production of cheese results in whey that is processed into different industrial ingredients. Further, a specific characteristic of cheese production is the ripening process, during which weight is being reduced, while value is being increased.

Multiple CODPs in dairy

Important factors impacting the CODPs positions in dairy are the broad range of end products for different markets and with different levels of decay, high interdependencies between product flows, high volume production, low volume flexibility (more or less fixed milk supply and capital intensive production). Due to these characteristics much diversity of CODP was found in the case study:

1. **CODPs per product or product-market combination**. Within the two main product categories, different CODP positions are found per specific customer segment. For fresh consumer products, including butter, Make to Stock (MTS) is most common, but also forms of Assemble to Order (ATO) exist. For example: specific health drinks that are produced on order from high concentrated liquids (thinning and adding specific ingredients). Most common in cheese is production of whole cheeses on forecast, whereas cutting and

packing is done on customer order. In the industrial ingredients segment, specialties are produced and sometimes even engineered on customer order. The remaining production capacity is used for bulk production.

2. **CODPs per product component.** A typical example of different CODPs per component is cheese production. Cheese is mostly cut and packaged on customer order, but on basis of standard package material. Another example is the production of specialty ingredients, whereas both standard and customer-specific powders are blended on customer-order.

3. **CODPs per level of customer commitment.** Contracts are widespread in dairy industry. Processing companies have long-term contracts with farmers (either as member of the cooperative or regular contracts), in which milk quality requirements and maximal quantities (including sanctions and bonuses) are specified (price is variable). Also transactions with suppliers of packaging and additional ingredients are based on contracts. Further, processing companies have several types of contracts with their customers, both of industrial ingredients and consumer products. In the consumer product segment, sometimes Vendor Managed Inventory contracts are found. At this, call-offs are not triggered by customers, but replenishment is the supplier responsibility.

4. **CODP per interface in the chain network.** Viewed from the processing industry as focal company, main actors of the dairy chain network are supermarkets, their purchasing companies or wholesalers (including DC's), second order industry, farmers and suppliers of additional ingredients and packaging. Each interface has its own CODPs.

Taking these dimensions into account shows that many chain network configurations exists in dairy. Figure 6 illustrates a dairy configuration that covers the different dimensions of CODP diversity.

The figure depicts basic processes of retailers, first order processing industry (focal actor) and farmers. It represents three different customer segments, with each multiple CODPs. In the middle of the diagram, production of fresh products is illustrated. Here, only distribution is on retail order. Up there, production and distribution of cheese are depicted. Here different CODPs exist for packaging and cheese cutting. Below the delivery of customer-specific industrial ingredients based on contracts is shown.

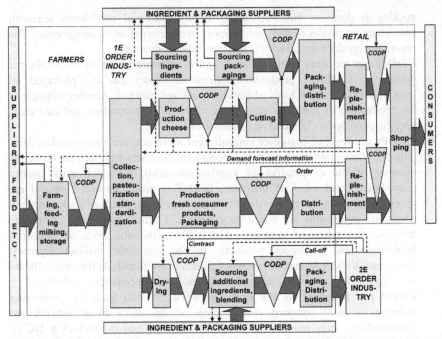

Fig. 6. Example of a chain network configuration with multiple CODPs in dairy

4   Discussion and conclusions

In this paper the generic CODP concept is expanded by modeling four main underlying factors of CODP diversity: the existence of different CODPs per product or product-market combination, per product component, per level of customer commitment (e.g. contracts versus specific call-offs), and per interface in the chain network (consumer-to-business orders and different business-to-business orders).

In the case study each dimension of CODP diversity was found in dairy. Many different CODP positions exist concurrently, even in this industry that is high volume, capital intensive, highly regulated and in which products decay.

This shows that taking the different dimensions of CODP diversity into account results in many concurrent chain network configurations. Detailed process models are an important mean to make this complexity manageable. Companies can develop their process models from scratch. However, disadvantages of this approach are high costs of the design process and long lead-times, which hinder rapid process (re)configuration and thus flexibility. An alternative approach is to start with predefined business process models that capture recommended practices and experiences of other companies. Such predefined models are called reference models.

The multiple CODP models as described in this paper provide the basic setup of a reference-process model for demand-driven chain networks. Further research is recommended to develop this into a formalized model that incorporates detailed implementation knowledge of different industries.

References

1. Aitken, J., P. Childerhouse, M. Christopher and D. Towill, 2005. Designing and Managing Multiple Pipelines. Journal of Business Logistics. 26, 2, 73-95.

2. Christopher, M. and D. Towill, 2001. An integrated model for the design of agile supply chains. International Journal of Physical Distribution & Logistics Management. 31, 4, 235-247.

3. Giesberts, P. M. J. and L. v. d. Tang, 1992. Dynamics of the customer order decoupling point: impact on information systems for production control. Production Planning & Control. 3, 3, 300-313.

4. Hoekstra, S. J. and J. M. Romme, 1992. Integral Logistic Structures: Developing Customer-oriented Goods Flow. McGraw Hill, London.

5. Holweg, M., 2005. The three dimensions of responsiveness. International Journal of Operations & Production Management. 25, 7, 603-622.

6. Lambert, D. M. and M. C. Cooper, 2000. Issues in supply chain management. Industrial Marketing Management. 29, 1, 65-83.

7. Mather, H., 1988. Competitive Manufacturing. Prentice-Hall, Englewood Cliffs, NJ.

8. Naylor, B., M. M. Naim and D. Berry, 1999. Leagility: interfacing the lean and agile manufacturing paradigm in the total supply chain. International Journal of Production Economics. 62, 107-118.

9. Olhager, J., 2003. Strategic positioning of the order penetration point. International Journal of Production Economics. 85, 3, 319.

10. Silvis, H. and K. de Bont, 2006. Prospects for the agricultural sector in The Netherlands. The Hague, Ministry of Agriculture, Nature and Food Quality.

11. Trienekens, J. H., 1999. Management of processes in chains: A research framework, PHD-thesis, Wageningen University.

12. Van der Vorst, J., A. Beulens and P. v. Beek, 2005. Innovations in Logistics and ICT in Food Supply Chain Networks. In: Innovations in agri-food systems: Product quality and consumer acceptance. W. M. F. Jongen and M. T. G. Meulenberg. Wageningen Academic Publishers.

13. Van der Vorst, J. G. A. J., 2000. Effective Food Supply Chains: Generating, modelling and evaluating supply chain scenarios. PHD-thesis, Wageningen University.

14. Van Donk, D. P., 2001. Make to stock or make to order: The decoupling point in the food processing industries. International Journal of Production Economics. 69, 3, 297-306.

15. Wikner, J. and M. Rudberg, 2005. Introducing a customer order decoupling zone in logistics decision-making. International Journal of Logistics. 8, 3, 211 - 224.

Critical Aspects of Information and Communication Technology in Vendor Managed Inventory

Astrid Vigtil, and Heidi C. Dreyer

NTNU, Norwegian University of Science and Technology,
Department of production and quality engineering,
NTNU Valgrinda,
N-7491 Trondheim, Norway

Abstract. The use of Information and communication technology (ICT) in supply chain collaboration has received substantial attention among researchers and practitioners. The multiple aspects of ICT offer a wide selection of research and application arenas. This paper discusses information sharing and takes a particular focus on the level of data integration when ICT is applied to support the replenishment process based on a Vendor Managed Inventory (VMI) principle, i.e. when the supplier is responsible for the replenishment process on the customer's behalf [1]. The findings conclude that it is not the capabilities of the computer technology and applications available that limit the level of data integration in the collaboration program. The most important limitation is the decision makers' competence and confidence in information sharing and computer systems, and the potential benefits these represent. The research methodology applied is a comparative case study where level of data integration and level of data utilization was studied in five cases of VMI collaboration.

1 Introduction

The aim of collaborative supply chains is to coordinate the supply, production and delivery processes, while balancing production and supply with customers' requirements and demand. Collaborative initiatives in the supply chain seek to gain real time information and to create a transparent, visible demand pattern that paces the entire supply chain [2]. Supply chain visibility offers higher predictability and insight into the demand situation which will dampen the "bullwhip" and artificial demand amplification [3, 4]. Information and communication technology (ICT) is considered an essential tool for obtaining demand visibility in the supply chain [5].

Please use the following format when citing this chapter:

Vigtil, A. and Dreyer, H.C., 2008, in IFIP International Federation for Information Processing, Volume 257, Lean Business Systems and Beyond, Tomasz Koch, ed.; (Boston: Springer), pp. 443–451.

Automated replenishment concepts such as vendor managed inventory (VMI) and collaborative planning, forecasting and replenishment (CPFR) are based on automation of administrative processes supporting the materials flows through transparent information flows in the supply chain [6, 7, 8]. By implementing such ICT supported concepts, companies can achieve benefits in terms of reduced inventory levels, increased flexibility and reduced lead-times.

VMI is a concept for supply chain collaboration where the supplier is responsible for the replenishment process [9, 10] and in order to undertake this responsibility the supplier will require some information about the customer's demand pattern. Different types of demand data are suggested, e.g. forecasts, inventory levels, production schedules, incoming orders, Point-of-sales data etc.

The purpose of this paper is to identify critical aspects regarding how this information is shared, integrated and utilized when information is used to create visibility and support the VMI replenishment process. The focus is on the automation of the information exchanging processes, and whether the choice of ICT system and level of data integration[3] is dependent on how much data should be transferred. More specifically is it important to reveal whether it is considered more important to increase level of data integration when the level of data interchange is high. Based on these objectives two research questions (RQ) is discussed.

RQ 1: *Is the selection of ICT solution dependent on how much data is exchanged?*

RQ 2: *Is it more important to increase level of data integration when level of data exchange is high?*

2   Research approach

A multiple case study strategy where chosen to support the presented research questions. The case study approach is preferred due to the need for a thorough and extensive study of how ICT is applied in a VMI relation [11, 12]. In this study the problem is related to critical aspects of ICT and information sharing. Gaining a rich picture has been essential in order to understand what variables could have affected the outcome, therefore a case study is found more valuable than a survey that would not embrace the context of the data. Furthermore, a survey would require far more respondents than a case study. Also this research strategy is valuable in our study due to both the lack of and unavailability of sufficient amounts of data and, thus a too comprehensive and expensive data collection process [13].

Five cases are studied in order to compare the gathered information. Comparison is a powerful mechanism, but when used in a case study strategy the comparison should be focused on a limited number of attributes. This is due to the information richness in case studies, where a single case study per se constitutes a sufficient information source [14]. Five cases of successful and unsuccessful VMI collaboration were studied; a manufacturer of damped boring bars and a distributor

---

[3] To what extent transferred data is automatically incorporated into the recipient's computer system. Low level of data integration implies high degree of manual data entry.

that assembles parts into a complete machining package for their customers; a manufacturer of cardboard packaging and a manufacturer that uses the cardboard boxes for packaging pipes and accessories for water, gas and electrical installations; a car manufacturer and its relations to a supplier of aluminum wheel extensions; the same car manufacturer and a supplier of aluminum bumpers; a supplier of fasteners and tools for general assembly and a manufacturer of agricultural and farming equipment.

The unit of analysis was the application of ICT systems for data exchange with focus on level of data integration, degree of data utilization[4] and frequency and volume of data exchange[5]. The data collection process was based on semi-structured interviews with representatives from the companies holding logistic manager positions or similar, and after every interview minutes were written by the researcher and signed by the interviewees. Only cases where the customer is a manufacturer were included in this study. For the analysis it is essential to be aware that case 3 and 5 are considered unsuccessful. Case 3 is terminated due to high costs at the VMI warehouse and in case 5 where the collaboration has been in place for four years the supplier has yet to benefit financially from the program.

3 Literature review

It is indicated that the most important benefits of VMI rest on transparency and demand visibility in the supply chain. Fundamental for obtaining transparency and demand visibility is the customer's willingness to supply demand data. Similarly the supplier must be able to apply this data for planning purpose, and these two elements are said to be essential for VMI success [10, 15, 16]. The following is a brief literature review on the three main elements encompassed by this study, level of data integration, level of data utilization and computer system properties and compatibility. It is observed that there are different opinions both on what solutions are required and what benefits will derive from adopting different levels of integration.

3.1 Data integration

The use of ICT for information sharing in VMI is discussed by several authors and perceptions of its vitality differ. Advanced information systems, electronic data transmission and collection, highly integrated with online inventory levels, production planning and control are claimed vital by [9, 17]. Others, e.g. [18, 19, 20, 21] recognize their opportunities but do not state their vitality. The use of advanced

---

[4] To what extent received data is utilized for planning purposes. In this study high level of data utilization implies that much of the data received is used to improve supplier's replenishment performance.

[5] To what extent data is a construct of many different types of information. High complexity implies there are multiple variables that must be interpreted separately.

information systems will increase level of data integration and as the perceptions on this subject differ this will be an essential element studied here.

3.2   Data utilization

In general, demand information sharing is considered a means to obtain transparency in the supply chain and thereby a means to dampen the bullwhip effect [22]. It has been claimed by some authors [22, 15, 16] that the success of VMI does not only rest on exchange technology but also to what extent the supplier is able to utilize the advance demand information received for planning purposes. Theoretically, the supplier could be able to utilize information about future demand both to smooth manufacturing capacity in his own production system, negotiate better purchasing agreements with his sub suppliers and plan for economic full truck load distribution [20]. Data must be reliable to benefit from data utilization [15]. If for instance forecasts are unreliable and inventory level status is old the supplier should not apply this data for planning purposes and [15] suggests that under these circumstances VMI would offer no more benefits than traditional replenishment.

3.3   Computer system properties

A computer system is a facilitator of data exchange as long as the sending and receiving systems are compatible and interpret the exchanged data similarly [23]. A survey performed by KPMG among Norwegian industry [24] revealed that many companies retained from sharing demand information to suppliers because the computer system applied did not facilitate such interaction. However, it has been argued that technological barriers are falling [25]. Basic technology for data scanning and exchange is readily available, technical aspects are routine and implementation costs are low. It has even been argued that we are closer to the end than the beginning of ICT buildout [23].

From this brief review it is observed a divergence between what practitioners believe restrict them from exploiting data exchange benefits and what ICT specialists find limiting. ICT properties are included in this work in order to study whether there are any technological aspects of ICT that are critical to information sharing in VMI.

4   Findings and discussion

In all the cases studied, the customers provide the information periodically to the suppliers who plan the replenishment in their internal computer systems. No online communication or direct planning in customers' computer systems is applied. **Table** shows frequency of data exchange from customer to supplier in every case and how large share of the supplier's total product range is affected by the particular VMI program. Share of total range is included to visualize how much of the total demand information is encompassed by the VMI program. This will indicate how important the information appears for the supplier.

Table 1. Case data on frequency of data update and share of supplier's total product range

Element	Case 1	Case 2	Case 3	Case 4	Case 5
Frequency	24 h	24 h	weekly	weekly	weekly
Share of total range	80 %	0,4 %	33 %	1 %	5 %

4.1   RQ 1: Selection of ICT solution and the volume of data exchange

From the cases studies it is found that it is rarely the capabilities of the ICT systems applied that limit the utilization of such systems in VMI relationships. The level of utilization rests on the extent to which the actors think they can benefit from applying ICT. This perception is based on two elements, namely the confidence in the transferred data, and the ability to understand the opportunities. Firstly it is based on the actors' experience in application of ICT for information sharing and to what extent they have previously been able to trust the data transferred. Secondly it is based on the actors' comprehension of opportunities inherent in information sharing. The consequence of this perception is that only when the actors truly understand the concepts and the opportunities they will know what data should be transferred, and only when the right type of data is transferred the recipient can apply it for further planning feeling confident that he is making good decisions. Additionally, when the sender is aware how important the input is for the recipient he will focus on maintaining high quality information.

The level of data utilization and level of data integration is considered interdependent. When the desire for data exploitation is pronounced, the need for data transfer is realized, and the more integrated means are applied the better they facilitate utilization and achieve experience and competence. In the cases studied an iterative evolving process was observed, where the initial need for data exchange initiated investments in ICT. The better the chosen technology facilitated integration the higher the level of data utilization. This process was however highly dependent on the actors' comprehension of the concept and the opportunities. This finding is in line with [2] who indicate that the slow progress of implementation of automated replenishment programs may be due to lack of common understanding of the concepts. **Fig. 1** illustrates how level of integration and utilization interacts while resting on a fundamental level of comprehension.

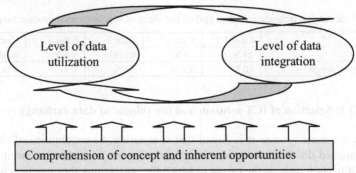

Fig. 1. Interdependency of level of integration and utilization, founded on comprehension

The conclusion of RQ 1 is that the selection and application of ICT solution does initially rest on how much data is expected to be transferred. However, as the relationship evolves and comprehension increases new opportunities are disclosed and there will be an interdependent increase in level of data integration and level of data utilization.

4.2   RQ 2: Data integration and data exchange

In all cases EDI or internet is used for information transfer but level of integration differs. Statements from all five cases indicate that the use of integrated communication systems have played a major part in the successfulness of their VMI programs. Even in the programs turning out not so favorable, the effect of the integrated automatic data transmission solutions are said to offer positive contributions. This supports [9] who state the vitality of advanced information systems but the evidence are not strong enough to contradict those who indicate that VMI can work with less integrated means [18, 20, 21].

For answering RQ 2 four specific variables were studied. Frequency of data transfer would indicate how often data is updated, level of product variants and level of shipped volumes would indicate the complexity of the data transferred and importance of ICT integration is a reflection on the interviewees perception of how beneficial integration has been to the supplier.

Table 2. Case data on variables for importance of data integration on a high-medium-low scale

Variables	Case 1	Case 2	Case 3	Case 4	Case 5
Information transfer Frequency	High	High	Low	Low	Low
Level of product variants	High	Low	Low	High	Low
Level of shipped volumes	Medium	Low	Medium	High	Medium
Importance of data integration	High	Low	Medium	High	Medium

From the empirical findings it can be concluded that it is the complexity of data that is the most important element. This is indicated by the fact that those cases where there were lots of product variants and lots of product specific data to handle the supplier benefited most from data integration. The fact that frequency and shipped volumes were high did not necessarily imply that the data was complex and difficult to handle.

Answering RQ 2 it could be argued that it is not the level of data exchange per se that is the critical aspect but the level of complexity in the set of data exchanged.

The findings of this study indicate that selection of ICT solution is a multifaceted decision. It is difficult to identify one specific critical variable because there are multiple elements influencing the selection process, both with respect to whether to apply ICT or not and the properties of the selected system.

5 Concluding remarks

The research reported in this paper has shown that the use of ICT for information sharing in VMI collaboration is not restricted by capabilities of the existing technology but by the level of competence among the applicants. It has also been shown that once a certain level of comprehension is obtained one will enter a loop of continuous enhancements to exploit the benefits inherent in the collaboration program. This loop will include a further utilization of ICT resources. From these findings one can argue that quality of exchanged data is critical because it builds confidence. Furthermore, understanding information needs of the partner and how exchanged data will be further utilised ensures emphasis on data quality. Even though the use of ICT for data exchange could be considered limited in the studied cases, positive effects were identified in terms of increased information quality, correct information and cost reductions from elimination of manual data entry.

These findings cannot be considered breaking news but they illustrate a gap between available and applied capabilities of existing ICT. It is necessary to educate practitioners to push them into the loop of continuous enhancements, simultaneously; further research on cutting edge capabilities to identify new technological potentials is required in order to stay ahead of application.

References

1. A. Harrison, and R. van Hoek, *Logistics management and strategy*, (Prentice Hall, Pearson Education, 2002).

2. M. Holweg, S. Disney, J. Holmström, and J. Småros, Supply chain collaboration: Making sense of the strategy continuum, *European management journal*, Vo. 23, No. 2, 170-181 (2005).

3. J.W. Forrester, *Industrial Dynamics* (MIT Press, Cambridge, MA, 1961).

4. H.L. Lee, V. Padmanabhan, and S. Whang, Information distortion in a supply chain: The Bullwhip effect, *Management Science,* Vol. 43, No. 4, April (1997).

5. Z. Yu, H. Yan, and T.C.E. Cheng, Benefits of information sharing with supply chain partnerships, *Industrial management & Data systems,* 101/3, 114-119 (2001).

6. P.J. Daugherty, M.B. Myers, and C.W. Autry, Automatic replenishment programs: An empirical examination, *Journal of Business Logistics,* Vol.20, No.2, 63-82 (1999).

7. E.A. Ellinger, C.J. Taylor, and J.P. Daugherty, Automatic replenishment programs and level of involvement: Performance implications, *The International Journal of Logistics Management,* Vol.10, No.1, 25 (1999).

8. R. Lohtia, T. Xie, and R. Subramaniam, Efficient consumer response in Japan Industry concerns, current status, benefits, and barriers to implementation, *Journal of Business Research*, Vol.57, 306-311 (2004).

9. D. Simchi-Levi, P. Kaminsky, and E. Simchi-Levi, *Designing and managing the supply chain, concepts, strategies and case studies* (McGraw Hill, 1st ed., 2000).

10. S.M. Disney and D.R. Towill, Vendor-managed inventory and bullwhip reduction in a two-level supply chain, *International journal of operation and production management,* Vol. 23, No. 6 (2003).

11. R.K. Yin, *Case study research, design and methods* (3rd ed., Sage publications, 2003).

12. K.M. Eisenhardt, Building Theories from Case Study Research, *Academy of Management Review,* Vol.14, No.4, 532-550 (1989).

13. S.S. Andersen, *Case-studier og generalisering, forskningsstrategi og design* (Fagbokforlaget, Bergen, 1997).

14. R.E. Stake, in: Handbook of Qualitative Research/ Case Studies, edited by N.K. Denzin, and Y.S. Lincoln (Thousand Oaks, CA, Sage Publications, Inc, 1994), pp. 236-247.

15. S.C. Kulp, The effect of information precision and information reliability on Manufacturer-Retailer Relationships, *The Accounting Review*, Vol. 77, No. 3, 653-677 (2002).

16. L. Lapide, New developments in business forecasting, *The Journal of Business Forecasting Methods & Systems,* Vol. 20, Iss. 4, 11-12 and 36. (2001).

17. T.L. Pohlen, and T.J. Goldsby, VMI and SMI programs, how economic value added can help sell the change, *International Journal of physical distribution and logistics management*, Vol. 33, no. 7, 565–581 (2003).

18. S-A. Mattson, *Logistik i försörjningskedjor* (Studentlitteratur, Lund, 2002).

19. R. Kaipia, J. Holmstöm, and K. Tanskanen, VMI: What are you loosing if you let your customer place orders, *Production planning and control*, Vol. 13, No. 1, (2002).

20. M. Waller, M.E. Johnson, and T. Davis, Vendor-managed inventory in the retail supply chain, *Journal of business logistics*, Vol. 20, No. 1 (1999).

21. J. Holmström, Business process innovation in the supply chain – a case study of implementing vendor managed inventory, *European journal of purchasing and supply management*, Vol. 4, 127-131 (1998).

22. J. Småros, J-M. Lehtonen, P. Appelqvist, and J. Holmström, The impact of increasing demand visibility on production and inventory control efficiency, *International Journal of Physical Distribution and Logistics Management*, Vol. 33, No. 4 (2003).

23. N.G. Carr, IT doesn't matter, *Harvard Business Review*, May (2003).

24.   KPMG,   Norsk   Logistikkbarometer   2003   (2003); http://www.logistikkbarometeret.no.

25. G. Kuk, Effectiveness of vendor-managed inventory in the electronics industry: determinant and outcomes, *Information & Management*, Vol. 41 (2004).

Hybrid Modeling Approach for Supply-Chain Simulation

Shigeki Umeda and Fang Zhang
Musashi University
1-26 Toyotama-kami Nerima Tokyo 176-8534 JAPAN

Abstract. This paper proposes a novel simulation-modeling framework that combines discrete-event simulations with system-dynamics simulations. The former represents both operational processes inside of a supply-chain, and the later represents management environment outside of a supply-chain. Further, the paper also discusses modeling capabilities of the proposed framework for supply-chain systems in real world by using several example simulation models.

1 Introduction

Supply chain management is one of the hottest topics in production planning and control areas. The primary goal of supply chains is to provide manufactured products to end-customers. Supply chain planning is, in a sense, restructuring a business system for supply chain members to collaborate with each other by exchanging information.

A supply-chain is a network of autonomous and semiautonomous business units collectively responsible for procurement, manufacturing, distribution activities associated with one or more families of products. Individual process in the chain can be affected by technology, marketing, and transportation. Such enterprise environment can also influence system performance of supply-chain. Supply chain managers, in both planning phases and operational phases, face various kinds of problems, such as capacity planning, production planning, inventory planning and others. Systematic approaches are needed to support planning and control of such supply chain systems.

Simulation is an effective tool to optimize designs and operations of manufacturing and logistics systems. Steady-state simulation can provide major system performance evaluation indexes, such as resource utilization, queuing length, and throughput. Terminated simulation also provides predictions of potential status

---

Please use the following format when citing this chapter:

Umeda, S. and Zhang, F., 2008, in IFIP International Federation for Information Processing, Volume 257, Lean Business Systems and Beyond, Tomasz Koch, ed.; (Boston: Springer), pp. 453–460.

by "what-if scenario", for examples, "What is the system throughput, if another machinery resources are added?", "What happens in picking server, if its queuing constraints are added?", and etc. [1].

Performances of supply-chain systems often depend on external factors such as marketability, traffic congestions, and other management environments. When simulation practitioners analyze supply-chain performance, these external factors are usually condensed into several parameters, which are independent on individual supply-chain components. For an example, an average demand volume is a very important simulation parameter. In this case, simulation practitioner condenses every marketing phenomenon into several numeric variables, probability distribution functions, and its statistical parameters such as means and variances. Once these variables are defined at simulation start time, they are kept as the constant values during simulation execution.

Consideration of external environment enables more realistic and detail simulations to system planner. Integration of discrete-based process simulation into external management environment will provide more realistic and detail simulation outputs. System dynamics model is applicable to represent such management environment, and it enables practitioners to analyze strategic scenarios as well as simulation of policies and operations.

This paper proposes a novel simulation-modeling framework that combines discrete-event simulations with system-dynamics simulations. The former represents both operational processes inside of a supply-chain, and the later represents management environment outside of a supply-chain. Further, the paper also discusses modeling capabilities of the proposed framework for supply-chain systems in real world by using several example simulation models.

2   Hybrid modeling for supply-chain simulation

2.1   Discrete-based simulation of supply-chain operations

(1)   Feature-elements models and modeling hierarchy
"Feature-elements model" defines the following members as elements of the top layer of the models. These models represent business processes of each member.

- Supplier: It provides materials, parts, or products in the chain.
- Source: It starts the material-flows in the chain. Parts and material suppliers, which material-flows start in the chain.
- Storage: It stores materials, parts, or products.
- Consumer: It sends purchase orders to the chain, and it acquires products.
- Deliverer: It transports products, parts, and/or materials between chain members.
- Planner: An organization that controls material-flows and information-flows in the chain.

The discrete-event simulator is composed of four-layered simulation models: "Feature Element Model", "Function Element Model", "Implementation Model", and "Execution modules". These represent supply chain members, major activities of business process activities in supply-chain systems, fundamental elements of discrete event simulation, and simulation programming codes using commercial simulation software, respectively.

(2) Control models

The major characteristic of this approach is an introduction of two types of common control method in supply chain systems: These are "stock-driven" control and "schedule-driven" control [2][3]. These are based on material management policies in discrete manufacturing systems [4].

- Schedule-driven control: It uses a production schedule, the so-called "Master Production Schedule" (MPS), which the supply chain planner generates.
- Stock-driven control: A stock-driven supplier autonomously replenishes material inventories based on parameters of input material stock volume.

Control models mainly represents business activities in a headquarters of the prime contractor controlling other supply-chain members. This model is an expansion of our previous research, supply-chain business activity model by using IDEF0 modeling method [5]. Figure.1 represents an example of hybrid schedule- and stock-driven supply chain.

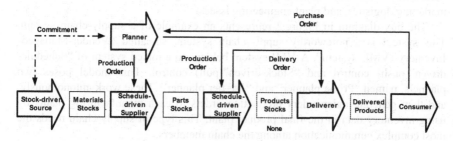

Fig. 1. A configuration example of hybrid schedule- and stock-driven supply chain

2.2　Dynamics of supply-chain enterprise environment

Supply-chain activities have relevance to its business environment. Suppose that a supply-chain system realizes a high performance and it shorten the consumers' purchase lead-time. In this case, the demand volume in market would increase because of the shortened purchase lead-time; the system would be busier by the increased demands. These activities give favorable or harmful influences to its external world, and their feedbacks can also give similar influences to the supply-chain. Similar scenarios would be applicable to relations between other supply-chain systems' activities and their feedbacks. They are, for examples, quality improvement programs in factories, manufacturing process automation programs, and operational improvement in parts/products transportation between suppliers.

System dynamics has been defined as 'a method of analyzing problems in which time is an important factor, and which involve the study of how the system can be defended against, or made benefit from, the shocks which fall upon it from outside world' [7]. This approach is useful to capture complex real-world situations, which include delays and feedback mechanisms. Practical applications include understanding market environments and assessing possible future scenarios. Dynamics complexity is not related to number of nodes or actors concerned, but the behavior they create when acting together [6].

Based on the above considerations, we defined the following dynamics models that represent supply-chain enterprise environment.

- Market dynamics represents market mechanisms, which produces, raises, and reduces the demand of the product provided by the supply-chain.
- Plant dynamics represents quality mechanisms, which represents a relationship between quality management and machining/assembling process control.
- Traffic dynamics represents traffic mechanisms, which provide supply-chain logistics.

2.3   Hybrid simulation-modeling framework for supply-chain

The proposed hybrid modeling method combines discrete-event models with system dynamics models. The formers represent business and operational processes such as manufacturing, inspections, shipping, transportation, and their planning. Meanwhile, the later represents external management environment such as marketing, logistics, and plant engineering issues.

The box diagram in Figure.2 represents an example of a supply-chain system. This system is a noteworthy supply-chain system, so-called "Vender-Managed-Inventory (VMI) system". A VMI system belongs to a mixed system of "Schedule-driven"(push) control and "Stock-driven"(pull) control. This model poses two planners, named "Prime planner" and "1st–tier planner". These work autonomously, and they generate independent production orders to each manufacturing plants by using inventory data in the final product plant. This type of supply-chain needs the most complex communication among the chain members.

The behaviors of market place are represented in "Market dynamics" model. The data, generated here, are for examples, selling status, customers' preference, competitive products trends, end etc. Both "Prime Planner" and "1st Tier Planner" receives marketing data in the market places, and use them to predict future demands and orders for production and shipment. Customers also receive these data and generate purchase orders. Dynamics model, simultaneously receives feedback data from these actors.

Other two dynamics models generate the similar data, and send/receive between supply-chain members. They also exchange feedback data, when it is required. The connections of chain members to dynamics models are generated dynamically according as simulation run.

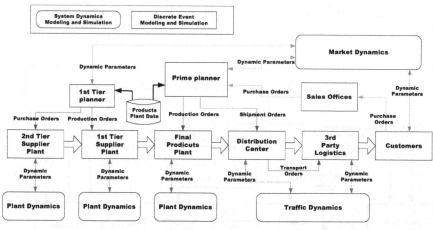

Fig. 2. Hybrid modeling framework for supply-chain simulation

3 An application example

3.1 A scenario of a simplified VMI model

Simulation scenario has been designed to verify the proposed hybrid simulation-modeling framework. As the first stage, we defined a simplified simulation model to clarify the relation between discrete-event business process models and a system dynamics business environment model.

Figure.3 represents the chain configuration and the data-flow among these chain members. The system is composed of five chain member models ("Planner", "Stock-driven Source", "Schedule-driven Supplier", "Schedule-driven Storage", "Consumer",). "Source", "Supplier", "Storage", and "Consumer" are connected with "Deliverer". The "Market dynamic" is an independent model of chain configuration.

Planner gives orders to a product factory ("Schedule-driven Supplier") and a distributor ("Schedule-driven Storage") according as the predicted demand by using past demands data. And, it also decides the stock-replenishment level and the stock-volume level for the "Stock-driven" members.

Stock-driven source continuously observes the stock volume of a particular chain member. Both stock-volume level and stock-replenishment level are critical variables to keep inventories to proper quantity. Assigning proper values to these variables enables to avoid both excessive and shortage of parts inventories. When the materials volume of the target supplier becomes lower than the stock-replenishment level, this source generates materials in its own buffer. Work continues until the stock volume reaches the stock-volume level. When it finishes a sourcing operation for a predefined lot-size, it sends a delivery order to the attached deliverer. This shipment will stop once the volume of materials at the specified supplier reaches or exceeds the stock volume level.

Outline of a dynamics model is shown in Figure.4. The role of Market dynamics model is to generate the average demand data, periodically. At that time, it uses feedback data from consumers ("Satisfaction" in Figure.4) to generate the demand data.

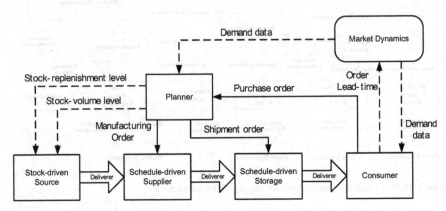

Fig. 3. Simplified VMI-based supply-chain simulation model

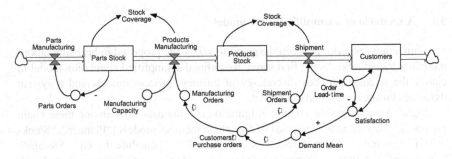

Fig. 4. Supply-chain business dynamics model

3.2 Simulation experiments

The objective of this experiment is to demonstrate that the proposed "Hybrid-modeling framework" is successful in representing characteristics of supply-chain system. We assigned a simplified form to "Satisfaction" function by the following formula, because the simulation shows an easy-to-understand result. When the satisfaction is greater than 0.5, the next-term "Demand-mean" increases. On the contrary, it decreases, when this is smaller than 0.5.

Satisfaction = c-a*Lead-time (a,c > 0)

(a: Decreasing index c: Constant) (0 ≤ Satisfaction ≤ 1)

Demand-mean(i) = Demand-mean(i-1)*(Satisfaction+0.5)

(Demand-mean ≤ Max(Demand-mean))

The transitions between discrete-event simulation and system-dynamics simulation are as follows.

(1) Discrete-event models generate consumers' order by using demand-mean as a random number parameter.
(2) Discrete-event models simulate production activities of ordering, manufacturing, shipping, and receiving, and etc.
(3) This simulation (2) calculates order lead-time to every ordering activity.
(4) The lead-time in (3) is input data to system dynamics model.
(5) Dynamics model estimates this lead-time.
(6) Dynamics model calculates demand-mean.
(7) This demand-mead (6) is used to the next random number generation.

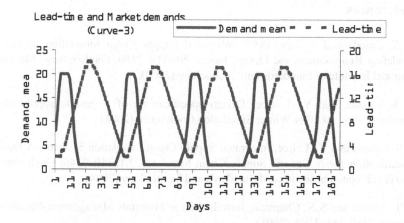

Fig. 5. Simulation output data transition (Lead-time and Market demand mean)

Figure.5 represents transitions of "Demand mean" that consumer generates and "Delivery lead-time" that consumer receives. At the initial stage, supply-chain system can provide products to consumer in very short lead-time, because the system is not so busy. Accordingly, the "Satisfaction" index and the demands (orders) increase. The system can affords to accept more orders at that time, and the system becomes gradually busy. The demand finally reaches full production status (the upper limit of the market). As the system becomes busy, the order lead-time becomes longer, and the "Satisfaction" decreases. This consequently makes down demand magnitude. The system becomes not so busy again.

4   Conclusion

This paper proposed a novel hybrid simulation-modeling framework combining supply-chain business process models and dynamics models representing enterprise management environment. This framework helps system analysts to evaluate system performance in a long-term period.

Supply-chain systems' activities and external phenomena give favorable or harmful influences each other. And, transition of supply-chain system performance has been performed. The effectiveness of the proposed framework has been confirmed.

A future direction of this research is development of a gaming methodology applied to supply-chain decision-making. Gaming is one of general-purpose methodologies to support management decision-making. Decision makers would play games by using the proposed hybrid- modeling simulator to make management decisions in supply-chain operations under various management hypotheses.

References

1. S. Umeda and S. Jain, ISSS: Integrated Supply Chain Simulation System -- Modeling Requirement and Design Issues, NISTIR 7180. Gaithersburg, Maryland National Institute of Standards and Technology (2004).

2. S. Umeda, and Y. T. Lee, Design specifications of a generic supply chain simulator, Proc. of 2004 Winter Simulation Conference (2004).

3. S. Umeda and Y. T. Lee, Integrated Supply Chain Simulation System --A Design Specification for A Generic Supply Chain Simulator, NISTIR 7146. Gaithersburg, Maryland: National Institute of Standards and Technology (2004).

4. T. Arnold and S.N. Chapman, Introduction to Materials Management 4th edition. Prentice Hall, Inc., USA (2001).

5. S. Umeda and B. Hu, Supply chain business reference model: a business process description using IDEF0, Proc. of the design of information infrastructure systems for manufacturing (DIISM) IFIP WG5.3 (2000).

6. A. Davis and J. O'donnell, Modeling complex problems: system dynamics and performance measurement, Management Accounting Today, May,18-20 (1977).

7. R.G. Coyle, System Dynamics Modeling – a Practical Approach (Chapman & Hall, London) (1996).

8. S. Umeda and F. Zhang, Supply chain simulation: generic models and application examples, Production Planning & Control, 17, 2, 155–166 (2006).

9. R. Broeckelmann: Inventory Classification Innovation: Paving the Way for Electronic Commerce and Vendor Managed Inventory, (The St. Lucie Press, APICS Series on Resource Management) (1998).

Concept for Quality Control Management Services in Distributed Design Networks – Conceptual Paper

Klaus-Dieter Thoben[1], Marcus Seifert[1], Patrick Sitek[1], Markus Emde[1],
Roberto Tarditi[2]

1 BIBA – Bremen Institute of Industrial Technology and Applied Work
Science at the University of Bremen
Hochschulring 20, 28359 Bremen, Germany
http://www.biba.uni-bremen.de

2 CRF – Centro Ricerche Fiat – Business Information Technologies Strada
Torino 50, 10043 Orbassano (TO), Italia
http://www.crf.it

Abstract. The actual situation is that partners in virtual organisations rely upon a great variety of tools, which are not integrated, difficult to use and often ineffective. High costs are sustained to train the people and acquire tools of different make as required by the OEMs. The objective of the proposed paper is to present a conceptual model of an integrated engineering environment specifically tailored to the needs of the suppliers operating in a design network. The focal point is to show how monitoring and control of projects in virtual organisations can be supported. Therefore a Quality Control Management (QCM) concept will be presented that is able to provide several services in order to trace and control project processes and performance in an effective, integrated, easy to understand and user-friendly way. The approach presented in the proposed paper is basing on the work carried out by the European funded research project E4 (Extended Enterprise management in enlarged Europe - EC Contract No. IST-FP6-027282).

1 Introduction

The continuous global and local economic fluctuations have increased the stress on manufacturing businesses. Companies' processes are challenged to provide operationally excellent, lean, cost-effective and rapid delivery of products and services globally. As a result of changed manufacturing businesses, companies must take business co-operation (Camarinha-Matos et. al., 2005). Facing a competitive global market, industrial manufacturers are hard pressed to adopt some strategies and technologies to enhance product quality, to cut manufacturing cost, and to reduce

Please use the following format when citing this chapter:

Thoben, K.-D., Seifert, M., Sitek, P., Emde, M. and Tarditi, R., 2008, in IFIP International Federation for Information Processing, Volume 257, Lean Business Systems and Beyond, Tomasz Koch, ed.; (Boston: Springer), pp. 461–471.

product lead-time. Of these strategies, agile manufacturing is being paid an increasingly important attention (Sheridan, 1993). In an agile manufacturing system, virtual organisations (VO) are one of the most important organisation manners (Reid et. al., 1996). In the context of emerging technologies and related knowledge-economy business models, linking stakeholders in dynamic clusters is believed to enhance competition and regional innovation (OECD, 1999).

International co-operation is also a vital strategy for the European companies in order to boost their competitiveness in the enlarged Internal Market and beyond. In all domains concerned with assembled products, the design is by now carried out by a network of enterprises (virtual organisations) (Müller et. al., 2006) which take responsibility of subsystems at the higher tier, and of simpler components at the lower tier. In such a context virtual organisations compete, as usual, on cost, quality and response time, whereby transparency and reliability are key components of process quality. The method presented in this paper is specifically addressing these needs targeting virtual organisations which operate in the product development/engineering area. From this point of view Quality Control Management (QCM) method provides several services in order to support project and network managers in virtual organisations tracing and monitoring engineering processes during manufacturing projects. The idea behind this method is to trace progress of work and to monitor also performance of project processes concerning several indicators like for example cost, time, resources, risks and other engineering critical issues (Aichele, 1997). Further on QCM supports the re-use of knowledge, experience and solutions gained as a result of tracing and monitoring and it provides this information for future projects. The method followed, QCM is an approach which is able to encompass stages of collaboration (initiation, management, operational life and dissolution) and also phases of extended products' development (conception, design, prototyping). The objective is to provide standardised, effective, easy to understand and low cost services to support project quality management for small partners in collaborations as they rely upon a great variety of tools, which are not integrated, difficult to use and perhaps even ineffective.

2   Quality Control Management Services

ISO9001 standard and Vision 2000 promote the adoption of a process-oriented approach in the development, use and improvement of the effectiveness of the quality management system, to increase the customer satisfaction by fully satisfying the customer requirements (ISO 9001:2000). As the approach of this paper traces the planning and execution of micro-processes the Quality Control Management builds on:

1. the list of project deliverables, linked to the person in charge and due date
2. user requirement on product performances, process quality and production costs

3. Traceability of the development process as the project plan is split up in micro-processes. Each micro-process will contain, moreover, all provided inputs and required outputs
4. KPIs on project costs and risks
5. data access history

Although current project management products prove very useful during project set up, they might prove not so useful when dealing with monitoring the progress of work. Data to calculate key performance indicators, which highlight the real progress of work, is rarely provided as well as the management of input/output deliverables of each phase (Böhnert, 1999). The Quality Control Management method tries to pursue a more comprehensive and integrated approach, where the user – either the customer, the project manager or specific development activity owner – gets all information to plan development activities and monitor the progress of work, keeping under control cost, time, quality and engineering critical issues, to deploy the activities internally and to view all relevant data at different levels of details.
The module provides three major functions:

o Deployment of planned activities with pre-defined micro-processes
o Monitoring capabilities over process and engineering performances indicators
o Levels of detail to represent information

Three levels of representation are envisioned to provide the different users with the proper level of detail, according to his/her role. Each level depicts a view of the project under development for different chores and with a varying degree of detail, from the "Negotiation level" where the customer and project manager agree on results, their deadlines and the path from one result to the next; to the "Deployment level" where each "tract" (part of the path) that will be travelled to get a certain result is split up in the micro-processes necessary to produce the result; to the "Execution level" where attributes of the micro-process must be computed and filled in. In this scenario several user profiles are working together on the same project, all are working to build the product. More project "dimension" are present a time: development, testing, prototypes building (virtual and physical), production scheduling, production tools and plants allocation, delivery, … and also time and costs. Quality target will be deployed in each of these dimensions. Only a taxonomical approach is able to manage a complex product project. Quality means that user target value (= vital parameters on the product) will be reached. Constant control of actual parameters respect the target value is necessary. The challenge is to obtain a dashboard with some KPI that permit to the project manager be able to respond a question like "is the project on time? Is it on cost?"

Approach
In QCM process control and monitoring is achieved thanks to an approach based upon a library of micro-processes, VCOR as process reference model and key performance indicators (KPI) which drive the steps and specify the required resources. The foundation provided by the process reference model and the KPI library allows the monitoring and quality evaluation of all parts of the project.

However it does not provide a complete way to monitor and evaluate the whole project. The missing linkage between single parts is the flow of goods/ information. Thus, focusing on such an approach it is important to realise a linkage between a product and the relevant engineering processes which are related to it in order to produce the required product. To fill those gaps, QCM uses the underlying bill of material (BOM) of the product to be produced in order to determine the links between the project partners and to create a project specific process chain as well as to derive a project plan (see figure 1).

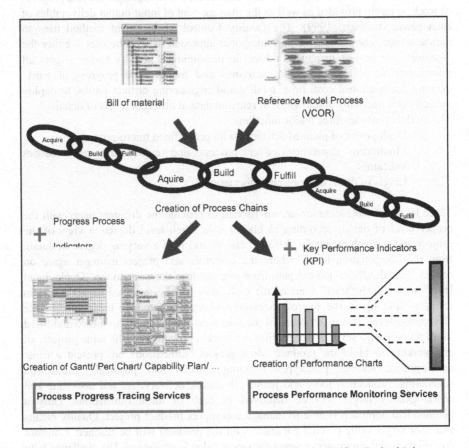

Fig. 1. Quality Control Management Services Approach (following Seifert, Eschenbächer, Thoben, 2004)

The idea to this approach is traced back to the fact that a BOM often turn out to be an initial point of a manufacturing project. It is a formally structured list for an object which lists all the component parts of the object with the name, reference number, quantity, and unit of measure of each component. A bill of material can only refer to a quantity greater than or equal to one of an object. It is a product data structure, which captures the end products, its assemblies, their quantities and relationships. QCM uses this product structure and relationships in order to generate engineering processes on which tracing and quality monitoring services are provided. The product structure shows the material, component parts subassemblies and other items in a hierarchical structure that represents the grouping of items on an assembly drawing or the grouping of items that come together at a stage in the manufacturing process. Further on it provides the understanding of the components which compose a product as well as their attributes.

This method is supported by the participating companies in a virtual organisation, who provide the required information by linking their products to the involved processes. The resulting ability, to identify all processes that are of relevance for the project in combination with having a database that provides information about who can provide the required process, allows QCM to generate highly customizable project partner configurations and at the end customer related services.

Global Process Reference Model (VCOR)

As already mentioned the process reference model is one part of the method. QCM uses VCOR due to a hierarchical description of processes as standards often simplify holistic approaches. To generally enable the monitoring of a project's quality, a method is needed to generalise a project and to transform it into a process based model. To support this modelling for each participating partner of any kind of projects, a generic process reference model should be integrated in the tool, which allows the description of any contribution to a project on a process basis. It is crucial to consider also service and design processes in the reference model.

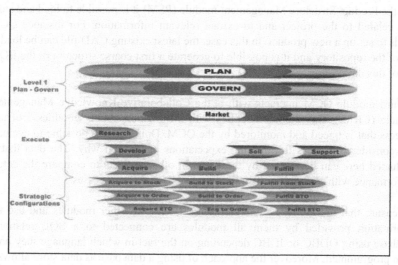

Fig. 2. VCOR model (www.value-chain.org)

Therefore it is foreseen to base the model on an existing standard as the VCOR (value chain operations reference model) which is more service oriented than manufacturing driven. The VCOR model supports the key issues and the gearing together of processes within and between the individual units of chains (networks, virtual organisations) for the benefit of the following

- Planning
- Governing
- Execution (information – financial – physical flows)

with the objective to increase the performance of the total chain (network, virtual organisation) and support the ongoing evolution. Figure 2 presents how VCOR, on executive level, is covering the whole value chain (Research→Develop→Acquire→Build→Sell→Fulfill→Support). The user will be able to input all his information regarding his own processes and at the end QCM generates charts in order to trace and control these processes.

QCM Module Architecture

QCM is embedded in a set of modules, each providing essential functionality supporting QCM (figure 3). The Collaborative Program Management module (CPM) as one of these appropriates a library of micro-processes which enables the QCM to deploy new products out of pre-defined micro-processes. Furthermore CPM puts QCM in a position to offer different levels of views. Doing so it is possible to focus to the execution level or summarise micro-processes and processes and have a view regarding only to results, their deadlines and the path from one result to the next.

Via the Product Structure Management module (PSM) it is possible to load and store files related to the project and to extract relevant information. For instance QCM needs to set up a new product. In this case, the latest existing CAD file can be loaded out of the repository and it is possible to generate a first coarse structure of the BOM out of this data.

A third module QCM interacts with is the Collaborative Knowledge Management module (CKM). This module supplies with information about "goodness" of any process that is traced and monitored by the QCM. Doing so it is possible to evaluate if a considered process fulfilled the expectations or not and why. The data that is evaluated here can be re-used by the CKM in other projects to compare the actual performance with stored data of similar products and their processes.

To ensure that the QCM module can interact with the other modules and use the information provided by them all modules are connected to a SQL relational database using ODBC or JDBC depending on the fact in which language they have been programmed. Moreover the approach of using a data base as data store allows it to exchange information with affiliated software like ERP- or PDM-systems in an easy way. QCM itself is written in the scripting language php to ensure that the module will be platform independent. Furthermore it is possible to set it up as a service reachable over Intra- or Internet using web technologies (http). No client or special software must be installed in order to use it.

Functionalities of the module and code regarding to the GUI, which is also provided, is separated as clear as possible to make it easy to reuse the implemented methods and GUI elements and to prevent redundant code. In this way it is also possible to generate web services and for instance automatically collect relevant performance indicators or other information by triggering data collection from connected ERP-systems. To do so the implemented methods provide functionalities to generate XML code interoperable to the WSDL standard. The GUI of the QCMS is designed to meet the highest requirements of user-friendliness. The other modules are integrated seamless and guarantee a smooth workflow.

Additional to the mentioned modules QCM reverts to common services and an enabling framework. These services provide functionalities like user management, access control or methods to generate web services and are sourced out to be available for all modules. This ensures the fact that functionalities do not have to be developed from scratch for each module. QCM itself is subdivided into four sub modules: QCM-Global, QCM-Process Progress Tracing, QCM-Process Performance Control and Lessons Learned (see figure 3)

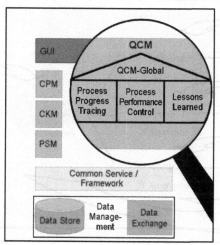

Fig. 3. Module Architecture

QCM-Global

In the very early phases of new product design, engineers begin the design by sketching out a structure for the product which identifies the major components and systems that will combine to create the desired product. For each component, existing standard parts and previously designed custom parts must be evaluated for their ability to provide the necessary function. In those cases for which no existing alternative can be identified, the engineer must specify that new parts should be created, and the details of the structure begin to emerge. QCM-Global, as a sub module of QCM, is devoted to functionalities in terms of building up the structure of a product and adapt it to the process reference model in order to customise a specific product (or project) oriented process chain. QCM enables each partner to define and model the own engineering processes, which are being supported by his company based on such global available process reference model. These single parts of a process chain from each partner can be connected to generate a project wide model with the ability to refine or to aggregate the view. While the network manager will get a top view of the network-wide activities, a process owner within a company will be able to have a detailed look into his processes.

As a first step QCM has to be customised in terms of a selected product which has to be manufactured (VCOR:"fulfilled") by using partner's capabilities that are organised in a virtual organisations. Therefore a network or project manager modifies the VCOR reference model by choosing relevant process out of the holistic VCOR (see figure 2) in regard to a special product's BOM. The result and approach of following scenario is presented in figure 4.

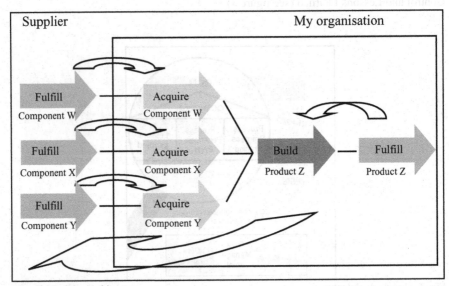

Fig. 4. Module Architecture

Due to own organisation, the network manger has the possibility to select those "acquire", "build" and "fulfill" (see chapter VCOR) process that are relevant regarding the chosen product. QCMS works top down, that means the modification starts at Level 1 and becomes more and more detailed down to strategic configurations. The next step is, regarding the chosen product, to identify all necessary components out of BOM and connect them to the already modified and customised reference model. Depending on the organisation some components are allocated to "build" others to "acquire" processes similarly to well known "make or buy" decisions. For this purpose a library provides all information concerning needed components. In case of missing components a manager is able to edit new one with all engineering descriptions needed and send a request to partners of a virtual organisation. All interested partners receive a message concerning a new "unverified component" and they are in the position to answer the request with all needed information like type of fulfill process (that automatically determines the acquire process of the virtual organisation manager), price and duration to deliver that component (or changing the view to the virtual organisation manager: duration of the "acquire" process). Starting from components allocated to "build" processes the manager also can send requests within his own organisation and ask for duration, costs and resources. These data are called progress process indicators (PPI). As soon as all relevant and required information about all needed components are available QCM creates a value chain at configuration level. Once QCM-Global is modified and configured it posses all process information needed in order to act as a basis for following trace and quality control services.

QCM-Process Progress Tracing

Based on the generated value chain QCM is now able provide Quality Control Management Services for virtual organisation partners who are part of that value chain. The Project Progress Tracing sub module is dedicated to generate and present charts out of available process progress information, like for example Pert-, Gant- and Capacity Charts. Further on each virtual organisation partner can trace costs, time and resources in terms of a specific date or a period. Depending on the role in the virtual organisation the manager has got a holistic view; a special process owner's view is limited to his field of activity or responsibility. There is also the possibility to connect information about costs etc. with selected "acquire, build and fulfill" processes. Progress process indicators (time, cost, resources) are computed from planned data, progress data and their difference; for example it is possible to monitor a project budget, the cumulated real expenditure and their balance over timeSo at the end QCM provides very detailed information about progress of engineering processes in virtual organisations and can give recommendations or warnings concerning any kind of course deviations.

QCM-Process Performance Control

The generated value chain does not only provide the idea to trace processes but also to monitor and evaluate quality based on the performance data of the involved processes. Management of key performance indicators (KPI) allows monitoring both process performance – such as time, costs, quality and risk (PPI) – as well as engineering performance – such as weight, stiffness and costs. Engineering indicators (for example weight, stiffness etc.) are computed from engineering outputs and are used as such or inside other formulas to build synthetic indicators. Some figures like "hours worked vs. hours billed" or "offers vs. realised offers per key account manager" are standard KPIs. The Project Quality Monitoring sub module supports the creation, modification, deletion and search of relevant key performance indicators. Further on it uses a method for acquisition of performance data for configured processes and to select and enter relevant KPIs out of an existing pool regarding selected processes. Using indicators QCM is able to evaluate processes in virtual organisations and visualise performance data in value chains.

Lessons Learned

Knowledge Management is becoming more and more important for achieving sustainable business success. Companies have started initiatives to be able to meet the challenges of the dynamic markets. Many Knowledge Management (KM) ideas like approaches or continuous learning are also fundamental ideas of Quality Management. The management of processes by which knowledge is created and applied is one of the main aspects. Information and experiences must be classified regarding indicators which are provided process improvement (Quintas et. al., 1997). From a QM perspective, an ideal model for evaluating KM should contain following elements, focus on processes, provide information for future activities/ projects, continuous learning and improvement and measurement and standardisation Wilson et. al., 1999).

Regarding Process Progress Tracing and Process Performance Control sub modules there is a lot of interesting information about process progress and performance that can be very fruitful for future projects. Focusing on this idea it makes sense to store project-oriented records like practices, targets, performance, arise unfeasibility a reactive alternatives. So QCM also provides information about good and bad case practices in virtual organisations in order to support re-use of knowledge, solutions and gained experience. The lessons learned sub module prepares all useful information concerning progress and performance that has been generated by QCM and provides it to the global Collaborative Knowledge Management module (CKM). Thus, there is a very close interaction between Lessons Learned and CKM.

3   Conclusions/ Outlook

It has been shown that tracing and monitoring of highly distributed processes in virtual organisations depends on the availability of production data from different perspectives such as design, planning and control or budgeting. The presented QCM functionalities will be implemented into a web-based platform to enable the single actor in the virtual organisation to access and to submit his own data. Integrating the data along the value chain and from different organisations allows the provision of new services to better manage the operations of SMEs in virtual organisations.

References

1. Aichele, C. (1997). Kennzahlenbasierte Geschäftsprozessanalyse, Wiesbaden.

2. Böhnert, A. (1999). Benchmarking: Charakteristik eines aktuellen Managementinstruments, Hamburg.

3. Camarinha-Matos; Afsarmanesh; Ollus (2005). Virtual Organisations – Systems and Practices, Springer.

4. http://www.crfproject-eu.org/frame.asp

5. http://www.value-chain.org

6. ISO 9001:2000 : Interpretation der Anforderungen der DIN EN ISO 9001 2000-12 unter Berücksichtigung der ISO 9004 2000; Normforderungen, Dokumentationsbeispiele, Effizienzhinweise, Kennzahlen (2002). TÜV Rheinland Berlin-Brandenburg, 4. überar. Aufl., Köln.

7. Müller, D.H., Gsell H., Kopfer H., Shigo N. (2006). Ein integriertes Produktdaten-/Prozessmodell für die Produkt-entwicklung im kooperativen Schiffbau. In: Industrie Management 22 (2006) 3, GITO-Verlag, S. 65-68.

8. OECD (1999). Boosting Innovation: The Cluster Approach. Retrieved 20 June, 2000, from http://www.oecd.org

9. Quintas, P.; Lefrere, P.; Jones, G. (1997). Knowledge Management, a Strategic Agenda, Long range Planning, 30, 385-391.

10 Reid, R.L.; Rogers, K.J.; Johnson, M.E.; Liles, D.H. (1996). Engineering the virtual enterprise, in: IERC Proceedings of 5th Annual Industrial Engineering Research Conference, pp. 485–490.

11. Seifert, M.; Eschenbächer, J; Thoben, K.D. (2004). A predictive Performance Measurement approach for adaptive Supply Chains, in: Logistics and global Outsourcing, Nottingham.

12. Sheridan, J.H. (1993). Agile manufacturing: stepping beyond lean production, Ind. Week 242 (8) 30–46.

13. Wilson, L.T.; Asay, D. (1999). Putting Quality in Knowledge Management, Quality Progress, 32, 25-31.

PART FOUR

Improving Service Processes

Need to Develop Best Practices for Business Related Services (BRS)

Amit Garg and Gerhard Gudergaan
Research Institute for Operations Management (FIR) at Aachen University
of Technology, Pontdriesch 14/16, D-52062 Aachen, Germany
Tel +49 241 47705-439, Fax:+49 241 47705-199

Abstract. Manufacturing organizations seek to effectively integrate diverse service participants and their resources into a synthesized activity and also to make use of available assets efficiently. In pursuit of these goals companies follow a common strategy of implementing what are called "Best Practices" in the supply chains. Our aim is to examine if the best practices proposed for the manufacturing sector serve to bring about a significant improvements in the service sector. With this objective, we first review some typical interaction characteristics of services and manufacturing functions in detail. Interaction characteristics are heavily influenced by four basic characteristics of services: intangibility, perishability, simultaneity and heterogeneity. Interaction analysis helps us to group these interaction characteristics under major groups. They are 1) Planning 2) Capacity management 3) Flexibility Management 4) Execution 5) Measurement Model 6) Decision Making 7) Transparency. Further we review best practices that have been proposed for the manufacturing sector and their feasibility for considered domain of BRS.

1 Manufacturing Supply Chain increasingly Outsource Services

As Manufacturing Supply Chain today strives to achieve minimum operating costs and lean operations, many in-house services have become potential targets for outsourcing [1]. Manufacturing organizations increasingly consider the option of outsourcing an important process associated with the goods they bring to the market to specialized service providers [2]. A recent global survey conducted by the Economist Intelligence Unit (EIU), found that a full 80 percent of respondents in the industries currently engage in some form of outsourcing [3]. Earlier outsourcing was confined to non-strategic business activities such as cleaning, transport or legal services, but now outsourcing is also predominant in business functions that are closer to the core. The past two decades have seen a growing trend towards the outsourcing of Business Related Services (BRS) such as R&D, Maintenance,

Please use the following format when citing this chapter:

Garg, A. and Gudergaan G., 2008, in IFIP International Federation for Information Processing, Volume 257, Lean Business Systems and Beyond, Tomasz Koch, ed.; (Boston: Springer), pp. 475–483.

Financing & Logistics [4]. Various services, as shown in Figure 1, are contracted out to specialized service providers to achieve lower cost and higher quality.

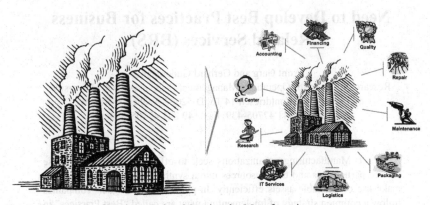

Fig. 1. Outsourcing of Business Related Services by Manufacturing

The relationship between services, particularly the BRS and the manufacturing is no more a substitutive relationship but rather it has become very complementary to each other [5]. The biggest challenge to manage complementary dependency is to enhance the use of standards, best practices, and common measure of performances as well as to ensure high visibility amongst all. The aim of this article is to examine if the best practices documented extensively in SCM literature are applicable to the service sector.

2 Methodology Proposed

Our aim is to examine if the best practices proposed for the manufacturing sector serve to bring about significant improvements in the service sector. With this end in view, the approach we adopt is outlined as follows: We first review some typical characteristics of services in detail. These typical characteristics have been well documented in literature. Based on these characteristics, we outline metrics in the service sector which are useful to measure the performance of a given service. Our next step is to review best practices that have been proposed for the manufacturing sector. The crucial step in our work is the matching of these two areas: the performance metrics of the services on one hand and the best practices in manufacturing on the other. We plot these two aspects on two axes, to evaluate if the best practices result in an improvement on the performance metrics. Two tools: the matching chart and the cluster relationship diagram are used for this purpose. We base our conclusions on the results from these two methodologies.

Characteristics of Services

We examine the four basic service characteristics: intangibility, perishability, simultaneity and heterogeneity, and performance metrics for these characteristics:

Intangibility

From the Manufacturer Perspective: Manufacturer often use the reputation of a service firm and its representatives to judge quality. Zeithaml observed that services often cannot be evaluated in advance of use [6]. Unlike goods they do not have many of what she called "search properties". *From the service provider perspective:* Service producers must take into account consumer psychology while making plans to launch and provide services.

Perishability

In general, services are not storable: this is yet another difference from manufactured goods. Manufacturing companies typically maintain safety stocks as a buffer against demand fluctuations, and work-in-process inventory serves as an additional buffer. However, it is not possible for a service provider to engage in a similar strategy: for example, a consultant cannot make recommendations in advance; neither can a maintenance service provider have a "buffer service": it must be real-time.

Simultaneity

A personal contact seems to be necessary in a majority of service operations, and customer participation is seen as playing a major role in the determination of a successful service-provider. Groenroos [7] stated that consumption and production are "broad overlapping processes".

Heterogeneity

Heterogeneity imposes many restrictions and demands on the service provider. Every consumer represents a unique case, in the sense that each service would have to be tailored the needs of the individual consumer. The needs of consumers are likely to be diverse, and often intangible. This inherent variability makes it difficult to set precise quantifiable standards for all of the elements of service.

Metrics Reviewed

Based on the characteristics of services, researchers have proposed several metrics to judge service quality. The SERVQUAL method proposed by Parasuraman et al. is one of the most widely used instruments for measuring the quality of services as perceived by the customer. This method evaluates service quality by performing a gap analysis of an organization's service quality performance against customer service quality needs [8]. Kettinger and Lee [9] modified the original model to adapt it to the software services sector.

Kaplan and Norton [10] proposed the Balanced Scorecard which details another approach towards measuring performance. It is a model of business performance evaluation that balances measures of financial performance, internal operations, innovation and learning, and customer satisfaction. These drivers encompass customers, the internal business process, growth and learning and the final measurement is the progress from an explicit and rigorous translation of the organization's strategy. Based on the metrics proposed in the above models, we propose the following list of metrics or indices to measure performance (Table 1). These may be tangible or intangible, with varying degrees of importance, depending on the given service.

Table 1. List of Metrics adequate to measure the appropriateness of best practices

Tangibles	Image
• Overall Equipment Effectiveness	• Appearance
• Accessibility (Uptime)	• Past Personal Experience
• Speed of Execution	• Past Experience of Customers
• Spatial Availability	• Brand Image due to Promotion
• Temporal Availability	• Effectiveness of Personal Contact
	• Trustworthiness
Quality, Reliability & Competence	**Security**
• Conformance to Expectations	• Integrity
• Guarantee	• Confidentiality

Existing Best Practices

Best practices are essentially methods or tools that leading firms use to carry out their business processes. As a result, this set of practices becomes a roadmap to improving business processes, hence the term best practices. Best practices are defined as methods, practices or process that when implemented in a pre-defined business environment; perform best on one or more pre-defined performance metrics. Hence a best practice must be specified with the business environment in which it is being implemented and the performance metrics that are used to evaluate it. Tremendous interest has been generated in the last two decades among business professionals and researchers alike in the area of Supply Chain Management (SCM) and the best practices therein. As a result, a plethora of research in the form of articles, whitepapers and journal publications has taken place, since SCM is seen as an effective way to create value for the trading partners and the customers. Two major initiatives namely SCOR Reference Model from the Supply Chain Council and the EU funded research project Prodchain deserve special reference owing to the key encapsulation and also classification of best practices for SCM.

The SCOR Model [11] classifies best practices in SCM into five process-building blocks: Plan, Source, Make, Deliver and Return and describes best practices for both technology and processes. SCOR has duly identified 12 best practices including Assess Supplier Performance, Cross Docking, Vendor Managed Inventory (VMI) to name a few.

On similar steps, Prodchain Project [12] aimed at the development of a decision support methodology to improve logistics performance in production networks. For their very specific needs to integrate SCM, Prodchain has analyzed and grouped best practices into Management Concepts, Software Solutions and Supportive Practices. All the existing best practices are primarily linked to one of these core groups. Combining the information on best practices from these two primary sources, the following Table (Table 2) epitomizes all the best practices relevant for manufacturing which are considered for further evaluation.

Table 2. List of Best Practices

Just-In-Time	Collaborative Efforts
• Inventory Management	• Collaborative Planning
• Inventory Management	• Collaborative Forecasting
• Continuous Replenishment	• Collaborative Replenishment
	• Co-located Procurement
Lean Manufacturing	• Supplier Relationship Management
• Inventory Management	• Continuous Replenishment
• Quick Changeover	• Efficient Consumer Response
• Continuous Replenishment	• Simultaneous Engineering
• Efficient Consumer Response	

These three focus areas were chosen because these represent the efforts of the industry towards making the supply chain more efficient thereby adding value to the consumer and the trading partners. Moreover, between them, these encompass activities and partners in the entire supply chain spectrum: from raw material provider to the end consumer.

Methodologies for Matching

Matching Chart

The first method we use is a matching chart: shown below (Table 3). On the vertical axis, the performance metrics for services are given. While on the horizontal axis, the planet concepts for the three clusters are plotted. If a direct improvement in the metric takes place due to the concept being considered, the corresponding entry is a darkened circle. In case there is a possibility of such an improvement, but not directly, then the corresponding entry is a circle with a half-dark part. In case the concept fails to address the performance metric totally, the entry is left blank.

To further elaborate the above concept, we present an example: Consider quick changeover and temporal availability. Quick changeover is a concept to reduce the downtime of equipment to the minimum possible, and further uses concepts like single minute exchange of die (SMED). If followed in a service environment, it would mean ensuring that downtime for a service is kept to a minimum. Temporal availability – the probability that the service is available at a given time - is then improved. Additionally, also take the case of efficient consumer response and brand image. Although brand management is not directly addressed by the concept of efficient consumer response, it contributes towards it by ensuring that every response by a consumer is efficiently met through improving internal processes.

An analysis of the above chart shows the inadequacy of the reviewed best practices towards the service sector. It's seen that although tangible measures of performances are covered by these best practices, the intangible ones: quality, reliability, security and image are not adequately addressed. Though indirect improvements do result on some measures, there are no direct best practices that addressed measures of performances in the service sector.

Table 3. Matching Chart

	Inventory Management	Quick Changeover	Continuous Replenishment	Efficient Consumer Response	Collaborative Planning	Collaborative Forecasting	Collaborative Replenishment	Co-located Procurement	Supplier Relationship Mgmt.	Simultaneous Engineering
Overall Equipment Effectiveness	●	●	●	◐	◐	◐	◐	◐		●
Accessibility (Uptime)		●								
Speed of Execution	◐	●	●	●			◐	◐	◐	●
Spatial Availability	◐		●	●	◐		●		◐	
Temporal Availability	◐	●	●	●	◐		●		◐	
Conformance to Expectations			◐		◐				◐	
Guarantee	◐	◐	◐	●			◐		◐	
Reliability	◐	◐	◐						◐	◐
Competence										
Integrity										
Confidentiality										
Appearance									◐	
Past Personal Experience	◐		◐						◐	
Past Experience of Other Customers	◐		◐						◐	
Effectiveness of Personal Contact										
Brand Image				◐						
Trustworthiness	◐		◐							

2.4.2 Cluster Relationship Diagram

These three groups of best practices (JIT, Lean manufacturing and Collaborative Efforts) are called *clusters*, while their components are called as planet *concepts*. Thus clusters are broad class names for a group of planet concepts.

Planet concepts themselves are composed of specific best practices, called *satellite concepts*. In the cluster relationship diagrams and the matching chart, we list the clusters and their planet concepts. The figure below (Figure 2), called the cluster relationship diagram shows the relationship between various clusters and their planet concepts. The colored dotted lines are used to mark each cluster and its planet concepts. Common planet concepts can be clearly seen through this diagram.

Superposed on this diagram is the supply chain: from the raw materials supplier to the end consumer. The role of service providers is also denoted – along this supply chain. The cluster relationship diagram also reiterates the conclusion in the matching chart. Best practices that cover the entire supply chain do not address the services. The service areas of transportation, maintenance, are missing from the clusters of the best practices. In other words, services are still outside the gamut of existing best practices.

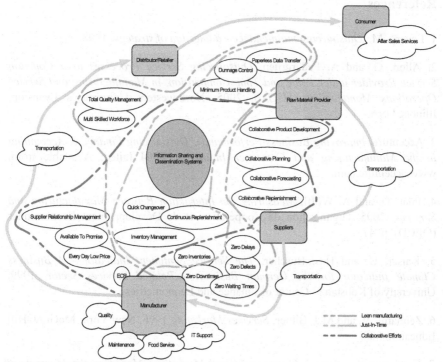

Fig. 2. Cluster Relationship Diagram

3   Conclusions

In the above article, we aim to throw some light on the understanding of best practices towards the service sector. With this goal, we have matched best practices in the industry being currently practiced against the performance metrics in the service sector. The clear conclusion that emerges from our exercise is that existing best practices are inadequate from the point of view of the service sector. The intangible issues pertaining to services are not addressed by these best practices. The best practices being currently practiced in the industry are under the assumption that the product relates to a good rather than a service. The basic difference between goods and services is responsible for this inadequacy. Services have already surpassed manufacturing both in terms of GDP generation and employment. Yet, this sector lacks a comprehensive set of best practices documentation, which is extensively available for the manufacturing sector. There is a great need to document best practices pertaining to the service sector, or re-align manufacturing best practices so that these are applicable to services too. This presents an opportunity for future work in this field.

References

1. Levery, M., *Outsourcing maintenance - a question of strategy*. 1998.

2. Allon, G. and A. Federgruen, *Outsourcing Service Processes to a Common Service Provider under Price and Time Competition, in Manufacturing and Service Operations Management (MSOM)*. 2005: Northwestern University's Evanston, Illinois, USA.

3. Accenture. *Improving Business Performance: Outsourcing Finance & Accounting in the Manufacturing and Consumer Industries*. 2004 [cited; Available from: www.accenture.com.

4. Pilat, D. and A. Wölfl, *Measuring the Interaction Between Manufacturing and Services*. 2005, Organisation de Coopération et de Développement Economiques (OECD). p. 47.

5. Kaiser, U. and H.S. Buscher, *The Service Sentiment Indicator - A Business Climate Indicator for the German Business - Related Services Sector*. 1999, University of Konstanz - Center of Finance and Econometrics.

6. Zeithaml, V. and M.J. Bitner, *Services Marketing* 1996, New York: McGraw-Hill Education 608.

7. Groenroos, C., *Service Management and Marketing: Managing the Moments of Truth in Service Competition* 1 ed. 1990: Prentice Hall 404.

8. Parasuraman, A., V. Zeithaml, and A. Berry, *SERVQUAL: A Multiple-Item Scale for Measuring Customer Perceptions of Service Quality.* Journal of Retailing, 1988. 64(1): p. 12-40.

9. Kettinger, W. and C. Lee, *Perceived service quality and user satisfaction with the information services function.* Decision Sciences, 1995. 25(5): p. 737-766.

10. Kaplan, R.S. and D.P. Norton. *The Balanced Scorecard: Measures That Drive Performance.* 2000 [cited; Available from: http://harvardbusinessonline.hbsp. harvard.edu/b01/en/common/item_detail.jhtml?referral=9421&id=92105.

11. Supply Chain Council. *SCOR Model Reference 7.0.* 2005 [cited; Available from: http://www.supply-chain.org.

12. PRODCHAIN, *Development of Decision Support Methodology to Improve Logistics Performance in Production Networks. EU Project IST-2000-61205.* 2003.

Lean Healthcare. An Experience in Italy

Alberto Portioli-Staudacher

1   Department of Management, Economics and Industrial
     engineering, Politecnico di Milano, Piazza L. da Vinci 32,
     I-20133 Milano, Italy.

Abstract. In this paper we present the experience of a lean implementation in
a Hospital. It all steamed out from a need to cut cost, and the focus on
inventory reduction. The methodology adopted and the peculiarities of an
implementation in a hospital are presented. A strong reduction in inventory has
been achieved but, more important, broken processes which lead to excessive
inventories have been identified so giving the possibility to remove the root
causes and avoid having the problem again. Finally, one of the best results has
been to make people in the hospital see differently about materials
management activities: best and faster results, with less effort, are not
achieved by batching (e.g. ordering 3 weeks consumption of a medicine
needed) rather by standardizing activities and levelling orders and activities
throughout the week (e.g. order every day all medicines consumed).

1   Introduction

Healthcare system in Italy is managed at a regional level, and 60% of Regions'
expenditures (and budget) are for healthcare system.
Population is aging and life expectation increasing, therefore healthcare expenditure
steadily increases, making cost reduction one of the main priorities for the Italian
government.
On the other hand, citizens ask for a higher and higher service level from the
healthcare system, and they are worried about decreases in healthcare budget
because they think this will unavoidably lead to a service level reduction.
Our experience is that healthcare, and most services in general, are at the very
beginning in the search for operational excellence, therefore much can be done to
decrease costs and at the same time to increase service level.
Many models and techniques of Industrial engineering are being transferred from
manufacturing to services, and books about service operations are starting to appear
(e.g. Johnston and Clark, 2002, Hill, 2002, Slack and Lewis, 2002, Chase et. al,
1998). Lean production approach also is being implemented in services, but

Please use the following format when citing this chapter:

Portioli-Staudacher, A., 2008, in IFIP International Federation for Information Processing, Volume
257, Lean Business Systems and Beyond, Tomasz Koch, ed.; (Boston: Springer), pp. 485–492.

experiences are at a very early stage, probably because lean approach is not widespread yet.

In this paper we present our experience in implementing a lean approach to material management in a leading hospital in Italy.

2   Materials and information management

In a hospital there are two main flow of materials: medicines and pharmaceutical, and other materials.

Medicines and pharmaceuticals are managed by a central Pharmacy, where the director is in charge of discussing with the medial doctors the best medicines, and alternatives for existing ones, also considering costs as a criteria. The director of the Pharmacy also selects suppliers, makes supply contracts, and sets stocks levels.

Most commonly used medicines are kept in stock and for a few of them there are contracts with suppliers setting prices over a period of 2-3 years.

Other medicines are not kept in stock but ordered when needed, for example because a person arrives who is already taking his/her medicines for a pre-existing disease, and the hospital usually carries on the same therapy.

Wards also have stock of most commonly used medicines, so to have them at hand. In the considered hospital Pharmacy delivers to wards twice a week, but medicines are not ordered so frequently. Because ordering takes time, medicines are ordered in lot quantities so to last for one week or two. If there are no orders for that ward, no delivery is done.

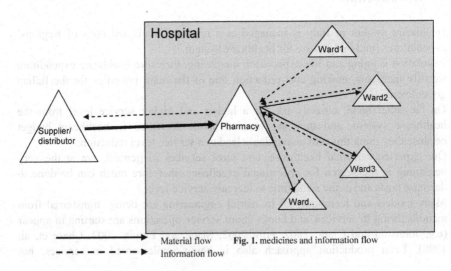

Material flow   **Fig. 1.** medicines and information flow
Information flow

Non pharmaceutical materials are not managed by the Pharmacy but by a common purchasing department, which takes care of buying everything, from syringes to napkins to X ray plates.

Most non pharmaceutical materials are not kept in stock in a central location, but managed directly by the wards, which store them and ask the purchasing department to order a new lot whenever inventory gests to low. In the considered hospital the lot quantity is about 4 months consumption, with an ordering level of 2-3 months, due to the uncertain lead time to get what ordered.

Every ward orders what needed independently from what other wards are doing.

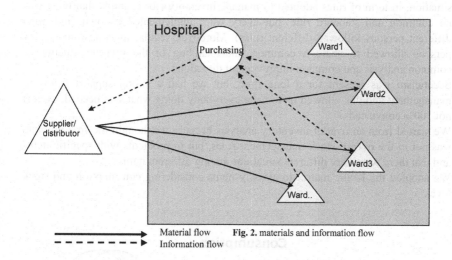

| ————————► | Material flow | **Fig. 2.** materials and information flow |
| – – – – – – – ► | Information flow | |

3   Inventory analysis

In the considered hospital, overall stocks, considering central stocks and stocks present in the wards, used to turn about 2,8 times a year.

We organised a kick off meeting with representatives of all people involved: director of purchasing, director of pharmacy, nurses director, IT director, and accounting director.

We were introduced by the top management of the hospital, and we presented the objectives of the work, and the methodology. In particular, the objective was to cut inventory without decreasing service level. Wherever possible, a reduction in expenditure was also an objective.

We described we wanted to map material and information flow, to highlight opportunities to decrease inventories. We made crystal clear we needed and wanted their collaboration, and no-one will be considered responsible for present situation, only for not improving it.

The first step has been to discover with them how things were actually working, to make clear we did not want to impose a one-fits-all recipe, but wanted to know their specific problems, and find specific solutions with their contribution.

Finally, we made clear we wanted to start the improvement process, to give them the tools to understand and improve, but we also wanted them to become independent from us as fast as possible,

The material and information flow description often highlighted an unknown situation. Our mapping had as a first result to make clear to everybody present situation, in term of rules adopted to manage inventory (for example that there was no common and standard rule, but every ward implemented its own, and often different persons followed different rules). Moreover, regular meetings among key persons allowed to share a common understanding of the present situation, a common analysis and common improvement directions.

Scepticism was present for a long time, but we had a strong support from top management and this allowed us to have everybody doing what was needed, even if not 100% convinced.

We started from an overall inventory analysis because we thought the first problem was not in the overall stock management rules, but in problems with specific items and that there were very different situations among different items.

We adopted the Kralic matrix to classify items considering consumption and stock level.

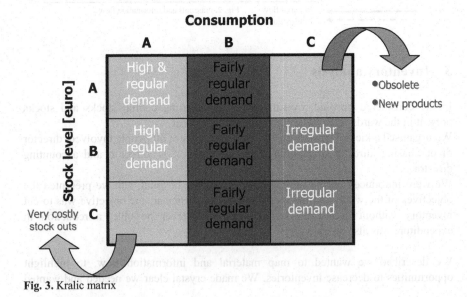

Fig. 3. Kralic matrix

In the A-C cell we found may products which were forgotten by everybody. For example, the medical doctor started using a new (and maybe less expensive) product, and nobody took the job of cancelling automatic reorders when stock fell under the set limit, and make sure that all remaining stock were consumed.

Starting from items with the highest value we could highlight about 300.000 euros of material which was about to become obsolete, with virtually no consumption.

We could even find items with no consumption and purchasing orders, and other materials with such a low consumption it would take years to finish stock (again risking to become obsolete befor being used).

This allowed not only to identify these items and arrange for a consumption, or a sale to other hospitals, but, most important, allowed to identify broken processes which allowed this situation to happen.

Repairing those processes will make impossible to have obsolete items again (and stocks remain low).

We found very few items in C-A cell. In a hospital there are many alarms and procedures to protect from stockout, or to react urgently in case of stockout, so to minimise the impact. But there are no procedure or alarm to highlight extra stock.

With an increased confidence in out methods, gained from the people of the hospital through the fast and clear results of our first analysis, we performed a second step considering all items in cells A-A, A-B, A-C, B-B and B-C and taking a few as an example, we questioned the stock management policy, the reorder point, the safety stock levels, the lot size, the frequency of orders etc. Lot size in many cases came out as constraint by the supplier. Thus on the one hand we invited to question with the supplier the constraint, on the other hand we sorted out all items which have been ordered in different quantities throughout the year: all purchase orders could be done with the minimum quantity ordered, how came it had been ordered in larger quantity?

4   First results

First result from this attack to inventory has been a tremendous decrease in overall inventory:

Pharmacy + wards :   45% reduction
Other materials: 24% reduction
for an overall reduction of   35%, out of the 6 million euros initial inventory.

This was not enough. The hospital was continuously decreasing inventory by fixing broken processes which were actively sought after, and by improving suppliers delivery. We found out that there was no formal records about supplier delivery performances. Probably suppliers knew this too, and both speed and on time delivery were low (from a sample we could witness). As a reaction, Pharmacy and wards increased the safety stocks and the ordering points. Now this has changed and there is a closer monitor of supplier performances and the hospital is questioning supplier constraints (if lot size is affected by the desire to have minimum delivery quantity, let's put together not larger quantities of a single item, but consider the whole bunch of materials the hospital orders from the supplier. Next step will be to pool with other hospital in the same region and reach a milkrun model).

Inventories were reduced much more in the central stores (mainly the Pharmacy) than in decentralised locations (i.e. wards). Therefore the next step has been to tackle the relationship (material and information flow) between the pharmacy and the wards.

5 Pharmacy – Wards relationship

Pharmacy and wards inventory management were carried out independently: both were looking at their own situation, and tried to improve their local performance.

We approached the problem for a different perspective. Once more the lean one.

We looked at the flow. Medicines had to flow from the supplier to the patient. Stocks at Pharmacy and at ward had only to cope with the fact that neither the Pharmacy nor the supplier were delivering every day, and with the fact that there is always a certain degree of uncertainty.

We made clear that Pharmacy was the one responsible for coping with uncertainty. Not the ward. Therefore, only the Pharmacy had to keep safety stock, the ward had to behave considering all medicines managed in stock, as always present at the Pharmacy.

The following actions have been undertaken with the sisters of two pilot wards:

⇒   get rid of all medicines that are not common use, by giving them back to the Pharmacy. A list of all non common use medicines that are requested by the ward, and that are not been used completely is passed to the Pharmacy every month. In case another ward needs a non common use medicine, it asks the Pharmacy which check on the list is another ward has any.

⇒   5S intervention for the positioning of the medicines

⇒   code coding medicines on the base of the type of use: Green for medicines that are common use (demand is high and regular), Yellow for medicines that are sometime used (demand is low and depends a lot on the number of patients treated with that medicine in that period), Red for medicines that are not common use. Have been ordered for a specific need of a specific patient, but it is quite improbable someboby else using it will arrive in the following weeks

⇒   revise reordering approach. Instead of lot ordering, when a certain stock level were reached, the following procedure was adopted: Green medicines were ordered twice a week (i.e. every time the Pharmacy was delivering), asking for the needed amount to replenish the stock to the desired level. Yellow medicines were ordered every time there had been a consumption (due to the low and irregular demand it may not be consumed for weeks), and the quantity was what needed for replenish the stock to the desired plus the amount needed to threat the patient that came in and started the consumption till the next delivery from the Pharmacy. Red one were not to be checked for reordering.

6   Results from the pilots

Here again we found scepticism. In particular the proposed method was perceived as leading to more time and effort devoted to medicine ordering (not perceived as an interesting activity).

But again we had the full support of top management, and as a first action we involved the sisters of the pilot wards in a run of the beer game. This helped them in seeing the impact of their actions on the Pharmacy (unpredictable demand also for high volume medicines) and how this was causing high inventory. Moreover, regular meeting with the sisters and the Director of the Pharmacy as the project was going on, allowed everybody to see a common objective and helped in destroying the walls and the wrong beliefs existing between Pharmacy (wards always keep a lot o stock) and wards (Pharmacy takes a long time to deliver, and not always has what has been ordered).

Inventory in wards was reduced by 10-15% (stock is decreased in Pharmacy also but this has not been quantified yet).

Space needed has been reduced by 15%.

Time required to check date on medicines dropped by 80% (much less medicines and faster turns).

To their surprise, the expected bad impact of more frequent orders did not arrived. On the contrary, making orders much more regular (an order is placed every Tuesday and Thursday), a good portion of the order is always the same (Green medicines) with small changes in quantity, so also receiving the medicines is more easy. Every time there is more or less the same amount, for a large portion it is always the same medicines, therefore more easy to check, and faster to put in place...

People in the Pharmacy's storehouse also were happy (a complaint was expected for more frequent orders of common use medicines): "when the order arrives we know already what you need". A large portion of the order is no surprise. They can more easily organise their activities.

Making orders more regular helped in standardise activities, and in reducing surprises (e.g. if one day a large quantity of medicines is ordered because many of them have reached the ordering level, then a lot of time is occupied in receiving, checking, storing these medicines. Then the following week very few medicines are ordered and much less time is occupied. Every week is different. It is much easier to allot every Tuesday and Thursday a defined amount if time, which with the new method will be constant, for these activities.)

For further decreasing stock at the wards, the Pharmacy illustrated again a procedure, made simpler than before, to get medicines from the Pharmacy in case an urgent need arises, so to make clear there is no need to have materials in the wards "just in case".

References

1. Chase, R., Aquilano, N., Jacobs, R., 1998, Production and Operations Management: Manufacturing and Services, Irwin.

2. Hill, T., 2002, Operations management, Palgrave.

3. Johnston, B., Clark, J., 2002, Service Operations Management, Prentice Hall.

4. Slack, N., Lewis, M., 2002, Operations Strategy, Prentice Hall.

5. Womack, J, Jones, D., 2004, Lean thinking, Free Press.

Working Time Configuration in Hospitals Using Personnel-oriented Simulation

Gert Zülch, Patricia Stock, and Jan Hrdina

ifab-Institute of Human and Industrial Engineering, University of Karlsruhe
Kaiserstrasse 12, D-76131 Karlsruhe, Germany,
WWW home page: http://www.ifab.uni-karlsruhe.de

Abstract. Current developments in Germany have led to severe consequences for the configuration of working times of medical and nursing personnel in hospitals. They underline the necessity to arrange work processes and personnel employment as efficiently as possible. In this context, the current project „Process Optimization and Efficient Personnel Employment in Hospitals" has set the goal of developing a simulation-based procedure for the analysis of working time model. This procedure shall which can be used to explore the advantages and possibilities of working time models in hospitals based on simulation investigations and to derive configuration recommendations. The flexible alignment of the personnel capacity with the capacity requirements for patient treatment is used to achieve a high degree of patient-oriented service in medical tasks in order to help hospitals efficiently employ available personnel resources as well as to realize personnel-oriented goals. This article will introduce the developed concept for a simulation-based configuration of working times.

1   Hospitals as Patient-oriented Enterprises

In 2001 hospitals in Germany account for approximately 62 bn Euro and 1.1 m employed persons ([1], pp. 13). In comparison to production enterprises or other service areas, hospitals are characterized by several structural particularities:

- The operating hours for hospitals are generally 24 hours a day and seven days a week. Additionally, a great deal of night-work must be carried out.
- As in other service industries, the workload fluctuates greatly since it is primarily determined by the stochastic arrival of patients. Furthermore, the patients must usually be treated immediately.
- Furthermore, decisions regarding treatment are often made based on incomplete information, causing operations to be highly individual and very difficult to plan.

- In comparison to production enterprises and many other service industries, which are dominated by organizational goals, patient-oriented goals are of primary concern in h ospitals
- The occupational health and safety as well as hygiene requirements of the medical and nursing personnel must be taken into account during treatment workflows.

In addition to these general conditions, hospitals have recently been experiencing serious changes, which are above all affected by three developments:

- Since 01.01.2004 the German hospital financing is a fixed-price system based on the "German Diagnosis Related Groups" (G-DRGs), in which only a fixed amount per patient case is paid by the health insurances under public law. The hospitals are thus forced to work in a highly cost-efficient and transparent manner in order to cope with the ever-increasing cost pressure. Therefore, the costs optimization of the personnel area of a hospital has a significant impact on the hospital's total costs since at least two thirds thereof can be ascribed to this area (cf. [2], p. 389).
- Since 31.08.2005 the hospitals are forced by legal regulations to provide quality reports. This leads to the necessity for internal an external quality assurance, often connected with the implementation of quality management systems. Therefore, the analysis of treatment processes as well as the revelation of rationalization potential in traditional hospital processes is gaining in significance.
- The European Court of Justice declared in its judgement from 09.09.2003 (C-151/02) that the guideline 93/104/EG of the European Council is to be interpreted that the stand-by duty of a doctor served by personal presence in the hospital represents in its entirety working time, even if said doctor is allowed, in times when he is not employed, to rest at his workplace. Since this decision the German working time law (Arbeitszeitgesetz - ArbZG) no longer corresponds with the cited EU guideline. This judgement has considerable effects on hospitals: Studies from the associations concerned assume that this creates a workforce deficit of 20,300 doctors and 12,900 other positions (all full-time) at least ([3], p. 9). This underlines the necessity to configure personnel employment more efficiently.

As a result of these far-reaching changes, hospitals find themselves confronted with fundamentally new organizational challenges. In order to meet the future challenges, hospitals must continue to redesign their structures and medical operations (cf. [4], p. 776). The same is true for the traditional working time configuration (i.e. shift and block models), which must be replaced by a more flexible and efficient task-oriented management of working time. The implementation of flexible working time models and their compliance with legal regulations represent one major prerequisite for the future alignment of personnel capacity and personnel requirements, since only then can patient-orientation and an economical personnel employment be achieved simultaneously (cf. e.g. [5], p. 43).

2   Problems in Working Time Configuration

Various general conditions must be taken into account in the configuration of appropriate working time models, in particular legal provisions, wage agreements, ergonomic recommendations as well as hospital-, patient-, and employee-oriented objectives, which are often competing ([6], p. 52). These result in numerous alternatives
or complementary applicable working time models. Thus, no "ideal" working time
model exists, rather a working time model must be aligned with the specific legal,
operational and personnel needs of each hospital department (cf. e.g. [7], p. 117).
The addressed general conditions can even change over time (as has recently been
the case in the hospital field; see chapter 1), thus creating the need for a periodic
evaluation of the adequacy of a working time model.
Traditional static planning and assessment methods (e.g. benefit analyses and
sensitivity analyses) only provide subjective statements regarding the expected
effects of working time systems since their results are dependent upon the specific
knowledge of the evaluator ([8], pp. 42). Furthermore, conventional assessment procedures do not sufficiently consider employee-related target criteria and in particular
do not provide a prognosis of the expected stress that be imposed on the employees
in certain working time models in hospitals with a fluctuating patient frequency
(following [8], p. 52). In contrast to the conventional assessment methods, a dynamic
analysis in a simulation model can provide comprehensive and prospective information regarding possible effects – both positive and negative – of envisaged working
time models ([8], p. 53).
For this purpose, personnel-oriented simulation can be used for prospective
evaluation. This approach has already proven to be highly effective in other fields of
planning and assessment of work organization ([9], p. 371). Since the parameters of
a working time configuration can be varied in a simulation model in nearly every
possible combination, an efficient analysis and assessment of various working time
models is thus made possible.

3   Simulation-based Working Time Configuration

For these reasons, the ifab-Institute for Human and Industrial Engineering of the
University of Karlsruhe (Germany) has developed a simulation-based procedure with
which working time models in hospitals can be assessed in an objective, efficient and
quantitative manner. Several concepts have been developed for modelling and assessment, which are elucidated in the following (see Fig. 1).

3.1   Modelling Concept for Working Time Models

First, a modelling concept for the working time models relevant to the hospital area
was developed. This concept was conceived to be capable of representing in particular working time models with on-call duty as well as flexible working time mod-

els. Many authors differentiate working time into two components following Teriet ([10], p. 10), namely
- chronology, meaning the placement and distribution of working times, and
- chronometry, the duration or volume of working time.

This principle was incorporated into the simulation procedure for working time configuration (e.g. see [11, 12]) and was refined for the hospital field of application (see Tab. 1; cf. also [8], pp. 55).

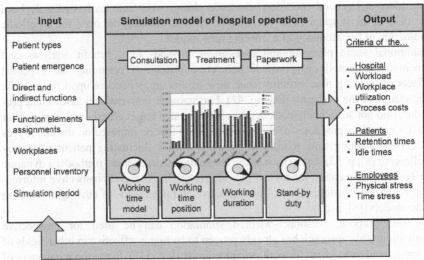

Fig. 1. Simulation of working time models for a hospital

Table 1. Modelling concept for working time models

Content configuration elements	Formal configuration elements

– Duration:
  • Weekly working time in hours
  • Minimum possible daily working time in hours
  • Maximum possible daily working time in hours
– Placement:
  • Number of working time corridors, meaning tuples with starting and ending times as well as availabilities and possible compensation bonuses
  • Cycle period in days
	– Reference time frame
	– Implementation time frame in days, meaning the time for which the working time model is valid
	– Compensation time frame in days, meaning the time in which the contractually agreed working time must be performed
	– Planning time frame in days, meaning the time in which the employment times for each employee of the organizational unit/organization are defined and binding

This modelling concept takes two aspects into account which are typical for hospitals:

- Hospitals often work with on-call duty. Therefore, the availability of on employee can be described with the following values:
  - Regular working time,
  - Work readiness, which forces the employee to stay on location of their employment (e.g. in the emergency room),
  - Stand-by duty, which forces the employee to stay at a location specified by his employer (e.g. in the rest room) in order to take-up his employment immediately, and
  - On-call duty, which allows the employee to choose his inhabitancy on his own as long as he is available in order to take-up his employment shortly.
- Wage agreements provide for varying compensation for night- and Sunday-shifts and also often for the compensation of overtime or various types of on-call duty. This can occur as a percentage or as a bonus, sometimes in combination.

Both individual working time models and even working time systems (meaning all the working time models implemented in an organizational unit/organization) can be described using these configuration elements. This takes the fact into account that, in practice, various working time models (e.g. differentiated for medical and nursing service or for various groups of practitioners) may be used within a hospital (or even within a hospital department).

3.2   Modelling Concept for Hospitals

Furthermore, a concept for modelling hospitals was developed. As a basis, the schemes developed by Heitz ([13], pp. 94) and Bogus ([8], pp. 102) for the description of manufacturing structures and service enterprises respectively have been used. The purely manufacturing- and service-specific attributes had to be eliminated from this scheme and supplemented with attributes for the description of hospital-specific requirements. The adjusted description scheme for hospitals includes the following elements:

- Patient structure and arrival patterns:
  - Patient type
    (characterized by the work operations to be carried out and their flow)
  - Patient arrival
    (characterized by the distribution of the arrival patterns per patient type)
- Functions:
  - Direct functions, meaning functions to be carried out specifically for a patient type (e.g. diagnosis or changing of bandages)
  - Indirect functions, meaning functions that are not carried out for the patients directly, rather usually of preparatory or wrap-up nature or carried out for several patients in common
    (e.g. preparation for the medicine distribution, shift hand-over, ward rounds)
- Resources:
  - Workplaces (e.g. treatment rooms, operating theatres)
  - Personnel (the workers employed and their qualifications)

- Equipment (e.g. medical devices)
- Material (e.g. medicine, medical supplies)

3.3 Evaluation Concept for Simulated Work Systems

Finally, a hospital-specific assessment concept was developed. The concept should include a system of meaningful key figures which are independent from each other while also being nondimensional and standardized. The assessment concept based on degrees of goal achievement (cf. e.g. [14], pp. 69), which has already proven to be advantageous in the assessment of simulation models (cf. e.g. [13], pp. 97; [8], pp. 126) was drawn upon for this reason. A degree of goal achievement can assume a value between 0 % and 100 %, where 100 % represents the ideal value of the assessment figure.

The assessment is carried out analogously to reality, in part with business management and financial key figures (e.g. service rate, duration of patient stay, patient handling costs, utilization of resources, simulated used capacity costs). In addition, also some employee-related criteria concentrating on the imposed stress were defined (e.g. degree of physical stress and time stress). These key figures were derived from existing assessment concepts from the manufacturing ([13], pp. 97) and service fields ([8], pp. 126). However, further hospital-specific figures still need to be developed. These comprise (following [15], p. 31) patient-related key figures, such as e.g. waiting times until a planned treatment, deviation from planned and simulated execution times or the degree of adherence to visiting hours on the one hand, as well as key figures regarding the quality of care, e.g. uncompleted tasks on the other hand.

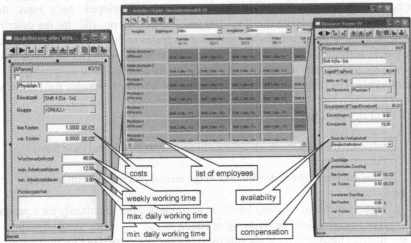

Fig. 2. Screenshot of the working times of one employees

4   The Simulation Procedure *OSim-GAM*

The modelling concept described here was integrated into the ifab-developed object-oriented simulation procedure *OSim* (Object simulator; [9, 16]), resulting in the simulation procedure *OSim-GAM* (Object simulator for working time configuration; [8]) for the analysis of working time models. In particular, each modelled employee or personnel type can be allocated to an individual working time model (see Fig. 2).

The modelling of the patient types is carried out using throughput diagrams in which the temporal-logistic dependencies of the patient treatment operations are repre-sented in a type of network diagram. A throughput diagram can be triggered either by internal or external events, e.g. the stochastic arrival of a patient. A hospital can thus be described by the pattern of incoming patients and the available personnel, workplaces and equipment as well as by the set of all throughput diagrams. As a trigger to initialize a throughput diagram the intermediate arrival times per patient type are used. Figure 3 shows an example of such a throughput diagram as well as its trigger. The ambulant patient type modelled therein requires a sequence of four work operations (examination, therapy, consultation, administration) whose execution times are subject to a beta distribution. The trigger describes the arrival of one patient belonging to this patient type.

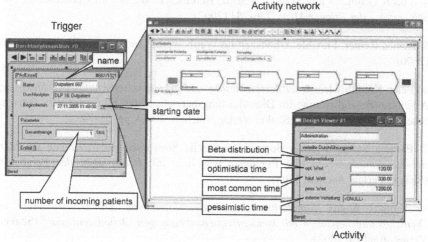

Fig. 3. Patient type and typical treatment illustrated through the example of an ambulant patient

5   Summary and Outlook

Working time configuration has proven to be an extremely complex problem, whose solution is influenced by myriad general conditions. In particular in hospitals, spe-cific working time models are necessary. Prevalent assessment procedures only pro-vide subjective results. For this purpose, the existing simulation procedure *OSim-GAM* was furthered for the objective and quantitative analysis of working time mod-els in the hospital area.

Simulation studies are currently being carried out in hospitals cooperating in this Project, which is supported by the German Research Association (DFG – Deutsche Forschungsgemeinschaft). The aim of theses studies is to verify the effectiveness of the procedure and to examine the effects of various working time models and systems on the defined goal criteria of the assessment concept.

References

1. Statistisches Bundesamt Deutschland (Edt.), *Gesundheit: Ausgaben und Personal 2001* (Wiesbaden, 2003). http://www.destatis.de/presse/deutsch/pk/2003/gbe_2003.pdf (May 29, 2006).

2. Christiane Rosenow and Anke Steinberg, *10 Jahre bundeseinheitliche Krankenhausstatistik*, in: Wirtschaft und Statistik 5/2002, edited by Statistisches Bundesamt Deutschland (Wiesbaden, 2002), pp. 383-391.

3. Martin Waiger, Flexible tarifliche Regelungen notwendig, *ku-Sonderheft* **04**(7), 8-9 (2004).

4. Volker Großkopf and Michael Schanz, Bereitschaftsdienste im Krankenhaus, *Die Schwester – der Pfleger* **41**(9), 776-784 (2002).

5. Bianca Reuter, Flexible Arbeitszeit im Wettbewerb, *Der Arbeitgeber* **52**(1), 43-46 (2000).

6. Peter Knauth, *Arbeitszeitflexiblisierung aus arbeitswissenschaftlicher Sicht*, in: Arbeitszeitflexibilisierung im Dienstleistungsbereich, edited by Gert Zülch, Patricia Stock, and Thomas Bogus (Shaker Verlag, Aachen, 2002), pp. 51-74.

7. Patricia Stock, Thomas Bogus, and Sascha Stowasser, *Auswirkungen flexibler Arbeitszeitmodelle auf den Personaleinsatz und die Belastungen des Personals* (Shaker Verlag, Aachen, 2004).

8. Thomas Bogus, *Simulationsbasierte Gestaltung von Arbeitszeitmodellen in Dienstleistungsbetrieben mit kundenfrequenzabhängigem Arbeitszeitbedarf* (Shaker Verlag, Aachen, 2002).

9. Gert Zülch, Jörg Fischer, and Uwe Jonsson, *An integrated object model for activity network based simulation,* in: Proceedings of the 2000 Winter Simulation Conference, Volume 1, edited by Jeffrey A. Joines, Russel R. Barton, Keebom Kang, and Paul A. Fishwick (The Institute of Electrical and Electronics Engineers et al., Piscatawy, NJ, 2000), pp. 371-380.

10. Bernhard Teriet, *Freie Arbeitszeitregelungen als Chance für Unternehmen und Mitarbeiter,* in: Freie Arbeitszeit. Neue Betriebliche Arbeitszeitmodelle (Gottlieb Duttweiler-Institut, Rüschlikon, 1979).

11. Gert Zülch, Patricia Stock, and Thomas Bogus, *Working time recommendations for the load reduction of employees in retail stores*, in: Human Performance and Aging, Proceedings of the XVth Triennial Congress of the International Ergonomics Association and The 7th Joint Conference of Ergonomics Society of Korea / Japan Ergonomics Society "Ergonomics in the Digital Age", Volume 4 (Ergonomics Society of Korea, Seoul, 2003), pp. 227-230.

12. Patricia Stock and Gert Zülch, *Reorganising the Working Time System of a Call-Centre with Personnel-oriented Simulation,* in: Integrating Human Aspects in Production Management., edited by Gert Zülch, Harinder S. Jagdev, and Patricia Stock (Springer, New York, 2005), pp. 57-69.

13. Max-Jürgen Heitz, *Ein engpaßorientierter Ansatz zur simulationsunterstützten Planung von Personalstrukturen* (Dissertation, Karlsruhe, 1994).

14. Hans-Georg von Wedemeyer, *Entscheidungsunterstützung in der Fertigungssteuerung mit Hilfe der Simulation* (VDI-Verlag, Düsseldorf, 1989).

15. Sven Warnke, *Entwicklung eines Systems computergestützter Planspiele zum Prozessmanagement im Krankenhaus* (Lehrstuhl für Betriebswirtschaftslehre und Operation Research der Universität Erlangen-Nürnberg, 2001).

16. Uwe Jonsson, *Ein integriertes Objektmodell zur durchlaufplanorientierten Simulation von Produktionssystemen* (Shaker Verlag, Aachen, 2000).

INDEX

Author	Page	Author	Page
Alfnes E.	129	Gudergaan G.	475
Alix T.	317	Hamacher B.	365
Andersen J.R.	285	Hayashi N.	3
Arai E.	41	Horbal R.	257
Badr Y.	373	Hrdina J.	493
Bandinelli R.	215	Hromada J.	175
Batsis A.	75	Huang H.	403
Bednarek M.	239	Hvolby H-H.	67
Beulens A.J.M.	433	Hvolby H-H.	383
Biennier F.	93	Hvolby H-H.	413
Biennier F.	373	Jaber M.	373
Bouras A.	337	Johansen J.	277
Bouwmeester D.	433	Johns R.	357
Carli D.	215	Jun H-B.	111
Cassina J.	101	Kagan R.	257
Crestan A. W.	337	Kaihara T.	3
Crute V.	357	Kanda Y.	121
Dreyer H.	129	Kehr M.	305
Dreyer H.	443	Kimura T.	121
Ducq Y.	165	Kiritsis D.	111
Emde M.	461	Koch T.	151
Falster P.	383	Koch T.	257
Falster P.	413	Koike M.	41
Fauske H.	231	Kurahashi M.	3
Freund R.	423	Lee H-L.	21
Frick J.	249	Legait A.	93
Fujii S.	3	Lindinger C.	305
Furmans K.	11	Lippolt C. R.	11
Garg A.	475	Macchi M.	143
Gocev P.	185	Marinescu P.	269
Goller I.	305	Marquard M.	101
Graves A.	357	Matta A.	101
Gregor M.	175	Matthiessen R.	277

...nor	Page	Author	Page
...ertins K.	185	Stock P.	493
...letin A.	101	Strandhagen J.O.	129
Mikkelsen H.	285	Strandhagen J.O.	231
Na H-B.	21	Strzelczak S.	393
Nakano M.	327	Strzelczak S.	403
Neubert G.	337	Svensson C.	347
Nielsen P.	57	Śliwiński T.	29
Nino Luna L.F.	239	Taisch M.	101
Noritake S.	327	Tarditi R	461
Ohashi T.	327	Tatsiopoulos I.	75
Olhager J.	195	Tezuka H.	121
Papadopoulos A.	75	Thoben K.D.	461
Papadopoulos G.	75	Toczyłowski E.	29
Park J.	21	Toma S. G.	269
Persson F.	195	Tomasella M.	101
Portioli-Staudacher A.	485	Trienekens J.H.	413
Rabe M.	185	Trienekens J.H.	433
Riis J.O.	285	Tsigkas A.	423
Rolstadaas A.	383	Tsumaya A.	41
Ruibal M.	111	Tucci M.	215
Rydzak F.	205	Umeda S.	453
Santarek K.	223	Vallespir B.	165
Sashio K.	3	Vallespir B.	317
Sawicka A.	205	Van Goubergen D.	295
Schwarz R.	49	Verdouw C.N.	433
Seifert M.	461	Vigtil A.	443
Semini M.	231	Wakamatsu H.	41
Sitek P.	461	Wickham A.	357
Sobczyk T.	151	Xirouchakis P.	111
Štefánik A.	175	Yokose H.	3
Steger-Jensen K.	57	Zhang F.	453
Steger-Jensen K.	67	Zülch G.	49
Steger-Jensen K.	413	Zülch G.	493